Translated Texts for]

This series is designed to meet the needs of stu(history and others who wish to broaden their study by reading source material, but whose knowledge of Latin or Greek is not sufficient to allow them to do so in the original language. Many important Late Imperial and Dark Age texts are currently unavailable in translation and it is hoped that TTH will help to fill this gap and to complement the secondary literature in English which already exists. The series relates principally to the period 300–800 AD and includes Late Imperial, Greek, Byzantine and Syriac texts as well as source books illustrating a particular period or theme. Each volume is a self-contained scholarly translation with an introductory essay on the text and its author and notes on the text indicating major problems of interpretation, including textual difficulties.

Editorial Committee
Sebastian Brock, Oriental Institute, University of Oxford
Averil Cameron, Keble College, Oxford
Henry Chadwick, Oxford
John Davies, University of Liverpool
Carlotta Dionisotti, King's College, London
Peter Heather, University College, London
William E. Klingshirn, The Catholic University of America
Michael Lapidge, Clare College, Cambridge
Robert Markus, University of Nottingham
John Matthews, Yale University
Claudia Rapp, University of California, Los Angeles
Raymond Van Dam, University of Michigan
Michael Whitby, University of Warwick
Ian Wood, University of Leeds

General Editors
Gillian Clark, University of Bristol
Mark Humphries, National University of Ireland, Maynooth
Mary Whitby, University of Liverpool

Front cover: An emperor (Diocletian?) and his courtiers worship a pagan god, perhaps Jupiter. Drawing by Roger Tomlin based on illumination from the first page of Book 1 of a fifteenth-century manuscript of Lactantius' *Divine Institutes*, MS Biblioteca Medicea Laurenziana Plut.21.6 f. 1r, Florence.

A full list of published titles in the Translated Texts for Historians series is available on request. The most recently published are shown below.

The Armenian History attributed to Sebeos
Translated with notes by R. W. THOMSON, Historical commentary by JAMES HOWARD-JOHNSTON. Assistance from TIM GREENWOOD
Volume 31 (in two parts): 240 pp., 224 pp., 1999, ISBN 0-85323-564-3

The Chronicle of Pseudo-Joshua the Stylite
Translated with notes and introduction by FRANK R. TROMBLEY and JOHN W. WATT
Volume 32: 240pp., including 3 maps and 2 plans, 2000, ISBN 0-85323-585-6

The Ecclesiastical History of Evagrius Scholasticus
Translated with an introduction and notes by MICHAEL WHITBY
Volume 33: 454pp., 2000, ISBN 0-85323-605-4

Antioch as a Centre of Hellenic Culture, as Observed by Libanius
Translated with an introduction and notes by A. F. NORMAN
Volume 34: 224pp., 2000, ISBN 0-85323-595-3

Neoplatonic Saints: The Lives of Plotinus and Proclus by their Students
Translated with an introduction and notes by MARK EDWARDS
Volume 35: 224pp., 2000, ISBN 0-85323-615-1

Politics, Philosophy and Empire in the Fourth Century: Select Orations of Themistius
Translated with an introduction by PETER HEATHER and DAVID MONCUR
Volume 36: 384pp., 2001, ISBN 0-85323-106-0

A Christian's Guide to Greek Culture: The Pseudo-Nonnus *Commentaries* on *Sermons* 4, 5, 39 and 43 of Gregory of Nazianzus
Translated with an introduction and notes by JENNIFER NIMMO SMITH
Volume 37: 208pp., 2001, ISBN 0-85323-917-7

Avitus of Vienne: Letters and Selected Prose
Translated with introduction and notes by DANUTA SHANZER and IAN WOOD
Volume 38: 472 pp., 2002, ISBN 0-85323-588-0

Constantine and Christendom: The Oration to the Saints, The Greek and Latin accounts of the Discovery of the Cross, The Edict of Constantine to Pope Silvester
Translated with introduction and notes by MARK EDWARDS
Volume 39: 192pp., 2003, ISBN 0-85323-648-8

For full details of Translated Texts for Historians, including prices and ordering information, please write to the following:
All countries, except the USA and Canada: Liverpool University Press, 4 Cambridge Street, Liverpool, L69 7ZU, UK (*Tel* +44-[0]151-794 2233 *Fax* +44-[0]151-794 2235, Email J.M. Smith@liv.ac.uk, http://www.liverpool-unipress.co.uk). **USA and Canada:** University of Pennsylvania Press, 4200 Pine Street, Philadelphia, PA 19104-6097, USA (*Tel* +1-215-898-6264, *Fax* +1-215-898-0404).

The resurrected worship Jesus. Illuminated first page of Book 7 of a fifteenth-century manuscript of Lactantius' *Divine Institutes*, MS Biblioteca Medicea Laurenziana Plut.21.6 f. 158r, Florence.

Translated Texts for Historians
Volume 40

Lactantius
Divine Institutes

Translated with an introduction and notes by
ANTHONY BOWEN and PETER GARNSEY

Liverpool
University
Press

First published 2003
Liverpool University Press
4 Cambridge Street
Liverpool, L69 7ZU

Copyright © 2003 Anthony Bowen and Peter Garnsey

Reprinted 2007

The right of Anthony Bowen and Peter Garnsey to be identified
as the authors of this work has been asserted by them in
accordance with the Copyright, Designs and Patents Act, 1988.

All rights reserved. No part of this book may be reproduced,
stored in a retrieval system, or transmitted, in any form or
by any means, electronic, mechanical, photocopying, recording,
or otherwise, without the prior written permission of the publisher.

British Library Cataloguing-in-Publication Data
A British Library CIP Record is available.

ISBN-13 978-0-85323-988-8

Set in Times by
Koinonia, Manchester
Printed in the European Union by
Bell and Bain Limited, Glasgow

Vir doctus, studio uerbis pietate refertus,
    hoc opus instituit quod tibi, lector, habe.
sic cultus delere malos, firmare fideles,
    omnibus illum unum conciliare deum,
omnibus et uitam uoluit suadere beatam
    quam bene per natum dat deus usque suum.
tam bene uerborum Lactanti lacteus amnis
    profluat atque animos irriget ipse pios.

A scholar's passion shaped in prose
    set up this work: take it, and read.
By it he meant false gods to expose,
    faith to grow strong, and all to heed
God's oneness and the life supreme
    which through his son he kindly extols.
Flow forth, Lactantius' milky stream:
    refresh all wisdom-seeking souls.

CONTENTS

Preface ix
Translator's Preface xi
List of Abbreviations xiii

Introduction 1

DIVINE INSTITUTES

Book 1 False Religion 57
Book 2 The Origin of Error 118
Book 3 False Wisdom 168
Book 4 True Wisdom and Religion 225
Book 5 Justice 281
Book 6 True Worship 330
Book 7 The Life of Bliss 389

Select Bibliography 443
Index of Topics 453
Index of Proper Names 460

PREFACE

This book has its origins in some lectures that I gave soon after my arrival in Cambridge in 1974, within the course in the history of political thought from antiquity to the modern era. I was initially asked to deliver the lectures in Greek Classical and Hellenistic thought, which Moses Finley (but not his audiences) considered he had given long enough, in tandem with my former colleague Richard Tuck, who was responsible (*inter alia*) for the period from Cicero to Augustine. In due course I passed the Greeks on to more expert practitioners than myself and took over the Romans and early Christians. That slice of the course, as designed by Richard Tuck – to whom I here acknowledge a longstanding intellectual debt – included lectures on Lactantius' *Divine Institutes*.

I discovered early on that Lactantius has interested predominantly French, German and Italian scholars, whose work is regrettably by and large unavailable to our own undergraduates and those of other English-speaking countries, and that in any case there was a need for a synthetic treatment of Lactantius and his *Divine Institutes*, composed with the concerns of students and scholars of intellectual history in mind. Eventually the present project emerged, an annotated translation of the work in question, prefaced by a discussion of Lactantius' thought. Our collaboration has been thoroughgoing and has touched every aspect of the project. However, primary responsibility for the introduction, the bulk of the annotation (together with the bibliography and the Index of Topics) lies with me, and for the translation (plus the textual and linguistic footnotes and the Index of Proper Names) with Anthony Bowen; it seemed entirely appropriate that the Orator of Cambridge University should take on the task of translating the most significant work of the Professor of Latin Rhetoric at the capital city of the emperor Diocletian. Two English translations already exist, but neither is both accurate and up-to-date; our own offers in addition an explanation of most of the numerous literary, philosophical, theological and historical references in the text, and an interpretation of the content of the work as a whole.

PREFACE

We have naturally leant on the work of other scholars, and are very happy to acknowledge our debt to them, more especially to S. Brandt, whose magnificent edition of the text appeared in 1890, and to P. Monat, whose excellent annotated French translation together with Latin text thus far runs to four of the seven books. Others whose work on Lactantius' thought has been of particular value to us include E. Heck, V. Loi, O. Nicholson, M. Perrin, R. Pichon, M. Spanneut and A. Wlosok. A number of colleagues have given us assistance at various stages: they include the members of seminars that we convened on Books 1 and 5. More particularly, we are extremely grateful to Timothy Barnes, Richard Finn, Caroline Humfress, Julia Kindt, Oliver Nicholson, Michael Reeve, Christopher Rowland, Malcolm Schofield and David Sedley. Above all, we are deeply indebted to Margaret Atkins, who read the whole work, saved us from many errors and offered numerous improvements and insights. Finally, our thanks are due to the Biblioteca Medicea Laurenziana, Firenze, for permitting us to reproduce an illuminated capital and a page from their manuscript of Lactantius, Biblioteca Medicea Laurenziana Plut.21.6.

PG

TRANSLATOR'S PREFACE

Manuscripts of *Diuinae Institutiones* are numerous, some are as early as the fifth or sixth century, and problems of text are seldom very serious. The text followed here is that of Samuel Brandt (Vienna, 1890) except where Pierre Monat's text in *Sources Chrétiennes* is available (Paris, 1973– ; so far Books 1, 2, 4 and 5 have appeared). Very occasionally Brandt's text has been preferred to Monat's. Two principal MSS (R and S) preserve text in various places throughout the work, some of it mere phrases but some of it whole paragraphs, that is not in the main tradition. The majority of this extra text contains passages that some have held to contain dualist thinking (see pp. 27–28 n. 106, however); most of the rest is directed at the emperor Constantine, invoking him at the start of a book or glorifying his power. These passages, relegated to the apparatus by Brandt and printed in italics by Monat, we have included without distinction; the paragraph numbering exposes the major passages.

Lactantius writes with an energy, wit and fullness reminiscent of Cicero in the Verrines. Lactantius' imitation of the great master and model of oratory is clear in vocabulary, syntax (see note on 5.17.30), sentence making, rhetoric and rhythm. Ciceronian Latin, which he had practised all his life, was clearly for him a comfortable and adequate idiom; so it would be for his intended audience also. To turn it into English that is comfortable and adequate itself is not a straightforward exercise. Sentence length and certain figures of speech such as apostrophe and rhetorical questions present problems well known to translators; this translation is literal (as it is called) only if it also makes good English. Priority has gone to Lactantius' sense and energy. A greater difficulty is presented by words such as *sapiens* and *innocens* or by word clusters such as *pius, impius, pietas, impietas* and *iustus, iniustus, iustitia, iniuria*. *Virtus*, here mostly translated 'virtue', is a particular problem. Lactantius was more of a moralist than a theologian, and the worth of his arguments varies greatly, even within a paragraph, for he measured worth more on a rhetorical than on an intellectual scale; he used his words carefully but generously; he played no small part in developing the Christian vocabulary. On the whole, such words have been rendered with consistency; but a total consistency is inimical to good English. Where Lactantius appears to have the Christian God in mind, the word is capitalised. When he uses *deus* so, he often gives it emphasis by putting it last in the sentence, even at the cost of a Ciceronian rhythm.

Attribution of Lactantius' quotations is not always easy: he patently quoted from memory, the plentifully stocked memory of a man well acquainted with the Bible, and at least as thoroughly acquainted with Classical authors, especially the Latin ones, as the best scholars of later ages have been. Mostly he quotes verbatim; sometimes local need causes small variations; sometimes he alludes in paraphrase. Where he is very close and the original survives, and the quotation is part of the argument, the reference is given in the text in square brackets; quotations that are ornamental are given their reference in a footnote. Where he is the only authority for the surviving text, reference has been given to a modern collection of such fragments where possible; so too, mostly, where he paraphrases or alludes; inverted commas mark certain or probable quotation. Lactantius' use of Greek is noted by G preceding the use, and readers are reminded of this by a note at its first occasion in each book. In the Index of Proper Names, references are underlined where text is quoted.

AJB

ABBREVIATIONS

AARC	Atti dell'Accademia romanistica costantiniana
Abel	Abel, E., *Orphica* (Leipzig, 1885)
AJP	American Journal of Philology
BICS	Bulletin of the Institute of Classical Studies
Breysig	Breysig, A., *Germanici Caesaris Aratea cum scholiis* (Hildesheim, 1967)
Charpin	Charpin, F., *Lucilii Saturae* 3 vols, Budé ed. (Paris, 1978–91)
Collatio	Mosaicarum et Romanarum Legum Collatio
CQ	Classical Quarterly
CSEL	Corpus Scriptorum Ecclesiasticorum Latinorum
Fontenrose	Fontenrose. J., *Didyma: Apollo's Oracle, Cult and Companions* (Berkeley, 1988)
Garbarino	Garbarino, I., *M. Tullii Ciceronis fragmenta ex libris philosophicis, ex aliis libris deperditis, ex scriptis incertis* (Mondadori, 1984)
HSCP	Harvard Studies in Classical Philology
Kern	Kern, O., *Orphica Fragmenta* (Berlin, 1922)
JAC	Jahrbuch für Antike und Christentum
JECS	Journal of Early Christian Studies
JRA	Journal of Roman Archaeology
JRS	Journal of Roman Studies
JThS	Journal of Theological Studies
LS	Long, A.A., and Sedley, D.N., *The Hellenistic Philosophers*, 2 vols (Cambridge, 1987)
Marx	Marx, F., *C. Lucilii Carminum Reliquiae*, 2 vols (Leipzig, 1904–05)
Maurenbrecher	Maurenbrecher, B., *C. Sallustii Crispi Historiarum Reliquiae* (Leipzig, 1891–93)
NF *Corp. Herm.*	Nock, A.D., and Festugière, A. J., *Corpus Hermeticum* (Paris, 1946–54)

Orac. Sib.	Geffcken, J., *Die Oracula Sibyllina* (Leipzig, 1902)
Peter	Peter, H., *Veterum historicum Romanorum reliquiae*, 2 vols (Leipzig, 1870–1906)
Plasberg	Plasberg, O., *Academicorum Reliquiae cum Lucullo* (Stuttgart, 1922)
Ritter	Ritter, C., *M. Fabii Quintiliani Declamationes quae supersunt cxlv* (Leipzig, 1884)
SC	Sources Chrétiennes
SDHI	*Scripta et documenta historiae iuris*
SO	*Symbolae Osloenses*
Straume-Zimmermann	Straume-Zimmerman, L., Broemser, F., and Gigon, O., *M. Tullius Cicero: Hortensius Lucullus Academici libri* (Darmstadt, 1990)
SVF	H.von Arnim, *Stoicorum veterum fragmenta*, 3 vols (Leipzig, 1903–05)
Usener	Usener, H., *Epicurea* (Leipzig, 1887)
Vahlen	Vahlen, J., *Enniae Poiesis Reliquiae* (Leipzig, 1928)
Vitelli	Vitelli, C., *M. Tullii Ciceronis Consolationis fragmenta* (Mondadori, 1979)
Vottero	Vottero, D., *Lucio Anneo Seneca: I Frammenti* (Bologna, 1998)
Warmington	Warmington, E.H., *Remains of Old Latin*, 4 vols (London, 1935–40)
Watt	Watt, W.S., *M. Tullii Ciceronis Epistulae*, vol. III (Oxford, 1958, 1965)
Weyssenhof	Weyssenhof, C., *Ciceronis epistularum fragmenta* (Warsaw, 1970)
WS	*Wiener Studien*
YCS	*Yale Classical Studies*
Ziegler, *leg.*	Ziegler, K., *M. Tullii Ciceronis De Legibus*, 3rd edn (Freiburg 1979)
Ziegler, *rep.*	Ziegler, K., *Cicero: de republica*, 6th edn (Leipzig, 1955)

INTRODUCTION

1. LIFE, WORKS, REPUTATION

L. Caecilius Firmianus Lactantius is thought to have lived c. 250–c. 325.[1] Of the little biographical information that we have, he himself releases some, Jerome (writing at the end of the fourth century) most of the rest. Lactantius was an African by birth. His city of origin is unknown. His instructor in rhetoric, Arnobius, came from Sicca Veneria, a regional centre in the Medjerda valley 100 or so miles south-west of Carthage. Arnobius was, like Lactantius, a convert to Christianity, and himself wrote seven books of Christian apologetic under the title *Adversus Nationes* (*Against the Nations*). Lactantius appears not to have known of the work when he composed *Divine Institutes*. There was an obvious place to refer to it and its author in *Divine Institutes*, namely, in Book 5 where three African apologists, Tertullian, Minucius Felix and Cyprian, are critically assessed.[2] Perhaps the two works were written more or less at the same time, and in places far apart.[3]

Lactantius made a reputation for himself teaching rhetoric in North Africa as his teacher had done. We do not know where, though it is hard not to believe, in view of his future career, that he was based in Carthage, provincial capital and centre of learning. Lactantius was always a teacher. As he says in an autobiographical aside: 'I have made efforts myself to achieve what little skill I could in speaking because of my career in teaching, but I have never been eloquent, because I never went into public life' (*quippe qui forum ne attigerim quidem*[4]). He is saying that he never became a career-

---

1 L's name is contested, as between Caelius and Caecilius. I follow Schanz-Hosius (1922), 414. A good brief introduction to Lactantius in English is lacking. See Wlosok (1993; French, translated from the German); Barnes (1981), 11–145, 291–92 nn. 96–99, is to be preferred on chronological matters. See Bryce (1999) for a full bibliographical catalogue of secondary literature on Lactantius. A shortlist of the more substantial works might include Pichon (1901), Wlosok (1960), Loi (1970), Fontaine and Perrin (1978), Perrin (1981), Monat (1982), Digeser (2000). Oliver Nicholson has made a singular contribution in a number of articles.

2 *D.I.* 5.1.21–28; 5.4.3–8.

3 *D.I.* belongs to 303–10. Simmons (1995), preface, dates *Adv. nat.* to 302–05, probably correctly.

4 3.13.12.

lawyer (though he inevitably taught forensic rhetoric); he was neither an advocate nor a jurist. He presumably produced a great many of both, particularly advocates, who always far outnumbered jurists. Advocacy was an established entrée into a career in administration and government. Lactantius may perhaps be seen as an African equivalent of Libanius of Antioch, peppering provincial governors with letters of recommendation for pupils seeking a job on their staff, typically as assessors in their courts. We have Libanius' correspondence but not Lactantius', so this is guesswork, but reasonable guesswork nonetheless. Lactantius after all was appointed to an official chair in Latin rhetoric in Nicomedia, Bithynia, the seat of the emperor Diocletian.[5] So he must have been, if not the best in the world at his profession, at least very well known and very well connected – someone with a network of people, especially ex-pupils and protégés, reaching into powerful places.[6]

Lactantius moved from North Africa to north-west Asia Minor to take up his post towards the end of the third century. The timing was unfortunate. The Great Persecution, launched in 303, was brewing when he arrived at court, and he was already a Christian. He encountered among others two zealous pagans, both unnamed, one a philosopher, the other a judge, who he says played leading roles in provoking the persecution.[7] The philosopher is sometimes, probably incorrectly, identified with Porphyry the Neoplatonic philosopher, well-known as a critic of Christianity. The identification of the judge with Sossianus Hierocles, governor of Bithynia in 303, is secure. Lactantius says that the philosopher was the author of three books *Against Religion and the Christian Name*, but he passes over any substantive criticisms of Christianity that they might have contained. We are treated rather to a destruction of his character and a scathing description of the bad reception that he received. Porphyry was notorious as a serious and effective critic of Christianity rather than as a moral reprobate. In contrast, a hostile airing is given to the judge's main criticisms: of Christianity, that its scriptures are full of contradictions, and of Christ, that he was a man who arrogantly claimed divine status and was outclassed as a miracle worker by Apollonius of Tyana. Lactantius refers to a tract called *Lover of Truth* which contained these criticisms. A work of that title is associated with Hierocles

---

5   5.2: *ego cum in Bithynia oratorias litteras accitus docerem.* According to Jerome, *Vir. Ill.* 80, he was 'summoned with the grammarian Fabius'.

6   See Nicholson (2001a), 184.

7   5.2–4.1. See Barnes (1976); (1981), 164–67, 174–78; (1994). Barnes argues against Porphyry, convincingly in my view. On the other side, see Digeser (1998; 2000).

INTRODUCTION

by a Eusebius (not Eusebius of Caesarea),[8] who answered him back in his *Against Hierocles*, just before the launching of the Great Persecution. Lactantius indicates that he was provoked into writing *Divine Institutes* by these men in particular, and by the Great Persecution in general.[9]

This was not his first work. It was preceded by a *Symposium*, an *Itinerary* of his journey from Africa to Bithynia composed in hexameters, a *Grammarian*, all lost, and the surviving *On the Workmanship of God* (*De Opificio Dei*), composed c. 303. We also have an (undatable) poem on the phoenix (*De ave phoenice*), which is presented as a symbol of the Christian who has achieved salvation. Other lost works, two books to Asclepiades, eight books of letters, four to Probus, two to Severus and two to a pupil Demetrianus, are not necessarily earlier than *Divine Institutes*.[10]

Lactantius' next movements, and his later literary works, are also not precisely dated. He probably left Nicomedia in about 305, passing to the West, perhaps to Italy, and was later employed by Constantine as tutor for his son Crispus in Trier, perhaps as early as 310.[11] To these years or later belong the introduction of minor changes in *Divine Institutes* – including invocations of Constantine – the composition of the triumphalist *On the Deaths of the Persecutors* (c. 313–15), followed by *On Anger* (c. 316), and the *Epitome of the Divine Institutes* (320 or later). He intended to write, but apparently never did, works against heretics and Jews.[12] During his extended stay at the court of Constantine, he was in theory in a position to make an impact on the emperor and his legislation. Whether he tried to exert influence, and how far it carried, is a matter for speculation.[13]

---

8 Hägg (1992).
9 For Lactantius as source for the history of the period, including the Great Persecution, historians normally turn, with justification, to his later work *De Mortibus Persecutorum* (*On the Deaths of the Persecutors*). On the Great Persecution, the content of the edicts and their consequences, see De Ste Croix (1954); also Barnes (1998), 274ff.
10 Perrin (1974), 11–17.
11 Barnes (1981), 13, and pers. comm., believes that Lactantius spent 305–08 somewhere in the West, perhaps in Africa. Italy appears more likely.
12 4.30.4; 7.1.26.
13 Amarelli (1978) thinks his influence was significant; others, e.g. Rougé (1983), 116, are more sceptical. Evans Grubbs (1995) argues persuasively for the limited impact of Christian thinking on Constantine's legislation as a whole (a conclusion that has implications for Lactantius), but thinks Constantine's *Oration to the Assembly of the Saints*, delivered at Easter, probably in 325 (cf. Barnes 2001a), does reflect Lactantius' influence (p. 35). For a recent contribution to the debate, with special reference to the matter of religious toleration, see Digeser (2000), 134–43.

Lactantius was famous in his own day and subsequently in late antiquity, not to mention the Renaissance,[14] as a teacher of rhetoric and for his own eloquence. As already noted, he attracted the attention, and was put on the payroll, of two emperors, Diocletian and Constantine. Jerome called him 'the most eloquent man of his time', and referred to the 'stream of Ciceronian eloquence'; his treatises were a kind of epitome of Cicero.[15] This remark could be read as something of a backhanded compliment, both because of 'epitome', and because Jerome, notoriously, had nightmares over whether his own exposure to Cicero in the past was preventing his being a good Christian in the present, and would be held against him at the Last Judgement in the future.[16] However, Jerome does also express admiration for the use to which Lactantius put his eloquence, and this is interesting, as involving an evaluation of *Divine Institutes*. In a letter to Paulinus of Nola he says he demolished his opponents with ease (*facile aliena destruxit*) and wrote very forcefully against the pagans (*contra gentes scripsit fortissime*).[17]

Up to this point Jerome was saying exactly what Lactantius would have wanted him to say. He knew his own strengths, and they lay in the ability to argue a persuasive case after the manner of the orators of old, above all Cicero. Lactantius set out to be an effective advocate for his new-found religion, superior to any of his predecessors. Jerome, however, in the same letter to Paulinus of Nola, mixes praise with criticism: 'Would that he had been as good at affirming our doctrines as he was at demolishing those of others' (*utinam tam nostra adfirmare potuisset quam facile aliena destruxit*). What is to be made of this? Is Jerome attacking his qualities as a theologian?[18] The context is significant. Jerome is finding fault with a whole string of Christian writers who wrote in Latin. Lactantius is one of them; the others are Tertullian, Cyprian, Victorinus, Arnobius and Hilary. Those are just about all the major players except Ambrose, who, unlike those on the list, was still alive.[19] Jerome's critique embraces both style and content. His remarks

---

14 See e.g. Panizza (1978). There are more than 150 manuscripts of *Divine Institutes*, mostly dating from the Renaissance. Pico de la Mirandola proclaimed him *Cicero Christianus*. See his *De studio divinae atque humanae philosophiae* (Basel, 1573), ch. 7.

15 Jerome, *Chron.* Ad 317 p.Chr. (p. 230 Helm): *vir omnium suo tempore eloquentissimus*; *Ep.* 58.10: *quasi flumen eloquentiae Tullianae*.

16 Jerome, *Ep.* 22.30.

17 Jerome, *Ep.* 58.10.

18 Jerome did find him lacking on the Trinity, see n. 23, below, but that is not at issue here.

19 In *Ep.* 60.10, Jerome lists as the source of quotations for the benefit of the learned Nepotianus, the following: Tertullian, Cyprian, Lactantius, Hilary, Minucius Felix, Victorinus and Arnobius.

about Cyprian and Lactantius run roughly along the same lines: Cyprian 'failed to expound the divine scriptures' (*scripturas divinas nequaquam disseruit*), Lactantius 'to affirm our doctrines' (*nostra adfirmare*). It may be that these barbed comments are to be read in the light of what was happening between Jerome and Augustine. The two men were competing for the attention of Paulinus, and the matter was argued, at least in part, over the use of pagan writings to preach the Gospel. This is the view of Jean Doignon, who thinks that Augustine was replying to Jerome in his *De doctrina christiana* (*On Christian Doctrine*) published two years later.[20] Augustine there names 'good men of the faith' who were refugees from Egypt, that is, paganism, and who put their experience with pagan letters to good use in preaching the Gospel. They are Cyprian, Lactantius, Victorinus, Optatus and Hilary.

The competition over Paulinus, if that is what it was, can only be part of the picture here. Lactantius' work was a forerunner of Augustine's much more ambitious counterblast to paganism in *De civitate dei* (*City of God*, composed c. 412–26). Augustine's implicit backing in *On Christian Doctrine* of Lactantius' project foreshadows at least a partial endorsement in *City of God* of his approach to pagan authorities, notably the use of the Sibyl as cited in Vergil's Fourth Eclogue and read by Augustine as prophesying the coming of Christ and his salvific role.[21] Jerome complained to Paulinus about the way some people flitted freely between sacred and profane writings and used Vergil as an interpreter of Scripture.[22]

Jerome's caveat about the way Lactantius (and others) expounded the Gospel should not therefore be read as a general attack on his (and their) deficiencies in the realm of theology.[23] In any case, modern criticisms of Lactantius are rather more serious. He has earned credit for preserving earlier literary material which we would not otherwise have from sources such as Cicero, Seneca, Ennius and the Corpus Hermeticum, and for structuring it in a reasonably intelligible way. But his work has been branded as essentially derivative and second-hand.[24] This assessment has been

---

20 Doignon (1963), on Augustine, *Doctr. Chr.* 2.40.60–61 (of 397).
21 *Civ.* 10.27; 18.23.
22 Jerome, *Ep.* 53.7.
23 In any case, Lactantius was writing a textbook, not a learned treatise. His alleged dualistic tendencies are to my mind heavily overplayed. See, briefly, Quasten (1950, repr. 1992), 406–07; in detail, Heck (1972), and n. 106, below. Jerome's charge that he denied the concept of the Trinity (especially in his lost *Letters of Demetrius*) carries little weight in view of the fact that the concept had yet to be developed. See Jerome, *Ep.* 84.7; *Comm. in Gal. ad* 4.6.
24 See e.g. Pichon (1901); Loi (1970). Both judge him to be a 'mediocrity'.

promoted by scholars with a dominant interest in the Classical sources of Lactantius and rather less concern for the quality of his argument. The first of the source-hunters was Brandt, who more than a century ago systematically mined *The Workmanship of God* for its literary ancestors. Pichon took up the subject of Lactantius' sources and treated it in some detail, though as a part of a much larger project. Works of *Quellenforschung* by de Labriolle and Hagendahl surveyed the whole field of early Christian writing. Perrin in his two-volume work on *The Workmanship of God* gave a lot of space to the discussion of possible literary relationships and parallels. The culmination of this approach was Ogilvie's project, which set out to identify the literature on which Lactantius drew, both his working library, and the books that he knew well enough to quote from memory.[25] Ogilvie managed to do this without any explicit evaluation of Lactantius, but the assumption permeating his book is that Lactantius' work was largely derivative. The conclusion, that Lactantius had read very little first-hand apart from Cicero and Vergil, is bound to affect one's view of him. That Augustine might have read no more, or even less, especially on the Greek side, is noted by Ogilvie at the end of his book, but nothing is made of the observation.[26]

The charge that Lactantius is not much more than his sources does not stand up to close scrutiny. A fairer and more accurate evaluation would focus on the effectiveness with which he argues the cause of Christianity against paganism before a putative audience of the educated classes of the Roman empire.[27] Such a project of rehabilitation cannot skirt the question of the influence of earlier and current literature and ideas, but it would demonstrate that Lactantius made creative use of such material; moreover, that his rhetorical strategy fashioned a kind of Christian apologetic that had never been seen before. Finally, a proper assessment of Lactantius would highlight his singular achievement in constructing a coherent body of Christian ethical thinking, against the background of and in critical dialogue with classical thought. We can at least initiate such a project now.[28]

25 Brandt (1891), Pichon (1901), de Labriolle (1924), Hagendahl (1958), Perrin (1974), Ogilvie (1978).

26 Bryce (1990) has the same title as Ogilvie's book, but is a constructive attempt to explore Lactantius' involvement with pagan writers, especially Cicero and Vergil. See Heck (1988) on Lactantius' use of the classics in general. Heck (1980) is a telling critique of Ogilvie.

27 The decline of Lactantius' stature since the Renaissance probably reflects the way the reputation of rhetoric has plummeted. See Crook (1995) for a timely defence of rhetoric. Lactantius in any case needs to be judged by the quality of his arguments as well as for his rhetoric.

28 See Roots (1987), and more fully (1988), for a parallel project based on *The Workmanship of God,* with an emphasis, however, on Lactantius' talents as a rhetorician.

INTRODUCTION 7

2. *DIVINE INSTITUTES*: CONTENTS, GENRE, AUTHORITIES

Contents

The work begins with a pair of books attacking the pagan gods, *De falsa religione* (*On false religion*) and *De Origine Erroris* (*The origin of error*). Lactantius contrives a consensus behind the proposition that God is one. The many 'gods' are no more than promoted men; indeed they represent debased humanity, to judge from their behaviour. Moreover, they are relatively new arrivals on the scene. Lactantius then (in Book 2) turns his attention to man, and the history of his worship of false gods. He explains how man, forgoing his special status in creation as the only creature which stands erect and faces the heavens, came to worship images and to persevere in this, even when it was obvious (and admitted) that it was stupid to do so. A second pair of books, *De falsa sapientia* (*False wisdom*) and *De vera sapientia et religione* (*True wisdom and religion*), are aimed at dethroning philosophers as self-appointed wise men, and at annexing wisdom for the Christian religion. Lactantius first turns the philosophers' own arguments against them, then confronts them with Christian weaponry, in the shape of the story of the life and death of Christ as foretold by the prophets. The fifth and sixth books, *De iustitia* (*Justice*) and *De vero cultu* (*True worship*), define the virtues, especially justice, and lay down the precepts for a Christian life. The seventh and final book *De beata vita* (*The life of bliss*) sets out his eschatology and the rewards that await those who follow the path of justice and virtue.

Book 1

Lactantius' mission is to free men from pagan religion and philosophy, and to point the way to the truth, which lies in Christianity. Christianity is the only religion to unite *sapientia* and *religio*. Educated men (*docti*), those who respect and seek wisdom, must be pointed towards the true wisdom. In following the philosophers they were on the wrong track. The philosophers might have believed that they were teaching how to live well (and the aim at least can be endorsed, making philosophy a more worthy profession than rhetoric), but they were hopelessly divided among themselves, and in any case did not possess the true religion, without which true wisdom is unattainable. The fundamental fact is that *sapientia* and *religio* are inseparable, and neither can be true independently of the other.

God is, and can only be, one. This is shown, in the first place, by the common belief in providence, backed up by reason and the evidence of poets, philosophers and oracles. The pagan gods, notably Hercules, Aesculapius and the benefactor-gods, Jupiter and Saturn, are not worthy of the name. In any case, as can be seen from the work of Euhemerus mediated through the translation of Ennius, Jupiter and Saturn (and the rest) were not gods, but men who were accorded divine status. The presence of women in the Pantheon (among other things) confirms that the so-called gods were promoted men. The Stoic allegorical interpretation of myths is to be rejected. The stupidities, barbarities and scandals connected with the gods and their cults are endless and despicable. Far from the Christian religion being new, it is the pagan gods who are *arrivistes*. Saturn was born only about 1800 years ago.

Book 2

What are the sources of religious error? Why did people think men were gods, and why did they persist in cult worship, even when like Cicero they could see the folly of it? The first part of the answer is ignorance, which is a property of the educated and the wise as much as of the masses. Human wisdom does not in itself enable us to perceive and embrace true religion: this is something which has to be taught. But it is a blind faith in ancestral tradition that above all maintains the cult of the gods. And who are the ancestors? Why, in the first place, Romulus' pack of primitive shepherds, from which he fashioned the first senate of Rome. We should not, however, like sheep follow old ideas, but instead use our brains and aim at wisdom, which is the realisation that God is one and the maker of all things. God created the world (according to the principle of opposing elements), and men and animals to live in it. Man was not made by Prometheus, nor did he spring from the earth, nor was he always there. Man's Fall issued in a world full of wickedness and crime, orchestrated by the fallen angels-turned-demons under their devilish leader. Oracles, astrology, augury, necromancy and magic are inventions of these bogus divinities, who usurp the worship of the true God. Their images, which are the object of cult, are impotent, mortal, man-made. It is sacrilege to worship them, but also an insult to our human reason and stature.

Book 3

Both religion and wisdom are necessary, and both are missed by the philosophers. The word philosophy gives the game away: it means pursuit of wisdom, so it can't be wisdom. Philosophy is in fact opinion, not wisdom, which is the property of God, not man. And there are as many opinions as there are philosophers. Socrates saw that nothing can be known – and the Academic Sceptics followed in his tracks – but in holding this view he was denying philosophy a raison d'être.

Of the three branches of philosophy, natural philosophy deals with matters beyond our grasp, while logic is to do with form, not substance. Ethics is concerned with how to live well, and thus must be primary. Yet moral philosophers have missed the end of man, the highest good. Whatever it is, it must be peculiar to man (and attainable by all men, not just a tiny elite), involve the soul rather than the body, and be grounded in knowledge and virtue. It is, in fact, immortality, the reward for the practice of true religion, that is, the recognition of God as father and the pious worship of him.

Philosophers were wrong both in thinking of this life as a great good, and in trusting in their capacity to teach happiness or achieve it. This is borne out by their behaviour – they do not practise what they preach – and by their false or scandalous ideas. Plato thought that equity, a central element in justice, could be achieved by the denial of private property and the family, the Stoics regarded pity as somewhere between a vice and a disease, and Cicero blamed evil on luck rather than on the devil. Philosophers have either stood by a false religion (like Socrates), or ruled religion out (like Epicurus). In so doing they have cut themselves off from true wisdom, which is knowing God and worshipping him.

Book 4

Wisdom and religion are inseparable; they come together only when the one God is worshipped. The worship of more than one god is against nature; it is also against reason, as is demonstrated by the unity of father and master in the *paterfamilias* according to the rules of the civil law. The authority of the prophets establishes the reality and truth of God and his works, in the first place the Son of God; he was born twice, once in the spirit (without a mother), once in the flesh (without a father). Prophetic authority and the mission of Christ are to be understood as part of a comprehensive understanding of the history of the world.

Christ was sent to earth in response to evil, the worship of false gods, and the desertion of God and his prophets by the Jews. He came to announce to all men that God is one, and to teach justice. Christ is the embodiment of both virtue and justice. He could have come in power and glory. This, however, would have been a denial of man's liberty, and would not have shown man that he could overcome sin. A good teacher will not convince unless he confirms his words with deeds. Where philosophers failed, Christ (alone) succeeded. Christ had to suffer, and to die the most degrading death, in order to teach man to endure pain and despise death; that is the way to virtue, perfect and complete.

How could God and Christ be one? A father cannot be called a father without a son, and vice versa. God and Christ are one just as father and son are one in civil law: the father controls the son; he may grant the son the name and power of master; in the law, however, there is only one house and one master.

Book 5

Christianity is under attack and has not been properly defended. The solution is to link justice to religion, and the correct strategy for winning over educated pagans and wavering Christians is to approach the Christian truth by way of the non-Christian authorities rather than Scripture.

Justice prevailed in the Golden Age. People lived in peace and harmony and worshipped the one true God. Jupiter's arrival wrecked this ideal society. Justice was put to flight, true religion was abandoned and *cupiditas* and the institutions to back it were installed. Justice returned to earth with the Incarnation, but only a few possess it; it goes unrecognised by the many, and is persecuted by the judicial authorities.

Why was justice not accepted when it was restored? God retained evil so that virtue could be identified and diversity kept, the essential condition for the existence and development of the mystery of the divine religion.

How are the just to be recognised? By their fruits. Polytheism goes with injustice, unholiness and persecution of the just, whereas the worship of the true God is the mark of the just – and virtuous.

What is justice? Justice embraces all the virtues, but especially *pietas* and *aequitas*. If you do not worship God you do not know justice. Greeks and Romans fail the test. Their practice of social inequality shows that they lack justice.

Why are the just thought foolish and why are they in fact wise? Carneades distinguished civil and natural justice: the former is wise but not just, the latter just but not wise. However, a just man escapes the situations imagined by Carneades, in which a choice has to be made between oneself and others often in a serious crisis, because he is not profit-seeking, but rather sociable and generous and knows the difference between good and

INTRODUCTION

evil. If he is caught up in such situations, he will be prepared to go without, or to die.

Why are so few just, and why do the unjust prosper? Human existence is spiritual not material, and its true goods are invisible and lasting. Some virtues (*patientia, innocentia*) can be exercised only in adversity. God's present priority is to test and discipline the faithful. Persecution adds to their numbers. God will judge and punish the unjust. In a digression Lactantius pleads for freedom of religious belief and practice, for the use of argument rather than force.

Book 6

Our duty (*officium*) is to worship God. True worship involves the mind and spirit, not earthbound objects. It issues from those on the path of virtue rather than of vice, aiming at heaven rather than hell. Virtue is not knowledge of good and evil, but doing good and not doing evil. It is necessarily preceded by knowledge, which is knowledge of God. First we must give God his due, then man (but this too is for God, as man is made in the likeness of God). These are the two *officia* of justice, which is the mother and head of the virtues. The second *officium* boils down to pity and humanity. Unlike those who follow the cults of the gods, who in giving invariably look for return, the just necessarily help those who are helpless and incapable of giving anything back. The Stoics were way off course in treating pity as a vice when it is man's distinctive virtue.

In general, the passions or emotions are not to be eradicated (Stoics) or merely controlled (Peripatetics), but directed on to the true path. They are not in themselves evil, but rather vicious if exercised badly and virtuous if exercised well. Even cupidity, lust and anger (the 'three Furies') have desirable ends, God having set bounds to them. Two key virtues are innocence and patience, which teach us not to cause injury, nor to seek redress for injury (*pace* Cicero), but to bear injury (and worse). The pleasures of the senses need to be recalled to their proper function. Ocular pleasure, such as experienced by spectators at the games, is polluting, especially when killing is part of the spectacle; but all killing is criminal, including soldiering, prosecuting for a capital penalty and exposure of children. The pleasure of touch, which amounts to lust, serves God's design to propagate the species and to enable the virtue of continence to emerge, but it too readily becomes a tool of the devil. In the matter of sexual behaviour, divine law rises above human law, in for example enjoining chastity on both husbands and wives and in condemning homosexuality. In sum, the proper sacrifice for God is a life of justice, patience, faith, innocence, chastity and abstinence. This is the true religion.

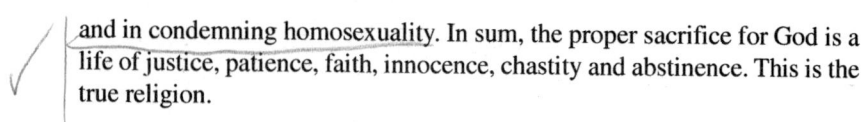

Book 7

Worshipping the true God through thick and thin would have no point were it not for the promised reward of perpetual bliss. To grasp the reality of this, one must understand why the world, and man, were made, and the timing of the end. The philosophers understood none of these things because they relied on human wisdom. They made contact with the truth, but could not see the whole picture, and were unable to mount a proper defence (e.g. in the face of Epicurean arguments against the immortality of the soul). Things were made for a purpose, there was a plan: the world was made for man (who alone has a divine element in him, and the capacity for virtue), and man was made for God (to worship him and honour him as father).

Why did God set up good and evil? Man is shaped out of opposed elements; he had to be offered both good to use and evil to shun. Virtue could not exist without vice: without an enemy there would be no victory. Man has two lives, one temporary and assigned to the body, the other eternal and related to the soul. We receive immortality in our second life as a reward for our labours in the first.

The end will come 6000 years after the beginning, which means rather soon – in 200 years at most. The destiny of Rome holds the key; by controlling the world Rome is putting off the end, which will be catastrophic. Society and morality will fall apart, justice will be put to flight. Christ will come again, however, to reign in the Holy City in justice and peace for 1000 years. At the end of the millennium, the release of the devil and his mustering of the nations and siege of the Holy City will usher in the final showdown, when God will conquer evil and transform the world and man. At the same time, the dead will be resurrected and God will decide the eternal fate of all mankind in the Last Judgement. Therefore, adopt the true religion with wisdom, opt for justice, fight for God and against evil, and win the prize for virtue!

Genre

This is Christian apologetic. It belongs in a succession of such works. On the Greek side, the line runs from Aristides through Melito, Athenagoras, Justin, Tatian and Theophilus, to Clement of Alexandria and Origen, and on the

INTRODUCTION 13

Latin side, from Tertullian, Minucius Felix and Cyprian to Arnobius and Lactantius. Lactantius mentions only the first three Latins. He makes most use of the *Octavius* of Minucius Felix.[29] A prime source of ammunition for his attack on pagan gods, however, is Cicero, *On the nature of the gods* (*De natura deorum*). Books 1 and 2 of Lactantius follow the first two books of Cicero's work.[30] Minucius Felix had used this work too, as a model of style, form and argument. There is a remark of Arnobius to the effect that zealous pagans thought that Cicero's treatise should be burned, because of the effective use that Christians were making of it.[31]

Christian apologetic is an umbrella term, covering a wide variety of examples. *Divine Institutes* is quite unlike any of its predecessors, though there is, unsurprisingly, some overlap in material, notably in the attacks on the pagan gods. The work is nothing less than the first attempt at a summary of Christian thought. The title is revealing: it evokes a manual of Roman law. The parallel with Roman law comes to the surface early in the first book.[32] Here Lactantius claims that although he has abandoned the education of advocates, all that pleading of imaginary cases was not without its uses for him,

---

29 See Pellegrino (1947). There is only one explicit quotation from Minucius Felix, but many borrowings and allusions. On Christian (and other) apologetics there is now Edwards (1999); see, however, the comments of Barnes (2001).

30 See Roots (1988), where in addition it is argued that Book 3 is to be aligned with the *Academics*, Book 5 with *Republic*, especially Book 3, Book 6 with *On Duties*, and Book 7 with the lost *Consolation*. The argument is plausible, and further confirms the already transparent special relationship between Cicero and Lactantius.

31 *Adv. nat.* 3.7: *haec scripta quibus Christiana religio comprobetur*. That the text of Cicero was deliberately manipulated and misinterpreted by Christian apologists needs no stress. See e.g. 1.17.4, where Book 3 of Cicero, *N.D.* (*On the Nature of the Gods*) is read as completely overturning Roman religion, rather than as a demonstration that Greek philosophy is not adequate to explain it.

32 1.1.8–12. There were Institutes, i.e. handbooks, of rhetoric too, most famously the *Institutio Oratoria* of Quintilian (c. 40–c. 96). Lactantius had Institutes of civil law in his sights, however – for example, those of the Classical jurists Marcianus, Florentinus, Ulpian and Paul. In the 6th century there appeared not only Justinian's *Institutes* (of 533), produced by a small committee headed by the quaestor Tribonian and a part of Justinian's grand project to codify the civil law; but also Cassiodorus' *Institutes* (c. 562), of which the first book is known in some manuscripts as *Institutiones Divinarum Litterarum* (with variants), and the second as *Institutiones saecularium litterarum* (with variants). This work in its name and purpose evokes Lactantius, of whom, however, Cassiodorus betrays no awareness. A more direct source is likely to have been *Instituta Regularia Divinae Legis* by Junillus, composed c. 542 by the successor to Tribonian as quaestor; this work is specifically recommended in Cassiodorus, *Inst.* 1.10.1, and was evidently promoted by him. I am indebted for this information to Mynors (1937), O'Donnell (1979), and Caroline Humfress (*per litt.*).

for it has equipped him to be an effective defence attorney for Christianity. He is in no doubt that a discourse that carries the bright sheen of rhetoric will make the greater impact on men's minds. The cause was incomparably more important. If lawyers can give the grand name of *Institutiones civilis iuris* to works designed to settle petty disputes between citizens 'over gutters or water-theft or common affray', how much better shall we be doing in composing *Institutiones divinae* about 'hope and life, salvation and immortality, and God, for the eternal settlement of superstition and error...?'[33] He offers further explanation in the context of a critique of his Latin predecessors in Book 5.[34] Among their inadequacies he counts the fact that their works were little more than broadsides against paganism. He is setting up (*instituere*) something new, making a positive and comprehensive statement about doctrine (*doctrinae totius substantia*): the nature of god and man, the beginning and end of the world, the life and mission of Christ, and Christian ethics. It would not be outlandish to see *Divine Institutes* as a forerunner of *City of God*, a (deservedly) more familiar work of Christian apologetic which doubles up as a *summa theologiae*. Augustine was familiar with his African predecessor's work, and self-consciously sought to improve on it and surpass it.[35]

Authorities

As an accomplished rhetorician Lactantius knew that the skilful deployment of evidence was crucial if he was to make a convincing case against the cult of the gods and for Christianity.[36] His choice of authorities is striking in a Christian apologist. He makes heavy use of non-Christian authorities, both human and divine, and relatively rarely cites Scripture.[37] The African apologist Minucius Felix had shown the way in his altogether slighter work *Octavius*, in avoiding Scripture and employing categories that went back to Cicero and Stoic philosophy. In Cicero's *On the Nature of the Gods*, human *testimonia* come down to the triad of the common man (*vulgus*), poets and philosophers. Minucius Felix reproduces this triad.[38] Lactantius is not

---

33 1.1.12; cf. Cic. *Leg.* 1.14.
34 5.4.3.
35 Lactantius and Augustine: O'Daly (1999), 40–52; Garnsey (2002).
36 To be noted also is his repeated insistence, against a backdrop of persecution, that matters of conscience and belief should be settled by argument rather than force. See esp. 5.19–20.
37 Monat (1982), 20, finds that there are 92 biblical citations, of which 73 are from the Old Testament.
38 *Oct.* 18.1. Clarke (1974) is an excellent commentary on this work.

entirely neglectful of the common man. Early in Book 1 he intimates that if he were to give the question of divine providence proper treatment, he would begin by using the evidence of ordinary people everywhere.[39] However, he is more inclined to lean on *auctores*, that is, on literature, poets and philosophers, to whom he will add, where it helps his case, historians and orators.[40] Cicero, his favourite author, is presented as both philosopher and orator. The relative sidelining of the *vulgus* in Lactantius is not unconnected with the fact that his target audience are *docti*, learned pagans, rather than the mass of *indocti*. His tactic is in line with the 'advice' given to Christians by the pagan critic of Christianity, Celsus, to turn for guidance to the divinely inspired poets, the wise men and the philosophers.[41]

When it comes to divine testimony, Lactantius makes a decisive move away from scriptural authority, specifically the prophets, early in Book 1. He goes back on this resolution only in Book 4, which is his exposition of the life and mission of Christ as foretold by the prophets. 'Their evidence', he says, 'is now relevant. In my earlier books I held off.'[42] In stressing prophecy, Lactantius is again working within the framework established in the rhetorical tradition: Cicero's category of 'divine testimony' begins with oracles and prophecy.[43] As Christian apologist, however, he has in mind for prophecy the special role of linking the Old and New Testaments. Thus in Book 5 he will claim, in refuting an unnamed pagan critic of Christianity (apparently Hierocles) who was comparing Christ unfavourably with the pagan wonder-worker Apollonius of Tyana, that Christ is proven to be the son of God not by his miracles, but by the fact that he fulfilled the predictions of the prophets.[44]

Pagan critics condemned the scriptures for being inferior literature, full of contradictions, and recent and novel. Lactantius tried to counter these charges.[45] But the crucial point for him in determining his rhetorical strategy was that his opponents refused to accept the testimony of the scriptures as divine. So an argument based on Scripture would never get off the ground.

---

39 1.2.4; cf. Cic. *N.D.* 1.24.61.

40 E.g. 1.11.33ff. (Euhemerus, Ennius); 1.14.1 (Ennius); cf. 5.4.6; 2.10.9ff. (historians etc.); 7.22.2 (orators).

41 E.g. 5.4.6: *docti homines ac diserti*; Celsus in Origen, *c. Cels.* 7.41.

42 4.5.3.

43 Cic. *Part. Orat.* 2.6.

44 5.3.18–21. The fact that pagan polemic had singled out the lack of education and alleged untrustworthiness of Christ's disciples, particularly Paul and Peter, would have only stiffened Lactantius' resolve not to argue from the New Testament (cf. n. 37, above). See 5.2.17–3.3.

45 4.5.9–10; 5.2.13–16.

As he says early in Book 1: 'Let us put the testimony of the prophets to one side, in case there is something unsatisfactory in a proof apparently dependent on sources which are wholly unacceptable.'[46] The implication of a passage in Book 3 is that the citing of Scripture is an *alternative* to producing 'fact and proof'.[47] In Book 5 he comments on the same issue at the expense of Cyprian, who had misguidedly attempted to refute Demetrianus from the scriptures: 'Demetrianus should have been rebutted with arguments based in logic, and not with quotations from scripture, which he simply saw as silly fiction and lies.'[48] The better strategy was 'to cite in evidence people who are often used against us'.[49] This means, in the first instance, poets and philosophers, but secondly, divine or quasi-divine testimony which also came from (or purported to come from) the pagan camp: the prophetic pronouncements of Hermes Trismegistus, the Sibylline Oracles, Apollo and others. The latter sources, he claims in Book 7, 'simply have to be believed by those who reject the truth'.[50]

Hermes was a popular divinity under whose name circulated two broad kinds of literature, technical treatises of magic and astrology, and philosophical books bringing together Egyptian and Greek religion and Hellenistic philosophy. Lactantius' interest was in the latter. He quoted from the Hermetica selectively to suit his argument. Thus, for example, we find that Hermes is judged to have said the right things about the nature of God, teaching the 'supremacy of the one and only God most high', who is 'lord and father', but himself without mother or father, and without name and the need of one, because unique.[51] In general, 'he said everything about God the father and much about the son which is contained in the divine secrets'.[52] Lactantius was uncertain how to classify Hermes: was he divine or human, his works revelation or speculation? At one point, he opts for the description *similis divino*; at another, he wonders whether he belongs among the philosophers, perhaps on a level with Plato and Pythagoras. He concedes that there are 'more reliable' testimonies, 'from oracular responses and sacred songs', meaning the Sibylline Oracles and Apollo.[53] Lactantius is unique among the

46 1.5.1.
47 3.1.10.
48 5.4.4.
49 1.5.2.
50 7.13.2.
51 1.6.4; cf. 4.7.3,13.2. See Festugière (1950) and (1967), esp. 28–99; Fowden (1986), 205–11.
52 4.27.19; cf. 4.9.3: 'somehow traced out almost all truth'; see also 2.15.6.
53 1.6.6; 7.13.4–5.

INTRODUCTION

major early Christian writers in trying to make constructive use of Hermes in the cause of Christianity.[54]

The Sibylline Oracles, as we have them, are 4230 lines of Greek hexameters divided into 14 books (but numbers 9 and 10 are lost, and 8 does duty for three books).[55] Books of prophecy were attributed to the prophetess Sibyl, along with other mythical or semi-mythical characters such as Orpheus, Epimenides, Bacis and Musaeus, at least as early as the sixth century BC. The Sibyl was already known to and cited by Heraclitus. The number of Sibyls grew thereafter, notably in the Hellenistic period. As Lactantius reports, ten were known to Varro.[56] The Romans placed a high value on the Sibylline Oracles from early days. In myth their acquisition is associated with Tarquin, and they come into Livy's narrative from the third decade. The collection at Rome seems to have contained predictions concerning prodigies and other strange or calamitous events such as natural disasters or foreign invasions. Using the present tense, Lactantius says they are still retained and used, presumably in Rome. He adds that the secrecy of the Cumaean Sibyl's oracles is respected. Julian the Apostate as emperor wrote to Rome to order the consultation of the Sibylline books. They were destroyed during the reign of Honorius by order of Stilicho in the first decade of the fifth century.[57]

The special value of the Sibylline Oracles to Lactantius is that they are (he claims) the *testimonia* of the pagans' own gods, and he can therefore quote them at his opponents with impunity. As he says in Book 1: 'what better than to rebut them with evidence from their own gods?'[58] In fact, the existing Sibylline books, especially numbers 3 to 5, bear the marks of the creative activity of Jewish and Christian writers. The collection Lactantius was using was probably put together in the third century AD, on the basis of earlier models. Augustine had access to still another version that was circulating in North Africa a century after Lactantius. Lactantius knew, and admits, that Christians were accused of fabricating such texts (Origen records a complaint of Celsus about the practice), but he hides behind Cicero and Varro, and applies what they say of the ancient oracles to the documents that he has.[59]

---

54 Contrast Augustine, *civ.* 8.23; *c. Faust.* 13.1.15 (Manichees use Hermes, among other authorities).
55 See Fontaine (1978); Guillaumin (1978). For the texts see Geffcken (1902), and for an English translation see Charlesworth (1983), vol.1, 335–472 (Collins).
56 1.6.6ff.
57 See Rut. Nam. *Red.* 2.52ff., 55ff. (Stilicho's act a worse crime than Nero's matricide).
58 1.6.17.
59 4.15.26–30; Origen, *c. Cels.* 7.53; cf. 5.62.

Lactantius uses the Sibylline Oracles extensively. There are 57 citations of one or more verses. Moreover, 37 citations appear in Books 4 and 7 where Lactantius is expounding Christian doctrine, and might have been expected to have used the testimony of Scripture almost exclusively. A lengthy prolegomenon at the beginning of Book 4 ends with the reinstatement of the testimony of the prophets. Then the doctrine of the Son of God is introduced. 'That he is the Son of God supreme and endowed with maximum power is demonstrated not just by what the prophets say, which is unanimous, but also by the predictions of Trismegistus and the prophecies of the Sybils.' A citation from Trismegistus, and three from the Sibyls precede one from Proverbs; the chapter is rounded off with two appropriate epithets for the son of God, one each from Trismegistus and the Sibyl.[60] In Book 7 the Sibyls are cited for (among other things) the Second Coming and the rule of the Great King, a Golden Age as conjured up in Vergil's Fourth Eclogue.[61] In Lactantius' view this age was wrongly attributed to the age of Saturn, but while Vergil was in this respect in error, he was nonetheless the privileged carrier of a correct and divinely inspired prophecy of the Sibyl. Lactantius started something here. In no time (that is, in the *Oration to the Assembly of the Saints* attributed to Constantine and dated to 325) the words of the Sibyl were read as foretelling the birth of Christ and the salvation of the Golden Age that he would bring.[62] A century later Augustine was crediting the Sibyl with 'utterances that are manifestly references to Christ', and speculating that she might be included among the citizens of the City of God.[63]

In presenting his wide variety of authorities Lactantius shows an intent to secure a wide consensus behind his arguments. In this he is pursuing a traditional and characteristically Stoic goal. He wanted (in Book 1) to bring together human and divine authorities in service of the argument for providence and a single god. Likewise (in Book 7) he sought to establish agreement on the end of things between 'prophets of this world and prophets of heaven', or as he engagingly puts it elsewhere, 'prophets who act on God's inspiration and of all seers who act at the instigation of demons'.[64]

---

60 4.6.
61 7.24.9–15.
62 *Oration to the Saints* 18. For the date, see Barnes (2001). For the Sibyl, Vergil and Christ, see Lane Fox (1986), 648–60, with bibliography; at 659–61 he treats the relation of Lactantius and Constantine. See also MacCormack (1998), 23.
63 *Civ.* 10.27; 18.23. On Apollo, see 1.7.8–11, 13; 4.3.11; 7.13.1. On Hystaspes, see 7.15.18–19. See Nicholson (2001b), on the 'foreign prophets'.
64 7.14.16, 18.1.

There is the further point, that these sources were sufficiently ancient to give access to a time of primeval innocence and justice when, Lactantius contends, God alone was worshipped.[65]

A consensus so broad could not be achieved without implausibilities and contradictions. No Christian apologist or Church Father after Lactantius was tempted to make Isaiah and Jeremiah share a bed with Apollo and Hystaspes. His harnessing of poetry to the cause was daring. His explanation for using poetry was that, like philosophy, it was 'often used against us';[66] but this does not explain his enthusiasm for the poets, in which he surpassed other Christian writers, and for that matter a number of pagan intellectuals. The appeal to poets had its roots in the old idea that poetic utterance was divinely inspired. There are traces of this still in Lactantius, in relation to verses that he particularly admires, in, for example, Terence and Vergil. He knows that philosophers were thought to have greater authority than poets. Still, it mattered to him to show that poets came before the philosophers; the oldest of them, Orpheus, was 'coeval with the gods'.[67] Poets, however, freely invented and fantasised. Lactantius admits that they produced lies and stupidities, but will not engage in diatribe against them, as Cicero did.[68] Instead he warns us against taking their words literally rather than seeking their deeper significance.[69] For 'no poetical work is a total fiction'.[70] In addition, he will lean on poetic authority, and couple it with that of Scripture, in the most unlikely places, as in the discussion of the Last Days (and, specifically, on the application of the divine fire to the pious and impious). This culminates in the following audacious passage:

> Some people think this is a poetic fabrication; they say it is impossible because they don't know the poets' sources. Their view is not surprising. What the poets report is inconsistent with reality; they may go much further back than historians and orators and other sorts of writers, but because they did not know the mystery of the divine promise, and mention of a future resurrection had reached them only as a faint rumour, they passed it on as a story without credibility, having heard it only casually. And yet they also

---

65 An observation of Nicholson (2001b), 372–74.
66 1.5.2.
67 1.5.4, 15.5; cf. *Epit.* 4.1; 5.5.1. On Orphic literature and the Orphics see West (1983); Graf (1993); Parker (1995).
68 Cic. *N.D.* 1.42ff., 2.70, with Pease's comm.
69 The principle of non-literal interpretation had already been employed by Stoics and Christians vis-à-vis, respectively, myths and the Old Testament.
70 1.11.30. See also 1.9.8–10; 1.11.23–25, 30, 36; 1.19.5, 21.44.

said they had no sure authority to follow, but only opinion; for instance, Vergil says: 'May it be right for me to say what I have heard.' Despite, then, their partial distortion of the secrets of truth, nevertheless the reality emerges all the more truly because of their partial agreement with the prophets, and that is sufficient for us as proof of the matter.[71]

Lactantius regularly exposes the deficiencies of his secular sources. Pagan prophecy, when it hits upon the truth, does so despite itself, and the best of the human authorities – Cicero, Seneca, Plato, Vergil – necessarily fall short because they lack knowledge of God. So how was the gap to be filled? The gap is illusory. Lactantius makes great play of taking Scripture out of the contest. It is regularly denied a voice and the best lines are usually given to others – so, for example, to the Sibyl, on the Fall.[72] Still, Scripture is often on stage as a mute actor, there to confirm the validity of those lesser authorities given the limelight. Thus in Book 2, where whether God made man is under discussion, Lactantius writes:

> Cicero, *despite his ignorance of holy writ*, saw it nevertheless; in book One of *On the Laws* he recorded *the same tradition as the prophets*. I supply his words [*On the Laws* 1.22 is then cited]. Can you see a man there who, for all his distance from a knowledge of the truth, yet, because he could gaze on an image of wisdom, did understand that man could not have been born except of God? Even so, we need divine evidence, in case the human evidence is inadequate. The Sibyl affirms that man is the work of God [a quotation follows]. *Holy writ says the same.*[73]

The audience is regularly made aware that Scripture could be invoked at any time to pronounce on and settle the matter, whatever is at issue. In practice he often decides that to do so would be unnecessary, since lesser authorities do an adequate job by themselves.[74] And he is not without the ambition to give his own exegesis of Scripture, which will sometimes act *as an alternative* to direct quotation.[75] A passage near the end of Book 7 is his last look at the matter of authorities, and nicely sums up his attitude. The

---

71 7.22.1–4.
72 2.12.17–20.
73 2.11.15–18.
74 Monat (1982), vol. 2, 19, n. 46, gives as examples 1.5.1; 3.1.10; 5.4.4–8; 7.5.21.
75 Note 'not my own words' in the citation that follows. Lactantius leaves himself something to do, and this is important. In some contexts, he will take a secular source as far as he can and himself supply what is missing. See e.g. 6.8.11: Cicero at his most inspired has to be supplemented by Lactantius himself. Here the author virtually assumes the role of a prophet, a role to which a mere philosopher could not aspire.

subject is the millennium, which he has just described with the aid of the Sibyls and Vergil. He goes on:

> This is what the prophets said would happen. I have not thought it necessary to set out what they say in evidence because it would go on for ever; my book could not manage so much material when so many people are saying the same things in the same spirit, and I would not want to bore my readers by piling up stuff gathered from all of them; besides, what I would be saying would simply be confirmation drawn from the writings of others, not my own words, and I would be pointing out that the truth is kept recorded not just with us, but also with those very people who keep persecuting us – though it is a truth which they refuse to acknowledge. Anyone wanting to know this more precisely should go to the fountainhead itself; they will discover more wonderful things than I have managed to get into these books of mine.[76]

There is therefore no genuine authority-gap: Scripture is forever hovering in the wings. When Lactantius wishes to use it, he deploys it with skill. It remains the case, however, that a *summa theologiae* which does not draw its strength from detailed and sustained biblical exegesis and interpretation is problematic. Lactantius sacrificed quite a lot (Jerome thought too much) in choosing to conduct a dialogue with the pagans as much as possible on their terms, in approaching them through Classical literature and philosophy. This was a medium to which he was very attached. He had been reading Cicero and Vergil and the rest all his working life.

3. WISDOM, RELIGION, AND JUSTICE

Lactantius is directing his message at men of education and culture, who were also, necessarily, prominent in society and politics. To win them over he must convince them that his religion is intellectually respectable and satisfying. He must in the process unseat the philosophers, the self-appointed champions and commonly accepted models of *sapientia*. He has to show that their idea of wisdom is empty and false, that true wisdom is not philosophy, but rather religion, which is knowledge and worship of the one true God. Fusing *religio* and *sapientia* and establishing the exclusive claim of Christianity to bring them together is a preoccupation with him, and holds the key to the structure of the *Divine Institutes*. He was the first Christian apologist to pursue such a project systematically. Justin Martyr labelled

---

[76] 7.25.1–2.

Christianity 'the divine philosophy', and searched for 'Christians before Christ' as part of a wider plan of reconciling philosophy and Christianity. Others, notably Tertullian and the Greek apologists Tatian and Theophilus of Antioch, viewed philosophy with hostility.[77] Lactantius takes up a middle position, using philosophy where he can to advance his case, but also refuting its claims and undermining its achievements. Augustine in *On True Religion* shows a similar interest in bringing together *religio* and *sapientia*, and shows himself to be in Lactantius' debt in other ways, even if without direct acknowledgement.[78]

Lactantius begins on a positive note, appearing to praise philosophers as men of genuine intelligence who devoted themselves to learning and the search for truth – even in some cases giving up their domestic life and renouncing all pleasure in the cause – rather than to piling up wealth and honours. They were absolutely right to do so, for these latter pursuits are fragile and earthly and have to do solely with the body; they cannot make us better people. He will shortly evoke the example of someone he genuinely admired, Cicero, when referring to great orators who 'have emerged from their life's work of pleading to turn in the end to philosophy'.[79] Cicero had abandoned public life (in fact he was forced off the political stage), and turned to philosophy. In the preambles of all the three books of *On Duties*, Cicero explains and justifies this choice, in terms of the desirability of seeking wisdom with the practical end in view of laying down canons of conduct (*praecepta vitae*). In Book 3 he writes to his son thus: 'Now, my dear Cicero, while the whole of philosophy is fertile and fruitful, and no part of it uncultivated and abandoned, still none of its topics is more productive and richer than that of duties; we derive from them advice for living with constancy and honour.'[80] Lactantius evidently regards his own experience, just presented, in changing from rhetorician into Christian apologist, as parallel to Cicero's (1.1.8–10), except that he, unlike Cicero, knows the way to true wisdom.

But the first paragraph in *Divine Institutes* also contains veiled criticism, in the allusion to 'some' philosophers who gave everything away. They are the same people who in Book 3 are called lesser figures (*minores*) as opposed

---

77 Justin, *II Apol.* 12.5. For Christianity and philosophy, see Spanneut (1957); Chadwick (1966); Osborn (1997). Lactantius had already called Christianity the true philosophy in the earlier work *Opif. dei*, 20.1.
78 Bochet (1998); Garnsey (2002).
79 1.1.11.
80 Cic. *Off.* 3.2.5; cf. 1.2.4; 2.2.4.

to the leaders in the field (*principes*), and are sharply criticised for their attitude to property. They boast of and are praised for contempt of money, but would more properly be accused of negligence for passing up the opportunity of giving to the poor. Democritus is one of them.[81]

Ambivalence towards philosophers is typical of Lactantius. Even when he praises them he will mention their deficiencies: 'It is enough for the moment to show that men of the greatest ability had reached the truth and had almost grasped it, except that they were hauled back by a deep-dyed habit of mistaken thinking.'[82] In any case, in this opening chapter he moves soon enough into a general criticism of all philosophers. They were all, to a man, ignorant. They did not realise that truth is secret, hidden and holy (*arcanum, sacramentum*), God's possession alone, beyond the ken of man, accessible only by revelation. Other faults stem from this central one. The philosophers are unsuitable guides, not surprisingly, because they are themselves ignorant. They also disagree among themselves, another sure sign that they do not know the truth, which is 'clear and lucid'.[83] The fact is that religion and wisdom are inseparable. With this he ends the introduction to the book, and to the whole work.[84]

The next step in the argument is to blame the philosophers for the divorce between wisdom and religion. Insofar as they exposed the errors of false religion, they gave the impression of being wise. But their wisdom turned out to be hollow, in that they were incapable of ushering in true religion in place of the false. This was because they did not know what it was like or where to locate it. Instead they either maintained their allegiance to a religion they knew to be false or they rejected religion entirely. This position is adumbrated in Book 2 and argued expansively in Book 3.[85] In the latter book he fills out his charge of ignorance, while 'admitting' that it was not much of an achievement to demonstrate this, as they 'perish on their own swords'.[86] The best of them (Socrates, Cicero as New Academician) confess

---

81 Lactantius was not predisposed to favour Democritus, as the co-founder of atomism, which became a central doctrine of his bête noire, Epicureanism. For the story of Democritus' abandoning of his property see Cic. *Fin.* 5.29.4; Sen. *Prov.* 6.2.

82 1.5.28.

83 1.1.21.

84 He returns to the same theme at the end of the book, with a reference to the *caelestis disciplinae sapientia*, 1.23.9.

85 2.3.12, 22; 3.28 (summary).

86 3.28.20. This, however, is overmodest of Lactantius. There is much to admire in the skill with which he uses the philosophers to undermine themselves.

that they can know nothing. Even this admission, he goes on to say, is off-beam. Wisdom is 'in not thinking you know everything, which is God's portion, and in not thinking you know nothing, which is an animal's portion. For in man's portion there is something in between, which is knowledge combined with and tempered by ignorance.'[87] In any case the philosophers condemn themselves in other ways, by their disagreements, their moral behaviour and their elitism. He promises to provide in the next book (Book 4) an elucidation of the nature of true wisdom and true religion.

Where is true wisdom to be found? Man is capable of seeking wisdom but will never find it under his own steam. He has to receive it from without, by divine revelation, in particular through the agency of Christ, who was sent into the world precisely to teach wisdom. Lactantius in treating the salvific role of the Son is less interested in the passion of Christ than in his function as teacher (*doctor*, *magister*) and as a model of virtue.[88] Where is true religion to be found? In a religion that recognises the stature and significance of man, improves his moral behaviour, and offers worshippers an intellectual and spiritual approach to their creator (rather than mere physical performance of sacrifice and ritual, as is the case with the cult of the gods). Wisdom and religion come together in the worship of the true God. It is the function of wisdom to understand and the function of religion to honour. They belong in this order, in that knowing God is the initial step that leads to the proper worship of him.

At this point in the argument the dualism *religio/sapientia* becomes a triad with the addition of *iustitia*, justice. How is God to be worshipped? That is the work of justice. Justice is giving God his due, that is, worshipping him, and then giving man his due, that is, treating him with fairness and humanity. Justice, in other words, has two component parts, *pietas* and *aequitas*. Books 5 and 6 are dominated by justice, its definition and elucidation. The trail is already being laid in the early books. In Book 2 the just are described as the worshippers of God.[89] In Book 3 Lactantius asks what the essence of man is, why we are here, and answers, in order to worship God who created us to serve him. What does this involve? The service of God is simply to guard and preserve justice by good actions. As to justice,

---

87 3.6.2.
88 In Augustine's *On True Religion* (e.g. at 55.110) Christ appears as *magister sapientiae* or *Sapientia*. The work was composed in 390, in a period where 'Augustine was still firmly rooted in the old world' (Brown 1967, 146). It reveals the influence of Lactantius. See Bochet (1998).
89 2.14.3 (*cultores dei*).

that is piety, and piety is the recognition of God as Father.[90] A little later Lactantius takes Plato to task. While he appreciated the other main aspect of justice, fairness or *aequitas*, he misread it disastrously in constructing his ideal state. For justice cannot be identified with any particular social arrangements, and certainly not with the sharing of wives and property.[91] Then in Book 4 Christ is described variously as teacher of wisdom, virtue and justice.[92]

4. THE SUPREME GOOD, VIRTUE AND JUSTICE

There is a second route to justice in *Divine Institutes*, leading through the proper definition and exposition of man's final end of happiness and the nature of virtuous living. In the course of his intellectual journey along this route, Lactantius will produce a systematic statement of Christian ethics, the first of its kind from a Christian thinker. This work is begun in Book 3, and reaches its consummation in Books 5 and 6.

Moral philosophy, Lactantius thinks, should serve as the guide for man in his search for self-improvement and a better life. Indeed, this is the only branch of philosophy worth engaging in, as alone concerned with producing happiness.[93] Unfortunately, its practitioners have let people down by their chronic inability to agree, their failure to offer anything to improve our lives, and their wrongheaded searching for happiness in our world. Lactantius could demonstrate this in laborious detail, but will choose instead a test-case, the item 'which is most important, the hinge on which all wisdom turns', namely, the supreme good (*summum bonum*).[94]

Supreme Good

The supreme good must fulfil three requirements. First, it has to be a property of man alone, and must not be shared with the lesser animals.[95] This knocks out such things as physical pleasure, release from pain, or living in accordance with nature (the claims of all of which had been advanced by some philosophers). The second criterion is closely associated with the first:

90 3.9.14–19.
91 3.21–22.
92 4.11.14, 12.15, 13.
93 3.7.1–3.
94 3.7.6.
95 3.8.3.

the supreme good is a property of the spirit, not the body. The body, at its best, as when it manifests physical courage, is striving for its survival, for 'life for a while', whereas the spirit 'wants life eternal'.[96] Thirdly, one must have knowledge and virtue in order to attain the supreme good. In fact, of the various candidates for the supreme good advanced by philosophers, knowledge and virtue are the most promising. Both are peculiar to man and involve the spirit. Knowledge, however, is sought for the sake of something else.[97] In any case, we have to ask, knowledge of what? The Christian answer must be knowledge of good and evil. But knowledge will only bring results, it will only lead to the *adoption* of good and the *avoidance* of evil, if it is accompanied by virtue. Similarly, virtue is not the supreme good itself, but is rather a necessary condition of attaining it. This last criterion, the need to have knowledge and virtue, eliminates the philosophers because of their intellectual and moral deficiencies. Knowledge means, in effect, knowledge of God. The philosophers did not know God, and so their wisdom was empty and false. As to virtue, here the philosophers missed out because they did not exercise justice, which is 'mother of all the virtues'.[98] Justice, we recall, is in the first instance piety, knowing and worshipping the true God. And God's gift to those who honour him is eternal life. The supreme good turns out to be, then, nothing less than immortality, which is 'the only thing that cannot be diminished, enlarged or changed'.[99] This is the conclusion that Augustine will reach more than a century later, following the trail blazed by Lactantius.[100]

Virtue

In *Divine Institutes,* Lactantius engages actively with Cicero's thinking on practical ethics. Cicero, especially in *On Duties* (*De Officiis*) set out actions that are morally justifiable, those that a *vir bonus* might perform, that is, his *officia,* and he analyses those actions in terms of the four cardinal virtues, courage, temperance, wisdom and justice. Lactantius too is centrally concerned with the duty of man,[101] but presents an account that diverges from Cicero's at a number of points. Crucially, the unifying idea in Cicero that

---

96 3.12.6.
97 3.8.24.
98 3.22.5
99 3.12.10; cf. 3.10: the *summum bonum* consists in religion alone.
100 *Civ.* 19.1–4.
101 3.8.3 (*cum de officio hominis agatur*). *Officium* is frequently coupled with *virtus*, or *iustitia*, e.g. 3.21.1; 4.24.7.

man's duties were played out in the public arena, and were owed to the social and political community, gives way to Lactantius' insistence on man's duty to God and his neighbours, including the most humble and poor. In the process, the virtues are overhauled, and a new understanding of the moral life, its character, its goals and its exemplary practitioners, is substituted for the old.

The groundwork is laid in Book 3. The pursuit of happiness, it is agreed, is the business of moral philosophy. But in Lactantius' view, ethical teaching and practice carry a serious health risk: any mistake can mean that one's whole life is wrecked.[102] With so much at stake it is not surprising to find that following the path of virtue is fraught with danger. Whereas the Stoics held that virtue was sufficient for a happy life, for Lactantius a virtuous life cannot be a state of bliss, for virtue is under constant siege from lust, vice and sin. 'All its natural energy goes in the endurance of evil.'[103] 'The only way in which we can know bliss in this life is to think ourselves minimally blissful, to shun the temptations of pleasure, to serve virtue alone, and to live with maximum toil and misery, for that is the training ground of virtue where virtue gets its strength...'[104] It's hard work to attain the supreme good.

At the root of these thoughts is an attempt to give a (non-Manichee) answer to the problem of evil. The result is bold and distinctively Lactantian: 'The purpose of evil is to test a man for virtue, because if his virtue is not stirred and strengthened by constant assault it cannot come to perfection; virtue is the brave and indomitable endurance of evils that have to be endured. Hence the fact that virtue cannot exist if it has no adversary.'[105] The idea of virtue and vice as mutually dependent opposites is a leitmotiv running through the whole work, linking up with other themes and sub-themes, and thoroughly integrated with the rest of his moral philosophy.[106]

---

102 3.7.37.
103 3.11.9.
104 3.12.35.
105 3.29.16. The origin of this doctrine may lie in Stoicism. For the argument that you can't have good without bad, see Gellius 7.1 = SVF 2.1169 = LS 54Q, quoting Chrysippus; cf. Plutarch 1050F, 1051A–B = SVF 2.1181 = LS 61R. I owe these references to Malcolm Schofield. However, no thinker, to my knowledge, develops the argument with reference to virtue as Lactantius does.
106 The doctrine of the interdependence of virtue and vice is associated with two passages that occur only in MSS R and S, and for this reason, and because of their alleged 'dualistic' character, are commonly thought to be later additions made by the author, revising his own text. The two passages in question are 2.8.6a–6i; and 7.5.27a–q, as printed here. See Heck (1972) for a full statement of the argument, and Heck (1975) for a brief summary; also, Perrin

The choice of *patientia* as an exemplary virtue follows naturally from the previous argument:

> With reference to the present enquiry it is sufficient to prove what we mean by taking one virtue. One important and principal virtue is certainly endurance. It wins high and frequent praise equally in the talk of ordinary people and from philosophers and orators. Its very high position among the virtues cannot be denied; but the just and wise have to be in the power of the unjust in order to develop it, endurance being the bearing with equanimity of ills whether imposed or accidental. Because a just and wise man is virtuous, so endurance is with him already: but it will be missing entirely if he suffers no adversity.[107]

Lactantius is leaning here on Seneca, whom he admired. 'He could have been a true worshipper of God if anyone had shown him how.'[108] It was Seneca who redefined the canonical virtue of *fortitudo* by shifting its focus from the display of physical courage on the battlefield to the endurance of suffering inflicted from without, as by a tyrant.[109] Lactantius cites Seneca in this section, but only for the further idea that the suffering of the good is part of God's plan to keep his people free from corruption: 'The good, whom he loves, he chastises quite often, and gives them constant troubles to exercise their virtue, not allowing them to become corrupt and depraved by goods that are perishable and mortal.'[110] The earlier African apologists for Christianity, Tertullian and Cyprian, had singled out *patientia* for brief, monographic treatment. It was left to Lactantius to give it the special twist that it

---

(1974), 86–94. The passage in Book 7 appears to be completely in tune with the other texts scattered through the work that deal with the relation of good and evil, virtue and vice; the passage in Book 2 discusses the creation of evil by God in more detail than elsewhere – but note that there is continuity with the passage immediately preceding, in 2.8. The case for L's dualism is greatly overstated. L. believed that evil came from God, in the sense that it was God who created a corruptible spirit (and later, mankind, similarly liable to corruption), which 'changed from good to evil and of its own choice'. God did this so that man could become virtuous, for without vice to pit oneself against, one cannot achieve virtue. This is a world away from the dualism of the Manichees, which involved an evil *principle* that rivalled the good Creator. That movement was very much a force at the time; indeed Diocletian attacked Manichaeism, in a rescript that survives, shortly before he turned his attention to Christianity. See *Collatio* 15.3 (= Stevenson 1968, 245).

107 5.22.2–4.
108 6.24.14.
109 See Shaw (1996).
110 5.22.12. Chastisement of the good is of course a repeated Old Testament idea, picked up in the New Testament. See e.g, Hebr. 12:1–11, citing Prov. 3:11–12.

was a virtue that can only appear in adversity, and to include it within a comprehensive account of the moral life of a Christian *bonus vir*.

Towards the end of Book 3, Lactantius considers the proposition that man can in fact achieve perfect bliss on earth, if he endures pain, torture, death, yes, even death on the cross, for his faith, for justice, for God.[111] The transition is easy to the presentation (in Book 4) of the suffering Christ as the only wise and virtuous man that the world has known.[112] Later, in Book 5, martyrs are marked out as the true models of virtue, displacing the heroes of old Rome. The comparison is the starker in that Lactantius chooses women and children for his exemplary martyrs. How did Rome's heroes fall short? Regulus opted to keep his oath and deliver himself up to his enemies in Carthage, and suffered in consequence. His choice was an honourable one, but it would still be completely misguided to imagine that he was 'happy in the blessedness of a virtuous soul', for he worshipped false gods. His patriotism, however, can function as a good example for Christians to follow in the service of their own, eternal fatherland.[113]

Finally, for those who suffer for Christ there is a reward in store, immortality, eternal life, the supreme good. Otherwise, Lactantius insists, a life of virtue would make no sense at all.[114]

Lactantius has saved for the end justice, 'the mother of the virtues', and that is the subject of Books 5 and 6.

Justice[115]

'Justice embraces all the virtues together, but there are two chief virtues which cannot be split off and separated from it, piety and fairness (*aequitas*).'[116] Elsewhere these central aspects of justice are defined in terminology taken over from Classical philosophy. Justice is giving what is due, first to God and then to humanity.[117] The principal ingredients of justice emerge in

---

111 3.27.4ff. It is not entirely clear whether Lactantius is conceding the possibility of happiness on earth; he seems to be using Stoic and Epicurean claims ironically here.

112 4.24.7, 12, 19; 26.24ff.

113 5.13.13–15. In treating martyrs as heroes, Lactantius is anticipating a favourite theme of Augustine.

114 3.27.

115 For Lactantius on justice, see Loi (1965; 1966); Heck (1978); Buchheit (1979b); Piccaluga (1996); Heim (1996).

116 5.14.9, 11.

117 6.10.1; cf. Augustine, *civ.* 19.21 (giving God his due).

outline from the 'brief history of justice' that comes early in Book 5.[118] The Golden Age of Saturn was an age of justice precisely because, in Lactantius' innovative reconstruction, the one God was worshipped and the *officia* of justice, namely, *humanitas*, *aequitas* and *misericordia*, operated among men. All this came to an abrupt end when Jupiter drove out his father Saturn and established a regime of violence, greed and gross inequality: in a word, injustice. God sent justice back into the world in the person of Christ, but no second Golden Age could ensue, for most people were (and are) ignorant of the one God, worshipping many gods, and they pursued self-aggrandisement rather than serving their neighbours, and, to cap it all, declared war on the few who were just (a war which at the time of writing was at its height).

To establish justice as uniquely Christian Lactantius sets out to demonstrate that it was absent in traditional Roman society. He begins with *pietas* and moves on to *aequitas*, but in fact these two aspects of justice are hardly separable in his analysis. In Book 6 we are told that what is granted to man as his due (namely *aequitas/humanitas*) is also granted to God, because man is made in God's likeness;[119] and the whole purpose of that book is to show 'how to worship God' in the context of social relationships. So, here in Book 5 Lactantius sets about demolishing 'their sort of piety' by looking at 'what they do in kindness and piety'. Aeneas, far from being the model pious man (as Vergil, who should have known better, represented him), was a ruthless killer who butchered captive enemies at the altar: 'Could anyone think he had a particle of virtue in him, when he blazed in frenzy like stubble, unable to bridle his wrath, forgetting the spirit of his father, in whose name he was entreated? Not pious, then, no way: he killed not only those who yielded without resistance but even those who prayed to him.'[120] The spotlight is on his behaviour towards other men rather than his religious affiliations, though Lactantius will go on to trace the morality of a society back to the values and behaviour of the gods that are worshipped. With gods like those that the Romans worshipped – bloodthirsty, patricidal, adulterous, cheating – they could hardly be good and just. Everything, therefore, stems from the worship of false gods. Lactantius' preferred way of dealing with pagan piety, however, is simply to eliminate it *by definition*: 'If then piety is to know God,

---

118 This runs parallel to, and is in a sense a rival to, the rather more elaborate history of religion of Book 1. The implications for the composition of the work are explored by Fredouille (1978) and Inglebert (1996).
119 6.10.
120 5.10.9.

and the nub of getting to know God is to worship him, anyone without a cult of God simply does not know justice... Plato said a great deal about a one and only god as the maker of the world, but he said nothing of his worship; he had dreamt his god: he did not know him.'[121]

If Lactantius was bold to attack the mythical founder of Rome,[122] he was venturing on truly dangerous ground in denying Romans (and Greeks) fairness on the grounds that they practised social inequality.[123] Christians were open to the same charge. In fact, Lactantius did not himself believe in a society in which all members were economically equal.[124] Here in Book 5 he beats a retreat and plumps for *spiritual* equality. Later, in Book 6, he pursues a different strategy – safer, but nonetheless carrying bite – which involves stressing the duty of the rich to distribute their surplus among those in dire need. This is part of a more general claim that Christianity breaks new ground in the realm of personal relationships.

In Book 6, Lactantius sets out, in clear rivalry with Cicero, the *officium* of man. A whole superstructure, he declares, is lacking from Cicero's account, and it will be his task to supply it by demonstrating how justice in the sense of *aequitas* works. The essence of justice-on-the-ground is, quite simply, to carry out God's commandment to love humanity. In interpreting this divine law Lactantius marks out the gap between Christian and pagan notions of charity, and does so more effectively than any other writer from antiquity. There are two basic principles that must be applied. First, help should go to those who most need it, which means those at the bottom of the pile, the blind, the sick, the lame, the destitute – not, in other words, 'the suitable', including the worthy poor, who might have something to offer in return. For, secondly, any hope or expectation of return must be discounted. 'Measure justice, which is mother and head of the virtues, at its own price and not by its advantage to you.'[125] 'The only true and certain *officium* of generosity is to feed the needy and the useless.'[126] 'The whole point (*ratio*) of justice consists precisely in our providing for others through humanity what we provide for our own family through affection.'[127]

---

121 5.14.12–13.
122 However, Tertullian had been ruder to Aeneas in *Adv. Nat.* 2.9.12ff.
123 5.14.15 and 15.
124 Cf. Garnsey and Humfress (2001), 203–07.
125 6.11.16. But there is a return. See 6.12.2: he will have his reward from God; cf. 6.13: his sins are wiped out.
126 6.11.28.
127 6.12.31.

The traditional value system, in contrast, is obsessed with *utilitas*, the pursuit of individual interests, and is blind to pity (*misericordia*). There are philosophers – the reference is to the Stoics – who actually treat pity as a vice, when it is man's distinctive virtue.[128] But then, the Stoics treat all emotions and passions that stir the soul as vices or maladies. This prompts Lactantius into laying out his general position on the emotions. The result is interesting. The emotions are natural, and it would be wrong as well as impossible to try to root them out, as the Stoics want us to do. At this point Lactantius' favourite argument from the interdependence of virtue and vice makes another appearance. If vice is removed from man, then virtue also makes an exit. If there is anyone with no vices to struggle against, then he will also be without virtues.[129] And again: the impulse to feel desire, joy, fear and sorrow needs to be present in order to keep us on the path of duty.[130] Lactantius has more sympathy with the Peripatetics, who thought that we should seek to control the emotions rather than to extirpate them. But in his view they should be not just controlled, but *directed towards a desirable end*: so, for example, fear towards God, pity towards men in need, anger, as in a *paterfamilias* towards a rebellious son, or in God over a sinner.[131] He is less indulgent towards the sensual pleasures (*voluptates*), but still talks in terms of recalling them to their proper purpose (*ratio*), rather than working for their outright suppression.[132] Even lust, the only aspect of the pleasure of touch that Lactantius is inclined to discuss, was implanted in man by God because of two desirable functions, the reproduction of the species and the winning of praise and glory for its containment.[133] In general, among early Christian thinkers Lactantius does not belong on the puritan wing.

One part of his exploration of justice remains to be discussed: Carneades' attack on justice and Lactantius' refutation of Carneades. This section has attracted attention mainly because it preserves more of the argument presented in the lost third book of Cicero's *Republic* than does any other ancient work. We learned from the discussion of the history of justice that justice has existed on earth since the incarnation, but has not been recognised, and the few who are just (and wise) are dismissed as fools. That

---

128 6.14.
129 6.15.5.
130 6.16.11.
131 Lactantius later composed a whole treatise *On Anger*.
132 6.20.
133 6.23.1–3. For Lactantius on the passions see Nicholson (1997); Ingremeau (1998). For a summary of Classical philosophical opinions, see Gill (1997), and in detail, Sorabji (2000).

INTRODUCTION

is not surprising, since those few have such a miserable time of it, suffering, as currently, persecution, torture and death. The persecution of the just was foretold in Cicero (in the missing third book), where Furius says that only the stupid would opt for justice if it carries misery in its train.[134] We don't, however, have to accept the argument of Furius. In particular, it is not the case that a wise man would rather be bad and well thought of than good and badly thought of. In any case, we can't be such fools if our numbers are growing all the time. Our opponents tacitly admit we are not fools by persecuting us. Lactantius spends a chapter pondering the significance of the Christian virtue of endurance in the story of the expansion of Christianity. Then he asks again why opponents of justice – and Carneades[135] has by now replaced his spokesman in Cicero's treatise, Furius – were able to get away with the assertion that the just are foolish. The short answer is that a justice that had no roots, and had in any case not yet returned to earth, simply could not be identified, let alone defended, by philosophers. This is the point at which Lactantius produces, and argues for, his summary definition of justice as piety plus fairness. That done, he is now ready to take on Carneades.

Carneades' thesis is as follows. People make laws useful to themselves. These laws are relative, not natural. Natural laws would be for the benefit of others. If people aimed at the benefit of others, they would be hurting themselves, which is folly. His first argument is from the public interest, from empire. If successful imperialists sought justice, they would have to return all their gains. Carneades next turns to private interest. Consider the dilemma of a good man trying to sell a runaway slave or a house with defects or copper pyrites for gold. It would be foolish for him to be honest, because a poor price would be the consequence. The wise move would be to make a dishonest profit. Or consider the good man's dilemma where his own life is at stake and he could save it, at the cost of another's. Suppose that a stronger man and a weaker man caught up in a storm at sea are in competition for a plank that will save one of their lives. A just man who is stronger will let the weak man have it, a wise man who is stronger will push him off. In a parallel example, two men are competing for the horse of a wounded man. In sum, justice loses out in both civil law and natural law. Civil law is wise but not just, while natural law is just but not wise.

In reply Lactantius is not unfriendly to Carneades, who, he says, got part of the way: he knew that justice is not folly, and that the truth is hidden, and

---

134 5.12.

135 Carneades is not, of course, a simple opponent of justice, but it is with his arguments against justice rather than his arguments in favour of justice that Lactantius wishes to engage.

he used this to confirm his Academic-Sceptic stance. For Carneades was bent on demonstrating that the truth was unknowable – hence he argued one day for justice and the next day against justice. Lactantius saves his barbs for Cicero, who fudged the issue by having the pro-justice Laelius confine his arguments to the action of communities rather than individuals. But Carneades still has to be refuted. Cicero couldn't do it, but I, Lactantius, can.

Lactantius refutes Carneades by taking a high moral stand, by redefining the key terms of folly and wisdom, and (the trump card) by introducing the notion of a reward for virtuous behaviour. First, the struggle over a horse or a plank would not happen to a just man, because he has no desire for anything belonging to another. Anyway, he wouldn't be at sea or at war, because he is not interested in gain, has enough food, and ranks murder as a sin. Secondly, it is not folly to die rather than kill, but innocence. Death for the sake of friendship or for a pledge is standardly taken as admirable. A life laid down in innocence, a death for God, is better. And we die for God, not just for other people. More generally, folly may be defined as straying in deed or in word as a result of ignorance of right and wrong. It would be a sin to deprive a wounded man of his horse or a shipwrecked man of his plank, and a wise man refrains from sin. Man, having knowledge of good and evil, is capable of refraining from harming his fellows. Animals lack this capacity. They harm people to help themselves. As for wisdom, Carneades 'wished us to see' that the man who stays mum over copper, slave or house is not wise (*sapiens*) but smart (*callidus et astutus*). Dumb animals can be smart too. Wisdom is something else: it is intelligence applied either to doing good and right or to refraining from unsound words and deeds. That is why a wise man does not seek profit, but is sociable and generous, herein displaying his kinship with God. Finally there are the consequences of virtuous action to be considered. It is not foolish to be in need, or to die. A good death is not the end. Virtue is not, *pace* Laelius, its own reward. A human reward for virtue is not possible, but a divine reward is. Without it, virtue would be the most useless and the most futile of things.[136]

Carneades would perhaps have made mincemeat of Lactantius: certainly the argument leaves much to be desired.[137] But let us put things into perspective.

---

136 Lactantius has not yet explained to his own satisfaction why God permitted justice to be construed as folly. He addresses this question briefly, at 5.18.11. God, he says, hid virtue as folly on purpose, to keep his truth secret, to condemn the things of this world, and to make the path to immortality difficult.

137 In general I am inclined to the view that Lactantius' intellectual sharpness and creativity has been underestimated, while acknowledging that the level of his argument is uneven, as in this section.

No other Christian writer attempted to refute Carneades' case against justice. Augustine in his skimpy treatment of the whole episode merely manipulates Laelius' defence of Roman imperialism for his own, theological, purposes. Thus, he agrees with Laelius that 'servitude' was advantageous 'to such men as provincials are... when dishonest men are deprived of their freedom to do wrong', and applauds the way Laelius brought into play a supporting argument from the 'natural' subordination of human to divine, body to soul and desires to reason. Augustine's inference is that some people gain from 'servitude' to other men, and everyone from 'servitude' to God.[138]

In general, we should not underrate the difficulty of constructing a Christian moral philosophy that could compete with and override Classical ethical systems. Lactantius' pioneering work in this area deserves to be recognised. Certainly Augustine's general debt to him is patent. There is a clear Lactantian base to his account of the supreme good, of virtue and of justice. The crucial idea that piety, the devoted worship of the Christian God, is a necessary condition of justice and the other virtues, was Lactantian long before it was Augustinian or Ambrosian.[139] The first substantial account of what just behaviour towards others involved came from Lactantius rather than one of his more illustrious successors. Meanwhile, there is much to admire in the cleverness of the way that Lactantius turns the philosophers against themselves by exploiting the sceptical arguments of Carneades.

5. SOCIAL AND POLITICAL IDEAS: THE GOLDEN AGE, OLD ROME, ROME UNDER THE TETRARCHS, LAST THOUGHTS

Cicero in *On Duties* professes to be addressing the whole of life and more particularly the behaviour of men in society. In fact he gives priority to *certain* social obligations involving a *restricted* class of men. Obligations to parents and to country come first, and the network of social relationships beyond the family involves men of property and status, and, marginally, others of lower standing judged to be capable and worthy (*idonei*) of some kind of exchange of services. In discussing the virtues, even the primarily intellectual virtue of wisdom, Cicero stresses the superiority of the life of action. For Cicero, justice, the social virtue par excellence, is best exercised in practical services

---

138 Augustine, *civ.* 19.21. Ambrose, *Off.* 1.43, says merely that Cicero in his *Republic* thought it important that a defence be presented against the argument against justice.
139 Ambrose, *Off.* 1.26.126: piety towards God is 'the foundation of all virtues'; cf. 127: 'the piety of justice'

to one's country. In Lactantius, the political or civic character of the virtues has been replaced by a strong religious and personal orientation. Justice gives everyone his due. But God has been left out of the equation by non-Christian thinkers: God has not been given his due. The first duty of a just man is towards God. The social dimension of justice that issues in the commandment to love your neighbour is an extension of this primary obligation: *pietas* flows into *aequitas*. This precept is to be acted out in entirely altruistic service of the rejects of society, not those capable of some kind of reciprocity. Given these preoccupations of our author, it is obvious that we should not expect to find in the work a systematic treatment of broader issues of social and political morality. It does not follow, however, that Lactantius had nothing coherent or interesting to say about such matters.

Lactantius' thoughts about society and politics fall into three main categories which flow into one another: a vision of an ideal society with an emphasis on moral values and social relationships rather than on political principles and institutions; criticism of the Roman state and its leadership in the past; and criticism of present policy of Diocletian and the Tetrarchy. All of this is more or less what might have been expected of a work written in the midst of persecution by someone with pronounced millenarianist tendencies. There is no fourth category of ideas, namely a programme of political and legal reforms put together for the benefit of Constantine, when he suddenly and unexpectedly arrived on the scene as a Christian emperor, after the composition of *Divine Institutes* and before the death of its author.

Golden Age[140]

In Book 5 Lactantius is working with, and correcting, the poets' vision of the Golden Age or the Age of Saturn. The main development is that in Lactantius' Golden Age there was no worship of the gods, only worship of

---

140 In Book 5 Lactantius countenances the historical existence in the past of a Golden Age society as envisaged by the poets (but with significant adjustments). In Book 7, he is at pains to assert that the Golden Age will occur, or rather, recur, in the future, following the return of Christ to earth. The poets were at fault in believing that the 'divine visions' they were seeing were of happenings that had a finite end (*quasi iam peractis... quasi fieri ac terminari*); their readers followed them in thinking that 'the events were things that were over and done with' (*completa esse iam veteribus saeculis illa omnia putaverunt*). For our purposes, the discussion of the earlier, Saturnian Golden Age, is the more useful because the more substantial, even if in the author's scheme of things it is of less consequence for the history of humanity than the time of the Second Coming, being an age of primeval innocence which 'took place in the reign of a mere man'. See 7.24.9–10; Nicholson (1985).

the one true God. 'He constantly assumes, and assumes his readers will agree, that Christianity, the Religion of the Most High God, is the original and natural religion of all mankind.'[141] Everything flows from the exclusive worship of God, first of all peace and harmony, the absence of foreign war and civil strife. 'There simply were no swords to be bared at all.'[142] 'What then is piety? Where is it? What is it like? It exists where people know nothing of wars, live in concord with all, are friendly even to enemies...'[143] Lactantius has just graphically described the treatment meted out by the 'pious' Aeneas to *his* enemies. In the Golden Age of Saturn – as distinct from the time of Jupiter, in whose reign Aeneas would presumably have been completely at home – there *were* no enemies, and no imperialism:

> Virtue: to believe your country's needs come first is, in the absence of human discord utterly without substance. What are a country's interests other than the disadvantage of some other community or people? Working land stolen from others by violence, for instance, expanding one's own power and levying heavier taxes: none of those is a virtue; they are the overthrow of virtue. First of all, the ties of human society are removed, and so is innocence, and abstention from property of others, and justice itself: justice cannot endure division in the human race. Wherever the weapons flash, there is her inevitable rout and expulsion.[144]

Justice reigned, without the need for magistrates to enforce it. 'Honours and purple robes and fasces' were an invention of Jupiter: 'When he had conquered his father in war and put him to flight, it was no kingship he then exercised but an impious tyranny, of violence and armies; the golden age of justice he removed...'[145] Lactantius is not impressed by political ambitions: 'Some he puffs up with ambition: they devote all their life's effort and energy to exercising public office, so that they stand in the annals and give their name to the year. Some in their greed aim higher, not wanting to be briefly military commander of some province, but to be called lords of the whole human race, with infinite and perpetual power.'[146] 'He' in the first sentence is the devil himself.

---

141 Nicholson (2001a), 185. As Barnes (1981), 126ff., 184ff., observes, Eusebius too held that the original religion of mankind was Christianity, which he thought of as identical with the religion of the patriarchs of the Old Testament. The idea was evidently current and 'in the air' c. AD 300.
142 5.5.4.
143 5.10.10.
144 6.6.18–20.
145 5.6.6.
146 6.4.21–22.

No formal legal system was (is) required where the law of God held (holds) sway:

> How blessed and how golden the state of humanity would be if all the world were civilised, pious, peaceful, innocent, self-controlled, fair and faithful! There would be no need for so many different laws for the government of mankind, because the one law of God would be enough for the accomplishment of innocence, nor would there be need for prisons and warders' swords, nor for the threat of punishment, since the wholesomeness of heavenly commandment would be working in human hearts, forming them freely to the practice of justice.[147] Civil law, which varies everywhere according to custom, is quite different from true justice, which is uniform and simple, being God's provision for us all...[148]

Laws are an instrument of expediency, not justice. They were introduced to serve the interests of Jupiter and his greedy men of property: 'In the name of justice they authorised for their own purposes laws of great unfairness and injustice, by which they could protect their greedy plunderings from mob violence.'[149]

Jupiter was also presumably responsible for the introduction of 'punishments, prisons, armed warders', in a word, penal law, as a weapon of coercion. For Lactantius, killing of any kind is incompatible with the divine law, and he specifies, among those kinds of killing that are permitted under the Roman civil law, levelling a capital charge. Passing and executing a capital sentence were apparently at least as reprehensible, in his view. The other officially lawful acts that are picked out for condemnation are soldiering, smothering the newborn and the exposure of babies. The list is not intended to be complete.[150]

Social relationships in the Golden Age were governed by the divine law of *humanitas, aequitas* and *misericordia*. But was there no private property, as the poets would have it? Vergil is pronounced to be wrong on this point. There *was* private property in the Golden Age, and the 'haves' shared their surplus generously with the 'have-nots'. It was not the existence of private property that marked out the tyranny of Jupiter from the Golden Age of Saturn, but rather the way the propertied were given free rein under Jupiter to build up their estates and exploit those economically and socially weaker:

147 5.8.8–9.
148 5.9.7.
149 5.6.3.
150 Presence at killing, e.g. at gladiatorial spectacles, is equally condemned: 6.20.15–26. For condemnation of killing in general, see 6.20.15 n. 69. Tertullian had similar views on soldiering: see 6.4.18, n. 13. On infanticide and exposure, see 6.20.18ff., with nn. 70–71.

INTRODUCTION

> The source of all these evils is greed, and greed presumably erupted out of contempt for the true superior power. Not merely did people of any prosperity fail to share with others, but they also seized the property of others, diverting everything to private gain, and what had previously been worked even by individuals for the benefit of everyone was now piled up in the houses of the few. To reduce the rest to servitude, they began first to withdraw the necessities of life, gathering them in and keeping them firmly locked up, so that the bounty of heaven became their bounty, not from any humanitarian impulse – they felt none – but to rake in the means of avarice and greed for themselves.[151]

Lactantius gets himself into a tangle over social inequality. A few chapters after his correction of Vergil over private property he interprets *aequitas* as *aequabilitas*, or arithmetic equality, attributes to God as creator the desire that all men should be 'on a level, that is... equal', and then asserts: 'Neither Romans nor Greeks could command justice, because they kept people distinct in different grades from poor to rich, from weak to strong, from lay power up to the sublime power of kings... Where people are not equal, there is no fairness: the inequality excludes justice itself. The whole force of justice lies in the fact that everyone who comes into this human estate on equal terms is made equal by it.'[152] Soon afterwards he will say that he was really talking about spiritual equality. This is not convincing. He has changed his tune. There is not much doubt, however, that he accepted at least economic inequality in the Golden Age and in his own society. *Gross* economic inequality, though, and slavery, were innovations of Jupiter. In Book 3 he scolds Plato for banishing private property from his ideal state. Having everything in common, says Lactantius, is 'tolerable' as concerns money (even if not women), but is nonetheless impossible *and unfair*, as he claims he could demonstrate in many ways.[153] After a tirade against having women in common, which 'produces adultery and lust', he identifies the source of Plato's mistake in his failure to appreciate that justice 'operates entirely in man's mind':

> Anyone wanting equality among mankind should remove not marriage and property but arrogance, pride and conceit, so that your men of power, the big ones, realise they are equal with the poorest. If the rich lose their haughtiness

---

151 5.6.1–2.
152 5.14.19–20.
153 3.21.2–3. In *Epit.* 33.2 there are the beginnings of a justification of private property in terms of the rewards for 'hard work', and the penalties for 'failure': *nec enim aut obesse cuiquam debet, si sua industria plus habet, aut prodesse, si sua culpa minus.*

and intolerance, it won't matter whether some are rich and others poor, because their souls will be at par, and the only thing capable of achieving that is the worship of God.[154]

This is a preview of his resolution of the dilemma of equality in Book 5. There is a final touch before he finishes with Plato, yet another invocation of the theory of the interdependence of virtue and vice of which he is so fond. When Plato abolished private property, he was also getting rid of the virtues of thrift and self-restraint, which meant that he was undermining justice, 'mother of the virtues'. 'Both virtue and vice take shape from the private ownership of things; common ownership simply gives licence to vice.'[155] Private property can be used well, as by the charitable rich under Saturn,[156] or badly, as by the greedy rich under Jupiter. Apparently Lactantius believed that justice could not exist, even in the Golden Age, unless both possibilities were present.[157]

Old Rome

There is an easy transition from Jupiter's destruction of the Golden Age to the story of early Rome. The mythical founder of Rome, the brutal rather than pious Aeneas, encapsulates the values of an unjust society. Jupiter as 'god' demanded human sacrifice, Aeneas performed it.[158] Then, King Romulus killed his brother and was in his turn assassinated by the senators whom he had himself assembled, a hundred 'skin-girt' old men, and nobody, however humble, would have wanted to marry their daughters to them. In order to stave off the inevitable charge of regicide, the senate through its spokesman, Julius Proculus, hoodwinked the citizenry into thinking that Romulus had become a god.[159] These same 'herdsmen' were themselves easily persuaded by a *foreign* king, Numa, to accept the whole apparatus of

---

154 3.22.3–4.
155 3.22.5–7
156 In 6.9.8 Lactantius uses as a model the Athenian statesman Cimon, 'who gave food to the needy, took in the poor, clothed the naked' – but all in vain, because he did not know God. Clearly, the generosity displayed by Cimon and the Golden Age 'haves' was compatible with lasting inequality.
157 See, however, 3.21.3: holding property in common is impossible and unfair. 'But let us allow its possibility: everyone is going to be wise and despise money.' Well, why not? And are the wise here introduced to be credited with virtue, or not?
158 5.10.3–9; 1.21; cf. *Epit.* 18.1–2.
159 1.15.29–33; 2.6.13–16.

pagan religion. Numa by this means 'soothed the savage temper of a new people and drew them away from war to the pursuit of peace'.[160] His achievement was ephemeral. Corruption set in quickly, through the agency of the very gods who were being worshipped. What kind of a model, after all, did Jupiter, who expelled his father, provide? Or Venus, 'the prostitute of Olympus'? What do you think happens to you if you have before you the example of 'gods of blood', Mars and Bellona?[161] In no time the Romans were manipulating religion in order to expand their territory at the expense of their neighbours and others further afield:

> The gap between justice and expediency is well demonstrated by the people of Rome, who got themselves control of the whole world by using Fetials to declare wars and by using forms of law to cover their wrongdoings and to seize and take other people's property. These Romans think they are just if they do nothing against their own laws; but that can be put down to fear, if they are kept from crime for fear of instant punishment.[162]

One might say that the Romans were operating as a nation in the way that Jupiter's men behaved at the private level in post-Golden Age society.

The passage just cited is as much about the exploitation of law as of religion for purposes of Realpolitik. Lactantius goes on to single out the Twelve Tables as a manifestation of how error-prone and unjust human creators of law can be. So much for the much-vaunted Roman civil law!

Lactantius was the first Christian writing in Latin to attempt a general account of the religious history of humanity and of Rome.[163] In line with his preoccupation with religion rather than politics, when key figures in Rome's history are presented as *exempla*, as they sporadically are, they are normally assessed on moral or religious grounds. The notices are brief: there is not much room for discussion or debate, once Lactantius has laid down the stringent requirement that only those 'educated by God with instruction from heaven' can be truly just and wise.[164] He does lower his guard once to concede that the apparently secondary virtues of *fides, temperantia, probitas* and *integritas* can exist without justice. Old Romans, then, were not necessarily completely without virtue. But heroes such as Mucius and Regulus lost

---

160 1.22.1–4.
161 5.10.15–18.
162 6.9.4–5; cf. 5.6.3.
163 See Fredouille (1978). See, however, 7.15.15, where Lactantius, following Seneca, presents a brief overview of the secular history of Rome in terms of its progress from infancy to old age.
164 6.6.28.

out in the comparison with Christian martyrs. As for Cato the younger, he was as wise as any Roman could be (*Romanae sapientiae princeps*), but is singled out for censure for his suicide, which is categorised as a foolish act of self-assassination.[165]

Politics gets short shrift from Lactantius. Still, from a few remarks that he makes in passing it seems that he was a republican in sympathy. In particular, there is the striking introduction of Pompey in heroic guise as an enemy of tyranny:

> Everyone knows, I take it, how often the losers are the better and the juster party. That is why communities have always been subject to vicious tyrannies. All history is full of examples, but we will be content with one. Pompey the Great set out to be defender of the good, since he took up arms on behalf of the republic, the senate and liberty. But he was conquered, and fell with liberty itself, and was left headless and graveless by Egyptian eunuchs.[166]

Pompey's opponent Julius Caesar receives a damning indictment as 'a man utterly remote from political and personal justice, never mind the justice of heaven'. The deification of Caesar, through the agency of the 'criminal' Mark Antony, was as scandalous as that of Romulus.[167] At least Caesar was a man of clemency, who sought his country's approval 'by the preservation of two fine citizens of it, Cicero and Cato'.[168] Clemency is however the virtue of a monarch.

There are few allusions to the Principate in *Divine Institutes*.[169] At one point, when talking of the ages of Rome, Lactantius represents the 'reversion' of Rome to one-man rule after civil war as a return to infancy. This is no compliment to monarchy.[170] Lactantius like everyone else would have

---

165 On the secondary virtues, see 5.14.10. For Roman exemplars see 5.13.13–15 (Mucius, Regulus); cf. 6.6.26–27 (Fabricius, Cato, Laelius); 3.18.8–11; cf. *Epit.* 34.9 (Cato; cf. 3.19.8: Cato and Catiline as moral opposites).

166 6.6.16–17. Cf. 7.15.16: Rome enters a second childhood with the loss of its liberty. Lactantius may have got his line on Pompey and Caesar from Lucan, with whose epic on the civil war he was familiar.

167 1.15.29.

168 3.18.12.

169 In his invocation of Constantine at 7.26.11–17, Lactantius compares him favourably with the 'good' emperors of the Principate. As patently an adjustment to the original text and an *ex post facto* judgement, this is more properly dealt with in a later section, along with the references to emperors of the Principate in *De Mort. Pers.*. See below, pp. 48–51.

170 7.15.16. He goes on to say that decline into old age inevitably followed the loss of the 'freedom' that Brutus had defended, *duce et auctore*. Being unable to sustain themselves, the Romans had to be propped up by 'rulers'.

taken the monarchical form of government for granted. Virtually from the start of the Principate there was no practical alternative to the rule of an emperor, unless it was the rule of two or more emperors. In places in Books 1 and 2 where he is arguing for the necessity of monotheism he might appear to be expressing a preference for one-man rule – but this may be merely a thinly disguised attack on the Tetrarchs. In any case, no special plea is made for the superiority of monarchy as a constitutional form, and the elaborate comparison of monotheism and monarchy that we find in Eusebius is lacking in Lactantius.[171] It is likely enough that Lactantius favoured emperors who had been (relatively) respectful of their upper-class subjects, that is, 'good' emperors of the Principate such as Augustus and Marcus Aurelius, over the more authoritarian emperors of the late third century and early fourth, but he does not advance their cause in *Divine Institutes*.[172] In any case, a good emperor for Lactantius is above all one who leaves Christians undisturbed. Again, if he thought, like Eusebius, that the birth of Christ in the reign of Augustus was providential, he kept it to himself.[173]

Rome under the Tetrarchs

Divine Institutes should be read as a product of and witness to the Great Persecution, and not as a response to the turnabout in the Church's fortunes that happened under Constantine. Lactantius, of course, lived on into the reign of Constantine. This is reflected in the dedication to Constantine and the several invocations of his name that occur in certain manuscripts, but in little else that is of significance for our purposes.[174] I therefore postpone discussion of those passages until the next section.

In *On the Deaths of the Persecutors* (*De mortibus persecutorum*) Lactantius offers a detailed account of the evolution of the Tetrarchy, relations between the Tetrarchs and the progress of the persecution. *Divine Institutes* contains nothing like this. It does, however, deal in pointed topical allusions.

---

171 For a different approach, treating together the responses to Constantine of Eusebius and Lactantius, see Young (2000), 650–57.

172 For another point of view, see Digeser (2000).

173 An opportunity was missed at 4.8.1, concerning the second birth of Christ. In *Epit.* 38.2, Christ's birth in the flesh is dated (but only that) to the reign of Augustus (*in carne ex homine Augusto imperante*). For Eusebius' position, see *Dem. Ev.* 3.7.30–35; *Prep. Ev.* 1.4.1–6; *Hist. Eccl.* 4.26.7–11 (citing Melito, bishop of Sardis); with Inglebert (1996), 164–68.

174 Alongside the invocations of Constantine, two allegedly dualistic passages are normally seen as late additions. But see n. 106, above.

Among the many pagan gods that are pilloried, Jupiter and Hercules are singled out for attack.[175] Their most conspicuous protégés in the author's day were Diocletian and his co-Augustus Maximian, who assumed the names Iovius and Herculius respectively. A contemporary panegyricist credited them with bringing back the Golden Age: 'The Golden Age which existed long ago when Saturn ruled [though not for a very long time] is now reborn under the eternal auspices of Jupiter and Hercules.'[176] Lactantius, as we saw, blames Jupiter for *destroying* the Golden Age. Far from seeking refuge with Jupiter, as the poets would have us believe, justice was a refugee from Jupiter. In *On the Deaths of the Persecutors* Lactantius paints a picture of misery and decline in the countryside under the Tetrarchs that is sharply at variance with his vision of plenitude and peace in the Golden Age of the Second Coming.[177] In general, Lactantius represented the rule of Diocletian-Jupiter and his colleagues as every bit as evil as the inaugural post-Golden Age regime of Jupiter.[178] His hostility to their regime dominates his thinking in *Divine Institutions*. He is totally engrossed in the struggle of the persecuted Church with a state whose values, he is persuaded, are topsy-turvy. At one point in Book 5[179] he cites Furius in Cicero's *Republic*, who is pressing the argument against justice advanced by the Athenian Academic philosopher Carneades during his famous visit to Rome in the mid-second century BC. Furius imagines a community that has gone off the rails, treating just men as wicked and wicked men as just. In such a situation, he asserts, only a madman would prefer the lot of the just man, 'harassed and seized, his hands cut off, his eyes put out, he himself condemned, imprisoned, branded, cast out, impoverished'. Lactantius goes on to refute Furius' prediction that the just and wise man would prefer to be bad and prosperous than good and miserable, but his first concern is to assert the applicability of Furius' paradigm to his own day:

---

175 As noticed long ago by Baynes (1944), 136. See Nicholson (1984a).

176 *Pan. Lat.* 9(4).18.5. According to Piccaluga (1996), the main function of Golden Age myth in the context of pagan Rome was the flattery of reigning emperors, whether we are talking of the Tetrarchs or Augustus.

177 *Mort. pers.* 7.3: '...with farmers' resources exhausted by the enormous size of the requisitions, fields became deserted and cultivated land was turned into forest'; cf. *D.I.* 7.24.7–8. For the later Christian writer Orosius, the *prosperity* of the period of the Tetrarchs is a problem requiring special attention and explanation: c. *Pag.* 7.26.5ff.

178 5.5.10–11 (Jupiter's actions provide a model for the Great Persecution); cf. 4.18.2 (persecution of Christ provides another model).

179 5.12.5ff.

When he proposed his model, Furius must have guessed what evils would be coming upon us, and how, because of justice. This is what our people suffer, all of it due to the wickedness of people confused. Here is our country, or rather, the whole wide world, in such a state of confusion that it persecutes good and just men, and does so as if they were evil and impious, torturing, condemning and killing them.[180]

The public authorities are applying the laws, to be sure, but those laws are utterly perverse. Lactantius cites the imperial rescripts against Christians assembled by the eminent jurist of the early third century Domitius (Ulpianus) in his treatise *On the Duties of a Proconsul*, at a time when Christians were yet to face a major persecution. In Lactantius' day judges everywhere (it is implied) were employing Ulpian's collection of rescripts as a weapon against the worshippers of God. These people 'call it law when elderly tyrants turn butcher and go rabid against the innocent'.[181]

Lactantius' thinking on political matters does not extend much further than this, though there is one possible exception to which we will come in a moment. There is no doctrine of citizenship, no ethic of participation, and in general an absence of constructive political thought. It is as if he envisages two alternatives, and no more, for the human race: the rule of injustice where crooked human law is administered and executed crookedly, or the rule of justice, where divine law prevails, rendering laws, prisons and punishments redundant.[182] Lactantius has not faced up to the challenge of sketching out the appropriate acts and attitudes of Christians in a state which is *not* bent on persecuting them. What we get instead is a radical criticism of central aspects of the traditional Roman way of life including war, empire, social inequality and the legal system – not to mention the cult of the gods, which is seen as the prime source of the evil permeating the public realm. The author's millenarianist tendencies, visible above all in the final book of *Divine Institutes*, and his experience of the Great Persecution, provoked him into voicing radical views against the political and legal establishment.[183]

---

180 5.12.7–8.
181 5.11.18–19; 12.1. In 6.12.21 Lactantius gives us a glimpse of how good judges (those who were applying the divine law) might interpret their responsibilities: 'A work of justice no less important is that of guarding and defending children and widows who are destitute and in need of aid. This is a universal prescription of divine law, since *all good judges* reckon it part of their duty to help such people and to try to do them good, from natural humanity.'
182 5.8.8–9. For Christ as the 'living law', see 4.25.
183 Lactantian apocalyptic is a synthesis of a variety of traditions, Jewish, Iranian and Christian. See especially Windisch (1929), Cumont (1931), Bidez and Cumont (1938), Daniélou

Tucked away in a digression in Book 5 is a call for religious toleration and the use of persuasion rather than force in matters of religion.[184] This was not the first time such opinions were expressed. Tertullian had briefly asserted the 'liberty of religion' (*libertas religionis*) and coined the phrase. Lactantius' plea for religious freedom, however, is the most elaborate and eloquent of its kind surviving from antiquity. Where did it come from? The argument is rooted in his specifically Christian understanding of God's purpose in creation and his salvific strategy for fallen man. He skirts this territory here, perhaps because he is purporting to be appealing to the highest authorities for a change in policy, and sees it as impolitic (or simply pointless) before such an audience to base his plea on overtly Christian doctrine. The full case, drawing also on material located elsewhere in the work, might be presented as follows:

Religion is, and should be, free and voluntary.[185] This was God's own prescription.[186] He created man to worship and honour him as father,[187] but will not accept devotion that is forced or unwilling, holding it to be empty and not deserving of his love in return: 'Since worship of God is an act of heavenly service, it needs the maximum of devotion and loyalty. How will God love a worshipper if the worshipper doesn't love him?...'[188]

The first man was free to sin if he wished, and unfortunately he used that freedom to make the wrong choice.[189] Again, God rejected the imposition of religion by force when he came to earth as Christ. The very reason he came as a man was to maintain man's freedom of choice. Christ came as a *teacher* to guide men towards the true religion. A consequence of this was that he was constrained to carry out his own advice. He therefore had to battle against evil, pursue virtue, in short, demonstrate by his own example that man could conquer sin. 'Every individual on the receiving end of advice is

---

(1948), Hinnels (1973), Fabrega (1974), Rowland (1982), Charlesworth (1983–85), Nicholson (1985), Daley (1991), Cohn (1993), Daley (1998), Frankfurter (1998), Hultgård (1998).

184 5.19.10–26; 20.5–11.

185 5.19.23: 'There is nothing that is so much a matter of willingness as religion.'

186 We may compare Tertullian's bald statement that 'It is ordained by both man-made *and natural law* that each person may worship whatever he wishes', insofar as 'natural law' is identical with divine law: *Ad Scap.* 2.2. By man-made law, Tertullian may have in mind Trajan's famous ruling that Christians were not to be hunted down (Pliny, *Ep.* 96–97), a ruling that was countermanded by persecuting emperors, but after Tertullian's time.

187 7.5.1–5, 27; 7.6.1–2.

188 5.19.26.

189 This is implied in Lactantius' version of the Fall as told in 2.12.

reluctant to accept the need to obey it, *rather as if his right to freedom were being denied him.*' And this attitude (says Lactantius) is entirely reasonable. 'It is an extraordinary desire of yours to want to impose laws on a free man that you don't obey yourself.'[190] Christ's strategy was to 'shame' rather than 'coerce' men into obeying him, 'and still leave them freedom'. This in turn entitled him to reward the obedient who 'could have disobeyed had they wanted', and punish the disobedient 'because they could have obeyed if they wished'.[191]

Now, however, we have a situation where men are denying the freedom of religion laid down by God, and in the most ruthless and brutal manner. Worse, it is precisely those who want to worship the true God who are being subjected to violence and death. This is sacrilegious and polluting.[192] There is another way, an alternative to the persecution of the innocent and just, namely, rational argument: 'Let them come out into the open, pontiffs great and lesser, flamens, augurs, kings of sacrifice, and all who are priests and spokesmen of the cults, and let them invite us to a meeting and encourage us to adopt cults of gods.'[193]

As it happens, brute force is not working. 'Worship of God increases the more they try to suppress it.' The defence of religion by endurance and death 'is acceptable to God and adds authority to the religion'. Finally, God, as a good general, will reward those who serve him well.[194] Conversely, he will eventually exact revenge from those who hate him, and will cast them into outer darkness. Even at the end, it seems, God will not compromise his principles and compel the unwilling to believe.

It had always been open to a Christian spokesman to put together an argument along these lines. Lactantius was the first to do it in style, having taken over the baton from Tertullian. It was persecution that forced it out of him. Conversely, the changed position of the Church, the fact that it was successively tolerated, favoured and established as the religion of the empire, helps to explain the failure of later leaders of the Church to restate or develop his arguments. One final thought: Lactantius argued that no one

---

190 4.23.3, 5, and in general.
191 4.24.7. See, briefly, Spanneut (1969) 146–47; Perrin (1981), 459–60.
192 Cf. 5.19.23: 'If you want to defend religion by bloodshed…, then at once it will not be so defended: it will be polluted and outraged.'
193 5.19.10. There is no sign, and no likelihood, that the arguments that were made publicly by the unknown philosopher and Hierocles on the eve of the Great Persecution were part of a debate with Christians.
194 5.19.9, 24 and 25.

should be forced to follow a particular religion; he might have made it even more embarrassing for succeeding Christian spokesman had he put the case (which he does not) for a community that was *pluralistic* and tolerant, in which minority beliefs would not be repressed or disadvantaged by a prevailing orthodox Christianity.

Last Thoughts

Lactantius until his late middle age was a faithful servant of Rome, a prime witness to the success of the Romans in spreading their culture and values among the provincial elites of the West. Conversion to Christianity (and to a brand of Christianity that eschewed political involvement and looked instead to the imminent arrival of the Kingdom of God), followed within a short space of time by the shock of the Great Persecution, profoundly transformed his outlook and attitudes. The Lactantius on view in *Divine Institutes* is in violent reaction against the Roman establishment and its value-system. Of course, Lactantius as Christian convert had not lost contact altogether with the Romanitas that had formed him and of which he had been a leading representative. Above all, his deep attachment to the Classical literary tradition shines through on every page of his written work.[195] It was thus in principle possible that, when a second revolution in his circumstances occurred with the arrival of a Christian emperor on the throne and the duty imposed on Lactantius by that emperor of educating his son,[196] he would seek ways of reconciling traditional Roman values, which might be represented as having been sidelined or overturned in the years of persecution, with those of the newly evolving Christian state. What indications are there, then, that he revised his attitude to politics and on the issue of the involvement of Christians in public life?

There is, first, a modest lifting of the veil on the period of the Principate, which he had passed over virtually without comment. In the invocation of Constantine inserted into Book 7 (but not in the shorter, parallel passage in Book 1), the emperor is said 'not just to equal but also, and most importantly, to surpass the glory of emperors of old, even though by reputation

---

[195] Note too the many references, not all of them casual, to Roman institutions, especially public administration, the civil law, the family and the army. See e.g. 2.16.7–8; 3.8.1; 4.3.15, 11.14; 6.4.17ff.; 7.7.25 (by implication favourable to the Roman empire).

[196] See Nicholson (2001a), 184: 'the earliest surviving Christian writer known to have been involved in the world of imperial politics'.

they are counted among the good emperors'. Those emperors could not have possessed more than 'a likeness of justice' because they did not know God as master of the universe.[197] Their shortcomings, in other words, are parallel to those of the more admirable philosophers and statesmen of classical antiquity – Plato, Cicero, Seneca, Cimon, Regulus and the like.

Traditionally, emperors were 'good' if the Roman aristocracy judged them to be so, because they did not lord it over the senate but treated it with relative respect. Lactantius might have made something of the senate's endorsement of Constantine following his victorious entry into Rome in 312, as indeed he did in *On the Deaths of the Persecutors*, the triumphalist tract written soon after the collapse of the persecution, and as Eusebius was to do more elaborately in his *Life of Constantine*.[198] The absence of this motif in the invocation to Constantine suggests that Lactantius' historical interests in *Divine Institutes* are still narrowly focused on religion – than which, he was convinced, 'nothing matters more in human affairs'.[199] If emperors were good, it was because they did not persecute Christians. This doctrine was laid down unambiguously in *On the Deaths of the Persecutors*. Nero and Domitian are there, predictably, singled out as enemies of the Church. It is true that in the case of Domitian it is mentioned that once he was dead the senate annulled his legislation and attacked his name. No special reason is given for this, beyond the general characterisation of the emperor as 'unpopular' and 'despotic', and Lactantius passes on to his real interest, which is how Domitian's death affected the fortunes of Christianity:

> The Church was not just restored to its previous state, it shone out with far more brilliance and success than before; and in the period that followed, when many good emperors guided and controlled the Roman empire, the Church suffered no attacks from her enemies while it extended its hands both to East and to West...[200]

---

197 *Mort. pers.* 2–3; *D.I.* 7.26.10e, pp. 668–69 Brandt. Augustine too bypassed the Principate in *City of God*. See Inglebert (1996), 445–48.

198 Eusebius, *Vita Const.* 39–41; Lactantius, *Mort. pers.* 44.10–12. Otherwise in this latter work the senate is noticed only at 3.3ff. (see below). See Nicholson (2001b), 180ff., for the re-use of old imperial portraits by Constantine, 'which might suggest an association with the "good emperors" of the past'. It would be too much to suggest that Lactantius was alluding to this practice in his invocation to Constantine.

199 5.19.21.

200 *Mort. pers.* 3.4–5. At 1.7 in a programmatic note, Lactantius announces that his aim in the work is 'to explain from the beginning, since the Church's foundation, who were its persecutors and with what penalties the severity of the heavenly Judge punished them.'

In general, the invocations to Constantine are empty of the political theology produced by Eusebius in his Christian version of Neopythagorean kingship theory.[201] What Lactantius furnishes is bare-bones panegyric: you are special, Constantine, you are the first emperor, the only emperor, to acknowledge the true God (thereby showing your superiority over 'good' emperors of the past). God is behind your success; with divine aid you have brought justice back to the world. May God continue to support you, as you protect the realm and punish the remaining enemies of religion.

The invocations to Constantine include no practical policy recommendations, beyond the advice, which Constantine hardly needed, to mop up the pockets of resistance to his rule and to the rehabilitation of the Church. The call for religious toleration is not restated; nor is there any indication that the original plea in Book 5, which was clearly aimed at the persecuting government of the Tetrarchs, was rewritten as a piece of advice for the new regime. Lactantius in his last years will have witnessed some at least of the government's actions against schism, heresy and paganism. 'This was not an era of tolerance, it was a time of revolution and conversion.'[202]

The *Epitome* to the *Divine Institutes*, composed around 320, is an obvious place in which to look for afterthoughts and adjustments. One catches the eye. Military service has been dropped from the catalogue of examples of unlawful killing, to be replaced by suicide, condemned as murder elsewhere in *Divine Institutes*. Constantine for much of his reign was heavily engaged in military activities, some of which at least Lactantius would probably have applauded, such as the war against Licinius who had renewed the policy of persecution of Christians in the East.[203]

Then again, in the late treatise *On Anger*, Lactantius seems to be taking a more constructive line on the duties of the judiciary: in *Divine Institutes* judges are merely the executors of injustice, and Christians are advised to stay away from the courts, leaving it to God to exercise judgement.[204] In one extended passage in *On Anger*, the following argument is presented, here summarised: it would be quite wrong to label all punishment as evil and

---

201 See Centrone (2000), 567–74 (Neopythagoreans); Inglebert (1996), 153–75 (Eusebius).
202 Nicholson (2001a), 184. Eusebius records these events with enthusiasm. See *Vita Const.* 3.63–6; 4.23–5; with Cameron and Hall (1999), *ad loc*; Barnes (1981), 54–61(persecution of Donatists).
203 *Epit.* 59.3; cf. *D.I.* 3.18.5. Lactantius' penchant for metaphors from the army and warfare, and in particular the extraordinary military imagery of his eschatology, already suggests a tension in *D.I.*
204 6.18.

malicious, for that would be tantamount to condemning as immoral laws that penalise criminals and judges who execute the laws and inflict capital punishment. Rather, the law is just that lays down for the offender the penalty that he merits, and the judge is good and upright who punishes crimes, because he protects the good in punishing the evil. The judge in this respect is like the head of household (*paterfamilias*), and indeed God. In one respect, however, the judge's position is different. God and a head of household are fully entitled to feel anger at the offences of those under their authority, but a judge is not. For he is merely a servant of the laws which he has not himself formed. Moreover, he has not himself witnessed the crime, and may even be dealing with someone who is innocent.[205]

Given time, Lactantius might have changed his position significantly on politics, citizenship, law and war. He certainly takes a hard line in *On Anger* against sinners and rebellious sons. The aim of that treatise is to argue, against various philosophical and religious positions, that God is justified in feeling angry at the sinful and wicked, and should in fact do so. As God, so his servants on earth. In the matter of the responsibility of judges and its limits, as with divine anger, Augustine's views happen to be very close to those of Lactantius.[206]

6. CONCLUSION

Lactantius was a famous teacher of Latin rhetoric who in late middle age discovered Christianity and used the skills he had perfected in the schoolroom to defend it in its darkest hours. There had been numerous earlier apologies for Christianity, but *Divine Institutes* was different, in two main ways. First, it makes extensive use of authorities that were pagan, or had a pagan past (the Sibylline Oracles), and was correspondingly sparing in its citation of Scripture. Secondly, it combined an attack on pagan religion and a comprehensive (if summary) account of the Christian faith. This was a calculated attempt to break down the barrier between Christianity and the educated classes of the Roman empire. With this end in view, Lactantius tapped into the Classical literary and philosophical literature, enlisting as unwitting allies writers such as Cicero, Seneca, Vergil and Terence. In an even bolder move, he used selective quotation from the Hermetic and

---

205 *De ira* esp. 17–18.
206 See e.g. Augustine, *civ.* 10.6; 1.21; 19.6; Mainz 54, in Dolbeau (1996), 269ff. See Micka (1943) for the opposing positions on divine anger of Arnobius and Lactantius. Who knows, Lactantius might have gone on to develop views on just wars similar to those of Augustine.

oracular literature, which (as he saw it) gave access to the earliest era of mankind's presence in the world, at a time when (he was persuaded) God was universally worshipped, to press the case for the fact of monotheism and the truth of Christianity. Having thus gone halfway to meet his target audience, he set before them a thinking man's faith, a *religio* that was the embodiment of *sapientia*. Christianity, he argued, gives access to the one true source of wisdom, unlike philosophy, with its umpteen conflicting theories and opinions, and unlike also the 'spokesmen of the cults', who seem quite unable to 'come out into the open' and argue the case for polytheism, its origins, 'the source and the system', the 'profit' and the 'penalty' for those who accept or reject it, with the aid of 'proofs from heaven'.[207]

Christianity in contrast affords an entrée to the knowledge of the nature of God, his reasons for creating man, man's essence, destiny and obligations. For man has definite, prescribed responsibilities that have to be met if he is achieve his designated end, eternal life, which is the highest good. For this purpose he must be equipped with the full armoury of virtues, in the first instance justice, at once the prime virtue and the sum of the virtues. We have here entered the sphere of ethics, flagged by Lactantius as the only department of philosophy worth involving oneself in, as alone concerned with human happiness. It is in this area that Lactantius makes his mark as pioneer and prophet. If his singular contribution as the first major Christian moral philosopher has gone more or less unnoticed, the reason lies in the shadows cast by the great Christian theologians of the late fourth and early fifth centuries.

An investigation of man's response to God takes one to the heart of justice. Taking the classical definition of justice as 'giving that which is due', Lactantius shows that there is, and always has been, a missing dimension: God has not received his due. One part of justice therefore is *pietas,* the honouring and worshipping of the creator and father of mankind. The other component of justice, hardly separable from *pietas* in his view, is *aequitas*, fairness, which is identified with the New Testament doctrine of loving your neighbour. A (typically) loosely structured argument leaves room for several striking cameos such as the Carneades debate, the attack on the social inequalities of ancient societies Greek and Roman, and the comparison of Christian and pagan giving. Arresting subsidiary themes include the necessary coexistence and interdependence of good and evil, the superiority of persuasion and debate over coercion in matters of religion, and the positive

---

[207] 5.19.10.

value of the emotions and passions. It is while treating the sense of sight and the feelings that it provokes that he launches his remarkable onslaught on killing in all its forms, including soldiering, bringing a capital charge and exposing unwanted babies.

The lengthy discussion of justice and the other virtues contains no instruction about duties to the fatherland, no doctrine of public service. Virtues that were predominantly public and civic in Cicero are private and religious in Lactantius. This is explicable enough in a spokesman for an unlawful religion. Once Christians were stripped of their civil rights by the Tetrarchs, participation in politics was of course completely out of the question. The several edicts against the Christians, and the anti-Christian measures of the political and legal authorities in general, gave Lactantius the incentive (if he needed it) not only to deny the authority of the law as presently embodied in the measures of the legal authorities, but also to press the argument for the superiority of natural over civil law. This explains the publicity he gives (unusually for a Christian author, indeed for any contemporary writer) to Carneades' notorious speeches for and against justice and to the attempt of Cicero to resolve the issue in the lost Third Book of his Republic. Lactantius shows, using Carneades as *his* spokesman, that civil law is enacted and enforced in the selfish interests of a community and the individuals. He then proceeds to prove, this time against Carneades (though he would like to think that Carneades is secretly on his side), that natural law is just *but also wise*.

It is to Augustine rather than to Lactantius that we must turn for the wider implications of the biblical instruction to love and serve one's neighbour, or for constructive thinking about the duties of a Christian citizen of the Roman empire. Lactantius' thought is on the one hand utopian and on the other destructive of established and traditional political and social values (and these two strands in his thinking are necessarily interwoven). We wonder how he might have set about picking up the pieces, if he had had the time, energy and inclination. Lactantius had once been a loyal servant of Rome, proud of the heights he had reached in his profession and of his achievement in launching the careers of a generation of leaders of North African and Roman society. Conversion to Christianity, closely followed by a punishing persecution, radicalised him and led him to write off the establishment and its system of values. Even so, there are glimpses of the old Lactantius in *Divine Institutes*, in his conspicuous attachment to the Classical literary tradition, his willingness to bring Roman law into play where it aided his argument, his acceptance of economic inequality, and his strong sense of the need for discipline in the household. And as we saw, there are some hints in his post-persecution writing that he was beginning to adjust his thinking. The indications are few, and we should not assume that his second thoughts would have been universally constructive. Would he have argued so strongly, or at all, for religious toleration in his contemplated works on Jews and on heretics? In any case, we have to work with what we have, and that is a Christian thinker trapped in the thought world of the pre-Constantinian era, and a singular work, which is at once a passionate, witty and sustained defence of his new-found faith, and an intelligent and individual interpretation of the religious history of man, the mission and teaching of Christ, and Christian precepts for living.

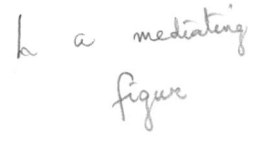

LACTANTIUS
DIVINE INSTITUTES

BOOK 1: FALSE RELIGION

Aims and methods

1.1 In the days when men of outstanding ability made a serious commitment to learning, they dropped every activity both public and private and devoted all the effort they could spend on it to the search for truth. They thought it far more glorious to investigate and understand the essence of things human and divine than to concentrate on piling up wealth and accumulating honours. 2 Those are fragile and earthly aims, and concern only the physical self, and so they cannot make anyone a more honest or a more just person. 3 These men certainly deserved their acquaintance with truth: their desire to know it was so strong that they wanted to put it before all else; 4 some abandoned all they had and renounced every pleasure, as is agreed, in order to strip themselves bare and follow virtue pure and simple.[1] The very word virtue and the power of it had so much weight with them that in their judgment it contained in itself the prize of the supreme good.

5 But they did not achieve their desire; they wasted their effort along with their energy, because truth (which is a secret of God most high, the creator of all things) cannot be grasped by the intelligence and the senses that serve it: there would otherwise be no difference between God and man if the planning and thinking of God's eternal greatness could be attained by human thought. 6 As it is impossible for divine thinking to become known to man by his own efforts, so God has not allowed man in his search for the light of wisdom to go astray any longer, wandering in inescapable darkness with nothing to show for his toil: eventually he opened man's eyes and made him a gift of the acquisition of truth, first to demonstrate that human wisdom is non-existent, and then to show the errant wanderer the path to immortality.

7 Few take advantage of this bountiful gift from heaven; the truth is wrapped in obscurity. Learned men despise it since it lacks suitable champions while the ignorant hate it because of its natural austerity, something that human nature, prone to vice, cannot bear. In all the virtues there is an admixture of bitterness, whereas the vices are spiced with pleasure, and so

---

1 L. probably has Democritus in mind (cf. 3.23.4); see Cic. *Fin.* 5.87, and note on 2.2 below.

people are put off by the one and beguiled by the other, and they plunge headlong into the embrace of evil rather than good because they are misled by a phantom of good. In this confusion I am sure that help is needed if the learned are to be directed towards true wisdom and the ignorant towards true religion, 8 and this is a much better calling, more useful and more worth boasting of, than the profession of rhetoric, in which we spent so long training young people not to be good but to be cleverly bad. We shall do much better now to discuss the precepts of heaven, which we can use to aim people's minds towards the worship of the true greatness; 9 offering knowledge of eloquence does not deserve as well of mankind as teaching the life of duty and innocence. That is why in Greece philosophers were held in greater esteem than orators: philosophers were reckoned to be teachers of how to live well, and that is a much more distinguished business, because speaking well concerns few, but living well concerns everyone. 10 Nevertheless, the practice of pleading imaginary cases has helped me considerably: I can now use my plentiful command of rhetoric to plead the cause of truth to its end. Though truth can be defended, as many often have defended it, without eloquence, nevertheless it ought to be illuminated and indeed maintained with clarity and splendour of utterance, so that it floods into people's minds more forcefully, with the equipment of its own power and religion and its own brilliance of rhetoric. It is upon religion and things divine, therefore, that our argument will focus.

11 Some of the greatest orators, veterans of their art, have emerged from their life's work of pleading to turn in the end to philosophy,[2] convinced it was the truest relief from toil that they could have: if torment of mind was all they got in searching for what could not be found (peace of mind seems not in fact to have been the aim of their search so much as trouble, and a much more irksome trouble than they were in to start with), then I shall be all the more right to aim for that haven of total sureness which is wisdom, the wisdom that is pious, true and of God, in which everything is readily uttered, sweet to hear, easy to grasp and honourable to do. 12 And if certain people who are professional experts in fairness have published Institutes of Civil Law for the settlement of lawsuits and quarrels between citizens in dispute, then we shall be all the more right to publish the Institutes of God, in which

---

2 L. is no doubt thinking of Cicero. Cicero's public career was effectively ended by the civil war and Caesar's brief supremacy (apart from the abortive attempt to have Mark Antony declared a public enemy in 44–43 BC). Most of his philosophical work was composed in 45–43 BC.

we shall not be discussing gutters or water-theft or common affray,[3] but hope and life, salvation and immortality, and God, for the eternal settlement of superstition and error, which are foul and lethal.

13 This work I now commence under the auspices of your name, Constantine, emperor most great:[4] you were the first of Roman emperors to repudiate falsehood and first to know and honour the greatness of the one true God. Ever since that day, the happiest to dawn upon the earth, when God most high raised you to the blessed peak of power, you inaugurated a reign that all desired for their salvation, and you began it outstandingly when you made amends for the abominable crime of others and brought back justice from her overthrow and exile. 14 For this, God will grant you happiness, virtue and long life, so that in your old age you may still keep the helm of state with the justice that you began with in your youth, and hand on the guardianship of the name of Rome to your children as you received it from your father.[5] 15 The wicked who still persecute the good in other parts of the world will pay full measure for their evil to the almighty one, and the later they do so, the fiercer the payment, because just as he is a most indulgent father to the pious, so he is a harsh judge of the impious. 16 In my desire to protect his faith and divine worship, whom should I sooner appeal to, whom sooner address, than him through whom justice and wisdom have been restored on earth?

17 Let us therefore leave to one side the inventors of this earth-based philosophy, who have nothing secure to offer, and go for the straight path. If I thought that they were sufficiently sound as guides to good living, I would both follow them myself and encourage others to do so. 18 But since they disagree violently with each other, and often with themselves, their route is plainly not a straight one at all; they have each followed the path of their own liking, leaving a great confusion for those who seek the truth. 19 We, however, who have received the sacrament of true religion have the truth by divine revelation, and we follow God as the teacher of wisdom and the guide to virtue: we therefore invite all people to the food of heaven with

---

3 L. is alluding to Cicero, *Leg.* 1.14, where the task of composing a treatise on universal justice and law is contrasted with that of writing on the law of 'gutters and housewalls', and other such humble matters.

4 For the invocations to Constantine see pp. 48–50.

5 Constantius was proclaimed Caesar with Galerius on 1 March 293, and Augustus, also with Galerius, on 1 May 305, following the abdication of Diocletian and Maximian. His responsibilities lay in the West. He died on 25 July 306, and was succeeded by his son Constantine. He was supposedly sympathetic to Christianity.

no distinction of age or sex; 20 there is no sweeter food for the soul than the knowledge of truth. We have devoted seven volumes to asserting and illuminating this truth; it could involve an almost endless, an infinite labour, since anyone wanting to develop the discussion to the full would find such lavish abundance of material that his volumes would have no number and his flow of words no stop. 21 We, however, shall manage it all in short form, because what we have to offer is clear and lucid (so much so, indeed, that it is surprising people found the truth so difficult to see, especially those with a reputation for intelligence), and our aim is anyway one of instruction, of redirecting people from the error that entangles them on to a straighter path.

22 If, as I hope, we achieve our purpose, then we can send them to the source of learning in all its richness and fullness and they can slake the thirst in their bellies and satisfy their ardour with great draughts of it; they will find everything is easy for them, all ready to hand and obvious, provided that in their aim of learning the teaching of wisdom they never tire of reading and listening. 23 Many cling stubbornly to vain superstitions and harden themselves against plain truth; they do no favour to the religions they assert so perversely and even less favour to themselves. They have the straight path, and yet they go a roundabout, devious course, abandoning the obvious line and tumbling over the edge; they shun the light, and collapse blind and enfeebled in darkness. 24 They need advice, to cease the fight against themselves and to will their tardy release from long-standing error; if they eventually come to see why they were born, they will do so anyway. 25 The cause of wickedness is ignorance of self. If a man can learn the truth and so sort out that ignorance, he will then know his life's purpose and how he should be living. I can summarise this knowledge as follows: no religion should be adopted without wisdom in it, and no wisdom should be accepted without religion in it.

Providence

2.1 In taking up the task of illuminating the truth I have not thought it necessary to start with the question which seems to be naturally first, whether all things are in the care of a thoughtful providence, or have been created or proceed by chance. 2 The latter theory was first set out by Democritus, and Epicurus supported it. But Protagoras had called the gods into doubt before that, and later Diagoras denied them altogether, and a number of others thought they did not exist: the result of which was simply the idea that providence did not exist.⁶ The other philosophers, however, and particularly all the Stoics, rebutted them with great vigour: the world could not have been made without a divine intention and could not survive unless governed by ultimate reason.⁷

3 Even Cicero, despite his defence of the teaching of the Academy, wrote at length on many occasions of providence as the guide of things, supporting the arguments of the Stoics and adding a great number of new ones himself; he does this in all his philosophical works, and particularly in *de Natura Deorum* [*N.D.* 2.73–153]. 4 It was certainly no problem to disprove the lies of the few, so mistaken in their thinking, by using the evidence of communities and peoples who on this one topic were in total accord. 5 No one, however ignorant and savage, can lift his eyes to heaven and fail to see, for all that he may not know whose providence it is that controls all that he sees, that some providence is there, simply because of the size of it all and its movement, its shape and stability, its use, beauty and system: anything constructed with such wonderful reason must have been put in place by some superior power of deliberation.

6 We certainly have no problem at all in developing this part of the argument at length: but since it has been much debated among philosophers, and since an adequate response to those who dismiss providence has clearly been made by people of shrewdness and eloquence, and since also we shall have to talk about the cleverness of divine providence here and there throughout this project of ours, let us for the moment leave the question to one side; it goes with the other questions in such a way that plainly none of them can be discussed without providence coming into the discussion too.

Unity of the divine

3.1 We must start our work then with the question that comes next, question two: is the world governed by the power of one god or many? No intelligent

---

6 Democritus of Abdera (*fl.* mid to late 5th cent.) developed the theory of atomism begun by Leucippus. Epicurus (341–271 BC) inherited the system from Democritus, and founded his own school of philosophy. He taught hedonism, man's mortality and the indifference of the gods to human affairs (L. picks out Epicureanism for special attack). Protagoras of Abdera (*fl.* later 5th cent.) was a famous sophist and agnostic, prosecuted by the Athenians for impiety in the 430s. Diagoras of Melos (*fl.* later 5th cent.) was a lyric poet and atheist, expelled from Athens c. 415 for mocking the Eleusinian mysteries. See also L. *de ira* 9.

7 For the Stoic concept of reason (*logos*, *ratio*), see Cic. *N.D.* 1.39: 'divine power resides in reason and in the mind and intellect of universal nature' (Chrysippus); cf. D.L. 7.134: of the two principles in the universe, 'that which acts is the reason in it, i.e., god'.

man who can do the sums would fail to see that there is only one, the God who founded it all in the first place and who now controls it with the same virtue with which he founded it.

2 What is the need for many gods to sustain the world's governance? – unless perhaps we are going to reckon that if there were more than one, each would have a reduced strength and power 3 (as the pluralists do reckon), on the grounds that if no one god could keep control of so great a mass without the assistance of the rest, they would have to be feeble. But God who is eternal mind is a being of perfect and consummate virtue simply in every respect: 4 if that is true, then there must be one god only. Absolute power, or absolute virtue, maintains its own strength; solidity is the quality of a thing which cannot be reduced, and perfection of a thing which cannot be extended. 5 A king who has command of the whole earth is beyond question the most powerful king, as he should be, since everything everywhere is his, and all resource from every source converges on him alone. 6 If the world were to be shared between more than one king, then each will certainly have a lesser portion of its wealth and strength, since each will abide within the bounds of his allotted share. 7 In like fashion, if there were more than one god, they will all have less power, since the others will have only so much for themselves. Virtue in its perfection is sooner to be found in a totality than in some small fraction of totality. If God is perfect, as he has to be, he cannot be so unless he is one, so that everything can be within him. 8 The virtues and powers of multiple gods must therefore be weak by comparison, because each individual god will lack what the rest possess: the more there are of them, the weaker they will be. 9 Nor can there even be division, not even once, of that totality of overall power and of that divine energy: anything that admits of division must also admit of death. If, however, death is far from god because god is incorruptible and eternal, it follows that the power of god cannot be divided.

10 God is therefore one, given that nothing else can exist with a power equivalent to his. And yet those who think there are many gods say that the divine functions are shared among them. We will argue all these issues in their proper place; 11 for the moment I stay with something relevant here: if there is a distribution of functions, we simply come back to the fact that no one of the gods can manage all the functions alone, and one who cannot control them all if the rest of the gods withdraw will not be perfect. In order to rule the world, therefore, we have to have the perfect virtue of one rather than the weakness of many. 12 It is a mistake to think that the world is too big to be controlled by one: it involves a failure to understand how great the

BOOK 1: FALSE RELIGION 63

power and energy of divine supremacy is; it means thinking that the one god who had the capacity to make the world lacks the capacity to control the world he has made. 13 If people could imagine the immensity of this divine work, and that though there was nothing there to begin with, yet it was forged from nothing by the virtue and vision of God – the work could not have been started and finished except by one and only one – then they will understand that it is much easier for something established by one to be controlled by one.

14 Someone may perhaps say that so great a work as the world could not even have been constructed except by more than one. However many makers he proposes, and however great he makes them, and whatever size and capacity, virtue and power he puts in all his gods, I attribute the whole thing to one God, and I say that its very existence is in him alone; thus the quantum of all the attributes in him will be beyond imagination and expression. 15 We lack both understanding and language for this because the human mind cannot cope with such a blaze of understanding nor the human tongue with its description: yet it is our duty to understand and to describe exactly that.

16 I realise what could be said in response, that the qualities we want for our one god are there in the many. But this is completely impossible, because the power of each one of them will not have the capacity to operate across the boundaries of the powers of the others where they clash. Each one must either be incapable of going outside its own limits or, if it does, must drive the other god from the territory. 17 Pluralists fail to see that it is possible for a multiplicity of gods to want different things, which leads to dispute and contest among them: hence Homer's fiction of gods at war with each other, some wanting Troy to be captured and others resisting. 18 Decisions about the world must therefore be made by one. If power over all the individual parts were not referable to one providence, the whole will not be able to abide as one; each individual god will care for no more than matters to him, as happens even in war without a unified strategic command. 19 If an army had as many commanders as it has legions and cohorts, wedges and wings, first it will be impossible to construct a line of battle if any one unit shirks the danger, nor will control and deployment be easy because they will all adopt their own plans, and the differences will do more harm than good. So it is with command of the world: if there were not to be one and only one to whom the care of the whole can be referred, it will all break up and collapse together. 20 To say that the world works by a mass vote is like asserting there are many minds in one body because there are many functions in the different limbs, so that people believe that one mind governs

each physical sensation, and the same goes for the emotions, those agents of our wrath or lust, our joy, fear or pity: people think there are separate minds at work in all of them too. If anyone were really to say that, plainly he wouldn't even have the one mind he does possess! 21 If, however, one mind does have the government of so much in one body, and if it does attend to everything at once, how could anyone think that the world could not be controlled by one, but could be controlled by more than one?

Those who argue for gods understand the point: they say that their many gods are in charge of individual areas, but in such a way that there is one overlord. 22 In that case the rest of them will not be gods, but subsidiaries and servants,[8] and the overlord, controlling everything, will put them in their posts and they will comply with his commands and wishes. If they are not all equal together, then they are not all gods: slave and master cannot be the same. 23 If god is the name of supreme power, he has to be incorruptible, perfect, the victim of no feelings and inferior to nothing. Those forced of necessity to obey one supreme god are therefore not gods. 24 People who think that they are, however, are not being fooled in vain, and we will soon reveal the cause of their error. Meantime let us set up the evidence for a single divine power.

Testimony: the prophets

4.1 The prophets, a rather numerous group, proclaim one god and speak of one god; filled as they are with the inspiration of one god, they have pronounced about the future with total unanimity. 2 Now, those who are ignorant of the truth think the prophets should not be believed: they say their voices were not divine but human; because their message concerns one god, evidently they must have been either lunatics or cheats! 3 We by contrast can see that their prophecies have been fulfilled, and are being fulfilled every day, and the way their divinations converge on one and the same idea shows that they were not mad. Who could be of disturbed mind and not only foretell the future but speak with one voice too? 4 So were they cheats? Nothing could be more unlikely than an intent to deceive when they were saving everyone from deception! That is why they were sent by God, to be heralds of his supremacy and to correct human wickedness.

5 Besides, the desire to invent and lie is typical of people who want to be rich and are looking for profit: these holy men were very far from that. 6 They

---

8 L.'s Latin, *satellites ac ministri*, is used frequently by Cicero in a sinister sense; see for example *Agr.* 2.32.

carried out their appointed duty in such fashion that they abandoned everything needful for preserving life and stopped toiling for the future, or even for the immediate day, content with the food that God supplied impromptu. They got not just zero profit out of it, but torture and death as well. 7 To men of vice and evil living, the precepts of justice taste bitter; hence the great bitterness they put into the torture and murder of those who tried to expose and prevent their wickedness. People with no urge for profit had therefore neither desire nor reason to deceive. 8 Why, some of them were princes or even kings, absolutely not people to be suspected of greed and deception, and yet they proclaimed the one God with the same divining power as the rest did.[9]

Pagan writers: poets and philosophers

5.1 Let us put the testimony of the prophets to one side, however, in case there is something unsatisfactory in a proof apparently dependent on sources which are wholly unacceptable. 2 Let us come to the writers, and to prove the truth let us cite in evidence people who are often used against us: I mean the poets and philosophers.[10] We must prove the oneness of god from them, not because they have a knowledge of the truth, but because the effect of the actual truth is too strong for even a blind man not to see divine brightness when it forces itself on his eyes.

3 Though the poets have devoted odes to the gods and have glorified the deeds of gods in paeans of praise, they are in frequent agreement that everything is held together and guided by a single spirit or mind. 4 Orpheus, oldest of the poets, and coeval with the gods (to go by the tradition that he sailed with the Argonauts in the company of Castor, Pollux and Hercules), calls the true and great God[G][11] 'first-born' because nothing was born before him and everything is descended from him. He also calls him[G] 'Appearer', because when there was still nothing in existence he came into being first and existed out of infinity.[12] 5 Because his nature and origin could not be comprehended, Orpheus said that he was born from immeasurable air:[G] 'Shining first-born son of enormous air'. There was nothing greater he could

---

9 L. is certainly stretching a point; on the other hand, the term prophet was applied quite widely by Christians, to include Abraham, Moses and David. See Jn 8:56; Mk 12:35ff.; Acts 2:29ff.

10 See pp. 14–16, 19 above.

11 G indicates that L. uses or quotes in Greek.

12 *Orph.* fr. 57 (Abel) = 73 (Kern).

say. 6 This is the one, he says, who is father of all the gods, and for their sake he made heaven and looked about for his children to have a place of common dwelling:[G] 'he founded for the immortals an imperishable home'.[13] Guided by nature and reason Orpheus realised that there was a pre-eminent power, the power which made heaven and earth. 7 He could not say that Jupiter was the prince of it all, who was born of Saturn, nor Saturn either, who was said to be born of heaven; and he did not dare set up heaven as a sort of first god, because he could see it was a part of the universe and that it needed a creator itself. This reasoning led him to the 'first-born' god, and to him he assigns and grants primacy.

8 Homer could not have given us anything which would be relevant to the truth: he wrote on a human rather than a divine level. Hesiod could, however; he covered the begetting of the gods in one book's work.[14] And yet he gave us nothing even so, because he took for his start not a founder god but chaos, which is a confused mass of unformed, disordered stuff; he ought instead to have clarified first where the chaos itself came from, and when, and how it began to take shape. 9 After all, the stuff of chaos has to be created by someone, just as everything is organised, arranged and effected by some competent power. So who did make the stuff of chaos if not God, to whose power all things are subject? 10 Hesiod retreats from that, however, scared of a truth he does not know. He did not reel off that poem on Helicon[15] at the prompting of the Muses, as he wanted people to think: he had done his thinking and came prepared.

11 Among our Roman poets Vergil stands first for closeness to the truth; for God most high, whom he calls 'mind' and 'spirit,' he has the following verses [A. 6.724–27]: 'In the beginning the sky and the lands and the liquid levels, the gleaming globe of the moon and the Titan stars, were fed within by a spirit; the whole mass was steeped through all its limbs, and its great body was suffused, by mind.' 12 To prevent ignorance of who that spirit was with so much power, he clarified it elsewhere [G. 4.221–24]: 'For god it is, they say, who goes through all lands and tracts of the sea, through lofty sky; he is the source of the slender life in every living thing, flocks, herds and men, and every sort of wild animal.'

13 Ovid too, at the start of his famous poem, acknowledges without any verbal subterfuge that the world was made by god, calling him 'craftsman of the world' and 'workman of it all' [*Met.* 1.57, 79]. 14 If only Orpheus or our

13 *Orph.* fr. 75 (Abel) = 89 (Kern).
14 Hesiod, *Theogonia*.
15 Hesiod, *Theogonia* 1–8.

BOOK 1: FALSE RELIGION

two Roman poets had persisted in standing by what nature led them to feel, they would have understood the truth and would have grasped the doctrine that we accept.

15 Enough of the poets. Let us come to the philosophers, whose impact is more authoritative and whose judgment is more sure, because people trust them to have pursued the search for truth rather than fiction. 16 Thales of Miletus, one of the Seven Sages,[16] is said to have been the first to investigate causation in nature: he declared that water is what everything is born from, and that god was the mind which turned water into everything else. Thus he based the substance of things in water while he established the basic cause of generation in god. 17 Pythagoras defined what god was as follows: it was a spirit going to and fro, diffusing itself through every part of the world and through all nature; all animals that are born take life from it. 18 Anaxagoras says that god is mind without limit, self-moving. Antisthenes says that there are popularly many gods, but only one in nature, the creator of the whole universe. 19 Cleanthes and Anaximenes say that aether[17] is supreme god, and our poet is in accord with that view [Verg. *G.* 2.325–27]: 'Then the omnipotent father comes down as aether in fruitful showers to the lap of his joyful wife, mingling his greatness in her great body and nurturing all her offspring.' 20 Chrysippus says god is the force of nature equipped with divine reason; sometimes he calls god divine necessity. Similarly Zeno calls god law natural and law divine.[18]

---

16 The Seven Sages flourished in the late 7th and early 6th centuries BC. They are first listed in Pl. *Prt.* 343a. Membership of the group varies; four seem to be constant, Thales of Miletus, Solon of Athens, Pittacus of Mytilene and Bias of Priene, and two others are frequent, Cleobulus of Lindos and Chilon of Sparta. They shared a reputation for practical and political skills; hence the original inclusion of Periander tyrant of Corinth, for whom Plato substituted Myson of Chen. L. owes most of 16–23 to Cic. *N.D.* 1.25–39.

17 The root of *aether* is the Greek verb to blaze; *aer* (whence air: root, to blow) was the atmosphere next to the earth and *aether* the layer beyond in which the heavenly bodies had their being.

18 Pythagoras of Samos, later of Croton, 6th cent. philosopher and forerunner of Plato, is an obscure figure. He founded a philosophical and religious movement which was highly influential in succeeding centuries. Anaxagoras of Clazomenae (*fl.* mid 5th cent.), a physical theorist, moved to Athens and was a friend of Pericles. He was prosecuted for impiety in the 430s. Antisthenes (*fl.* late 5th cent.) was an associate of Socrates and a prolific writer. Critical of conventional religion, he tended towards monotheism. Cleanthes (331–232 BC), Stoic philosopher and poet, headed the Stoa from 262. Anaximenes of Miletus (*fl.* c. 546–525 BC) was a physical theorist and a monist. Chrysippus (c. 280–c. 206 BC) was a leading Stoic philosopher and head of the school from 232. Zeno of Citium (334–262 BC) was the founder of Stoicism. For philosophers and monotheism see Athanassiadi and Frede (1999).

21 The ideas of all these philosophers may be inconclusive but they do point in the same direction in agreeing there is one providence. Whether you call it nature or aether, reason or mind, the necessity of fate or divine law or whatever, they are all the same as what is called God by us. The difference of label is no problem, since in their meaning they all come back to one and the same thing. 22 Despite being at odds with himself in saying and thinking things that contradict each other, Aristotle acknowledges in the end that the world is in the charge of one mind. 23 Plato, considered the wisest of them all, backs monarchy quite openly: he does not call god aether or reason or nature, but god, as he is, and this perfect and wonderful world, he says, was made by god.[19]

24 Cicero follows him closely, acknowledging god's existence in many of his writings on many occasions: in the *Laws* [*Leg.* 1.22] he calls him supreme; in the argument in *de Natura Deorum* he shows that the world is governed by god as follows [*N.D.* 2.77]: 'Nothing is more remarkable than god. The world must therefore be governed by god. God is therefore not obedient to or subject to any natural force. Therefore he controls all nature himself.' 25 He defines what god is in his *Consolatio*: 'God himself, the god whom we understand, cannot be understood otherwise than as mind untrammeled and free, distinct from all perishable accretion, perceiving all things and setting them all in motion.'[20]

26 Seneca too, who was the sharpest Stoic of all Romans,[21] time and again gives god most high the praise he deserves. In his work *On Premature Death* he says: 'Do you not comprehend the authority and supremacy of your judge, that he is governor of the earth and sky and god of all gods, on whom depend those powers which one by one we worship and adore?'[22] 27 So too in his *Exhortationes*: 'When he was laying the first foundations of this beautiful world, and when he was beginning this work of a size and quality unknown to nature, god extended himself throughout its whole body; nevertheless, so that every part of it should proceed under its own proper guidance, he still created servants of his kingship.'[23] 28 He said a great deal

---

19 Cic. *Ac.* fr. 25.5 (Plasberg).
20 Part of a larger fragment cited in Cic. *Tusc.* 1.66 (= fr. 21 Vitelli, in part).
21 *Acerrimus Stoicus*; cf. 1.7.13, 2.8.23 and 6.24.14 (he could have been a Christian). L. Annaeus Seneca (c. 4 BC–AD 65) was born in Cordoba in Spain, pursued a political career in Rome and was forced to commit suicide by Nero.
22 Sen. F61, 176 (Vottero).
23 Sen. F86a, 200 (Vottero).

more too on the subject of god similar to what we say, but I postpone it for the moment because it comes better elsewhere.

It is enough for the moment to show that men of the greatest ability had reached the truth and had almost grasped it, except that they were hauled back by a deep-dyed habit of mistaken thinking: they supposed that other gods existed as well, and they believed that the things God made for man to use should themselves be thought of as gods and worshipped as gods as if *they* were endowed with sense.

Divine testimony: Trismegistus and the Sibyls

6.1 Let us now pass to evidence from the gods. First, however, I will put forward one item which is like divine evidence in two respects: it is exceedingly old, and the human being whom I shall name has been translated to the gods.

2 In Cicero the pontifex C. Cotta is in dispute with the Stoics on the subject of religions and the variety of ideas that there usually are about the gods; in order, like a typical Academic, to keep things undecided, he says [*N.D.* 3.56] that 'there are five Mercuries' and, after listing four of them in a row, that 'the fifth is the killer of Argus; that is why he fled to Egypt and established laws and literature among the people there. 3 The Egyptians call him Thoyth; from him the first month of their year' (which is September) 'got its name.' He also founded a town, which in Greek is still called Mercury's city,[24] and the people of Faenia[25] worship him devoutly. Though he was a man, nevertheless he was so very old and so very learned in all manner of scholarship that his knowledge of many facts and skills gave him the extra name of Trismegistus.[26] 4 He wrote books in great quantity which are relevant to knowledge of things divine; in them he asserts the supremacy of the one and only God most high, and calls him by the same titles that we do, 'lord and father'.[27] And in case anyone should ask God's name, he said that he was nameless, on the grounds that God needs no proper name precisely because of his uniqueness. These are Trismegistus' words:[G] 'God is one, and what is one needs no name. He that is is nameless.' 5 God therefore has no[28] name because he is unique; a proper name is only needed when

---

24 Hermopolis, that is. Two are known, one in the Delta and one in the Thebaid.
25 Faenia was in N.E. Arcadia (Paus. 8.14.6–15.4, there called Pheneos).
26 *Trismégistos*: Greek for thrice greatest. For Hermes Trismegistus see pp. 16–17 above.
27 The first of many references in this work to God as *dominus et pater*.
28 Brandt's addition of the negative is accepted.

a multitude of people needs to be distinguished, so that each individual can be marked with his own distinctive appellation. Because god is unique, his proper name is God.[29]

6 It remains to present the much more reliable evidence from oracular responses and sacred songs. Possibly our opponents think that poets are not to be believed because they construct empty fictions, nor are philosophers because they can make mistakes, being human themselves. 7 Even in Greece no more learned man ever lived than M. Varro:[30] in his books on things divine which he dedicated to Julius Caesar, pontifex maximus, in speaking of the quindecimvirs[31] he says that[32] 'the Sibylline books were not the product of one single Sibyl but were given the one title Sibylline, because all female prophets are called Sibyls by the ancients, either after the one Sibyl of Delphi or from their delivery of god's advice.[33] In Aeolic dialect gods are called *sioí*, not *theoí*, and advice is *boúlla*, not *boulé*: hence Sibyl, meaning god's advice.[34] 8 The Sibyls were ten in number (he listed them all, under the writers who dealt with them individually); 'the first was from Persia, and is mentioned by Nicanor, who wrote a history of Alexander of Macedon; the second was a Libyan, as recorded by Euripides in the prologue to his *Lamia*; 9 the third was from Delphi, and Chrysippus speaks of her in his book *de Divinatione*; the fourth was a Cimmerian, in Italy, as named by Naevius in his *Punic War* and by Piso in his *Annales*; the fifth was from Erythrae, confirmed by Apollodorus of Erythrae as his own fellow-citizen, who foretold to the Greeks as they set out for Ilium both the fall of Troy and Homer's fictions about it; the sixth was a Samian: Eratosthenes says he found her discussed in some ancient Samian records;[35] 10 the seventh was

---

29 NF *Corp. Herm.* vol. 4, fr. 3a. Cf. Exod. 3:13–15.

30 M. Terentius Varro (116–27 BC), exhaustive scholar, prolific writer, reported author of 75 different works, was used by Christian writers as an authority on classical religion and philosophy.

31 The *quindecimuiri sacris faciundis* were one of the four main colleges of Roman priests. They were responsible for the Sibylline books, which were kept on the Capitol and consulted in moments of crisis by order of the senate.

32 L. reports him first in indirect speech, then briefly in direct speech, and finally at length in indirect speech. He is probably quoting from memory, as usual.

33 For the Sibylline Oracles see pp. 17–21 above.

34 This sort of etymology was long established; cf. Aesch. *Ch.* 949, where *Díke*, Justice, is derived from *Diòs kóre*, 'Zeus' daughter'. But *siós* (for *theós*) is Laconian, not Aeolic, and *boúlla* would give -bul-, not -byl-. The Aeolic form of *boulé* is *bólla* (the change of accent appears to be right). It is unlikely that Sibyl is a Greek word at all.

35 Nicanor was a friend of Aristotle and served with Alexander the Great. For Chrysippus see n. 18. Naevius (*fl.* mid to late 3rd cent.) wrote a narrative poem on the First Carthaginian

from Cumae, and was called Amalthea (or by others Herophile, or Demophile): she it was who brought the nine books to king Tarquinius Priscus, demanding 300 philips for them, and he mocked the huge price and laughed at the woman's madness; in the sight of the king she then burnt three of them and asked the same price for the remainder; Tarquin thought the woman madder still; 11 when she burnt three more and still stuck to her price, the king was persuaded and bought the rest for 300 gold pieces.[36] Their number was later increased when the Capitol was rebuilt, because books were gathered and brought to Rome from all communities of Italy and Greece and especially from Erythrae, under the name of any Sibyl; 12 the eighth, from the Hellespont, was born in Trojan territory in the village of Marmessus[37] near the town of Gergithium, and Heraclides of Pontus[38] writes of her that she belonged to the era of Solon and Cyrus; the ninth was Phrygian, and she uttered at Ancyra; the tenth was from Tibur and was called Albunea, and was worshipped as a goddess at Tibur by the banks of the river Anio, in whose waters an image of her is said to have been found, holding a book in her hand. Her oracles were moved to the Capitol by the senate.' 13 The utterances of all these Sibyls are still rehearsed and kept, except for those of the Sibyl of Cumae: her books are Roman state secrets and no one has the right to see them except the quindecimviri. Each book is the book of an individual Sibyl, but because they are all labelled Sibylline people think that they are all by one Sibyl, and the books have become confused; it is not possible to distinguish them and to establish the authorship of each, except for the Erythrean one; that Sibyl has put her true name in the verse, saying in her preface that she will be called Erythrean despite being born in Babylon. 14 We too will say Sibyl indiscriminately, however, any time their evidence is needed.

All these Sibyls, then, proclaim one god, but the Erythrean one does so pre-eminently; she is considered more celebrated than the rest, and more distinguished, inasmuch as Fenestella, a most careful author, in speaking of

---

War (264–241 BC). L. Calpurnius Piso, consul in 133 BC, was an annalistic historian. For Apollodorus of Erythrae, cited elsewhere by L. himself (*de ira* 22) and by the scholiast on Pl. *Phdr.* 244b, see Jacoby *FGrH* 3b 422. Eratosthenes of Cyrene (c. 285–194 BC) presided over the library at Alexandria in succession to Apollonius of Rhodes. Versatile and learned, he wrote *inter alia* on chronology, mathematics, geography and philosophy.

36 The story is told, but with much less detail, in D.H. 4.62 and in Zonaras 7.11.
37 Properly Marpessus; the error seems to be the author's.
38 Heraclides of Pontus, 4th cent. philosopher, studied in Plato's Academy with Speusippus and Aristotle, and wrote extensively in dialogue form.

the quindecimviri says that 'when the Capitol was restored, C. Curio the consul proposed in the senate that a mission should go to Erythrae to obtain the oracles of the Sibyl and bring them back to Rome; so P. Gabinius, M. Otacilius and L. Valerius were sent, and they brought back to Rome about a thousand verses which had been copied down by private individuals.'[39] Varro relates the same, as I said earlier. 15 The evidence for one god in the verses that the mission brought to Rome is as follows:[G] 'One god ruling alone, supremely great, unbegotten.' This is the one supreme God who made the heavens and marked them out with the heavenly bodies, for it continues:[G] 'God is one and single, utterly above all; he made the sky and sun and stars and moon, and the fruitful earth and the swell of the water of the sea.'[40] 16 Since he is the sole constructor of the world and maker of the things which either constitute it or exist in it, he is alone to be worshipped, as follows:[G] 'Worship him who is the only governor of the world, who alone was made from eternity and for eternity.'[41] Another Sibyl (which one I do not know), in saying that she conveyed the word of god to man, said:[G] 'I am the only god and there is no other.'[42]

17 I might now proceed to the evidence of all the others, but these will suffice here, and I will keep the rest for better moments. But since we are defending the cause of truth before people who are astray from it in the service of false religions, what sort of proof could we better use against them than to rebut them with evidence from their own gods?

Apollo: objections answered

7.1 Apollo is seen as divine, and especially as oracular, more than all other gods; when he spoke at Colophon (where he went from Delphi because, I suppose, of the charm of Asia Minor), upon being asked who or what god really was, he replied in twenty-one verses. Here are the first three:[G] 'He is self-born, untaught, unmothered, unaffectable, unnameable by any word, dwelling in fire, god thus, and we his messengers are a little fraction of him.'[43] 2 Can anyone imagine that said of Jupiter? Jupiter has both a mother

---

39 Fenestella, *Ann.* fr. 18* (Peter). A historian of the early principate (d. c. 35), he was used by Pliny the Elder, and cited by L. in *de ira* 22.5–6. C. Scribonius Curio was consul in 76 BC, and the three men named were apparently *quindecimuiri* (there is a shorter notice in *de ira* 22).
40 Cf. *Orac. Sib.* 8.7 and 3.3–5.
41 *Orac. Sib.* 8.15ff., 17.
42 Cf. *Orac. Sib.* fr. 1, 15–16.
43 *Orac. Apoll.* fr. 51, 223–5 (Fontenrose).

BOOK 1: FALSE RELIGION

and a name. And what about the famous 'thrice greatest'[44] Mercury, whom I mentioned earlier? Does he not call god not only unmothered, as Apollo says, but also unfathered, because he has no origins anywhere at all?[45] 3 It is impossible for the power that created all things of itself to be created by anyone.

That is sufficient demonstration by argument, I think, and sufficient confirmation by evidence of a fact that is clear enough by itself, that the world has one king, one father and one lord only. 4 Someone may possibly ask of us the same question that Hortensius asked in Cicero:[46] 'If god is one and only one, what happiness can he have in his solitude?' We might as well say that because he is unique he is on his own, solitary! Why, he has servants, whom we call messengers.[47] 5 Seneca's phrase in his *Exhortationes* which I noted earlier is also true, that 'god created servants of his kingship.'[48] The servants are not gods nor do they expect to be called gods or worshipped so, since they do nothing contrary to the instructions and will of god. They are anyway not the ones popularly worshipped, whose number is very limited and known. 6 If those who worship gods think they are worshipping the same creatures that we call servants of God most high, that is no reason why they should get cross with us for saying there is one god and for denying there are many. 7 If they like having many, we say there are not just twelve of them, or three hundred and sixty-five, as Orpheus says, but that they are countless.[49] We maintain that their error goes in the wrong direction if they think the gods so few! They ought to know the proper appellation of their gods, however, to avoid offending the true God: it is his name they use when they apply it to their lot. 8 They should heed their Apollo: in the response quoted, in denying Jupiter pre-eminence he also denied the rest of them the name of god. The third verse shows that servants of God should not be called gods, but angels. 9 On the subject of himself Apollo has told a lie: though he belongs among the demons, he has attached himself to the angels of God. In other responses he admitted that he was a demon. When he was asked how he wanted to be addressed in prayer, he answered as follows:[G] 'All-wise, all-

---

44 L. uses the word *termaximus*, a Latinisation of *trismégistos*, just as he turns Hermes into Mercury.

45 Cf. 4.8.4–5.

46 Cic. *Hort*. fr. 62 (Straume-Zimmermann). L. refers to a lost work of Cicero in which Q. Hortensius Hortalus was the chief speaker. Hortensius (114–49 BC) was the leading orator of the period until Cicero bested him in the trial of Verres in 70 BC.

47 Here L. uses *nuntius* as the translation of *ángelos* used in 1 above. In 8 and 9 below he transliterates the Greek into *angelus*.

48 Sen. F86a, 200 (Vottero).

49 *Orph*. fr. 4 (Abel) = pp. 225–26 (Kern).

learnèd, most variable demon, hear us'. When he was asked for a prayer for Apollo Sminthius, he made a similar proposal starting as follows:[G] 'Harmony of the world, light-bearer, all-wise spirit'. 10 What is left, then, except surrender by his own admission to chastisement and eternal punishment from the true god? For in another reply he said:[G] 'The demons who roam by land and sea are subdued by the whip of the unwearying god.'[50]

11 For the time being we can be content with the fact that in his desire to glorify himself and take a place in heaven he has acknowledged the reality about the proper naming of those who share God's presence. 12 Mankind should therefore retreat from its errors, discard its evil cults, and recognise its lord and father: his excellence cannot be measured nor his greatness be perceived nor his beginning be understood. When the human mind, with all its capacity for focus and penetration, reaches as far as God, it halts, as if every path were eroded and gone; it pauses and quails, and there is no further progress it can make. 13 But because it is impossible for anything created[51] not to have started its existence at some time, it follows that because there was nothing preceding him he himself was created by himself before everything else, and that is why he is called[G] 'self-grown' by Apollo and[G] 'self-generated', 'unbegotten' and 'unmade' by the Sibyl.[52] That is what Seneca in his shrewdness saw, in his *Exhortationes*. 'Our origins lie elsewhere,' he said. 'Hence, we look towards someone whom we may credit with what is best in us. We were produced and informed by someone else, whereas God was created by God himself.'[53]

Gods were born

8.1 This then is the evidence, the very considerable evidence, which shows that the world is governed by the power and foresight of one god, 'whose energy and superiority are so great' (says Plato in *Timaeus*) 'that no one can conceive them intellectually nor express them in words, because his power is too great and beyond measure.'[54] 2 Could anyone doubt for a moment

---

50 *Orac. Apoll.* fr.: see Monat (1986), 89 n. 2. For Sminthius, see *Iliad* i 39. The epithet is probably from a word for mouse: Apollo mouse-god, i.e., plague-god. For demons, see 2.14.5–9 and n. 63 there.
51 Reading *fit* (as in ms M), not *sit*.
52 *Orac. Sib.* 8.7, 15ff; cf. fr. 1.17, and 7.
53 Sen. F87, 202 (Vottero).
54 The quotation is in Latin, but the sense is some way from the original (Plato, *Ti.* 28c); the passage quoted was something of a commonplace.

whether God would find anything difficult or impossible when he has planned all these wonderful works with his providence, has established them with his virtue and has perfected them with his plan, or whether he would now sustain them with his spirit and control them with his power, he the incomprehensible, the ineffable, known to no other as he is to himself? 3 As I meditate more and more upon this greatness of his, worshippers of gods have come to seem to me so blind, so mindless, so thoughtless, so like the dumb beasts, in believing that people born of the coition of male and female could have had any element of superiority and divine excellence. Why, the Sibyl of Erythrae says,[G] 'A man's thighs and a womb cannot create a god.'[55] 4 If that is true, which it is, plainly Hercules, Apollo, Bacchus, Mercury and Jupiter himself were also merely men, since they were born of a pairing of the sexes. 5 Is there anything quite so remote from God as the activity which he himself gave to mankind for the procreation of its offspring and which simply has to be physical to work at all? If the gods are therefore immortal, eternal and everlasting, what is the point of a second sex? To procreate? Of course! And what is the point of progeny? Those who live for ever do not need successors. 6 In human beings and in the other animals, obviously, difference of sex, copulation and procreation exist simply so that all living species, doomed by the condition of their mortality to die, can live on through their successors; whereas God who lives for ever needs neither a second sex nor a succession. 7 'What about providing himself with servants,' it will be suggested, 'or people to exercise his power on?' What is the point in that case of the female sex, since God who is all-powerful, as people say, could produce children without using the labour of a female? 8 If certain very small creatures have the power of 'picking themselves children off leaves and off sweet plants with their mouths' [Verg. *G.* 4.200–01], why should anyone think that God himself could not procreate except by copulation with a second sex? Even a fool must realise the mortality of those who are addressed and worshipped as gods by the ignorant and stupid. 'Then how are they thought to be gods?' someone will say. It's obvious: they were kings, very great and powerful kings; their virtues, their service and skills became well known, their subjects loved them for the worth of those qualities, and to remember them they treated them as holy. Anyone in doubt should look at their achievements, recorded in their entirety by both the poets and the early historians.

---

55 *Orac. Sib.* 3.1ff; cf. fr. 3.1f.

Hercules

9.1 Hercules is renowned for his virtues; he is seen as a sort of Africanus among the gods.[56] Yet his rapes and adulteries and other sexual exploits fouled the very earth that his travels are said to have cleansed. No wonder: he was the product of Alcmena's adultery. What divinity could there be in a man who was the slave of his own vices and broke all laws in bringing infamy, shame and disgrace on male and female alike? 2 Even the great and wonderful deeds he did ought not to compel the judgment that they must be attributed plainly to divine virtues in him. What is so very remarkable after all about overcoming a lion and a boar, about shooting down birds with arrows, about cleaning out a king's stable, about conquering an Amazon and wrenching off her girdle, or killing some wild horses together with their owner?[57] Those are the deeds of a brave man, but of a man, be it noted: 3 his victims were frail and mortal. As Cicero observes [*Marc.* 8], 'There is no power so great that it cannot be weakened and broken by weapons of strength; 4 to tame one's own spirit and contain one's own passions' takes a very brave man. Hercules never did that, and never could have. 'I don't compare anyone who can do that with even the greatest of men: I think him very like a god.'

I wish Cicero had added something about lust and self-indulgence, and greed and contempt, in order to complete the tale of virtue in the man he thought to be godlike. 5 The man who gets the better of a lion is not to be thought braver than the man who tames that wild beast within him of irascibility; picking off gluttonous birds is not braver than conquering a ravening greed; beating a warrior Amazon or cleaning the muck from a stable is not braver than subduing the lust that wars against self-respect and reputation, or cleaning vice from one's own heart: these vices are more destructive for being one's own personal wickedness than are those which can with due care be avoided. 6 Hence, the only man who ought to be judged brave is the one who is self-controlled, temperate and just. Anyone who pondered the works of God would soon think all these things that stupid people gape at ludicrous. People think of them as they do because of the weakness of their own

---

56 P. Cornelius Scipio Africanus, conqueror of Hannibal. For the comparison with Hercules see 18.11–13 below. L. picks out Hercules for criticism together with Jupiter. It is no coincidence that Maximian called himself Herculius and Diocletian was known as Jovius, after Jupiter. See pp. 43–44 above.

57 L. refers to six of Hercules' labours: the Nemean lion, the Erymanthian boar, the Stymphalian birds, the Augean stables, Hippolyta's belt and Diomedes and his mares. In 5 below he repeats four of them.

BOOK 1: FALSE RELIGION

powers, and not for any divine virtues in them, which they know nothing of anyhow. 7 No one has denied the fact that Hercules was slave not only to king Eurystheus (which could be seen as honourable up to a point) but also to Omphale, a woman of great impropriety, who dressed him up in her own clothes and made him sit at her feet spinning wool. Revolting! Degenerate! But that was the price of pleasure.

8 'What about you?' they'll say. 'Do you think poets are credible?' Why shouldn't I? It's not a story by Lucilius, or by Lucian,[58] who spared neither gods nor men; it is told especially by those who sang their gods' praises, 9 and if we have no confidence in them, whom shall we believe? Anyone who thinks they are liars should offer us some other believable authors to tell us who those gods are, how they were created and where from, what their strength, number and capacity is, what is wonderful about them and worth worship, and what mystery they hold of special truth and reliability. There won't be a single one. 10 So let's believe those poets: they did not speak to rebuke their gods, but to proclaim them.

Hercules sailed off therefore with the Argonauts and sacked Troy in his fury with Laomedon, who had denied him his reward for saving his daughter. That makes it plain when he lived. He also killed his wife and children in a fit of mad passion. 11 Yet people think he is a god! His heir Philoctetes did not think so: he put the torch to his pyre, and watched his limbs and muscles burn and disintegrate; he buried his bones and ashes on Mount Oeta, for which kindness he received the hero's bow and arrows.

Sundry gods

10.1 Aesculapius is another whose birth was Apollo's fault. What did he do to earn divine honours except for healing Hippolytus? At least his death was more distinguished: he earned a god's thunderbolt. 2 In his *Famous Men* Tarquitius says 'he was born of unknown parents; he was exposed, and found by huntsmen; he was reared on dog milk and handed over to Chiron who taught him healing; he had been a Messenian but lived at Epidaurus.'[59] Cicero adds [*N.D.* 3.57] that he was buried at Cynosura.

3 What about his father Apollo? He disgracefully rustled another man's herd because of a love affair that inflamed him; he built walls for Laomedon

---

[58] Lucilius was a Roman poet and satirist of the 2nd century BC. The reference to Lucian, a Greek writer of the 2nd century AD, is seen by some as an interpolation.

[59] Tarquitius Priscus (an eminent Etruscan of the mid 1st cent. BC) translated or adapted Etruscan books into Latin.

under a contract he could bilk him of without redress; and he was the first to teach that faithless king to default on his agreements with the gods. He also molested a pretty boy[60] while kissing him, and killed him as he played with him. 4 Mars was a murderer. The Athenians in gratitude acquitted him on the charge. To avoid appearing too fierce and savage, he then committed adultery with Venus. 5 Castor and Pollux, busy grabbing other men's wives, left off being twins. One of them was slain by a swordthrust from Idas, who was provoked to anger by the liberties being taken, and the poets say they then lived and died in alternation. That makes them the most miserable of men, as well as of gods: they are not permitted to die once and for all. 6 Homer, however, records them both simply as dead (which is not the standard story): when he sat Helen on the walls beside Priam, recognising all the Greek leaders and missing only her own brothers, he added a line to her speech as follows: 'So she spoke, but they were kept buried in earth.'[61] 7 As for that thief and trickster Mercury, what has he left to his name and fame except the record of his deceptions? He earns his place in the sky, no doubt, for inventing wrestling schools and being first to construct a lyre!

8 Of supreme authority in the senate of the gods, with right to speak first in debate, must be father Bacchus, the only one of them all, Jupiter apart, to win a triumph, after leading his army to victory in India. Yet our invincible general, Indicus the greatest, became the shameful victim of passion and lust.[62] 9 He landed in Crete 'with his semi-male retinue',[63] and found a loose woman on the shore; in the confidence of his Indian victory, and wanting to play the man (in case he looked too effeminate), he bound himself in marriage to a woman who had betrayed her father, had killed her brother and had already been ditched and disowned by another man. Side by side Bacchus and she, now 'liberated' herself,[64] ascended into heaven.

10 And what of Jupiter, the father of all these others, who is solemnly invoked as Best and Greatest? From his earliest boyhood he can be accused of disrespect and virtual parricide, when he drove his father off the throne and chased him out, unable in his desire to be king to wait for the feeble old

60 Hyacinthus is meant. See Ovid, *Met.* 10.162–219.
61 L. quotes the line (*Il.* 3.243) in a Latin version.
62 Cf. V. Max. 3.6.6 for Bacchus. L. makes play with several Roman practices in this section: the order in which a presiding consul called senators to speak, the title '*pater*', the right to triumphs, and the adoption of extra names (like Indicus) to mark them.
63 Verg. *A.* 4.215.
64 Bacchus was commonly called Liber in Latin, as L. calls him here. He calls Ariadne Libera to work the pun on name and status.

BOOK 1: FALSE RELIGION

fellow's death. Once he had seized his father's throne by force of arms, the Titans provoked him to a war: and that was the beginning of trouble for the human race. After the Titans' defeat and the establishment of a lasting peace, he spent the rest of his life in debauch and adultery. 11 I omit the girls he abused, since that tends to pass for tolerable; I cannot, however, pass by Amphitryo and Tyndarus; their homes he filled quite full of shame and dishonour. 12 But the crown of his impiety and wickedness was the seizure of a king's son for sex.[65] Fouling and shaming himself with assaults on the honour of women was plainly of little note if he failed to abuse his own sex: real adultery has to be unnatural. 13 We have to wonder whether such a performer can be called Greatest; Best, certainly not. That title has nothing to do with corruption, adultery and unchastity, unless perhaps we human beings are wrong in calling people who do such things wicked and desperate, and in condemning them to every penalty they deserve. 14 But then, Cicero was silly to attack Verres for his adulteries: Jupiter too committed adultery, and Cicero worshipped Jupiter. So too when he attacked P. Clodius for incest with his sister:[66] Jupiter Best and Greatest had the same woman 'for sister and wife.'[67]

Jupiter (continued) and Saturn

11.1 Who can be so witless, then, as to think that someone is reigning in heaven who would not deserve to reign on earth? The poet who wrote the *Triumph of Cupid* was no fool; in it he makes Cupid not only the most powerful of the gods but also their conqueror.[68] 2 One by one he listed the love affairs that had brought them under Cupid's power and control, and he created a procession in which Jupiter is led in chains, together with the rest of the gods, in front of the victor's chariot. It makes a pretty enough picture, and without being far from the truth, either. 3 Anyone devoid of goodness, anyone prisoner to the evils of greed and lust, is the victim not of Cupid, as the poet put it, but of everlasting death.

---

65 Amphitryo and Tyndarus were both cuckolded by Zeus; Amphitryo's wife Alcmena produced twins, Hercules being Zeus' son and Iphicles the son of Amphitryo, while Tyndarus' wife Leda, seduced by Zeus in the guise of a swan, produced Castor, Pollux, Helen and Clytemnestra. The king's son mentioned is Ganymede, son of a king of Troy.

66 For C. Verres see 2.4.27–37 below. P. Clodius (c. 92–52 BC), a maverick politician of the late Republic, was accused of violating the Bona Dea ceremony in December 62 by attending dressed as a woman. Cicero broke his alibi, but Clodius had his revenge in 58 when he secured Cicero's exile.

67 Verg. *A.* 1.47.

68 Ovid, *Am.* 1.2.23ff describes a triumph of Cupid, but without Olympians in it.

4 Let us talk no more of their behaviour and study the facts instead, so that people can understand the errors that make them so miserable. 5 The mass of people thinks that Jupiter reigns in the sky; this is the conviction of learned and ignorant alike, and it is seen in all their religion, in their prayers and hymns, and in their shrines and images. 6 They also say, however, that he was born of Saturn and Rhea. How can he be seen as a god, or, as the poet says [A. 12.829], 'inventor of people and things', when there were countless thousands of people in existence before he was, the ones who lived when Saturn was king and who saw the light sooner than Jupiter did? 7 I observe that there was one god who was king in early times, and another in the period following. It is possible, therefore, that there is yet another still to come. If the kingship changed before, why should we despair of it changing later? – unless, perhaps, Saturn had the power to produce a stronger successor but Jupiter does not? 8 And yet, either divine authority is immutable for ever, or, if it can change hands (which is impossible), it can do so at any time. Can Jupiter then lose his kingship, just as his father did? 9 Of course he can. Though he failed to spare maidens and married women, he did refrain from Thetis, and only Thetis, because of the oracle that any child born of her would be greater than his father. 10 That argues first a lack of foresight in Jupiter not proper in a god: had Themis[69] not told him the future, he would not have known it; and if he were not to be divine, he would not even be a god (divinity is so called from god, as humanity is from man[70]); 11 second, it argues his awareness of his weakness: he was afraid of a greater. Anyone with that fear must know he is not the 'Greatest' since something greater is capable of existing. 12 Then there is his solemn oath, sworn on the waters of Styx, 'the only oath of might granted to the gods above.'[71] What is this oath of might, and who granted it? Is there some very great power which can punish gods who commit perjury? Why are they so scared of the waters below if they themselves are immortal? Why should they fear something which will only be seen by those who have to die? 13 And why in that case should human beings raise their eyes to the sky, and why should they swear by the gods above when those very gods above look down to the gods below to find *their* objects of worship and adoration? What does it mean for there to be fates obeyed by all the gods, including Jupiter himself? 14 If the power

69 Themis, traditionally the child of Uranus (Heaven) and Gaia (Earth), was seen as an oracular goddess, preceding Apollo at Delphi.
70 L.'s argument is etymological: the adjective of *deus*, god, is *diuinus*, and the adjective of *homo*, man, is *humanus*; he is right in both pairs.
71 Verg. *A.* 12.817.

of the fates is so strong that they can do more than all the celestial beings together and more than their ruler and lord, why should *they* not be said to hold sway, since necessity compels their laws and statutes to be obeyed by every god? Can anyone doubt that 'greatest' is not the word for anyone who accepts the superiority of something else? If it were, that 'greatest' person would not accept fate: he would cause it.

15 I return now to a point passed over before. That self-restraint which Jupiter accepted in the case of one woman, despite his passion for her, was due to no good instinct but to fear of his own successor. 16 That panic is absolutely typical of someone who is mortal, weak and worthless: after all, the child could have been destroyed at birth, as Jupiter's own elder brother was; if that child had lived, he would never have yielded power to his younger brother. But Jupiter was preserved by stealth and reared in secret, and was named Zeus or Zen, not as certain people think from the 'seething of celestial fire' or because he is 'giver of life' and puts breath in the creatures that breathe, which is a power of god alone – what breath could be created in them by someone receiving his own from elsewhere? – but because he was the first of Saturn's male children who 'lived.'[72] 17 If Saturn had not been tricked by his wife, mankind could have had a different god as ruler. Oh, but that's a poetical fiction! Not so: anyone thinking that is wrong. The poets were talking about men, but they used the word god of them in order to mark out the ones whose memories they recorded with approval. Fiction is thus a better label for what they said of them as gods than for what they said of them as men, as will become clear from the example I shall now present.

18 When he was going to rape Danae, he showered her lap with gold coins as payment for his lust. The poets were unwilling to talk down the power of the divine greatness which people believed in; they were speaking in effect about a god; they contrived a descent of Jupiter in a shower of gold, using the same metaphor as in the showers of iron they talk of when describing volleys of missiles and arrows. 19 They say he stole Ganymede[73] on an eagle: that is also poetical embellishment. In fact, either he stole him using soldiers – the legionary standard is an eagle – or the ship on which he put him had an eagle as its guardian image, like the bull when he stole Europa and carried her away. 20 In the same fashion they say that he turned

---

72 Zen (Zan in Doric Greek: see 46 below) is Zeus. L. is etymologising again. *zên* or *zân* was the Greek for to live; *zeîn* meant to seethe.

73 L. uses the Latin form of his name, Catamitus.

Io daughter of Inachus into a cow; in order to escape the anger of Juno, she is said to have swum across the sea and come to Egypt 'now beset with bristles, now a cow'[74] and there, regaining her original shape, she became the goddess now called Isis. 21 So what argument is there to prove that Europa did not sit on a bull and Io was not made into a cow? This: there is a special day in the calendar when the 'Voyage of Isis' is celebrated.[75] That shows that she did not swim but went by boat. 22 People with any sense of their own intelligence realise that a living and earthly body cannot exist in the sky, and so they dismiss the whole tale of Ganymede as false; but they fail to see that it all happened on earth, matter and lust being earthly things. 23 The poets have thus not created events – if they did they would be impostors – but they have added a certain colour to events. They were not writing in denigration but in a desire to embellish. 24 That is what deceives people, especially because all the while that they think of these things as poetical fictions they are worshipping what they do not recognise. They do not know the limits of poetical licence and how far one may go in a fiction, since a poet's business lies in transposing reality into something else with metaphor and allusion and in covering up the misrepresentation with charm. 25 To misrepresent the whole of one's subject matter is merely inept, however; to do that argues a liar, not a poet.

26 Suppose, however, that the poets did create the works we think of as fables: would that be true also of their writings on female gods and their marriages with gods? Why are they so depicted and so worshipped? Perhaps it is not only the poets who lie, but also the painters and the statue makers. 27 If Jupiter is this god that people say he is and not the child of Saturn and Ops, there ought to be no statue in all the temples except his alone. 28 What is the point of likenesses of women? Why the weaker sex at all? If this Jupiter did fall for them, the very stone of his statues will declare him a man. 29 People say the poets are liars and yet they believe them: but in fact they prove that they were not liars. They make their images of gods in such a way that the truth of the poets' tales is demonstrated by precisely the difference of sex. What other message is there in a statue of Ganymede and the image of an eagle set before Jupiter's feet in temples and worshipped equally with him, except the perpetuation for ever of the record of a foul deed of rape?

30 No poetical work is a total fiction. There is some element perhaps of adaptation and concealment by metaphor so that the truth can be hidden in

---

74 Verg. *A.* 7.790.
75 5 March, when the seas are open again to navigation.

wraps, like the tale of the allotment of kingdoms. Jupiter got the sky, they say, Neptune got the sea and Pluto the underworld. Why was the third lot not the earth? Perhaps because it all took place on earth. 31 The truth of the matter is that kingship of the world was divided and allotted in such a way that control over the east went to Jupiter and the western share fell to Pluto, also called Agesilaus,[76] on the grounds that the eastern shore, the source of light for mortals, is the upper one, whereas the western shore appears to be lower. That is how they veiled the truth in falsehood, so that the truth should not of itself upset popular belief. 32 The matter of Neptune's share is plain: his kingship we reckon to be the same as M. Antonius' command without limit, when the senate gave him power over every coastal area so that he could pursue the pirates and bring peace to the whole Mediterranean;[77] that was Neptune's share: all the coasts with the islands.

33 How can that be proved? It is the plain lesson of ancient history. Euhemerus,[78] a long dead writer who came from Messene, gathered together the deeds of Jupiter and of the others thought to be gods and stitched together his *History* out of sacred dedications and inscriptions which were kept in the oldest temples and especially in the temple of Jupiter Triphylius: the dedication there indicated that a gold column had been put in place by Jupiter himself, and he inscribed his achievements on it to be a memorial of his deeds for posterity. 34 This is the *History* that Ennius took up and followed, and these are Ennius' words: 'When Jupiter gave Neptune command of the sea, and kingship over all islands and all areas by the sea...'[79] The poets thus got it right, but obscured it with a sort of veil. 35 Mount Olympus is also capable of giving the poets an image: they could say that Jupiter was allotted kingship of the sky, because Olympus is an ambiguous word meaning both mountain and sky. The *History* already cited says that Jupiter had lived on Olympus: 'At that period Jupiter was spending most of his time on Mount Olympus, and people came to him there for justice in cases of controversy. So too, people who discovered something of useful application

---

[76] An epithet for Hades, referring to his role as leader or host of the dead. See Aeschylus, fr. 406 (Nauck); Call. *Lav. Pall.* 130.

[77] Not the famous Mark Antony, but his father M. Antonius Creticus, who for his campaign against the pirates in 74 BC received powers equal to those of any governors he encountered.

[78] Euhemerus of Messene (either the Peloponnesian or the Sicilian town) lived in the early 3rd century BC, and wrote a work of fiction, the *Sacred Record*, in which he argued that the Olympian gods were promoted mortals. Ennius translated or adapted his work about a hundred years later, and L. drew on that composition probably through an intermediary, who may have been Varro. See conveniently Bosworth (1999), 10–13.

[79] Enn. *Euhem.* fr. 7 (Vahlen) = Warmington p. 424.

to human life would come there and show it to Jupiter.'[80] 36 The poets shift a great deal in this fashion, not in order to misrepresent the gods (whom they worship, after all) but to increase the grace and charm of their poetry with a variety of images. People who fail to understand how and why each detail is thus represented attack the poets for lies and sacrilege. 37 This is the mistake that misled philosophers: they could see the inappropriateness in a god of the things being said about Jupiter, and they assumed two Jupiters, one natural and the other mythological. 38 They saw the truth in part: the person the poets spoke of was a human being, of course, but they went wrong about the natural Jupiter: popular religious custom persuaded them to transfer a man's name to a god, and, as said above, god needs no proper name because he is on his own. But Jupiter is the child of Ops and Saturn, and that is undeniable.

39 People who attribute the name Jupiter to God most high are thus victims of a vain belief. Some of them try to defend their errors with the following explanation: persuaded of one god and unable to deny it, they say firmly that it is him they worship, but that they decided to call him Jupiter. What could be sillier than that? Jupiter cannot be worshipped without his household of wife and daughter, and that makes it plain who he is, and it is improper to switch his name where there is no Minerva or Juno. 40 What about the fact that the meaning of the name indicates a human, and not a divine, capacity? 'Jupiter and Juno are so named from helping,'[81] says Cicero by way of explanation [*N.D.* 2.64, 66]; 'Jupiter is a version of helpful father.' The name is particularly unsuitable for a god, since help is a human activity: one person brings some element of assistance to another who is a stranger, and the benefit is slight. 41 Nobody prays to god for help, but to be saved, and to have life and salvation: that is much more than mere help, and much more important. And since we are speaking of a father, no father is said to 'help' his sons when he creates them or brings them up. The word is too trivial to express the importance of a father's generosity. 42 How much more inappropriate it is for God, who is the true father, through whom we exist and whose possession we all are; he makes us, inspirits us, illuminates us; he gives us life, health and all manner of food. 43 People who think they are only *helped* by God fail to understand his acts of virtue. People who reduce the excellence of supreme power by calling it Jupiter are not just ignorant but irreligious.

80 Enn. *Euhem.* fr. 8 (Vahlen) = Warmington p. 424.
81 To help is *iuuare* (Jupiter and Juno were then spelt with i, not j, a letter form developed much later). Varro, *L.* 5.65, quotes Ennius for the same point.

44 If we have grasped that Jupiter was a man both in his deeds and in his behaviour and that he was a king on earth, it remains for us to investigate his death. 45 Ennius in his *Sacred History* described all that he did in his life and finally said:[82] 'After Jupiter had gone five times round the earth and had divided and willed his powers among all his friends and relations, while for men he prepared laws, customs and food and did many other good things, then stirred by the undying glamour of his record he left memorials to his people that would last for ever. 46 As his life went into decline, he removed to Crete and departed to the gods, and his sons the Curetes looked after him[83] and did him honour. His tomb is in Crete, in the town of Cnossos, which Vesta is said to have founded; on the tomb is an inscription in ancient Greek lettering, *'Zan Kronou'*, which means in Latin Jupiter son of Saturn.' 47 This is certainly not what the poets say; it is in the writers upon antiquities. But it is true enough to be confirmed by the Sibylline verses which go as follows:[G] 'Gods without souls, looking like exhausted corpses, whose tombs will be the boast of sorry Crete.'[84] 48 When Cicero in *de Natura Deorum* [*N.D.* 3.53] said 'three Jupiters are counted by the theologians' he added that 'the third was Cretan, the son of Saturn, and his tomb is on display in the island.' 49 So how can god be alive in one place and dead in another, and have a temple in one place and a tomb in another? The Romans need to realise that their Capitol, the capital, that is,[85] of all their state religion, is simply a meaningless memorial.

50 Now let us come to his father who reigned before him, and who may perhaps have something extra in him, since he is said to have been born of the meeting of remarkable elements. Let us see what there is in him worthy of a god. First, there is the fact that he is said to have enjoyed a golden age and that under him there was justice on earth. 51 I note something in him which did not exist in his son: what could be so appropriate to a god as a rule of justice and a time of piety? 52 But when I stop to think that he was born in the usual fashion, I cannot imagine as god most high someone whose superior in age I can see: sky and earth, that is. I want a god with absolutely nothing beyond him, a god who is the original source of everything; such

---

82 Enn. *Euhem.* fr. 11 (Vahlen) = Warmington p. 428.
83 The Curetes are divine warriors of Crete who attend upon Zeus; or, in other myth, they protect the newborn Zeus from his father Cronus by clashing shields. L.'s word for 'looked after' is *curauerunt*: in its first syllable he sees a meaningful repetition of the first syllable of Curetes. But Curetes is Greek and related to a Greek word for youth.
84 *Orac. Sib.* 8.47ff.
85 For the pun see Livy 5.54.7.

must be the creator of heaven itself and the founder of the earth. 53 If Saturn was born of these, as he is thought to be, how can he be the original god and also owe his birth to others? Alternatively, who was in charge of the world before Saturn was born? 54 As I said a little while ago, this is a poetical fiction. It was impossible for elements without any senses and widely separated from each other to meet in one place and produce a son, or for the son that was born not to be very like his parents rather than have an appearance which his own parents did not have.

55 Let us therefore seek the element of truth which lurks beneath this image. In his book entitled *Octavius* Minucius Felix argues as follows [23.10–12]: 'When Saturn had been forced by his son to flee and had come to Italy, he was called son of the sky because we usually say that people whose virtue we admire or who arrive all of a sudden have arrived out of the blue; he was called son of the earth, however, because that is our title for children of parents unknown.'[86] 56 That is close to the truth, but not the actual truth, because Saturn was already so called, as is generally agreed, when he was still on the throne. 57 The argument could have gone thus: when Saturn was in full regal authority, he bestowed his parents' names on sky and earth in order to preserve their memory, sky and earth being previously called something else; it is on the same basis, as we know, that mountains and rivers get named. 58 When the poets speak of the offspring of Atlas or of the river Inachus, they are absolutely not saying that human beings were able to be created from things lacking the senses; they are simply remarking on people born of those human beings who in their lifetime or after death have given their names to mountains or rivers. 59 It was a common practice in ancient time, particularly with the Greeks. We hear tell of seas named after people who fell into them, like the Aegean and the Icarian sea and the Hellespont, and in Latium Aventinus gave his name to the mountain where he was buried, and Tiberinus or Thybris did so to the river in which he was drowned. 60 It should be no surprise that the names of men who were ancestors of great kings were attached to earth and sky. 61 Thus it is clear that Saturn was not born of the sky, which is impossible, but from a man whose name was Uranus.[87] Trismegistus is our authority for the truth of

---

86 This is the first of two citations of Minucius Felix by name (see also 5.1.2ff.); L. uses him extensively. Minucius was apparently an advocate who practised in Rome. His *Octavius* (composed between 197 and 248) is a dialogue, set in Ostia and conducted after the manner of Cicero, between two friends of his, a pagan, Caecilius, and a Christian, Octavius. It ends with the conversion of Caecilius. See Clarke (1974).

87 Uranus is the transliteration of a Greek word for heaven.

BOOK 1: FALSE RELIGION

this: when he observed that 'there were very few whose learning was perfect,' he named among them 'Uranus, with Saturn and Mercury his kinsmen.'[88] 62 This is what Minucius Felix failed to understand; hence the misdirection of his history.

I have shown how it could have been argued. I will now explain how and where the naming was done and who did it. It was not the work of Saturn but of Jupiter. 63 Ennius in his *Sacred History* reports as follows: 'Then he was taken to the Panchaean mountain[89] which is called the Pillar of Heaven.[90] When Jupiter had climbed it, he gazed all over the lands, and there on the mountain he built an altar to heaven, and he was the first to sacrifice on the altar. There he looked up at what we now call heaven, and he gave the name heaven to what is above the world, which used to be called aether, naming it after his grandfather, and Jupiter was the first to call what used to be called aether heaven, doing so in a placatory spirit; the sacrificial victim that he offered there he burnt entire.'[91] This is not the only place where Jupiter can be found making sacrifice. 64 In his *Aratus* Germanicus reports Aglaosthene as saying that 'when Jupiter set out from the island of Naxos against the Titans, and was making sacrifice on the shore, an eagle flew towards him by way of omen; once Jupiter was victorious, he took the eagle under his protection in acknowledgement of its good omen.'[92] 65 Earlier the *Sacred History* says that 'an eagle settled on his head as a portent of his kingship.'[93] Who else could Jupiter sacrifice to except to his grandfather heaven, of whom Euhemerus says that 'he died in Oceania and was buried in the town of Aulacia'?[94]

---

88 NF *Corp. Herm.* vol. 4, fr. 5a.
89 Reading not *Pan eum* but *Panchaeum*; see Warmington n. *ad loc.* So too Bryce (1990), 333, citing Jacoby, *RE* 6.957.
90 Alternatively (reading not *stela* but *stella*), the Star of Heaven.
91 Enn. *Euhem.* fr. 6 (Vahlen) = Warmington pp. 422–24.
92 Germ. schol. fr. on 318–20, pp. 91, 19 (Breysig). Germanicus (15 BC–AD 19) translated into Latin the *Phaenomena* of Aratus of Sicyon (271–213 BC), and wrote comedies in Greek and epigrams in Greek and Latin. Advanced by Augustus, he led Roman armies in Germany under Tiberius, whose nephew and adopted son (AD 4) he was, but fell out with him and died mysteriously in Syria, convinced that he had been poisoned by the governor of the province Calpurnius Piso. The information quoted is not in Germanicus' text but in a commentary on it.
93 Enn. *Euhem.* fr. 5 end (Vahlen) = Warmington p. 422.
94 Enn. *Euhem.* fr. 2 (Vahlen) = Warmington p. 418.

Stoic explanation

12.1 Now that we have exposed the mysteries of the poets and found Saturn's parents, let us return to his virtues and deeds. 'He was just in his kingship.' 2 First, because he *was*, for that very reason he *is* not god; second, he was not even just, but wicked, not merely towards his sons, whom he killed, but also towards his father, whose genitals he is said to have cut off – which it is probable did happen. 3 Out of respect for the element called sky, however, people dismiss the whole story as a very clumsy fiction, though the Stoics, as usual, try to give it a physical explanation. In his discussion in *de Natura Deorum* Cicero sets their theory out. 4 He says [*N.D.* 2.64]: 'They wished that organ of the body which needed contact with another body for procreation to be no part of the heavenly, utterly superior nature of aether – the fiery nature, that is – which could generate everything on its own.'

This logic could have fitted Vesta, if she were declared male. 5 People think of Vesta as a virgin because fire is an inviolable element and nothing can be born of it since it consumes everything it seizes. 6 Ovid in his *Fasti* says [6.291–94]: 'Do not think of Vesta as anything other than living flame; you can see that no creatures are born of flame. She is therefore rightly a virgin who neither gives nor takes any seed and whose love is for the companions of her virginity.' 7 The same could have been said of Vulcan: he is thought of as god of fire, and yet the poets have not castrated him. It could also have been said of the sun: all growth is dependent on the sun and without the sun's fiery heat nothing can be born or develop; no other element needs genitals as much as heat does, since all conception, birth and nurture require that cherishing warmth. 8 Finally, even if the sky were to be as people want it, why should we think of it as castrated rather than just born without sexual organs at all? If it creates of itself, then it never needed genitals, even when creating Saturn. But if it did have the organs and they were cut off by its son, the creation of everything, all nature, would have failed.

9 What about people depriving Saturn himself not only of his divinity but also of his humanity, when they assert that 'it is Saturn who contains the circular course of space and time, and his Greek name means exactly that?[95] He is called[G] Cronos, which is the same as[G] Chronos, which means extent of time; and he is called Saturn because he is saturated with years.' 10 Those are Cicero's words [*N.D.* 2.64] setting out Stoic theory; its emptiness is

---

95 At this point L. switches from indirect to direct speech. Neither etymology is sound.

BOOK 1: FALSE RELIGION   89

readily intelligible to anyone. If Saturn is son of Sky,[96] how could Time be born of Sky, or how after that could Time be deprived of his authority by his son Jupiter? Or how could Jupiter be born of Time? Or how many years would it take to saturate eternity which has no end?

Euhemerist explanation

13.1 If then the theories of the philosophers are a waste of time, what are we left with except to believe that one man's castration by another really did happen? Or does anyone think you can have a god who fears a co-heir? If he had had some godly quality, he ought to have cut off his own genitals, not his father's, to prevent the birth of Jupiter, who deprived him of his possession of the kingship. 2 When he took his sister Rhea to wife (in Latin we call her Ops), he is said to have been told by an oracle not to rear male children because he was going to be driven out by a son. Fearful of the prospect he did not just swallow the sons born to him, as the stories say, but killed them, despite it being written in the *Sacred History* that 'Saturn and Ops and the rest of their contemporaries were used to eating human flesh; it was Jupiter who first, in creating laws and customs for mankind, banned by edict their freedom to feed on such food.'[97] If that is true, what justice can there be in Saturn? 3 Saturn devouring his sons we are certainly to see as fictitious, and not without reason: are we to think that he ate his sons just because people say so, when he followed them to their graves and committed them to burial?

When Ops gave birth to Jupiter, she smuggled the infant out and sent him to Crete in secret for his rearing. 4 Once again I must attack such unintelligence. Why did Saturn take an oracle from someone else? There he was in the sky: could he not see on earth? 5 Why did the Corybantes deceive him with cymbals?[98] And finally, why did some greater power emerge which could outdo his power? Ah, of course: an older man is easily defeated and stripped of his authority by a younger man.

6 So Saturn was driven into exile, and after prolonged diversions he came to Italy by boat, as Ovid reports in *Fasti* [1.233–34]. 'It remains to explain the boat. After roaming all over the world, it was by boat that the sickle-bearing god came to the Tuscan river.' 7 He was taken in by Janus

---

96 For Sky L. uses Caelus: see 13.14 below. The word for sky is *caelum* (neuter): L. is taking advantage of the similarity of declension. He also puns on Saturn with saturate.
97 Enn. *Euhem.* fr. 9 (Vahlen) = Warmington p. 426.
98 The Corybantes are sometimes confused with the Curetes (see note on 11.46 above). They are spirits of nature who protected the newborn Zeus (and the infant Dionysus).

poverty-stricken from his wanderings, and there are ancient coins to prove the fact, on which there is Janus with his double face, and on the reverse a ship, just as Ovid also says [239–40] in supplement: 'Posterity in its piety stamped a boat upon its coppers, in witness of the arrival of this guest turned god.' 8 Thus all writers, not just poets but historians and antiquarians too, agree that he was a man, and the deeds he did in Italy have been recorded by the Greeks Diodorus and Thallus and by the Romans Nepos, Cassius and Varro.[99] 9 In the days when life in Italy was rather rustic in style, 'He united a stubborn stock scattered among high hills, gave laws to them, and had the place called Latium because he once had lurked safely in these lands.' [Verg. A. 8.321–23] 10 Does anyone think that one who got kicked out, who ran away, and lay low, is a god? No one is so silly. People who run away and hide must be scared – scared of being beaten up and killed.

11 Orpheus, a rather more recent figure, records plainly that Saturn was a king on earth, among men:[G] 'First king of all over terrestrial men was Cronos, and from Cronos was born the great king far-thundering Zeus.'[100] 12 Likewise our own Vergil [G. 2.538]: 'Such was the life that golden Saturn lived upon earth,' and in another place [A. 8.324–25]: 'His reign was the period called in legend the Golden Age, so favourable the peace in which he ruled his peoples.' 13 He does not say in the first quotation that Saturn spent his life in heaven, nor in the second that he ruled the gods in peace. Hence it is obvious that he was a king on earth, which is what he says more plainly elsewhere [A. 6.793–95]: 'he shall restore the Golden Age in Latium, in the land where Saturn ruled of old.'

14 Ennius in his *Euhemerus* does not give priority to Saturn's reign, but to that of his father Uranus. 'In the beginning,' he says, 'first Caelus held supreme sway on earth. He established and organised that kingship for himself together with his brothers.'[101] 15 A difference of father and son between two very considerable authors is no great matter. In any case, each is a possibility: Uranus could begin to outdo the rest in power and get himself the

---

99 Diodorus of Sicily, who lived in Rome from 56 to 30 BC, wrote a universal history down to 60. Fifteen of the 40 books survive in their entirety, the others in fragments. Thallus was a Greek chronographer who lived under the early principate; Theophilus (see note on 23.2 below), *Autol.* 3.29, points to Thallus' euhemerist tendencies. Cornelius Nepos (c. 99–24 BC) was a minor historian and biographer; 25 biographies are extant. Cassius Hemina was a Latin annalist of the 2nd. cent. BC. The same four are mentioned in Min. Fel. 23.9. See also Tert. *apol.* 10.7 (but he surnames Cassius Severus: see Quint. *Inst.* 11.1.57); *nat.* 2.12.26 (with Tacitus for Thallus). The ultimate source is Varro.

100 Orph. fr. 243 (Abel) = 139 (Kern).

101 Enn. *Euhem.* fr. 1 (Vahlen) = Warmington p. 418.

leadership but not the kingship, and then Saturn could accumulate greater resources for himself and claim the title of king.

Euhemerist explanation (continued)

14.1 Since there is a certain difference between the *Sacred History* and what I have quoted, let us now lay out the contents of truthful literature, to prevent any idea that in attacking religions we follow poets and approve of their stupidities. 2 Here are Ennius' words: 'Then Saturn took Ops to wife. Titan, the elder brother, demanded the kingship for himself. Vesta their mother, with their sisters Ceres and Ops, persuaded Saturn not to give way to his brother in the matter. 3 Titan was less good-looking than Saturn; for that reason, and also because he could see his mother and sisters working to have it so, he conceded the kingship to Saturn, and came to terms with him: if Saturn had a male child born to him, it would not be reared. This was done to secure reversion of the kingship to Titan's children. 4 They then killed the first son that was born to Saturn. Next came twin children, Jupiter and Juno. Juno was given to Saturn to see while Jupiter was secretly removed and given to Vesta to be brought up without Saturn's knowledge. 5 In the same way without Saturn knowing, Ops bore Neptune and hid him away. In her third[102] labour Ops bore another set of twins, Pluto and Glauce. (Pluto in Latin is Diespiter; some call him Orcus.) Saturn was shown his daughter Glauce but his son Pluto was hidden and removed. Glauce then died young. 6 That is the pedigree, as written, of Jupiter and his brothers; that is how it has been passed down to us in holy scripture.'[103] 7 A little later he adds in similar fashion: 'Next, when Titan realised Saturn had sons who had been born and brought up without his knowledge, he gathered his own sons about him (they are called Titani), seized his brother Saturn and Ops, built a wall around them and set a guard over them.'[104] 8 The truth of this account is upheld by the Erythrean Sibyl's nearly identical version; only in a few, irrelevant details is there any difference.[105] 9 Jupiter is thus acquitted of the very great crime of (as is alleged) putting his father in fetters. That was the act of his uncle Titan, done because Saturn had reared male children in contravention of their agreement and his oath.

---

102 Fourth: Ennius has either disallowed the first birth or miscounted.
103 Enn. *Euhem.* fr. 3 (Vahlen) = Warmington pp. 418–20.
104 Enn. *Euhem.* fr. 4 (Vahlen) = Warmington p. 420.
105 *Orac. Sib.* 3.110ff, 199ff.

10 The remainder of the *History* goes as follows: 'When Jupiter grew up and heard that his father and mother were ringed about with guards and had been thrown into chains, he came with a great host of Cretans and conquered Titan and his sons in battle; he released his parents, restored his father to the kingship, and then went back to Crete. 11 After that Saturn was warned by an oracle to beware of his son driving him off the throne. To remove the threat of the oracle and to avoid the danger, he plotted to have Jupiter killed; Jupiter learnt of the plot, reclaimed his right to rule, and put Saturn to flight. 12 Saturn was chased from land to land, pursued by armed men sent by Jupiter to seize him or kill him; with difficulty he found a place in Italy where he could hide.'[106]

Deification in history

15.1 That makes it clear that they were men; it is also clear why they began to be called gods. 2 If there were no kings before Saturn or Uranus, because of the lack of population – life was rustic, and people lived without rulers – then no doubt that was the time when people began to honour a particular king and all his family with special adoration and new distinctions, to the point of actually calling them gods, either for their remarkable good qualities (an opinion which would be honestly held by people still rough and simple) or, as tends to be the case, in deference to their actual power, or because of their welcome promotion of civilisation. 3 Since those kings were highly regarded by the people whose lives they had civilised, at their deaths a great yearning ensued for them. 4 Hence the statues of them that people put up, so that by gazing at the likenesses they could find some consolation; taking it a bit further, out of their affection they began to cultivate a memory of the dead, partly to show their gratitude to men who had served them well and partly to spur their successors to a desire to be good rulers themselves.

5 This is what Cicero says in *de Natura Deorum* [*N.D.* 2.62]: 'Human life and its pattern of communality developed to a point where men notable for their good deeds were raised to the skies in popular report and in popular wish. Hence Hercules, Castor and Pollux, Aesculapius and Bacchus.' 6 Elsewhere he says [3.50]: 'It can be seen in many communities that the memory of brave men was made into something holy by honouring them like immortal gods, either to sharpen people's courage or to persuade all good

---

106 Enn. *Euhem.* fr. 5 (Vahlen) = Warmington pp. 420–22.

BOOK 1: FALSE RELIGION   93

citizens to take risks willingly for the sake of the community.' This is the reason, no doubt, why the Romans treated their Caesars as holy, and so did the Moors their kings. 7 In this way, little by little cults came into being; the original generation that knew them instilled the ritual into their children and grandchildren, and so into all their descendants, and finally these great kings were worshipped in every land because of the fame of their names. 8 In individual communities, on the other hand, separate cults of great veneration developed for the founders of particular clans or towns, whether those founders were men of notable courage or women of wonderful chastity: so Egypt worships Isis, the Moors worship Juba, the Macedonians Cabirus, the Carthaginians Urania, the people of Latium Faunus, the Sabines Sancus, and the Romans Quirinus; 9 in exactly the same way Athens worships Minerva, Samos Juno, Paphos Venus, Lemnos Vulcan, Naxos Bacchus, and Delos worships Apollo. 10 Thus among different peoples and territories different rites get instituted for as long as people want to give thanks to their leaders and cannot discover what other marks of honour to offer their dead.[107]

11 The biggest contribution to error came in any case from the piety of their successors: they offered, and required others to offer, divine honours to their ancestors precisely in order to seem to be born of divine stock themselves. 12 No one can have any doubts about how the worship of these gods began when they read in Vergil Aeneas' instructions to his companions [*A.* 7.133–34]: 'Now make libation with bowls to Jupiter and call in prayer upon my father Anchises'. It was not just immortality that he granted him, but power over the winds as well [5.59–60]: 'Let us pray for favourable winds: may he grant me, my city once founded, to hold these rites each year at a shrine dedicated to him'. 13 That is patently what Bacchus, Pan, Mercury and Apollo did about Jupiter, and what their descendants then did about them. The poets joined in, writing their poetry in compliment, and lauding them to the skies, as happens now when bad kings are extolled in dishonest panegyrics.

14 The corruption began with the Greeks; it is incredible what clouds of falsehood have been whipped up out of irresponsibility plentifully equipped with facile rhetoric. They started the institution of the cults and also passed them on to everyone else, out of mere admiration. 15 This is the vain nonsense that the Sibyl attacked them for:[G] 'O Greece, why have you put your faith in men as leaders? Why do you offer the dead gifts that are empty? Are you

---

107 A list of gods and the peoples who worshipped them is a commonplace. See e.g. Ovid, *Fast.* 3.81ff.; Tert. *apol.* 24.7; Min. Fel. 6.2.

sacrificing to images? Who set your wits a-roaming after these mysteries, abandoning the face of almighty God?'[108] 16 In the book that he wrote to console himself for his daughter's death, Cicero, who was not just a perfect orator but also a philosopher (the only philosopher, in fact, to follow Plato closely) declared unhesitatingly that the gods who were worshipped in public had been men.[109] 17 His testimony deserves to be taken very seriously because he not only held a priesthood in the college of augurs but also attests his own worship and veneration of those gods. 18 In a few lines he has thus given us two points: when he said that he was going to consecrate an image of his daughter in the same way that gods were consecrated by earlier generations, first he has exposed the fact that those gods had died and second he has revealed the origin of the empty superstition. 19 'Since we can see in the sum of the gods,' he says, 'great numbers of human beings both male and female, and since we venerate their most holy shrines in city and in country, let us acknowledge the wisdom of those whose inventive talents have organised and established the laws and institutions that govern our whole lives. 20 If consecration ought ever to have happened to any living being, it certainly belongs to her. If a reputation in heaven was deserved by the offspring of Cadmus, Amphitryo or Tyndarus, for sure the same distinction ought to be hers, and I will see that it happens. You were the best and most learned of all daughters; I will put you among the gods with the gods' own approval, and I will make you sacred in the thinking of all mortals.'

21 It may perhaps be said that excess of grief had sent Cicero mad. On the contrary: the whole of that work, perfect in its learning, illustration and style, marks a temperament and judgment not ailing but resolute, and the passage quoted offers no sign of anguish at all. 22 Indeed, I am sure he could not have written with such variety, fullness and control if his grief had not been tempered by his own reason, by the comfort of his friends and the passage of time. 23 What about the fact that he says the same in *de Republica* and in *de Gloria*? In *Laws*, where he followed Plato in the desire to write the laws which he thought a fair and sensible state would have, he prescribed as follows for religion [2.19]: 'Let them worship as gods both those who have always been treated as celestial and those whose deserts have placed them in heaven, Hercules, Bacchus, Aesculapius, Castor, Pollux and Quirinus.' 24 So too in his *Tusculan Disputations*, in remarking that virtually the whole of heaven was occupied by humankind, he said [1.29]: 'If I tried to examine the

---

108 *Orac. Sib.* 3.545, 547–49.
109 Cic. *Consol.* fr. 23 (Vitelli).

BOOK 1: FALSE RELIGION

tradition and then to pick from it the instances given by the writers of Greece, precisely those who are held to be gods of most ancient stock will be found to have started out for heaven from here, from us. 25 Since their[110] tombs are pointed out in Greece, remember, initiate as you are, the lore imparted in the mysteries: then you will come to realise the huge extent of it.' 26 He has relied, of course, on Atticus' understanding that the mysteries could be taken as showing by themselves the human origins of all those who are particular objects of worship; he said this about Hercules, Bacchus, Aesculapius, Castor and Pollux without hesitation, but in the case of their fathers Apollo and Jupiter, and also Neptune, Vulcan, Mars and Mercury (the gods of most ancient stock, as he called them), he was scared to say it openly. 27 Hence his phrase 'the huge extent of it': we are to understand that Jupiter and the rest of the older gods are included; if the ancients made the memory of them sacred in the same way that Cicero says he would make the image and name of his daughter sacred, in their grief they can be forgiven, but not in their faith. 28 Who is so stupid as to think that heaven opens up for the dead at the consent and determination of a host of idiots, or that anyone can give to another what he does not possess himself?

29 Julius Caesar became a god in Rome because that criminal Mark Antony so decided; Quirinus became a god because some shepherds liked the idea. Yet one of the two men killed his brother and the other one killed his country. 30 But if Antony had not been consul, Caesar would not have had the honour for his service to the state that even a dead man gets; that was indeed the advice of his father-in-law Piso and his kinsman L. Caesar, who tried to ban his funeral from taking place, and of the other consul Dolabella, who pulled down his column in the forum (his tomb, that is) and cleansed the area.[111] 31 Ennius says Romulus was much missed by his people. He makes them speak as follows in their grief for their lost king:[112] 'O Romulus, divine Romulus, what a guardian of your country the gods created in you! You led us forth within the shores of light, o father, o begetter, o blood born of the gods!' 32 Because of this feeling of loss the lie of Julius Proculus was more easily believed. He had been suborned by the senate to announce to the

---

110 'From us' is in L.'s text but not in Cicero's, and for L.'s 'Since their', Cicero has 'Ask whose'. L. is probably quoting from memory.

111 L. is inaccurate here. According to Appian (*B.C.* 2.135–36; cf. 129–30), who probably drew on a contemporary and participant, Asinius Pollio, Piso pressed for a public funeral for Caesar while Dolabella at first backed the conspirators but then changed sides. See Weinstock (1971), 346–55.

112 Enn. *Ann.* 111–14. See Skutsch (1985), 79.

people that he had seen the king dressed in more than human magnificence, and that the king had appointed him to have the people build him a shrine; for he was a god, and his name was Quirinus. 33 This he did, and he convinced the people that Romulus had departed to the gods, so freeing the senate from suspicion of regicide.

Additional arguments

16.1 I could rest content with what I have quoted, but much still remains which is necessary to the task I have taken on. 2 Although in destroying the chief of the cults itself I have destroyed them all, nevertheless I would like to hunt down the rest and confute this inveterate belief more fully, so that people may eventually be ashamed of their mistakes and repent of them. 3 It is a great task, and worth a man's while, that 'I proceed to release men's minds from the knots of superstition', as Lucretius puts it [1.932] – though he could not, since he had no truth to offer. That task belongs to us because we maintain a true god and disprove false ones.

4 People therefore who think that stories about the gods are a poets' creation both believe in the existence of female gods and worship them; without realising it they are brought round to admitting what they denied, that gods copulate and give birth. 5 Two sexes can only have been instituted for the sake of producing offspring. People accept the distinction of sexes and fail to realise the consequence of it, which is conception. That is not possible for a god, but they think it is, since they claim children both for Jupiter and for all the other gods. 6 Thus new gods get born every day (gods are not inferior to human beings in fertility) and everywhere is full of innumerable gods, since none dies. 7 Human energy is unbelievable, and human numbers are beyond count, but at least human birth is inevitably followed by death; but what sum total of gods are we to think of as existing in the end? Generation by generation they get born, and they never lose their immortality. 8 Why are there so few being worshipped? Or do we think that there are two sexes of gods simply for pleasure, and not procreation, and they are busy at things which we poor mortals are ashamed to do and to have done to us? 9 But since certain particular gods are said to be born of certain particular gods, it follows that if births occur at any time they occur at all times, or if they have stopped, we ought to know the cause and time of their stopping. 10 Seneca's observation in his books of Moral Philosophy is quite witty: 'What is the reason then,' he asks, 'that in the poets that sex-fiend Jupiter has stopped producing children? Is he over sixty, and infibulated by

the Papian law? Or has he appealed successfully to the three children law?[113] Or has he understood at last "Be done by as you did", and is he scared of someone doing to him what he did to Saturn?'

11 Those who maintain these gods' existence should look to the reply they will make to this argument we bring: if there are two sexes of gods, then copulation follows; if that happens, then they will have to have houses, for they are not so lacking in decency and modesty as to do it all together or in public, as we see the dumb beasts do. 12 If they have houses, it follows that they have towns, which is indeed what Ovid says [*Met.* 1.173–74]: 'The plebeian gods live apart from the famous and important ones, who have set up their household gods in front.' 13 If they have towns, they will therefore also have land. It is easy to see what follows now: they plough the land and plant it, which is done for the sake of food. Therefore they are mortal.

14 This argument also works in the other direction. For if they don't have land, then they don't have towns either, and if no towns, then no houses, and if no houses, then no copulation, and if no copulation, then no female sex. But we see that among the gods there are females. Therefore they are not gods. 15 Undo the logic if you can! The propositions go in such a sequence that this simply has to be the conclusion.

16 No one will undo the following argument either: of the two sexes, one is stronger and one weaker (the stronger ones are the males, and the feebler the females). But feebleness is not a feature of a god: neither therefore is the female sex. 17 To this can be added the conclusion of the previous chain of logic above, that because there are females among the gods, they are not gods.

Stoic allegory; divine misfortune and scandal

17.1 This is why the Stoics understand the gods differently, and because they do not entirely see what is really involved, they try to link the gods with their theory of the natural world. Cicero adopted that line, expressing the following view upon the gods and their cults [*N.D.* 2.70]: 2 'Do you see then how our thinking has been diverted from things physical, where good and useful discoveries can be made, to gods which are bogus and factitious? This has

---

113 Sen. F93, 206 (Vottero). In AD 9 Augustus enacted through the consuls M. Papius and Q. Poppaeus *inter alia* that men over sixty should not marry women of child-bearing age; in Roman law fathers and mothers of three or more children were favoured in a number of ways. For the details see Treggiari (1991), 60–80. For infibulation (the closing of the sexual organs by a clasp or buckle) see Celsus 7.25.3.

made for mistakes in opinion, disturbing errors, and superstitions fit for old women. We know gods by their shape and age and by their dress and decoration, not to mention their families, marriages and kinships; the whole thing has been reduced to the measure of human frailty.' 3 Nothing could be put more plainly and soundly. The prince of Roman philosophy, the holder of a most important priesthood, maintains that the gods are bogus and factitious, testifying that their cults are superstitions fit for old women, and he protests that people are entangled in mistaken opinions and disturbing errors. 4 The whole of book Three of *de Natura Deorum* is a total subversion of all cults. What more can we do? Have we the power to outdo Cicero in eloquence? Scarcely; but because he did not know the truth, he lacked faith, something he admits quite straightforwardly when he says [*N.D.* 1.60] he could more easily say what does not exist than what does: that is, that he knows what is false and does not know what is true. 5 It is plain therefore that those considered to be gods were men; consecration of their memory came after death. Hence their diversity of age and the individuality of their images, because they all had their likenesses done in the clothes and at the age of the moment when death took them.

6 Let us please consider the anguish of the gods who were unlucky. Isis lost her son,[114] and Ceres her daughter; Latona was driven out and harried all over the world, only with difficulty finding a little island to give birth on. 7 The mother of the gods fell in love with a pretty youth, and when she caught him with a paramour, she castrated him and made him a eunuch, and that is why his ritual is celebrated even now by the priests called Galli.[115] Juno persecuted her brother's paramours so fiercely because she could not get pregnant by him herself. 8 'The island of Samos,' writes Varro, 'was previously called Parthenia because there Juno grew up and there she married Jupiter. Hence her very famous and ancient temple on Samos and the statue that shows her in wedding dress, and the annual ceremony in her honour conducted like a wedding.' If then she grew up, if she was first a girl and then a wife, anyone who fails to realise she was human is admitting a bovine stupidity. 9 The indecency of Venus is beyond words, prostituting herself to the lust of one and all, not only gods but also men. She it was who bore Harmonia as a result of Mars' famous rape of her, and by Mercury she had Hermaphroditus, who was born bisexual. By Jupiter she had Cupid, by Anchises Aeneas, by

114 Her husband. L. repeats the error of Minucius Felix (22.1).
115 L. refers to the tale of Cybele, whom Romans identified with Rhea, and Attis. The Galli are the eunuch cult officials of the Great Mother. No Roman citizen was permitted to hold these posts. See D.H. 2.19.3–5; see also 21.16 below.

Butes Eryx; only with Adonis did she fail, because he was gored to death by a boar while still a boy. 10 As it says in the *Sacred History*, she started prostitution, and promoted it on Cyprus as a way the women could make money from public hire of their bodies: she required it of them to avoid herself being seen as the only wicked woman, with a gross appetite for men.[116] 11 Is there a sacred element in her at all, when her liaisons are more numerous than her bastards?

Even the virgin goddesses were unable to preserve their virginity intact. Who are we to think of as mother of Erichthonius? The earth, as the poets want it to appear? The truth is blatant. 12 When Vulcan had made weapons for the gods, and Jupiter had given him the chance to ask for the reward he wanted, swearing, as he usually did, by the lake below that he would refuse him nothing, the lame smith asked for wedding with Minerva. 13 Jupiter Best and Greatest, bound by the force of his oath, could not at this point say no, but he did advise Minerva to object and defend her chastity. In the struggle that developed they say that Vulcan ejaculated on to the soil, and so Erichthonius was born, and his name was given him[G] 'from Eris and Chthon', strife and soil, that is. 14 Then why did the virgin goddess entrust the three virgin daughters of Cecrops with that child, shut up with a snake in a sealed box?[117] Patent incest, in my opinion, which simply could not be glossed over. 15 The other goddess had almost lost her admirer when he was 'torn to bits by bolting horses' [Verg. *A.* 7.767]; to heal the youth she called on that expert doctor Asclepius, and when he was healed, she hid him [774–77] 'in a secret place, removing him to the grove of the nymph Egeria, where he could live out his days alone and unknown in Italian woods, having changed his name to Virbius.'[118] 16 What is the meaning of all this loving care and attention? Why the 'secret place'? Why the distant banishment, whether to a woman or to solitude? And why the change of name? Finally, why such a fierce anathema on the horses? What does all this indicate except consciousness of rape and a very unmaidenly passion? 17 That was plainly the reason why she went to so much trouble for so faithful a youth who had refused to serve his amorous stepmother.

---

116 Enn. *Euhem.* fr. 12 (Vahlen) = Warmington p. 430.
117 The story first occurs in Eur. *Ion,* 267–74.
118 The 'other goddess' is Artemis, or Diana, and the 'admirer' Hippolytus. After his death (see Eur. *Hipp.*) he was translated to Italy and identified with a minor local deity, Virbius, at Nemi, as narrated in Callimachus' *Aetia.* L. presumably derived the story from Varro's *Aetia.* See Horsfall (2000), *ad loc.*

Deification of benefactors

18.1 At this point we must also rebut those who do not just admit that gods were made out of men but even glory in it, in order to praise them, either, like Hercules, because of his virtue, or for their gifts, like Ceres and Bacchus, or for the skills they make available, like Aesculapius and Minerva. 2 The silliness and impropriety of all this – of people staining themselves with wickedness they could not remove and becoming enemies of the true God, and spurning him to take up cults of the dead – I will demonstrate item by item.

3 They say it is virtue that lifts a man to heaven: not the virtue that the philosophers speak of, which is a spiritual good, but our physical virtue, often called bravery. Since it was outstanding in Hercules, they think he deserved immortality. 4 No one is so stupidly silly as to think physical force is a divine, or even a human, good, when mere animals have greater, and when it is often undone by a single illness or brought to collapse by mere old age. 5 That is why Hercules himself did not want to be healed and to grow old when he saw his muscles deformed by ulcers, in case he should ever look reduced or misshapen compared with his former self. 6 People thought he had ascended into heaven off the pyre on which he cremated himself alive, and in utterly witless admiration of his deeds they recorded and commemorated them in statuary and pictures so that reminders should live on for ever of the stupidity of those who believed that murder of wild animals made gods.

7 Perhaps, however, this is the fault of the Greeks. They have always exaggerated the importance of trivialities. 8 But are our Romans any wiser? They despise athletic excellence because it doesn't impinge anyway, but a king's power, because of its tendency to cut a broad swathe, they so admire that they think bold and belligerent leaders belong in the company of the gods, and the only path to immortality is leading armies, ravaging other people's land, wiping out cities, destroying towns and either slaughtering free people or forcing them into slavery.[119] 9 Presumably the more people they have oppressed, robbed and killed, the more famous and glorious they think they are: they are deceived by a sort of sham glory and label their wicked deeds with a tag saying virtue. 10 I would rather people made gods for themselves from the slaughter of animals than have them endorse an immortality as bloodily got as that. If you cut the throat of one man, you are treated as contagiously evil, and no one thinks it right for you to be admitted

---

119 Cf. 6.6.18–20 below.

into a god's house here on earth; but the man who has slain his tens of thousands, soaking the fields in gore and fouling rivers, is let into heaven, not just into temples. 11 In Ennius Africanus speaks as follows [*var.* 23]: 'If it is right for any man to climb to the tracts of the heavenly ones, then the great gate of heaven lies open for me alone'[120] – because, of course, he had wiped out a large fraction of humanity. 12 O what a darkness for you to work in, Africanus – or rather, for you the poet! For it was the poet who thought that ascent into heaven lay open to men by way of blood and slaughter. 13 Even Cicero allied himself to such nonsense. 'It is so indeed, Africanus,' he said; 'that same door lay open also to Hercules.'[121] As if he himself were doorkeeper of heaven when it happened, of course!

14 I cannot make up my mind whether I think it lamentable or ludicrous to see serious, educated men, men wise in their own eyes, bobbing up and down in such a sorry storm of error. 15 If this is the virtue that makes us immortal, I'd rather die than be cause of death to as many as possible. 16 If immortality can only be delivered through blood, what will happen in a universal concord? That will certainly be a possibility if people are willing to abandon their destructive and wicked passions and become innocent and just. 17 Will no one be worthy of heaven then? Will virtue perish because man has no chance to ruin his fellow? Those whose greatest boast is the wrecking of civilisations won't endure a general peace: they will smash and bash and do acts of untold violence, breaking the terms on which human society works, in order to be able to have some enemy they can wipe out with more cruelty than they persecuted him in the first place.

Let us now proceed to the rest of it. 18 The title of gods came to Ceres and Bacchus for the gifts they gave. I can show from sacred literature that people were using wine and bread before those offspring of Caelus and Saturn existed; nevertheless, let us pretend that they discovered them. 19 Can it really seem that gathering grain, grinding it and teaching bread-making, or picking grapes, pressing them and making wine, is greater or more significant than creating the very grain and vines and making them sprout from the soil? 20 Even if God had left creation for men to discover, all things are still his, inevitably: he it is who gave mankind both the wisdom to discover and the things to be discovered.

21 The arts are also said to have produced immortality for their discoverers, as medicine has for Aesculapius and metalwork for Vulcan. In that

---

120 Because Seneca, *Ep.* 108.33, cites these words and ascribes them to Cicero, they are normally classed as a fragment of Cic. *Rep.* (Ziegler, *rep.*).
121 See Monat (1986), 185 n.2.

case we should also be worshipping the teachers of dry-cleaning and cobbling. Why is the inventor of pottery not honoured? Is it because your rich men do not esteem Samian ware? 22 There are other arts too whose inventors have greatly benefited human life: why have temples not been granted also to them? 23 Oh but of course – Minerva invented all them, and that is why craftsmen pray to her. So theirs are the grubby hands that have raised her into heaven. 24 Is there good reason why anyone should neglect him who set out the earth with living creatures and set the sky with stars and lights, to worship instead the one who taught the setting of a loom? 25 What about the one who taught the healing of bodily wounds? Can he be more significant than the one who gave those very bodies their form and their pattern of sense and sight, and even planned and grew the very herbs and the other material that constitute the art of healing?

19.1 Someone will doubtless argue that both this God most high who created all things and those gods who helped a bit each deserve their own due veneration. 2 First: it never has happened, and it never can happen, that one who worships them also worships him; because if he is granted the same distinction of worship that other gods have, then he is not being worshipped at all: worship of him entails the belief that he is the one and only God. 3 The master poet proclaims [Verg. A. 6.663, 7.772–73] a place in the underworld for all those who 'civilised life by the skills they discovered' including the one who 'discovered that potent art of healing and was thrust down to the waters of Styx with a lightning-stroke', so that we recognise how powerful the father is who can wipe out even gods with his thunderbolts. 4 Perhaps some clever people were using the following argument: since a god cannot be destroyed by thunderbolt, clearly it did not happen. Rather, since it did happen, clearly he was not a god but a man. 5 The lie the poets tell is one of category, not fact: they were afraid of bad reactions if they affronted public opinion with admission of the truth. 6 But if people are themselves agreed that gods were made out of men, why do they not then believe their poets whenever they tell them of gods being exiled, wounded and killed, and fighting and committing adulteries? 7 Thus we may understand that they could not have become gods on any terms at all because they weren't good even as men and they did in their lives those deeds which give birth to everlasting death.

Gods of Rome

20.1 Now that I have spoken of international cults, I come to those of the Romans. The she-wolf that suckled Romulus is the recipient of divine honours. I could put up with that if she was the animal whose shape she takes. 2 But Livy is our source for the fact that she is a representation of Larentina, and not of Larentina's physical form but of her intentions and behaviour.[122] She was the wife of Faustulus, and because she made her body cheaply available the countryfolk called her She-wolf: that is, prostitute. (Hence the word for a brothel.[123]) 3 The Romans presumably followed the Athenian example in shaping her so; in Athens the tyrant was killed by a prostitute called Lioness; because it was forbidden for a statue of a prostitute to be erected in a temple, they set up a likeness of the animal whose name she bore.[124] 4 The Athenians made their memorial out of the woman's name, and the Romans theirs out of her profession. There is even a day devoted to her name, and a festival called the Larentinalia.

5 She is not the only prostitute the Romans worship. There is also Faula, who, writes Verrius,[125] was Hercules' moll. What is our opinion to be now of an immortality that even prostitutes can achieve? 6 Flora made a great fortune plying as a prostitute; she made the people her heirs and left them a sum of money: out of the annual interest on it her birthday was to be celebrated by provision of games, called the Floralia.[126] 7 The senate thought it wicked, and so resolved to make an interpretation of her name which would lend some respectability to a matter of shame. They pretended she was the goddess in charge of flowers, and that she was to be propitiated so that the fruit on trees or vines would set and develop successfully. 8 Working to the same pattern, Ovid in *Fasti* [5.195ff.] told of a notable nymph called Chloris: she was married to Zephyrus and received as her husband's wedding gift the privilege of power over all the flowers. 9 The tale is told fairly enough, but belief in it is not right or proper; when we are looking for truth, pretence of that sort ought not to deceive us. 10 So, the games are celebrated in obedience to the memory of a strumpet with all manner of loose behaviour. Apart from a verbal licence which lets off a torrent of obscenity, at popular entreaty the women even take off their clothes; they

---

122 Cf. Livy 1.4.
123 She-wolf: in Latin, *lupa*. Brothel: in Latin, *lupanar*.
124 Cf. Pliny, *Nat.* 7.87.
125 M. Verrius Flaccus (c. 55 BC–AD 20), a freedman hired by Augustus as tutor to his grandsons, was a distinguished scholar; his major work was *de Verborum Significatione*.
126 See Scullard (1981), 110–11.

then perform like actors on stage, making suggestive movements of their bodies in public view till the eyes of lust are satisfied.

11 The image of Cloacina was found in the Great Drain[127] and was dedicated by Tatius. He named it from the place of its discovery because he did not know whose statue it was. Panic and Paleness were given a form and cult by Tullus Hostilius. 12 I can only say of him that he deserved to have his gods 'very present' – as the prayer is usually put. What M. Marcellus did in his dedication of Honour and Virtue[128] differs from Tullus' consecration in decency of title, but it is the same in fact. 13 With a similar empty-headedness the senate gave divine status to Mind. If they had had a mind between them, they would never have set up that sort of cult.

14 Cicero says that 'Greece adopted the big, bold idea of installing images of Cupids and Loves in the gymnasia.'[129] Obviously he was flattering Atticus, or else teasing him as a close friend. 15 'Big idea' is not the proper phrase for it, nor even 'idea' at all. It was the disgracefully and deplorably immoral scheme of people prostituting their own sons, in whom they ought to have been developing a sense of decency, to the lusts of young men; in effect, they wanted their sons to worship gods of debauchery, in places moreover where their naked bodies are in full view of perverts and at a time of life when in their innocence and ignorance they can tumble into traps and get ensnared before they can look after themselves. 16 Is it any surprise that Greece is a source of universal corruption, when vice itself is a part of religion, and is not shunned but actually worshipped? That is why he added his own opinion, as if he were outdoing the Greeks in good sense [*Leg.* 2.28]: 'it is virtue, and not vice, that should be held sacred.' 17 If you accept that, my dear Cicero, don't you see that the vices will gatecrash the virtues because bad clings to good and has greater influence on human minds? If you say vices are not to be treated as holy, the reply will be – Greece does not change – that gods are worshipped some for the good they do and some against the bad they do. That is the regular argument of people who treat their evils as gods, as the Romans treat mildew and fever.[130] 18 If then vices are not to be made holy, and I agree with you, then neither are

---

127 Drain: in Latin *cloaca*.

128 L. refers to the temple of Honor et Virtus just outside the Porta Capena. It was first dedicated by a Fabius Maximus and later rededicated by M. Claudius Marcellus in 205 BC, after being vowed by his father M. Claudius Marcellus the conqueror of Syracuse.

129 Cic. *Leg.* fr. 3 (Ziegler, *leg.*).

130 Robigo, the mildew on wheat, is warded off by the ceremonies of 25 April (Ovid, *Fast.* 4.905ff.); Febris, fever, had a temple on the Palatine (Cic. *Leg.* 2.28; *N.D.* 3.63; Sen. *Apoc.* 6.1).

virtues. Virtues have no intelligence or sensations of their own, and they are not for confinement within a house or shrine of mud: they belong in the heart, and are to be kept within; if they were outside, they might prove false. 19 I therefore reject with scorn that famous rule of yours expressed as follows [*Leg.* 2.19]: 'Including those qualities that granted them though human their rise to heaven: mind, virtue, piety and trust; and let there be shrines to those glories.' But these qualities are inseparable from a person. If they are to have a cult, it must happen inside the person, 20 whereas if they are outside you, what is the point of a cult of what you do not have? It is virtue, not an image of virtue, that needs cultivation, and the cultivation is not to be done through sacrifice of any sort or incense or regular litanies, but by the will alone and by determination. 21 What else is a cult of virtue than getting it by heart and holding on to it? As soon as an individual starts to want it, he achieves it, and this is the only cultivation of virtue that there is: the only religion and worship to keep to is that of the one and only God.

22 What is the point, my dear clever Cicero, of dumping superfluous buildings on land that could serve human need? Why appoint priests to worship things empty of all response? Why sacrifice victims? Why spend so much money on making or worshipping images? 23 A temple of greater strength and pureness is the human heart: so give that temple what it needs; fill that temple with true divinity. 24 These bogus dedications entail an inevitable consequence: people who worship virtues in that way, who go for images and shadows of virtues, that is, cannot obtain the things that are really true.

25 There is thus no virtue in anyone; vice is master everywhere. There is no trust, since people grab what they can for themselves; there is no sense of duty, since greed spares neither parents nor family and lust resorts to poison and the knife; there is no peace and concord, since war rages openly and even private enmities are mad enough for blood; there is no shame, since lust runs loose in man and woman alike, corrupting every act of the body. 26 And even so, people continue to worship what they shun and hate. They worship with incense and fingertips what they ought to worship with their inmost hearts, and the whole mistake arises from their ignorance of the chief and supreme good.

27 When the Gauls took Rome, and the people were under siege on the Capitol, they strung their catapults with their womenfolk's hair; then they dedicated a temple to Venus the Bald.[131] 28 They do not see how stupid their

---

131 Vegetius, *mil.* 4.9. The traditional date for the capture of Rome by the Gauls is 390 BC. See Livy 5.35.4–49.7.

cults are even from the fact that they mock them with such silliness. 29 Perhaps the Spartans were their example for making gods out of events. The Messenians were under siege; they tricked their besiegers, slipped out without being noticed, and sped off to plunder Sparta, but were routed and put to flight by the Spartan women. 30 The Spartan men meantime had realised their enemies' deception and were in pursuit. But their womenfolk, duly armed, had come out a considerable way. They met. When the women saw their menfolk preparing to fight, they thought they were the Messenians, and stripped themselves naked. 31 The men then recognised their wives, and the sight aroused them sexually. Armed as they were, they grappled with them, quite promiscuously, since there was no time to make distinctions, 32 just as they had done as young men on a previous mission when their wives were girls, and the Partheniae were born as a consequence.[132] To record the event they erected a temple and a statue to Venus under Arms; though the cause was still poor, it seems a little better to dedicate a Venus under Arms than a Venus Bald.

33 At the same time too, an altar was built for Jupiter the Baker. Jupiter had advised the besieged Romans in a moment of rest to take all the grain they had, to make it into bread and to throw the bread into the enemies' camp; if that were done, the siege would be raised, as the Gauls would despair of bringing Rome down by starvation.[133] 34 This is a mockery of religion. If I were speaking in defence of it all, I should make a fierce protest about the contempt of the divine spirit which is produced by these vulgar labels, and about the ridicule it leads to. 35 You have to laugh at a goddess Fornax – or at least, at educated people busy celebrating a Fornacalia.[134] You have to guffaw when you hear of a goddess Muta. This is the one, they say, who is mother of the Lares, called Lara or Larunda.[135] What possible use to a worshipper is a goddess who cannot speak?

36 There is also the cult of Caca, who told Hercules his cattle had been stolen: she achieved divinity by betraying her brother; and there is Cunina, who watches babies in their cradles and wards off the evil eye; and there is Stercutus,[136] who introduced the practice of dunging the fields; and there is Tutinus, on whose lap sit blushing brides-to-be, so that it looks as if Tutinus

---

132 For the Partheniae, see Strabo 6.3.2–3.
133 Cf. Livy 5.48.4; Ovid, *Fast.* 6.349ff.
134 Ovid, *Fast.* 2.525–32.
135 Ovid, *Fast.* 2.583–616.
136 So spelt in MSS R and S (and in Pliny, *Nat.* 17.50); Sterculus in most others. The three names Caca, Cunina and Stercutus all evoke excrement.

had first go at their sexual charms; and there are a thousand other wonders of the religious world: the people who adopt them for worship are sillier than we say the Egyptians are, and the Egyptians worship some really monstrous and ludicrous images. 37 Yet even those images have some form. What about worshipping a rough and shapeless stone and calling it Terminus? This is the stone that Saturn ate instead of eating Jupiter, so they say. It deserves its distinction. 38 When Tarquin wanted to build the Capitol, numerous gods had little shrines there already. He inquired of them by augury whether they would give place to Jupiter. All the rest did; only Terminus stayed put. Hence the poet's phrase 'the Capitol's unmoving rock.'[137] 39 That is a good measure of the might of Jupiter: he was resisted by a stone. Perhaps it relied upon the fact that it had freed him from the paternal throat. 40 That is why, when the Capitol was built, a hole was left in the roof over Terminus, so that for not giving way he had a free sight of the heavens, something not enjoyed by those who thought a stone enjoyed it. 41 Terminus is also the object of public prayer as the god who guards territory, being not just a stone but from time to time a fencepost. What can you say of people who worship that sort of thing, except that they themselves are the sticks and stones?

Cults bloody and comic

21.1 So much for the gods who get worshipped: now for a few words on their rituals and their mysteries. In Cyprus Teucer sacrificed a human victim to Jupiter, and passed the practice on to his descendants;[138] on Hadrian's orders it has lately been suppressed. 2 Among the Tauri, a savage and inhuman race, there was a law that foreign arrivals should be sacrificed to Diana, and that persisted for a long period of time. 3 The Gauls used to placate Esus and Teutates with human blood.[139] Even the people of Latium were not exempt from this cruelty: in our own day Jupiter Latiaris is still worshipped with human blood.[140] 4 What good can these gods be asked for by people who sacrifice like that? What can such gods give to the people whose sufferings

---

137 Verg. *A.* 9.448.
138 Cf. Verg. *A.* 3.118.
139 Cf. Caes. *Gal.* 6.16; Lucan 1.444–46.
140 Cf. Porph. *abst.* 2.56.9, close to L. in time: see Clark (2000), 161 n. 362. More probably, however, L. had in mind Tert. *apol.* 9.5ff.; *Scorp.* 7.6; Min. Fel. 30.4. The theme was a common one in Christian apologetic: see Rives (1995), esp. 75–77. The attribution of human sacrifice to the worship of Jupiter Latiaris probably arose out of a (deliberate?) confusion with the gladiatorial games held in his honour in the context of the great Latin festival. So Rose (1927).

are the offering? In the case of barbarians there is no great surprise: their religion goes with their morality; but we have always boasted of our civilised and humane ways with special emphasis: are we not shown up by these sacrilegious offerings as even nastier? 5 People who give up on their humanity despite the advantage of a liberal education deserve their name for wickedness far more than those whose lack of education tips them into wicked deeds from ignorance of good. 6 It appears, however, that the ritual of sacrificing human beings is old, since Saturn has been worshipped in Latium with the same sort of offering; the man was not in fact killed at the altar but was thrown into the Tiber off the Mulvian bridge.[141] 7 It was done, according to Varro, in obedience to an oracle: the last verse of the response goes as follows,[G] 'Send heads to Hades and to Father, man' (that is, a human being). Because of the obvious ambiguity, Saturn is usually sent both a torch and a human being.[142] 8 Sacrifice of that sort is said to have been abolished by Hercules on his way back from Spain, but the ceremony survived, with model men of straw being thrown in instead of real, as Ovid explains in *Fasti* [5.629–32]. 'Until the Tirynthian hero came to these lands, the dismal rite was performed every year, it is said, in the Leucadian manner. He flung Romans of straw into the water; following Hercules' example unreal bodies are still thrown in.' 9 The ceremony is performed by the Vestal Virgins, as Ovid also says [621–22]: 'At that time the priestess also observes the custom of flinging from the wooden bridge bulrush models of men of olden time.' As for the children who also used to be sacrificed to Saturn because of his hatred of Jupiter, I cannot think what to say: 10 how could men be so barbarously cruel as to use the word sacrifice for child murder, which is a foul and accursed crime throughout humanity? Without any regard for the duty of love they destroyed lives of tenderest innocence, a time of life especially dear to parents, and in their savagery they outdid the cruelty of all wild beasts – and yet animals love their young! 11 What incurable folly! What more could those gods of theirs do for them in their greatest wrath than they do already when feeling favourable? They stain their worshippers with

---

141 The bridge was the Pons Sublicius. See Le Gall (1953), 83. Constantine's victory in 312 happens to have been won at Rome's Mulvian or Milvian bridge.

142 *Orac. Apoll.* fr. This oracle is given in fuller form in D.H. 1.19 and in Macr. *Sat.* 1.7.28. Both sources attribute it to Dodona, and Macrobius (at least) derived it from Varro. In the Greek man, human being, is *phôta* (acc. sing.). There is also a word *phôs*, light, light of a torch, with a different declension. Confusion of the two was helped by the fact that *skótos*, darkness, has an adjective *skoteinós*; *phôs* has *photeinós*, probably formed analogically. The adjectives may be found paired as early as Xenophon: *Mem.* 3.10.1 and 4.3.4.

BOOK 1: FALSE RELIGION

murder, they stun them with loss of their children, and they strip them of human sensibility. 12 What can be sacred to these people? If they commit such awful crimes at the altars of their gods, what would they do in places not sacred? 13 In his *Satirical Stories* Pescennius Festus[143] says that 'the Carthaginians used to make human sacrifices to Saturn, and when they were conquered by Agathocles king of Sicily they assumed the god was angry with them; they therefore sacrificed two hundred children of noble birth in extra careful expiation.' 14 'Such evil has it been within the power of religion to inspire: criminal and ungodly deeds have been its frequent product' [Lucr. 1.101, 83]. 15 Whose interests were the madmen serving with such a sacrifice? They killed as great a fraction of the community as even the victorious Agathocles probably did.

16 No less mad in comparison with that sort of offering must surely be those public ceremonies, some of them belonging to the Great Mother, in which men slice off their own manhood – by amputation of sex they become neither men nor women[144] – and some of them belonging to Virtus (also called Bellona), in which the priests offer not others' blood in sacrifice but their own. 17 They cut their upper arms and run round in a trance, completely mad, waving a drawn sword in either hand. Quintilian in his *Fanatic* puts it very well: 'If a god wants that, he's an angry god.'[145] 18 Are these offerings at all? Isn't it better to live like animals than to worship gods so godless, so profane and bloodthirsty? 19 We will discuss in their proper place, however, the sources of such mistaken and wicked enormities.

Meantime let us look also at all the other practices which are not criminal, in case our enthusiasm to attack makes it look as if we are picking out the bad bits. 20 There are ceremonies in honour of Egyptian Isis to deal with the loss of her young son[146] and his finding. Her priests first depilate their bodies, and then beat their breasts and wail, just as she did herself when she lost the boy. Then a boy is produced, as if he had been found, and the grief turns into joy. So Lucan:[147] 'Osiris, never searched for long enough.' They are always losing and finding him. 21 In the ritual, then, an image is produced of an event that actually happened, which shows (if we have our

---

143 Otherwise unknown. Agathocles was king of Syracuse from 361/0 until his assassination in 289/8.
144 See note on 17.7 above.
145 [Quint.] *Decl.* fr.; cf. Ritter pref. III n.
146 See note on 17.6 above. Her husband's name was Osiris.
147 Not Lucan: L. is mistaken. The phrase is from Ovid, *Met.* 9.693; but see Lucan 8.831–33.

wits about us) that she was a mortal, a woman without family unless she found her only son. That particular point was not lost on the poet: when young Pompey hears of his father's death, he speaks as follows [Luc. 9.158–9]: 'I shall unwind Isis, that deity of the nations, from her tomb, and I shall scatter Osiris abroad in his linen wraps.' 22 This is the Osiris whom people call Serapis, or Serapides. Names usually get changed when the dead are deified, in case anybody should think they were human, I suppose. 23 After his death Romulus became Quirinus, Leda became Nemesis, Circe Marica; after her plunge into the sea, Ino became Leucothea and also Mater Matuta, while her son Melicertes became Palaemon and Portunus.[148]

24 The ceremonies for Ceres at Eleusis are not very different. In Egypt the boy Osiris is pursued by his mother's lamentations and at Eleusis Proserpina is seized for an incestuous wedding with her uncle, and her ritual is celebrated with tossing of lighted torches because Ceres is said to have sought Proserpina in Sicily with brands lit from the summit of Etna.[149] 25 In Lampsacus the propitiatory victim for Priapus is a donkey; the reason for the sacrifice is given in *Fasti* as follows:[150] all the gods had met for the festival of the Great Mother; they had eaten their fill and were spending the night in fun. Vesta lay down on the ground and fell asleep. Priapus laid siege to her sleep and to her honour, but she was woken by an untimely bray from the donkey ridden by Silenus, and her attacker's desires were disappointed; 26 that is why the people of Lampsacus have their custom of sacrificing a donkey to Priapus, to give the god his revenge, while in Rome the donkey is crowned with bread in a ceremony of the Vestals to celebrate honour preserved. 27 What could be more shameful and scandalous than to have Vesta's virginity owed to an ass? Oh, but the story is a poet's invention, they say. 28 Then is there more truth in the story told by the authors[151] of *Phaenomena* when in

---

148 Quirinus is thought to be a deity of Sabine origin: he is both a war god and a founding god associated with agriculture. The word comes from *co-uiri-um*, assembly of men; hence *Quirites* as a name for the citizens of Rome. Leda, a figure of myth, and divine Nemesis were each fertilised by Zeus. Circe, daughter of the Sun, is identified with Marica, mother of Latinus: cf. Verg. *A.* 12.164 with Serv. *ad loc.* Ino, or Leucothea, is associated with Mater Matuta, mother of the Dawn, whose temple was in the forum boarium at Rome; her son Melicertes, flung into the sea when she was pursued by Athamas, was rescued by a dolphin, secured a new name Palaemon and was honoured with the Isthmian games; Portunus was worshipped in the Tiber harbour near Rome.

149 Cf. Cic. *Ver.* 5.106.

150 6.319–48.

151 The authors probably known to L. who wrote *Phaenomena* were Aratus, Cicero and Germanicus; see note on 11.64 above. None of the works survives entire.

speaking of the two stars of the sign of the Crab which the Greeks call Donkeys they say they were the donkeys ridden by father Bacchus when he could not cross the river, and as a reward he gave one of them the power of human speech? And so a competition developed between him and Priapus over the size of their members, and Priapus lost, and killed the winner in his anger! 29 That is a much sillier story. Oh, but the poets can do what they like, they say. Well, I'm not going to open up so ugly a mystery, nor strip Priapus naked, in case something worth a laugh shows up. Let's call it poetical fancy then. Yes, but contrived of a necessity, to cover up some greater nastiness. 30 So let's find out what it is. Oh, it's plain enough, surely. A bull is sacrificed to the Moon because it has horns like the moon, and [Ov. *Fast.* 1.385–86] 'Hyperion girt with sunbeams is given a horse by Persis so that a speedy god is not offered a laggard victim.' So, because a donkey has a sexual organ of enormous size, no fitter victim could be found for that prodigy Priapus than one which could mimic the god to whom it is sacrificed.

31 Near Lindos, a town on Rhodes, there is a ceremony for Hercules, and its ritual is very different from all others, since it is conducted not amid what the Greeks call[G] goodspeech[152] but with curses and execrations, and if at any point during the solemn ritual someone lets fall a good word, even unawares, it is treated as profanation. 32 The reason given for this (if, of course, there can be any reason in such nonsense) is as follows: 33 Hercules had arrived in Lindos and was starving; he spied a ploughman at work, and started to ask him to sell him an ox. The ploughman said that it was quite impossible; all his hopes of tilling the soil depended upon the pair of oxen. 34 So Hercules exercised his usual violence: because he had been unable to get one of the oxen, he took both. When the poor ploughman saw his oxen being sacrificed, he avenged his loss with curses, which was very acceptable to our refined and urbane hero; 35 as he prepared the feast for his companions and devoured someone else's cattle, he listened to the man's bitterest objurgations with hoots of laughter. 36 But when the decision was made to offer divine honours to Hercules in admiration of his virtue, an altar was set up for him by the people of Lindos, and he called it the Ox-yoke, from what he had done; a yoke of oxen was to be sacrificed at it, just like the ones he stole from the ploughman, and the ploughman was himself appointed priest by Hercules, and told always to use the same curses in carrying out the sacrifice: he had never dined, he said, with more enjoyment. 37 This is now no sacred ceremony but sacrilege. People are treating as

---

152 *Euphemía*, 'goodspeech': the safest speech in the presence of the gods was silence.

holy something which, if it were to occur in any other ceremony, is very severely punished.

38 As for the rites of Cretan Jupiter himself, what else do they reveal except the way in which he was either stolen from his father or fed? There is a nanny goat belonging to the nymph Amalthea, which fed the child from its own udder. Germanicus speaks of the animal in his Aratean poem as follows [165–68]: 'It is thought to be Jupiter's nurse; if the infant Jupiter really did suck the trusty teats of a Cretan goat, she can prove her suckling's gratitude with a bright constellation.' 39 Musaeus says that 'Jupiter used this goat's hide as his shield when fighting against the Titans.'[153] Hence the poets' title for him of 'goatskin-bearing'.[154] Whatever was done in spiriting the child away is done in imitation at the ceremony. 40 But his mother's rites also operate similarly, as Ovid says in *Fasti* [4.207–14]: 'Steep Ida had been resounding a long while with clamourings so that the child could wail in safety from its infant mouth. Some beat shields with sticks and others beat empty helmets: the Curetes had the one task and the Corybantes the other. The deed went unobserved, but a replay of it survives: the goddess's devotees shake rattles of bronze and leather. Instead of helmets they thump cymbals and instead of shields drums, and a pipe plays Phrygian tunes as it did on the first occasion.' 41 Sallust rejected this view in its entirety as a fiction of the poets; he proposed an ingenious interpretation of why the Curetes are said to have been 'Jupiter's rearers'. It is as follows: 'because they were the first to grasp divinity, so antiquity, exaggerating as it always does, celebrated them as Jupiter's rearers.'[155] 42 How wrong the learned man was is now clear from the event: if Jupiter is the startpoint of the gods and their cults, and if there were no gods of popular worship before him because the gods to worship had not yet been born, it is plain that the Curetes were, conversely, the first *not* to grasp divinity; they were the cause of the whole mistake and of the record of the true god disappearing. 43 People ought to have realised from the mysteries and ceremonies themselves that they were praying to dead men.

44 I therefore put no pressure on anyone to believe the fictions of the poets. Anyone who thinks they are lying should consider what the priests

---

153 Musaeus was often associated with Orpheus; Diodorus Siculus calls him son of Orpheus (4.25), but Pausanias says son of Antiophemus (10.5.6). Various poems of mystic inspiration were attributed to him.

154 In Greek *aigíochos*; the word has probably been misunderstood from early times; of Zeus it meant 'cloud-driving' or 'storm-riding'.

155 Sal. *Hist.* 3.60 (Maurenbrecher).

BOOK 1: FALSE RELIGION 113

themselves have recorded, and should ponder the literature that relates to the ceremonies. He will perhaps find more there than I am mentioning from which to realise the emptiness, stupidity and falsehood of everything that is being treated as holy. 45 Anyone who can see what is sense and can lay aside error will surely laugh at the idiocies of virtual madmen: I mean the people who prance about in obscene dances or run naked, oiled and garlanded, and either masked or smeared in mud. 46 What can one say about shields now rotted with age? When they carry them, they think they bear very gods upon their shoulders. 47 One of the principal examples of pious behaviour is reckoned to be Furius Bibaculus:[156] though he was praetor, he carried a shield as his lictors went before him even though by virtue of office he had exemption from the duty. 48 He wasn't Furius, but simply raving, if he thought he did his office any good by such behaviour, and when these things get done by men of some experience and education, Lucretius is right to exclaim [2.14–16], 'O foolish[157] human minds, o hearts of blindness! What a dark and dangerous world it is that encompasses this little lifespan of ours!' 49 No one even faintly sane could fail to laugh at such rubbish if he saw people apparently bereft of their wits treating stuff as serious which done for a joke would mark the doer as stupid and depraved.

Origin of cults

22.1 All this nonsense was started and established in Rome by that Sabine king, grossly entangling a simple and inexperienced folk in new-fangled superstitions. In order to do so with some authority, he pretended he had nocturnal meetings with the goddess Egeria.[158] 2 There was a cave of great obscurity in the Arician wood, from which a stream of water flowed all year round. Here he used to withdraw, with no witnesses present, so that he could make his bogus claim that he was passing to the people, on the advice of his goddess wife, rituals that the gods would find very acceptable. 3 No doubt he

---

156 Furius Bibaculus was praetor in 219 or shortly before. At the bidding of his father, head of the brotherhood of the Salii, he carried the sacred shields though exempt by virtue of his office. These twelve shields, of figure-of-eight shape, were replicas of the shields that fell from heaven into the hands of king Numa in a time of plague. They were kept by the Salii in the shrine of Mars. See Livy 1.20.4 (with Ogilvie, *Comm.*); V. Max. 1.1.9 (with clear verbal echoes in L.).

157 Lucretius' MSS have *miseras*, 'wretched', not *stultas*. So too some of L.'s MSS, probably in correction. *Stultas* suited L.'s argument better.

158 For Numa, Romulus' successor who reigned by tradition from 715 to 673, for his religious reforms, and for his association with Egeria, see Livy 1.21.3.

wanted to copy the shrewdness of Minos, who withdrew to Jupiter's cave, spent a long time there and then produced his laws as a gift to him from Jupiter, so that he could enforce the people's obedience not merely by command but by religious sanction also. 4 It was certainly not difficult to persuade herdsmen. So he created priests, flamens, Salii and augurs, and sorted the gods into families, and thus he soothed the savage temper of a new people and drew them away from war to the pursuit of peace. 5 But though he fooled others he did not deceive himself. A good many years later, when Cornelius and Baebius were consuls,[159] two stone coffers were found in an excavation on land belonging to the scribe Petilius under the Janiculum. In one of them was the body of Numa, and in the other, seven books in Latin on the rights of the priesthood and seven in Greek on the study of wisdom, in which he completely undid all religious cults whatever, including the ones he had set up himself. 6 The matter came before the senate, and the senate voted for the destruction of the books. The praetor urbanus Q. Petilius therefore burnt them at an assembly of the people. 7 That was an unintelligent act. What was the point of the books being burnt when the doubt they cast on cults was now preserved as the cause of their burning? 8 Every member of the senate at the time was obviously very stupid: it was quite possible for the books to be burnt without their content being remembered. The senators meant to commend to their heirs the piety with which they protected the religious cults, but their actual legacy was to weaken the authority of the cults.

9 Before Numa gave the Romans their stupid religions, Faunus was at it in Latium. He established a wicked rite for his grandfather Saturn, honoured his father Picus along with the gods and declared holy his sister Fenta Fauna, who was also his wife. Gavius Bassus records[160] that she was 'called Fatua because she had the same practice of telling the future to women as Faunus did to men'. 10 Varro writes of her that she 'was of such great modesty that no male ever saw her or heard her name as long as she lived except her husband. 11 That is why women sacrifice to her in private and call her the Good Goddess.'[161] In the book he wrote in Greek, Sextus Clodius reports[162]

---

159 See Livy 40.29, under 181 BC.

160 He was a late Republican writer on etymology (*de Origine Verborum*) and on religion (*de Diis*). He relates the name Fatua to the root *fa-*, speak, whence also *fatum*, fate; L. follows him in the etymology.

161 Cf. Macr. *Sat.* 1.12.27.

162 Sex. Clodius is probably the grammarian from Sicily who taught Mark Antony. See Suet. *Gramm.* 29. For Clodius on Fatua see, more fully, Arnobius *adv. nat.* 5.18.

BOOK 1: FALSE RELIGION

that 'she was the wife of Faunus; because she had secretly downed a pitcher of wine and become drunk, contrary to royal custom and decency, she was beaten to death by her husband with sticks of myrtle; later, however, he was sorry for what he had done and could not endure his longing for her, and so he gave her divine honours; that is why at her ceremony a jar of wine is offered all wrapped up.' 12 So Faunus too has bequeathed no small sum of error to posterity; but sensible folk understand. 13 Lucilius mocks the stupidity of the people who think images are gods in the following lines: 'He shudders at these terrifying Lamias, the inventions of Faunus and Pompilius Numa: for him everything depends on them. Just as young children believe that all statues of bronze are alive and are people, so those people think all fiction is true, believing that statues of bronze have a heart. It is a painter's studio, nothing true in it at all, all fiction.' 14 The poet compares stupid people to children, but I say they are much more short-sighted than that. Children think that statues are people, whereas the adults think they are gods. Children take for true what is not so because of their age; adults do so from stupidity. And children will soon leave off being deceived, whereas adult folly lasts for ever and expands.

15 The rites of father Bacchus were first brought into Greece by Orpheus, and he was also first to celebrate them on a mountain in Boeotia near to Thebes where Bacchus was born; it is called Cithaeron because it used often to resound to the music of the cithara. 16 The rites in which the poet himself is torn apart and broken into pieces are still called Orphic; he lived at much the same time as Faunus. 17 The question of which was the elder is open to doubt, since Latinus and Priam were kings in the same period; the same is true of their fathers Faunus and Laomedon. It was in Laomedon's reign that Orpheus came to the coast of Ilium with the Argonauts.

18 Let us go further, and ask who was the absolutely first inventor of worshipping the gods. 19 In his books of commentary on Pindar, Didymus says[163] that 'Melisseus king of the Cretans was the first to make sacrifice to the gods and to introduce new rituals and processions of holy objects; he had two daughters, Amalthea and Melissa, who fed the child Jupiter with goat's milk and honey' 20 (that is the source of the poet's tale that bees flew down and filled the child's mouth with honey); 'Melissa was appointed by her father as first priestess of the Great Mother, and to this day those who attend to the Great Mother are all called Melissa.' 21 The *Sacred History* says that

163 A learned scholar of Alexandria in the 1st cent. BC.

'after Jupiter attained power,' he developed such an arrogance that 'he set up shrines to himself all over the place.'[164] 22 As he went round his lands, in every region that he came to he bound the kings and princes of the peoples to him by the tie of hospitality and friendship, and when he departed from them he gave orders for a shrine to be built to him in the name of his host, as if a memory of the friendship and agreement could be so preserved. 23 On that basis temples were set up to Jupiter Ataburius and Jupiter Labryandius (Ataburus and Labryandus were his hosts and his helpers in a war); so too to Jupiter Laprius, Jupiter Molio and Jupiter Casius and all the others of like title. It was a very clever idea of his: he acquired for himself divine honours and for his hosts a name for ever, linked with a religious cult. 24 The kings were glad therefore, and readily obeyed his rule; in gratitude for the perpetuation of their names they celebrated the festival with its ritual every year. 25 Something similar was done in Sicily by Aeneas, when he founded a city and named it after his host Acestes, so that in after time Acestes would gladly and readily love it, expand it and beautify it.[165] 26 In this way Jupiter spread the celebration of his cult throughout the world and made it an example for everyone else to follow.

27 Whether the ritual of worshipping gods issued from Melisseus, as Didymus reports, or from Jupiter himself, as Euhemerus says, there is nevertheless agreement on the time at which gods began to be worshipped. 28 Melisseus was very much the earlier: he brought up Jupiter as his grandson, and for that reason it is possible that he established godworship either before Jupiter's childhood or while he was still a child, the gods being his charge's mother, his grandmother Tellus (who was wife of Uranus) and his father Saturn. The example and pattern he set encouraged Jupiter to such pride in himself that he later had the arrogance to give himself divine honours.

Gods are recent

23.1 Now we have understood the origin of these silly superstitions, it remains to compare the lifetimes of those whose memory is so fostered. 2 Theophilus in his book *On Times*, written for Autolycus, says[166] that 'in his

---

164 Enn. *Euhem.* fr. 10 (Vahlen) = Warmington pp. 426–28.
165 See Verg. *A.* 5.746–61.
166 Theoph. *Autol.* 3.29. He was a Christian apologist of the 2nd century.

History Thallus says that Belus, worshipped by Babylonians and Assyrians, turns out to have been 322 years older than the Trojan war; he was also contemporary with Saturn, and both grew up at the same time.' 3 That is sufficiently sound for a rational comparison to be made. Agamemnon who conducted the Trojan war was Jupiter's great-great-grandson, and Achilles and Ajax were Jupiter's great-grandsons; Ulysses was related in the same degree, while Priam was more distant <...>.[167] There is a tradition in certain authors, however, that Dardanus and Iasius were sons of Corythus, not of Jupiter; if it were so, he could not have indulged in unnatural practices with Ganymede as his own great-grandson. 4 If then you allow the appropriate number of years to the ancestors of those named above, the sum will work. Since the fall of Troy, there have been 1470 years. 5 From our calculation of the preceding generations it is plain that Saturn's birth occurred not more than 1800 years ago, and he was the source of all the gods. Since origin, reason and duration of all their ceremonies are thus known, proud boasts of cultic antiquity are not for them to make.[168]

6 A few points still remain which would be very effective in proving the falseness of the cults, but I have decided to end this book now in order not to exceed the limit. 7 The points need to be developed more fully if we are to rebut all the apparent obstacles to the truth and be able to bring people who roam uncertainly in ignorance of good to the way of true worship. 8 The first step to knowledge is to understand what is wrong, and the second is to learn what is right. 9 In this first *Institute* then, we have exposed what is wrong. Anyone who has found that useful will now be stimulated to the learning of what is right, and there is no pleasure for a human being more enjoyable than that. If he goes forward willing and ready to learn what remains, he will soon be worthy of the wisdom which abides in heavenly learning.

---

167 Loss of text is suspected; Priam's relationship needed to be spelt out.
168 For L. on dates, and their derivation from Theophilus, see Nicholson (1985).

BOOK 2: THE ORIGIN OF ERROR

Aim: to expose and refute error

1.1 In Book 1, I showed that the cults of the gods were mistaken on the grounds that the gods were mortals, and when they finished life they yielded to god-given necessity by dying; the adoption of their various different cults all over the earth was due to a stupid piece of collaborative self-deception by men. In case any doubt may remain, however, this second book will expose the actual source of the errors and will unfold all the reasons why people were deceived, first into thinking that these men were gods, and then, when the belief had become inveterate, into persisting in the cults they had so wickedly adopted.

2 My desire, O emperor Constantine, is to refute these nonsenses and to lay bare man's irreligious folly, and so to assert the greatness of the one and only God by taking on the greater and more useful task of recalling people from their wicked ways and restoring them to a state of grace with themselves; otherwise they may copy certain philosophers in rating themselves too low, and in thinking that they were born weak, superfluous, worthless and utterly futile, a view which drives many to vice.

3 For as long as men think that we are the concern of no god at all, or else that we shall be nothing after death, they surrender themselves completely to their desires, and as long as they think they are free to do so, they settle into deep and thirsty draughts of those pleasures which may run them unaware into the snares of death. 4 They do not know the point of being human. If they wanted to grasp it, they would first acknowledge their lord, practise virtue and justice, not bewilder their souls with earthly fictions, not pursue the lethal sweetness of their lusts, and they would finally put high value on themselves and understand that there is more in human beings than appears: that their power and position cannot be maintained at all without laying aside wickedness and worshipping their true father. 5 When I meditate, as I often and properly do, upon the sum of things, I am always astonished that the greatness of the one and only God, which embraces and governs all things, has fallen into such oblivion that when it ought to be the only thing worshipped it is the one thing most neglected, and people themselves have

been reduced to such blindness that the true and living God takes second place to the dead: he who is creator of the earth itself yields place to gods made of earth and buried in earth.

6 This impiety of man could be forgiven even so if the error came entirely from ignorance of God's name. But since we often see the worshippers of gods themselves both acknowledging and preaching a god supreme, what forgiveness could they possibly expect for their wickedness in failing to observe the rites of the God whom it is plain wrong of man not to know? 7 When they swear an oath, when they utter a prayer, when they offer thanks, it is not Jupiter or strings of gods they name, but God: even from reluctant hearts the truth will out when nature says! 8 But they don't do that when things are going well. God most slips from mind precisely when men are in receipt of his goodness and ought to be honouring his divine indulgence. 9 In fact, they remember God only when some pressing need is upon them: if threat of war is rumbling, if plague and pest are taking hold, if prolonged drought denies sustenance to crops, if fierce storms and hail set in, then they fly to God and ask his help, and pray for him to rescue them. 10 When tossing at sea in a raging wind, him it is they invoke, him they implore when victims of some violence, him alone they call to witness when they are reduced to the ultimate necessity of begging, and plead for food with prayers; when people ask for the pity of men, they do it in his divine and unique name. 11 So it is that they never remember God except when in trouble; once fear departs and their perils recede, off they go with alacrity to the temples of the gods, pouring them libations, giving them sacrifices and garlands, 12 without even a word of thanks to the god whom they besought in their necessity. Prosperity revives their spirit of self-indulgence, and all vices come of that, including impiety to God. 13 Why should we think this happens unless we believe there is a perverse power which is always hostile to truth, which rejoices in human error, whose one perpetual task it is to spread darkness in the way and to dim people's minds so that they cannot see the light, and cannot even look up to heaven and maintain the nature they were born with?

14 Other living creatures gaze at the ground with their bodies face down because they have not been granted reason and intelligence. We stand upright and gaze aloft by the gift of God our maker. These cults of gods plainly have no part in human reason because they bend a being of the sky to worship things of earth. 15 When our one and only father was making man as an intelligent being capable of reason, he raised him up from the ground and elevated him to contemplation of his maker. This was very well put by a

gifted poet [Ovid, *Met.* 1.84–86]: 'Though all the other animals gaze at the ground face down, he gave man a visage which faced aloft, and bade him behold the skies, and uplift his face to the stars.' 16 This is why the Greeks call man 'anthropos', because he looks upwards.[1] Those who look down and not up thus deny themselves and forfeit their title of man – unless perhaps our upright stance is something they think granted to man without a reason. 17 Our heavenwards gaze is simply the will of God unobstructed. The birds can see the sky, and so can virtually all of dumb creation, but our special gift is to gaze at it standing upright, so that we can seek our faith there, and can contemplate god whose abode it is in our minds though we cannot with our eyes. That is certainly not the act of one who worships bronze and stone, things of earth. 18 It is very wrong that the human mind which is eternal should be made low when the body which is time-bound is upright; the whole meaning of our form and stance is simply that the human mind should look in the same direction as the face, and the human spirit's duty is to be as upright as the body is, in imitation of what it is due to command. 19 But human beings forget their own name and purpose; they cast their gaze down from on high, and fix it on the ground and fear creations of their own fingers, as if anything can be greater than its own maker.

Worship of statues is demeaning

2.1 What a madness it is then for people either to create what they come to fear or to fear what they create! 'Oh, it's not the things themselves that we fear,' they say; 'we fear the things in whose image they are created and in whose names they are dedicated.' You fear them, no doubt, because you think they exist in heaven; indeed, if they are gods, nothing else can be the case. 2 Why then do you not raise your eyes to heaven and call upon their names and worship them with sacrifice openly? Why must you gaze at walls and timber and stone all the time rather than towards where you think they are? What is the point of your temples and altars, and of the images themselves, which are only memorials of men dead or absent? 3 The whole point of the invention of image-making was precisely to preserve the memory of those who had been removed by death or distanced by absence.

4 In which group then shall we put the gods? If we put them with the dead, only a fool would worship them. If we put them with the absent, they

---

1 L. implies that *anthropos* was made from the three Greek roots *ana*, *athre-* and *op-*: up-look-face. See Perrin (1981), 73ff., for the theme (on which L. is very keen); 408 n. 146, on the etymology.

BOOK 2: THE ORIGIN OF ERROR   121

are still not fit for worship if they cannot see our acts or hear our prayers. 5 And if absence is impossible for gods who can see and hear everything wherever they are because they are divine, then their ubiquity makes images of them superfluous: praying by name to gods who can hear is enough. 6 Oh, but they are only present when they are by their images. Oh yes? Exactly the popular belief, that the souls of the dead haunt their graves and their own physical relics! 7 But once God begins to be around, there is no need of his image. I mean, if someone gazed a good many times at the picture of a man living abroad in order to get comfort from it in his absence, if he then went on gazing at it when the fellow had returned and was around again, would he seem sane in wanting a picture of him rather than sight of him in person? Surely not! 8 The picture of a person is plainly needed when he's not around and it is superfluous when he is, but in the case of God, whose power and spirit spread everywhere and can never be absent, a picture is superfluous at any time.

9 People are actually afraid that if they see nothing there to adore, all their worship of these gods is vain and empty; that is why they set up statues, which being likenesses of the dead resemble the dead in lacking the capacity to feel, 10 whereas the likeness of God who lives for ever should be alive and capable of feeling. But if that word likeness comes from 'being like',[2] how can those likenesses be thought like god when they have neither feeling nor emotion? A likeness of god is not the thing crafted by human hand from stone or bronze or any other material: man is himself that likeness, because he feels and reacts and can do so many great deeds.

11 People in their stupidity do not realise that if statues could feel and react, they would of their own accord adore the person by whom they were made and finished: had they not been shaped by man, they would still be rough and untended stone or raw and shapeless wood. 12 Man is therefore to be considered their virtual father: his is the handiwork that gave them birth; through him they slowly took on form, features and beauty; 13 hence the craftman's superiority over his creations. And yet, no one looks up to the craftsman or reveres him for himself: people fear his creations, as if there could possibly be more in the work than in the workman. 14 Seneca was right to say in his books on Morality, 'They worship images of gods, they pray to them on bended knee, they adore them, they sit or stand by them all the day long, they throw them a coin or kill them a victim; and though they

---

2 L. is correctly linking *simulacrum*, image, with *similis*, like, resembling, and its noun *similitudo*.

look up at them with such concentration, they despise the craftsmen who made them. 15 How contrary can you be, to despise the statuary and worship his statue, not even admitting to table with you the man who made you your gods!'[3]

So what force, what power can the statues have when their maker doesn't? He couldn't even give them the powers he did have, of sight, sound, speech and emotion. 16 Surely no one can be so stupid as to think that a statue of a god has something in it when the only human thing about it is its outline anyway. But people don't think of that; they succumb to popular fancy, and their minds absorb the dye of folly. 17 So sentience reveres the senseless and wisdom reveres the irrational; life adores the lifeless, and the heaven-born worship the earthly. 18 What a pleasure then, to stand on some high eminence where everyone can hear you and shout out that line of Persius [2.61], 'O spirits bent to earth, empty of heaven', look at the sky instead! Your own maker God has roused you up to do so! 19 He gave you your upturned faces, and you bend yourselves to the ground; he set your minds on high and raised them with their bodies towards their father, and you force them ever lower, as if you were sorry you weren't born quadruped. 20 It is not right for a heavenly being to be levelled with earthly beings that aim at the ground. Why strip yourselves of your heavenly blessings and fall flat on the ground of your own deliberate will? You roll on the earth in your wretchedness, hunting down below for what you ought to seek above. 21 Those ludicrous, feeble artefacts of the human hand, shaped out of all manner of stuff, are nothing but the earth of which they were made. 22 Why grovel to things beneath you? Why heap earth upon your heads? Every time you fall to the ground and humiliate yourselves, you are deliberately drowning yourselves, condemning yourselves to death, because lower than the earth there is nothing except death and the underworld.

23 If you were willing to escape that, you would trample the earth in contempt of it and preserve your natural posture: you were given your upright stance in order that you could level eyes and mind at your maker. 24 Spurning and trampling the earth is simply refusal to worship images because they are made of earth; so too it is refusal to covet wealth, it is spurning the pleasures of the body because wealth is earth and so is the body itself whose guest we are. In order to live, worship what lives; anyone who consigns himself and his soul to the dead must die.

---

3 Sen. F94, 208 (Vottero).

Even Sceptics participate in cult worship

3.1 But what is the point of haranguing a rough, uneducated mob in this fashion when we see that even learned and sensible men, despite perceiving the emptiness of the cults, nevertheless out of some perversity persist in worshipping those very images they condemn? 2 Cicero realised that people were praying to deceptions; though he said much of value for the overthrow of cults, even so he says, 'It should not be argued in public, in case such argument does away with cults that have been publicly adopted.'[4] 3 What is to be done with a fellow who knows he is off course and then deliberately trips on the rocks so that all the people stumble, and plucks out his own eyes so that everyone is blind? He deserves well neither of those he lets go astray nor of himself in straying on to the paths of others; above all he fails to use the gift of his own intelligence to fulfil in action what he realises in his mind: he sets his foot in the trap in full knowledge and awareness, so that he too is caught along with all the rest, when his superior understanding should have been their liberation.

4 If there is any virtue in you, Cicero, why not try to make the people understand too? It is a task worth all your powers of eloquence: no need to fear that speech may fail you when the cause is so good; you have often enough taken on bad causes with fluency and courage. 5 But you fear the cell of Socrates, and no wonder: that is why you dare not take on advocacy of the truth. Even so it was your duty as a wise man to despise death; it would be much finer to die for something blessed than for something accursed; even your Philippics could not have brought you more glory than sorting out the error of the human race and recalling the minds of men to health with argument of yours. 6 Suppose, however, we concede a timidity which ought not to occur in a wise man: why then persist in the same error yourself? I see you venerating earthly things, things made by human hand; you know they are empty, and yet you do exactly what is done by people you say are utterly stupid. 7 What use was it to have seen the truth if you were not going to defend it or accept it?

Yet even those who know their error are happy in it; all the more so the ignorant masses, who rejoice in meaningless ceremonies and gawp at everything like children, delighted by frivolities and enchanted by pretty images. Being incapable of thinking each thing out for themselves, they fail to see that nothing visible to mortal eyes is worth worship because it is

---

4 Cic. *N.D.* fr. 1, p. 1229 (Pease); the sentence is thought to come from a passage lost at 3.65.

bound to be mortal too, 8 and it's no wonder they don't see God when they can't even see the man they think they see! This object before their eyes is not man but man's container, and a man's quality and form are not visible in the shape of the vessel that contains him but in his acts and in the quality of his behaviour. 9 People who worship images are bodies lacking man because they have given themselves over to things of the body, and they see no more intellectually than they do physically, even though it is the business of the brain to sort out with greater precision what physical sight cannot observe.

10 These are the people so fiercely attacked for their dim and abject attitude in prostrating themselves in unnatural worship of earthly things by that same philosopher poet who says [Lucr. 6.52–53], 'In terror of the gods they abase their minds and flatten them to the ground', though when he said that he meant something else: since his gods have no care for mankind, there was nothing there to worship at all. 11 Finally, he says elsewhere [5.1198–1202] that religions and cults of gods are a meaningless activity: 'It is no piety at all to be seen in public[5] bowing time and again to a stone and visiting all the altars, falling prostrate to the ground and spreading one's hands before the shrines of the gods, nor is it piety to drench altars in animal blood and tack prayer on to prayer.' If these things are vain, then surely so lofty and sublime a thing as the mind must not be distracted and forced to the ground? It should be thinking only of heavenly things.

12 Wise men therefore attacked false religions because they realised they were false, but that did not bring in true religion because they did not know what sort of a thing or where it was. 13 Because they could not find the true religion, they thought of all religions as void, and so fell into a much greater error than the people who kept up a false one. 14 Those people are certainly foolish to worship such frail stuff, assuming there is something heavenly in what is earthly and corruptible; but they have some sense, and they can be forgiven for grasping man's supreme business in theory if not in full fact, given that the only, or at least the most important, distinction between man and the dumb creation is in religion.

15 But the wiser these people were in recognising the error of false religion, the stupider they were for not thinking that there was a true religion. 16 Because it is easier to criticise other people's ideas than one's own, they saw the precipice in front of others but failed to see what lay

---

5 In public: *uulgatum*; some of L.'s MSS have *uelatum*, which is Lucretius' text, meaning veiled.

before their own feet. 17 On either side then, there is great stupidity to be found and a certain smack of wisdom, so that you can be in doubt which ones to call the stupider, the ones who adopt a bogus religion or the ones who adopt none at all.

18 As I said, however, the inexpert and the ones who do not claim to be clever can be forgiven, but those who claim wisdom and display stupidity instead cannot. 19 I am not so unfair as to think that they ought to have guessed how to find the truth on their own, since I acknowledge it can't be done, but I do require of them what they could have achieved by just thinking. 20 If they realised that there was a true religion and attacked the false ones, declaring openly that people were not observing the true one, that would have been more sensible of them. Perhaps, however, they were influenced by the idea that if there were a true religion, it would declare itself and make its own claim, and not let anything else exist. 21 They simply could not see by whom or what, or how, a true religion might get suppressed: but that is a matter of God's promise and the mystery of heaven; without being taught it no one can know it at all.

22 The main point is this. The inexpert and the ignorant treat false religions as true because they do not know the true one and they do not understand the false ones, whereas better informed people, in their ignorance of the true religion, either persist in the ones they know to be false so as to look as if they abide by something, or they worship absolutely nothing in case they fall into error, even though it is the greatest error of all to copy the life of the beasts in the form of man. 23 To realise that something is wrong is a mark of wisdom, but of mere human wisdom; man cannot go beyond this stage, and so, as I have explained, many philosophers have excluded religions. To know the truth, on the other hand, is a mark of divine wisdom; man cannot attain this knowledge without being taught it by God. 24 In realising what is not the case the philosophers have thus achieved the height of human wisdom, but they have not been able to reach the point of saying what is. Cicero's remark is well known [*N.D.* 1.91]: 'If only I could discover the truth as easily as I can expose falsehood.' 25 Since that is beyond our power to achieve as humans, we have been granted the opportunity for it by god: he has given us knowledge of the truth. The four final books will serve to set that forth; meantime, let us continue to uncover falsehood as we began.

Statues are impotent, and sacrilege is unpunished

4.1 What importance can images have then, when it was up to a mere man whether they turned into something else or didn't get made at all?[6] This is why Priapus, in Horace, speaks thus [*Sat.* 1.8.1–4]: 'Once I was a fig-tree trunk, a useless bit of timber, when the carpenter, uncertain whether to make a stool or a Priapus, preferred to have the god. So a god am I, the great terror of thieves and birds.' 2 Now there's a protector to make a man feel safe! I mean, are thieves so stupid that they fear Priapus' erection when the very birds which they suppose are kept off for fear of his scythe or his sex perch on artificial images, on statues just like men, that is, and make their nests and their messes on them? 3 Satirical poet that he was, Horace mocked the vanity of mankind, but image-makers think they are engaged on serious business. 4 The greatest poet of them all, despite his common sense in other respects, goes soft on this topic, more like an old woman than a poet,[7] when in his most perfect books he gives the following advice [Verg. *G.* 4.110–11]: 'Let the protection of Priapus of the Hellespont, who watches against birds and thieves, keep all safe with his willow scythe.' 5 People are thus worshipping things mortal or mortally made, things that can be broken, burnt and destroyed. When shrines collapse from age their statues frequently get shattered; they can go up in flames and be reduced to ash, and they often fall prey to thieves, unless their size saves them or some diligent watch keeps guard. 6 We're scared they may get smashed, or burnt, or ruined: what lunacy it is to be scared of them themselves! What stupidity to hope for any protection from things which cannot protect themselves! What perversity, to run for safety to things which have no power of restoration when damaged unless their own worshippers see to it!

7 Where then is the truth? It is where no hurt can be done to worship, where nothing capable of being hurt is to be seen, where sacrilege cannot happen. Anything dependent on human hand or eye is because of that frailty in it utterly remote from immortality in any form.

8 People waste their time when they adorn and deck their gods with gold, ivory and jewels, as if their gods could get any pleasure from such things. 9 There is as much use in precious gifts to those who cannot perceive them as there is in gifts to the dead. People lay dead bodies in the ground, daubing them with spices and wrapping them in precious garments, with as

---

6 On the lack of images among Christians see Min. Fel. 10.2, with Clarke (1974), 226, n. 129.

7 An unusually sharp criticism of L.'s favourite poet.

BOOK 2: THE ORIGIN OF ERROR

much reason as they honour their gods, who did not notice when they were made and do not know of their own worship (they got no sense of it from their consecration).

10 Persius[8] did not agree with gold vases being brought into temples: he thought it otiose to have anything in religion that was more a means of expressing greed than piety. 11 It is better to bring as a gift to the god whom you mean to worship properly [2.73–74] 'a soul where rights human and divine combine, a mind all hallowed within, and a heart steeped in old-fashioned honour.' That is a notably wise perception. 12 But the continuation is ridiculous [2.69–70]: 'Gold in temples is the same as the dolls which girls offer up to Venus.' Perhaps he despised them for their tiny size. 13 He failed to see that the very images and statues of gods all made of gold and ivory by the hands of Polyclitus, Euphranor and Phidias[9] were no more than big dolls, dedicated not by girls at play, which can be excused, but by bearded men. 14 Seneca is right therefore to mock the folly of the old: 'We are not children twice, as the saying is, but for ever; the difference is that we play bigger games.'[10] 15 So it is that they bring to these great silly decorated dolls ointments, incense and perfumes, offering fine fat victims to this lot, who have mouths but lack the service of teeth, and a peplos[11] and precious clothes to that lot, who have no need of veiling, and gold and silver to another lot, who are less the owners of the stuff than the givers are.

16 When Dionysius the tyrant of Sicily occupied Greece[12] after his victory, he was right to despise, despoil and taunt such gods (he did indeed follow up his acts of sacrilege with words of mockery).[13] 17 He took a golden cloak off Olympian Jupiter, and ordered a woollen one to replace it, saying that a golden cloak was heavy in summer and cold in winter, whereas a woollen one suited either season. 18 He also tore a golden beard off

---

8 Cf. 6.2.11–12 below. Augustine, *civ.* 2.6–7, also used Persius to attack paganism.

9 Three famous Greek sculptors: Polyclitus (of Argos, active c. 460–400 BC) was best known for his Doryphorus (Spearbearer) in bronze, Euphranor (active c. 370–330 BC) for his colossal marble Apollo Patrous, and Phidias (active c. 465–425 BC), friend of Pericles, for directing the Parthenon's exterior sculpture and for sculpting the Zeus at Olympia.

10 Sen. F95, 208 (Vottero).

11 Peplos: Greek for robe or dress. The most famous was the one woven new and presented to Athena every fourth year at the Great Panathenaea for the statue of her which was eventually kept in the Erechtheum on the Acropolis.

12 L. probably means Magna Graecia, the parts of Sicily and south Italy of heavy Greek population. During the time of his power (405–367 BC), Dionysius I of Syracuse extended his area of control across the straits of Messina.

13 See Cic. *N.D.* 3.83.

Aesculapius, saying it was incongruous and unfair that his father Apollo should still be beardless and smooth-skinned and that son should be seen with a beard before his father. 19 He would pull away plates and processional goods too, and certain small figurines held in the outstretched hands of statues, saying he was accepting them, not removing them: it was particularly silly and ungrateful to refuse gifts so freely offered by those to whom people were already praying for good. 20 Because he was a victorious king, he got away with it, and his usual success stayed with him too; he lived on into old age and passed his kingship on to his son in person. In his case, since people could not avenge his acts of sacrilege, the gods themselves should have been their own avengers.

21 If a poor man does things like that, he gets the whips and flames, the rack, crucifixion, anything that men maddened to anger can think of, 22 but in punishing people caught in sacrilege they mistrust the power of their own gods: if they think their gods do have power, why not leave the space for revenge to them? 23 They assume of course that thieves of sacred objects get caught and held by divine will, and their own cruelty has less to do with their anger than their fear that if they fail to avenge the assault upon the gods, then punishment will seek them out. What an incredible fantasy! They think the gods will get at them for the crimes of other people, when those very gods themselves have been quite unable to get at their own attackers and despoilers! 24 Oh, but the gods have often taken revenge upon the sacrilegious, they say. That could be mere accident, in that it is occasional and not consistent; but I will show how it happens a little later on.

25 For the moment I am asking why they did not take revenge on Dionysius for all his acts of great sacrilege, when he treated the gods as a joke not privately, but quite openly. Why did they not keep this vigorous sinner away from their temples, rites and statues? Why did he put to sea without disaster after he had stolen sacred objects (something he acknowledged himself with a joke, in his usual way)? 26 'Do you see,' he said to his companions, scared as they were of a shipwreck, 'how fair a voyage we sacrilegious folk are being granted by the immortal gods themselves?' Perhaps he had learnt from Plato that the immortal gods are nothing.[14] 27 What about C. Verres? Cicero, his prosecutor, compared him not only to Dionysius

14 Plato probably visited Sicily first in 388/7; he may have been invited to Syracuse by its ruler; the visit was ended, according to the story, by Dionysius having him sold into slavery (see 3.25.16 below). After Dionysius' death Plato visited again, probably in 367 and in 361, to educate the new ruler, Dionysius' son. L. may be confusing the two; the son was also called Dionysius.

BOOK 2: THE ORIGIN OF ERROR

but also to Phalaris,[15] and to every other tyrant. Verres stripped the whole of Sicily of its gods' statues and their shrine furniture. 28 It would be tedious to work through all the cases: one will do, where the prosecutor used all his powers of eloquence and every vocal and physical effort to weep for Ceres, whether of Catina or of Henna.[16] Traditional scruples were so strong at Catina that it was forbidden for men to approach her temple's secret sanctuary; at Henna the cult of Ceres was so ancient that all the histories say she was the goddess who first found grain in the soil there and it was her daughter who was abducted from there as a girl. 29 In the time of the Gracchi, when Rome was racked with plots and portents, and it had been discovered in the Sibylline books that Ceres 'most ancient' should be placated, it was to Henna that the delegation was sent.[17] 30 This is the Ceres, either holiest Ceres not to be seen by men even for the sake of prayer, or the most ancient one, placated by the senate and people of Rome with sacrifices and offerings, who was stolen from her secret and ancient sanctuary by a posse of thieving slaves at the instigation of C. Verres, and he got away with it. 31 When Cicero declared that the Sicilians had begged him to take up their cause, he used these words [*Div. Caec.* 3]: 'The people now had no gods in their cities to turn to because C. Verres had stolen their holiest statues out of their most sacred shrines', as if by stealing them from their towns and temples Verres had also stolen them from heaven. 32 Thus it becomes plain that those gods had no more in them than the stuff they were made of.

33 The Sicilians were not wrong to turn to you, Cicero, to a man, that is, after three years' experience of the impotence of their gods. They would be stupid indeed to have turned to them to ward off human wickedness when the gods could vent no wrath on Verres even on their own behalf. 34 Oh, but Verres was found guilty of those deeds, they say. But it wasn't the gods who restored justice: it was the hard work of Cicero, whether in beating down Verres' protectors or in fighting against their influence. 35 After all, in Verres' case there was no guilty verdict: he got away.[18] The immortal gods apparently gave him peace and quiet in which to enjoy the fruits of his

---

15 See Cic. *Ver.* 5.145. Phalaris was tyrant of Agrigentum (7–6 cent. BC); Pindar mentions him (*Pyth.* 1.95). For comparison with the Roman governor of Sicily C. Verres, prosecuted by Cicero in 70 BC, see *Off.* 2.26 and 3.29–32.

16 The cult statues of Ceres were allegedly stolen by order of Verres: Cic. *Ver.* 4.99–102, 106–12.

17 See Cic. *Ver.* 4.108.

18 Anticipating a verdict against him, Verres withdrew to Marseilles to escape any penalty of the court. He lived there in voluntary exile for over 25 years.

sacrilege in tranquillity just as they gave Dionysius a fair wind for his cargo of divine plunder. 36 Later, when civil war was raging, Verres was far away from all peril and fear, protected by his defeat: he merely heard of other people's hard times and wretched deaths. When all the rest stood tall he seemed the only failure, but when all the rest were failing, he alone stayed on his feet; only when the profits of his sacrilege were gone and he was sated with life and weary with age did triumviral proscription carry him off, just as it also did Cicero, avenger of the gods' slighted majesty. 37 Even then Verres had the luck, in hearing how miserably his prosecutor had died before his own death occurred. No doubt the gods took care that one so good at sacrilege and plunder of their cults should not die till he had some solace for their vengeance.

Errors of the Stoics

5.1 It is far better then to set aside things incapable of meaningful response and to direct one's gaze where the seat and habitation of the true god is, who has poised the earth with a sure steadiness, who has picked out the heaven with flashing stars, who has lit up the sun, that unique and brightest light of humanity, to prove his own unique greatness, and has poured the waters round the lands and taught the rivers to flow with unceasing stream: he 'bade the fields stretch out, the valleys sink, the woods be clothed with leaf, the stony mountains rise' [Ovid, *Met.* 1.43–44]. 2 And not a bit of it was the work of Jupiter, born seventeen hundred years ago: it was all done by 'that great craftsman, the starter of a better world' [Ovid, *Met.* 1.79] whose name is God, whose own beginning is not to be sought because it cannot be understood. 3 It is enough for a full and perfect wisdom in man if he understand that God exists, and the full power of that understanding is this, that he look up and do honour to him who is both father of the human race and creator of all wonders.

4 Hence some people of dull and blunted perception adore as if they were gods elements that are mere creations and lack all capacity to feel. 5 These people marvelled at the works of god, the sky, that is, with its different stars, the earth with its fields and hills, the seas with their rivers, lakes and springs, until their wonder bewildered them; they forgot the creator himself whom they could not see, and began to venerate and worship his works, and never could understand how much greater and more marvellous is he who created them from nothing. 6 Though they see these things obeying God's laws and serving the needs of man as such things ever must, they still think of them as

gods, which is ingratitude towards God's goodness: they have put the works of God in front of God, their most indulgent father.[19]

7 It is not surprising, however, that rude and ignorant people go wrong when even philosophers of the Stoic school are of the same opinion, thinking that every moving thing in the sky is to be counted among the gods. In Cicero the Stoic Lucilius speaks as follows [*N.D.* 2.54]: 8 'This regularity among the stars then, this extraordinary punctuality throughout all eternity of their timing in their very different courses, is something I cannot imagine occurring without a mind, a purpose, a plan. Since we see it in the stars, we cannot fail to count them too among the number of the gods.' 9 A little earlier he also says [*N.D.* 2.44]: 'The movements of the stars must be voluntary. Once see that, and it would not only be stupid but also wicked to deny their divinity.'

10 We, however, do deny it consistently, and we can also show that you philosophers are not just stupid and wicked, but also blind, inept and mad: you have outdone the ignorance of the ignorant with nonsense.[20] They think the sun and moon are gods, while you think the stars are too. 11 Teach us the mysteries of the stars, so that we can raise altars and temples to each of them, and know the rites and the day for the worship of each, and the titles and prayers with which to address them – unless perhaps we should be worshipping such numerous and diminutive gods collectively, with no distinctions between them!

12 What about the fact that the proof by which they conclude all things in the sky are gods works to the opposite effect? If they think that the heavenly bodies are gods because they have fixed and analysable courses, they are wrong. This is the proof that they are not gods, because they cannot diverge from their ordered orbits. 13 If they were gods, they could move this way and that all over the place without any need to do so, like animals on earth, whose wills are free, and so they roam hither and thither as they please, each one going where its inclination takes it. 14 The movement of the stars is therefore not 'voluntary' but inevitable: they simply obey the rules and duties assigned to them. 15 When Lucilius was detailing the orbits of the stars, however, and he realised they could not be fortuitous because of the way that times and events fitted together, he concluded that they were voluntary presumably because they could not move in such regular order unless they had some intelligent awareness of their proper business. 16 Truth

---

19 For Stoic pantheism see e.g. Cic. *N.D.* 1.39; 2.37–39.
20 See Cic. *N.D.* 3.39–40.

is so very difficult for the ignorant, and so easy for those who know! 'If,' he says, 'the movements of the stars are not fortuitous, then they can only be voluntary.' No no! It is as plain that they are not voluntary as it is that they are not haphazard. 17 'How can they stay constant in completing their courses then?' God the creator of the universe so arranged it, of course; he contrived for them to hurtle through the spaces of heaven by his divine and marvellous plan so that they should accomplish the alternations of the seasons in their succession. 18 Could Archimedes in Sicily make a model of the world from a bronze sphere, and fix the sun and moon in it so that they could carry out their different movements on the pattern of their celestial rotations virtually day by day, and the sphere in its rotation show not only the rising and setting of the sun and the waxing and waning of the moon but also the separate courses of the fixed and the wandering stars, and yet God could not construct the original, and bring about what human skill can only copy? 19 If a Stoic had seen the representations of the stars marked in paint on that piece of bronze, would he say that they moved of their own will and not by contrivance of their maker? The stars do have a plan for the performance of their movements, but the plan belongs to God who made and governs all things, and not to the stars that move by it.

20 Had he wanted the sun to stay still, there would be day for ever and ever. So too, if the stars made no movements, who doubts there would be night eternal? 21 He willed them to move in order to have alternation of day and night and he willed their variety of movement so that there should be mutual exchange not only of day and night, setting up different times for work and rest, but also of cold and heat so that the power of the different seasons could serve for the sowing and ripening of crops. 22 Because the philosophers failed to see this clever application of God's power in arranging the courses of the stars, so they thought that the stars were living things, as if they marched of their own accord and not to God's plan. 23 As for why God planned it so, anyone can tell that. It was to prevent too black a night with its grim and shuddering darkness lying heavy on living things and harming them if the light of the sun withdrew. So too he marked the sky with marvellous variation and tempered the darkness with many tiny lights.

24 Ovid saw it so much more shrewdly than those who think they study wisdom: he knew those lights were put there by God to dispel the horror of darkness. He closed his abridgement of *Phaenomena* with these three verses: 'Such in form, and so many, were the signs god set upon heaven, and he bade them spread through the gloomy darkness and give a clear light to the frosty night.'

25 If it is impossible for stars to be gods, then sun and moon cannot be gods either, since their light differs from starlight not in kind but in intensity. But if these are not gods, then neither is the sky in which they all have their being. 26 Similarly, if the earth which we tread and which we work and till for food is not a god, neither will the lowlands and the highlands be gods, and if they are not gods, then neither can the whole earth be seen as a god. 27 So too, if water which serves living things for drinking and washing is not a god, then neither are its sources the springs; and if springs are not gods, neither are the rivers that accumulate from them; if rivers too are not gods, then even the sea, the product of the rivers, cannot be counted a god. 28 But if neither sky nor earth nor sea, which are parts of the world, can be gods, then neither is the whole world a god, as those Stoics say, arguing that it has both life and wisdom and so is a god. They have been so inconsistent in all this that there is nothing they have said that they have not also unsaid. 29 They argue as follows: it is impossible for senses to be missing in anything which generates things with senses. The world generates man, who is endowed with senses; therefore, they say, the world itself must have senses. 30 Likewise, senses cannot be missing in something of which a part has senses; since therefore man has senses, there must be sense also in the world of which man is part. 31 The two basic propositions are sound enough, that anything generating something endowed with senses also has senses and that senses exist in anything of which a part has senses, but the minor premises which round off the process of argument are wrong, because the world does not generate man and man is not part of the world. The same God made man in the beginning as made the world, and man is not a part of the world as a limb is of a body: 32 the world can exist without man as a town can, or a house. In fact, however, just as a house is the habitation of one human and a town is the habitation of one people, so the world is the domicile of the whole human race; the habitation is one thing, the inhabitant another.

33 But while they strove to validate the theory they had mistakenly adopted, that the world has senses and is god, they failed to see the consequences of their arguments. 34 For if man is part of the world and the world has senses because man has, then because man is mortal the earth is bound to be mortal too, and not just mortal but subject to every disease and emotion. 35 Contrarily, if the world is a god and its parts are immortal, then man is a god too, because he is (I quote) a part of the world. And if man, then the beasts of burden and the farm animals and all the other varieties of beast and bird and fish, since they too have senses in the same way and are parts of the world. 36 Oh, but that's all right, they say: the Egyptians worship them

too. But we get to a point where frogs and fleas and ants are apparently gods, because they too have senses and are a part of the world. Arguments based in error always have inept and absurd conclusions. 37 What about these same people saying that the world was constructed for the sake of gods and men, to be their common home? If the world was constructed, then it is neither a god nor alive; living things get born, not constructed, and if it was built, then it is just like a house or a ship. There is then a maker of the world, God; on one side will be the world that was made and on the other he who made it.

38 Now there is the absurd contradiction of asserting the divinity of the fires in the sky and of all the other elements in the world while also saying that the world itself is a god. How can one god be constructed out of a pile of many gods? 39 If the stars are gods, then the world is not a god but the home of gods. If on the other hand the world is a god, then all the things in it are not gods but limbs of the god; they simply cannot take the name god on their own. 40 No one can sensibly say that the limbs of one man are many men. Anyway, there is no precise comparison between a living thing and the world. Because a living being is endowed with senses, so are its limbs; they don't lose that unless sundered from the body. 41 What then does the world bear comparison with? They tell us themselves when they agree that it was made to be a sort of joint home for gods and men. If it was constructed as a home, then it is not a god and neither are the elements that are its parts, because a house cannot exercise mastery over itself, nor can the things the house is built of. 42 Thus they are defeated not only by the truth but also by their own words. Just as a house built to be lived in has no sentience of its own and is subject to the master who made it or inhabits it, so the world has no sentience of itself and is subject to God its maker, who made it for his own use.

God's creations are worshipped rather than God

6.1 They are wrong, then, these fools, and doubly wrong: first, they put the elements, that is, the creations of God, before God, and second, they worship representations of those very elements, giving them human form. 2 They make images of the sun and moon in human shape, and of fire, earth and sea too, which they call Vulcan, Vesta and Neptune, instead of sacrificing in the open to the actual elements. People are so gripped with a desire for likenesses that the real thing is now thought less valuable; what really makes them happy is gold, jewels and ivory. 3 Their beauty and brightness catch the eye, and where they don't gleam people think no religion exists. Thus greed and lust get exercised under cover of gods. They think the gods love what they themselves desire, anything that makes theft, murder and robbery the daily madness, anything that uproots people and towns in wars throughout the world. 4 They dedicate their loot and plunder to the gods, who must be feeble things, bereft of any virtue, if they submit to such acts of greed. 5 Why should we think of them as heavenly beings if they want something from earth, or as blessed if they have needs, or as pure if they take pleasure in things that the covetousness of men is rightly condemned for seeking?

6 So people come to the gods not for worship's sake, which cannot exist in a context of ill-gotten gains and dishonesty, but to glut their eyes with gold, to gaze at the sheen of polished marble and ivory, to handle clothes rich in jewels and colours or drinking cups picked out with gleaming gems, gazing on them insatiably. The more elaborate their temples and the prettier their statues, the more effective the gods are thought to be; their worship is no more than the admiration of greedy humans.

7 This is the religion handed down to them by their ancestors which they strive so fiercely to protect and sustain. They don't stop to think what sort of religion it is; they trust it is sound and true from the fact that old men passed it on, and such is the authority of age that they think it a crime to question it. Hence the belief in it everywhere as if it were the certain truth. 8 In Cicero for instance [*N.D.* 3.6], Cotta says to Lucilius: 'There, Balbus, you've got Cotta's views, a priest's views. Now let me know what your views are; you're a philosopher, and I ought to get a reason for religion from you, though I must accept our ancestors' views without one.' 9 If you believe, why do you want reason, which can cause unbelief? But if you think you ought to look for a reason, then you don't believe; you're asking for one so as to follow it when you find it. 10 Suppose reason instructs you that no true religions of gods exist: what will you do? Will you follow your ancestors or reason, a reason not fed into you by someone else but found and raised on high by you yourself when you plucked up all religion by the roots? 11 If you prefer reason, you have to withdraw from the institutions and authority of your ancestors because the only right thing is what reason prescribes; if piety persuades you to follow your ancestors, then you admit two things: they were stupid for accepting irrational religions, and you are a fool for observing what you are sure is false. 12 Since, however, the word ancestor is coming up so much, it is high time to look at who these people were whose authority it is thought so wicked to reject.

13 When Romulus was about to found his city, he called together the shepherds among whom he had grown up, and since their number seemed

inadequate for the foundation, he declared asylum. All the worst types sought refuge with him from the neighbouring areas without any distinction of status. 14 Out of the sum of them he welded together a people, choosing for the senate those that were the oldest and calling them fathers: he would go on their advice in everything. Propertius the elegist speaks of that senate as follows [4.1.13–14, 11–12]: 'A cowhorn called the first Quirites to debate; often the senate was a hundred men in a field. Nowadays the senate house gleams on high with its senators in robes; in the old days the fathers wore skins: what rustic wits they were!' 15 Those are the fathers whose decisions are to be observed so devotedly by wise and learned men, and all posterity must judge that what a hundred skin-girt elders decided to enact is true and immutable; and yet, as was said in Book 1 [22.1–8], Numa got them to accept as true rituals which he himself installed. 16 Are later generations really to think so highly of the authority of people whom no one in their own day, highest or lowest, thought fit to have as in-laws?

Reason to be used, not tradition, in assessing the power of gods

7.1 In the context of living life intelligently it is every man's especial duty to have confidence in himself and to rely on his own judgment and perceptions in order to search out and weigh up the truth, rather than be credulous and get deceived by other people's mistakes as if bereft of wits oneself. 2 God gave all men wisdom to the extent that was proper to each so that they could search out things not heard of and weigh up the things they did hear. They may have preceded us in time, but they have not therefore preceded us in wisdom, and if wisdom is granted equally to all, our predecessors cannot have taken it all. 3 Like the light and brightness of the sun, it is undiminishable, because wisdom is the light of the human heart as the sun is the illumination of our eyes. 4 Since everybody has the innate capacity to be wise – to seek the truth, that is – people who exercise no judgment in accepting the ideas of their ancestors are reducing their own intelligence; they are being led by others like sheep. 5 The mistake is this: they think that if the word 'greater' is there, then they themselves cannot be more intelligent because the word for them is 'lesser', nor can the others be stupid since they are the 'greater' ones.[21] 6 So what prevents us using their example? They

---

21 L. is playing on the use of *maior*, greater and *minor*, lesser, which also mean (usually with *natu*, by birth) older and younger. *Maiores* was in common use to mean ancestors, as in 6.7–12 above.

BOOK 2: THE ORIGIN OF ERROR   137

passed on to their successors the falsehoods they found; let us pass on to our successors something better, the truth that we have found.

7 That leaves a massive problem, and discussion of it depends not on common sense but on knowledge. It will take some time to set it out so that nothing is left at all doubtful. People may perhaps have recourse to the very considerable and unambiguous tradition which says that those who, according to our analysis, are not gods have nevertheless made frequent demonstration of their power by way of prodigies, dreams, auguries and oracles. 8 A long list could certainly be made[22] of things which deserve our wonder, most notably the advice of the chief augur Attus Navius to Tarquinius Priscus, to start on nothing new without first taking an augury; the king, mocking people's faith in the art, told him to consult the birds and then tell him whether it was possible for him to do what he had in mind, and when Navius said it was, 'Then take this whetstone,' he said, 'and slice it in two with a razor.' Without a pause the augur took the stone and split it. 9 Second comes the appearance of Castor and Pollux by the water of Juturna in the Latin war, washing the sweat off their horses when their temple attached to the fountain had opened of its own accord.[23] 10 It is said that they also revealed themselves in the Macedonian war, sitting on white horses, to P. Vatienus on his way to Rome by night; they declared that king Perseus had been conquered and made prisoner that very day. A few days later despatches from Paulus confirmed the truth of it.[24] 11 There is also the miracle of the statue of Fortuna Muliebris, which is said to have spoken, and more than once; so too the statue of Juno Moneta: when Veii was captured,[25] one of the soldiers detailed to move the statue to Rome asked in jest, for fun, whether she wanted to come to Rome, and she said yes. 12 Another example of a miracle is Claudia. When the Idean Mother had been brought to Rome in accordance with the Sibylline books,[26] and the ship conveying her got stuck on a shoal in the Tiber and no force could shift it, they say that Claudia, who had always

---

22 See Min. Fel. 7 for a shorter list. L. appears to have used Valerius Maximus (1.1.8). The tale of Attus Navius is told in Livy 1.36.3–4.
23 Cic. *N.D.* 2.6; V. Max. 1.8.1; D.H. 6.13.
24 The reference is to the Third Macedonian War of 171–168 BC. The Roman army was led by L. Aemilius Paullus (L.'s MSS show one 'l' only; see 16.17 below for an earlier member of the same family).
25 Traditionally dated to 396 BC. For the anecdote, see Livy 5.22. For the ceremony of *euocatio* to which allusion is made, see Macrobius, *Sat.* 3.9.7–8: the tutelary god of the doomed city passes over to the Romans at their invitation.
26 For the arrival of Magna Mater (= Cybele), see Livy 29.10.4–11.8; 14.5; Min. Fel. 7.3; with Beard, North and Price (1998), vol. 1, 96–99; vol. 2, 44–47.

been considered immodest for overmuch attention to her person, begged the goddess on bended knee to follow her girdle if she believed in her modesty, and a single woman shifted a ship which all the young men of Rome could not. 13 Equally remarkable is the story of Aesculapius: he was summoned from Epidaurus to Rome when a plague was raging, and freed the city from prolonged pestilence.[27]

14 A list can also be made of those whose prompt punishment for sacrilege makes people think the gods avenged the wrong done them.[28] 15 Appius Claudius the censor transferred the ritual of Hercules to the care of public slaves and lost his sight; the Potitius family, which surrendered the cult, was wiped out within the space of one year. 16 So too the censor Fulvius removed some marble tiles from the temple of Juno Lacinia to roof the temple of Fortuna Equestris which he had built at Rome: he lost his wits, he lost his two sons fighting in Illyrium, and died of an extremity of grief. 17 Mark Antony's prefect Turullius cut down a grove of Aesculapius on Cos to build a fleet: he was later killed by soldiers of Caesar on the spot. 18 The example of Pyrrhus can be added to these: he stole money from the treasury of Proserpina at Locri, and suffered shipwreck; after the smash, which occurred close by the goddess' temple, nothing was found intact except the money. 19 Ceres of Miletus also earned herself much veneration: the town had been captured by Alexander; his soldiers broke in to plunder her shrine, and suddenly a flash of light left every man blind.

20 Even dreams are found which seem to reveal the power of the gods. Jupiter is said to have appeared in the peace of the night to a plebeian named Tiberius Atinius,[29] bidding him tell the consuls and senate that at the most recent games in the Circus the dance-leader had offended him: a certain Autronius Maximus had flogged a slave, and had brought him to punishment in mid circus under the fork; the games should therefore be started again. 21 When Atinius failed to give the message, the same day he lost his son and was himself taken by a serious illness; when he had the same vision again, asking him whether he had paid penalty enough for his neglect of instructions, he had himself carried to the consuls on a litter, and upon declaring everything in the senate received his physical strength back and went home on his own two feet. 22 Of no less remark is the dream which is said to have saved Augustus. When in the civil war with Brutus he fell gravely ill and

---

27 See Livy 10.47.6–7 (293 BC), with Beard, North and Price (1998), vol. 1, 69; vol. 2, 43.
28 For a different list of casualties, see Min. Fel. 7.4.
29 See Livy 2.36 (who calls him T. Latinius); Macr. *Sat.* 1.11 (Annius).

decided to miss the battle, his doctor Artorius was visited by a likeness of Minerva recommending that because of his infirmity Augustus should not stay in camp. He was therefore taken to the fight on a litter, and the same day his camp was captured by Brutus.

23 Many similar examples can be presented besides, but I fear that if I dwell too long upon the presentation of the other side, either I may seem to have forgotten my purpose, or else I may incur a charge of prolixity.

God created the world – and the potential for evil

8.1 I will therefore set out the reason for all these incidents so that their difficulties and obscurities can be more readily understood, and I will expose all those tricks of bogus divinity which seduce people too far from the path of truth. 2 I will cast back a long way, however, so that any who come to read this with no experience or knowledge of the truth may be informed and understand what is the 'head and cause of these evils',[30] and in that light may see their own errors and those of the whole human race.

3 Since God was very alert in his preparations and very skilful in execution, before he began this task of the world he created good and evil. What that is I will explain more clearly, in case anyone thinks I am talking the way poets usually talk, who embrace the abstract in images that are virtually visible. Since nothing existed at the time apart from himself, because the source of full and perfect good was in himself, as it always is, in order that good should spring from him like a stream and flow forth on and on, he produced a spirit like himself, which was to be endowed with all the virtues of God his father. How he did it when there was only himself I will try to explain in my fourth book. 4 Then by means of the one he made first he made another, liable to corruption. In this one the divine inheritance was not to abide. This spirit was poisoned by its own envy; it changed from good to evil, and of its own choice, a free choice granted it by God, it claimed for itself a contradictory name.[31] 5 The source of all evil can consequently be seen as jealousy. The spirit was jealous of the one that came before it, which consistently earned the favour and affection of God its father. I will be brief about that spirit here, because its virtue, name and purpose are to be set out elsewhere; I will deal with the other more extensively, so that the pattern of God's purpose may be known: good cannot be understood without evil, nor

---

30 Verg. A. 11.361.
31 Lucifer: bringer of light.

can evil without good, and wisdom is the knowledge of good and evil. 6 This evil spirit, which made itself evil instead of good, the Greeks therefore call the slanderer;[G32] we call it the prosecutor, because it brings before God the prosecution of crimes which it inspires itself.

6a[33] Why God wanted it to be like that I will now explain, as far as my modest perception can manage. 6b When God was about to make this world, which was to be composed of diverse and discordant elements, he established and created in advance of that diversity, in advance of everything indeed, two sources for these elements which were to oppose and quarrel with each other; these are the two spirits right and wrong, the one serving as God's right hand, as it were, and the other as his left, so that they should have control of the contrarieties out of whose combination and blending the world and everything in it would be composed. 6c And when he was about to make man, whose rule for living was to be virtue through which he would achieve immortality, he made good and evil so that there could be virtue; if virtue were not beset with evils, it will either lose its potency or else not exist at all. 6d It is the sharpness of need which makes wealth look good, it is the gloom of darkness which commends the grace of light, and the pleasures of health and strength are learnt from sickness and pain. Just so, good cannot exist without evil in this life, and though each is opposed to the other, yet they so stick together that if you remove one, you remove both. 6e Good cannot be grasped and understood without the effort to escape from evil, and evil cannot be watched and overcome without the help of good duly grasped and understood. Evil therefore had to be created, so that there could be good. 6f Because it was not right for evil to proceed from God – God will not act against himself – he set up this inventor of evils, and when he created him, he gave him the talent and wit to think up evil things, so that he should be the home of depravity of will and of perfect wickedness. God wanted him to be the source of all that was the opposite of his own virtues, and he wanted competition with him over whether he himself could cause more good than the other could cause evil. 6g But then again, since there can be no successsful fight against God supreme, he passed control of his own good to his champion, who we said above was good and perfect. So he set up a pair to fight, and equipped them, but the one of them he loved like a good son and the other he disowned as a bad son. Later he created many more agents to carry out his tasks, whom the Greeks

---

32 The Greek word, which L. quotes (hence the G), is *diábolos*: whence 'devil'.
33 Sections 6a to 6i Brandt regarded as interpolated; hence the numbering. See pp. 27–28n.

BOOK 2: THE ORIGIN OF ERROR

call angels and..[34] 6h Though corruptible, they were not corrupted straight-away, from the moment of their creation; they opted out of the strength of their heavenly being perversely and deliberately after the world had been made and organised, as I will explain shortly, but in the beginning they were all equal, and existed with God on equal terms, and were therefore all angels, but led by the two above. 6i[35] When God had put one of these two in charge of good and the other in charge of evil, then he started on the fabric of the world, with all those he had created serving him in specific offices as arranged. 7 When he had thus begun the making of the world, he put his eldest and most important son in charge of the whole work, using him as his adviser and craftsman in thinking things out and in arranging and completing them, since he was perfect in foresight, planning and power. I will be brief on the topic here, since his virtue, name and purpose are to be set out elsewhere.

8 No one need ask after the materials from which God created those great and wonderful works. He made them all from nothing. The poets are not to be heeded either: they say that in the beginning there was chaos, a confusion of bits and pieces, and God sorted the whole heap out later, picking bits out of the pile of confusion one by one and allotting each its place, and so he fitted out the world at the same time as he made it. 9 Replying to them is easy: they do not understand the power of God; they think he can make nothing unless material is lying there ready.

Even the philosophers have made that mistake. 10 Cicero, discussing the nature of the gods, says: 'First then, it is not demonstrable that the stuff of things, from which everything has arisen, was brought into being by divine providence; it is more likely that it has, and always has had, its own power and nature. 11 A craftsman about to build something does not create the material himself but uses what is ready there; likewise a modeller in wax; so for your divine providence material ought to have been at hand, available for use and not for him still to make. But if the basic material is not made by god, then neither are earth, air, fire and water made by god.'[36]

12 What a lot of errors in those ten lines! First is the fact that Cicero, who was always a supporter of providence in virtually all his other debates and works, deploying the most penetrating of arguments against those who denied the existence of providence, now becomes a sort of traitor or turncoat

---

34 The MSS do not yield translatable text at this point.
35 This section, 6i, is to some extent a doublet of the next one, 7.
36 Cic. *N.D.* fr. 2, p. 1229 (Pease).

trying to abolish providence himself. 13 If you wanted to argue against him, there is no need to rack your brains: read him some of his own writings; Cicero can't be refuted by anyone more forcefully than by Cicero.

14 The freedom of truly free people to say and think what they like is something we can acknowledge in the tradition of the Academics, but we must still ponder what they do think. 'It is not demonstrable,' he says, 'that the stuff of things was made by god.' 15 What is your proof of that? You have offered no reason why it can't be shown. 16 My view is quite the opposite, that it very much can be shown, and I do not think it a rash view of mine that God, reduced by you to the feeble level of man when you grant him only craftsmanship, has something extra in him. 17 In what way will God's power differ from man's power if God needs others' aid as much as man does? And he does need it if he can achieve nothing unless someone else supplies him material. If that is the case, then his virtue is simply flawed, and the supplier of the material will have to be judged the stronger. 18 What will the name be for addressing the one who outdoes God in power (on the assumption that it is greater to make your own material than apply someone else's)? 19 If it is impossible for anything to be more powerful than God, who is by necessity a being of perfect virtue, power and reason, then he is as much the maker of the basic material as he is the maker of things composed of it. For without god's creative will nothing can exist, nor should it.

20 'It is demonstrable, however, that the stuff of things has, and always has had, its own power and nature.' What power could it have with no one to give it the power, and what nature if no one created it? If it had power, it got it from someone. Who could that be except God? If it had a nature (and the word nature comes simply from the word for being born), then it was born. But who could be the cause of its birth except God? 21 If nature, which you people say is the source of everything, has no power of planning, it can achieve nothing. If it is capable of generation and creation, it has a power of planning and therefore must be God, 22 and there is no other name to employ for that power in which there exists both the providence for thinking things out and the skill and capacity to create. 23 Seneca put it better. Sharpest of all the Stoics,[37] he saw that nature was simply god. 'Shall we not therefore praise god,' he said, 'whose virtue is natural? No one taught him his virtue. Yes, we will praise him. Natural as it is to him, he gave himself the virtue, for god is nature himself.' 24 Every time you attribute the beginning of things to nature and deny it to God, then 'You're stuck in the same old

37 Cf. 1.5.26 above. The citation is from Sen. F84, 198 (Vottero).

mud, Geta: you'll only get out by borrowing.'[38] First you say it isn't his creation and then you admit it is, by changing the name you give him.

25 A really inept comparison follows. 'A craftsman,' he says, 'about to build something does not create the material himself but uses what is ready there; likewise a modeller in wax; so for your divine providence material ought to have been at hand, available for use and not for him still to make.' 26 Ought is the wrong word! God will be a creature of inferior competence if he works from stuff available; that is man's competence. A carpenter without timber will make nothing, because he cannot make the timber itself, and incompetence is the mark of human feebleness. 27 God makes his own material because he can: that competence is the mark of God; if he can't he's not God. 28 Man makes from what is there because thanks to his mortality he is weak and thanks to his weakness he is of limited and modest capacity; God makes from what is not there because thanks to his eternity he is strong and thanks to his strength he has power immeasurable, power which lacks end and limit as does the creator's life. 29 No wonder then that God, when about to make the world, first prepared the material with which to make it and prepared it from what was not there. It is wrong for God to be borrowing from some other source, since he himself is the source and place of everything. 30 If anything at all precedes him, if there is anything at all created but not by him, at once he will forfeit the name and power of God.

Oh, but, they may say, the creation of matter is not like God's creation of this world out of matter. 31 In that case two things eternal are being set up diametrically opposed to each other, which cannot occur without discord and destruction; things whose power and aim are opposed are bound to be on a collision course. They cannot thus both be eternal if they come to collision, because one is bound to win. 32 The nature of anything eternal is bound to be simple, so that everything comes from it like waters from a spring. Either God is made from matter or matter from God, and it is easy to see which proposition is true, 33 for as between God and matter one has sense and the other does not. The capacity to create can only exist in something which has sense, wits, thought and motion. 34 Nothing can start, continue or end existence unless before its existence there was a plan both for its making and for its continuance after making. 35 Finally, making is the act of someone who has the will to make and the hands to effect his will. Anything without sense is doomed to inertia and torpidity for ever; nothing

---

38 Ter. *Ph.* 780. Geta is a common slave name.

can originate where there is no deliberate motion. 36 If all living things have reason built into them, then no living thing can originate from something without reason in it, and there can be no alternative source for something which is not in the place where it was sought. 37 There should be no problem, however, in some living things apparently originating in the earth. They are not born of the actual earth but of the spirit of God, without which nothing is born. 38 Thus matter is not the source of God because it is impossible for something with sense to come from something without, nor something wise from something brute, nor something that cannot suffer from something that can, nor the bodiless from the corporeal: rather, God is the source of matter.

39 Anything of solid and palpable body is liable to external forces; anything exposed to a force is liable to collapse; anything liable to collapse will die; anything that dies must have been born; anything born had its source of birth, a source that is some sentient, thinking creator, expert in creation. That is surely God. 40 And since God is endowed with sense, reason, foresight, power and virtue, he can invent and create things both animate and inanimate because he grasps how each thing should be made. 41 Matter on the other hand cannot have existed for ever: if it had, it would not undergo change. Anything that has existed for ever continues to exist for ever, and anything lacking a start must lack an end. It is in fact easier for something with a beginning to have no end than for an end to exist of something with no beginning. 42 If then matter is not a created thing, nothing can be made from it either, and if creation from it is impossible, it will not even be matter, for matter is what things are made of. Everything moves from its start to its destruction and to the start of being something else because it is subject to the hand of its maker. 43 Since therefore matter had its ending from the moment when the world was made of it, so too it had its beginning. Any destruction entails a construction, any undoing a doing up, and any ending a beginning. If we conclude that from its changing and ending matter had a beginning, who else could have caused it but God? 44 God then is the only thing not made: he can undo other stuff but he cannot be undone himself. He will persist for ever in the state he has always been in because he has no other source of being: his origin and birth depend on nothing else which could undo him by its alteration. He exists of himself, as I said in Book 1 [7.13], and for that reason he is as he wished to be, impassible, unchangeable, unmarred, blessed and eternal.

45 The conclusion that Cicero came to now looks much more absurd. 'If the basic material,' he says, 'is not made by god, then earth, water, air and

fire were also not made by god.'[39] 46 There's a clever evasion of peril! He made his first assumption as if it needed no proof, though it was much more insecure than the point it was made for. 'If matter was not made by god,' he says, 'then neither was the world made by god.' 47 He has preferred a false conclusion from a false premise to a sound conclusion from a sound premise: uncertainties should be tested against certainties, but he has taken his proof off an uncertainty in order to overthrow a certainty. 48 The world was made by divine providence: Trismegistus says so, but I will omit him, and the Sibylline verses say it, but I will omit them;[40] the prophets attest the making of the world and god's making of it with one breath and one voice, but I will not mention them; it is even agreed among virtually all the philosophers: the Pythagoreans, the Stoics and the Peripatetics all say it, and they are the chief schools of philosophy. 49 It was also an accepted and undoubted fact from the Seven Sages in the early days right down to Socrates and Plato, until after many generations came the lone lunatic Epicurus, who presumed to deny what was absolutely obvious, no doubt from a desire to be original, in order to establish a school with his own name on it. 50 Because he could not discover a new line, he decided to chuck out the old ones, simply to look different from everyone else: but philosophers have all come yapping round to prove him wrong. It is a surer thing that the world was constructed by providence than that its material got stuck together by providence. 51 It is not to be thought that the world was not made by divine providence just because its matter was not so made; rather, because the world was made by divine providence, so also the stuff of it was made divinely. 52 It is more credible that matter was made by God because of his omnipotence than that the world was not made by God, because nothing can be made without purpose, system and plan.

53 This is not Cicero's fault, however, but his school's. When he developed his discussion against the nature of the gods, about which the philosophers were jabbering on, he thought in his ignorance of the truth that all divinity had to go. 54 He could do away with the gods because they did not exist anyway, but when he tried to abolish divine providence, which does exist in the one and only God, proof failed him, and inevitably he got into a hole which he could not get out of, because he was fighting against the truth. That is where I've got him pinned down and stuck, because Lucilius, who was arguing the contrary, fell silent. 55 This is the hinge of the argument,

---

39 Cf. 11 above.
40 NF *Corp. Herm.* vol. 4, fr. 6; *orac. Sib.* fr. 1.11.

and everything turns on it. If Cotta can get himself out of the whirlpool, let him: he must bring forward arguments to explain that matter has always existed and no providence made it; he must show how anything of mass and weight could either exist without a maker, or manage to change and leave off being what it had always been so as to start being what it never was. 56 If he can prove that, then I will indeed agree that the world too was not made by divine providence: but my agreement will merely catch him in a different trap. 57 He'll find himself back where he won't want to be, saying that matter, the stuff of the world, is there by nature, and so is the world too, which is made of matter, while I shall contend that nature itself is God. 58 No one can do wonderful things, things consistent with supreme reason, that is, unless he has the mind, the foresight and the capacity for it. 59 It will therefore be the case that God made everything and that nothing can exist at all that does not derive its origin from God.

60 Every time our friend Cicero plays the Epicurean and doesn't want the world to be made by God, he usually asks[41] with what hands, machinery and levers, and with what effort god accomplished the great work. If you could have been there at the time when he did it, perhaps you would have seen! 61 But to prevent man seeing his works, God refused to bring him into the world until everything was ready. 62 Not that he could have been brought in: how would he subsist when the sky above was still being made and the earth below was still being built, when wet things were going solid perhaps, paralysed by too much stiffness, or were going hard in the solidifying cooking of a fiery heat? How would he live with no sun in place, and no food, or animals in being? Man had to be last: by then the last touch had been given to the world and to everything else. 63 Finally, holy scripture teaches that man was the last work of God: he was brought into this world as if into a house ready prepared; everything had been made for his sake. 64 Even the poets acknowledge it: after dealing with the making of the world and the forming of all its animals, Ovid then wrote as follows [*Met.* 1.76–78]: 'An animal more sacred than these, more capable of lofty thought and of dominion over the rest, was missing: man was born.' We must reckon it very wrong to investigate what God wanted hidden.

65 Cicero didn't ask his question from a desire to listen and learn, however, but to carry his point, sure that none could respond: as if, just because we can't see how it happened, that should make us think creation was not divine. 66 If you had been brought up in a house built and furnished by an

---

41 Cic. *N.D.* 1.19.

architect and had never seen building materials, would you have thought the house had not been built by someone just because you didn't know how it was built? You'd be asking the same question about the house that you are asking about the world, with what hands, with what tools a man could have constructed so massive a work, especially if you saw huge blocks of stone, quantities of concrete, vast columns, and the whole thing towering to the sky. Plainly, you would think it went beyond the limit of human might only because you did not know that it was not made by might as much as by thought and skill.[42] 67 But if man, not a perfect creature at all, achieves more even so by exercise of thought than his slender physical strength permits, why should you think it incredible when people say the world was made by God? He is perfect: in him wisdom can have no limit and might no measure.

68 His works are visible to the eye, but how he made them is not visible even to the mind's eye, because, as Hermes says, mortal cannot approach immortal, nor temporal perpetual, nor corruptible incorruptible; cannot get close, that is, and pursue it intellectually.[43] That is why no creature on earth has yet obtained a sight of things in heaven, because its body is a sort of guarding fence about it stopping it seeing everything with a free and easy perception. 69 Anyone who wants to know what cannot be explained must realise his folly, which is to reach beyond the limit of his nature and not to understand how far a man may reach. 70 Finally, when God revealed the truth to man, he wanted man to know only those things that were relevant to man to know for the conduct of his life; on anything referable to a profane and inquisitive curiosity he said nothing, so that it should be secret. 71 Why then seek a knowledge you cannot have? It wouldn't make you happier if you could. Wisdom is perfect in man if he learns that God is one, and that everything was made by him.

The stages of creation

9.1 Now that we have refuted those who think otherwise than the truth has it about the world and God its maker, let us return to the divine making of the world. The record is in the hidden writings of holy religion.

2 First of all things God made the heavens, and suspended them on high to be his own place, the seat of God the founder. Then he built the earth, and set it below the heavens, for man to inhabit with the rest of the animal

---

42 Cf. Cic. *N.D.* 2.15.
43 NF *Corp. Herm.* vol. 4, fr. 7.

species. He decided that water should wash around it and contain it. 3 His own dwelling place he marked and filled with bright lights, the sun, that is, and the gleaming orb of the moon and the radiant signs of the twinkling stars; on earth he set a darkness, because it is the opposite of these; it has no light of itself unless it receive some from the heavens. In the heavens he set a lasting light, and the higher beings and perpetual life; on earth, in contrast, he set darkness, lower beings and death. 4 These are as far distant from those above as evil is from good and vice from virtue.

5 He also arranged for two parts of the earth itself to be set against each other and to differ from each other, east and west, that is.[44] The east is attached to God because he is the source of light and the illuminator of the world and he makes us rise toward eternal life, whereas the west belongs to that disturbed and depraved intent, because it hides the light away and ever brings on darkness, and it makes people fall and perish in their sins. 6 Just as light belongs to the east and just as light is the context of a rational life, so darkness belongs to the west, and darkness is the context of death and destruction. 7 Then he measured out the other areas on the same basis, south and north, which are connected to the first two areas. 8 The one that is more ablaze with the heat of the sun is close to the east and sticks with it, while the one that is stiff with cold and perpetual frost belongs with the furthest west. Cold is the contrary of heat just as light is of darkness. 9 As heat is close to light, then, so south is to east, and as cold is close to dark, so the north zone is to the west. To each area he allotted its own weather, spring to the orient, that is, and summer to the southern quarter; autumn belongs to the west, and winter to the north. 10 In the two second areas of south and north there is a metaphor of life and death, because life depends on warmth but cold is the context of death. Warmth comes from fire, moreover, but cold from water.

11 Day and night he also made to the pattern of the four quarters: they were to produce a length and cycle of seasons to roll round in alternating succession for ever, in periods which we call years. Day, which is brought to us by sunrise, necessarily belongs to God, like all things whatsoever that are good, while night, brought on by sunset, belongs of course to the one we called God's rival. Well aware of the future as he was in this matter, God created these two deliberately so that true religion and bogus superstitions should both have some visible image. 12 The sun which rises every day may do so in solitude (which Cicero wants to see as the origin of its name,

---

44 L. constructs the story of creation around his theory of opposing elements. See Perrin (1981), 352–56.

BOOK 2: THE ORIGIN OF ERROR   149

because in blocking out the other stars it alone is visible[45]), but just as it is the true light, of perfect plenitude, illuminating everything with its powerful heat and flashing brightness, so too in God, alone though he is, there is perfect supremacy, virtue and brightness. 13 Night, however, which we say belongs to the wicked anti-god, reveals his own many different cults by way of image: 14 although there appear to be countless stars winking and twinkling, nevertheless, because their lights are not full and steady, they cannot promote any heat nor overcome darkness by their quantity.

15 Duality is thus the principle of it: two things have opposed and contrary powers, heat and wet, and God planned them wonderfully well for the sustenance and regeneration of everything. 16 Though God's virtue is in fire and heat, if he had not tempered his burning energy with an admixture of wet and cold, nothing could have come to birth and held its own without perishing in instant conflagration at the point of starting to be whatever it was. 17 Hence certain philosophers, and poets too, have said that the world exists in a 'concord of discord'; but they failed to see through to the plan.

18 Heraclitus said that the source of everything was fire; Thales said it was water. Each man saw something, but each was also wrong, because if either thing had been the only thing in existence, water could not have come from fire, nor fire from water: it is sounder to say that all things have been brought into being from a simultaneous combination of the two. 19 True, fire cannot be combined with water because they have a hostility for each other, and if they do come together, whichever gets the better of the other will necessarily destroy it; but their substances can be combined: the substance of fire is heat, and the substance of water is wetness. 20 Ovid was right [*Met.* 1.430–33]: 'When wet and heat have established a good blend, they conceive, and everything arises from those two. Though fire is in conflict with water, a hot wet steam is the creator of everything; for birth, a concord of discord is appropriate.' 21 One element is masculine, so to speak, and the other feminine, one active, the other passive. Hence the arrangement of our ancestors, that a sacrament of fire and water should sanctify the bonds of marriage, because it is by heat and wet that the offspring of living things become incarnate and animate for their lives. 22 Every living thing is made of spirit and flesh: wet is the corporeal context, and heat is the spiritual. We can learn this from the offspring of birds: eggs are full of a viscous liquid; if they are not nursed with creative warmth, the wet cannot become body nor

---

45 Any connection between *sol*, sun, and *solus*, alone, such as L. attributes to Cicero here, is mistaken. The two words have different roots.

can the body become animate. 23 People sent into exile used to be banned from fire and water; wicked as they were, they were human beings, and as it still seemed wrong in those days to exercise capital punishment, 24 banning the use of what human life is made of was thus a virtual death penalty for anyone so sentenced. These two things are considered so primary that people do not believe that human birth or life are possible without them. 25 One of them we share with all the rest of the animals, but the other has been vouchsafed to humankind alone. We have the use of fire because we are a heavenly and immortal animal, and it has been granted us in proof of our immortality, because fire is of heaven; it is by nature never still and always striving upwards, and that is the pattern of life. 26 Because all the other animals are totally mortal, they have the use only of water, which is a corporeal and earthly thing; it is by nature never still and is always seeking its lowest level, and that is a figure of death. Animals do not look up to heaven and are not acquainted with religion because the use of fire is foreign to them. 27 Only God who made them can know the origin of his two primary elements and how he kindled fire and distilled water.

Creation of animals and man

10.1 Upon completion of the world, he ordered animals of different species with different shapes to be made, both greater and lesser. They were made in pairs, one each of either sex, that is, and the sky, the earth and the seas were filled with their offspring, and God gave them all food from the earth according to their sort so that they could be of use to mankind, some for food, of course, and some for clothing, and those that were of great strength to help in the tilling of the soil: hence their title, beasts of burden.[46]

2 When everything was thus organised in an admirable arrangement, he decided to set up for himself an eternal kingship and to procreate countless souls whom he would endow with immortality. 3 Of his own act he made himself something which had senses and understanding; something, that is, in the shape of his own form [*Gen.* 127], which is the ultimate in perfection: he made man out of the mud of the earth; hence the name 'man', because man was made of soil.[47] 4 Notably, Plato says that the human form is godlike [*Rep.* 501b]; so too the Sibyl:[G] 'Man is an icon of me, possessing true

---

[46] L. makes play with the first syllables of *iuuare*, to help, and *iumentum*, beast of burden, but again, the two words do not have a common root.

[47] L. now makes play with the first three letters of *homo*, man, and *humus*, soil. Again, there is no connection.

reason.'[48] 5 The same tradition about the making of man is also, despite some corruption, in the poets: man was made from mud they say, by Prometheus. They are wrong not about the event but about its agent. 6 They had had no contact with literature containing the truth; they had merely absorbed into their own poetry what had been handed down in the predictions of the prophets and kept in a god's shrine, despite its corrupt derivation from fantasies and vague prejudice; truth usually gets diluted like that, and corrupted in popular talk, with everybody adding their bit to the tradition. It was certainly stupid of them to attribute to man something so wonderfully and divinely wrought. 7 What need was there for man to be made from mud when he could have been created in the same way that Prometheus was born of Iapetus? If Prometheus was a man, then he could have procreated a man but could not have made one; the fact that he was not born of the gods is shown by his punishment on Mount Caucasus. 8 But no one calls his father Iapetus or his uncle Titan gods, because the lofty height of kingship belonged to Saturn alone, and Saturn achieved divine honours, together with all his posterity, because of that supremacy. There are plenty of arguments with which to refute this fiction of the poets.

9 There is general agreement that the flood was produced in order to root out and destroy the great wickedness in the world. Philosophers, poets and historians of antiquity all say so, and they particularly agree on the point with what the prophets say. 10 So if the flood was brought about deliberately so that evil which had developed amongst too great a number of people could be destroyed, how can Prometheus be a maker of man when his son Deucalion was, according to those same authorities, the only man to be saved because of his sense of justice? How can the earth have been filled with people so swiftly from one family in one generation? 11 They must have muddled this point as they did the earlier one, because they did not know when the cataclysm occurred on earth, or who for his sense of justice deserved to be saved when the human race was perishing, or how or with whom he was saved: yet all of it is explained in prophetic literature. It is plain, therefore, that what they say about Prometheus' creativity is false.

12 I said, however, that the poets did not usually tell total lies: they wrapped what they were saying in figures of speech, and so kept it obscure. I do not say that they have lied: rather, Prometheus was the first person ever to shape a likeness of man from soft and squeezy mud; the art of making statues and likenesses started with him; he lived in the time of Jupiter, when

[48] *Orac. Sib.* 8.402.

temples were first being built and the new patterns of worship were developing. 13 The truth has thus been stained with falsehood; what was being called God's creation came to be attributed to a man who copied God's work. The creation of a true and living man out of mud is God's work. 14 So says Hermes too; he did not merely say that man was made in God's image, but tried also to explain the subtlety of the plan for the shaping of every individual limb of the human body, since every limb is just as important for its use as for its beauty.[49] 15 Even the Stoics are trying to do this when they talk of providence, and Cicero has followed them in several places;[50] but he touches only lightly on a topic of abundant richness. I shall pass it by for the moment, because I have recently written a book devoted to the topic for my reader Demetrianus.[51] 16 What I cannot pass by in this context is the statement of certain mistaken philosophers who say human beings and the other animals sprang from the earth without any creator. Hence Vergil's observation [*G.* 2.430–31]: 'the iron progeny of men upreared their heads from the hard fields.' The people most insistent on this idea are the ones who say there is no providence: the Stoics attribute the making of living things to divine skill.

17 Aristotle freed himself from the toil and trouble of this by saying that the world had always existed; there was therefore no beginning for the human race nor for the other creatures: they always had existed and always would.[52] 18 But since we can see every individual creature not already present both beginning its existence and ending it, it is inevitable that the whole species began to exist at some point in time, and that because it began it will cease to exist at some point in time. 19 All things are necessarily contained within three times, past, present and future. Beginning belongs to the past, existence to the present, and break-up to the future. 20 All three are visible in every single human being: we begin when we get born, we exist when we are alive, and we cease when we die. Hence people's desire for the Three Fates, one to cast on man's life, a second to weave it, and a third to break the thread and end it. 21 Within the whole human race only time present is visible: yet from it we can grasp both time past (the beginning, that is) and time to come (the break-up). 22 Because man exists, it is plain that he began some time: nothing can exist without a beginning; and because he begins, some time it is plain he will cease: any one thing constructed of mortal elements cannot be immortal.

49 NF *Corp. Herm.* 1.12 and vol. 4 fr. 8a.
50 See *Leg.* 1.27; *N.D.* 2.133; *Rep.* 4.1.
51 *De Opificio Dei*, composed shortly before this work.
52 Cf. Arist. *Cael.* 1.10; *G.A.* 2.1; perhaps derived from Cic. *Ac.* 2.119; *Tusc.* 1.70.

23 We all die, but we do it individually: it is possible that we may all die in some chance event together, from a universal dearth perhaps, a thing that tends to ravage particular areas, or from a plague worldwide (plague usually devastates particular towns or regions), or from a fire striking the earth, such as is said to have occurred under Phaethon, or from a great flood, like that under Deucalion, when apart from one man the whole human race was wiped out. 24 If that flood was accidental, it could have happened that even he, the only survivor, perished; but if he was reserved by the will of divine providence, which cannot be denied, to regenerate mankind, then it is plain that the life and death of the human race are in the power of God. But if death can befall the whole of a species because it can befall it here and there, it is plain that a species came into being at a certain point, and its end is declared by its frailty as much as its beginning is. 25 If that is true, Aristotle will not be able to resist the conclusion that the world too had its beginning. And if Plato and Epicurus can win that much from Aristotle, then Plato and Aristotle, who thought that the world would exist for ever, will, for all their eloquence, reluctantly yield to Epicurus the consequence that it also has an end. 26 This will be treated at greater length in the final book. For the moment let us return to the beginning of man.[53]

Against spontaneous generation

11.1 They say that at particular rotations of heaven and at particular shifts of the constellations a moment of ripeness arrives for sowing living things; when the earth was new, it kept the procreative seed in little pouches which it produced in the likeness of wombs: Lucretius says on the subject [5.808]: 'Wombs developed, attached to the earth by roots.' When they were ripe, at the instance of nature they burst, and poured forth living things in a delicate state. 2 Then the earth itself overflowed with a liquid like milk, and the living things were fed by its nourishment. How could they have endured or avoided the effects of heat and cold, or even get born at all when the sun was burning them or the cold chilling them? Oh, at the beginning of the world, they say, there was neither winter nor summer but a perpetual and even-tempered springtime. 3 Then why do we see none of this going on now? Because, they say, for animals to get born it only needed to happen once; after they had started on their existence, the earth left off producing because the animals had been given the power of procreation, and the climate changed.

---

[53] See 7.14.5ff.

4 How easy it is to disprove rubbish! First, nothing can exist in this world which does not stay as it begins. Sun, moon and stars did not fail to be there at the start, and when they were there they did not fail to have their orbits, and the divine control which moderates and regulates their courses was also there with them. 5 Second, if things were to be as they say, the existence of divine providence is inevitable, and they tumble into the pit they most seek to avoid. 6 For when the animals were not yet born, someone simply arranged for it to happen, so that the world should not be empty and bristling untended. But for them to be able to be born of the earth with no parents to do their bit, great foresight and preparation were needed; further, for the liquid that came out of the earth to be turned into bodies of all the different sorts, and for those bodies to pour forth out of the pouches which had protected them, as if they were coming out of a maternal womb now that they had their programme for life and sentience, miraculous and intricate foresight was needed. 7 Let us suppose, however, that it too was an accidental event; what followed could not possibly be haphazard, for the earth to ooze with instant milk, I mean, and for the climate to be so equable. 8 If it is agreed that all this did happen so that the new-born animals could have their food or not be at risk, then someone with a divine intelligence must have foreseen it all. Now, who has that power of foresight except God?

9 Let us see, nevertheless, whether what they say, birth of people out of earth, could have happened. If anyone stopped to think for a moment about the length of time and the ways in which a child is brought up, he will surely realise that those children born of the earth could not have been reared without someone to see to them. 10 They would have had to lie where they were dropped many months, until their muscles developed and they could move and change place, which scarcely happens within a year. 11 Do ask yourself whether a child can lie for months and months in the same place and posture it was in when born without dying half-drowned and half-rotted in a mixture of the liquid which the earth was offering for its sustenance and the excretions of its own body! 12 It is wholly impossible for someone not to have taken it up – unless perhaps all animals are not born weak but tough – but they never thought of saying that. 13 The whole train of thought is impossibly futile, if indeed it can be called a train of thought when its aim is no thinking at all. Anyone who says that everything was born spontaneously and who makes no allowance for divine providence is not pursuing but destroying a train of thought. 14 But if nothing can be made or get born without an act of thought, then the existence of divine providence is obvious: thought is exactly its mode.

God who made all things therefore made man. 15 Cicero, despite his ignorance of holy writ, saw it nevertheless; in book One of *Laws* he recorded the same tradition as the prophets. I supply his words [*Leg.* 1.22]. 16 'This living creature, with its foresight, wisdom, and variety, its shrewdness, its memory, its abundance of thought and decision, which we call man, was produced by god most high on some exceptional basis. It is the only one of all the species and types of living things which partakes of reason and thought; all the rest are quite without.' 17 Can you see a man there who, for all his distance from a knowledge of the truth, yet, because he could gaze on an image of wisdom, did understand that man could not have been born except of God? 18 Even so, we need divine evidence, in case the human evidence is inadequate. The Sibyl affirms that man is the work of God[G], 'who is god alone, founder, unconquerable, initiator, and he in person made fast the stamp of his shape, and he in person composed the nature of all mortals, he the begetter of life.'[54] Holy writ says the same.

19 God has therefore performed the task of a real father, himself creating our body, himself infusing the spirit by which we breathe; all that we are is his. 20 How he did it he would have told us if we needed to know, just as he has told us all the other things that have brought us knowledge both of our original error and of the true light.

Contrary elements in man; Paradise, Fall

12.1 When he had shaped the first male to his own likeness, then he shaped a female after the likeness of the man, so that the two sexes could combine together and procreate offspring and fill the whole earth with their number. 2 It was in the making of the human being that he brought together and fulfilled his plan for the two materials which we said were at odds with each other, fire and water.[55] 3 When the body was made, he breathed spirit into it from the living source of his own spirit (which is everlasting), so that it could bear a likeness to the world itself, which is also constructed of contrary elements. For it is composed of spirit and body, or virtually of heaven and earth, since the spirit by which we live in coming from God comes from heaven, and the body comes from the earth, being shaped, as we said, from its mud.

4 You may not be sure whether to count Empedocles with the poets or with the philosophers, because he wrote upon the nature of things in verse,

---

54 *Orac. Sib.* fr. 5.
55 See 9.19ff. above.

as did Lucretius and Varro in Rome;[56] anyway, he proposed four basic elements, fire, air, water and earth, possibly following Trismegistus, who said that 'our bodies were composed out of these four elements by god: 5 they had some element of fire, air, earth and water in them without actually being fire, air, earth or water.'[57] That is not wrong, for there is a measure of earth in our flesh, of liquid in our blood, of air in our breath, and of fire in our vital warmth. 6 But blood cannot be separated from the body as water can from earth, nor can our vital warmth be separated from our breath as fire can from air. That is the extent to which, out of all the elements, there are only two whose whole purpose is fulfilled in the making of our body.

7 Man is therefore composed of elements which are contrary and hostile just as the world is composed of good and bad, light and dark and life and death; and god arranged for these two to fight it out in man so that if the spirit which springs from god is victorious man will be immortal and live in perpetual light, but if the body conquers the soul and brings it under its control, man will be in everlasting darkness and death. 8 Its power is not such that it can wholly destroy unjust souls, but it can keep them punished for ever. That punishment we call 'second death'; it is itself everlasting, just as immortality is too. 9 We define first death thus: it is the undoing of the nature of living things; or thus: it is the separation of body and soul. Second death is as follows: it is the suffering of eternal pain; or thus: it is the damnation of souls to eternal torment according to their deserts. This does not affect the dumb creation: their souls break up at death because they are derived from the air which all living things have in common and not from God.

10 In this association of heaven and earth, which is given expression in the figure of man, a superior role is taken by what belongs to God, which is, of course, the soul; it has command of the body. An inferior role is taken by what belongs to the devil, which is simply the body: because it is of the earth, it must be subject to the soul as earth is to heaven, 11 for the body is a sort of container, to be used by our heavenly spirit as its temporal home. There are duties for either: what comes of heaven and God has a duty to command, and what comes of earth and the devil has a duty to perform accordingly.

12 The point did not escape that bad man Sallust,[58] who says [*Cat.* 1.2]: 'All our energy lies in soul and body. 13 We employ the soul to command

56 See Quint. *Inst.* 1.4.4.
57 NF *Corp. Herm.* vol. 3, p. 4.
58 For Sallust's poor reputation, see Dio Cassius 43.9.2 (maladministration) and A. Gellius 17.18 citing Varro (adultery). Syme (1964), 269–73, is sceptical. In 1.21.42, Sallust is called 'learned', and in 3.29.8 simply 'the historian'.

and the body to serve.' Fine, had he lived as he spoke. 14 In fact, he served his pleasures, most disgustingly, and undid his understanding by the depravity of his life. If the soul is fire, as we have shown, then like fire it should aim for heaven, so as not to be extinguished; it should aim for immortality, that is, whose place is heaven; and just as fire cannot burn and live unless sustained by some rich stuff off which it can feed, so the food and stuff of the soul is justice and by justice alone is it kept alive.

15 After God had created man to the pattern I have set forth, he put him in Paradise, in a garden, that is, of great fertility and beauty. He planted the garden in its eastern parts with every sort of timber and tree so that man could be fed from their various fruits and serve God the father with total devotion, free from any labour. 16 Then he gave man precise commandments; if he observed them, he would remain immortal, but if he transgressed them he would suffer death. There was also this instruction, that he should not taste of one tree, which was in the middle of Paradise, in which God had put the knowledge of good and evil.

17 Then that accuser, jealous of God's works, aimed all his deceit and cunning at bringing man down, in order to lose him his immortality. 18 First he deceitfully lured the woman to pick the forbidden fruit, and through her he persuaded the man too to transgress god's law. Once man had the knowledge of good and evil, he became ashamed of his nakedness, and hid himself from the face of God, which he had not done previously. 19 Then God gave sentence on the sinners and ejected man from Paradise to get his food by toil, and he walled off Paradise with fire, to prevent man getting in until the final judgment is given on earth and God calls the good men who worship him back to the same place, death being now removed, as holy writ tells us, and so does the Sibyl of Erythrae when she says,[G] 'Those who honour the true and everlasting god inherit life, and they dwell together in the fertile garden of Paradise for the whole span of time.'[59] 20 Because these things belong at the end, I will deal with them in the final part of this work; for the moment let me explain what comes first.

Death thus followed man in accordance with God's judgment, which is what the Sibyl also says in her poem as follows:[G] 'Man, formed by the holy hands of god, was treacherously sent wandering by the snake to go to his fate of death and to gain the knowledge of good and evil.'[60] 21 Thus man's life became limited, but long: it was to last a thousand years. This is set forth in

---

59 *Orac. Sib.* fr. 3.46–48.
60 *Orac. Sib.* 8.260–62.

holy scripture and is generally known to all; Varro could not ignore it, and strove instead to prove by argument 'why the ancients were thought to have lived a thousand years. 22 In Egypt,' he says, 'they count months instead of years: it is not the circuit of the sun through the twelve signs which makes up a year, but the moon, which works through that circle of signs in the space of thirty days.' That argument is transparently bogus; no one exceeded a thousand years then, 23 but nowadays, people who make it to a hundred (a very frequent occurrence) obviously live twelve hundred months. We have it on good authority that a hundred and twenty is often reached. 24 But because Varro did not know why or when human life was shortened, he shortened it himself, even though he knew that a life of fourteen hundred months was possible.

Flood, Hebrews, Canaanites, Gentiles

13.1 Later, when God saw that the world was full of wickedness and crime, he decided to destroy the human race in a flood. But in order to restore the population he picked out one man, the unique surviving example, amid the corruption, of a just man. 2 Though this man was six hundred years old, he built an ark, as God had required, in which he, his wife, his three sons and three daughters-in-law were all preserved, even though the water covered every mountain top. 3 When the world was dry again, God cursed the injustice of the previous generation, and in case length of life should again be cause for evil machinations, slowly, generation by generation, he reduced the human lifespan and set its limit at a hundred and twenty years, not to be exceeded. 4 When Noah came out of the ark, as holy scripture tells, he tilled the soil with care and planted a vine with his own hand. That is the rebuttal of those who think wine was invented by Bacchus. Noah was many ages older, not only than Bacchus, but also than Saturn and Uranus.

5 When he took the first fruit off that vine, he was happy, and drank till he was drunk, and lay there naked. He was seen by one of his sons, called Ham. Ham did not cover up his father's nakedness, but went off and told his brothers. They took a cloak, went in with their eyes averted and covered him up. 6 When their father recognised what they had done, he disinherited his son Ham and banished him. Ham fled, and settled in the part of the earth now called Arabia; it is called Canaan, and its people Canaanites, from his name.[61] 7 These were the first people not to know God, because their leader

---

61 L. spells Ham Cham and Canaan Chanaan.

and founder, after the curse upon him, did not follow his father in the worship of God, thus bequeathing to his descendants ignorance of the godhead.

8 From this nation came all the neighbouring peoples in ever growing numbers. Noah's own descendants were called Hebrews: worship of God became their abiding thing. 9 Later, even they multiplied beyond measure, and when their land became too small for them, the young men went off, on their parents' instructions or of their own accord, to look for new homes for themselves, forced to it by need, and they spread this way and that, occupying every island and the whole earth; they lost contact with their original holy stock, and set up new ways of life for themselves and new institutions of their choice.

10 Those who occupied Egypt were first to start gazing at the skies and worshipping what they saw there. Because they lived without roofs overhead, the climate being what it is, and because no clouds obscure the sky in those parts, they could mark the orbits of the stars and what they brought to pass; frequent worship increased the care and the scope of their watching. 11 In due course, persuaded by certain portents whose actual authors we will reveal in a moment, they devised figures of animals for worship, to generate portents.

12 The rest of them, once spread all over the earth, came to wonder at elements of the world, worshipping sky, sun, earth and sea, but without statues and temples, and they made sacrifice to them in the open, until in the process of time they made temples and statues for their most powerful kings and began to worship the statues with animal sacrifice and incense. Separation from knowledge of God thus began to produce the Gentiles. 13 It is a mistake to claim that worship of gods has existed from the start of things, and that worship of God came only after pagan rites; it is only thought to be a later invention because the fountainhead of truth was unknown. Let us now go back to the beginning of the world.

On angels and demons, good and bad

14.1 When the number of people began to grow again, God did what he had done in the beginning: he sent his angels to guard and tend the human race; he foresaw that the devil, to whom he had given control of the earth at the start, might corrupt or even destroy man with his deceptions, and he told the angels before all else not to lose the worth of their celestial substance by letting contact with earth stain them. Presumably he warned them not to do what he knew they would do in order to deny them hope of pardon. 2 As they continued to spend time with humans, that treacherous lord of the earth little by little habituated them to the lure of wickedness, and sullied them by unions with women. 3 Then, when they were not acceptable in heaven because of the sins in which they had plunged themselves, they fell to earth, and thus out of angels of God the devil made them henchmen and servants of his own.

4 Because their offspring were neither angels nor men, but had a half and half nature, they were no more acceptable below than their parents were above. 5 So two sorts of demon were created, one celestial and one earthly. The earthly ones are the unclean spirits, authors of all wickedness that occurs, and the devil is their chief. 6 Hence Trismegistus' name for him, demoniarch.[62] Philologists say they are called demons from[G] 'daëmon', 'expert', that is, and 'knowing',[63] for they think of them as gods. They do know much of the future, but not all of it, since they cannot know God's thinking from within, and that is why they usually arrange for their responses to emerge in ambiguous form.

7 The poets know that they are demons and they say so too. Hesiod puts it as follows [*Op.* 122–23]: 'Some are demons by will of great Zeus, good spirits of earth, guardians of mortal men.' 8 That was said because God had sent them as guardians of the human race; yet even they, destroyers of people as they are, still want to be seen as guardians, so that they are worshipped and God is not.

9 The philosophers also discuss them. Plato attempted to express their natures in his *Symposium*,[64] and Socrates used to say that he was attended by a constant demon, which had stuck to him since his boyhood; his life was governed by its every wish and whim.

10 All the skill and power of the Magi depend upon the influence of these beings also; they summon the Magi, who then falsify what people see, hoodwinking and blinding them so that they don't see what is there and think they see what isn't. 11 They are, as I say, defiled and desperate spirits which roam all over the earth and work for the perdition of people as solace for their own perdition: 12 they fill everything with treachery, fraud, deceit and misguidance; they attach themselves to individuals, they occupy the

---

62 *Asclep.* 28, in NF *Corp. Herm.* vol. 2, p. 334.
63 L. takes as equivalent (so had Archilochus and Plato earlier) two different Greek roots, *da-*, learn, and *da-/dai-*, distribute (hence probably *daímon* as distributor of people's fates, a word often used by the Greek poets as a rough synonym for *theós*, god).
64 202e.

gates of every household, and they get themselves called genii (that is the Latin for demons). 13 People worship them in their shrines at home, they pour wine to them every day, they are wittingly venerating demons as if they were earthly gods, the dispellers of those evils which the demons themselves are doing and causing. 14 Because these spirits are slender and hard to grasp, they work themselves into people's bodies and secretly get at their guts, wrecking their health, causing illness, scaring their wits with dreams, unsettling their minds with madness, till people are forced to run for help to them in troubles of their making.

The pious have nothing to fear from demons

15.1 The explanation of all these misunderstandings is a puzzle for those who lack the truth. They think that when gods lay off doing harm (and harm is all they have the power to do), then they are doing good. 2 Since, it may perhaps be said, they have this capacity to do harm, they ought to be worshipped to prevent them doing it. They certainly do harm, but only to people who fear them, people unprotected by the sublime and powerful hand of God, people unacquainted with the sacrament of truth. 3 But they are frightened of just people, worshippers of God, that is: when adjured in his name they leave the bodies they occupy, and the words of the good are like whips, flogging them not only into admission that they are demons but also into revealing the cult titles that are used for them in their temples. This they often do in the presence of their own worshippers, to the shame not simply of their cult but also of their own position in it, because they cannot lie to God in whose name they are being adjured nor can they lie to the just whose words torment them. 4 Hence the howls and cries they often utter, saying they are being beaten and are on fire and are dying any moment: 5 such is the power of the knowledge of God, and such the power of his justice. The only people to whom they can do bad are the ones they have in their own power. 6 Hermes says conclusively that those who know God are not only safe from the attacks of demons but are not even in the grip of fate.[G] 'Piety,' he says, 'is the one safe guard. The pious are not in the power of any evil demon nor of fate. God protects the pious from all evil. The one and only good within man's power is piety.' What he means by piety he explains elsewhere as follows:[G] 'Piety is the knowledge of god.'[65] 7 His disciple Asclepius has also explained the idea at greater length in that *Perfect Discourse* which he wrote

---

65 NF *Corp. Herm.* vol. 4, fr. 10; *Corp. Herm. (Poem.)* 9.4.

to the king.⁶⁶ 8 They each declare 'Demons are enemies and tormentors of men', which is why Trismegistus calls them^G 'wicked angels'; he was well aware that they turned into earthly creatures upon corruption of their celestial nature.⁶⁷

Evil works of demons

16.1 Their inventions include astrology, entrail inspection, augury, anything called an oracle, necromancy, and magic, together with any other evil that people practise openly or secretly. All are bogus on their own terms, as the Sibyl of Erythrae says:^G 'All the things that mindless men chase after in the daylight, all are deceptive.'⁶⁸ 2 But people think it is true because of the presence of exactly those inventors of it, who put on a false divinity (it would not suit to reveal the truth), and use people's own credulity to fool them. 3 These are the ones who taught people to make statues and likenesses; in order to divert attention away from worship of the true God, they copied the features of dead kings, giving them a special attractiveness, and had them set up and consecrated, and took on their names themselves, like a sort of mask. 4 But when the Magi and those popularly and rightly called evildoers are practising their accursed arts, they invoke them by their real names, the heavenly names that can be read in holy scripture.

5 In order to create confusion and to fill human hearts with error, these unclean vagabond spirits sow falsehood mixed with truth. Because there are many angel spirits in heaven and God is the one lord and father of them all, so they have pretended that there are many heavenly beings and one king Jupiter over them all: but they have wrapped the truth up in bogus names and kept it out of sight. 6 As I explained in the beginning, God needs no name because he is the only god, and though the angels are immortal, they do not allow themselves to be called gods nor do they want to be: their one and only duty is to attend to the wishes of God and to do absolutely nothing without his command. 7 The world is governed by God, we say, as a province is by its governor;⁶⁹ no one would say that in governing the province a governor's staff are his equals, despite the fact that their work keeps it going. 8 Indeed,

---

66 The most commonly cited of the Hermetic works, it was available to L. in both the Greek version and in a Latin translation. The translation available to L. was not, however, the same as the one used by Augustine over a century later in *civ.* 8.23–24, 26.
67 *Asclep.* 25 in NF *Corp. Herm.* vol. 2, pp. 329ff.
68 *Orac. Sib.* 3.228ff.
69 Here speaks a Roman provincial.

because of his ignorance, which is a piece of his human condition, a governor's staff do have some powers beyond their instructions; but he who presides over the world and governs the universe, he who knows all things, he from whose divine eyes nothing is hid, has power over all things on his own, and his angels have no need to do anything but obey. 9 That is why they want no honour for themselves: all their honour is in God. Those who abandoned God's service, however, being enemies of the truth and in collusion against God, try to secure divine worship for themselves, together with the title of gods, not because they want any honour – what honour could they have in their abandoned state? – nor to hurt God, who cannot be hurt, but to hurt man: it is man they are striving so hard to divert from knowledge and worship of the true greatness, in case man gains the immortality which they have lost by their own wickedness.

10 So they pour down darkness and blot out the truth with obscurity to prevent knowledge of their lord and father, and so as to lure men in easily they hide in temples, attending every sacrifice and often producing prodigies to astonish mankind and make them give credit to mere images of divinity and power. 11 Hence the stone carved in two by an augur with a razor, and Juno of Veii saying she wanted to move to Rome, and Fortuna Muliebris declaring her peril, and the ship obedient to Claudia's pull, and the revenge for sacrilege on the part of Juno Naked, Proserpina of Locri and Ceres of Miletus, and of Hercules on Appius, of Jupiter on Atinius and of Minerva on Caesar; hence also the snake summoned from Epidaurus and its liberation of Rome from plague.[70] 12 The prince of demons himself was brought to Rome in his own likeness, without any attempt to pretend otherwise, if, that is, the delegation sent for the purpose did bring back with them a snake of wondrous size.

13 Their greatest deception is done in oracles; irreligious people cannot tell their tricks from the truth, and so they think that power, victory, wealth and a happy outcome to all their affairs is granted by the oracles themselves; they even think that their country has often been saved from threats of danger by oracular will: after all, oracular response exposed the peril, and placatory sacrifice averted it. 14 But all that sort of thing is a deception. Since, having once been his servants, they understand God's purposes already, they intervene in a situation so that whatever God has done or is doing, it appears that *they* are the agents, and any time some good is due to a people or a city in accordance with God's will, they promise that *they* will

---

70 See 7.8–19 above.

bring it about, using prodigies or dreams or oracles, provided that they are given temples, honours and sacrifices. The gifts are made; what was going to happen happens; and great veneration for them is the result. 15 Temples are dedicated and new statues are consecrated; flocks of victims are put to the knife; but when all that is done, the real sacrifice is still the life and health of the people who have done it. 16 Every time danger threatens, the demons claim they are angry on some stupid and trivial ground, as Juno said she was with Varro, because he put a pretty boy in Jupiter's cart to carry his relics, and that was why the name of Rome was nearly wiped out at Cannae.[71] 17 But if Juno was scared of a second Ganymede, why did young Rome pay the price? Or if gods neglect the infantry in favour of the generals, why did Varro escape, who was responsible for the disaster, while the undeserving Paulus got killed? No doubt at the time when a pair of the republic's armies fell to Hannibal's skill and virtue, the 'decree of unjust Juno' was not operative in Rome. 18 Juno 'had her arms and her chariot' at Carthage, but she could not raise her nerve to protect it or to hurt Rome, for 'she had heard a future race was forming of Trojan blood, which one day would topple that Tyrian stronghold.'[72]

19 That is, however, the sort of game they play, as they lurk under names of dead men and set their nets for the living. If the danger that threatens can be avoided, they want it to appear that placating them diverts it; if not, they arrange for it to look as if it happened because they were despised. Thus they develop in people who do not know them a sense of their authority and of their power to scare. 20 This is the artful cunning with which they have made knowledge of the one true god something barely remembered among the nations. Destroyed by their own wickedness they prowl savagely around to destroy others. 21 That is why, in their hostility towards the human race, they have even thought up human sacrifice, to swallow up as many souls as they can.

God permits demons to test man; summary of Book 2

17.1 It will be asked 'Then why does God let these things happen and not come to the rescue of such awful mistakes?' So that evil may fight with good, so that vice may be set against virtue, so that he may have some to punish and some to honour. He has appointed the end of time for his

---

71 See V. Max. 1.1.16.
72 Verg. *A.* 8.292; 1.16; 1.19–20.

BOOK 2: THE ORIGIN OF ERROR

judgment upon the living and the dead; I shall discuss that judgment in my final book. 2 He is therefore postponing to the end of time the effusion of his wrath in heavenly power and might; we shall 'recall presages, dread forewarnings of the prophets of old, with horror.'[73]

3 For the time being he suffers men to stray and to fail in duty even to himself while he remains just, gentle and patient. In him is perfect virtue: perfect patience is necessarily in him also. 4 Hence the view of some people that God does not even get angry, because he is not subject to emotions, which are disturbances of the mind: all creatures liable to emotional affect are frail. That belief destroys truth and religion utterly. 5 Let us set aside for the moment, however, this topic of the wrath of God, because the material for it is quite large and needs to be treated more broadly in its own right.[74] Anyone, then, who venerates those wickedest of spirits and follows them will gain neither heaven nor light, which are God's: instead that man will go down into what we argued was granted in the distribution of things to the prince of evil himself: into darkness, that is, into the underworld and into torment eternal.

6 I have explained that worship of gods is triply vain. First, the images which are worshipped are effigies of men long dead, and it is perverse and topsy-turvy for the image of a man to be worshipped by the image of God, since he is worshipping what is worse and weaker; 7 it is further an unforgivable crime to abandon the living God in order to serve memorials of the dead, who cannot bestow on anyone the life and light they lack themselves; and there is no other god at all except the one God to whose arbitrament and power every soul is subject.

8 Second, the holy images themselves which people serve in their stupidity lack all sense of it, because they are of earth. 9 Anyone can see that it is wrong for an upright creature to bend down to adore the earth. That is why the earth has been set beneath our feet, to be trampled on, not worshipped; we were raised out of it and given our lofty stature, in contrast with all other living creatures, precisely in order not to collapse back down and prostrate our heavenly features to the ground, but to direct our eyes where they are directed by their own natural condition, and there is nothing else for our adoration and worship except the single name of our sole maker and parent, who has made man straight and tall so that we may know that we are called to things on high in heaven.

---

73 Verg. *A* 4.464–5.
74 L. would deal with this in his work *de ira*.

10 Third, the spirits which preside over the actual ceremonies have been condemned and discarded by God to wallow on the earth; not only can they do no good to their worshippers because power over all things is in the control of the one, but they even destroy them with deadly temptations and distractions: it is their daily task to cloak man in darkness in case he should seek the true god. 11 They are therefore not to be worshipped because they are subject to the verdict of god. It is a very great sin to submit yourself to their power when you could if you followed justice surpass them; by using God's name against them you could drive them out and put them to flight.

12 If it is clear that cults of that sort are empty in all the ways I have pointed out, then it is clear that people who supplicate the dead or venerate the earth or shackle their souls to unclean spirits are not sustaining human reason, and people who in rebellion against God the father of the human race adopt unforgivable rituals and violate all that is right and proper will pay the penalty for their crime of impiety.

Religion raises man's gaze to the heavens

18.1 Any man therefore who strives to protect the mystery of man and to possess the reason for human nature must raise himself from the ground and direct his gaze to the heavens with mind erect. He must not look for god beneath his feet nor wrest something to worship from his own footprints: anything below a man must be beneath him. Instead he must look aloft and search on high: nothing can be greater than man except what is above him. God is greater than man: God is therefore above him, not below him, and he must not be sought in the lowest parts, but in the highest. 2 That is why there can be no religion anywhere there is an image: that is indubitable. If worship issues from things divine, and if there is nothing divine except in things celestial, then images have nothing to worship in them because nothing celestial can exist in something made of earth. A wise man could see that from the very vocabulary. 3 Anything copied must be false; nothing can ever be called true which fakes the truth by dye and imitation. If all imitation is absolutely not serious, but a sort of comic game, then there is no religion in images but only a pantomime of it. 4 The truth must therefore take preference over all falsehoods, and things earthly must be trampled under so that we achieve the things celestial. 5 The situation is such that anyone who bows his soul, a thing of heavenly origin, to the depths below falls where he casts himself; he should therefore remember his reason and his stature, and direct all his efforts and energy towards the things above. 6 He who does that will plainly be judged a wise man, a just man, a human; above all, a man worthy of heaven, and his father will know him as he made him, not lowly and stooped to the ground like a four-footed beast, but standing tall and straight.

Preview of Book 3

19.1 I think I have now completed a large and difficult portion of the work I have undertaken, and with the support of heaven for my powers of expression I have dispelled mistakes of long standing. 2 Now, however, a greater and more difficult struggle is before me as I wrestle with the philosophers, whose great learning and eloquence loom like a mountain in my path. 3 Previously I was beset by mass, by the near unanimity of popular opinion; now I am beset by men of authority, whose reputation is outstanding in every way. 4 Everyone knows that there is more weight in a handful of scholars than in hosts of the ignorant. 5 But we must not despair. With God and truth to guide us they too can be shifted from their views; I think they will not be so obstinate as to deny they see the sun in its full brightness when their eyes are healthily opened. 6 Just let their usual claim hold good, that their controlling passion is the search for truth, and I will surely bring them to believe that the truth they seek was discovered long ago, and to admit that it could not have been discovered by human wit alone.

BOOK 3: FALSE WISDOM

Truth, rhetoric and philosophy

1.1 Because truth, O emperor Constantine, is still thought to lurk in obscurity, whether from the ignorance and inexperience of ordinary men who are slaves to a variety of silly superstitions, or from the attempts of philosophers in their intellectual wickedness to muddy things rather than clarify them, I wish I had a faculty of eloquence which, if not the same as Cicero's – that was something quite specially remarkable – was at least close to it; then truth could lean on my powers of intelligence as much as it does on its own strength, and one day it could rise up and shake off confusions, whether general or peculiar to those thought wise, dispelling them all, and it could bring its light of great brightness upon all mankind. 2 I have two reasons for my wish: one is that since a dressing of rhetoric and some seductive vocabulary make ordinary people such ready victims of falsehood, the embellishment of truth would make them all the more able to believe in it; secondly, in vanquishing the philosophers themselves, we ought to make prime use of their own weapons, in which they typically have such a contented confidence. 3 But it is as it is by God's will; truth is to be the more glorious by being plain and unadorned, for it is well enough equipped as it is, and addition of extraneous ornament only masks and corrupts it, whereas a lie would only please by looking other than it is, for lies are self-corrupting and they break up and vanish unless painted and polished with adornments sought from elsewhere. Hence I bear with equanimity the fact that I have been granted an average talent.

4 This task that I have taken on, too great perhaps for my own strength to sustain, I have undertaken out of no confidence in rhetoric: my confidence lies in the truth of it. Even if I am inadequate to it, any deficiencies will, with God's help whose task it is, be fully made up by truth. 5 All the greatest speakers, as I well know, have often lost to average pleaders: the power of truth, even when things are difficult, is strong enough to see to its own defence by its own light; why should I think that it will be overwhelmed now, in a cause as great as this, by men who for all their ability and eloquence are nevertheless telling lies? 6 Why should it not shine out bright and

glorious in its own light whatever the shortcomings of my rhetoric, which is a thin stream from a slender source at best? There have been philosophers of remarkable literary learning, but I would not yield place to them for knowledge and understanding of truth: no one can achieve truth simply by thinking and arguing. 7 I cast no slur on their desire to know the truth, since man's great greed to acquire it is the doing of God; what I object to, after all that fine and excellent intention of theirs, is the utter lack of product due to their complete ignorance of what truth is, and of how, where, and in what frame of mind to seek it. 8 In the midst of their desire to rescue people from delusion they thus plunge into the greatest of traps and confusion themselves.

It is the sequence itself of the material under consideration which has brought me to this task of refuting philosophy. 9 Since all error arises either from wrong worship or from wrong understanding, in order to prove error wrong both must be undone. 10 Though we have the tradition of holy scripture that the thinking of philosophers is futile, it is fact and proof that we must use to divert people from a preference for belief in things human rather than in things divine, whether they are persuaded by the fair name of philosophy or tricked by the glitter of empty rhetoric.

11 The scriptural tradition is short and stark:[1] when God was addressing man, addition of argument to his words, as if he would not otherwise be believed, was not appropriate; he spoke as the supreme judge of all creation ought to speak, his business being not discussion but declaration. 12 He is, being God, the truth himself; since the evidence of his divine utterance is available to us for every single thing, we shall certainly show how much more secure the arguments are that can defend the truth, since even falsehood can be defended till it often looks like truth.

13 There is thus no reason for us to hold philosophers in such esteem that we grow scared of their eloquence. 14 They have the educated man's capacity to speak well, but no capacity at all to speak truth, because they never learnt it from him who is lord of it. 15 We shall not, of course, be doing anything notable in convicting them of ignorance: they often admit to ignorance themselves. 16 Since they lack credibility in the one thing in which alone they ought to be credible, I shall endeavour to show that they never spoke a truer word than in delivering the verdict on their own ignorance.

---

1 L. is sensitive to the charge, commonly levelled, that the scriptures lack literary merit. See 5.1.10–21, and 5.3.1–3.

Pursuit of wisdom is not wisdom

2.1 In the first two books the falseness of cults was demonstrated, together with analysis of the origin of the whole mistake. The task of this book is to demonstrate the emptiness and error of philosophy as well, so that all mistakes may be removed and the revelation of truth may shine forth. 2 Let us start therefore with the word philosophy in its usual sense; if we can destroy its head, we shall have an easier path to destruction of its whole body, if indeed body is the right word when all its parts and limbs are in conflict, with nothing binding them coherently together; they seem in their disconnection to be twitching rather than living.

3 Philosophy is, as its name shows and as its practitioners define it, the pursuit of wisdom. I can make no better proof that philosophy is not wisdom than from the meaning of the word itself. Anyone in pursuit of wisdom is obviously not wise yet; he studies to become capable of wisdom. 4 In other skills it is clear what study does and what its aim is; when people arrive at mastery through learning, they are not called students of the craft any longer, but craftsmen. 5 Philosophers have called themselves students of wisdom rather than wise out of modesty, it may be said. 6 Pythagoras, inventor of the word, disproves that; his predecessors had thought of themselves as wise, but he was a little bit wiser, for he realised that wisdom could not be attained through any human pursuit of it, and therefore it was wrong to apply so absolute a word to something beyond our grasp and achievement. Hence his answer when people asked him what he claimed to be, and he said 'A philosopher'; a seeker after wisdom, that is. 7 If then philosophy is a search for wisdom, it is not wisdom itself, because seeker and sought are necessarily distinct, nor is the search itself sound, because it is incapable of finding anything. I would not myself allow that even those in pursuit of wisdom are philosophers, because their pursuit does not bring them to wisdom. 8 If the chance of discovering truth were obedient to the desire for it, and if the desire were a sort of pathway to truth, then truth would have been found at some point. Yet it has not happened, for all the time and talent spent in search of it; plainly, there is no wisdom in philosophy. 9 Those who philosophize, therefore, are not in pursuit of wisdom, although they think they are, because they do not know the nature or the whereabouts of what they seek. 10 Whether they are, therefore, or are not in pursuit of wisdom, they are not wise, because what is not being correctly sought or is not being sought at all can never be found. Nevertheless, let us see whether anything or nothing can be discovered by this process of search.

Divine knowledge, human opinion

3.1 There seem to be two elements in philosophy, knowledge and opinion, and no others. 2 Knowledge cannot come from one's ability nor can it be grasped by thought, because to have any particular knowledge in oneself is a property of God, not of man, 3 and mortal nature only takes in knowledge which comes from outside. Eyes, ears and the other senses have been opened up in the body by divine skill deliberately so that knowledge could percolate into the mind by those channels. 4 To investigate the causes of natural phenomena – to want to know whether the sun is as big as it looks or many times bigger than this whole earth of ours, whether the moon is spherical or concave, whether the stars stick to the sky or travel freely through the atmosphere, what size the sky is and what it is made of, whether it is still and motionless or spins at very high speed, how thick the earth is or what foundations it is poised and hung upon – 5 to want, I repeat, to understand all that by arguing and guessing is surely best compared with wanting to discuss what we think a city of some far distant folk is like which we have never seen and whose name is the only thing we know of it. 6 If we laid claim to knowledge of something which cannot be known, we would surely seem mad for daring to assert what we could be proved wrong about. So when there are people who think they know things about nature which cannot be humanly known, how much madder and more demented they must be! 7 Socrates and the Academics who followed him were quite right to reject as knowledge what belongs to intuition, not to debate.

8 The conclusion is that only opinion constitutes philosophy: where knowledge fails opinion takes over, and what you don't know you suppose. People discussing natural phenomena suppose that the phenomena correspond to their opinions about them. So they do not know the truth about them, because knowing entails certainty and opinion uncertainty. 9 Let us return to the instance mentioned above: let's play 'Let's suppose' about the state and style of a city of which we know nothing at all but its name. Very probably it is on level ground, with stone walls, lofty buildings, numerous streets and wonderfully decorated temples. 10 Now let's write down the lifestyle and behaviour of its citizens. But as soon as we do all that, someone else will maintain a different version, and when he's finished, a third party will get up, and others after him, and they will suppose things very different from what we supposed. 11 So which version out of them all will be nearer the truth? Possibly none. Oh, but everything contingent to the nature of things has been said, so one version must be true! 12 Ah, but there won't be

any knowing whose version that is. It is possible that they were all wrong at some point in their description, and that they all got it right at some point. We would be stupid, then, if we made discussion our method of search: someone could turn up to scoff at our opinions and take us for fools in wanting to have opinions about the nature of something we know nothing of.

13 There is no need to go after distant objects, where probably no one will emerge to put us down. 14 Let's play 'Let's suppose' about what's happening at this moment in the market or town hall. But that's remote stuff too. So let's say what's going on through the wall next door. But no one can know that without hearing it and seeing it. That's why no one ventures to say it, because he will be proved wrong on the spot, not verbally but by instant evidence. 15 And yet that is what the philosophers do, discussing what's going on in the sky; they think they get away with it because there is no one around to expose their mistakes, 16 whereas if they thought someone would come down to show how mad and mendacious they are, they would never discuss any item at all on the list of impossible knowledge! Not that they get away with their cheek and presumption by not being put down: don't think it! God puts them down, who alone knows the truth, even though he may seem to wink at them; he takes the wisdom of men for the height of folly.

Ignorance of philosophers

4.1 Zeno and the Stoics were thus right to reject supposition. To suppose you know what you don't is not the mark of a wise man but rather of a reckless fool. 2 If, then, nothing can be known, as Socrates held, and nothing should be supposed, as Zeno held, philosophy disappears *in toto*, overthrown not only by these two, who were princes of philosophy, but by everybody; by now it looks as though it fell victim to its own weapons long ago.

3 Philosophy has split into a multiplicity of sects, and they all think differently. Which one do we go to for truth? It can't be in them all, for sure. 4 Let's pick a particular one: wisdom will then obviously fail to exist in all the others. Let's work through them one by one: again, whatever we grant to one we shall deny to the rest. Any one sect dismisses all others in order to confirm itself and its own ideas, and it admits wisdom in no other sect in case it concedes error of its own; but its process of dismissing other sects is the same process by which they dismiss it, 5 for those who condemn a sect for its folly are philosophers none the less: praise any one sect and call it true, and philosophers condemn it as false. 6 Shall we put our faith in a single sect, then, which extols itself and its teaching, or in lots of them, all

busy attacking each other's ignorance? The views of a majority must be sounder than a lone voice, 7 for no one can form a sound view of himself, as that great poet attests [Ter. *Hau.* 503]:

> How human nature is so featly made,
> that others' ways are better seen and judged
> than one's own!

8 Since then everything is uncertain, either all must be believed, or no one. If no one, then wise men don't exist because each one thinks he alone is wise; if all, then wise men still don't exist because each one is denied his wisdom by all the rest. 9 This way they all perish together: like the Sparti of the poets, they kill each other in turn till none survive at all, and that happens because they have swords but no shields. 10 If then individual sects are found guilty of folly on the verdict of the many, then they all turn out to be vain and futile. Thus philosophy works its own end and destruction itself.

11 This was the understanding of Arcesilaus, founder of the Academy;[2] he combined everybody's attacks on everybody else together with confession of ignorance on the part of some notable philosophers, and armed himself against everyone, constructing a novel philosophy of non-philosophizing. 12 His initiative brought two sorts of philosophy into existence, one being the original one, asserting its claim to knowledge, and the other the new one, fighting the claim down. In these two I see the division of a truly civil war: 13 wisdom cannot be divided; so on which side shall we post it? If the nature of things can be known, our squad of novices will perish; if it cannot, then the veterans will die; if the fight is a draw, philosophy the commander in chief will still perish because it is torn in two: nothing can be in contradiction of itself without perishing. 14 If the weakness of the human condition precludes the existence in man of any special knowledge from within at all, as I have explained, then victory goes to Arcesilaus' troop. Even he will not stand his ground, however, since it is not possible for absolutely nothing to be known.

The new academy self-destructs

5.1 There are indeed plenty of things we are compelled to know either naturally or experientially or from the pressure to survive. If you don't know

---

2 Arcesilaus (c. 315–240 BC), founded the new Academy, turning the school that Plato had founded in a sceptical direction. Cf. 5.3ff. and 6.7ff. below.

how to find what is useful for survival or how to avoid and shun what is dangerous, you perish necessarily. 2 There are plenty of things besides which are the fruits of experience. The varying courses of sun and moon, and the transit of the planets and the system of seasons have been grasped; doctors have learnt about the nature of bodies and the power of herbs, and farmers have learnt about types of soil and indicators of rain and storms brewing. There is no skill not founded in knowledge. 3 If Arcesilaus had had any sense, he should have sorted out what could be known from what couldn't; but if he had done that, he would have reduced himself to the level of ordinary men, 4 who are sometimes the wiser for knowing only as much as they need to know. Ask one of them whether he knows something or nothing, and he'll tell you he knows what he knows and he'll admit he doesn't know what he doesn't know. 5 Arcesilaus was right to dismiss other people's teaching but wrong in the basing of his own. Total ignorance cannot be wisdom: wisdom's business is knowing. When he routed the philosophers and demonstrated they knew nothing, he also lost his own claim to be a philosopher, because his teaching was that nothing was known. 6 Anyone attacking others for ignorance needs to be knowledgeable himself, but when he isn't, it is an odd piece of perversity to set himself up as a philosopher on the grounds that he can dismiss the rest! They could reply, 7 'If you prove that we know nothing and are not wise because we know nothing, then you aren't wise either because you acknowledge that you know nothing too.' 8 Arcesilaus' achievement is to finish off all the philosophers and to perish on the same sword himself!

Human knowledge is tempered by ignorance: the case of natural philosophy

6.1 Does wisdom exist nowhere then? Oh no! It was there in their midst all the time, but nobody saw it. Some thought everything could be known: plainly they were not wise; some thought nothing could be known: they were not wise either, attributing too little to man just as the others attributed too much. Each party overstated its case.

2 So where is wisdom? In not thinking you know everything, which is God's portion, and in not thinking you know nothing, which is an animal's portion. For in man's portion there is something in between, which is knowledge combined with and tempered by ignorance. 3 What we know comes from the soul, which comes from heaven, and our ignorance comes from the body, which comes from the earth: we thus have something in common both

with God and with the animals. 4 Since we are composed of these two elements, the one endowed with light and the other with darkness, we have some share of knowledge and some share of ignorance. This is our bridge; it is possible to cross it without risk of falling because all who lean to one side or the other tumble off, either to right or to left. I will explain how each party has gone astray.

5 Academics in dispute with natural philosophers, in order to show that there was no knowledge, used items of some obscurity; they were content with instances of a few very difficult items, and they plumped for ignorance as if they had abolished all knowledge by abolishing it in part. 6 The natural philosophers developed the contrasting case, that everything could be known from material that was transparent, and they maintained the possibility of knowledge content with these obvious examples, as if by defending knowledge in part they had defended it all. The one lot failed to see what was obvious and the others failed to see what was difficult; in the middle of their fisticuffs to retain or reject knowledge as a whole, they failed to see the doorway in between which would let them through to wisdom.

7 In criticising Zeno the leader of the Stoics in order to overthrow philosophy in its entirety, Arcesilaus, the champion of ignorance, took the view, following Socrates, that knowledge should be declared wholly impossible. 8 He therefore argued against the thinking of those philosophers who would have attributed the unearthing and discovery of truth to their own talents. Now, since such wisdom was plainly mortal and had reached its peak of growth a few generations after its start, for it to grow old and die as by now it had to, up comes the Academy all of a sudden to be philosophy's old age and to finish it off as its bloomtime passed, 9 and Arcesilaus was right to see that people who thought knowledge of truth could be grasped by guessing were claiming too much, or rather, were being stupid.

10 Things said in error, however, cannot be rebutted except by someone who knows the truth already. Arcesilaus was trying to act without knowing the truth; hence his introduction of the 'asystatic' system of philosophy (asystatic we may render as inconsistent or unsystematic).[3] 11 For nothing to be knowable, something has to be known; if you knew absolutely nothing at all, the fact that nothing can be known would itself be removed. 12 Anyone who declares *ex cathedra*, as it were, that nothing is known makes his declaration as something itself known and understood: therefore something can be

3 The word *asystatus* is not otherwise known; the sense unsystematic appears to fit Arcesilaus' philosophy quite well. In creating a Latin loan-word from Greek L. is following Ciceronian practice.

known. 13 Something similar to the following is often put forward in the schools as an example of asystaticism; it is the case of the man who dreamt he was not to trust in dreams. If he trusts his dream, then it will follow that it is not to be trusted, whereas if he does not trust it, it will follow that it is to be trusted. 14 So too, if nothing can be known, the fact that nothing can be known has to be known itself, but if it is known that nothing can be known, then it is an error to say that nothing can be known. Thus we have a doctrine at odds with itself and self-destructive. 15 It is a crafty fellow who wants to deny knowledge to all other philosophers in order to hide it at home for himself – anyone affirming something in order to deny knowledge to the rest is obviously not denying it to himself – but it doesn't work: people observe his legerdemain. 16 He would be acting more wisely and more truly if he made an exception and said that the causes and reasons at least for celestial and natural phenomena could not be known because they were concealed (no one explains them), and should not be investigated because investigation could not reveal them. 17 With that exception he would have warned the natural philosophers not to investigate things beyond the bounds of human thought, and he would also have freed himself from jealous criticism and would certainly have given us something to follow. 18 As it is, in preventing us from following others in case we should want to know more than we can, he stopped us from following him too. 19 Who would want to toil away to know nothing? Who would adopt a theory of a sort that would even undo standard knowledge? If such a theory exists, it must be composed of knowledge; if not, it would be very silly to think something worth learning where there is no advance towards learning, and possibly even a retreat from it. 20 And that is why if it is impossible to know everything, as the natural philosophers think, and equally if it is impossible to know anything, as the Academics think, philosophy is utterly wiped out.

Moral philosophers disagree

7.1 Now let us pass to the other area of philosophy, which philosophers call moral. The justification for the whole of philosophy lies in moral philosophy, since natural philosophy is merely of interest while moral philosophy is also useful. 2 Since mistakes made in sorting out one's life and in developing one's morality are comparatively dangerous, a greater care must be taken to know how we should live. 3 In natural philosophy allowances can be made: if people talk sense, they do no good, and if they talk rubbish they do no harm; in moral philosophy, however, there is no room for division of opinion and

BOOK 3: FALSE WISDOM

no room for error. All should think the same, and the philosophy should be presented as from one mouth, since any error means the wrecking of all life. 4 In that first area of philosophy, its lack of danger was balanced by its greater difficulty: problems of analysis led to diversity and difference of opinion; here, the extra danger is balance by reduced difficulty, because daily experience and practice show us what is better and sounder. 5 So let us see whether people do agree, or else what they offer for the improvement of our lives. 6 There is no need for a full survey; let us pick out one item, and best of all, the one which is most important, the hinge on which all wisdom turns.

7[4] Epicurus considers that our greatest good lies in mental pleasure; Aristippus thinks it is in physical pleasure; Callipho and Dinomachus combine pleasure with good repute. Diodorus locates it in removal of pain, Hieronymus in absence of pain, and the Peripatetics in the joint good of mind, body and fortune. 8 Herillus' supreme good is knowledge, Zeno's is to live in accord with nature, and for certain Stoics it is to follow virtue. Aristotle locates it in good repute and virtue combined. Those are virtually all the views of everybody.[5]

9 Who is to be followed in such diversity? Who is to be believed? They all have an equal authority. If we can select something which is better, then we don't need philosophy: we are wise already, because we are in judgment of wise men's ideas. 10 But since our purpose is to learn wisdom, how can we judge when we have not yet begun to be wise, especially with the great Academic[6] beside us to tug at our cloaks and prevent us believing anyone, while offering nothing for us to follow himself?

Supreme good: erroneous theories

8.1 It only remains to leave the litigants to their lunatic quarrels and to turn to a judge.[7] He will of course be a judge offering a straightforward and

---

4 For 7–8, cf. Cic. *Ac.* 2.129, 131; *Tusc.* 5.84ff.; for Epicurus, see Usener p. 294, 14, *ad fr.* 452.

5 For similar catalogues, see Cic. *Fin.* 5.73; *Ac.* 2.139. Aristippus founded the Cyrenaic school, which flourished in the late 4th and early 3rd centuries. Callipho and Dinomachus are hardly known of otherwise. Diodorus (Cronus; died c. 284 BC) was leader of the Dialectical school, which specialised in logic. Hieronymus of Rhodes lived in Athens c. 290–230 BC; he abandoned the Peripatetics to found an eclectic school. Herillus of Carthage was a pupil of Zeno of Citium, but his brand of Stoicism deviated from mainline Stoicism, which continued under Chrysippus.

6 L. means Socrates.

7 L., whose teaching encompassed forensic rhetoric, slips easily into the language of legal process.

peaceable wisdom which will have power not only to shape us and bring us on course but also to give a verdsict on the differences of those philosophers. 2 This is the wisdom which shows us what man's true and supreme good is. Before I start to discuss it, however, all those other ideas must be rebutted, so that it is quite clear that none of those philosophers ever was wise.

3 We are discussing the duty of man: the supreme good of the supreme animal ought to consist in something quite distinct from that of the other animals. 4 Wild beasts have fangs, cattle have horns, birds have wings as their specific instrument: so man must have something allotted him without which he would lose any sense of his own condition. What all animals have for their survival or procreation is a natural good, but not a supreme good unless it is specific to each individual species. 5 The philosopher who thought that pleasure of mind was the supreme good was not wise because whether pleasure of mind is a relief or a joy, it is shared by all. 6 Aristippus I don't think worth an answer; someone for ever resorting to physical pleasures, in thrall to belly and sex, cannot be thought of as a man at all. Except for the fact that he talked, he lived a life indistinguishable from that of an animal. 7 If donkeys, pigs or dogs had a power of speech and were asked what they want when they pursue females so fiercely that they can scarcely be pulled apart and they forget about food and drink, why they either drive off other males with violence or don't keep away even when beaten but persist in their pursuit despite frequent drubbings from their betters, why they don't fear rain and frost, why they accept the burden and don't reject the danger, they will respond by saying simply that physical pleasure is the supreme good, and they go for it in order to have sensations of supreme delight, and those sensations are so precious that they think no hardship or damage or even death worth evading in pursuit of them. 8 Will these be the people to go to for advice on life when they think the same as animals[8] bereft of reason?

9 Cyrenaics give the glory to virtue on the grounds that virtue is effective of pleasure.[9] 'True,' says the scratching dog, or your filthy pig; 'that's why I fight with my rival with all the strength I've got, so that my virtue brings me pleasure; if I go away the loser I'm bound to have no pleasure.' 10 So are those the people to be our source of wisdom, when they are distinct from animals in speech only, and not in thought? The view that the supreme good is the removal of pain belongs obviously not to the Peripatetics or Stoics but

---

8 Brandt's proposal to read *animantes* for *animae* is accepted.
9 The characteristic doctrine of the Cyrenaic school founded by Aristippus was hedonism.

to the 'Clinic' philosophers.[10] 11 It is a position maintained by people who are ill or in some pain, as is clear, but it is ludicrous to have as your supreme good something a doctor can offer. For the enjoyment of good, pain is necessary, and frequent pain and great pain at that, so as to increase the pleasure when the pain leaves off. 12 Someone who has never felt pain is in a very sorry case, because he is missing a good; we used to think such a man very happy because he did miss out on evil. 13 Anyone saying that the supreme good is to have absolutely no pain is rather close to that sort of silliness. Quite apart from every animal being shy of pain, who can make a good for himself out of something whose occurrence we can only hope for? 14 A supreme good cannot bring anyone to bliss unless it was always within his reach, and that does not come to man by any virtue or learning or labour of his own: nature herself makes it available to every living creature.

15 As for those who linked pleasure with honesty, despite their wish to avoid such a combination they have achieved a contradictory good: anyone devoted to pleasure is bound to miss out on honesty, and anyone keen on honesty is bound to miss out on pleasure. 16 The Peripatetics' good is over-complex; apart from the goods of the mind (and there is quarrel enough what they are), their good seems one shared with animals. 17 Physical goods such as freedom from injury, pain and illness are no less necessary to dumb beasts than to man, and perhaps more so, since a man can be restored by treatment and care but they cannot. 18 So too with the goods of luck, as they are called: animals need prey and pasture to keep life going just as man needs his resources. 19 By proposing as a good something not within human grasp they put all mankind under an alien control.

20 Let's hear what Zeno says. Even he can dream his way to virtue from time to time. 'The supreme good,' he says, 'is to live in accord with nature.' In that case we must live in the manner of wild beasts, 21 since in them are found all the things which ought to be far from man: they seek pleasure, they suffer fear, they trick, they lurk, they kill, and (most relevant) they do not know God. 22 So why does Zeno recommend I live according to nature when she herself is prone to the slippery slope and topples into vice at the prompting of a few temptations? 23 If he is saying that the nature of beasts is one thing and the nature of man another because man is born to virtue, that's something; but even so it won't be a definition of supreme good because there is no animal that doesn't live according to its nature.

10 Cf. Cypr. *Ep.* 69.16.2 (with 13.1–2), where *Peripatetici* ('the Walkers') and *Clinici* ('the Bedridden') are jokingly juxtaposed. L. might be aiming his barbs at the Epicureans, or at some other philosophical group or groups.

24 The philosopher who made knowledge the supreme good did offer something which is peculiar to man, but people seek knowledge for the sake of something else and not for itself. 25 No one is content to know without getting some profit from his knowledge. Skills are learnt to be practised, and they are practised either to sustain life, or for pleasure, or for glory. Knowledge is not therefore the supreme good because it is not sought for itself. 26 So what is the difference between thinking the supreme good is knowledge and thinking it is what knowledge produces, food, glory and pleasure? But those things are not peculiar to man and therefore are not supreme goods: an appetite for pleasure and food occurs not only in man but also in beasts. 27 As for the desire for glory, that can be found in horses, who rejoice as winners and grieve as losers. 'So keen they are for the laurels, and victory means so much.' The supreme poet rightly says there needs to be a test for 'what anguish each one feels when beaten, and what pride in victory's palm.'[11] If other animals share in the products of knowledge, then knowledge is not the supreme good. 28 There is in any case a considerable fault in this definition: 'knowledge' is used too starkly. People who have any skill at all will start to have a claim on bliss, including those with evil skills; an expert at poison will seem as entitled as a healer. 29 The question is what the knowledge is to be related to. If it is related to the causes of natural phenomena, what bliss am I being offered if I know the source of the Nile or some mad theory about the sky? There is no knowledge of such stuff, only opinion, which varies with ability.

30 The remaining theory is that the supreme good is the knowledge of good and evil. So why did our philosopher prefer to say the supreme good was knowing rather than plain wisdom? The effective meaning of each word is the same. So far, however, no one has said that the supreme good was wisdom because better can be said. 31 Knowledge is inadequate for the adoption of good and the avoidance of evil unless it is accompanied by virtue. Though many philosophers debated good and evil, under the compulsion of nature they lived their lives differently from what they said because they lacked virtue. Virtue is wisdom if combined with knowledge.

32 It remains to rebut the people who think that virtue itself is the supreme good, one of whom was actually Cicero; they have been very injudicious. Virtue is not itself the supreme good but it is the effector and mother of it, because without virtue the supreme good cannot be attained. Each point is easy to understand. 33 Do they think, I ask, that such a glorious

---

11 Verg. *G.* 3.112 and 102.

good can be reached easily, or only with toil and trouble? They must sharpen their wits and defend their mistake. 34 If its attainment is easy and free from toil, then it is not the supreme good. Why should we torture ourselves to death, struggling night and day, when what we seek is so readily available that anyone could grasp it without any effort of mind? 35 But if there is no good we achieve without effort, even a common or garden good, it being the nature of good to go steeply up while evil goes steeply down, so the supreme good is bound to be attained only with supreme effort. If that is very true, then a second virtue is needed in order to reach the virtue which is said to be the supreme good, and it is utterly absurd that all virtue's efforts should only arrive at itself. 36 If there is no attainment of any good without effort, plainly virtue is the means of attainment, since the effective business of virtue lies in taking on hard work and carrying it through. The supreme good therefore cannot be the means necessary for arriving at something else. 37 As they did not know what virtue could do and where it aimed but they failed to find anything better, they stuck to the word virtue itself, saying that it should be the aim but without declaring its reward; in consequence they set up as their good something which lacked a good.

38 Aristotle was not far from this position: he thought the supreme good was virtue with good repute – as if a disreputable virtue could even exist! It would simply cease to be a virtue if it had any taint of vice. 39 But he did see the possibility of virtue being misjudged out of perversity; hence his view that public opinion should be heeded. But anyone doing that will go way off what is right and good, because it is not within our power to give virtue the repute that matches its deserts. That sort of honour is simply a distinction conferred on someone over time in accord with popular approval. 40 What will happen if human error or perversity causes a mistaken opinion to develop? Shall we abandon virtue just because ignorant people think it wicked and vicious? 41 Virtue can be sorely subjected to envy: in order for it to be a particular and perpetual good it must have no need of extraneous help; it must depend upon its own strength and stand firm by itself. 42 It must not look for any good from man, nor decline any evil.

Recognition of God leads to the supreme good

9.1 I come now to the supreme good of true wisdom. Its nature must be determined as follows: first, it must belong to man alone and not be available to any other animal; second, it must belong to spirit alone and not permit the body to partake of it; finally, no one must be able to attain it without knowledge and virtue. 2 That limitation shuts out and undoes all philosophers' opinions: nothing that they said is anything like it.

3 I will now say what it is, in order to show, as I intended, that all philosophers have been blind and ignorant; at no time could they see or understand or even suspect what was set up as man's supreme good. 4 When Anaxagoras was asked why he had been born, he said it was to see the sky and the sun. This has won universal admiration, as an answer worthy of a philosopher. 5 I think, however, that he couldn't work out what to say, and rather than say nothing answered at random. Had he been wise he should have pondered it privately and meditated upon it; anyone who does not know the reason for his own existence is no man. Let us assume the remark was not uttered casually, however. 6 Let us see what a massive mistake he has made in only three words: first, he located all man's business in the eyes alone, referring everything to the body and nothing to the mind. 7 Suppose him blind: will he lose his function as a man? That cannot happen without the failure of the soul. What about the other parts of the body? 8 Will they each lose their functions? What about the superior importance of the ears over the eyes? Learning and wisdom can be got by the ears alone but not by the eyes alone. 9 You were born to see the sky and the sun, were you? Who brought you to the spectacle? What does your gaze contribute to the sky and the realm of nature? Surely you are meant to praise this vast and wonderful work! 10 Admit the existence of God, then, the creator of all things, who brought you into this world to witness his colossal work and to praise it. 11 You think it's great to see the sky and sun, do you? Why not give thanks to him who is the creator of this great kindness? You admire his works? Why not take mental measure of God's virtue, foresight and power? Anyone who has brought such wonders into being is bound to be much more wonderful himself.

12 Suppose you had been invited to dine and had been very well entertained, would people think you sane if you treated the pleasure as more important than its creator? That is the extent to which philosophers refer everything to the body and nothing at all to the mind, seeing no more than what's within sight. 13 And yet, when all the functions of the body are set aside, the purpose of man must be seen in his mind alone. We are not then born in order to see what has been made, but to gaze upon the maker of all things himself: to see him in the mind, that is. 14 If then a man of true wisdom were asked why he was born, he will reply fearlessly and promptly that he was born to worship God who created us to serve him. 15 The service of God is simply to guard and preserve justice by good actions. Anaxagoras, being a novice in things divine, reduced something of great importance to a

minimum by picking two things only which he said he was to contemplate. 16 If he had said he was born to gaze on the world, though he would be taking in everything and speaking more comprehensively, he would still not have fully described man's business because world is less important than God to the same extent that body is less than soul, because the world was made and is guided by God. 17 The world is thus not for ocular contemplation, both world and eyes being corporeal, but God is for contemplation by the soul because God, in accordance with his own immortality, has deliberately made soul eternal. Contemplation of God is veneration and worship of the common parent of the human species. 18 If that has escaped philosophers, and they have cast themselves to the ground in ignorance of the divine, Anaxagoras must be considered to have seen neither sky nor sun, for all his claim to have been born to that end! 19 The purpose of man's existence is thus made plain, if he were wise; humanity is man's special thing. But what is humanity, except justice? And what is justice, except piety? And piety is simply recognition of God our parent.

Man's special capacity for worshipping God

10.1 Man's supreme good consists thus in religion alone. Everything else, including items thought peculiar to man, can be found in the other animals too. 2 Whenever animals pick out their own utterances and sort them out according to their particular noises, they appear to be in conversation with each other. They also appear to have some sort of smile when they relax their ears, compress the mouth and roll their eyes in play, jesting at man or at their own kind. As for their own mates and offspring, they surely share with them some sort of mutual love and sympathy. 3 Animals which look to their future and lay up food are certainly exercising foresight, and signs of thought can be seen in many. When they look for what will be useful to them, when they take precautions against hurt and avoid danger, when they arrange their lairs with plenty of exits, they are obviously showing intelligence. 4 A power of thought in them is undeniable, since they often fool man himself. There is perhaps a perfect foresight in the ones with a duty of making honey: they occupy allotted sites, build defensive works, construct their houses with unbelievable skill, and serve their king. 5 It is not clear, therefore, whether capacities granted to man are shared with other creatures, but a religious capacity is certainly missing. 6 In my view, all animals have been given a power of thought, but the dumb ones were given it only to preserve life whereas man was given it to extend life. Because reason is perfected in man, it is called wisdom: wisdom makes man special through the unique gift to him of understanding things divine.

7 Cicero's view on this is sound. 'Of all the species, there is no animal,' he says [*Leg.* 1.24], 'apart from man which has any knowledge of god, and among men themselves there is no race either so civilised or so savage as not to know that some sort of god must be entertained even if his proper nature is not known. 8 Consideration of one's own origins thus entails acknowledgement of god.' 9 Philosophers who want to set souls free of all fear remove religion as well, and deprive man of his own unique good, causing separation from the good life and from all humanity; for just as God made all living things subject to man, so he made man subject to himself. 10 What reason have these fellows for disputing the need to aim the mind where the face is lifted up?[12] If we have no other reason for gazing at heaven than religion, then if religion is removed we have no rational link with heaven at all. 11 We must either gaze at heaven or fall to the ground. Falling to the ground is impossible even if we wanted it, since we stand erect. 12 We must therefore gaze at heaven: our physical estate requires it. If there is agreement on that, then it must be done either in the service of religion or to give us knowledge of things celestial. 13 But knowledge of things celestial is something we cannot attain, because nothing of that sort can be got by thinking, as I explained above. 14 It is religion then that we must serve. Anyone not accepting that plunges himself to the ground and lives the life of animals, abandoning his humanity. 15 The ignorant thus have the greater wisdom: they may err in their choice of religion, but they do take note of their own nature and estate.

Religion, wisdom, and the claims of virtue to be the supreme good

11.1 The whole human race is therefore united in agreeing that religion ought to be upheld. Now to explain how it goes wrong.

2 God deliberately created man with such a nature that a pair of things would be his great desire, and these are religion and wisdom. People go wrong either in taking up religion and forgetting wisdom or in going for wisdom alone and forgetting religion. One without the other cannot be sound. 3 Thus they fall for a multiplicity of religions, all false, however, because they leave out the wisdom which could teach them that a multiplicity of gods is impossible. Alternatively they go for wisdom, but then that is false because they leave out worship of God most high who could guide them towards knowledge of

---

12 Cic. *Leg.* 1.26; *N.D.* 2.140.

the truth. 4 People adopting one or the other thus lead a life that deviates and is full of massive error, since it is in the inseparable combination of the two that the duty of man and the whole of truth are found united.

5 The complete failure of any philosopher to find the hearth and home of the supreme good puzzles me. 6 They could have enquired as follows: whatever the supreme good is, it must be available to all. Pleasure is something which all seek, but it is shared with animals, it has no force for good, it causes satiety, in excess it does damage, it diminishes with the passage of time, and many miss out on it; people short on wealth, who are the majority, are bound to be short on pleasure too. Pleasure therefore is not the supreme good, and it is not even a good. 7 The same is even truer of wealth. Even fewer achieve wealth; it generally comes by accident, and often without effort, and sometimes through crime; it is notably desired by people who have it already. 8 Kingship? No: not even kingship. All men cannot be king, and everybody must be capable of the supreme good.

9 So let us look for something available to everybody. Virtue? Virtue is undeniably a good, and certainly a universal good, but because all its natural energy goes in the endurance of evil, it cannot be a state of bliss, and so it is plainly not the supreme good. Let us look for something else. 10 Oh, but there's nothing as attractive as virtue, nothing as worthy of a wise man! If vices are to be shunned because of their ugliness, then virtue is to be sought for its beauty! So what? Is it possible for something agreed to be good and reputable to have no reward or prize, to be such a dead end that no benefit comes of it? 11 All that toil and trouble, all that wrestling with evil which life is so full of, must surely result in some great good. 12 What shall we say it is? Pleasure? But nothing disreputable can come from what is reputable. Wealth? Power? But those are fragile and transitory things. Glory? Honour? A name that lives on? Those have no place in virtue itself: they all depend on the opinion and judgment of others. 13 Virtue is often envied, and affected by evil. The good that comes of virtue ought to stick with it so closely that it cannot be split apart and torn away, and it cannot be seen as the supreme good unless it is both peculiar to virtue and incapable of addition or subtraction itself. 14 What of the fact that the duties of virtue consist in despising all these things? Pleasure, wealth, power, honours and all the things that are treated as goods are exactly what it is the mark of virtue not to desire, not to seek and not to love the way all other people do, who are victims of their lust. 15 Virtue thus achieves something loftier and more glorious, and its struggle against these immediate goods is not in vain, except that its real desire is for things greater and truer still. Let us not

despair of it ever being found, then, provided our investigation looks in every direction: the prizes on offer are neither slight nor contemptible.

The supreme good is immortality, not virtue

12.1 If the question is what we get born for and what virtue does, we can investigate as follows. There are two constituents of man, spirit and body. There are many things specific to the spirit and many specific to the body and many common to both, like virtue itself; when virtue is related to the body, for the sake of distinction it is called courage. 2 Since courage underlies each constituent, each has fighting in front of it, and in the fighting each can be victorious. Because the body is material and graspable, it is bound to compete with material and graspable things, whereas the spirit, being slight and invisible, grapples with those enemies which cannot be seen and touched. 3 The obvious enemies of spirit are lust, vice and sin. If virtue conquers them and puts them to rout, the spirit will emerge unblemished and pure. 4 What spiritual courage achieves can only be understood by comparison with what is linked to it and equal with it, which is physical courage; when it comes to grappling and fighting, the only prize for winning is survival. Whether you fight with man or with beast, the fight is for your life. 5 In winning, the body achieves its aim of not dying; likewise the spirit in winning achieves its aim of living on. Defeat by its enemies costs the body its life; likewise, defeat by vice entails the death of the spirit. 6 The only difference between the spirit's fight and the body's fight will be that the body wants life for a while and the spirit wants life eternal. 7 If then virtue is not a state of bliss itself (since, as I said, all its energy goes in enduring evil), if it ignores everything that people lust for as if they were goods, if its supreme manifestation exposes it to death (since it mostly rejects life that everyone else wants and bravely takes on death that everyone else fears), if some great good must needs be the product of it (since labours undertaken and overcome even unto death cannot be without reward), 8 if no reward worthy of it is found on earth (since it spurns all things that are feeble and transitory), then the only option left is to achieve something celestial since it despises all things earthly, and to strive for the heights since it despises the depths; that achievement can only be immortality.

9 Euclides the founder of the Megarian school,[13] no nonentity among

---

13 Euclides (c. 450–c. 380 BC) was an associate of Socrates and Plato. His school blended Socratic and Cynic ethics. See D.L. 10.106–112.

philosophers, was right in his disagreement with all the others to say the supreme good was something consistently the same. 10 He saw, presumably, what the nature of the supreme good is even though he could not explain what it is. It is immortality, and absolutely nothing else, because immortality is the only thing that cannot be diminished, enlarged or changed. 11 Seneca also happened to admit, unawares, that immortality was the only prize of virtue. In praising virtue in the book he wrote on *Premature Death*, he says 'Virtue is the one thing which could give us immortality and make us the equals of the gods.'[14] 12 Even the Stoics, however, whom he followed, say that no one can achieve bliss without virtue. The reward of virtue is a life of bliss therefore if, as is rightly said, a life of bliss is the creation of virtue. 13 So virtue does not have to be sought for itself, as they say, but for the life of bliss, which is the necessary consequence of virtue. 14 That argument could have shown them what the supreme good was. This present, corporeal life cannot be bliss because it is subject through the body to evil. 15 Epicurus calls god blessed and incorrupt because he is eternal.[15] Bliss ought to be perfect, so that there can be nothing to upset, diminish or change it; 16 nothing can be thought of as blessed if it is not incorruptible, and anything incorruptible must be immortal. Only immortality is blessed, because it cannot be undone or corrupted. 17 If virtue occurs in a man, and undeniably it does, then bliss occurs also: no one with virtue can possibly be miserable. If bliss occurs, then immortality also occurs, which is bliss. 18 Thus the supreme good is revealed as immortality, because no other animal or body attains it, and it cannot reach anyone without the exercise of knowledge and virtue, without, that is, the acknowledgement of God and the exercise of justice. 19 The right and truth of the search for it is revealed by our greed for this life: temporary it may be and very full of trouble, but everybody has an earnest desire for it; it is the wish of old and young, of kings and beggars, of wise and stupid. 20 Contemplation of the sky and of light itself is, as Anaxagoras saw, so prized that any miseries you like can be endured. 21 Since then this brief and troublesome life is thought to be a great good by common consent not only of people but also of all other creatures, it is plain that it also becomes the supreme and perfect good if it is free of termination and all evil.

22 Finally, there would never have been anyone to despise this life in its brevity or to undergo death unless in hope of a longer life. Those who have willingly sacrificed themselves to save their fellow citizens, like Menoeceus

---

14 Sen. F62, 176 (Vottero).
15 Epic. *ad fr.* 360, p. 241, 15 (Usener)

in Thebes, Codrus at Athens, and Curtius and the Decii at Rome, would never have put death before the benefits of life if they had not thought they were achieving immortality in the esteem of their fellows.[16] They did not know the path of immortality, but the event did not deceive them. 23 If virtue despises riches and wealth because they are fragile, and if it despises pleasures because they are short-lived, then it despises a short and fragile life in order to achieve one which is secure and long-lasting.

24 Thus analysis, proceeding step by step and taking everything into account, brings us to that unique and wonderful good which is the reason for our birth. 25 If philosophers had done that instead of preferring a jealous protection of their one moment of understanding they would surely have arrived at this truth as I showed it just now. And if that was not the interest of those who destroy celestial souls together with their bodies, then those who discuss the immortality of the soul ought at least to have understood that virtue has been made available to us so that our lusts may be tamed, our desire for earthly things be subdued, and our souls return pure and victorious to God who is their origin.

26 Alone among living creatures we are erect to behold the sky so that we may have faith that our highest good is in the heights, 27 and we alone practise religion so that we may know the human spirit is not mortal because it yearns for God who is immortal and because it acknowledges him. 28 Of all philosophers, those who have accepted either knowledge or virtue as the supreme good have at least got on to the path of truth, but have not reached its summit. 29 These are the two things which together can achieve what's wanted: knowledge provides that we know how and where we are to go, and virtue ensures that we get there. One without the other is useless: from knowledge comes virtue, and from virtue the supreme good.

30 The life of bliss which philosophers have always sought and do so still, whether in worship of gods or in philosophy, is non-existent: they could never have found it because they looked for the highest good in the depths and not in the heights. 31 What is highest if not heaven and God the source of spirit? What is lowest if not earth the source of body? 32 Granted, some philosophers may have attributed the supreme good to spirit and not body, but because they related it to this life which ends when the body ends, so they were back with body, to which belongs all this span of time passed on earth. 33 Their failure to grasp the supreme good is well deserved: anything

---

16 For Menoeceus son of Creon, see Eur. *Ph.* 905–1012, 1090–92; for Codrus king of Athens (11th cent? BC), see Pherec. *FGrH* 3 F 154; for M. Curtius (d. 362 BC), see Livy 7.6.3–5; for the Decii (340 and 295 BC), see Livy 8.9 and 10.28.6–18; with Min. Fel. 7.3.

focussed on body and ignorant of immortality must belong on the lowest level. 34 Bliss does not come to a man in the way philosophers have assumed therefore; it is timed to come not when he is living in his body, which has to be corrupted in order to be undone, but when his soul has been freed of the body's company and lives in the spirit alone. 35 The only way in which we can know bliss in this life is to think ourselves minimally blissful, to shun the temptations of pleasure, to serve virtue alone, and to live with maximum toil and misery, for that is the training ground of virtue where virtue gets its strength; we must cling to that rough and arduous path which has been shown us leading to beatitude. 36 The supreme good which brings us bliss can exist only in the religion and the learning that is linked to hope of immortality.

Moral philosophy alone important; moral philosophers disastrously in error

13.1 At this point, now that we have shown that the supreme good is immortality, the situation seems to demand that we prove the immortality of the soul. 2 On this there is enormous disagreement among philosophers; even those with a true sentiment about it have nevertheless been unable to demonstrate their understanding to a point of establishing it. 3 They lack the relevant learning about God; they have failed to present arguments sound enough to prevail or evidence sound enough as proof. We will deal with this problem more conveniently in the final book, when our business will be to discuss the life of bliss.

4 There remains a third area of philosophy, called[G17] 'logic'. It contains all dialectic and all systematic utterance. 5 Learning about God has no need of this because wisdom lives in the heart, not the tongue, and it does not matter what form of utterance you employ. The stuff of utterance is in question, and not its form. Our business too is not with professional linguists or orators, whose knowledge lies in how one ought to speak; we are discussing the wise man, whose learning lies in how one ought to live. 6 If neither natural philosophy nor logic are necessary, however, because they cannot produce bliss, then the effective contribution of all philosophy must be confined to ethics; that is what Socrates is said to have studied, abandoning everything else.

7 Even within ethics, now that I have shown the error of those philosophers who failed to grasp the supreme good which we were born to aim

---

17 G indicates that L. uses or quotes Greek.

for, it is plain that all philosophy is hopelessly mistaken because it neither prepares us for the practice of justice nor brings the duty and purpose of man to joint fulfilment. 8 Those who think philosophy is wisdom need to know their mistake; they must not be led astray by anyone, however authoritative: instead they must back the truth and support it. There is no room for adventurousness: punishment for folly lasts for ever, whether the error was caused by a stupid person or a mistaken opinion. 9 As for an individual human being of whatever sort trusting in himself – trusting in a human being, that is – I won't say he's a fool for not seeing his mistake, but he's certainly over-confident in daring to claim for himself what his human condition disallows. 10 Even the greatest exponent of the Latin language went wrong, as can be seen from a passage in his *de Officiis* [2.5]: 'Philosophy is simply the pursuit of wisdom,' he said, 'and wisdom itself is knowledge of things divine and things human;' then he added, 'I really don't understand what someone who reviles the pursuit can think worth praising in it at all. 11 If the aim is refreshment of the mind and respite from anxieties, what can be compared with the pursuits of people who are always looking for something powerfully focussed on a life of bliss? If note is taken of persistence and virtue, then either this is the system by which we can attain them or there is no system at all. To say that there is no system where matters of the utmost importance are concerned when there is no unimportant matter without its system is the language of people speaking without proper reflection, people much astray on matters of the utmost importance. If any training in virtue exists, where shall it be sought when you withdraw from that sort of learning?' 12 I have made efforts myself to achieve what little skill I could in speaking because of my career in teaching, but I have never been eloquent, because I never went into public life;[18] nevertheless, where a knowledge of things divine together with the truth itself is enough for an eloquent and abundant defence of a case, then the very excellence of that case is bound to make me eloquent.

13 I wish that Cicero could rise, even briefly, from the underworld, so that such a giant of eloquence could be instructed by a pigmy of no eloquence. First, I would ask him what a man who reviles the pursuit called philosophy would think worth praise at all; second, I should tell him that philosophy is not the skill by which virtue and justice get learnt, as he thought it was, nor is it any other kind of skill; finally, since a training in

---

18 L. produced advocates, administrators and politicians, but did not himself pursue a public career.

virtue does exist, I should ask him where to look for it once you move away from that sort of learning; not that he put his question with a view to listening and learning: who could have given him an answer when nobody knew? 14 He followed his usual court practice, putting on pressure through cross-examination and trying to force a confession as if he were sure there was simply no other response possible except that philosophy was the teacher of virtue. He made this very obvious in his *Tusculan Disputations* [5.5], in a speech devoted to philosophy, virtually boasting in declamatory style, 15 'O philosophy, guide of life, searcher out of virtue, driver out of vice! What could I, what could human life, have done without you! O philosophy, you have been our inventor of laws, our teacher of morality and discipline!' 16 as if it were sentient of itself and the praise didn't belong instead to the one who provided it. Cicero could just as well have said thankyou to food and drink, on the grounds that without them life can't exist; but there's no more benevolence in them than sentience. Yet there is an analogy: food feeds the body, and the soul is fed on wisdom.

Philosophy cannot teach how to live

14.1 Lucretius put it better: he praises the inventor of wisdom, but his praise was clumsy because he thought it was invented by a man – as if the man he praises found it lying around like pipes at a spring, to quote the poets. 2 Lucretius praised the inventor of wisdom as if he were a god: his words are [5.6–8]: 'He will be no one in my opinion born of mortal body. If I must put it as is demanded by the very greatness of the world once understood, he was a god, most noble Memmius, a god.' 3 Even so, God was not to be praised like that for inventing wisdom but for inventing man with the capacity to get wisdom. Praising part for whole is a diminution of the praise. 4 He praised him, in fact, as a man, but as a man who ought to be treated as a god for his invention of wisdom; as he says [5.50–51], 'Will it not be right for this man to be counted in the number of the gods?' 5 It is clear from this that his intention was to praise either Pythagoras, the first person, as I said, to call himself philosopher, or Thales of Miletus, who is said to have been the first to discuss natural phenomena. 6 In seeking to praise a man he downgraded the invention: it can't be much of a thing if it can be invented by a man. 7 But we can grant him the indulgence proper to a poet.

As for Cicero, at once perfect orator and supreme philosopher (and I don't want to get at the Greeks: he's always at them for trivialising things, though he follows them none the less), sometimes he calls wisdom a gift and sometimes a discovery of the gods [*Tusc.* 1.64]; either way in presenting its essence metaphorically he praises it to its face. 8 He even complains bitterly of the existence of some who attacked it. 'Has anyone the nerve,' he says [5.6], 'to criticise the parent of his life, befouling himself with parricide and being so wickedly ungrateful?' 9 Does that make me a parricide, my dear Cicero, and should I be sewn up in a sack[19] on your verdict for denying that philosophy is parent of my life, 10 or should you be, for being so wickedly ungrateful towards God, not the god whose image you worship as it sits upon the Capitol, but the one who made the world and created man, and bestowed upon him wisdom too, among all his other celestial kindnesses? You call philosophy teacher of virtue, do you, or parent of life? Anyone who grapples with philosophy is bound to become much more confused than he was before. 11 Which virtue is meant? Philosophers still can't sort out its location. Which life? The experts will be worn out by old age or death before they have decided how life should be lived themselves. Which truth can you claim that philosophy is searching out, when you say so often that 'though there have been so many philosophers, there has never yet been a wise man'?[20]

12 So what has this teacher of life taught you then? How to fling curses at a powerful consul, and to dub him the enemy of his country with speeches of venom?[21] But let's leave out what can be excused under the heading of luck. 13 After all, you pursued philosophy, Cicero, none more diligently; you learnt all its disciplines, as you say with such frequent pride, you set it out in lucid Latin and proved yourself a follower of Plato.[22] 14 So come, tell us what you learnt, or in what school you caught up with truth. In the Academy, no doubt: you followed the Academy and held it up for approval. 15 But all the Academy teaches is to know one's own ignorance. So it is your own works which prove how non-existent philosophy's teaching is for life. Here are your own words: 'In my view we are not only blind as regards wisdom, but dim and dull about the very things that can to some extent be seen.'[23] 16 If philosophy is the teacher of life, why did you see yourself as

---

19 Parricides were traditionally drowned in a leather sack. See also 5.9.16.

20 L. seems to have in mind *de Orat.* 1.94, where Cicero has Antonius say that though he has known a number of skilled speakers, he has not yet known anyone of real eloquence.

21 L. refers to Cicero's *Philippics*, delivered against Mark Antony the triumvir in 44–43 BC. They take their name from those delivered by Demosthenes in defence of Athens against Philip of Macedon.

22 See Cic. *Leg.* 3.1; cf. *Rep.* 1.36. Cicero's works which are named after Plato's *Laws* and *Republic* have similarities with them in both structure and content.

23 Cic. *Ac.* fr. 25.5 (Plasberg).

blind, dim and dull? Under her instruction you should have become wise, sensitive and thoroughly illuminated! 17 How much you trusted in the truth of philosophy comes clear in the advice you gave your son, where you tell him that 'the precepts of philosophy must be learnt, but life is to be lived conventionally.'[24] 18 What could be more contradictory? If the precepts of philosophy are something to be learnt, that is simply so that we may live life properly and wisely; alternatively, if we must live conventionally, then philosophy is not wisdom, since it's better to live conventionally than as a philosopher. 19 If wisdom is what is called philosophy, anyone not living in accordance with philosophy will plainly be living stupidly, whereas if anyone living conventionally is not living stupidly, it follows that anyone living by philosophy is living stupidly. Philosophy is thus condemned for stupidity and futility on your own judgment. 20 You came to that conclusion about philosophy in your *Consolatio* too, not a work of humour: 'I don't know; some confusion, some wretched ignorance of the truth gets hold of us.'[25] So where is philosophy's teaching role, and what have you learnt from the parent of life, if you are so wretchedly ignorant of the truth? 21 If this admission of confusion and ignorance has been wrung from the depths of your heart against your will, you should tell yourself the truth some time, that philosophy, which you have praised to the skies though it taught you nothing, cannot be the teacher of virtue.

Philosophers are not good men

15.1 Seneca made the same mistake (when Cicero strayed, who could keep straight?). 'Philosophy,' he said, 'is simply the right system of life, or the knowledge of how to live honestly, or the skill of living uprightly. We shall not be wrong if we say that philosophy is a law for living a good and honest life; anyone calling it the rule of life gives it its due.'[26] 2 Seneca clearly had no regard for the usual meaning of the word. Philosophy is split into numbers of sects and schools, and has nothing fixed about it; nothing, that is, which everyone can agree to with unanimity. It is a complete mistake to call it either the rule of life when the diversity of guidance in it obstructs the true path and confuses it, or a law for living well when its chapter headings are all in disagreement, or the knowledge of how to run one's life when repetition

---

24 Cic. *Ep.* fr. 6 p. 95 (Weyssenhof) (= VIII 4 Watt).
25 Cic. *consol.* fr. 2 (Vitelli).
26 Sen. F82, 182 (Vottero).

of views that contradict each other leads only to no one knowing anything at all. 3 Does he think the Academy is philosophy, I wonder, or not? I don't think he'll say it isn't. If it is, then none of his phrases belongs: the Academy's aim is to maximise uncertainty; hence its abrogation of law, its denial of skill, its overthrow of reason, its twisting of the rules and its utter destruction of knowledge. All his phrases are thus untrue, because they cannot work with an uncertainty that is persistently unproductive. 4 There is therefore no system or knowledge or law of living well except in this wisdom of ours, which is unique, true and celestial, and quite unkown to philosophers. 5 Earthly philosophy is wrong; hence its variety and multiplicity and total self-contradiction. There is only one maker and ruler of this world, and there is only one truth; wisdom is bound also to be single and simple, because anything good and true cannot be perfectly so unless it is uniquely so.

6 If philosophy could teach life, only philosophers would be good; any non-philosophers would all be utterly bad. 7 But since there are countless people, and always have been, who are or were good without learning, whereas among philosophers there were very seldom any who did anything praiseworthy in their lives, everybody can see that in the end those people aren't teachers of virtue: they haven't got it to start with. 8 Anyone investigating their behaviour carefully will find them bad-tempered people, greedy, lustful, proud, shameless, and hiding their faults under a mask of wisdom while doing at home what they would have slated in school.

9 My desire to attack makes me exaggerate, you think? Cicero allows my claim, and makes his own complaint [*Tusc.* 2.11–12]. 'How often do you find a philosopher,' he says, 'who has lived his life in the spirit and form that reason demands, who thinks his learning is not a show of knowledge but a law for living, who controls himself and obeys his own instructions? You can see some so full of trivial self-glorification that they'd have done better not to study at all, some greedy for money, some for glory, many the slaves of their lusts, so that what they say is in wondrous conflict with how they live.' 10 Cornelius Nepos, too, in a letter to Cicero says: 'I am so far from thinking philosophy the teacher of life and perfecter of bliss that I think no one needs teachers of living more than those who discuss the topic so busily. Of all those who give such shrewd advice in school on modesty and self-control I see the majority living on their passions, living in lust.'[27] 11 So too Seneca; he says in his *Exhortations*:[28] 'Many a philosopher is the sort of man who is

---

27 Cic. *Ep.* fr. 1, VIIB, p. 31 (Weyssenhof) (= IIA Watt).
28 Sen. F77, 194 (Vottero).

eloquent to his own reproof. If you heard them denouncing greed, lust and ambition, you would think they had turned informer, the attacks they once launched at the public now so rebound upon themselves. They ought to be thought of like doctors; there's a cure on the label, but there's poison in the bottle. 12 Some are not restrained by shame even; they construct defences for their disgraceful behaviour, so that it will look as if they erred in good faith. 13 A wise man,' he continues, 'will even do what he disapproves of to gain access to more important things; he won't desert his principles but he will adapt them to the situation; what others employ for their glory or their pleasure he will employ to achieve his aim.'[29] 14 A little further on: 'A wise man will do all the things that the extravagant and the ignorant do, but not in the same way and not on the same basis.'[30] And yet, the intention with which you do something that is wrong is immaterial: it is what is done that gets seen, and not the intention. 15 Aristippus, head of the Cyrenaics, had a relationship with Lais, the famous prostitute. This distinguished professor of philosophy used to defend such scandalous behaviour by claiming there was a world of difference between himself and Lais' other lovers: she kept them, but he kept her. 16 That is a wonderful model of wisdom for good men! Would you give him your sons to teach, to become expert in keeping a mistress? He claimed a difference between himself and mere wastrels; they were wasting their goods, while he was indulging for free, 17 but the advantage of wisdom lay rather with Lais; she had a philosopher for her pimp, so that all the young would rush to her with no feelings of shame, corrupted by the example and the authority of their teacher.

18 So what difference did it make what intention the philosopher had in visiting his infamous mistress, when everyone, including his rivals, could see he was worse than all the wastrels? 19 Even living like that wasn't enough, either; he began to give classes on lust, transferring his own behaviour from brothel to schoolroom, and arguing that physical pleasure was the supreme good. That is a loathsome and disgusting doctrine; no philosopher's mind produced it: only a tart's embrace.

20 What can I say of the Cynics,[31] who have a habit of intercourse with their wives on the doorstep? Is it any wonder that they get their nickname

29 Sen. F79, 196 (Vottero).
30 Sen. F80, 196 (Vottero).
31 Cynicism (lit. Doggishness) was a way of life rather than a philosophy, but it made philosophical claims, in particular that virtue consists in living in accordance with primitive nature. The most famous Cynic was Diogenes of Sinope (c. 412/403–c. 324/321), but the first may have been Antisthenes, a devotee of Socrates.

from the dogs whose lifestyle they imitate? 21 There is no instruction in virtue in this sect; even those who give comparatively good advice either don't practise what they preach, or if they do, which is rare, it is not their learning which directs them towards right but nature, which commonly causes even the uninstructed to do what is admirable.

Opt for wisdom, dispense with philosophy

16.1 They surrender themselves to perpetual sloth, they make no attempt at virtue at all, and they spend all their lives in fine talk: the only reputation they deserve is one for laziness. 2 Wisdom is futile and bogus if it is not active in some way that puts its power to work, and Cicero was quite right to put teachers of philosophy below people in public life who guide affairs of state, who set up new communities or sustain old ones with equity, and who preserve the lives and liberties of citizens with good laws, sound advice and sober judgment.[32] 3 It is better that good men act than shut themselves up in a corner, recommending action they would not take themselves; they have withdrawn from real action, and they have plainly lit upon the game of philosophy either to keep their tongues going or to withdraw altogether. People who only teach and don't act diminish the substance of their advice. Who is to obey, when the lesson of those very teachers is to disobey? 4 It is good to recommend what is right and reputable, but if you do not act accordingly, what you say is a lie, and it is contradictory and stupid to keep goodness on your lips and not in your heart.

5 Their aim in philosophy is not something useful but pleasure, as Cicero bears witness. 'In all their controversy,' he says, 'there are rich seams of virtue and knowledge, but when comparison is made with their actions and achievements, I'm afraid it may seem more a contribution to the amusement of their idleness than to serious business.'[33] 6 Cicero should not have been afraid of telling the truth, but perhaps he feared being summoned by the philosophers to answer a charge of betraying a mystery, and so failed to tell the truth boldly, that philosophers do not argue for the sake of their teaching but for the amusement of their idleness. They press for action but do nothing themselves; treatment of them as mere talkers is inevitable. 7 They were contributing nothing to the quality of life: no wonder they disobeyed their own commands, and no wonder that no one has been found in all these centuries to live life by their laws.

32 Cf. Cic. *de Orat.* 1.33ff., 219; *Off.* 1.43–44.
33 Cic. *Hort.* fr. 18 (Straume-Zimmermann).

All philosophy must therefore be discarded: what is needed is not the pursuit of wisdom, which lacks aim and limit, but wisdom itself, and soon, too: 8 we have no second life allowed us so that we can look for wisdom in this one and be wise in the next; this life must suffice for both. The finding of wisdom must be quick, so that its adoption can be quick, in case we waste any part of our unknown span of life.

9 Cicero's Hortensius gets caught in a shrewd argument in speaking against philosophy.[34] He said that there was no need for it; but he appeared to be using it nevertheless because it is a philosopher's business to debate what should and should not be done in life. 10 Now I dispense altogether with philosophy, as a construct of the human mind, and I defend wisdom[35] as a gift of God, and I say that everyone should take it up: so I am immune from such attack. 11 When Hortensius dispensed with philosophy and put nothing in its place, he was thought to be dispensing with wisdom, and he was easily shifted from that ground, because of the general acceptance that man was born to wisdom and not stupidity. 12 There is, besides, the very powerful argument against philosophy used by Hortensius also: 'It can be understood that philosophy is not wisdom from the fact that its origin and startpoint are obvious. 13 When,' he asks, 'did philosophers come into existence? Thales was the first, I think. That is quite recent. So where did the passion for investigating truth hide itself in earlier generations?'[36] 14 Lucretius says the same [5.335–37]: 'Finally, this is the system of natural phenomena lately revealed, and I am first among the first to be revealed with the power to present it in my native tongue.' 15 Seneca says: 'It is not a thousand years since the first stirrings of wisdom.'[37] The human race therefore lived many centuries without reason; hence the mockery of Persius [6.38–39], 'After wisdom came to town, together with pepper and dates,' as if wisdom was some savoury exotic. If wisdom is natural in man, then it must have begun with man, and if it is not, then human nature could not acquire it anyway. 16 Since it does acquire it, however, it must have been there from the start; and since philosophy was not there from the start, then it is not the same thing as true wisdom. Because the Greeks had made no contact with the sacred literature of truth, plainly they did not know the way in which wisdom had been

---

34 On 7–11, see Straume-Zimmermann 49.
35 Wisdom: L. uses here not his usual Latin word *sapientia* but the Greek word (transliterated) *sophía*, to emphasise its relationship with *philosophía*, the love, or pursuit, of wisdom. See 3.2.3 above.
36 On 12–16, see Straume-Zimmermann 52.
37 Sen. F83, 198 (Vottero).

distorted; they fabricated philosophy thinking that human life was devoid of wisdom, but the truth was there all the time, unknown to them, and they wilfully wrecked it by debate, calling their pursuit of it wisdom, in ignorance of the truth.

Errors of Epicurus

17.1 I have spoken of philosophy itself as briefly as I could. Let us now turn to the philosophers, not to fight them – they cannot resist anyway – but to see them off our territory in abject flight.

2 Much the best known of all the philosophies has always been Epicureanism,[38] not for any contribution to truth it makes, but because its great name for hedonism lures so many to it. Everyone is prone to vice, 3 and anyway, in order to attract the masses, Epicureanism speaks to the lifestyles of individuals. It recommends the lazy not to study, it liberates the mean from public benefactions, it advises the coward against politics, the slothful against exercise and the scared against a military career. 4 The irreligious are told that the gods take no interest, and the selfish and unkind are instructed to make no gifts, because the wise man does everything for his own sake.[39] 5 Those who shun the bustle of life find solitude praised, and the overthrifty learn that life can be sustained on bread and water.[40] Wife-haters are told the benefits of celibacy, and parents with bad children hear well of childlessness, while undutiful offspring are told that nature knows no ties. The soft and sensitive understand that the worst of all evils is pain, and the brave that even in agony the wise man is in bliss.[41] 6 Those ambitious for fame and power are encouraged to cultivate kings, and those who dislike trouble are told to shun the court.[42] 7 A shrewd fellow thus constructs himself a round of behaviour of very great diversity, but in his anxiety to please the world he goes to a bitterer war with himself than the world does with itself.

We must explain where all Epicurus' learning comes from and what its origin is. 8 He saw that good men are always liable to misery, in the shape of poverty, toil, exile and loss of loved ones, whereas bad men flourish with ever more power and influence; he saw that innocence is insecure while crimes can be committed with impunity; he saw that death rages without

---

38 Epic. fr. 553 (Usener).
39 Epic. *ad fr.* 581 (p. 333, 15 Usener).
40 Epic. fr. 571; 471.
41 Epic. *ad fr.* 526 (p. 320, 4 Usener); fr. 529; *ad fr.* 401 (p. 276, 20; cf. p. 339, 8).
42 Epic. fr. 557 (Usener).

regard for morality, rank or age, some people reaching old age and others being taken in infancy, some dying in their full maturity and others removed in the first flower of youth with untimely deaths, and in war the best particularly being conquered and killed.[43] 9 He was most moved by the fact that people of notable piety suffered very grievously, whereas the completely irreligious or casual worshippers had few troubles or none; even temples themselves would often go up in flames. 10 This is Lucretius' objection, when he says of god [2.1101–04]: 'Let him fire his thunderbolts then, and wreck his own temples, and withdraw to a wilderness, furiously practising a weapon which so often misses the guilty and destroys the undeserving.' 11 If he'd had even a breath of the truth, however, he would never say 'wreck his own temples' because their wrecking was due to their not being God's. 12 The Capitol, which is the chief thing in the city of Rome and its religion, has been struck by lightning and gone up in flames not once but several times. 13 The opinion of learned men on this can be seen in what Cicero says [*Ver.* 4.69]: 'The fire had a divine origin; its purpose was not to destroy Jupiter's domicile on earth but to demand one more sublime and more magnificent.' 14 In *de Consulatu* he echoes Lucretius' words: 'Jupiter thundering on high leant on starry Olympus and aimed for his own citadel with its famous temples, and flung his fire on the shrines of the Capitol.'[44] 15 By their persistent stupidity they not only failed to understand the power and majesty of the true god but also exacerbated the impiety of their own mistakes in striving, against all propriety, to restore a temple so often damned by judgment of heaven.

16 Such was the view of Epicurus, encouraged by the unfairness of things, as it seemed to him in his ignorance of the real reason.[45] Hence his opinion that there is no providence. Having convinced himself of this, he undertook to defend his conviction, and got himself tied up inextricably. 17 If there is no providence, how come the world is so organised and ordered? 'There is no order,' says Epicurus. 'Much occurs otherwise than it ought.'[46] Clever fellow! He even found some points of attack. 18 If there were time to reject them one by one, I would easily show that he was neither wise nor

---

43 Epic. fr. 370 (Usener).

44 The lines are quoted twice in Cic. *Div.* 1.19; 2.45. The wording of the second line, however, is slightly different. The idea occurs in Lucr. 6.379–422, and more briefly in 2.1093–1104, of which the key words are cited in 10 above. Lucretius is likely to have taken it over from earlier Epicurean writers.

45 Epic. fr. 370. This is based simply on Lucr. 4.823–57.

46 Cf. Lucr. 5.195–234.

sane. Again, if there is no providence, how come the bodies of animals are formed so providently that every single limb is designed with wonderful sense to sustain its functions? 19 'In the generation of animals,' he says, 'no system of providence is at work. Eyes were not made for seeing nor ears for hearing nor tongue for speech nor feet for walking because these organs were all created before there was seeing, hearing, talk or walking. They were therefore not created for use: use developed from them.'[47] 20 If there is no providence, why does rain fall or fruit grow or trees burst into leaf? 'Those things do not happen for the sake of the animals,' he says, 'because they are no use to providence; everything necessarily happens of its own accord.'[48] 21 So where do they come from, or how does everything happen that does happen? 'It is not the work of providence,' he says; 'there are seeds of things which float through space, and it is from their accidental combination that everything gets born and grows.'[49] 22 So why don't we perceive or see these seeds? 'Because they have no colour,' he says, 'nor warmth or smell. They are also devoid of flavour and moisture, and are so small that they cannot be cut or split.'[50] 23 That is the madness inevitably produced in consequence of a false premiss at the start. Where are those tiny bodies, or where do they come from? Why did they never enter anyone's dreams except uniquely those of Leucippus, who taught Democritus, who left the inheritance of folly to Epicurus? 24 If there are tiny bodies, and they are as solid as is said, surely they can get seen. If they are all identical in nature, how are things created different? 'They come together,' he says, 'in different sequences, like letters of the alphabet, which are few in number but create countless different words by shifts of position.'[51] 25 But letters have different shapes. 'So do the basic elements,' says he. 'There are rough ones, barbed ones and smooth ones.'[52] But if there is anything in them which projects, then they can be cut and split. And if there are smooth ones without barbs, they cannot cohere. They ought to be barbed then, in order to make combinations in their turn. 26 But when they are said to be so small that they cannot be split by any metal edge, how come they have barbs and projections? Barbs and projections stand out, and so must be detachable. 27 What are the terms, the plan, on which they meet to create something out of themselves? If they lack sense they cannot come

47 See note on 16 above.
48 Cf. Lucr. 5.156–94.
49 See especially Lucr. 2.1048–66; 5.187–94, 416–31.
50 For 22–27, see Epic. fr. 287 (Usener).
51 Cf. Lucr. 2.478ff., 660ff., 688–99.
52 Cf. Lucr. 2.333ff., 381–477.

together in any organised fashion: only reason can create something rational.

28 What a wealth of refutation this stupidity produces! On with the debate, however. Epicurus is the man 'who outdid the human race in genius and quelled them all as the rising sun in the sky puts out the stars' [Lucr. 3.1043–3]. I can never read those verses without a laugh. 29 He wasn't speaking of Socrates, or of Plato, who are treated as the kings of philosophy, but of someone who in his fullest sanity was more crazily mad than any sick man. Leonine praise like that from the idiot poet has not distinguished his mouse, but destroyed him and wiped him out. 30 Yet Epicurus is also the man who frees us from fear of death. Here are his own express words on it (D.L. 10.125): 'When we exist, death does not. When death exists, we do not. Death is therefore nothing to us.'[53] 31 What a shrewdly bogus piece of reasoning! As if death were to be feared when it has done its work of taking sense away, rather than the process of dying when sense is being taken away. There is a point of time when we no longer exist and death does not yet exist either, and that is what seems so sad, because death's existence is beginning and our existence is failing. 32 There is also sense in his remark 'Death is not sad; the onset of death is sad:'[54] fading from illness, that is, suffering a stroke, being stabbed, burning to death, being eaten alive; 33 that is what men fear, not the onset of death but the onset of great pain. Better to hold that pain is not an evil. 'It is the worst of all evils,' he says.[55] How then can I fail to be afraid, if what precedes death and causes it is evil? And what about the utter nonsense of the argument anyway, because souls do not perish? 34 'Oh yes, they do,' says he: 'what is born with the body must necessarily die with the body.'[56] I observed earlier that I am postponing this topic and keeping it for the final book, to refute both by argument and with God's evidence this conviction of Epicurus – unless it belongs to Democritus, or else to Dicaearchus.[57] 35 Epicurus, however, perhaps promised himself impunity for his faults: he was the champion of hedonism in all its horror; indeed, he thought man was born for pleasure. 36 Who would keep from vice and wickedness on hearing that asserted? If souls are due to perish, let's go for wealth, so that

---

53 = Usener p. 61, 6ff.
54 The origin of this is unclear, but cf. Sen. *Ep.* 30.9.
55 Epic. *ad fr.* 401 (p. 276, 18 Usener).
56 Cf. Lucr. 3.445–48, 634–39.
57 Dicaearchus of Messana (*fl.* 320–300 BC), a pupil of Aristotle, wrote extensively over a wide range of subjects, including philosophy, politics, geography and literary and cultural history.

we can command all the pleasures, and if we have no wealth, let's take it from those who do, secretly, by treachery, by force, and if there's no god who cares what men do, then let us plunder and kill all the more, whenever the hope of impunity smiles upon us. 37 A wise man should do evil if it is both advantageous and safe for him, because no god who may exist in heaven gets cross with anyone. Equally, it is a fool's errand to do good, because divine favour is as slow to stir as divine wrath is. 38 Let us indulge our pleasures in whatever way we can: in a little while we shall exist no more at all. We must not let a single day, a single moment of time, slip past us without its pleasure, in case we lose our life while living it just because we shall lose it in the end.[58]

39 That may not be word for word, but it is in effect his message. Whenever he argues that wise men always act in their own interests, he is relating everything wise men do to its usefulness.[59] 40 Anyone listening to such outrageous stuff will think that no good needs to be done since good deeds look to the benefit of someone else, and no crime need be ducked because bad deeds bring reward. 41 If some pirate chief or king of thieves were to urge his men on to violence, what words can he employ other than those of Epicurus, repeating them precisely? 42 The gods are not interested, he will say; no wrath or gratitude stir them; there are no penalties underworld to fear, because after death souls die and there simply is no underworld; the supreme good is pleasure; human society does not exist; each man consults his own interest; no one loves his neighbour except for his own purposes; no brave man need fear death or pain, since even if he is being tortured or burnt, he can say he does not care.[60] 43 Is there any good reason for anyone to think that talk like that is the mark of a wise man when it best befits brigands?

Errors of Pythagoreans and Stoics and the criminality of suicide

18.1 Some support the contrary position and argue for the survival of souls after death.[61] Here the leaders are the Pythagoreans and the Stoics. The correctness of their view earns some indulgence, but I cannot refrain from criticism, in that they have tumbled upon the truth accidentally and not intelligently. Hence some errors even in the basic soundness of their view.

---

58 Cf. Epic. *ad fr.* 491 (p. 308, 3 Usener).
59 Epic. fr. 581 (Usener).
60 Epic. *ad fr.* 341 (p. 228, 18 Usener); fr. 523; *ad fr.* 540 (p. 324, 16); *ad fr.* 601 (p. 339, 13).
61 L. deals with this subject at length in 7.3–13.

2 They were scared of the argument which concludes that souls must die with their bodies because they are born with the bodies; so they said instead that souls do not get born but are rather inserted into bodies and transfer from one to another. 3 They could not conceive a survival of souls after death unless souls had apparently pre-existed bodies. Both parties have come to a parallel and virtually identical error, but this lot are wrong about the past and the Epicureans are wrong about the future. 4 None of them saw the obvious truth, that souls get born and also do not die; why that should happen, or what the purpose of man was, they did not know. 5 Many of those who guessed that souls were eternal committed suicide as if they would then transfer to heaven: Cleanthes, for instance, Chrysippus and Zeno, and Empedocles, who flung himself into a fissure when Etna was erupting, at dead of night, so that people would think from his sudden disappearance he had gone to join the gods. On the Roman side there is Cato, who modelled himself all his life on Stoic stupidity.[62] 6 Democritus was of a different persuasion, but even so 'he put himself in the pathway of death of his own accord' [Lucr. 3.1041], and there is nothing that can be worse than that. If a murderer is, by being destroyer of a man, a criminal, then the man who kills himself comes under the same heading because he too kills a man. 7 In fact, suicide should be considered the greater crime because the avenging of it belongs to god alone. We do not come into this life of our own accord; we should correspondingly retire from this corporeal abode, given us to guard, at the word of that same one who put us in this body to abide there till he bids us be gone. At the occurrence of any violence at all, we must be calm and endure it, because souls of the innocent destroyed cannot go unavenged, and vengeance is pure only when exacted by our own great judge alone.

8 All those philosophers are murderers, then, including the prince of Roman wisdom Cato; before he killed himself, so it is said, he read through Plato's work on the everlasting nature of the soul, and he resorted to the supreme wickedness on the word of a philosopher. And yet he had some reason apparently for dying, the hatred of enslavement. 9 Then there is the fellow from Ambracia:[63] he read the selfsame work and flung himself off a

---

[62] The first three named, and Cato, were Stoics. For a statement of the Stoic attitude to suicide, see Sen. *Ep.* 77. M. Porcius Cato (95–46 BC), great-grandson of Cato the Censor, was prominent in late Republican politics; hostile to Julius Caesar, in peace and in war, he committed suicide rather than accept Caesar's pardon. Augustine's discussion of suicide, in *civ.* 1.17–27, features Cato (23–24). For suicide in antiquity, see Van Hooff (1990).

[63] Theombrotus – his name is revealed in two sentences' time – was a Cynic philosopher (end of 4th/beginning of 3rd cent.).

cliff simply because he trusted Plato. It is a doctrine to be cursed and shunned if it drives men out of life. 10 If Plato had known and said by whom immortality is granted and how and to whom and why and when, he would not have driven Theombrotus and Cato to their wilful deaths; he would have educated them instead to life and justice. 11 It seems to me that Cato hunted up his excuse for dying not to escape Caesar as much as to satisfy the requirements of his chosen sect the Stoics, and to promote his own reputation by some crime of great note; what evil could have befallen him had he lived I can't imagine. 12 Caesar was a man of clemency: all he wanted, even amid the passions of a civil war, was to earn his country's approval by the preservation of two fine citizens of it, Cicero and Cato.[64] Let us return however, to those who praise death as a good.

13 You complain of life as if it were over, or as if you had ever established a reason for being born at all. That justifies a retort from the true father of us all in the language of Terence: 'First learn what it is to live; if you don't like it, try the other then.'[65] 14 You are offended at being the victim of evil, as if you deserved anything good when you don't know your father, your lord or your king; you gaze at the brightest light there is, and yet your mind is blind, face down in the darkest depths of ignorance. That ignorance has made some people not ashamed to say that we were born to pay for our crimes. I cannot imagine anything more crazy. 15 What could our crimes have been, and where could we have committed them when we simply didn't exist, unless we believe that silly old fool who claimed he had been Euphorbus in a previous life? He got himself a family from verses of Homer because he had no pedigree of his own, I suppose. 16 What a uniquely miraculous memory Pythagoras had, and how hopelessly forgetful we all are in not knowing who we were before! Perhaps it is a mistake, or else an act of favour, that only Pythagoras failed to reach the whirlpool of Lethe and taste the water of oblivion. Obviously the old fool fabricated stories, like old women without enough to do, for an audience of gullible children. 17 If he had thought well of his audience, if he had thought of them as men, he would never have claimed the right to lie so impudently. No: you have to despise such a trifler's emptiness. 18 What shall we do with Cicero? At the start of his *Consolatio* he said that men were born to pay for their crimes, and he repeated it later, as if protesting against the view that life is not a

---

64 L. is less complimentary to Caesar at 1.15.29, where he calls him *patriae parricida*, murderer of his fatherland.
65 *Hau.* 971–72.

BOOK 3: FALSE WISDOM 205

punishment. His first remark of all was right, that he was 'subject to confusion, and to a wretched ignorance of the truth.'

Death not a good if life was evil

19.1 It is ignorance of the truth which makes those who discuss the good of death argue their case as follows: if there is nothing after death, death is not an evil because it takes away perception of evil. If on the other hand souls survive, it is even a good, because immortality ensues. 2 This view is put by Cicero in *de Legibus*: 'Let us congratulate ourselves, because death will bring about a situation either better than there is in life or certainly no worse; life in a living soul without a body is divine, and with no perception there is certainly no evil.'[66] 3 Shrewd words, it seems: as if there were no other possibility. And yet, both the conclusions are wrong. Sacred literature says that souls are not extinguished; they are either rewarded for just behaviour or punished for ever for their wickedness. 4 It is not right that anyone successfully wicked in life should escape what he deserves, or that anyone who has suffered for his justice should be deprived of his reward. 5 The truth of that is borne out by Cicero in his *Consolatio*: he says the just do not occupy the same area as the wicked. 6 'Those same wise persons,' he says, 'have concluded that the same path to heaven is not open to all. People with the stain of vice and crime upon them are sent down to darkness, they say, and lie in filth, while clean souls of purity, integrity and honesty, models of good ambitions and good practice, fly up to the gods, to a nature like their own, that is, in a smooth and comfortable glide.'[67] 7 That view is at odds with the case put previous to it. The assumption made is as if every man born must be granted immortality. 8 Where is the distinction between virtue and vice if it makes no difference whether someone was an Aristides[68] or a Phalaris, or a Cato instead of a Catiline?[69] This conflict between facts and opinions is impenetrable to anyone without the truth. 9 If I were asked whether death is a good thing or a bad thing, my answer will be that its quality depends on the

---

66 Cic. *Leg.* fr. 1 (Ziegler, *Leg.*).
67 Cic. *Consol.* fr. 22 (Vitelli).
68 Aristides of Athens, nicknamed 'The Just'; *cf.* Cic. *Off.* 3.16, 49, 87. For Phalaris the notorious tyrant of Agrigentum, see 2.4.27n.
69 L. Sergius Catilina: frustrated in politics, he turned to revolution, and died in battle against the forces of the state in January 62 BC. Cato was his fierce opponent in politics, as well as being seen later as his moral antithesis; Cato forced through a senatorial decree which ordered the execution of Catiline's followers in Rome.

sort of life led. A life is a good thing if conducted virtuously and a bad thing if wickedly; so too a death must be measured by the preceding acts of the life. 10 Hence the fact that if the life were spent in worship of God, its death would not be bad, because there is a transfer to immortality; if not, it would be bad of course, since, as I said, there is transfer to eternal torment.

11 I can only conclude that people who seek death out as a good or who shun it as an evil are wrong (not to mention their great iniquity in not weighing the paucity of evil against the greater tally of good). 12 They spend their whole life in a choice round of diverse pleasures and then they want to die as soon as something nasty supervenes; they think they've never had it good if they've once had it bad. They thus damn the whole of life and conclude that it is utterly full of evil. 13 Hence the silly view that what we think is life is death and what we fear will be death is life; the prime good then is not to get born and the next is to die soon. 14 To improve its credibility the view is attributed to Silenus.[70] Cicero says in his *Consolatio* that 'not to be born is best, not to crash upon these rocks of life; next best, if you do get born, is to escape as fast as possible from the blaze of misfortune.'[71] His belief in so stupid a dictum is made plain by the embellishment he adds to it of his own making. 15 Whose advantage does he think it is, I wonder, not to be born? There would be absolutely no one to know. The good or bad of something is a construct of our perception. 16 Second: why did he think the whole of life is rocks or inferno? As if either we had power not to be born, or else our life were a gift of luck and not of god, or as if the reason for being alive could have any similarity to fire.

17 Plato said much the same, where he says 'he thanked nature first that he was born a human and not a dumb beast, second that he was born a man and not a woman, <third> that he was born a Greek and not a barbarian, and lastly that he was born in Athens and in the time of Socrates.'[72] 18 The degree of mental blindness, the size of error in such ignorance of the truth, is beyond expression. Let me simply say that nothing more crazy has ever been said in human history; as if being born a barbarian or a woman or a donkey would have left him the same Plato and not what he was born as. 19 No doubt he put his faith in Pythagoras, who tried to prevent people feeding on animals by saying that souls transferred from their bodies into the bodies of other animals, which is both stupid and impossible: stupid, because there

---

70 Cf. Cic. *Tusc.* 1.114.
71 Cic. *Consol.* fr. 9 (Vitelli). The ultimate source was doubtless Soph. *OC* 1224–8.
72 Plu. *Mar.* 46.1.

was no need to switch old souls into new bodies when the creator who once made the first souls could always make new ones, and impossible, because a soul of the right pattern can no more change its natural state than fire can work downwards or make its flames flow sideways like a river. 20 So, a wise man thought it possible that the soul then in Plato could be put into some dumb beast and keep its human perceptions, and could understand to its sorrow that it was burdened with an inappropriate body. 21 He would have done better to give thanks for being born clever and teachable, so that he could be so richly and so liberally educated. 22 What was the benefit of being born in Athens? There have been lots of people in other states of outstanding talent and learning who were every one a better man than all the Athenians. 23 How many thousands of people are we to think were born in Athens in the time of Socrates who were uneducated and stupid? It is not walls, or the place a man emerges from the womb in, that make him apt for wisdom. 24 Why be so pleased to be born in the time of Socrates? Could Socrates equip his pupils with brains? Did it not occur to Plato that Alcibiades too, and Critias, were regular in attendance upon that same Socrates, and one of them was his country's bitterest foe and the other the cruellest of all tyrants?[73]

On Socrates: his strengths and weaknesses

20.1 Let us now consider what was so great about Socrates himself that a wise man could fairly give thanks for being born in his time. 2 I do not deny he was a little more shrewd than the others who thought the nature of things could be comprehended intellectually, but in my view they were not just mad, but also wicked, for wanting to set their prying eyes upon the secrets of heavenly providence.

3 At Rome, and in a number of cities, we know that there are sacred items which it is thought wrong for men to see. People without licence to pollute them therefore keep from seeing them, and if by chance, mistake or accident a man does see them, the impiety is expiated first by punishment of the man and then by repetition of the ceremony. 4 What is one to do to these people who want to gaze on what is forbidden? Those who seek to profane the secrets of the world and this celestial temple with their impious investigations are much more wicked for sure than anyone who entered the temple

---

[73] Alcibiades was the maverick Athenian statesman prominent in the last two decades of the Peloponnesian War. Critias was chief of the Thirty Tyrants, who were permitted by Sparta to rule Athens after her defeat in 404.

of Vesta or Bona Dea or Ceres. Those shrines may be unapproachable by men, but they were built by men. 5 These people, however, are not just evading a charge of impiety; they are after something which is much less respectable, a reputation for eloquence and a great name for cleverness. 6 What if they had the power to investigate anything? They are as stupid in professing to as they are wrong in trying to, since they cannot discover anything, and if they do, they cannot justify it. 7 If they do see the truth, even by chance, which is not uncommon, they simply arrange for others to dismiss it as false.

Someone does not come down from heaven to deliver a verdict on the views of individuals. 8 No one should have any doubt about the stupidity, the ineptitude and the insanity of people who pursue such questions. 9 Socrates thus had a fair measure of common sense: when he realised there was no discovery to made in the field, he withdrew from investigation of that sort. I regret it was the only sort. There is much he did not just undeserving of praise but strongly deserving of censure; he was very much a child of his times. 10 I will select just one item for universal approval. He held the following saying in high esteem, 'What is above us is irrelevant to us.'[74] 11 Let's fall to the ground then, and turn the hands that were given us for doing great works into feet: let the heaven we are urged to gaze at be irrelevant, and so too the very light of heaven. Yet the cause of our sustenance is in heaven. 12 If Socrates saw that discussion of things in heaven was not on, he still couldn't grasp the system in what was at his feet. Well? Was his confusion verbal? Probably not: surely he understood his own observation, that religion needed no attention. If he had said that openly, however, no one would have put up with it.

13 Anyone would see that this world of such wondrous and perfect formation is governed by some sort of providence, because there is nothing which can successfully exist without some guide and controller. 14 A house abandoned by its occupant falls down, a ship without a helmsman comes to grief, and a body left without a soul disintegrates: we cannot think that a world as big as ours could have been constructed without an architect, or could have lasted so long without a ruler. 15 If Socrates meant to destroy his city's religious rituals, I don't disapprove and I will even applaud – if he himself comes up with something better. In his oaths, however, he invoked the dog and the goose.[75] What a buffoon, as Zeno the Epicurean[76] says of

74 Cf. Min. Fel. 13.1. But Tertullian, *nat.* 2.4.15, ascribes the saying to Epicurus. It was proverbial.
75 Variants may be found in Tert. *nat.* 1.10.42; *apol.* 14.7; Aug. *vera relig.* 2.2.
76 This Zeno came from Sidon. He taught Philodemus, and lived c. 155–75 BC. L. derives his reference from Cic. *N.D.* 1.93; Min. Fel. 38.5 has Socrates as *scurra*, buffoon.

him! What a silly, sorry fool if he meant to mock religion, and if he meant it seriously, what a lunatic, to treat an unclean animal as a god! 16 Who would dare attack the superstitions of Egypt when Socrates has personally endorsed them in Athens? And what about that piece of supreme futility, when before his death he asked his friends to sacrifice a cock he had promised to Aesculapius?[77] 17 Obviously he was scared Asclepius would haul him up before Rhadamanthus the assessor for non-performance.[78] If he had died in consequence of a disease, I would reckon he died insane. But since he acted in full health, anyone who thinks him wise is mad himself. And that's the man in whose time a wise man should be glad to be born!

Plato's warped view of fairness

21.1 Let us consider instead what Plato learnt off Socrates. After his rejection of scientific inquiry, Socrates concentrated on investigating virtue and duty. Doubtless therefore, he enlightened his listeners with his advice on justice. 2 Under Socrates' tuition, Plato surely saw that the power of justice consists in fairness, since all men are born on the same terms. 'Let them therefore have nothing private of their own,' he says [*Rep.* 416d], 'and so that equality is possible, which justice logically requires, let them have everything in common.' 3 That is tolerable as long as it is clear that the topic is money. How impossible it actually is and how unfair, I could demonstrate in many ways, but let us allow its possibility: everyone is going to be wise and despise money.[79] 4 So where does this idea of 'in common' take him? 'Marriages,' he says [457c], 'will also need to be collective.' Presumably he means lots of men flocking round the same woman like dogs, and the one with the most strength winning her; alternatively, if they are patient men, like philosophers, they can wait, and take their turn like men in a brothel. 5 What a remarkable notion of fairness Plato has! Where is the virtue of chastity? Where is conjugal fidelity? Take them away, and all justice is gone! 6 Yet Plato also said [473d] that 'cities would be in bliss if either philosophers

---

77 These were Socrates' last words, as recorded by Plato (*Phd.* 118). Cf. Tert. *apol.* 46.5; *nat.* 1.6, 2.2.12.

78 At 7.22.5, L. links Rhadamanthus with Minos and Aeacus in giving judgement in the underworld. Plato adds Triptolemus (*Grg.* 524a); Vergil omits Aeacus (*A.* 6.540). Tertullian mocks pagans for imagining (following Plato and the poets) that they would be judged at the tribunal of Rhadamanthus or Minos, rather than by Christ. See *apol.* 23.13; *nat.* 1.19.5; *spect.* 30.4.

79 For L. on private property, see pp. 38–40.

became kings or kings turned philosopher.' Would you give kingship to a man so just and fair, a man who would have taken away people's property and bestowed it on others, and would have prostituted the women? Never mind any king, no tyrant ever did that!

7 What grounds did he offer for this disgusting advice? 'The community will be harmonious,' he says [463c], 'and tightly bonded in mutual affection, if everyone is husband, father, wife and child of everyone.' 8 What a mishmash of humanity! How can love survive where there is no certainty who to love? What husband will love his wife or wife her husband unless they have always lived as one, unless deliberate devotion and steadfast exchange of loyalty have produced a mutuality of love? That is a virtue for which Plato's promiscuous pleasuring allows no room. 9 So too, if everyone is a child of everyone, who will love children as they would their own children when they either do not know or else are not sure that they are their own? Who will honour his father, as it might be, when he does not know whose son he is himself? The result is not just that he treats some outsider as his father: he may also treat his father as some outsider. 10 What about the fact that a wife can be in common but a son cannot? Any child's conception is necessarily unique: the child is uniquely incompetent to be a common property; nature itself objects. 11 All that Plato is left with is communality of wives for the sake of harmony. But there is no fiercer cause of quarrels than pursuit of one female by a host of males. 12 If Plato couldn't get the advice from reason, he could certainly have had it from the example not only of dumb animals, whose bitterest battles are so caused, but also of human beings, who have always fought their worst wars with each other for that reason.

Critique of Plato (continued)

22.1 Communality of that sort simply produces adultery and lust, and to get those out by the roots you need virtue most of all. 2 Plato didn't find the harmony he sought because he didn't see where it comes from. Justice has no impact if it is way off centre, or lodged in the body even; it operates entirely in man's mind. 3 Anyone wanting equality among mankind should remove not marriage and property but arrogance, pride and conceit, so that your men of power, the big ones, realise they are equal with the poorest. 4 If the rich lose their haughtiness and intolerance, it won't matter whether some are rich and others poor, because their souls will be at par, and the only thing capable of achieving that is the worship of God.

5 Plato thought he had found justice when he was simply overthrowing

it: it is minds that need to be in common, not breakable things. If justice is mother of all the virtues, then whenever a single virtue is removed, justice itself is undone. 6 Plato removed thrift first of all, which simply doesn't exist when there is nothing of one's own; he removed self-restraint since there was nothing of anyone else's to keep from; he removed self-control and chastity, which are the greatest sexual virtues on either side; he removed modesty, shame and deference – if, that is, right and proper begin to be the words for what is usually seen as scandalous and shameful. 7 He wanted to bestow virtue all round, and he took it away all round. Both vice and virtue take shape from private ownership of things; common ownership simply gives licence to vice. 8 Men owning lots of women can only be called self-indulgent prodigals. So too, women owned by lots of men are not exactly adulteresses, since marriage does not apply, but they are certainly prostitutes and harlots. 9 Plato has thus reduced the life of man to something like that not of dumb things, but of beasts and cattle. Virtually all birds form unions and stay paired, defending their nests with one accord like marriage beds, and loving their offspring because their parentage is sure; if you foist others on them, they turf them out. 10 And yet Plato in all his wisdom, rejecting both human custom and nature, chose rather stupid examples to follow: seeing that in the other animals the duties of male and female are not distinct, he concluded that women should also take on soldiering, be concerned in political debate and exercise office both civil and military. So he assigned them weapons and horses. The consequence is wool and spindles for men, and the bearing of children! 11 He did not see the impossibility of his ideas; there simply has never yet been a nation on earth either so stupid or so wise as to live like that.

Some bizarre beliefs of philosophers

23.1 When the leading lights of philosophy can be caught out in such silliness, what shall we think of the lesser ones? Contempt for money is what usually gives them their noisy self-esteem as wise. 'The spirit is strong.' I keep my eye on what they do, on where the contempt for money takes them. 2 Parental inheritance they reject and shun as an evil: to avoid shipwreck in a storm they venture boldly out in calm conditions, their bravery coming not of courage but of a perverse fear, like the people who kill themselves rather than be killed by the enemy, avoiding death by death! 3 They could have acquired a great name for liberality, but they throw the means away, earning neither distinction nor gratitude. 4 Democritus is praised for abandoning his fields and letting them become public pasture. If he had made a gift of them, fine: but there is no wisdom in an act which if done universally is useless and bad. 5 Even so, that carelessness is tolerable compared with turning one's inheritance into cash and chucking it in the sea. I wonder whether such a man is sane or mad. 'Begone to the depths,' he said, 'you evil desires; I shall drown you to prevent being drowned by you myself.' 6 If your contempt for money is so great, turn it to good, put it to humane use, give to the poor: what you propose to throw away you can use to help a great host of people not to die of hunger, thirst or nakedness. 7 At least copy Tuditanus' mad frenzy: scatter it for the people to grab.[80] Then you can be free of it and yet bestow it well: anything that helps so many is a good thing.

8 Zeno's idea of the parity of faults is also unacceptable.[81] Let us omit, however, what has always excited universal derision, and prove the lunatic's confusion well enough by reference to his classing of pity between vice and disease.[82] He thus deprives us of the emotion which embraces almost all human life. 9 Human beings are naturally weaker than the rest of the animals, animals being equipped by heavenly providence with natural safeguards for withstanding the elements or fending off physical attacks, whereas man has none of them: in their place he has the emotion of pity, more simply called humanity, for our mutual protection of each other. 10 If man went mad at the sight of another man, which we see happen in animals of a solitary nature, there would be no society of men, no interest in founding cities and no reason to either, and so life itself would not be safe, since man would be exposed in all his weakness to the other animals, and would also attack his own fellow men as the wild beasts do.

11 Other philosophers are just as crazy. What can be said of the one who claimed snow was black? The consequence of that was the claim that pitch was white! This is the philosopher who said he was born in order to see the sky and the sun, though he saw nothing at all on earth, even in broad

---

80 This man appears to be C. Sempronius Tuditanus, consul of 129 BC, and the context is the distribution of land to colonists under the agrarian law of Tiberius Gracchus of 133/2. L. seems to have misunderstood Tuditanus' role, for by refusing the senate's request to adjudicate between the agrarian commission and Italian allies who stood to lose by its work, he was holding up rather than promoting the distribution of land. See Appian, *B.C.* 1.18.

81 Stoics believed that there were no degrees of virtue or vice. See D.L. 7.127; cf. Plutarch, *On Common Perceptions* (*Mor.* 1063 A–B): the man under water one arm's length down and the man 500 fathoms down are equally drowning.

82 Pity is classifiable under the passion of distress (cf. Stobaeus 2.90.19–91.9 = LS I, p412E). The central place of pity in L.'s Christian vision is given a full discussion in 6.10–16.

daylight.[83] 12 Xenophanes[84] very foolishly believed mathematicians who said that the moon's orb was eighteen times larger than the earth's; in keeping with his silliness there he said there was another earth within the hollow curve of the moon, and another race of men lived on it in the same way that we live on this earth. 13 That gives those loony folk a second moon to shed nocturnal light upon them as ours does on us, and perhaps this earth of ours is moon to another earth below. 14 'Among the Stoics,' says Seneca, 'there was one who considered attributing a population to the sun.'[85] Patently, a silly consideration. What would he be losing if he had made the attribution? The heat put him off, I believe. He was afraid to put such a multitude in peril, in case the great disaster of their death in such heat might come to be blamed on him.

On the Antipodes

24.1 Well now: when philosophers opine there are people beneath our feet in the antipodes, are they talking sense?[86] Is anyone so silly as to believe there are people whose feet are above their heads? Or that things on the ground with us hang the other way there, and crops and trees grow downwards, and rain, snow and hail fall upwards to the ground? No wonder the Hanging Gardens are counted among the seven wonders of the world when philosophers produce hanging fields, cities, seas and mountains! We must expose the origin of this confusion too. 2 They always get confused the same way. They pick up as a first premise something wrong which looks right, and then proceed to its consequences necessarily. Thus they tumble into lots of ludicrous stuff, because anything in agreement with what's in error is bound to be in error itself. 3 Once they trust a premise, they don't examine the nature of what follows; they just defend it every way, though they ought to be judging the truth or falsehood of their premises from the consequences.

4 So what persuaded them to think of antipodean people? They could see the stars in their courses travelling to their settings, and the sun and moon always setting in the same direction and rising from the same place, 5 but since they couldn't see what mechanism controlled their courses or how they returned from setting to rising, and they thought that the sky itself sloped

83 See 9.4ff. above.
84 Cf. Cic. *Ac.* 2.82 (18 times larger); 123 (moon inhabited, says Xenophanes). Xenophanes of Colophon was a poet and philosopher of the late 6th cent. BC.
85 Sen. F76, 194 (Vottero).
86 L.'s critique was picked up by Augustine: see *civ.* 16.9.

down in all directions, which it is bound to appear to do given its huge breadth, they considered the world to be round like a ball, and from the movement of the stars they concluded that the sky revolved; the stars and sun upon setting were thus brought back to their startpoint simply by the revolution of the world. 6 They then built spheres in the air after the model of the world, and engraved them with fantastic devices which they said were the stars. 7 The consequence of this sphericity of the sky was that the earth was shut in at the heart of it, and if that were so, then the earth itself was like a sphere: anything enclosed by something spherical was bound to be spherical itself. 8 But if the earth were round, then it would have to present the same appearance to all quarters of the sky, rearing up mountains, laying out plains and flattening oceans on all sides. And if that were so, the ultimate consequence was that no part of the earth would go uninhabited by men and the other animals. Thus those pendent antipodeans were the final inference of the roundness of the sky. 9 If you were to ask the people who defend these fantasies how everything avoids tumbling into the bottom of the sky, they reply that it is the nature of things for weight to be drawn to the centre, and for everything to be centrally bound, like the spokes of a wheel, while light things, like cloud, smoke and fire, are diffused from the centre to seek the sky.

10 I don't know what to say about them; they make that initial mistake, and then they stick faithfully to their folly, defending nonsense with nonsense, though I sometimes think they are either philosophising for fun or else knowingly and wittingly taking up the defence of untruth to practise and display their talents on rubbish. 11 I could prove the impossibility of sky being under the earth with plenty of arguments, except for needing to bring this book to its end and still having some things to say more immediately necessary. Since it is not the task of a single book to deal with the mistakes of individual philosophers, enumeration of a few mistakes should be enough from which to understand the nature of the rest.

If philosophy is for an elite, it is not wisdom

25.1 I must now say a word or two about philosophy in general, in order to end with my case well made. Our friend the great imitator of Plato thought that philosophy was not for ordinary people because only educated people could attain it. 2 'Philosophy,' he says [*Tusc.* 2.4], 'is well content to have few critics; it deliberately eschews the masses.' If philosophy abhors a crowd, it is not wisdom, because if wisdom is granted to man then it is granted to all men without distinction, so that there is simply no one who cannot acquire it.

BOOK 3: FALSE WISDOM

3 Philosophers welcome virtue, a gift to the human race, in such a way that they apparently want to be the only ones in enjoyment of a public good. Such jealousy! As if they wanted to put blinds over everyone else's eyes, or even to put their eyes out, to prevent them seeing the sun! 4 Denying men wisdom is simply depriving men's minds of the true light of God. 5 If man is naturally competent to be wise, then wisdom ought to be teachable to craftsmen, peasants and women, indeed, to all of human shape, and the population of the wise should be a mix of every tongue, condition, sex and age.

6 The best proof that philosophy neither leads to wisdom nor is wisdom is the celebration of its secret by beard and gown alone. 7 The Stoics realised as much; they said philosophy was both for slaves and for women;[87] so did Epicurus, who invites people of no education at all to philosophy; so did Plato, who wanted to build his community from the wise. 8 They tried to do what truth required, but could not get beyond the wording, 9 firstly because many skills are needed for the attainment of philosophy to be possible. There are the standard letters of the alphabet to learn, to enable reading, because the great variety of topics prevents all details being learnt by listening or by rote. 10 Much time has to be spent with the language teachers too, to learn the right patterns of utterance, and that is bound to take up years. 11 Even rhetoric cannot be omitted, for the projection and enunciation of what has been learnt. Geometry, music and astrology are also needed: these are all skills associated with philosophy. 12 It is all quite beyond a woman's capacity, because in her adolescent years she must learn the tasks soon to serve her in housekeeping; it is also beyond slaves, because all the years in which they could be learning are entirely devoted to service; and it is also beyond the poor, craftsmen or peasants, as they have to spend each day working for their food. That is why Cicero said that philosophy abhors a crowd.[88] 13 Oh, but Epicurus will accept the uneducated.[89] Then how will they understand his stuff about atoms, which is cryptic and intricate, and scarcely intelligible even to educated folk? 14 What room is there for the non-expert, the innocent, on matters so wrapped in obscurity, so complicated by different minds at work, and so thick with the rhetoric of fine talkers? 15 As for women, there isn't one in the whole record whom the Epicureans ever taught to philosophize except Themiste,[90] and among slaves

---

87 The Stoic Musonius Rufus (c. 30–100) wrote a treatise 'that women too should study philosophy'. See Lutz (1947), 38–43.
88 *Tusc.* 2.4; see 2 above.
89 For this, and for 4–5 above, cf. Epic. fr. 227a (p. 171, 19 Usener).
90 See D.L. 10.5 (Epicurus taught her himself, and wrote her letters); cf. Cic. *Pis.* 63; *Fin.* 2.68.

there is only Phaedo, educated, it is said, after being bought out of evil slavery.[91] 16 They try to count Plato and Diogenes, but they were not slaves: they came into slavery by capture, and Plato at least is said to have been bought out of it by a certain Anniceris, for eight sesterces.[92] Seneca made a ferocious attack on the buyer for rating Plato so cheap; 17 I think he was enraged out of anger with the fellow for not wasting loads of money, as if he should have been paying a Hector's ransom of gold, or heaping up coins way beyond the seller's demand. 18 Among barbarians there is only Anacharsis the Scythian,[93] who would never have dreamt of philosophy had he not already learnt language and literature.

Wisdom comes from God

26.1 The philosophers realised under pressure from nature what had to be done, but they could not do it themselves and they did not see it could not be done by philosophers: the only thing that can do it is the teaching of heaven, for that alone is wisdom. 2 Can people who fail even to persuade themselves of something manage to persuade anyone? Alternatively, will philosophers suppress desires, cool wrath or control lust in anyone when they surrender to vice themselves and admit that natural forces are superior? 3 Because the precepts of God are true and simple, their power in the souls of men is clear from daily experience. 4 Give me a man who is wrathful, bad-mouthed and uncontrolled: with a few words of God 'I will make him as quiet as a sheep.'[94] 5 Give me someone greedy, mean and grasping: I will return him to you generous and distributing great handfuls of his own coin. 6 Give me someone scared of pain and death: in no time at all he will despise the cross, the fire and Perillus' bull.[95] 7 Give me a debauchee, an adulterer, a glutton: soon you will see him sober, chaste and continent. 8 Give me someone cruel and hungry for blood: soon his frenzy will change into merest kindness. 9 Give me someone unfair, stupid and sinful, and at once he will be fair, sensible and innocent: all his wickedness will be drained out in one washing.

10 The power of divine wisdom is so great that when it has steeped a

---

91 He associated with Socrates and founded a philosophical school at Elis.

92 See Sen. F85, 200 (Vottero). For Plato, see D.L. 3.20, and 2 4.26n above; Anniceris was a philosopher of the Cyrenaic school; for Diogenes the Cynic, see D.L. 9.20; cf. Epict. 4.1.114.

93 A largely legendary figure, exemplifying the wise barbarian. See Hdt. 4.76, and Hartog (1988), 61–84.

94 Ter. *Ad.* 534.

95 Perillus designed Phalaris' bull. See V. Max. 9.2.ext.9; Pliny, *Nat.* 34.89.

man's heart it can drive out stupidity the mother of crime in one single surge, and to achieve that there is no need of payment or books or study in the small hours. 11 It happens for free, with ease and at speed, provided one's ears are open and one's heart is athirst for wisdom. No one need be afraid: we are not selling water or offering the sun for a fee. The fountain of God is supremely rich and full, and is available to all; the light of heaven we see rises for all who have eyes. 12 Has any philosopher ever provided that? If he wanted to, can he? They waste the days of their life in pursuit of philosophy, but if nature is at all resistant, they cannot improve anyone, not even themselves. The greatest achievement of their wisdom is not to cut out vice but merely to cover it up. 13 A few words from God change a man so entirely, stripping off the old and remaking him new, that you would not know him for the same.[96]

Philosophers may come close to the truth, but lack authority

27.1 Well? Don't the philosophers give like advice? Yes, in plenty, and they often get near the truth, but their advice has no weight because it is merely human and lacks a greater – that is, a divine – authority. 2 Hence no one believes it, because the listener thinks he is as much of a man as the giver is. 3 In addition, philosophers' advice has no certitude since nothing is said from knowledge; since it is all based on conjecture and much of it diverges, only an utter fool would willingly obey advice whose soundness or error is doubtful. No one obeys it because no one willingly puts in hard work for no clear end.

4 The Stoics say that only virtue produces a life of bliss. Nothing can be truer. Imagine someone on a cross, however, or being tortured: can anyone be in bliss in the midst of his executioners? Yes: pain applied to the body is the very stuff of virtue; even in torment there is no misery. 5 Epicurus puts it much more bravely: 'A wise man is always in bliss, and even when caught in Phalaris' bull he'll cry, It's lovely; I don't mind it at all!'[97] That's asking for mockery, especially since it's our man of pleasure who has adopted the rôle of hero for himself and gone right over the top. No one could possibly think that the torture of his body was a pleasure. The duty of virtue is quite adequately met by mere endurance. 6 What do you Stoics say, and you too, Epicurus? 'The wise man is in bliss even when under torture.' If he's in bliss

---

96 Cf. Eph. 4:22ff.; Tert. *resurr.* 45.
97 For this saying, see Cic. *Tusc.* 2.17; cf. 5.31, 75. In the following sections, L. is following the same source; see *Tusc.* 2.18; 5.73ff., 88. In L.'s version only the key words are the same. See Epic. *ad fr.* 601 (p. 339, 8 Usener).

from pride in his endurance, he'll have no joy of that: under torture he may die. If he's in bliss from thinking of future fame, either he won't know of it (if souls perish), or if he does, he'll gain nothing from it. 7 So what other benefit of virtue is there, or what bliss in one's lifetime? 'Let a man die calm,' they say. You offer me a good which lasts an hour, or perhaps a minute, and there would be no point in a whole life spent in toil and misery for that. 8 How long does death take? When it comes, whether you endure it calmly or not is by then of no importance at all. There is thus nothing to be got from virtue except glory, 9 but glory is either brief and superfluous or, popular opinion being perverse, non-existent. Where virtue is mortal and fleeting, it has no fruits. 10 People who claimed that it did were seeing a shadow of virtue, and not the thing itself. They were head down to the ground, and didn't raise their gaze on high to see the virtue which 'displayed itself across the heavens.'[98] 11 This is the reason why nobody heeds philosophers' advice: if they defend pleasure they are training us up for vice; if they promote virtue, they put no penalty on sin except the penalty of its mere nastiness, and they promise no prize for virtue except good repute and praise alone, since they say that virtue is only to be pursued for its own sake.

12 The wise man under torture is therefore in bliss; when he is being tortured for his faith, or for justice, or God, it is that endurance of pain which puts him in perfect bliss. 13 Only God can honour virtue: the reward of virtue is immortality alone. The power of virtue is all unknown to those who do not seek it or who have no religion, which is the link with eternal life: they do not know the reward of it and they are not focussed on heaven, though they think that in tracking the untrackable they are, because the whole point of contemplating heaven is either adoption of religion or belief in the immortality of one's soul. 14 Anyone who either understands that God is to be worshipped or keeps the hope of immortality set before him has his mind on heaven: he may not see it with his eyes, but he does see it with the light of his soul. 15 Those who do not adopt religion are earthbound, because religion is from heaven, and those who think the soul dies with the body are equally focussed on earth because they see nothing beyond the body, which is earth – nothing, that is, which might be immortal. 16 It is therefore no use for man to be so created that he can gaze at the sky erect unless he gazes at God with mind erect too and has all his thinking fixed on the hope of perpetual life.

---

98 Lucr. 1.64.

Philosophy has missed wisdom, rejected truth and promoted luck

28.1 The only basis of reason in life, and the only ground of our being, is recognition of the God who made us, and a true and religious worship of him. Because the philosophers missed it, so they were not wise. 2 Wisdom was what they sought, but they did not search for it rightly, and so their failure was the greater; they got into such confusion that they even failed to keep hold of ordinary wisdom. 3 They did not just refuse to promote religion; they actually abolished it. Beguiled by the appearance of a bogus virtue, they tried to release men's minds from all fear. This overthrow of religion has earned the label 'natural'. 4 Either they did not know by whom the world was made, or they wanted to convince people that no divine intelligence had been at work on it; hence their statement that nature is mother of all things, as if to say that everything comes into being spontaneously. They admit their folly in that one word. Without a divine providence and power, nature simply fails to exist. 5 If by nature they mean god, it is merely perverse to use that word instead of god; if on the other hand nature means the reason or necessity or condition of coming into being, then since it has no senses of itself, a divine mind must exist to give all things their start in life through its providence. If, again, nature is sky and earth and all that has ever been created, nature is not god but the work of god.

6 It is much the same mistake which makes them think of luck as a sort of god who mocks humanity with a variety of accidents. They do not know where their good and evil come from; 7 they think they are paired with luck in a fight, but they offer no analysis of the agent or the cause of the pairing, and simply boast at every moment that their duel is with luck. 8 Anyone offering consolation to another at the death or loss of dear ones lashes the name of luck with the most ferocious invective; in fact, there is no discussion of virtue at all on their part in which luck doesn't get hammered. 9 In his *Consolatio* Cicero says that he always fought against luck, and always had her beaten when he was brave and stood up to his enemies' attacks. Even when driven from home and deprived of his citizenship he was not broken by her; but when he lost his darling daughter, then (he says, to his shame) he was the victim of luck. 'I give in,' he says, 'I put my hands up.'[99] 10 How wretched to lie down like that! He calls his action foolish, and yet he professes to be wise! So what's the point of using the word? What's the point

---

[99] See Cic. *Consol.* fr. 3, 3a (Vitelli). The death of Tullia in February 45 BC dominated Cicero's letters to Atticus between March and August (*Att.* 12.13ff.). His plan for a shrine in her memory (*Att.* 12.18 *et al.*) was eventually abandoned.

of all that superiority, so eloquently expressed? Why present yourselves so differently dressed from the rest? Or more simply, why do you offer advice on wisdom if no one has yet been found who is wise? Philosophers admit themselves that they know nothing and aren't wise: how can they carp at us for saying so too?

11 Only if their failings get so great that they cannot even pretend to wisdom (which they do in all other cases) are they eventually alerted to their ignorance; then they jump about like lunatics, proclaiming their blindness and stupidity. 12[100] Anaxagoras says that everything is shrouded in darkness; Empedocles laments the narrowness of the paths of perception as if he needed a four-wheeled carriage or a four-horse chariot in order to think; 13 Democritus thinks that truth lies sunk down a well-shaft so deep that it has no bottom, which is as stupid as the rest of his stuff, of course. 14 Truth is not sunk in a well which he could climb down, or even fall into: imagine it on the topmost tip of a lofty mountain, or, better, in the sky, which is absolutely true. 15 Why should he go saying it is down at the lowest level rather than raised on high? – unless he'd rather lodge his own mind in his feet perhaps, or in the soles of his shoes, rather than in heart or head. 16 They were so very far from the truth that even their own body posture failed to warn them to look for truth on high. 17 This is the desperate context for Socrates' famous claim, when he said he knew nothing except for the one thing that he knew nothing, and that was the source of the Academy's teaching, if teaching is what to call it when only ignorance is taught and learnt. 18 Even the ones who claimed knowledge for themselves could not consistently argue the case for what they thought they knew, 19 and because their ignorance of things divine barred their theories from making sense, they were so diverse and imprecise, and often so at odds with themselves in their arguments, that what they taught and meant you simply couldn't sort out and decide.

20 So why fight with people who perish on their own swords? Why labour to overthrow people who are overthrown and brought low by their own utterance? 'Aristotle,' says Cicero [*Tusc.* 3.69], 'in attacking previous philosophers says that they were either very stupid or else very arrogant in thinking that philosophy was brought to perfection by their talents, whereas he could see that philosophy would soon be made perfect given its great and speedy improvement recently.' 21 So what did he mean by 'soon'? When was philosophy perfected, and by whom? In saying they were very stupid in thinking wisdom had been brought to perfection by their talents he was

---

100 For the following sections, cf. Cic. *Ac.* 1.44–45.

right, but even Aristotle was incautious in thinking that what had been begun by his predecessors or had been improved recently would be perfected in the next generation. 22 There can be no investigation where the search is on the wrong track.

Luck is nothing, evil a reality which tests the virtuous

29.1 Let us go back to what we left out. Luck by itself is nothing, and we must not think of it existing perceptibly at all, as it is simply the sudden and unexpected outcome of things contingent. 2 Philosophers, however, are willing to be wise on a silly point (in case they fail to go wrong eventually): they change its gender, and say it is not a goddess (the popular view) but a god. 3 But they also call it sometimes nature and sometimes luck, 'because,' as Cicero says [*Ac.* 1.29], 'it causes much to happen that we do not expect, thanks to the obscurity of the causation and our ignorance of it.' Since they do not know why things happen, they are bound not to know who makes them happen.

4 In a very serious work in which he drew on philosophy to give his son advice about life, Cicero also says [*Off.* 2.19], 'The great power of luck in either direction is well known. When its wind blows fair and we take our chance, we reach our desired results, and when it blows against us, we are shipwrecked.' 5 First: he speaks as though the item were one of both personal and general knowledge, despite denying that anything can be known. Second, despite his efforts to cast doubt even on things that are obvious, he thinks clear something which he ought to treat as extremely doubtful: to a wise man it is utterly false. 6 'It is well known,' he says. Not to me. Let him tell me if he can what that power is of blowing this way and blowing that way. It is disgraceful of a clever man to assert something which he cannot prove if challenged.

7 Finally, though he says that 'we must withhold assent, because it is folly to agree to things unknown too soon',[101] he has obviously put his faith in ideas of the ignorant mob, who think that good and evil are bestowed on mankind by luck. They give her icon a horn of plenty and a steering oar, as if she bestows prosperity and has control of human affairs. 8 Even Vergil agrees with that, calling luck 'omnipotent' [*A.* 8.33], and so does the historian [Sal. *Cat.* 8.1] who says 'Assuredly, luck is the dominant factor in all things.' 9 What space does that leave for the rest of the gods? Why is luck not said to

---

101 Cf. Cic. *Ac.* 1.45; *N.D.* 1.1.1.

rule if luck has superior power? Alternatively, why is luck not worshipped alone if luck has all the power? Or if it is only evil she bestows, let them produce some reason why, if she is a goddess, she is so ill-disposed towards men and wants them ruined, despite their faithful worship of her, why she is fair to bad men and unfair to good men, why she lurks in ambush to wreck, deceive and destroy, 10 who made her the perpetual tormentor of the human race, and why, finally, she controls a power so evil that 'she brings all things in and out of fame according to whim rather than truth.' [Sal. *Cat.* 8.1] 11 Those are the questions I say philosophers should be asking, rather than make intemperate attacks on luck which is innocent. Even if luck did exist in some form, they can offer no reason for it being as hostile to mankind as it is thought to be.

12 All those speeches in which they lash the unfairness of luck and make such proud boast of their own virtues in opposing it are simply the ravings of ill-considered triviality. 13 They need not be jealous of us who have god's revelation of the truth: we know that luck is nothing, and likewise we know that there is an evil and treacherous spirit which is hostile to good men and is the enemy of justice; it does the opposite of God, and we have given the explanation of its jealous temper in book 2. 14 It lays its traps for everyone. Those who do not know God stumble in confusion and stagger in folly, surrounded by darkness, so that none may come to knowledge of the name of God in whom alone wisdom and life perpetual are contained. 15 Those who do know God, on the other hand, are assailed with clever deceptions, to enmesh them in desire and lust, to deprave them with beguiling sins, and to drive them towards death; if deception will not do the work, their overthrow is attempted by force and violence. 16 The first steps in transgression do not thrust a man away from God and into punishment immediately: the purpose of evil is to test a man for virtue, because if his virtue is not stirred and strengthened by constant assault it cannot come to perfection; virtue is the brave and indomitable endurance of evils that have to be endured. Hence the fact that virtue cannot exist if it has no adversary. 17 So when they perceived that the energy of this perverse power was in conflict with virtue and they did not know its name, they invented for themselves the empty word luck; how far that word is from wisdom is clear in these verses of Juvenal [10.365–66]: 'You have, or should have, no power, if providence existed. It is we who make a goddess of you, luck, and we who set you in the sky.' 18 The words 'nature' and 'luck' were thus brought in by folly, error and blindness, and, as Cicero says, by ignorance of things and their causes. 19 Philosophers do not know the adversary; by the same token they do not even

BOOK 3: FALSE WISDOM

know virtue, knowledge of which is derived from knowledge of the adversary. If virtue is linked with wisdom or if it is itself wisdom, as they say themselves, then they are bound not to know where it is. 20 No one can be equipped with true weapons if he does not know the foe he is to be equipped to fight, and no one can conquer an adversary who strikes at a shadow in the fighting and not at his true foe. If a fighter is looking elsewhere and fails to see in time the blow launched at his vitals or to guard against it, he will fall prostrate.

Philosophy is false wisdom: abandon it

30.1 I have explained as far as my average ability can manage that the path taken by the philosophers is very far from the truth; I know how much, however, I have left out in not engaging in the argument they deserved. 2 But the diversion was one which had to be made, in order to show how many fine philosophical talents have been wasted on bogus stuff, in case anyone cut off from worthless cults might think of turning to them to find something reliable. 3 For men there is one hope and one salvation, to be found in the teaching we argue for; all human wisdom rests in the requirement to know God and worship him. That is our doctrine, and that is our judgment.

4 As loudly as I can, therefore, I pronounce, proclaim and bear witness: this is the thing which all the philosophers looked for all their lives and yet never could find, grasp or hold, because they either maintained a false religion or abolished religion entirely. 5 Away with them, therefore, all those philosophers who bring no system to human life but merely confound it. Whom can they teach? Who can learn off them? They have not learnt off themselves yet. Whom can a sick man heal? Whom can a blind man guide? All who mind about wisdom must rally to the call, 6 or we shall be waiting until Socrates knows something, or Anaxagoras finds light in his darkness, or Democritus hauls up truth from its well, or Empedocles widens the paths of his mind, or Arcesilaus and Carneades[102] can see, think and understand. 7 Behold, a voice from heaven, teaching truth and showing us a light brighter than the sun itself! Why are we so hard on ourselves? Why do we hesitate to take up the wisdom which learned men have wasted all their lives in seeking and have never been able to find? 8 Let anyone who wishes to be wise and in

---

[102] Carneades (c. 214/3–129/8 BC) was head of the new Academy in the mid-2nd century. Sent by the Athenians, together with the Stoic Diogenes and the Peripatetic Critolaus, on a mission to Rome c. 155, he stunned his audience by arguing for justice and against justice on successive days. See 5.16.2ff.

bliss hear the word of God and learn justice; let him know the mystery of his birth, despise things human and take up things divine, so that he may achieve that supreme good for which he was born.

9 When all religions have been undone and everything that used to be said or could be said in their defence has been refuted, and when the teachings of philosophy have been disproved, then we must come to true religion and wisdom. The two are bound together, as I shall explain, so that we can support wisdom with proofs, examples and satisfactory evidence while we show that stupidity, a charge which those worshippers of gods never cease to fling at us, is entirely in their province and not in ours at all. 10 I have demonstrated where truth lies both in the previous books, where I was proving the falseness of religions, and in this, where I was getting rid of false wisdom; the next book will demonstrate more clearly, however, what true religion and true wisdom are.

BOOK 4: TRUE WISDOM AND RELIGION[1]

Birth of paganism

1.1 When I consider the previous state of the human race, O emperor Constantine, and turn it over in my mind as often as I do, it usually seems to me as remarkable as it is disgraceful that one generation[2] in its folly could adopt a variety of religions, believing that there were many gods, and suddenly plunge into such ignorance of its own self that once truth was out of sight, neither worship of the true God nor an understanding of humanity could be sustained, as people sought the supreme God not in heaven but on earth. 2 That, no doubt, is why the happiness of earlier generations is gone. When people had once abandoned God the father and founder of all, they began to venerate the inanimate creations of their own fingers. What this wickedness has achieved, or what evil it has produced, is evident from the event.

3 The supreme good is something blessed and everlasting precisely because it cannot be seen, touched or understood, and yet people turned away from it, and away too from the virtues which go with that good, which are equally immortal, and they fell for these corrupt and feeble gods, and grew keen for those things which adorn, feed and rejoice only the body; they thus sought out a perpetual death for themselves, together with the gods and the goods of the body; for the whole body is liable to death. 4 Worship of that sort was followed by injustice and wickedness, as was inevitable. They left off raising their faces to heaven; instead, people's minds were bent downwards, and they concentrated on terrestrial religions and terrestrial good. 5 Then came division in the human race, and cheating, and all manner of wickedness, because people despised the goods that are eternal and incorruptible, which ought to be the only ones desired, and preferred things of a short life in this world; faith in evil grew strong: people preferred bad to good, because bad was more immediate. 6 So human life, spent by previous generations in the brightest of light, fell into the grip of shadow and darkness.

---

1 The theological positions taken up by L. are best pursued with the aid of Loi (1970) and Monat (1982).
2 The generation that L. has in mind is that of Jupiter, as indicated in 1.11ff; cf. 5.5.

Once wisdom had gone, people then began to claim the title of wise for themselves, which was an act consistent with the new depravity. 7 When every one was wise, however, no one was called so: if only a word once so widespread could regain its proper value, however few it properly described! 8 Perhaps those few might be able, by their talents or authority or persistent encouragement, to release people from their vice and error. But wisdom had collapsed so totally that from their very claim to the title it is plain that none of those called wise really was wise.

9 And yet, before what is called philosophy was invented, there were seven, it is said, who for their courage in investigating and debating the natural world were the first of all men to deserve the reputation as well as the name of wise.[3] 10 What a wretched and disastrous time, when in all the world there were only seven people who could claim the name of man! Only a wise man can rightly be called a man; 11 yet if all the rest bar them were fools, even they were not wise, for no one can truly be wise if fools are the judges. 12 They were so very remote from wisdom that even later, when learning expanded and there were many great minds ever intent on its development, it could not be brought to perfection and the truth be grasped.

After the renown of the seven sages, it is extraordinary what an enthusiasm for searching out truth flared up all over Greece. 13 To begin with, the very word 'wise' seemed to claim too much, and people refused it and called themselves merely pursuers of wisdom. In doing so, they condemned the error and folly of those who had claimed the title of wise too readily, and they also condemned the ignorance in themselves, an ignorance which they didn't try to deny; 14 for wherever nature set her hand, as it were, against their understanding, to prevent them from producing any explanation at all of something, they declared they knew nothing and perceived nothing. Hence the much greater wisdom attributed to those who saw their own unwisdom in part compared with those who were sure they were wise.

Wisdom hides behind folly

2.1 If then those called wise were not wise, and their successors, unhesitating in confession of their ignorance, were not wise either, it remains to look for wisdom elsewhere, since it has not been found where it was sought. 2 There is only one reason for something not being found when so much time and talent has been spent searching for it so enthusiastically

---

3 For the Seven Sages, see 1.5.16; cf. Cic. *Off.* 3.16.

and laboriously: philosophers have looked for it outside its proper territory. 3 Since they have hunted for wisdom everywhere without finding it anywhere, and since it has to be somewhere, plainly it is best to look for it where the label of folly appears:[4] this was the veil under which God hid his treasure of truth and wisdom, so that the secret of his divine work should not be open to all. 4 I am regularly amazed that Pythagoras and later Plato were so fired with a passion for pursuing truth that they went as far as the Egyptians, the Magi and the Persians to learn the religious practices of those nations (they had a suspicion that wisdom belonged in a religious context) while the Jews alone received no visit, though they were its only abode of truth at the time and it was easier to get to them. 5 I think that they were diverted from the chance to learn the truth by divine providence because it was not yet right for people of another race than the Jews to get to know the religion and justice of the true God. 6 God's plan was to send his great leader from heaven only as the end of time was approaching, so that he could reveal to other nations what had been taken away from a faithless and ungrateful people.

This is the topic that I shall now proceed to discuss in this book, once I have shown that wisdom goes so closely with religion that neither can be torn from the other.

Vanity of paganism

3.1 As I explained in book 1, there is no wisdom in worship of gods not just because it subordinates a divine being, man, to things earthly and perishable, but because it contains no discourse which might help in improving one's behaviour and giving shape to one's life, nor is there any investigation of truth in it, but simply a system of worship which consists in a physical performance and not in a service of the mind.[5] 2 It is not to be considered a true religion because it does not educate people or improve them by instruction in justice or virtue. So, because philosophy contains no religion, no ultimate piety, it is not true wisdom. 3 If the godhead which governs this world sustains the human race with an incredible generosity and cherishes it with a virtually paternal kindness, it surely wants thanks and honour in return, and no pattern of piety can hold good for man if he remains ungrateful for the benevolence of heaven; that is not the behaviour of a wise man.

---

4 Cf. I Cor. 1:20–25. The nature of Christian 'folly' is explored in 5.14–18.
5 The message of 3.1–3 is further developed in 5.19.27–34.

4 Since therefore philosophy and a religion of gods are, as I have said, different things and far apart, in that those who profess the philosophy are one thing, offering no access to gods, and champions of the religion are another, making no pretence to learning, the one is plainly no true wisdom and the other no true religion. 5 That is why philosophy has not been able to understand the truth, nor has the religion of gods been able to give the logical account of itself which it lacks. 6 Where, however, wisdom is linked with religion in an inseparable bond, each is bound to be true, because in worship we need to exercise intelligence – we must, that is, know what we are to worship and how – and in exercise of our intelligence we must worship – that is, we must fulfil what we know in real earnest.

7 Where then is wisdom linked with religion? Where the one God is worshipped, of course, and all life and action is related to one beginning and one end: then masters of learning and priests of God are one and the same people. 8 No one should be worried at a philosopher taking up a priesthood of the gods: it is a frequent event, and a possible one; but when it happens, philosophy is not united with religion; instead, philosophy will pause amid the ritual, as will religion when the philosophy is being practised. 9 Religion is dumb not only because it is a religion of the dumb but because the ritual is all a matter of hands and fingers, not of heart and tongue, as ours is, which is the true religion.

10 Religion is thus within wisdom, and wisdom within religion. Wisdom cannot be separated from religion because wisdom is simply honouring the true God with worship that is just and holy. 11 The fact that a ritual of many gods is contrary to nature can be well understood from the following argument: every god worshipped by mankind is bound in the course of the due rituals and prayers to be called father, not just as a mark of honour but logically, because he antedates man and provides life, health and food like a father. 12 So Jupiter is called father by his worshippers, and so are Saturn, Janus, Bacchus and all the rest of them, which is what Lucilius mocks in his 'Council of the Gods', noting 'how there isn't one of us who isn't either Best father of the gods, or father Neptune, or father Liber or Saturn, or father Mars, Janus or Quirinus: father we get called every one!'[6]

13 But if, procreation being a unique act, nature forbids one person to have many fathers, so it is unnatural and unholy to worship many gods. 14 Worship must be given therefore to the one who alone can truly be named father; he is bound also to be lord, because he has a power to punish

---

6 Lucil. 1.24–27 (Warmington) = 16 (Charpin) = 19–22 (Marx).

matching his power to indulge. 15 He is to be called father because he makes us so many great gifts, and lord because he has the supreme power of reproof and punishment. Even the reasoning of the civil law shows that a father must also be a master.[7] Who will be able to bring up sons unless he has a master's power over them? 16 A man is properly called 'father of a family', provided he has sons; obviously, 'father' includes slaves too because 'of a family' follows,[8] and 'family' includes sons because 'father' precedes. Hence it is clear that one and the same person is both father of his slaves and master of his sons.[9] 17 Finally, a son is manumitted like a slave, and a slave when freed takes his master's name like a son. If, further, a 'father of a family' is so named in order to clarify the fact that he has a double power, in that as a father he must be kind and as a master he must control, so a son is also a slave and a father is also a master. 18 As therefore by the law of nature there can only be one father, so too there can only be one master. What will a servant do if a multiplicity of masters gives a diversity of orders?

19 Worship of many gods is therefore contrary both to reason and to nature, since neither fathers nor lords can be plural and gods are bound to be entitled lords and fathers. 20 It is thus impossible to keep hold of the truth in a situation where one and the same person is subject to a multitude of lords and fathers and his attention is diverted in all directions, wandering this way and that, 21 and religion can have no stability when it lacks a sure and lasting home.

22 Worship of gods cannot therefore be true in exactly the same way that marriage is not the word where one woman has many husbands: she will be called either whore or adulteress; when modesty, chastity and faith are missing, there is bound to be a lack of virtue. A religion of gods is thus indecent and impure as well, because it lacks faith in serving many, and the devotion intended, being unfocussed and unclear, has no head or derivation.

---

[7] This striking introduction of Roman law in the service of a theological argument (that God is one) is revealing about L.'s interests and those of his intended audience.

[8] The *paterfamilias* presides over the *familia*, by which is meant all those under the same authority and not just those related by blood or marriage.

[9] Roman *patria potestas* was unique (see Gaius *Inst.* 1.55) for the power conferred on fathers over their children. Hence the comparison of a son with a slave (as pursued here by L. for his own purposes) was in principle feasible. L. is technically correct in indicating that sons too had to be emancipated (by a ritualised sale thrice over) in order to be *sui iuris*, and free from their father's *potestas*.

Wisdom and religion unite in God the father and master

4.1 That makes it plain how close the link is between wisdom and religion. Wisdom looks to sons in demanding love, and religion looks to slaves in demanding fear. Just as sons should love and honour a father, so slaves should fear and respect a master. 2 God is one: since he sustains the role of both father and master, we should love him as sons and fear him as slaves.

Religion thus cannot be severed from wisdom nor wisdom divorced from religion, because it is one and the same God who should be both understood, which is the work of wisdom, and honoured, which is the work of religion. 3 But wisdom goes first and religion follows because knowing God comes first and worship of him is the consequence. Thus there is a single force in the two words, despite the apparent diversity: the one belongs in perception and the other in action; 4 they are like two streams sourced by one spring: the spring of wisdom and of religion is God, and if these two streams lose their link with him, they are bound to run dry. Those who don't know God can be neither wise nor religious.

5 So it is that both philosophers and worshippers of gods are like disinherited sons or runaway slaves: the sons are not looking for father nor the slaves for master.[10] And just as disinherited sons cannot win a legacy from their father nor can runaway slaves win impunity, so philosophers will not receive a legacy from heaven of immortality – the supreme good, that is, which is what they are after most of all – nor will worshippers of gods escape the penalty of everlasting death, which is the verdict of the true lord on those who flee his power and name. 6 God's status as father and lord was not known to either group, whether worshippers of gods or people professing wisdom, that is; either they thought there was no one to be worshipped, or they endorsed religions that were false, or, despite understanding the power and potential of a supreme god (like Plato, who says there is only one god who made the world,[11] and Cicero, who says [*Leg.* 1.22] that 'man was given a remarkable status by the supreme god who created him'), yet they made him no offer of the worship that was owed him as supreme father, though it was both consequent and necessary. 7 The impossibility of gods plural being lords and fathers is proved not only by their numbers, as I pointed out above, but by logic: there is no story of man being created by gods and no discovery that gods preceded the arrival of man, 8 since it is clear that there were people on earth before the births of Vulcan, Bacchus, Apollo and Jupiter

---

10 For bad slaves and sons, see 5.18.12–16; *de ira* 18.9ff., 20.1ff.
11 Plato, *Ti.* 28c. Cf. 1.8.1n.

BOOK 4: TRUE WISDOM AND RELIGION   231

himself, and yet creation of man is not usually attributed to Saturn or to his father Caelus.

9 But if there is no tradition of man being formed and established from the start by any of the gods who get worshipped, then none of them can have the name of father of man, and so not even the name of god. Veneration is therefore wholly wrong for such as could not create man, and his creation was beyond them because he could not be created either <by those whom he pre-existed or>[12] by a multiplicity of them. 10 Thus the one to whom worship is uniquely due is the one who preceded Jupiter and Saturn, and preceded heaven and earth too. The one who created heaven and earth before man is necessarily the one who shaped man. 11 Only a creator can properly be called father, and only a ruler, one who has a true and lasting power of life and death, can properly be named lord; anyone who does not worship him is both a stupid slave, for either fleeing his master or not recognising him, and an undutiful son, for hating his own true father or not knowing him.

True religion

5.1 Now that I have explained that wisdom and religion cannot be separated, it remains to discuss them for themselves. 2 I am well aware how difficult discussion is of things celestial, but the attempt must be made so that the truth may be available in full clarity and many may be freed from error and death who despise and reject it as long as it lurks beneath a veil of stupidity. 3 But before I start to speak of God and his works, I must say a few words on the prophets: their evidence is now relevant. In my earlier books I held off.[13]

4 Above all, anyone eager to grasp the truth should not only attend to understanding what the prophets say but also find out with great care what period they each lived in, so as to know both the future they predicted and the lapse of time before its fulfilment. 5 There is no difficulty in gathering this information at all. Each has named the reign in which he experienced the coming of God's spirit, 6 and many writers[14] have produced books on the chronology; they start with the prophet Moses, who lived about 900 years before the Trojan war.[15] When he had guided his people for 40 years, he took Joshua as his successor, and Joshua was their leader for 27 years. 7 They

---

12 The bracketed text is owed to a suggestion by Brandt.
13 See 1.4–5.1.
14 See the list in Tert. *Apol.* 19.6.
15 L. follows Theophilus, *Autol.* 3.21, 29. See Nicholson (1985), 306. Some MSS say 700, not 900, years, but neither figure allows a reasonable chronology.

were then under judges for 370 years. After a change of constitution they took to having kings. Kings held power for 450 years, down to the reign of Zedekiah, when the Jews were conquered by the king of Babylon and endured a long captivity as slaves, until after 70 years Cyrus the Great restored them to their lands; he came to authority over the Persians at the same time as Tarquin the Proud was king in Rome. 8 Since a whole chronology can be collated from Jewish history and Greek and Roman history, even the dates of individual prophets can be fitted in; the last of the prophets was Zechariah,[16] and it is agreed that he prophesied in the time of king Darius, in the eighth month of the second year of his reign. That is the extent to which the prophets turn out to predate even Greek writers.

9 I set all that out so that people who try to discredit holy scripture as something new and recently constructed can see their error;[17] they do not know the source from which our divine religion starts its stream. 10 If people will only lay a sound basis for understanding by collating and considering the datings, they will develop a thorough grasp of the truth, and when they know the truth they can also abandon their error.

Father and son

6.1 God, then, who invented and constructed all things, as we said in book 2, before approaching the remarkable task of making this world created a holy and incorruptible spirit whom he called his son,[18] 2 and though he later created countless others, whom we call angels, this, his first-born, was the only one he distinguished with a name of divine significance, presumably because he had his father's qualities of power and supremacy. 3 That he is the son of God supreme and endowed with maximum power is demonstrated not just by what the prophets say, which is unanimous, but also by the predictions of Trismegistus and the prophecies of the Sibyls.

4 In his book called[G19] *Perfect Discourse*, Hermes uses these words:[G] 'The lord and maker of all things, whom we usually call God, created the second God visible and sensible (when I say sensible, I do not mean it actively – whether he has sensations or not will be dealt with later – but that

---

16 This is incorrect. L. is following Theophilus, *Autol.* 1.27.

17 Antiquity was important to Romans. See Cic. *Leg.* 2.27; Min. Fel. 6.1–3. Christians, like Jews, argued that Moses predated and inspired the Greek philosophers. See e.g. Justin, *apol.* 1.44.9; 59.1.

18 See ch. 8 below; L.'s thinking smacks of Arianism.

19 G indicates that L. uses or quotes Greek.

God submitted him to perception and sight); when he had created him as his first and unique creation, and thought him fine and full of all good, he loved and cherished him as his only son.'[20]

5 At the beginning of the poem in which the Erythraean Sibyl opens with God supreme, she declares the son of God to be guide and commander of all men in the following verses:[G] 'Feeder, founder of all, who put the sweet breath of life in all, and made god guide of all men.' Then again at the end, 'God gave another one for the faithful to honour.' Another Sibyl also recommends his recognition:[G] 'Know that the son of God is himself your God.'[21]

6 Plainly it is also the very son of God who spoke through Solomon, the wisest of kings and full of the holy spirit, saying as follows [Prov. 8:22–31]: 'God made me[22] as the start of his path towards his works; before time he founded me; in the beginning, before he made the earth and established its depths, before springs of water came forth, before all the hills he fathered me. God made the lands and countries habitable under the sky. 7 I was beside him when he made the sky, and when he marked his own seat; when he set strong clouds upon the winds, when he appointed settled springs beneath the sky, when he fortified earth's foundations, I was with him arranging them. 8 It was I in whom he rejoiced, and I was his daily delight before his face, when he was gladdened by the world he had made.'

9 Trismegistus calls him[G] 'God's craftsman' and the Sibyl calls him[G] 'God's adviser' because he was given all that wisdom and virtue by God his father so that God could use his counsel and his handiwork in the making of the world.[23]

The word

7.1 Someone may perhaps inquire at this point who he is, with such power and so precious to God, and what his name is whose first nativity not only preceded the world but also planned it with care and built it by his virtue.

2 We need to know first that his name is not known even to the angels who dwell in heaven but only to himself and God his father, nor will it be made known until God's arrangements are completed, as is reported in holy scripture; 3 secondly, that it cannot even be uttered by human tongue, as Hermes explains, saying:[G] 'The cause of this cause is the will of God the

---

20 NF *Corp. Herm.* 5.1. Cf. *Ascl.* 8.
21 *Orac. Sib.* 3.775; 8.329; fr. 1.5ff.
22 *Sc.* Wisdom, as the feminine in the Latin shows.
23 Cf. NF *Corp. Herm. Ascl.* 26; *Orac. Sib.* 8.264.

good God, whose name cannot be uttered by human mouth,' and a little further on (to his son): 'There is, my child, an account of wisdom, unspeakable and holy, concerning God who is the sole lord of all, the God who foresees all, whose naming is beyond mankind.'[24] 4 But though the name given to him from the start by his supreme father is known to no other than himself, he has another name among the angels and yet another among men. Amongst men he is called Jesus. For Christ is not a proper name but a title, expressing power and kingship; the Jews used to call their kings so. 5 The meaning of the title needs to be explained because of the error of ignorant people who tend to change one letter and call him Chrest.[25] 6 The Jews had been advised earlier to prepare a holy ointment with which to anoint those called to priesthood or kingship; for Romans today, putting on the purple is a sign that royal status has been assumed, and for the Jews the name and powers of kingship were conferred by an anointing with holy ointment. 7 The ancient Greeks used the word *khríesthai* for being anointed (nowadays they say *aleíphesthai*), as the following line of Homer indicates: 'When the servant girls had washed them and anointed them with oil;'[G26] so we call him Christ, that is, 'the anointed', which in Hebrew is 'Messiah'. Hence in some Greek texts, where the Hebrew has been misinterpreted, *eleimménos* is found written, from *aleíphesthai*.[27]

8 But the meaning is 'king', by whichever word, not because he has taken up this earthly kingship, for which the time has not yet come, but because of his celestial and eternal kingship, of which we shall speak in our final book.[28] For the moment let us speak about his first birth.

Two births

8.1 First we affirm that he was born twice, in the spirit and then in the flesh.[29] Hence the sentence in Jeremiah [1:5]: 'Before I formed you in the womb I knew you'. So too: 'Blessed is he who lived before he was born'. That has happened only to Christ. 2 Though he was son of God from the beginning,

---

24 NF *Corp. Herm.* vol. 4, fr. 11a; 12a.
25 L.'s comment is taken over from earlier apologists. See Justin, *apol.* 1.4.1–5, Theophilus, *Autol.* 1.1, 12. *Chrestos* properly means useful; then good, especially of people. In L.'s day *khristós* and *khrestós* would have been pronounced identically.
26 L. conflates *Od.* 4.59 and 17.88.
27 *Eleimménos* is perf. part. pass.: literally, having been smeared.
28 7.20.24.
29 See Monat (1982), 112–15.

he was reborn anew in the flesh. This double birth of his has caused great confusion in human hearts, and has shed darkness even on people who kept the mysteries of the true religion. 3 We will explain it, however, plainly and clearly, so that lovers of wisdom can inform themselves with greater ease and care.

No one hearing the phrase 'son of God' should admit such evil into his mind as to think that God procreated as a result of marriage and intercourse with a female: only animals with bodies do that, who are liable to death. 4 And since God was still alone, with whom could he have intercourse? Alternatively, since he commanded such power that he could do whatever he wanted, he simply did not need anyone else's company in creating: unless perhaps we are going to reckon, as Orpheus did,[30] that God is both male and female, on the grounds that he could not procreate unless he had the capacity of both sexes – as if he could have intercourse with himself, or could not procreate without intercourse. 5 Hermes, however, was also of Orpheus' opinion in calling God[G] 'autofather' and 'automother'.[31] But if that were so, he would be called mother by the prophets just as he is called father.

6 How then did he procreate?[32] First: the actions of God can neither be known nor fully reported by anyone; there is information, however, in holy scripture, where we are warned that the son of God is the word of God, and also that the other angels are the breath of God. Speech is an expiration of breath with significant noise. 7 But since breath and speech emerge from different areas, in that breathing comes from the nostrils and speech from the mouth, there is a great difference between this son of God and the other angels. They went forth from God as silent breath, since they were not created to pass on God's teaching but to do his bidding, 8 but the son of God, despite being also a spirit, came forth vocalised from the mouth of God like a word, presumably on the basis that he was to use his voice for the people; that is, he was going to be the master of God's teaching and of bringing the secret of heaven to mankind. God uttered him in the first place so that he himself could speak to us through him, and so that his son could unveil for us the word and will of God.

9 He is rightly therefore called the word of God because in having him proceed from his mouth as a talking spirit, conceived not in a womb but in a mind, God with his unimaginable virtue and his majesty's power shaped him

---

30 *Orph. fr.* 178 (Abel) = 145 (Kern).
31 NF *Corp. Herm.* vol. 4, fr. 13.
32 For the blending of Stoic and Platonic doctrine in this passage, see Loi (1970), 167–71, and Monat (1982), 173–75.

into a form which could thrive with its own senses and wisdom; likewise he shaped the rest of his breath into angels. 10 Our breath is evanescent because we are mortal, whereas the breaths of God live, last and think because he himself is immortal and the giver of sense and life. 11 What we say may well be carried off on the breeze and disappear, but when put in writing it survives to a considerable extent: which is all the more reason for trusting that God's word abides for ever, full of the power and sense which it draws from God the father like a river from its source.

12 If anyone is surprised that God could be born of God by emission of word and breath, he will surely abandon his surprise once he knows the holy utterances of the prophets. 13 That Solomon and his father David were kings of great power and also prophets will perhaps be known even to people who have had no contact with holy scripture; Solomon, the second of the two to be king, preceded the fall of Troy by 140 years. 14 His father, composer of the holy hymns, says in psalm 32 [33:6]:[33] 'By the word of God the heavens were fixed, and all their virtue by his breath.' So too in psalm 44 he says [45:1]: 'My heart has disgorged a good word: I tell of my works to the king,' proving of course that God's works are known only to his only son, who is the word of God and whose reign must last for ever. 15 So too Solomon demonstrates that the son is the word of God by whose hands all those works of the world were made [Eccl. 24:3–4]. 'I proceeded,' he says, 'from the mouth of the most high before all creation. I made an unfailing light arise in the heavens, and as a cloud I covered all the earth. I dwelt in the heights and my throne was on a column of cloud.' 16 John also says [1:1–3]: 'In the beginning was the word, and the word was with God and the word was God. It was with God in the beginning. All things were made through him, and nothing was made without him.'

Logos

9.1 The Greeks express it better than we do as 'word' or 'talk': they say[G] 'logos'. Logos means both talk and reason; it is both God's word and God's wisdom.[34] 2 Even the philosophers know of this divine account, since Zeno

---

33 L. was working from a text akin to the Septuagint; users of King James' Bible and its successors should not expect to find close verbal correspondence. The references in square brackets are to the Psalms as divided and numbered in King James' Bible. The difference begins with Ps. 9 and ends with Ps. 147.

34 See Tert. *Prax.* 5.2–3; *Apol.* 21.10: a combination of Stoic and biblical *logos*. See Spanneut (1957), 310ff.

declares that the arranger of everything in nature and the craftsman of the universe is logos, which he calls both fate and the necessity of things, and god, and the mind of Jupiter (following the custom they had of saying Jupiter for God). 3 But the words are no problem since the meaning coincides with the truth. What he called mind of Jupiter is the spirit of God. Trismegistus, who somehow traced out almost all the truth, often described the virtue and majesty of the word, as in the text quoted earlier where he says that there is an account, unspeakable and holy, whose utterance is beyond man's limit.[35]

4 I have spoken briefly, according to my ability, of the first birth. I must now speak at greater length of the second birth, which is very controversial, so that all who desire to know the truth may receive the light of understanding.

The divine law

10.1 People ought principally to know that the arrangements of God most high proceeded from the beginning in such a way that as the end of time approached it would be necessary for the son of God to descend to earth in order to establish God's temple[36] and to teach his justice, neither with an angel's virtue nor in heavenly power but in a man's shape, in a mortal condition; and when he had completed his teaching he would pass into the hands of impious men and undergo death, so that when death too had been tamed by his virtue, he would rise again, offering the hope of overcoming death to man whose condition he had adopted and borne, and also admitting him into the rewards of immortality. 2 To prevent any ignorance of this arrangement, we will explain that everything which we see fulfilled in Christ had been foretold. 3 No one is to believe this assertion of ours unless I show that a long passage of time followed the prophets' prediction that a son of God would eventually be born as man and would do wonderful things and would sow the worship of God throughout the earth, and would finally be nailed to a cross and rise again two days later, 4 and when I have proved it all from the writings of those very people who did violence to their God when he was using mortal form, there will be no more obstruction whatever of the plain fact that true wisdom abides in this religion alone.

5 The origin of the whole sacred mystery must now be narrated from the beginning. Our ancestors, the leaders of the Hebrews, were in trouble from

---

35 NF *Corp. Herm.* vol. 4, fr. 12b.
36 The Church, that is.

famine and helplessness; they crossed into Egypt for the sake of grain. There they stayed a considerable time, and came under the pressure of an intolerable yoke of slavery. 6 God then took pity on them and brought them out of Egypt, delivering them from the king's hand after 430 years; their leader was Moses, through whom God later gave them the law. In bringing them out, God showed the virtue of his majesty. 7 He carried the people through the midst of the Red Sea with an angel going before them parting the water, so that they could go through on dry ground (or as the poet puts it more accurately, 'The water stood up on end in a mountainous curve all round'[37]). 8 When the despot of Egypt heard of it, he pursued with a great band of his people; the sea was still wide open when he rashly entered, but then the waters met and he was destroyed with all his army.

The Hebrews proceeded into a desert and saw many wonders. 9 When they were suffering from thirst, at the blow of a stick upon a rock a spring of water burst forth and restored them. 10 Again, when they were in hunger, a rain of heavenly nourishment descended; a wind even brought quails into their camp, so that they were filled not only with bread of heaven but also with something fancier. 11 Even so, they gave God no honour for his acts of divine kindness; after being freed from slavery and rid of thirst and hunger, they relapsed into a life of luxury and switched attention to the profane rituals of the Egyptians. 12 When their leader Moses climbed a mountain and stayed there forty days, they made a calf's head of gold, calling it Apis, to go before them on a pole. 13 This sinful crime offended God, and he inflicted severe punishment upon his impious and ungrateful people, as they deserved, and put them under the law which he had given to Moses. 14 Later, when they had settled in a deserted part of Syria, they lost their old name of Hebrews: because the leader of their host was Judah, they were called Judaeans,[38] and the land they inhabited Judaea.

15 At first they were not subject to the rule of kings; citizen judges presided over the people and the law, not appointed annually like the Roman consuls but sustained in their jurisdiction for life. Then the title of judge was abolished and a king's power introduced. 16 While the judges had power over them, the people had often taken up wicked religions, and God in umbrage had equally often put them under the control of foreigners, until their penitence softened him and he liberated them from their servitude. 17 In the time of the kings they were also harassed for their sins by wars with their

---

37 Verg. *G.* 4.361.
38 *Iudaei* is Latin for both Judaeans and Jews.

neighbours, and finally were taken captive and led away to Babylon, there to pay grim penalty for their impiety as slaves, until Cyrus came into his kingship and at once restored them by edict. 18 After that they had tetrarchs until Herod, who lived in the emperorship of Tiberius; in Tiberius' fifteenth year, in the consulship of the two Gemini, on 23rd March, the Jews put Christ on the cross.[39]

19 That account of events, in that sequence, is to be found in the mysteries of holy writ. First, however, I will explain why Christ came to earth, so that the fundamental thinking in divine religion may be clear.

Rejection of prophets and Christ

11.1 As the Jews kept rebelling against advice given them for their good and kept breaking with God's law, wandering off to wicked cults of gods,[40] so God would fill some just and chosen men with the holy spirit and put them as prophets in the midst of the people; through them he would then attack his ungrateful people with threatening words for their sins, and, just as much, exhort them to be penitent; 2 if they were not penitent, but failed to abandon their stupidity and return to their god, he would change his covenant – that is, he would switch the inheritance of immortal life to other nations and would recruit himself another people of greater loyalty from among foreigners. 3 When the Jews were attacked like that by the prophets, however, they not only rejected their warnings but in annoyance at having their sins rebuked they killed them with studied cruelty.

All this is kept sealed in holy scripture. 4 The prophet Jeremiah says [25:4–6]: 'I have sent you my servants the prophets. Before daybreak I sent them, and you did not listen, nor did you give ear when I said to you, Let each one of you be converted from his wicked way and from your most evil tendencies, and you shall live in the land that I gave to you and your fathers from generation to generation. Do not walk after alien gods, to serve them; do not provoke me with the works of your hands to scatter you abroad.' 5 The prophet Esdras, who was a contemporary of the Cyrus who restored the Jews, speaks as follows [Neh. 9:26]: 'They have broken with you, and they have thrown your law behind them and have killed your prophets who

---

39 L. derives the year (AD 29) from Tert. *Iud.* 8, but not the day, which Tertullian sets at 25 March; this occurs, in the Latin tradition, only in Gaul. Did L. compose at least this book in Gaul? See Loi (1973); cf. Barnes (1981), 291; Nicholson (1985), 304–05.

40 L.'s account is close to Cyprian *Test.* 1.2ff.; see Monat (1982), 178–80.

testified that they should turn back to you.' 6 So too Elijah in the third book of Kings[41] [1 Kgs 19:10]: 'I have been zealous with great zeal for the lord God almighty, because the children of Israel have left you; they have demolished your altars and have killed your prophets with a sword, and I alone have remained, and they seek to take away my life.'

7 Because of these wicked deeds of theirs he abandoned them for ever, and left off sending them prophets. Instead he gave orders for his first-born son, the craftsman of the world and his counsellor, to descend from heaven to pass the holy worship of God to the Gentiles, to people, that is, who did not know God, and to teach them the justice which his disloyal people had rejected. 8 He had declared he would do this long before, as the prophet Malachi points out, saying [1:10–11]: 'I have no pleasure in you, says the lord, and I will not accept sacrifice from your hands, because from the rising of the sun to its setting my name shall be glorified among the Gentiles.' 9 So too David in psalm 17 [18:43]: 'You shall set me at the head of the Gentiles; a people whom I have not known has served me.' 10 Isaiah also speaks as follows [66:18–19]: 'I come to gather all peoples and tongues, and they shall come and shall see my brilliance. And I will send a sign over them, and I will send from among them those that are saved to go to distant nations who have not heard of my glory, and they shall report my brilliance among the peoples.'

11 In wanting to send the architect of his temple to earth, God did not want to send him in power and celestial brilliance: the people for their ingratitude towards God were to be led into maximum error, paying the penalty for their wickedness in not receiving their lord and God – as the prophets had previously declared would happen. 12 Isaiah, whom the Jews themselves killed with great cruelty, sawing him in half,[42] speaks thus [1:2–3]: 'Hearken, o heaven, and hear with your ears, o earth, for the lord has spoken: I have created sons and have raised them on high, but they have spurned me. The ox knows his master and the ass his master's stall, but Israel has not acknowledged me and its people have not understood me.' Jeremiah says likewise [8:7–9]: 13 'The turtle dove and swallow know their time, and the birds of the field have watched for the time of their migration, but my people have not known the judgment of the lord. How will you say, We are wise, and the law of the lord is with us? The measure of the false scribe has

---

41 1 and 2 Samuel are also known as 1 and 2 Kings in the Vulgate. Hence the numbering.

42 The story of the brutal killing of Isaiah by Manasseh, king of Judah, is told in the apocryphal *Lives of the Prophets* and in *Ascension of Isaiah*. It appears in the Talmud of Jerusalem 28c, and in several Christian writers prior to L., including Justin, *dial.* 120, and Tertullian, *Pat.* 14; *Scorp.* 8.

been made in vain, the wise are in confusion; they trembled and were captured, because they rejected the word of the lord.'

14 Therefore, as I had begun to say, when God decided to send a teacher of virtue to mankind, he arranged for his second birth to be in flesh; he was to be made like a human being, to be man's guide, companion and master. 15 But since God is kind and good towards his people, he sent his son to exactly those people that he hated, so as not to close off their path to salvation for ever but to give them a clear opportunity of following him; thus they could obtain the reward of life if they did follow, which many of them do and have done, but if they repudiated their king, then by their own fault they would incur the penalty of death. 16 God's command was therefore for his son to be reborn as one of them, and of their seed, so that they could not claim with justification in law that they had not accepted him because he was of alien birth; equally, God wanted the hope of immortality to be denied to no nation on earth at all.

Incarnation

12.1[43] The holy spirit of God descended therefore from heaven and chose a pious girl in whose womb to put himself. She, being filled with the intake of the holy spirit, conceived, and without any touch from man her womb suddenly swelled. 2 It is common knowledge that certain animals often conceive from the wind and the breeze: why should anyone think it odd when we say that a girl became pregnant from the breath of God? Every wish of his is easily fulfilled. 3 It certainly could seem unbelievable, had the prophets not foretold the event many generations earlier. Solomon in song 19[44] says as follows: 'The virgin's womb was opened and received a fetus, and the virgin became pregnant and was made a mother amid great pity.' 4 So too the prophet Isaiah, who speaks as follows [7:14]: 'Because of this God will give you a sign: behold, a virgin will receive in her womb and bring forth a son, and you shall call his name Emmanuel.' 5 What can be put more plainly than that? That was a text of the Jews, who killed him. If anyone thinks this is a fiction of ours, let him ask them: they would be the best source; what one's enemies say is evidence of strength enough to prove a truth.

---

43 For L. on the Incarnation, see Monat (1982), 180–84.

44 A Syriac version of an original Greek text, discovered in 1905, confirms the authenticity of this text, otherwise unrecorded. See Harris and Mingana (1916–20). L. uses this and the following text here as proofs of the possibility of virgin birth; in *Epit.* 44, they revert to the role of prophetic utterances.

6 He has in fact never been called Emmanuel, but Jesus, which means salutary or saviour, because he came bringing salvation to all people; but the prophet announced him as Emmanuel because God would come to mankind in the flesh. 7 Emmanuel means 'God with us', obviously because once he was born of the girl people ought to acknowledge that God was with them: on earth, that is, and in mortal flesh. Hence David says in psalm 84 [85:11] 'Truth has arisen from the earth' because God, who contains the truth, received an earthly body to open the way of salvation to the people of earth. 8 So too Isaiah [63:10–11]: 'But they have not believed, and have embittered the holy spirit; he has turned hostile towards them, taking them by storm himself; once he raised up a shepherd of his sheep from the earth, and he has remembered the days of old.' 9 Who that shepherd was going to be he made plain elsewhere, saying [45:8] 'Let the heavens above exult, and let the clouds put on justice and earth be opened, and let a saviour come up: for I the lord God have created him.' The saviour is, as we said above, Jesus.

10 In another place the same prophet said [9:6]: 'Behold, a boy is born to you, a son is given to you; his power is upon his shoulders, and his name is Messenger of Great Counsel.' 11 For he was sent by God his father on purpose to reveal to all nations under the heavens the holy mystery of the one true God, a mystery which was taken away from a faithless people who often sinned against God.

12 Daniel also made the same prediction [7:13–14]. 'I saw,' he says, 'in a dream of the night, and behold, in the clouds of heaven as it were the son of man coming, and he came right to the ancient of days. And those who stood there presented him, and he was given kingship, honour and power, and all peoples, tribes and tongues shall serve him, and his power shall be eternal: it will never pass away and his kingship shall not be broken.' 13 How do the Jews both confess God's anointed and hope for him when they had rejected him precisely because he was born a human? 14 Although it has been established by God that this Christ will come to earth twice, once to announce to the Gentiles that God is one and the second time to reign, how do people who don't believe in his first coming believe in his second coming? 15 And yet each of his comings was covered by the prophet quite briefly: 'Behold,' he said, 'in the clouds of heaven, as it were a son of man coming.' He did not say son of God but son of man, to show that he had to take on flesh on earth, so that when he had taken on human form and this mortal estate he could teach men justice, and when he had done the bidding of God and revealed the truth to the Gentiles he could even be punished with death, so as to conquer the underworld too and seal it up, and so at last could

rise again and reach his father, borne up on a cloud. 16 The prophet also said: 'And he came right to the ancient of days and was presented to him.' By ancient of days he meant God most high, whose age and origin cannot be grasped, because he alone has existed since before time just as he will continue to exist for all time.

17 That Christ would rise to God his father after his passion and resurrection is declared by David in psalm 109 as follows [110:1]: 'The lord said to my lord: sit at my right hand, until I make your enemies a footstool for your feet.' That prophet was a king: who else could he call his lord, to sit at the right hand of God, except Christ the son of God, who is king of kings and lord of lords? [1 Tim. 6:15] 18 Isaiah demonstrates the point more obviously when he says [45:1–3]: 'Thus says the lord God to Christ my lord, whose right hand I have held for the nations to bow before him, and I will break up the bravery of kings, I will open the gates before him and the cities shall not be closed. I will go before you and lay the mountains flat; bronze gates will I wear away and iron bolts will I smash. I will give you hidden treasures, invisible treasures, so that you may know that I am the lord God who call you by name.'

19 Finally, for the virtue and faith he showed to God on earth, 'he has been given kingship, honour and power, and all peoples, tribes and tongues serve him, and his power is eternal: it will never pass away, and his kingship shall not be broken.' 20 There are two ways of understanding that: first, he has perpetual power now; all peoples and all tongues venerate his name, admit his supremacy, follow his teaching and imitate his virtue; he has power and honour whenever all the tribes of the earth comply with his behests. 21 Second, when he comes again in brilliance and power to judge every soul and restore the just to life, then in truth he will have control of the whole earth: then all evil will be removed from human affairs and the golden age, as the poets call it, will arise: a time, that is, of justice and peace. 22 We will discuss this more fully, however, in the final book when we speak of the second coming; for the moment let us explain the first coming, as we had begun to do.

Virgin birth and Christ's humanity

13.1[45] When God most high, parent of all, wished to transmit the worship of himself, he sent a teacher of justice from heaven so that the new worshippers received the new law in him, or through him, which was not what he had

---

45 On this chapter, see Monat (1982), 137–40, 188–90.

done before, when he did it through a man; this time he wanted his teacher to be born like a man, so that he would be like his supreme father in all respects. 2 God the father himself, the origin and start of all things and having no parents, is most accurately called[G] 'fatherless' and 'motherless' by Trismegistus because he was born of no one.[46] It was right therefore for his son to be born twice, so that he too should be fatherless and motherless. 3 At his first birth, in the spirit, he was motherless because he was generated by God the father alone with no role for a mother, 4 but at his second birth, in the flesh, he was fatherless because he came from a virginal womb with no role for a father, so that in assuming a substance midway between God and man he could guide this fragile, feeble nature of ours in the direction of immortality as it were by hand. 5 He was made son of God through the spirit and son of man through the flesh: both God and man, that is. The strength of God appears in him in the deeds which he did and the weakness of man in the suffering he endured: why he undertook it I will explain in a moment.[47]

6 Meantime we learn from the declarations of the prophets that he was both God and man in both sorts. 7 Isaiah attests his divinity in these words [45:14–16]: 'Egypt is exhausted, and the trade of the Ethiopians and the great men of Sheba will cross over to you and will be your slaves; they will walk behind you bound in fetters, and will worship and pray to you. For God is in you, and there is no other god beside you. You are God and we did not know you, saviour God of Israel. All shall be confounded who opposed you; they will turn to awe, and fall to confession.' 8 So too the prophet Jeremiah says [*Bar.* 3:35–37]: 'This is our God, and no other shall be so considered apart from him, who found the whole path of wisdom and gave it to Jacob his son and to Israel his beloved. After that, he was seen on earth and conversed with men.' 9 So too David in psalm 44 [45:6–7]: 'Your throne, o God, is for ever and ever; the rod of equity is the rod of your rule. You have loved justice and have hated injustice. Besides, the lord your God has anointed you with the oil of exultation.' In that word he revealed his name, since (as I said above) Christ is named from his anointing.

10 Then Jeremiah explains that he was also human, saying [17:9]: 'He is a man, and who knows him?' So too Isaiah [19:20]: 'And the lord shall send them a man who shall save them and heal them by his judgment.' Moses too in Numbers says as follows [24:17]: 'A star shall arise from Jacob, and a man shall rise up from Israel.'

---

46 Cf. 1.7.2.
47 See ch. 16 below.

BOOK 4: TRUE WISDOM AND RELIGION

11 Besides, Apollo of Miletus[48] when asked whether he was god or man replied in this fashion:[G] 'He was mortal in the flesh, wise in miraculous deeds, but he was made prisoner by the Chaldean lawgivers and nailed to stakes, and came to a painful death.'[49] 12 The truth is there in the first line, but Apollo has cleverly deceived his questioner, who knew absolutely nothing of the sacred mystery of truth: he seems to have denied that he was God. But when he admits that he was mortal in the flesh, which is what we too claim, it follows that he was God in the spirit, which we assert. 13 What need to mention the flesh when it was enough to say that he was mortal? Forced by the truth, however, he could not deny how things were.

So too with calling him wise. 14 What is your response to that, Apollo? If he was wise, then his teaching is wisdom, and nothing else is, and those who follow it are wise, and no one else is. Why then are we popularly taken for silly, stupid fools when we follow a master who is wise on the admission of even the gods themselves? 15 As for the observation that he did miraculous deeds (a very good reason for believing in his divinity), it is plain by now that Apollo agrees with us: he is saying exactly what we make boast of.

16 Nevertheless, he recovers his nerve and returns to his nonsense about demons. He had spoken the truth perforce; now he was clearly betraying his fellow gods and himself, except insofar as he had obscured with a deceptive mendacity what truth had forced out of him. Hence he says Jesus did do wonderful works, but by virtue of being a magician and not as God. 17 It is no wonder that Apollo convinced ignorant people of the truth of this, when the Jews, clearly worshippers of God most high, have also thought exactly the same, despite those wonders being done daily before their eyes. Even then they could not be forced to believe that the man they saw was God, for all their contemplation of his great miracles. 18 Besides, David says (they read him most, far more than the other prophets) in psalm 27, in condemnation of them [28:4–5]: 'Give them what they are owed: they have had no understanding in the works of the lord.' Both David and other prophets announced that Christ would be born according to the flesh from the house of David himself. 19 In Isaiah it is written [11:10]: 'And on that day there will be a root of Jesse, and he who rises up from it will be chief among the peoples; in him the nations will hope, and his peace will be in honour'. 20 And elsewhere [11:1–3]: 'There will come forth a rod from the root of Jesse, and a flower will rise up from the root; and the spirit of the lord

---

48 L. refers to the Oracle at Didyma, ten miles south of Miletus.
49 *Orac. Apoll.* fr. 49, 222 (Fontenrose).

will rest upon it, the spirit of wisdom and understanding, the spirit of counsel and courage, the spirit of learning and piety; and the spirit of the fear of the lord will fill him.' 21 Jesse was the father of David: it was from his root that David declared a flower would rise up, clearly meaning the one the Sibyl speaks of saying[G] 'a pure flower will blossom'.[50]

22 So too in the second book of Kings Nathan the prophet was sent to David when he wished to build a temple for god [2 Sam. 7:4, 5, 12–14, 16]: 'And the word of the lord was with Nathan, saying, Go and say to my servant David: thus says the lord your God the almighty: you shall not build me a house to dwell in, but when your days are fulfilled and you sleep with your fathers I will raise up your seed after you and I will prepare its kingship. 23 He shall build me a house in my name, and I will lift up his throne for ever, and I shall be his in the father and he shall be mine in the son. And his house shall achieve faith and so shall his kingdom, for ever.'

24 The reason for the Jews' incomprehension of this was the fact that Solomon, David's son, built God a temple and a city, which he called Jerusalem, after his own name.[51] Hence they referred what was said by the prophet to Solomon, but he received his authority to rule from his father, 25 whereas the prophets were speaking of him who was to be born when David was at rest with his fathers. Furthermore the rule of Solomon did not last for ever: he reigned for forty years. 26 Then there is the fact that he was never called son of God but son of David, and the house which he built did not keep faith as the church does; the church is the true temple of God because it does not consist of walls but of the faithful hearts of those who believe in him and are called the faithful, whereas Solomon's temple was made by hand and fell by the hand. 27 Finally, his father prophesied about his son's works in psalm 126 in this fashion [127:1]: 'Except the lord build the house, vain is the labour of those who built it; except the lord guard the city, empty is the watch of him who guarded it.'

Christ as high priest

14.1[52] From all this it is plain that every prophet has declared of Christ that he would be born in the flesh one day of the family of David and would establish an eternal temple for God, called the church, and would invite all

---

50 *Orac. Sib.* 6.8.
51 L. appears to be alone in deriving -salem from Solomon.
52 On this chapter, see Monat (1982), 141–49.

the nations to God's true religion. 2 This is the house of faith, and this the immortal temple: if any fail to sacrifice in it, they shall not have the reward of immortality. 3 Since Christ was the maker of the temple, a temple both great and everlasting, so inevitably he holds an eternal priesthood in it, nor can the temple or the sight of God be reached except through him who established it.

4 Exactly this point is made by David in psalm 109, saying [110:3–4]: 'Before the morning star I created you. The lord has sworn and will not repent: you are his priest for ever.' 5 So too in the first book of Kings [1 Sam. 2:35]: 'And I will raise me up a faithful priest who will do all the things that are in my heart, and I will build him a faithful house and he shall walk in my sight all his days.'

6 Who was to be the recipient of God's eternal priesthood was made clear by Zechariah, who named him [3:1–8]: 'And the lord has shown me Jesus[53] standing tall before the face of the angel of the lord, and the devil stood at his right hand to speak against him. 7 And the lord said to the devil: Let the lord who chose Jerusalem command you. And behold, a firebrand rejected by the fire. And Jesus was dressed in filthy clothes, and he stood before the face of the angel. And he replied to those standing before his face, 8 Take the filthy garments off him, and put a tunic on him down to his ankles and put a clean headdress upon his head. And they clothed him with garments and put a headdress on his head. 9 And the angel of the lord stood and testified to Jesus, saying, Thus says the lord almighty: If you have walked in my ways and have kept my commandments, you shall judge my house, and I will give you people to converse with you amid these bystanders. Hear therefore, Jesus, great priest.'

10 Who could fail to think the Jews were out of their minds, laying wicked hands on their own God after reading and hearing that? 11 And yet from the time of Zechariah to the fifteenth year of the reign of the emperor Tiberius when Jesus was crucified, there is a span of nearly 500 years; for Zechariah grew up in the time of Darius and Alexander,[54] who lived not long after Tarquin the Proud was driven out. 12 But the Jews were tricked and deceived in the same way again, thinking the words were said of Jesus son of Nun who came after Moses, or of Jesus son of Josedech the priest, though none of what the prophet said fitted them. 13 Those two were never filthily

---

53 Jesus is the form in L.'s text and in the Vulgate, but in King James' Bible it is Joshua: different forms of the same name. Iosue is another Vulgate form.

54 Not Alexander the Great, but an earlier king of Macedon, Alexander I, who figures in the pages of Herodotus, and reigned c. 495–452 BC.

dressed, since one was a most powerful prince and the other a priest, nor did they ever endure adversity, to be thought of as brands ejected from the burning, nor did they stand in the sight of God and his angels at any time, nor did the prophet speak about the past rather than the future. 14 He spoke of Jesus son of God, to show that he would first come in lowliness and in the flesh (for flesh is the filthy garment), to prepare a temple for God and to be burnt like a brand in the fire: to endure from men the torture of crucifixion, that is, and to be killed in the end. (A brand is what people call a log taken off the fire half-burnt and out.)

15 As for the way in which he was sent to earth by God and the instructions with which he was sent, the spirit of God working through the prophet made it plain that when he had faithfully and steadfastly fulfilled the will of his father on high he would receive judgment and eternal power. 16 'If you walk in my ways,' he says, 'keeping my commandments, you shall judge my house.' What the ways of God and his commandments are is neither ambiguous nor obscure.

17 When God saw that evil and the worship of false gods had grown so strong all over the world that his name by now had been almost removed from people's memories – even the Jews, the sole repository of God's secret, had abandoned the living God and had strayed into worshipping things of their own making, snared by the deceits of demons, and though warned by their prophets were unwilling to return to God – he sent them his own son, the prince of the angels, to turn them from wicked and empty patterns of worship to knowing and worshipping the true God, and also to draw their minds away from folly to wisdom and from iniquity to works of justice. 18 Those are the ways of God in which he bade him walk, and those are the commandments which he instructed him to keep.

He also demonstrated his faith to God: he taught that there is one God and that he alone is to be worshipped, and he never said that he was God himself: he would not have kept faith if after being sent to get rid of gods and to assert a single God he had introduced another one besides. 19 That would not have been proclamation of a single God, but conducting his own private business and separating himself from the one he had come to illuminate. 20 Because he proved himself so faithful and because he took nothing at all for himself, in order to fulfil the instructions of the one who sent him, so he received the dignity of eternal priesthood, the honour of supreme kingship, the power to judge and the name of God.

Public life of Christ

15.1 Since we spoke of a second birth, in which he revealed himself to mankind in the flesh, let us now come to those wonderful works for which the Jews thought him a wizard, though they were actually the signs of celestial virtue.

2 At the beginning of his youth, he was dipped by the prophet John in the river Jordan, in order to wipe out with a spiritual washing sins that were not his own – he simply had none – but which were sins of the flesh he had adopted, so that by baptism, by the pouring over him of purifying water, that is, he could save the Gentiles in the same way that by receiving circumcision he could save the Jews. 3 Then 'a voice was heard from heaven: you are my son; I have begotten you today'. The utterance may be found foretold by David [Lk. 3:22 with Ps. 2:7]. And the spirit of god descended upon him shaped in the image of a white dove. 4 Thereupon he began to work very great miracles, not by magician's tricks, which have nothing solid and true to reveal, but by the force and power of heaven; these works had been long foretold by the prophets in their pronouncements, 5 and they are so numerous that a whole book would not be enough to contain them. I will list them briefly and generically, therefore, without identifying people or places, so that I can arrive at the reasoned exposition of his suffering and crucifixion, the goal to which my work has long been hastening.

6 His miracles were those called 'portentific' by Apollo,[55] because wherever he went he could make the sick and the weak and those troubled by every sort of disease well again with one word, in one moment, so much so that even when deprived of every limb they could suddenly regain their strength and take up their beds themselves, when a little while beforehand they had been brought to him on them. 7 To the lame and those with problems in the feet he gave the power not just of walking but of running. The eyes of those whose light was blind and in deep darkness he restored to their previous sight. 8 The tongues of the dumb he released into speech and talk. He also opened the ears of the deaf and instilled hearing, and people covered in filthy sores he made clean again. 9 And all this he did not with his hands or with any ointment but by a word of command, as the Sibyl had even predicted:[G] 'Doing well and healing all disease with a word.'[56] 10 It is wholly unsurprising that he did miracles with a word, since he was the word of God himself, sustained by the virtue and power of heaven. 11 Nor was it

---
55 Cf. 13.11 above.
56 *Orac. Sib.* 8.272.

enough to give strength back to the weak, wholeness to the feeble and health to the sick and suffering if he could not also raise the dead, releasing them from sleep as it were, and recalling them to life.

12 When the Jews saw that, they then tried to prove that it was the work of demonic power, even though their own secret literature contained the promise that all would be done as it was done. 13 They could read for instance the words of the prophet Isaiah in particular, saying [35:3–6]: 'Grow strong, exhausted hands and weakened knees; you that are faint of heart, be comforted, be not afraid, do not be scared. Our god will grant you judgment; he himself will come and make us whole. 14 Then the eyes of the blind will be opened and the ears of the deaf will hear; then the lame man will leap like a stag and the tongue of the dumb will be clear, because water has broken out in the desert and there is a river in thirsty ground.' 15 The Sibyl had the same to say in these verses:^{G} 'There shall be resurrection of the dead and swift running of the lame, and the deaf man will hear, and blind men will see and non-talkers will talk.'[57]

16 Because of these miracles and divine works of his, a great host began to follow him of the weak and sick and of those who wished to present their own sick for healing; so he went up a deserted hill, to pray there. When he had been there three days and the people were beginning to suffer from hunger, he summoned his disciples, asking how much food they had with them. They said they had five loaves of bread and two fishes in a bag. He bade them be brought and told the people to sit down in groups of five hundred. 17 While the disciples saw to that, he broke up the bread himself into small pieces and divided the flesh of the fish, and in his hands both were increased. When he told the disciples to give the food to the people, five thousand of them were fed and twelve baskets over and above were filled with the fragments left.[58] What could be more wonderful than that? 18 Yet the Sibyl had declared it would happen; her verses go like this:^{G} 'From five loaves of bread and fish of the sea he will satisfy five thousand men in a desert place, and he will take the left-overs with all the fragments and fill twelve baskets, for the hope of the nations.'[59] 19 I put the question: what could the art of magic have done here, when its only expertise lies in confounding people's sight?

20 Again, when he was about to go off to a hill to pray, as he used to, he told his disciples to take a small boat and to precede him. They set out as

57 *Orac.Sib.* 8.205–07.
58 Mk 8:5ff.; Mt. 14:16ff.
59 *Orac. Sib.* 8.275–78.

BOOK 4: TRUE WISDOM AND RELIGION

evening began to fall, but were soon in trouble from an adverse wind. 21 When they were in the middle of open water, he entered the sea on foot and caught them up as if he were walking on solid ground – not like the poet's false picture of Orion walking on the sea, when most of his body was submerged and 'only his head and shoulders stood out.'[60] 22 On another occasion he went to sleep in a boat, and the wind rose, with very dangerous gusts; they woke him from his sleep, and he told the wind to be silent forthwith, and the waves, which were coming in great size, to be still: and at his word tranquillity at once ensued.

23 Perhaps sacred literature lies when it says his power was so great that at a word from him he could make winds obey him and waters serve him, disease depart and the underworld submit. 24 What about the fact that the Sibyls had set all this out in their verses long before? One of them, whom we mentioned above, says as follows:[G] 'He could check the winds with a word and level the raging sea, walking on feet of peace in confidence.'[61] 25 Another one says:[G] 'He will trample the waves, undo the sickness of mankind, raise up the dead, drive off many pains, and from a single bag there will be more than enough bread for men.'[62]

26 This evidence is overwhelming; some people in reaction go so far as to say that those verses are not Sibylline, but invented and compiled by our people.[63] 27 That will not be the opinion of those who read Cicero and Varro and other old writers who mention the Erythraean Sibyl and other Sibyls whose books are our source for those examples, and those writers were all dead before Christ was born in the flesh. 28 I have no doubt that those verses were treated as mad in earlier generations, since no one could understand them. They were proclaiming wonders of a fantastic sort, for which no reason, time or author was given. 29 The Erythraean Sibyl even said that she would be called mad and mendacious. She said:[G] 'They will call the Sibyl mad and a liar. But you will remember me when it all happens, and no one will call me mad any longer: me, prophetess of the great God.'[64] 30 So they lay low for many generations, to be heeded only later, after Christ's birth and passion had opened up the secrets, just as the prophets' words were then also

---

60 Verg. A. 10.764.
61 Orac. Sib. 8.273–74.
62 Orac. Sib. 6.13–15.
63 See Origen, c. Cels. 7.53, with Guillaumin (1978), at 198–200. Celsus' critique is the one that survives; L. may well have heard the anti-Christian Hierocles (see 5.2.2 and 12ff.) argue along similar lines. His riposte is hardly convincing.
64 Orac. Sib. 3.815–18.

heeded. These words had been read by the Jews for over 1500 years, but even so they were not understood until after Christ had interpreted them in word and deed, for he was the one the prophets had proclaimed; but what they said could not be understood without everything being fulfilled.

Seeds of the passion

16.1[65] I now come to the passion itself, which is often made a cause of fierce attack upon us (on the grounds that we worship someone who was a man himself and who suffered notable punishment at the hands of other men, and was crucified), in order to explain that the suffering was accepted in accordance with God's great plan, and that virtue, truth and wisdom are contained in it alone.

2 If he had spent his life on earth in happiness and had been a king throughout it in the utmost prosperity, no wise man would either have thought him a god or judged him worth honour as a god. That is what people with no knowledge of true divinity do: they don't just admire wealth that fails, power that is fragile and goods that only serve others, but they even consecrate these things, knowingly tending the memory of dead men and worshipping a luck already exhausted, which wise men never thought worth worship even when it was around. 3 Among the things of this world there cannot be one worth heaven and veneration; it is only virtue, only justice, which can be considered a true, heavenly and eternal good, because it is neither granted to nor taken from anyone. 4 Since Christ came to earth equipped with that virtue and justice, or rather, since he himself is virtue and he himself is justice, he came down in order to teach it and to form man. When he had done his teaching, fulfilling his instructions from God, then because of the virtue which he had both taught and exemplified in action he not only earned the belief of all people in his divinity but also made it possible.

5 Huge numbers therefore flocked around him, either because of the justice which he taught or the miracles which he performed, and they listened to his advice and believed he was sent by God and was the son of God. As a result, the leaders of the Jews and their priests grew angry because they were being attacked by him as sinners; they became corroded with envy because they saw themselves despised and abandoned as the multitudes went his way, and (the chief point of their wickedness) they were blinded by their stupid mistakes, and they forgot the advice of heaven and their prophets,

---

65 See Monat (1982), 196–98.

and combined against him, forming a wicked plan to remove him and have him crucified.

6 This the prophets had described long before. David, at the start of his psalms, with spiritual foresight of how great a crime was going to be committed, said [1:1]: 'Blessed is the man who has not gone astray amid the counsel of the ungodly.' 7 Solomon in the book of Wisdom used these words [2:12–22]: 'Let us compass the just man about, as he is unpleasing to us and attacks us for breaking the law. He promises he has knowledge of God and names himself son of God. He has been created for the destruction of our thinking and he is painful for us even to behold, since his life is different from others and his ways are altered. 8 We are trifles in his estimation; he keeps himself from our paths as from dirt; he prefers the latest deeds of the just and brags that the lord is his father. Let us see therefore if his words are true, and let us test their outcome for him. 9 Let us question him with insult and torture, let us learn his obedience and try his patience. 10 Such were their thoughts, and they were wrong, for he blinded them with their own stupidity and they did not know God's mysteries.' Solomon has described the wicked plan made against god by impious men so well that it seems as if he took part in it: and yet between Solomon who described it and the time at which it happened, 1010 years went by. 11 There is nothing in that text of our own invention or addition: it is the text the perpetrators had, and they could read who it was aimed at, and the heirs of their name and crime still have the text now and give voice in their readings every day to their own damnation as the prophets foretold it; and yet they never admit it in their hearts – which is a piece of their damnation.

12 Under frequent attack, therefore, from Christ's disapproval of their sins and injustice, and virtually abandoned by the people, the Jews were provoked into killing him: their nerve to do that came from his humility. 13 They read in the texts of the power and glory with which the son of God would come from heaven, and yet the Jesus they saw was humble, common and undistinguished: so they did not believe he was son of God, not realising that two comings had been foretold by the prophets, his first being shrouded in the weakness of the flesh and the second bright in the bravery of his majesty. 14 About the first coming David says in psalm 71 [72:6–7]: 'He will descend like rain on a fleece, and in his days there will arise justice and abundance of peace for as long as the moon rises.' Rain falling on a fleece makes no noise and cannot be noticed; Christ would come to earth, said David, to teach justice and peace, without anyone suspecting. 15 Isaiah said [53:1–6]: 'Lord, who has believed what they hear of us? To whom has the arm of the lord

been shown? We have made announcements in his presence like children, like a root in the thirsty earth. There is no beauty or brilliance in him: we saw him, and he had no looks or beauty; he was without distinction, and deficient beside the rest. He is a man under a beating, knowing how to endure weakness because he was rejected and left out of the reckoning. 16 This man bears our sins and grieves on our behalf, and we thought him to be in pain and torment from blows; he was wounded because of our wickedness, and he was weakened because of our sins. Teaching us peace is his task, and we have been healed by his bruises. We have all strayed like sheep, and the lord has handed him over for our sins.' 17 In like fashion the Sibyl says:[G] 'He is pitiable, without distinction or looks, so that he can give hope to the pitiable.'[66] This humility prevented them recognising their God, and so they formed their loathsome plan to deprive of life the one who had come to give them life.

Jewish grievances

17.1 The reasons they put forward, however, for the anger and jealousy which they kept close in their hearts were different: Christ was trying to do away with the law of God given them by Moses – that is, he would not give up working for people's health on the sabbath, he emptied circumcision of meaning, he removed the ban on pork (these are the constituents of the sacraments of Judaism). 2 All those who had not yet gone over to him were thus stirred up by the priests on these counts to judge him impious, because he was undoing God's law, even though he did what he did not of his own design but following God's will and in accordance with the predictions of the prophets.

3 Micah declared that a new law would be given in this fashion [4:2–3]: 'The law shall go forth from Sion, and the word of the lord from Jerusalem, and it shall give judgment among the multitude of peoples and shall rebuke and expose mighty nations.' 4 The first law given by Moses was given on Mount Horeb, not on Mount Sion; that is the law which the Sibyl made plain would be undone by the son of God:[G] 'When all these things that I have spoken are accomplished, then in him is all the law undone.'[67]

5 Even Moses himself, through whom they fell away from God and failed to recognise him even while strenuously observing the law given them, had foretold that a very great prophet would be sent by God to be

---

66 *Orac. Sib.* 8.257.
67 *Orac. Sib.* 8.299–300.

above the law to bring God's will to men. 6 In Deuteronomy he left the following [18:17–19]: 'And the lord said to me: I will raise up a prophet for them from amongst their brethren as I have raised up you, and I will put my word in his mouth and he shall say to them what I tell him. And whoever fails to hear what that prophet says in my name will know my vengeance upon him.' 7 God was obviously using the law-giver himself to convey the fact that he was about to send his son – living, immediate law, that is, – and was about to undo the old law given by a mortal, so that he could ratify the eternal law anew through him who was eternal himself.

8 On the abolition of circumcision Isaiah prophesied as follows [Jer. 4:3–4]: 'Thus says the lord to the men of Judah and the inhabitants of Jerusalem: renew the newness among yourselves; do not sow among thorns. Circumcise yourselves to your God, and circumcise the foreskin of your heart, in case my wrath go abroad like fire and there be none to extinguish it.' 9 So too Moses himself [Deut. 30:6)]: 'In the latter days God will circumcise your heart for the loving of the lord your God.' So too Jesus[68] son of Nun his successor [Josh. 5:2]: 'And the lord said to Jesus, Make your knives of stone very sharp, and sit and circumcise the sons of Israel again.' 10 He said that the second circumcision would be not of the flesh, which the first was (a custom the Jews maintain even now), but of the heart and spirit, which Christ brought, who was the true Jesus. 11 The prophet does not say 'And the lord said to me' but 'to Jesus', in order to show that he was not speaking of himself but of Christ, to whom God was then speaking, 12 for that earlier Jesus prefigured Christ; he was first called Auses,[69] but Moses foresaw what would be and said he was to be called Jesus, so that as chosen leader of the army against Amalek who was attacking the sons of Israel he could beat his adversary in battle through the form of his name and lead the people into the land of promise. 13 Hence his succession to Moses, to reveal the fact that a new law given by Jesus Christ would succeed to the old law given by Moses.

14 That circumcision of the flesh is entirely without reason: if God had wanted it, he would have made man without a foreskin from the start; but the meaning of the second circumcision was a metaphor for the heart being bared – that is, we must live with an openness and simplicity of heart, because the part of the body which is circumcised has a certain similarity to the heart and is a matter for due modesty. 15 God said that it was to be bared so that he could warn us by the metaphor not to keep our hearts wrapped up

---

68 See note on 15.6 above.
69 Spelt Osee in the Vulgate and Oshea in King James' Bible (Num. 13: 9 and 17).

– that is, not to keep any shaming crime veiled amongst the secrets of our consciences. 16 That is the circumcision of the heart of which the prophets speak: God has transferred it from mortal flesh to the soul, which alone will abide. 17 In his desire to give us good advice for our life and health, consistently with his eternal goodness, he has offered us in that image of circumcision repentance, so that if we bare our hearts – that is, if we satisfy God with confession of our sins –, we can obtain mercy, which those who stubbornly conceal their crimes are denied: for he gazes not upon the face, as we do, but upon the inmost and secret places of the heart.

18 The ban on pork is to the same effect. When God told them to abstain from it, he wanted it to be understood in particular that they should abstain from sin and uncleanness. 19 The pig is a dirty, unclean animal and never looks up to heaven: body and face it hugs the ground, and it serves its belly and its feeding all the time; while it lives it provides no other service as the other living creatures do, which offer a means of sitting or riding or help in working the land, or pull carts by the neck or take loads on their back or give clothing with their pelts or supply milk in abundance or keep watch guarding houses. 20 Hence the ban on using pigflesh; it is a ban on copying the life of pigs, who are fed merely to die, so that people should not, in obedience to belly and pleasure, become useless at acting justly and be subjected to death; 21 they should not sink into filthy lusts either, like the pig which wallows in mud, or serve images made of earth, and befoul themselves with mud. Mud is what defiles the people who worship gods: they worship mud and earth.

Every single precept of Jewish law is aimed at the display of justice, because they are delivered with a double meaning, so that things spiritual can be learnt from the form of things carnal.

The passion

18.1[70] Christ was fulfilling what God wanted done and what he had foretold many generations earlier through his prophets; yet despite that spur, in their ignorance of holy scripture people continued to condemn their own God.

2 He knew that would happen, and said repeatedly that it was his duty to suffer and be killed for the salvation of many; nevertheless he withdrew with his disciples, not to avoid the inevitable endurance and suffering, but to show that this was the proper behaviour in any persecution, in case a man should

---

70 There are original touches in L.'s account of the Passion. See Monat (1982), 198–211.

apparently fall by his own fault;[71] and he told them his betrayal would be by one of them. 3 So Judas betrayed him to the Jews, lured on by the reward.

4 When he had been arrested and brought before Pontius Pilate (who was then legate of Syria[72]), they demanded his crucifixion, objecting to him simply for saying he was son of God and king of the Jews, and also for having said [Mk 14:58] 'If you undo this temple, which was 46 years in the building, I will raise it up without hands within three days', meaning that his suffering would be short and that he would rise again, two days after the Jews had killed him. He was himself the true temple of God. 5 These words of his they attacked for their ill omen and impiety. When Pilate heard it, and when Jesus offered nothing in his own defence, Pilate declared that there seemed to be nothing in him worthy of condemnation. But they, in all the injustice of their accusation, began to cry out with the people, whom they were egging on, and to demand the cross with shouts and yells. 6 Then Pilate gave way, not only to their clamour but also to the prodding of the tetrarch Herod, who was afraid of losing his throne; even so, Pilate did not deliver sentence himself but handed him over to the Jews, so that they could judge him according to their law.

7 So they beat him with whips and led him off, and before they put him on the cross they mocked him: they dressed him in a garment of purple and crowned him with thorns and hailed him as king, and gave him bitter-tasting food and mixed him a drink of vinegar. 8 After this they spat in his face and struck him with the flat of their hands. When his executioners were in dispute over his garments, they drew lots for his tunic and cloak. 9 And while all this was being done, not a word did he utter from his mouth, as if he were dumb. Then they hoisted him up between two criminals condemned for robbery, and put him on the cross.

10 What can my sorrow be now for so great a crime? What words can I employ to lament so great a wickedness? I depict no Gavian cross, such as Cicero did, with every muscle and fibre of his eloquence and the wellsprings of his genius in full flow, crying out [*Ver.* 5.170] 'that it was a deed of disgrace that a Roman citizen had been put on a cross in defiance of all the

---

71 On the controversial issue of how to respond to persecution, L. states boldly that Christ himself had withdrawn, flight was a way of imitating him, and he had intended Christians to follow his example. L. presumably did so too. See Nicholson (1989).

72 An error. Pilate was governor (prefect) of Judaea, a minor province with no garrison, such as was held by a lesser aristocrat (of equestrian status) or, on occasion, a freedman. Syria was a major province, governed by a leading aristocrat (*legatus Augusti pro praetore*, senatorial in status), with three legions.

laws.' 11 Yet though Gavius was innocent and undeserving of the punishment, he was a mere man, suffering under a bad man who had no time for justice. 12 What shall we say of the unworthiness of this cross, on which God was hanged, put there by the very worshippers of God? Who will there be so eloquent, so equipped with good store of words and facts, and what speech will go speeding in such rich abundance, that that cross can be bewailed as it deserves, a cross that was bewailed by the world itself and all its elements?

13 Yet that is what was foretold in the words of the prophets and in the verses of the Sibyl. In Isaiah we find written [50:5–6] 'I am no rebel and I do not answer back: I have submitted my back to their whips and my cheeks to their hands, and I have not turned my face away from the filth of their spitting.' 14 Likewise David in psalm 34 [35:15–16]: 'They massed their whips against me and knew me not; they were wicked and impenitent; they tried me and mocked me with derision, and gnashed at me with their teeth.' 15 The Sibyl also revealed that this would happen:[G] 'He will come in the end into lawless hands, the hands of the faithless, and they will give blows to God with unclean hands, and with filthy mouths they will deliver poisonous spit, and he will give his spotless back in simplicity to their whips.'[73]

16 Isaiah spoke further, about the silence which he stubbornly maintained until his death, as follows [53:7]: 'He was brought like a sheep to the sacrifice, and like a lamb among the shearers without a noise; so he opened not his mouth.' 17 So too the Sibyl mentioned above:[G] 'While they flog him he will be silent, lest anyone know what his utterance is or whence it came, so that he may speak to the dead and wear his crown of thorns.'[74]

18 As for the food and drink which they offered him before they crucified him, David says as follows in psalm 68 [69:21]: 'They gave me gall for my food and in my thirst they gave me vinegar to drink.' 19 The Sibyl also declared that this would happen:[G] 'Into my food they put gall and into my drink vinegar; this is the table of inhospitality they will reveal.'[75] 20 Another Sibyl attacks the land of Judah in these verses:[G] 'In your malignity you did not see that your God was playing with mortal ideas; instead you crowned him with a crown of thorns and you mixed him fearful gall.'[76]

21 In prophesying that the Jews would lay hands on their own God and

---

[73] *Orac. Sib.* 8.287–90.
[74] *Orac. Sib.* 8.292–94.
[75] *Orac. Sib.* 8.303–04.
[76] *Orac. Sib.* 6.22–24.

kill him, these words precede the testimony of the prophets. 22 In Esdras it is written:[77] 'And Esdras spoke to the people: this passion is our saviour and our refuge. Consider, and let it climb into your heart, since we shall set him low by way of a sign, and after this we shall hope in him, so that this place is not deserted for all eternity, says the lord god of all virtues. If you do not believe in him and hear his announcement, you will be the laughing-stock of the nations.' 23 It is obvious from this that the Jews had no other hope unless they cleansed themselves from his blood and put their hope in precisely the man they had killed. 24 Isaiah also points out their crime, saying [53:8, 9, 12] 'Judgment of him was disabled in the face of his humility. Who will tell of his birth? Because his life will be removed from earth he has been led away to death by the wickedness of my people. I will offer up the wicked for his burial and the rich for his death, because he has committed no crime and has spoken no lies. 25 Besides, he will overtake many himself and will divide the spoils of the brave, because he was handed over to death and was counted among criminals, and has borne the sins of many himself, and has been handed over for their wickedness.' 26 David also says in psalm 93 [94:21–22]: 'They will attack the just man's soul and condemn innocent blood, and the lord has been made my refuge.' 27 So too Jeremiah [11:18–19]: 'Lord, tell me and I shall know. Then I saw their intentions: I was led like a lamb without evil to become a victim; they made their plans against me, saying, Come, let us send timber after his bread, and let us uproot his life from the earth, and his name will be remembered no more'. 28 By timber he means the cross and by bread his body, because he is himself the food and life of all who believe in the flesh in which he was clothed and in the cross on which he hung.

29 Moses himself was even more clear in his prophecy on this, in Deuteronomy [28:66]: 'Your life will be hanging before your eyes, and day and night you will be afraid and will not trust your life.' In Numbers he says [23:19]: 'God does not hang like a man, and he does not endure threats like a son of man.' Zechariah has reported thus [12:10]: 'They shall gaze upon me whom they have pierced.'

30 So too David in psalm 21 [22:17–19]: 'They have pierced my hands and my feet, they have counted all my bones; they have watched me themselves and seen me, and have split my garments among them and have cast lots for my clothes.' 31 The prophet did not speak of himself: he was king, and he never suffered like that; the spirit of God spoke through him, of the

---

77 The words are not in Esdras and have not been traced.

one who would endure all those things 1050 years later. That is the sum of the years from the reign of David to the crucifixion of Christ. 32 Solomon also, David's son and founder of Jerusalem, prophesied that it too would perish to avenge the holy cross [1 Kgs 9:6–9]: 'But if you turn away from me, says the lord, and do not guard my truth, I will uproot Israel from the land I gave it, and this house which I have built for them in my name I will cast out utterly, and Israel will be a target for people's abuse and condemnation. This house will be abandoned, and all who pass by it will marvel and say, Why has God done these evils to this land and to this house? 33 And they will say, Because they forsook the lord their God and persecuted their king who was God's beloved, and crucified him in great humiliation: that is why God has brought these evils upon them.'

Death and resurrection

19.1[78] What more can now be said about the crime of the Jews? They were blinded, and overwhelmed by an incurable madness; though they read these things every day they neither understood them nor could they take precautions against themselves.

2 As he hung there nailed to the cross, he cried out to God in a great voice and freely gave up the spirit. And at the same moment there was an earthquake, and the veil of the temple which divided the two tabernacles was split in two pieces and the sun was suddenly eclipsed, and from the sixth hour to the ninth there was darkness. 3 The prophet Amos bears witness of this [8:9–10]: 'And it shall be on that day, says the lord, the sun will fail at midday and the day shall be darkened of light; and I will turn your days of joy into grief and your songs into lament.' 4 So too Jeremiah [15:9]: 'The soul that gave birth was terrified and became weary, and the sun gave way to her though it was yet midday; she was bruised and accursed; their remnants I will give to the sword in the sight of their enemies.' 5 The Sibyl also says:[G] 'The veil of the temple is to be rent, and at midday there shall be monstrous dark night for three hours.'[79]

6 Though that was what happened, they could not understand their wickedness even from celestial portents; rather, because he had said that he would rise again from the underworld two days later, for fear that his disciples would steal and remove his body and everyone would think that he

---

78 For L.'s deviations in this chapter from tradition, see Monat (1982), 212–17.
79 *Orac. Sib.* 8.305–06.

had risen and confusion among the people would be still greater, they took him down from the cross and shut him in a tomb and set a guard of soldiers close about it. 7 Two days later, however, there was a sudden earthquake before dawn, and the place of burial opened; though the guards in their panic and astonishment saw nothing, he emerged from the tomb alive and whole, and set off to Galilee to look for his disciples. In the tomb there was nothing to be found except the graveclothes in which they had wrapped and covered his body.

8 Yet the prophets had foretold that he would not remain in the underworld but would rise again two days later. David says in psalm 15 [16:10]: 'You will not abandon my soul to the underworld, nor will you allow your holy one to see death.' So too in psalm 3 [3:6]: 'I have slept and have been asleep, and I have risen because the lord has aided me.' 9 Hosea also, the first of the twelve prophets, has testified to his rising again [13:13–14]: 'This my son is wise because now he will not pause long in the place of his sons' tribulation; and I will wrest him from the hand of the underworld. O death, where is your judgment, or where is your sting?' In another place he says [6:3]: 'He will restore us to life in two days, on the third day.' 10 That is why the Sibyl said that after three days' sleep he would put an end to death:[G] 'Death's portion also he will complete when he has slept a third day; he will come into the light released from the dead, being first to outline for the elect the start of resurrection.'[80] For by overcoming death he has won life for us.

11 No other hope is thus granted to man of achieving immortality unless he believes in him and takes up that cross of his to bear and to endure.

Return to Galilee and the meaning of the testament

20.1[81] He set out therefore for Galilee, loath to reveal himself to the Jews in case he should bring them to repentance and rescue them from their impiety, and when his disciples were gathered together again, he explained the words of holy scripture – the secrets of the prophets, that is – which could not be understood at all until he had suffered, because they gave notice of him and his suffering.

2 That is why Moses and all those prophets call the law which was given to the Jews a testament: unless the testator is dead, his testament cannot be confirmed, and what he wrote cannot be known, because it is closed with his

---

80 *Orac. Sib.* 8.312–14.
81 On this chapter, see Monat (1982), 75–85.

seal. 3 If Christ had not endured death, his testament could not have been opened – revealed, that is – nor could the mystery of God have been understood.

4 All scripture is divided into two testaments. The one which came before the advent and passion of Christ, which is the law and the prophets, is called the old testament, and what was written after his resurrection is called the new testament. 5 The Jews use the old testament, and we use the new one: but they are not different, because the new one is the fulfilment of the old, and the testator is the same in each, namely Christ, who took on death for our sake and makes us the heirs of his eternal kingship, since the Jewish people have been stood down and disinherited, as the prophet Jeremiah attests when he says as follows [31:31–32]: 6 'Behold, the days come, says the lord, and I will consummate a new testament for the house of Israel and for the house of Judah, not in accord with the testament which I gave their fathers in the day when I took them by the hand to lead them out of the land of Egypt, because they did not abide by my testament, and I discounted them, says the lord.' 7 He puts it similarly in another place [12:7–8]: 'I abandoned my house, I let my inheritance go into the hands of its enemies. My inheritance became like a lion in the forest; it uttered its words over me itself, and therefore I hated it.' 8 Since its inheritance is kingship in heaven, he does not mean simply that he hates the inheritance itself, but the heirs, for showing ingratitude and impiety towards him. 9 'My inheritance,' he says, 'became to me like a lion': that is, 'I became the prey and the devouring of my heirs, who sacrificed me like a cow.' 'It uttered its word over me': that is, 'They uttered sentences of death and crucifixion against me.'

10 As for his earlier remarks, that he would 'consummate a new testament for the house of Judah', he showed thereby that the old testament which was given through Moses was not perfect, and he would consummate the one which he was keeping to be given through Christ. 11 As for the house of Judah and of Israel, he does not mean the Jews: he had deposed them; he means us, whom he summoned from among the nations to be adopted in their place, and we are called the sons of the Jews. That is what the Sibyl declares when she says:[G] 'The divine race of the blessed Jews, the heavenly ones.'[82]

12 The future of that race is explained to us by Isaiah, in whom the supreme father addresses his son saying [42:6]: 'I the lord God have summoned you to justice, and I will hold your hand and strengthen you, and

---

82 *Orac. Sib.* 5.249.

I have given you as a testament to my people, as a light to the nations, to open the eyes of the blind, to bring forth prisoners from their chains and those sitting in darkness from the house of gaol.' 13 Though once we sat in darkness, as if blind and incarcerated in stupidity, ignorant of God and truth, we have been illuminated by him who adopted us in his testament; now that we are freed of the evil chains and have been brought into the light of wisdom, he has made us heirs of the kingship of heaven.

Ascension

21.1[83] When he had appointed his disciples to preach the good news and his own name, a cloud suddenly wrapped itself round him and bore him up to heaven, on the fortieth day after his passion, as Daniel foretold, saying [7:13]: 'And behold, in the clouds of the sky as it were the son of man coming, and he came to the ancient of days.'

2 His disciples spread through the provinces, to lay the foundations of the church in every area, themselves doing important and almost incredible miracles in the name of God their master; when he went, he had equipped them with virtue and power in order that the pattern of the new annunciation could be established in strength. He also revealed them all the future: that is what Peter and Paul preached at Rome, and their preaching remains on record. In it 'they said among many remarkable things that this too would be the case: after a short while God would send a king to take the Jews by storm and to raze their cities to the ground while he beset them with the ultimate pangs of hunger and thirst. 3 Then it would come about that they fed on their own people and consumed them in turn, 4 and finally they would fall captive into the hands of their enemies, and they would see before their own eyes their wives most grievously assailed, their girls violated and prostituted, their boys taken as loot, their babies smashed, and everything given over to the wasting of fire and sword; the captives would be driven from their lands for ever, all because they had exulted over God's beloved and most upright son.'[84] 5 After the death of Peter and Paul, when Nero had killed them,[85]

---

83 On this chapter, see Monat (1982), 219–23.
84 Cited from the apocryphal *Preaching of Peter and Paul*.
85 It was commonly believed in the early Church that Peter and Paul were martyred in Rome at the same time, in Nero's reign. See Euseb. *Hist. Eccl.* 2.25.7, citing earlier sources; cf. Chron., where he places their deaths in AD 68, under Nero. Scholars prefer AD 64, when Nero is known to have ordered the deaths of some Christians; see Tac. *Ann.* 15.44.3ff.

Vespasian brought to an end the name and people of the Jews, and did all those things that Peter and Paul had foretold.[86]

The need for argument

22.1 It may seem false and incredible, but it is confirmed in my view by people not imbued with the true teaching of holy scripture. Even so, to complete our rebuttal of those who are too clever by half (to their own hurt), and who refuse their faith to things divine, let us expose their error with their own arguments, so that in the end they do eventually see that it had to happen as we say it did. 2 In front of good judges, either evidence without argument or argument without evidence can be strong enough, but we are not content with one or other since we have both available, and need not leave room for anyone of a twisted ingenuity either not to understand or to argue the opposite.

3 They say that nothing could possibly make space for a nature that was immortal; they also say that it was not worthy of god to want to become man and to burden himself with the infirmity of flesh, to subject himself to feeling, pain and death of his own accord – as if it were not easy for him, since he wanted it so, to reveal himself to mankind this side of the weakness of the flesh and to teach them justice, with all the extra authority of a self-acknowledged God; 4 everyone would then have obeyed his heavenly precepts if they had been supported by the virtue and power of God the preceptor. 5 'Why then,' they say, 'did he not come to teach men as God? Why did he make himself so low and feeble that he could be despised by man and punished? Why did he submit to the violence of weak, mortal men? Why did he not drive off their assaults with his virtue, or evade them with his divinity? Why did he not reveal his majesty at least at the moment of death, instead of being led off to judgment like a weakling, sentenced as if guilty and put to death as if mortal?'

6 I will rebut these charges with care and allow no one to be mistaken. It was all done for a great and remarkable reason: anyone who understands will not just cease to wonder that God was crucified by men but will also easily see that belief in him as God would not even have been possible if what he intended had not been done.

---

86 Vespasian was sent by Nero in AD 66 to quell the Jewish revolts. The war was pursued only sporadically after Nero's death, because of the eruption of civil war between the various contenders for the succession, until AD 70, when Titus, the elder son of Vespasian, now emperor, took Jerusalem and destroyed the temple.

BOOK 4: TRUE WISDOM AND RELIGION

A teacher who lived by his precepts

23.1 Anyone giving people advice shapes it to suit the life and habits of others. My question is, should he himself do what he recommends or not? 2 If he does not, his advice is undone. If it is good advice that he gives, raising the life of man to its best possible state, then the preceptor should not detach himself from the company of those amongst whom he is operating, and he should live in exactly the same way himself that he teaches others to live, so that he doesn't lessen confidence in his precepts by living differently, trivialising his teaching by undoing in action what he tries to assert in his sayings.

3 Every individual on the receiving end of advice is reluctant to accept the need to obey it, rather as if his right to freedom were being denied him.[87] 4 His answer to his adviser goes thus: 'I cannot do what you want because it is impossible. You tell me not to be angry, not to be greedy, not to be lustful, not to fear pain or death, but this is all unnatural; why, all the animals are subject to such feelings. Or if you think that nature can be resisted like that, do what you say yourself, so that I can know it can be done. 5 Since you don't, however, it is an extraordinary desire of yours to impose laws on a free man that you don't obey yourself. Learn first, teacher, and put your own behaviour right before you put others' right.' 6 That's a very fair reply, I think you'll agree. Why, a teacher of that sort will even fall into contempt, and he'll be misled himself because he will plainly be misleading others. 7 So what will our adviser do in response to these objections? How will he deny these mules their evasions except by showing, with immediate action, that his advice can be taken? 8 Hence the result that no one submits to the teaching of philosophers. People prefer example before talk, because talk is easy and example is hard. If only there were as many people of good behaviour as there are of good advice! But advisers who can't perform have no credibility: if they are human beings, they will be despised as frivolous, and if they are God, then the excuse of human weakness will be offered. 9 In sum, words must be confirmed by deeds, and philosophers can't do it. Since the advisers are themselves overcome by the emotions which they declare should be overcome, they cannot educate anyone to the virtue they proclaim so falsely, and that is why they think that no perfectly wise man has yet existed – a man, that is, in whom supreme virtue and perfect justice are consistent with supreme learning and knowledge – which is true. 10 No such person

---

87 Representing Christ as teacher (rather than, e.g., saviour) furnishes L. with another argument for the freedom of which he is such an active advocate in this work. See 5.19.

ever has existed since the world was made except Christ, who has offered us wisdom in his words and has reinforced his teaching with his ever present virtue.

The teacher had to be perfect and human

24.1 Let us now consider whether a teacher sent from heaven could possibly not be perfect. I am not now speaking of the one they say did not come from god. Let us imagine that someone is to be sent from heaven to give human life the rudiments of virtue and to conform it to justice. 2 No one can possibly doubt that this teacher sent from heaven must be as perfect in knowledge of everything as he is in virtue; otherwise there would be no distinction between earthly and heavenly. 3 In a human being there can be no learning that is private and peculiar to him: a mind enclosed in earthly tissue and impeded by bodily decay can neither comprehend things itself nor grasp the truth without instruction from elsewhere. 4 Even if it were to have a very great power, it still could not grasp ultimate virtue and stand up to all the vices whose substance is contained within its tissue. So it is that an earthly teacher cannot be perfect.

5 A heavenly teacher, on the other hand, who is granted knowledge by his divinity and virtue by his immortality is bound to be as consummately perfect in his teaching as in everything else. But that absolutely could not happen unless he took on a mortal body. The reason for the impossibility is obvious. 6 If he came among mankind as God (I omit the fact that mortal eyes cannot endure the sight of the brightness of his majesty), he will certainly not be able to teach virtue in the person of God because without a body he will not act as he teaches, and thus his teaching won't be perfect. 7 In any case, if perfect virtue is to endure pain with patience in accordance with justice and duty, if perfect virtue is to be fearless in the face of impending death and to endure it bravely when it comes, then a teacher of that perfection has a double duty, to teach it all by precept and to substantiate it in action, because anyone offering precepts for living must cut off all his escape routes in order to press on people the need to obey not perforce but for shame, and still leave them freedom: thus those who obey have their reward since they could have disobeyed had they wanted, and the disobedient have their punishment because they could have obeyed if they wished.

8 How then will the escape routes be cut off unless the teacher acts as he teaches, and goes the path in advance, reaching out a hand to his follower? And how can he act as he teaches unless he is like his pupil? 9 If he were not

susceptible to any suffering, his teaching could be answered as follows: 'I certainly don't want to sin, but I get overcome; I'm dressed in weak and feeble flesh, and it is the flesh which gets lustful and passionate, and scared of pain and dying. I am led against my will, and I sin not because I want to but because I am compelled to. I'm well aware that I'm sinning, but I'm driven by a weakness that's inevitable, and I can't resist.' 10 What will the teacher of justice reply to that? How will he beat down in argument a human being who can offer the excuse of his own flesh for his sins unless he himself is clothed in flesh, to show that even the flesh can achieve virtue? That sort of resistance cannot be beaten down except by example. 11 Teaching can have no authority unless the teacher can take the lead in acting it out: because human nature with all its proclivity to vice wants not just indulgence for its patent sinning but some grounds as well, 12 so the master and teacher of virtue must be very like man, so that by conquering sin he can teach man that sin can be conquered by man as well.

13 If he were immortal, on the other hand, he could not possibly set man an example. There will be some faithful fellow and he will say, 'You don't sin because you're free of this body, and you have no lusts because an immortal has no needs at all, whereas I need all sorts of things to keep this life of mine going. You don't fear death because death can have no power over you, and you despise pain because no act of violence can touch you, 14 whereas I'm mortal and I fear both, because they bring me the most excruciating agonies, which the weakness of the flesh cannot withstand.' 15 The teacher of virtue must remove this escape route too to prevent people attributing sin to necessity rather than to personal failing. 16 One measure of his perfection must be a complete impossibility of objection by the pupil, so that if the pupil says 'Your advice is impossible to take' he can reply 'But I take it.' 'Yes, but I'm clothed in flesh, whose peculiarity it is to sin.' 'I too have that same flesh, but sin has no mastery over me.' 17 'It is hard for me to despise wealth because I cannot live in this body without it.' 'I too have a body, and yet I fight against all desires.' 'I cannot endure pain or death in the cause of justice because I'm weak.' 'Pain and death also have power over me, and yet what scares you I overcome, in order to make you too a winner over pain and death. I lead the way through things that you claim cannot be endured: if you cannot follow advice, follow example.' Thus every excuse is pre-empted, and people are bound to admit that they are unjust by their own fault in not following their teacher of virtue who is also their guide.

You can now see how much more perfect a mortal teacher is in being able to guide other mortals than an immortal teacher would be: he could not teach endurance because he would not be susceptible to suffering. 18 This does not lead me to put man before God; I simply point out that perfect teaching is not within human competence unless the human being is also God, so that he can force people to obedience with all the authority of heaven, and it is not within God's competence unless he puts on a mortal body, so that by fulfilling his own advice in his own actions he puts the rest of us under the necessity of obeying him.

19 It is therefore as clear as water that anyone due to be the leader of living and the teacher of justice must be incarnate; otherwise his teaching cannot be full and perfect, and have fundamental roots and abide sure and stable among men, and he himself must endure the feebleness of flesh and body and take upon himself the virtue which he teaches in order to demonstrate it in deed and word together. So too he must be susceptible to death and all manner of suffering, since it is in the endurance of suffering and in enduring death that the requirements of virtue are exercised. All these things are, as I have said, what the perfect teacher must endure, to show that they can be endured.

The teacher had to be God and man

25.1 People should therefore learn, and understand why God most high in sending his deputy and messenger to educate mortality in the precepts of justice wanted him to take on flesh, to be crucified and to be punished with death.

2 Since there was no justice on earth, he sent his teacher like a living law, to establish his name and found a new temple, and to sow true and pious worship throughout the earth by word and by example. 3 So that it should be certain, however, that he was sent from God, he was not to be born as humans are, the product of two mortals; so that it should be plain that even as a man he was of heaven, he was made without the intervention of a begetter. 4 He had a spiritual father in God, and just as God was father of his spirit without a mother, so a virgin was mother of his body without a father. 5 He was therefore both God and man, being constituted midway between the two (which is why Greeks call him[G] middleman), so that he could bring man to God: that is, to immortality.

If he had only been God, then as said above he could not have presented man with examples of virtue, and if he had only been man, he could not drive people towards justice without the addition of a superhuman authority and virtue. 6 For even though man is composed of flesh and spirit, and the spirit should earn its eternity with works of justice, since the flesh is earthy and therefore mortal, so it takes the spirit with it, linked together as they are, and draws it away from immortality towards death.

7 Spirit which had no part in flesh could not possibly be man's guide to immortality, since flesh prevents spirit from following God. It is feeble, and liable to sin, and sin is the sustenance of death. 8 Hence the coming of the mediator – God, that is – in flesh, so that the flesh could follow him and snatch man from death whose dominion is in the flesh. He put on flesh so that by taming its lusts he could show that sin is no necessity but a matter of determination and will. 9 The one great and pre-eminent fight we fight is with the flesh: our infinite carnal lusts oppress the soul and prevent it from retaining its mastery; they enslave it with the sweetness of pleasure and temptation, and they work on it with everlasting death. 10 God revealed and declared to us the means of overcoming the flesh so that we could fight against those lusts. When our virtue is perfect, and is released from all calculation, it bestows upon the winners the crowning reward of immortality.

Meaning of miracles and of the passion

26.1[88] I have said why God preferred to adopt lowliness, feebleness and suffering; now the reason for the cross must be given and its importance laid out. 2 Not only the divination of the prophets (which came out true for Christ) but also the point of his suffering itself demonstrate the supreme father's dispositions from the beginning and his organisation of everything that has happened since. 3 What Christ suffered was none of it in vain; it had as great a symbolic significance as all the divine works he did, and their power and importance were clearly considerable at the time and were also pointing to something for the future.

4 He opened the eyes of the blind. It is a heavenly virtue to restore light to those without it, but in doing so he was indicating that when he turned to the people who did not know God he would enlighten the hearts of the ignorant with the light of wisdom and would open the eyes of the heart to behold virtue. 5 The truly blind are those who do not see heaven and worship fragile things of earth, plunged in the darkness of ignorance.

6 He opened the ears of the deaf. That was not all that his heavenly power was doing in the matter; he was also indicating that in a short while the divine words of God would become both audible and intelligible to those

---

88 On this chapter, see Monat (1982), 229–38.

deprived of the truth. True deafness you may attribute to those who do not heed both the truth and the feasibility of things celestial.

7 He released the tongues of the dumb into speech. That is a wonderful act of power, even when it was the only thing done; but in this virtue of his there was another meaning, which was to show that those ignorant hitherto of things celestial would soon understand the teaching of wisdom and would soon be speaking of God and truth. 8 It is someone with no understanding of the godhead who is truly tongueless and dumb, even if he is the world's best orator otherwise. For when the tongue begins to speak the truth, which is to interpret the virtue and majesty of the one and only God, then at last it is performing the task it was made for, but as long as it tells lies it is out of its path. He who cannot set forth God's words had better be dumb.

9 He also restored the feet of the lame to their task of walking. The robustness of God's work there is praiseworthy, but as metaphor it contained the fact that if the aberrations of our straying, secular life were checked, the path of truth would be revealed, and people could travel on it to win God's grace. 10 The man to be thought of as truly lame is the one wrapped in the gloom and dark of ignorance; he does not know where he is going, and he treads the path of death with steps that stumble and falter.

11 He also cleansed bodies that were foul with blisters and sores. That was no slight operation of his immortal power itself, but his energy portended the fact that his teaching was going to purify those stained with the blisters of sin and the blotches of vice by teaching justice. 12 True leprosy or elephantiasis must be considered the disease of those who are driven to crime by numberless lusts or to acts of outrage by their insatiable need for pleasure: they are branded with blisters of shame and marked with an eternal scar.

13 He revived the bodies of the dead; he called on them by their own names and retrieved them from death. What act could fit God better? What could be more worth a miracle in every generation than to re-register a life expired, to add to the fullness of its mortal span, and to expose the mysteries of death? 14 But this inexpressible power of his was the sign of a greater virtue: it showed that his teaching was going to have such force that all the people on earth who were lost to God and subject to death would be inspired by knowledge of the true light and would come to the rewards of immortality. 15 The truly dead you may reckon are those who do not know the God who gave them life and who debase their spirits from heaven to earth and tumble into the snares of eternal death. 16 The things that he did for them were thus images of things to be; what he revealed in bodies maimed and damaged bore the shape of things spiritual, so that in this world he could

display the work of a non-earthly virtue, and for the future he could show the power of his own heavenly greatness.

17 If then his deeds had a further significance, the signification of a greater power, so too his suffering was not simple or superfluous, and it did not come about by chance. 18 Just as his deeds revealed the great virtue and power of his teaching, so too his sufferings proclaimed the fact that his wisdom would be a thing to hate. The drink of vinegar and the food of gall promised sharpness and bitterness in this life for the persecutors of truth. 19 Though his actual suffering, sharp and bitter in itself, gave us an indication of those torments yet to come that are set up by virtue itself for those who abide in this generation, nevertheless our model for persecution, toil and misery was the arrival in our teacher's mouth of food and drink of that sort. 20 All these things must be endured to the end by those who follow truth, because truth is sharp and loathsome to all who have no virtue, who surrender their lives to pleasures that are lethal. 21 The crown of thorns that was set upon his head made it plain that he would gather himself a people of God from among sinners: for crown means people standing in a ring.[89] 22 Before we knew God, when we were unjust people, we were thorns: bad, that is, and sinful, ignorant of good; we were strangers to any notion of justice and its works, and we mucked up everything with our crimes of lust. 23 Picked as we therefore are from the briars and thorns, we are the ring round God's holy head, because we have been summoned by him in person, we have flocked to him from all sides, and we stand by God as our master and teacher, and we crown him king of the world and lord of all things living.

24 As for the cross, there is a great power in it, and great reason, which I will now attempt to demonstrate. 25 When God decided to set man free, as I explained above, he sent a teacher of virtue to earth, to shape man for innocence through precepts of salvation, and also to open the road to justice by his immediate works and deeds: man could step on that road and by following his teacher could come to eternal life. 26 That teacher was given a body and clothed in flesh so that he could present man, for whose instruction he had come, with examples of virtue and with encouragement thereto. 27 But when he had applied his pattern of justice to all the obligations of life, in order to pass on to man endurance of pain and contempt for death (by which virtue is made perfect and complete), he came into the hands of an impious nation, even though he could have avoided it through his knowledge of the

---

89 L. has in mind the use of *corona*, crown, to be seen in e.g. Cic. *Brut.* 192, *Ver.* 3.49 and *Tusc.* 1.10, and in other classical authors.

future, and could have repelled it with the same virtue that worked his miracles. So he endured the torture, the wounds and the thorns. 28 Finally he did not refuse to undertake even death, so that man could triumph over death and all its terrors as a thing suppressed and put in chains under the leadership of Christ.

29 Why the supreme father chose the particular sort of death for him to die that he did allow is explained as follows. Someone may possibly say, 'If he was God and he wanted to die, why did he not at least suffer some decent form of death? Why crucifixion of all things? Why go for humiliation in a sort of penalty that even a free man, however guilty, wouldn't obviously deserve?' 30 First: he who came in humility to bring help to the lowest in society and to reveal the hope of salvation to all had to die the sort of death that is common among the lowest in society, in case there were even one who could not imitate him. 31 Second: his body had to be kept whole, since he was due to rise from the dead two days later. No one should be unaware of the fact that he himself in speaking of his suffering had already made it known that he had the power of laying down and taking up his spirit when he wanted.[90] 32 Because he gave up his spirit while crucified, his executioners did not think it necessary to break his bones, as the custom was; instead, they merely pierced his side. 33 Thus his body was taken down from the cross and carefully laid in its tomb still whole. That was all done so that his body should not be so wounded or damaged that it was unsuitable for resurrection.

Another important reason for God preferring crucifixion was that on a cross he would necessarily be raised on high, and God's suffering would be visible to all nations. 34 A man who hangs on a cross is conspicuous to all and higher than everyone else: hence the choice of crucifixion, to indicate that he would be so conspicuous and so high up that all nations would converge from all over the world both to recognise him and to worship him. 35 Finally, no nation is so savage and no region so remote that either his suffering or the sublimity of his greatness could be unknown. 36 In his suffering he stretched out his hands and spanned the world, to show even then that a great gathering of people from all tongues and tribes would come beneath his wings, from the rising of the sun to its setting, and would accept upon every forehead that great and lofty mark of baptism.

37 The Jews offer a symbol of this even now, when they mark their thresholds with the blood of a lamb. When God was about to strike the Egyptians, he told the Hebrews (in order to keep them safe from the blow) to

90 L. alludes to Jn 10:17–18.

sacrifice a white lamb without blemish, and to make a mark on their thresholds with its blood. 38 So when the first-born of Egypt all died in one night, the Hebrews alone were safe because of the mark of blood, not because the blood of an animal has power enough in itself to save people but because it was an image of things to be. 39 The white lamb without blemish was Christ, innocent, just and holy, that is, and his sacrifice by those same Jews has been the salvation of all who make upon their foreheads the mark of blood, the mark of the cross, that is, on which he shed that blood. The forehead is man's highest threshold, and wood wetted with blood signifies the cross. 40 Finally, the sacrifice of an animal is called by those who do it Pascha, from the Greek *páskhein*, because it is the symbol of suffering, and God with his foreknowledge of the future passed it down to his people, through Moses, for their celebration. 41 At the time, the power of the image lay in its ability to thrust away danger then, so that it would be plain how strong truth itself would be in protecting God's people in the whole world's ultimate need. 42 In what way, or at what point of peril, there would be safety for all who put this sign of the true and God-given blood upon the high point of their bodies I will explain in my final book.

Power of the cross over demons

27.1 For the moment it is enough to lay out how great the mark's potency is. The terror it causes to demons will be known to anyone who has seen how far those conjured in the name of Christ flee from the bodies they beset.[91] 2 When he was at work among men, he could rout all demons with a word and could restore minds disturbed and maddened by evil attacks to their former senses himself; now it is his followers who free people from the same spirits of defilement in the name of their master and the sign of his suffering. 3 Proof of this is not difficult. If someone with his forehead duly marked is present at a sacrifice to gods, the sacrifice simply doesn't work, 'nor can the priest when asked interpret the response,'[92] and this has often been a main cause for bad kings to persecute justice. 4 When certain servants of our persuasion were with their masters at a sacrifice, through the mark made on their foreheads they put their masters' gods to flight, so that the future could not be made out in the victims' entrails.[93] 5 When the diviners realised it, at

---

91 For L. on demons, see 2.14; and Schneweis (1944).
92 Verg. *G.* 3.491.
93 The incident is described in the later work *de mort. persec.* 10.

the instigation of the demons for whom they divine they complained that profane people were taking part in the ritual, and they drove their bosses into a frenzy to make them storm the temple of God and foul themselves with real sacrilege, to be expiated with very fierce punishment of the persecutors.

6 Even after that, people in their blindness cannot understand either that this is the true religion, with so great a power of victory in it, or that theirs is false, in its incompetence to meet the challenge. 7 They claim that their gods act thus from hatred, not fear: as though hatred is possible in any gods unless they cause harm or have that power. It would better suit their supposed superiority to visit those they hate with immediate punishment rather than run away, 8 but because they cannot approach people on whom they see the mark of heaven, nor can they harm people who are protected by the immortal sign as if by an impregnable wall, they use people to attack them, and persecute them by other men's hands.

9 If people admit the existence of gods like that, then we have won. You simply cannot escape the truth of a religion which knows the demons' system, understands their cleverness, blunts their violence, tames and subdues them with the weapons of the spirit, and forces them into surrender. 10 If people deny the existence of such gods, on the other hand, they will be rebutted by the evidence of the poets and philosophers. But if they don't deny their existence and don't deny their evil, what else can they say except that some are gods and others are demons? 11 So let them tell us the difference between the two types, and then we can know which to worship and which to curse, and whether they have some link between them or are truly hostile to each other. If there is some necessary link, how far shall we distinguish them? How shall we avoid muddling the honour and worship that belong to each? If they are enemies, on the other hand, why don't the demons fear the gods, or, alternatively, why can't the gods scare off the demons? 12 Imagine someone under the influence of a demon's touch going mad and raving like a lunatic: let's take him into the temple of Jupiter Best and Greatest – or, since Jupiter doesn't know about healing people, into a shrine of Aesculapius or Apollo. Then let the priest of either god bid the harmful spirit come out of the man in his god's name: there is no way it can happen. 13 So what is the gods' power if they cannot keep demons under control, yet when those same demons are adjured in the name of the true God they exit straightaway? 14 What is their reason for fearing Christ and not fearing Jupiter, unless what the people think are gods are actually demons? Suppose finally there were a public confrontation between someone generally agreed to be suffering a demonic attack and the priest of Apollo at

Delphi: they will both shudder at the name of God in like fashion, and Apollo will come out of his priest as smartly as the demon out of the man, and once his god has been adjured and put to flight, the priest will be silent for ever. So: the demons that people say should be cursed and what they pray to as gods are one and the same thing. 15 If they don't think we can be trusted, let them trust Homer, who counts great Jupiter with the demons,[94] and let them trust other poets and philosophers too, who sometimes say demon and sometimes god, but only one of the words is true, and the other is false.

16 When those evil spirits are called to account, they admit that they are demons, but when they are worshipped they lie and say they are gods, so as to send people astray and distract them from knowledge of the true God, through whom alone eternal death can be avoided. 17 They are also the ones who have established a variety of worship for themselves in different regions in order to bring man down, and they do it under false names in order to deceive. Because they could not achieve divinity on their own, they assumed the names of great kings in order to get themselves divine honours under those titles. 18 This error can be dispelled, and the truth can be brought into the light. Anyone wanting to investigate further should call a meeting of those skilled in summoning up spirits from the underworld. Let them call up Jupiter, Neptune, Vulcan, Mercury, Apollo, and the father of them all, Saturn: they will all respond from the underworld, and will answer questions and come clean about themselves and God. 19 After that let them call up Christ: he won't attend, he won't appear, because he was no more than two days down there. You can't have proof more certain than that. I have no doubt myself that Trismegistus arrived at the truth by some such analysis; he said everything about God the father and much about the son which is contained in the divine secrets.

Meaning of religion

28.1 Since things are as we have explained, it is plain that man can have no hope of life unless he casts away his silliness and his miserable mistakes and recognises and serves God; he must renounce this temporal life and teach himself the rudiments of justice in order to cultivate true religion. 2 We are born on the following terms, that we present our just and due obedience to God who creates us, and that we acknowledge and follow him alone.

3 This is the chain of piety that ties and binds us to God: hence the word

---

94 See note on 2.14.6.

religion, and not as Cicero takes it, from re-reading.[95] In book 2 *de Natura Deorum* he says [71–72], 4 'It is not only philosophers who distinguished superstition from religion but also our own ancestors. People who spent whole days in prayer and sacrifice to ensure their own children would survive[96] were called superstitious, 5 while people who reviewed and rethought everything of relevance to the worship of gods were called religious, from *relegere*, just as the elegant are so called from *eligere* and the diligent from *diligere* and the intelligent from *intellegere*.[97] In all these words there is the same vital element of *legere* as there is in religious. In the case of superstitious and religious, one is a word of reproof and the other a word of praise.' 6 The ineptitude of this interpretation can be learnt from the facts. If both superstition and religion are being practised in the worship of the same gods, then there is little or no difference between them. 7 What good reason will there be, frankly, for thinking that to pray once for the health of one's children is the mark of a religious man and to do so ten times is superstitious? If to do so once is very good, it must be better still to do so more often. If prayer at prime is good, all day is better, and if one victim serves to appease, more will appease more, because acts of obedience multiplied gain favour rather than offend. 8 We don't think servants a nuisance who are ever present to assist and obey; we prize them rather. So why should a man come in for reproach, and get a bad name for loving his sons or honouring God too much, while one who doesn't is to be praised?

9 This argument works the other way round too. If praying and sacrificing all day every day is a matter for accusation, so it is to do so once. If to pray regularly for surviving children is a vice, then the man who does so only occasionally is superstitious too. Alternatively, why should the label of vice be applied to a deed that is peerless for its honesty and justice? 10 As for Cicero's remark that 'those who carefully reviewed everything of relevance to the worship of gods were called religious from *relegere*', why should those who act so many times a day lose the title of religious when as a result of their concentration they are simply making a much more careful review of the ways in which gods are worshipped? 11 Well? Religion is of course worship of what is true, and superstition is worship of what is false. And

---

95 L. relates *religio* to *religare*, to tie down; in the passage quoted Cicero relates it to *relegere* or *religere*, to pick over or re-read.
96 Literally 'should be survivors'; survivors in the Latin is *superstites*.
97 The basic sense of *legere* is to pick; the prefixes *e-*, *di/dis-* and *inter-* give to pick out, to pick through and to pick between.

what you worship is absolutely important, more so than how you worship or what you should pray. But because worshippers of gods think they are religious when in fact they are superstitious, so they cannot distinguish religion from superstition or explain the meaning of the words. 12 We have observed that the word religion comes from the bond of piety because God has bound man to him and tied him with piety: we simply have to serve him as master and obey him as father. 13 Lucretius interpreted the word much better when he said [1.932] he was 'untying religious knots'. People are called superstitious, on the other hand, not for praying for surviving chldren – we all pray for that – but either for cultivating a surviving memory of the dead or for surviving their own parents and worshipping images of them at home like household gods. 14 Superstitious was the word for people who used to develop novel rituals to divert honours from gods to dead people who they thought had been elevated above human rank to a place in heaven; 15 religious was kept for those who worshipped the long-established public gods. Hence Vergil's line [*A.* 8.187]: 'A superstition vain, and ignorant of the ancient gods.' 16 But since we find that the ancient gods were also consecrated after death in the same fashion, superstitious is the word for those who worship quantities of false gods, and religious is for us who pray to the one true God.

Father and son are one

29.1 It may be asked how we can assert two gods, God the father and God the son, when we say we worship one God. This assertion puts a good number of people into confusion. 2 What we say seems probable enough to them except on this one point, where they reckon we are on slippery ground in admitting to a second god who is also mortal. His mortality has been discussed; let us now explain the oneness of God.

3 When we talk of God the father and God the son, we do not mean different gods and we do not separate one from the other, because the father cannot be separated from the son nor the son from the father, since a father cannot be called a father without a son and a son cannot be created without a father. 4 Since father creates son and son creates father, there is one and the same mind in each, one and the same spirit and one and the same substance. But the father is like a spring in full flow and the son like a stream derived from it; the father is like the sun and the son like a ray projected from it. 5 Because the son is loyal to the supreme father and precious to him, he is never separated from him, just as a river cannot be cut off from its source nor a sunbeam from the sun; the water of a source is in the river, and

the light of the sun is in a sunbeam. Equally, a voice cannot be divorced from a mouth, nor can virtue or an act of virtue be detached from a body. 6 When prophets speak of the handiwork of God, his virtue and his utterance as one and the same thing, the lack of distinction is due to the fact that a tongue, the instrument of utterance, and a hand, the agent of virtue, are individual pieces of one body. 7 A more immediate example may be better. When a man has a son whom he loves especially but the son lives in the house, under the hand of his father, father may grant son the name and power of master, but in civil law there is said to be only the one house and one master of it. 8 So this world is God's one and only house, and father and son who occupy the world in total unanimity are one God: one is as two and two as one. 9 There is no cause for surprise in this, since son is in father because father loves son and father is in son because son obeys father's will faithfully, and never does nor ever has done anything except what father wished or required.

10 Finally, Isaiah explained that there was one God, as much father as son, in the text quoted earlier,[98] when he said 'They will adore you and pray to you, because God is in you, and there is no other god apart from you.' In another place [44:6] he says likewise, 'Thus says God the king of Israel, the eternal God who rescued him: I am first and I am last, and there is no God beside me.' 11 Though he put forward a pair of persons, God the king – Christ, that is – and God the father who raised him from the dead after his passion, just as we said[99] the prophet Hosea claimed in saying 'I will wrest him from the hand of the underworld,' nevertheless he added 'and there is no God beside me' with reference to each person, since he could have said 'beside us'. But it simply would not have been proper to split a unit so close knit and use a plural of it. 12 For the supreme God is one God, the only God, free and without origin, because he himself is the origin of everything and in him are contained at one and the same time both the son and everything else. 13 Since, then, the mind and will of the one is in the other, or rather, since there is one and the same mind in each, each is rightly called the one God, because whatever is in father flows through to son and whatever is in son comes through from father. 14 God most high, the one and only God, cannot therefore be worshipped except through his son. Anyone who thinks he is worshipping only God the father in failing to worship the son fails even to worship the father, 15 whereas anyone who adopts the son and wears his name is worshipping father at the same time as he worships son, because son is

---

98 13.7 above.
99 19.9 above.

representative, messenger and priest of God most high. The son is the door of the great temple, the path of light, the guide to salvation and the entry into life.

Heresy

30.1 Because of the existence of many heresies and division among God's people from the attack of demons, truth must be given a brief definition and placed in its proper home; then, if anyone desires to drink the water of life, he need not go to 'polluted pools which have no channel' [Jer. 2:13] but can become acquainted with its richest source, and when he has drunk of that he can have perennial light. 2 We need to know above all that he and his representatives foretold the inevitability of many sects which would break the concord of the holy body, and that they warned us to take great care never to fall into the traps and tricks of that adversary of ours, with whom God wished us to fight; 3 at that point certain commands were given, which we must keep for ever, but many people forget them; abandoning the road to heaven they have made paths off track for themselves, by winding and precipitous ways, in order to draw careless and simple folk towards darkness and death. I will explain the present extent of this.

4 There have been some amongst us either less firm in their faith, or less knowledgeable or less careful, who caused a split in our unity and sent the church different ways. 5 There were some people who, despite a dodgy faith, pretended they knew God and worshipped him; by building up their resources and concentrating on office they tried to gain the top priesthood. When put down by people more powerful, they then preferred to withdraw with their supporters rather than have over them the people they had wanted to dominate themselves. 6 Then there were people not adequately instructed in holy scripture; they were unable to meet the attacks on truth made by objectors saying that it was impossible or inappropriate for God to shut himself in the womb of a woman, and that his heavenly majesty could not be reduced to such feebleness that he became the butt of mankind, mocked, despised and insulted, in the end enduring torture and being nailed to an accursed cross. 7 Since they lacked the ability or the knowledge to fight off all these arguments – they could not see the powerful reason for events in any depth – they were tempted off the true path, and corrupted holy scripture to give themselves a new doctrine, without root or stability. 8 Some again were attracted by the utterance of false prophets (the true prophets and God himself had both given warning of them), and they fell away from God's teaching and abandoned the true tradition.

9 All those groups of people were trapped by the deceptions of demons; they should have looked out for them and taken care, but they failed to do so and lost the name and the worship of God. 10 For when they are called Phrygians or Novatians or Valentinians or Marcionites or Anthropians or whatever else they get called, they have stopped being Christians; they have lost the name of Christ and have put on titles that are human and external.

11 It is only the catholic church that keeps true worship. It is the source of truth, the home of faith and the temple of God: anyone who does not enter it, or who walks out from it, is estranged from hope of life and salvation. No one should preen himself on his pertinacity in argument: 12 it is a matter of life and salvation, and if life and salvation are not most carefully and cautiously considered, then they will be lost and gone. 13 Nevertheless, because certain particular groups of heretics each think that they are specially Christian and theirs is the catholic church, it must be realised that the true church is the one where confession and repentance exist, the one which cares in healing fashion for the sins and wounds to which the flesh in its weakness is susceptible.

14 I have set this forth briefly for the moment by way of warning: no one seeking to escape error should get entangled in greater error by failing to understand the innermost truth. We shall fight more fully and more extensively later against all the sects and their lies, but this will be in a separate work with its own focus.

15 Since we have now spoken adequately about true religion and wisdom, it follows that in the next book we will speak of justice.

BOOK 5: JUSTICE

Supposing debate is allowed, the cause demands appropriate strategies and skilled advocates

1.1[1] There is no doubt on my part, emperor Constantine, that if this work of mine which asserts the oneness of that founder of all things and ruler of this vast world comes into the hands of those whose religions are all wrong, then, intolerant as they are because of their gross superstition, they will assail it with curses, and though they may scarcely read its prologue, they will attack it, reject it and curse it; if they had the patience either to read it or to hear it read, they would think they were smeared and besmirched by an act of evil beyond expiation. 2 We beg these people, nevertheless, by the law of humanity, if possible not to condemn before they know the whole story. If opportunity for self-defence is granted to those who commit sacrilege, to traitors and to poisoners, and if no one may be found guilty case unheard, then the justice of our request is plain: anyone who comes upon these words should read right through if he reads at all, and if he hears them read he should postpone his verdict till the end. 3 I am well aware of their stubbornness, however;[2] our wish will never be achieved. They are scared that defeat by us will compel them to yield in the end; the truth itself will cry out. 4 So they make noisy interruptions to avoid hearing, and they cover up their eyes to keep them from seeing the light we offer, plainly revealing in this their lack of faith in their own hopeless system: they don't dare learn, and they don't dare come to grips with us, because they know they are easy losers.

5 Debate is thus ruled out. As Ennius says,[3] 'Wisdom is driven forth, force reigns instead'. And because they are keen to condemn as guilty people they know very well are innocent, they refuse to accept the innocence; to condemn innocence proven would be even more unfair, no doubt, than to condemn it unheard! 6 But, as I said, they are frightened that if they do listen they will

---

1 The first four chapters of this book are tantamount to a re-introduction to the whole work.
2 L. follows the strategy of earlier Christian apologists in throwing back at pagans charges conventionally levelled at Christians. For *superstitio*, see 4.28.3ff.; for *pertinacia*, see Pliny, *Ep. Tra.* 10.96.
3 *Ann.* 263.

not be able to condemn: hence their torture, murder and banishment of those who worship the supreme God, the just people, that is. Their hatred is so strong that they cannot even account for it: 7 their loathing of those on the true path is a measure of their own aberrance, and though they could put themselves right by themselves, they heap up their confusions on top of their cruelties, and go staining themselves with innocent blood, wrenching from disembowelled bodies hearts given to God. 8 These are the people we now want to grapple with in argument, and to guide from a stupid belief to the truth, these people who find the blood of just men more palatable than their words.

9 So: shall we be wasting our time? Not at all. Even if we cannot win them back from a death they speed towards, nor restore them to life and light from their deviations (they are fighting against their own salvation), at least we shall strengthen those of our own folk whose understanding is wobbly and not firmly based on solid foundations.

Most people waver, especially those of any attainment in literature.[4] 10 Philosophy, oratory and poetry are all pernicious for the ease with which they ensnare incautious souls in beguiling prose and the nice modulations of poetical flow. 11 They are honey, hiding poison, and that is why I wish to combine wisdom with religion, so that all that empty learning is no obstruction to enthusiasts, and the scholarship of letters not only does no harm to religion and justice but actually assists them as far as possible – provided the scholar of literature becomes more learned in the virtues and wiser in the truth. 12 Besides, even if it benefits no one else, it will benefit me: my conscience will rejoice, and my mind will be glad to be working in the light of truth, which is the food of the soul and steeped in unbelievable delight. 13 This is no case for despair, of course; perhaps 'we sing not to the deaf'.[5] Things are not so bad – or else unclean spirits have more licence than the holy spirit – that sound minds do not exist to take pleasure in truth and to see and follow the right path once it is shown them. 14 Simply rim the cup of wisdom with honey from heaven,[6] so that bitter medicine can be drunk unawares with no hostile reaction: the initial sweetness beguiles, and the

---

4 A hint that L. is targeting doubting Christians, not only confirmed pagans, among the educated classes.

5 Verg. *Ecl.* 10.8.

6 The image first occurs in Plato, *Lg.* 659e–660a: legislators dealing with poets are compared with doctors who give children medicine disguised as 'food and drink to enjoy'. As L.'s words show, however, it was Lucretius (1.936ff., repeated at 4.11ff.) who made it memorable. Quintilian (*Inst.* 3.1.4) confirms Lucretius' success.

harshness of the bitter flavour is concealed beneath the covering of sugar.

15 This is the principal reason why holy scripture lacks the trust of the wise,[7] both scholars and princes of this world: its prophets have spoken to suit ordinary folk, in plain and ordinary language; 16 they thus earn the contempt of people who will not read or hear anything not polished and eloquent. Nothing sticks in such people's minds unless it soothes their ears with its smoothness, and anything seeming coarse they think is stuff for old women, stupid and vulgar. 17 Anything rough on the ears they assume is untrue, and nothing is credible unless it provides aesthetic pleasure; they weigh by garb and not by truth. 18 Hence their disbelief in God's word, because it wears no make-up, and the disbelief extends to its interpreters, because they are not educated men, or only slightly so, themselves, and it is exceedingly rare for such people to have good powers of expression. The reason is obvious. 19 Eloquence serves this world; it likes a public to show off to and to please with its mischief, since it often tries to oust the truth to prove its own effectiveness; it seeks out wealth, it covets distinction, and it demands top place in public esteem. 20 Hence its contempt for this humble stuff of ours, and its flight from mysteries that seem to oppose it: it likes publicity, of course, and looks for crowds to throng around it; 21 wisdom and truth in consequence have no proper champions, and scholars who came to their rescue were inadequate to defend them.[8]

22 Among those known to me in this capacity, one notable advocate was Minucius Felix.[9] His book, called *Octavius*, makes plain how good a vindication of truth he could have made if he had devoted himself totally to the subject. 23 Septimius Tertullian[10] also had skill in every sort of writing, but his eloquence was uneven, and he was rather rough and not at all lucid: even he failed to win enough publicity. 24 The only one of real distinction was

---

[7] The problem is the medium: Christian literature does not appeal because it lacks eloquence and polish; cf. 3.1–3 below, and 6.21.4–5.

[8] The list which follows of L.'s predecessors omits, notoriously, Arnobius of Sicca Veneria in North Africa. Arnobius was L.'s teacher, and composer of *Against the Nations*, a work of Christian apologetic in seven books. It has been thought that this omission was deliberate, but if Arnobius' work was composed around the same time as this work and in Africa, L. may not have known of it.

[9] Minucius Felix flourished in the first third of the 3rd century (after Tertullian and before Cyprian). African by birth, he was an advocate at the Roman bar. He wrote *Octavius* in clear and direct imitation of Cicero.

[10] Tertullian wrote works of Christian theology, morality and apologetic in the reigns of Septimius Severus and Caracalla (datable works are between 196/7 and 212).

thus Cyprian:[11] he won himself considerable fame as a professor of rhetoric, and he also wrote a great deal worth admiring for itself. 25 He had an easy talent, a sweet flow of words, and (the greatest of virtues in exposition) he was clear; you could not tell with him whether elegance of language, success in explanation or power of persuasion came first. 26 Beyond a power of words, however, Cyprian cannot go in satisfying those who do not know God's sacred mystery, because what he spoke of is both mystical and prepared for the ears of the faithful alone. Scholars of this world who become acquainted with his writings usually mock them. 27 I have heard of one, certainly a man of eloquence, who changed one letter and called him Coprian,[12] on the grounds that he employed on old wives' tales a literary talent that deserved better. 28 If that can happen to a man of some charm with words, what can we think is the fate of those whose prose is thin and ugly, who have never had an ability to persuade in them, or a skill in argumentation, or even a power of plain rebuttal?

The opposition: a philosopher and a judge

2.1 We have thus not had scholars of adequate expertise to undo popular error with energy and precision, and to plead the whole case for truth in choice and fluent fashion, and this deficiency has been taken by some as a good chance to try their pens against a truth they do not understand. 2 I omit those who attacked to no avail in earlier times; I quote my experience in Bithynia, where I had been invited to teach rhetoric.[13] It happened that a temple of God was reduced to rubble,[14] which caused a pair of people to jeer at the utter prostration of truth; whether their mockery owed more to disdain or perversity I cannot say.

3 One of them[15] claimed to be a spokesman for philosophy, but he was so wicked in his ways, this professor of self-control, that he glowed with greed no less than with lust, and so luxurious was his lifestyle that for all his profession of virtue in school and for all his praise of thrift and poverty, his

---

11 Cyprian was a rhetor before his conversion. He was bishop of Carthage from 248/9, fled the Decian persecution (250) and was martyred in that of Valerian; he died in September 258. Numerous treatises and a considerable corpus of letters survive.

12 *Kópros* is the Greek for dung.

13 A rare autobiographical detail.

14 Cf. *de mort. pers.* 12.5.

15 He is thought to be Porphyry, but is probably not; L. perhaps conceals his name to reduce his substance. See p. 2.

dinner at home was better than dinner at the palace. Nevertheless he masked his vices under his long hair and Greek gown, and (best mask of all) under his wealth, and to increase his wealth he would go to remarkable lengths to make friends with the judiciary; using the prestige of his bogus title he would suddenly put them under an obligation to him, not just in order to trade their verdicts, but also, using this power of his, to stop his neighbours from recovering lands and homes from which he was expelling them. 4 At the same time as the just people were being wickedly persecuted, this fellow ruined his arguments by his own behaviour, or alternatively, exposed his behaviour by his own arguments (he was his own worst critic and fiercest prosecutor): he spewed out three volumes attacking the name and faith of Christians, 5 claiming that 'it was the philosopher's pre-eminent duty to rescue people from error and to redirect them to the true path, to worship of the gods, that is, by whose superior power the world was governed; he would not let the inexperienced be taken in by certain persons' frauds in case honesty should become prey and provender for the clever; 6 he had therefore taken on this task, a task very proper to philosophy, of presenting the light of wisdom to non-beholders, not simply for them to resume worship of the gods and so regain their health, but also to have them drop their determined refusal of it, escape physical torture and abandon their willingness to endure ferocious bodily pains to no purpose.' 7 To clarify why this task had so absorbed his efforts, he launched into praise of the emperors 'whose piety and foresight', to quote his own words, 'had been revealed most notably in their defence of worship of the gods; for the good of mankind they had eventually decided to control a wicked and maudlin superstition in order to free all people for legitimate religion and the experience of divine goodwill.'

8 His wish to undermine the logic of the faith he was speaking against turned him, however, into a laughing-stock for folly and incompetence. Our worthy and altruistic adviser simply did not know what he was saying, never mind what he was attacking. 9 Any of our folk there would wink to meet the occasion, but in their own minds they laughed to see the fellow claiming he would enlighten others when he was the blind one, he would rescue others from error when he didn't know himself where he was putting his own feet, and he would teach others the truth when he had never seen a single spark of the stuff himself, being a professor of wisdom whose every effort was all aimed at wasting it. 10 As everyone else pointed out, he chose the moment to launch his attack when a loathsome bout of cruelty was raging. What a fawning, time-serving philosopher! 11 He earned the contempt his self-

conceit deserved in failing to win the thanks he hoped for, and the infamy he did achieve turned into reproach and disapproval.

12 The other man[16] wrote similarly, but more caustically; he was at the time one of the judiciary, and a prime mover of the persecution, but not content with that crime he even pursued his victims with his pen. 13 He wrote a pair of pamphlets, not 'against' the Christians, to avoid seeming too hostile in his attack, but 'to' them, to give the impression of a humane and kindly adviser. In them he attempted to prove the falsity of holy scripture on the basis that it entirely contradicted itself. 14 In listing certain headings which gave the semblance of self-contradiction, he laid them out in such intimate detail that it looked in the end as if he had once been one of our persuasion. 15 If he was so, then even Demosthenes will be incapable of defending him on a charge of impiety, since he has turned traitor to the religion that inspired him, traitor to the faith whose name he adopted, and traitor to the sacred mysteries he accepted – unless, of course, mere chance had put the holy writings in his hands. 16 In which case, what a nerve, to dare to undo what no one had explained to him – well, what he had either not learnt or not understood. Self-contradiction is as remote from holy scripture as he was from faith and truth, 17 and yet, he laid into Paul and Peter especially, and into the other disciples, as 'disseminators of falsehood', claiming that they were also 'untrained and uneducated,[17] since some of them made a living as fishermen': was he put out because fishing had had no commentary from an Aristophanes or an Aristarchus?[18]

Scripture does not contradict itself; Christ was no magician

3.1 Since Peter and Paul were uneducated, they clearly had neither the will nor the wit for fiction. Alternatively, who without an education could put together anything coherent and self-consistent when philosophers of great learning, Plato and Aristotle, Epicurus and Zeno, could themselves produce stuff that is self-contradictory and incompatible? Incoherence is the very essence of falsehood, 2 but what the disciples have passed down to us

---

16 He is to be identified with Sossianus Hierocles, governor of Bithynia. See Barnes (1976); *PIR¹* 432.

17 An old charge against Christians; see Acts 4:13; Origen, *c. Cels.* 1.27, 29; 3.18, 44; etc.

18 Aristophanes of Byzantium (c. 257–180 BC) was head of the library of Alexandria from c. 194, and a scholar of language, texts, literature and science. Aristarchus of Samothrace (c. 216–144) was also head librarian (from c. 153) and author of many critical editions, commentaries and treatises.

squares on every side because it is true, being wholly consistent with itself, and persuasive because it is based on sound reason. 3 They did not fabricate this religion of ours for profit or advantage: after all, they followed a path of life, for real as well as in theory, which eschews pleasure and despises all that is commonly held to be good, and they not only endured death for their beliefs, but also knew that they were going to die and said so quite openly, saying also that all who followed their teaching would endure unspeakable agonies after them.

4 'Christ himself,' the fellow declared, 'when forced out by the Jews gathered a band of 900 men and resorted to brigandage.' 5 Such authoritativeness! Unchallengeable! We had better accept it; perhaps it was vouchsafed him by some Apollo in a dream. Robbers have always perished in plenty, and do so every day, and you yourself have passed sentence on many: but which of them has been called 'man' after his crucifixion, never mind 'God'? 6 Presumably this belief of yours is based on the fact that you people made a god out of the murderer Mars, which you'd never have done if the court of the Areopagus had sentenced him to crucifixion!

7 When this fellow was pulling Christ's miracles to pieces and even so couldn't deny them, nevertheless he tried to show that 'Apollonius did the like, or even greater.'[19] (It is surprising he left out Apuleius, who tends to come very high in the miracle count.[20]) 8 So why does nobody worship Apollonius as a god? You're crazy – or are you out on your own perhaps, the sort of fan such a so-called god deserves, and the true God will punish you and him together for eternity?

9 If Christ was a magician 'because he did miracles', Apollonius was simply cleverer 'who', as you write, 'suddenly wasn't there in the courtroom when Domitian wanted to punish him', whereas Christ was both arrested and crucified. 10 Ah, but he probably wanted to use Christ's claim to be God to contrast the outrageousness of Christ with the apparent modesty of Apollonius: though Apollonius did the greater miracles (so he thinks!), nevertheless that was not his great claim.

11 I omit any comparison here of their actual deeds, because I have dealt with the deceptive illusions of magic in Books 2 and 4. 12 I say there is no

---

19 Apollonius of Tyana (1st cent. AD): his *Life* was written by Philostratus in c. 217. Despite L., there were some who worshipped him. See Dio 77.18.4; *SHA S. Al.* 29.

20 Apuleius of Madauros in Numidia, author of *The Golden Ass*. He defended himself against charges of magic in his *Apologia* c. 157. He is linked with Apollonius also in Aug. *Ep.* 136.1; 138.18.

one who would not make it his first choice after death to have the same as even the greatest kings desire. 13 Why do people prepare magnificent tombs for themselves, and statues and portraits? Why are they anxious to earn the good opinion of others by glorious deeds, or even by dying for their fellow-citizens? And why have you sought to establish this monument of your intelligence – though it's as revoltingly stupid as if it were made of mud – unless you hope for immortality through remembrance of your name? 14 It is stupid to think that Apollonius refused what he certainly wanted to have if he could; there is nobody who would refuse immortality, especially when you say 'he was also worshipped as a god by certain people, and a statue of him, set up under the name of Hercules Averter of Evil, is honoured by the people of Ephesus to this day.' 15 He could not be taken for a god after his death because everyone agreed he had been a man and a magician, and he tried for divine status under a name not his own because under his own he neither could try nor dared to try. Our God, however, can be taken as God because he was not a magician, and he is so taken because he was truly God. 16 'I am not saying that Apollonius was not considered a god because he refused to be', says our fellow; 'I say it to reveal our own greater wisdom in not instantly attaching to miraculous deeds a belief in their doer's divinity. You people, by contrast, have believed in a god on flimsy showings.' 17 You are so unacquainted with the wisdom of God! No wonder you understand nothing of what you have read, when even the Jews, long practised in reading the prophets and entrusted with God's sacred mystery, did not understand what they were reading.

18 Please understand therefore, if you can manage it, that we do not believe in him as God 'because he did miracles', but because we have seen accomplished in him all those things foretold us in the predictions of the prophets. 19 'He did miracles': we would have thought him a mere magician, as you do now and as the Jews did at the time, had not all the prophets predicted with one breath that he would do exactly so. 20 We think of him as God, therefore, not for his miraculous deeds and works but rather for that cross, which you lick like dogs, because that too was one of the predictions. 21 It is not therefore his own testimony that makes us believe in his divinity – who can be believed when speaking of himself? – but the testimony of the prophets, who uttered all that he did and suffered long before the event. That is not something which could ever have happened to Apollonius or Apuleius or any magician at all, nor can it.

22 After unloading himself like that with the delusions of his ignorance, in his efforts to wipe out truth altogether he then had the nerve to label those

wicked and God-hating books of his[G21] 'Truth-loving'! 23 What blindness of mind! What a more than Cimmerian darkness (to quote)! Perhaps he was a student of Anaxagoras, and snow was ink for him.[22] And yet it is one and the same blindness, to label falsehood truth and truth falsehood. Obviously this trickster was intending to create a wolf in sheep's clothing, so that he could ensnare the reader with a bogus title.

24 Never mind: you did it in ignorance, we will say, not in malice. So what truth have you finally brought us, if not that in defending your gods you have in the end been their betrayer? 25 In pressing the 'glorification of god most high', a god whom you claim to be 'king, the greatest, the maker of all things, the source of good, father of all, creator and nourisher of living things', you have deprived your Jupiter of his kingship, you have driven him from power and you have reduced him to the rank of servant. Thus your own epilogue convicts you of stupidity, futility and error. 26 You declare that there are gods, and yet you subject and enslave them to the God whose worship you are trying to overthrow.

Previous defenders were inadequate

4.1 When these two of whom I have spoken had set forth their wicked works in my presence (and to my grief), I was stimulated to undertake this task, of exposing their attack upon justice with all the intelligence I could, both by my presumption of their impiety and by my awareness of the truth, and also, as I believe, by God. My aim in writing was not to put down people who could be eliminated in a few words but to wipe out in one single attack all those people everywhere who are attacking justice or who have done so.

2 I have no doubt that plenty of others in plenty of places have constructed a record of their own injustice, not only in Greek but also in Latin. Since I could not respond to them all individually, I decided I had to argue my case in such a way that previous writers would be undone together with all their works, and future writers would lose all opportunity of writing or of replying themselves. They have only to give ear, and I can ensure that all who think like that will either adopt what they previously condemned or (which is much the same) will eventually leave off their scorn and derision.

3 A version of this was argued by Tertullian in his book called

---

21 G indicates that L. uses or quotes Greek.
22 Sextus, *Pyrrh*. 1.33 (DK 59A97): 'Anaxagoras used to oppose to the view that snow is white the argument that snow is frozen water, water is black, and so snow is black.'

Apologia;[23] even so, because there is a difference between merely responding to attacks, when defence and denial is the sole form, and setting up something new,[24] which is what I am doing, when the full doctrinal content[25] has to be in place, I have not shrunk from the labour of developing in full material which Cyprian failed to develop in the speech where he tried to refute Demetrianus 'barking and barracking', as he put it, 'against the truth.' 4 He failed to exploit the material as he should have done, because Demetrianus should have been rebutted with arguments based in logic, and not with quotations from scripture, which he simply saw as silly fiction and lies. 5 Since he was arguing against a man ignorant of the truth, Cyprian should have kept his scriptural texts back a while; he should have given the fellow some primary training, as if he were a beginner, showing him the elements of illumination little by little to avoid blinding him with all the light at once. 6 Children cannot take food in all its strength when their digestive powers are still weak; they are nourished instead with milk, which is liquid and bland, until their powers develop and they can feed on stronger stuff:[26] so Demetrianus should first have been offered men's evidence since he could not yet take God's evidence, the evidence of philosophers and historians, that is; then he could be refuted as far as possible by authorities which he himself acknowledged. 7 Cyprian failed to do this because he was swept away by his own remarkable knowledge of divine literature; indeed, he was content with only those things which are the substance of our faith. Hence my own approach to the task, under the inspiration of God, and my approach also to preparation of a path for others to follow. 8 If men of learning and eloquence begin to muster at my encouragement, willing to engage their talents and powers of utterance on this battlefield of truth, then beyond all doubt false religions will swiftly vanish and all philosophy will go down, provided only that all are convinced that this is as much the only true wisdom as it is the only religion. But I have strayed further from my path than I intended.

Justice under Saturn expelled by Jupiter

5.1 Now for the discussion of justice which I proposed.[27] Justice is itself either the supreme virtue or the source of virtue,[28] and I mean the virtue sought not

23 L. returns to the subject of the deficiencies of preceding apologists.
24 L.'s Latin picks up the title of his work: *instituere*, to set up.
25 *Doctrinae totius substantiam*: a kind of *Summa Theologiae*.
26 Cf. I Cor. 3:2; Hebr. 5:12.
27 The matter for discussion (*disputatio*) is the presence or absence of justice in the world.
28 Cf. Cic. *Off.* 3.2; elsewhere in L., 14.7 below; 3.22.5.

BOOK 5: JUSTICE

only by the philosophers but also by the poets who preceded them, who had a name for wisdom long before the word philosophy was born. 2 The poets clearly understood that justice was remote from human activities, and they created a story that it had fled the earth and migrated to heaven because it was offended at people's wickedness. In order to explain what it is to live in justice, they go back for examples of it – poets' advice is usually given obliquely – to the age of Saturn, the so-called golden age, and they tell of the state in which human life existed when justice still dwelt on earth.

3 This is not to be treated as poetical fiction but as truth. When Saturn was king, and worship of gods had not yet been instituted and no nation was yet committed to a view of divine status, God was certainly being worshipped.[29] 4 Hence the lack of discord, and of enmity or war; 'Passion had not yet bared the swords of madness', as Germanicus says in his translation of Aratus [112–13], 'nor was discord known to kinsmen', nor even between different families; there simply were no swords to be bared at all. 5 In a context where justice was thriving, who would think of protecting himself when no one lay in wait for him, and who would think of another's ruin when no one coveted anything? 'They preferred to live content with slender means', as Cicero says in his translation [*Arat.* 21]; that is a particular feature of our religion. 'It was not even right to mark the land or portion it with boundaries: all need was met in common' [Verg. *G.* 1.126–27]: 6 God, after all, had given the land for all to share, so that life should be lived in common, not so that a ravenous, raging greed should claim everything for itself; what was produced for all should not be denied to any. 7 We are not to take these poet's words to mean that there was no private property at all in those days;[30] they are rather a poetical image of people being so generous that they did not fence off fruits of the earth as their own, nor did they stow them away and sit on them; instead, they laboured themselves and also allowed the poor a share of the harvest. 'Streams of milk were flowing now, and streams of nectar too' [Ovid, *Met.* 1.111], 8 and no wonder when the storerooms of the just were open in goodwill to all, and the flow of God's bounty was not diverted by greed, causing hunger and thirst among the people, but all were equally well off because abundant and generous giving was done by those with to those without.

9 Once Saturn had been driven out by his son, however, and had landed

---

29 It was a feature of L.'s Golden Age that God alone was worshipped. The end of his worship, and the introduction of pagan deities, thus spelt the end of the Golden Age. Cf. 6.2 below.

30 For L. on private property, see pp. 38–40.

up in Latium 'fleeing the weapons of Jupiter and in exile, his kingdom stolen' [Verg. *A.* 8.320], and the people left off worshipping God, whether for fear of the new king or from a natural depravity, and began to treat the king as God, and the king himself, a virtual parricide, was a model for the abuse of piety to everyone else, then 'swiftly the lady of justice left the earth' [Germ. *Arat.* 137], but she did not, as Cicero says [*Arat.* 23], 'settle in Jupiter's kingdom in a region of the sky.' 10 How could she settle or abide in the kingdom of someone who had driven his own father out of it, waging war against him and harrying him in his exile all over the earth? 'He put the evil poison in black snakes, and bid the wolves go hunt' [Verg. *G.* 1.129–30]; that is, Jupiter put envy, hatred and cheating into human beings so that they should be as venomous as snakes and as rapacious as wolves. 11 That is exactly the performance of those who persecute the just, the people loyal to God, and give licence to judges to treat the innocent with savagery. 12 Perhaps Jupiter did that sort of thing to drive out justice and abolish it, and that is why he is recorded to have sent snakes mad and to have sharpened wolves. 'Then came the savageness of war, and love of owning' [Verg. *A.* 8.327] – deservedly. 13 For once the worship of God was gone, 'knowledge of good and evil' [Gen. 2:17] was lost as well. The communality of life dropped away, and the social contract was undone. 14 Then people began to fight with each other, and to plot, and to seek their self-esteem in human blood.

Jupiter instals the apparatus of injustice

6.1 The source of all these evils is greed,[31] and greed presumably erupted out of contempt for the true superior power. Not merely did people of any prosperity fail to share with others, but they also seized the property of others, diverting everything to private gain, and what had previously been worked even by individuals for the benefit of everyone was now piled up in the houses of a few.

2 To reduce the rest to servitude, they began first to withdraw the necessities of life, gathering them in and keeping them firmly locked up, so that the bounty of heaven became their bounty, not from any humanitarian impulse – they felt none – but to rake in the means of avarice and greed for themselves. 3 In the name of justice they authorised for their own purposes

---

31 *Cupiditas* and the closely allied *auaritia* (cf. 5.8 above) are regularly attacked by pagan and Christian authors alike. See Cic. *Tusc.* 3.24; 4.11; Sen. *Ep.* 90.3, 36; I Tim. 6:10; Aug. *civ.* 19.1; etc.

laws of great unfairness and injustice, by which they could protect their greedy plunderings from mob violence. Their advantage thus came from sheer position as much as it did from their muscle, money and malice, 4 and since there was no trace at all in them of justice, whose due expression is fairness, kindness and pity,[32] the inequality they now rejoiced in swelled their sense of superiority; they raised themselves above the rest with trains of henchmen, weaponry and special dress. 5 Hence their invention of office for themselves, and purple and maces: they could use the threat of sword and axe to lord it over a cowed and petrified people with all the authority of a tyrant.[33]

6 That was the state of human life under king Jupiter: when he had conquered his father in war and put him to flight, it was no kingship he then exercised but an impious tyranny, of violence and armies; the golden age of justice he removed, forcing people into evil and impiety precisely by turning them away from truth and diverting them from worshipping God to worshipping him, such was the terror produced by his extraordinary power. 7 Who would not be scared of a man girt about with weapons, or ringed with the unprecedented gleam of iron swords? What stranger would be spared by a man who had not spared his own father? Who could alarm a man who had conquered the sturdy race of Titans in war, a people of outstanding strength, and then murdered them out of existence? 8 Can we be surprised if a whole people under pressure of exceptional panic gave way to adulation of a single individual? All their veneration and highest regard went to him. 9 And since imitation of a king's misbehaviour passes for a species of obedience, they all abandoned their piety, in case by living so they might seem to disapprove of their king's badness. 10 The constant imitation thus corrupted them; they left off what God sanctioned, and little by little a habit of evil living became the custom. Nothing now survived of the previous generation's piety and excellence: justice had been driven away, and taking truth with her she left the human race to error, ignorance and blindness.

11 The poets had thus got it wrong in saying justice had fled to the kingdom of Jupiter. If justice was on earth in the age they call golden, then quite simply it was driven out by Jupiter: he ended the golden age. 12 But ending the golden age and driving out justice has to be seen, as I said, as the abandonment of worship of God, which is the only cause of humans cherishing

---

32 An early (and incomplete) description of justice; piety is soon added (6.10 and 7.2 etc.).

33 Institutions and symbols of magisterial authority in Rome are here provocatively associated with the power of a king or slave owner (here *dominus*; *tyrannus* and *rex* are sometimes also used).

one another and of knowing the bond of brotherhood that binds them: since God is 'father equally to all' [Lucr. 2.992], so people are to share with those denied it the bounty of the God and father whom they all share, harming none, oppressing none, shutting their doors to no caller and their ears to no entreaty, but being 'generous, bountiful, liberal: which is the glory of a king', as Cicero thought [*Deiot.* 26]. 13 That is what justice really means; that is the golden age. But it went wrong at the outset of Jupiter's reign, and when he and all his family were deified and worship of many gods ensued, it was soon all gone.

Justice returns for the few, and evil remains to test them

7.1 God is like a most indulgent parent, however: when the latter days were approaching,[34] he sent a messenger to restore that time long gone and to bring back justice from exile, so that mankind should be wracked no more by its huge and persistent errors. 2 Back came the golden age in its beauty, and justice – which is nothing other than pious and worshipful attention to the one and only God – was restored to earth, though few were given it. 3 If that is what justice is, however, some may perhaps be puzzled why it was not granted to the whole human race and why people were not all united in accepting it. That is matter for a long debate: when God put justice back on earth, why was difference kept? I have given an explanation elsewhere, and the explanation will continue to be given wherever good occasion arises.[35] 4 For the moment, a very brief exposition will suffice: virtue either cannot be seen without the contrast of vice or is not perfected without the test of adversity.

5 That is the gap that God wanted to have between good and bad, so that we may know the quality of good from bad and likewise of bad from good: the nature of the one cannot be understood if the other is not there too. When about to restore justice, God did not exclude evil, in order that a reason for virtue could be constructed. 6 How could endurance[36] sustain its name and meaning if there were nothing we were forced to endure? How could a faithful devotion to God win praise unless there were someone with a purpose of turning us away from God? He deliberately let the unjust have the advantage of power so that they could try to force us to evil, and he let them

---

34 L.'s chronology of the end of the world is set out in 7.14.11.

35 See 2.17.1; 3.29.13–16; with 22.1–10 below and 6.15, 20.

36 *Patientia*, in time of persecution the defining Christian virtue. See 13.11ff., 22.2–3; 6.18.19, 30; and pp. 28–29.

have the advantage of numbers so that virtue should be prized for its rarity.

This is precisely what Quintilian showed so well and briefly in his *Covered Head*.[37] 7 'What sort of virtue would innocence be', he says, 'unless its rarity gave it value? But because things are naturally so organised that hatred, greed and anger drive men blindly to what they covet, it seems superhuman to be free of fault. On the other hand, if nature had given everybody similar impulses, piety would mean nothing.' 8 The truth of this is shown by the very inevitability of the logic. If virtue is a sturdy resistance to vice and evil, then it is obvious that without some vice and evil there is no virtue. God preserved its contrary for it to wrestle with to give it the chance of achieving perfection: 9 it arrives at stability when battered by the blows of evil, and the frequency of the assaults is the measure of its firmness and solidity. 10 This is no doubt the reason why, despite the despatch of justice to earth, the existence of a golden age cannot be claimed: God sustained evil in order to sustain difference, which is the only context for the sacred mystery of divine worship.

Justice cannot reign in the presence of false religion

8.1 People who think that no just man exists have justice in front of their eyes but will not see it. Why is it that in their poetry and in all their prose they depict it by lamenting its absence, even though it would be very easy for people to be good if they wished? 2 Why picture a justice for yourselves which is impossible? Why hope for it to fall from heaven, like something statue-shaped? Look: it's well within your sights! Adopt it if you can, and house it in your hearts; do not think it difficult, or alien to the times. 3 Be fair and be good, and the justice you seek will attend you of its own accord. Drop all evil thoughts from your hearts, and the golden age will return to you at once; but you cannot have it back unless you start to worship the true God.

4 You people want justice on earth in the middle of worship of gods, which is utterly impossible. It was utterly impossible even in the circumstances you think it was possible in; before the birth of those gods you worship with such impiety, worship of one God existed on earth necessarily. I mean of course the God who curses wickedness and demands goodness, whose temple is not stone and mud, but man himself who bears the form of God, and that temple is not furnished with the evanescent gifts of gold and jewelry but with the eternal endowment of the virtues. 5 Use your surviving intelligence, then, and understand that people are bad and unjust because

37 [Quint.] *decl.* fr. (Ritter pref. 111n).

they worship gods, and evil grows daily more heavy on human affairs because God, creator and controller of this world, has been neglected and religions of impiety have been adopted contrary to what is right, and lastly because you do not even allow worship of God, or only to a few.

6 If one God were worshipped, there would be no discord and no war; people would know that they were children of the one God and so were bound together by a holy, inviolable chain of divine kinship; there would be no secret plots, since they would know what sort of penalties God had ready for those who kill the soul: he perceives their covert wickedness, and even their very thinking; there would be no treachery and theft if they had learnt from God's advice and were 'content with what they had, however small' [Cic. *Off.* 1.70], so that things solid and permanent had preference over things fragile and fleeting; 7 there would be no adultery or other wrongful intercourse, and no prostitution of women, if everybody knew that God condemns all lustful appetite beyond procreation; no need would force a woman to profane her honour and seek a loathsome living, since men would contain their lust and people of means would contribute to those without as in religion duly bound. 8 All these evils, as I have said, would thus not exist on earth if everyone took an oath in the name of God's law, if all people did what only our people do.

How blessed and how golden the state of humanity would be if all the world were civilised, pious, peaceful, innocent, self-controlled, fair and faithful! 9 There would be no need for so many different laws for the government of mankind, because the one law of God would be enough for the accomplishment of innocence, nor would there be need for prisons and warders' swords, nor for the threat of punishment, since the wholesomeness of heavenly commandment[38] would be working in human hearts, forming them freely to the practice of justice.

10 As it is, people are bad from ignorance of what is right and good. That is what Cicero saw. In discussion of the laws he says[39] 'Just as the world is of one and the same nature, and coheres in and depends on all its parts in their mutual congruence, so all mankind is naturally compact of itself but in discord by depravity; people do not see that they share one blood and they all come under one and the same protective power; if that were grasped, they would very soon be living the life of the gods'. 11 All the ills, therefore, with

---

38 Divine laws in L. are in competition with secular laws, which are also described as *salubres*, health-giving, as in *Not. Dig.* 12.1 (ed. Seeck p. 34).

39 Cic. *Leg.* fr.2 (Ziegler, *leg.*).

which the human race exhausts itself in every generation are brought on by the injustice and impiety of worshipping gods. Piety simply could not be sustained by people who, like prodigal and rebellious children, had denied God's common fatherhood of them all.

The just are not recognised as such, but are persecuted

9.1 Sometimes, however, people feel their wickedness; they praise the way things were in times past, and conclude in the light of their own behaviour and worth that justice has gone. And though justice is there before their eyes, they not only fail to adopt and acknowledge it but even hate and persecute it energetically, striving to drive it out. 2 Let us imagine for a moment that the justice we pursue is not justice: what will be their reception of the justice they think true if it ever arrives, when they maim and murder the very people whom they themselves admit to be models of it because of their good works and their deeds of justice? If they killed only the wicked, they might deserve not to have justice come among them: bloodshed was the only reason for justice abandoning the earth in the first place. 3 But since they kill the pious and treat supporters of justice as enemies, indeed, as even worse than enemies, the neglect of them by justice is all the more deserved. Even though they go for the lives, fortunes and children of the pious with fire and sword, nevertheless, losers do get spared, and mercy has a place in war; alternatively, if savagery is the rule, the victims suffer merely death, or merely enslavement. 4 Yet what is done to these people so ignorant of evildoing is beyond description, and none are treated as more dangerous than those who are the most innocent of all. It is outrageous that men so wicked talk of justice when they outdo wild beasts in their ferocity, and lay waste God's peaceful flock 'like wolves hunting in a dark cloud, driven blindly by a wicked belly rage'.[40] 5 But in the case of these men, it is no belly rage but heart rage that maddened them: they don't go plundering 'in a dark cloud' but in broad daylight, and no conscience about their crimes ever restrains them from violating the pious and holy name of justice in language which drips with the blood of the innocent like animals' jaws.

6 What can we best claim as cause for this huge, persistent hatred? Is it the case that 'truth gives birth to hatred', as the poet says,[41] filled with some divine inspiration, or do they blush to be so evil in the presence of the just

---

40 Verg. *A.* 2.355–57.
41 Ter. *An.* 68.

and good, or is it both at once? Truth is often hated precisely because the sinner wants ample space for his sinning, reckoning he cannot have a comfortable enjoyment of his misdeeds unless they have everyone's approval. 7 Hence their great efforts to be rid of those they see as witnesses to their wickedness: they want such people out; they think of them as enemies as if their own lives were being exposed; 8 why should anyone so unseasonably good exist, to show up the world of corruption to reproach by the goodness of their own lives? Why shouldn't everyone be equally bad, greedy, immoral, adulterous, perjured, lustful and deceitful? Why not be rid of people whose presence shames the evil doer? They don't browbeat the sinner verbally, for they never say a word, but they do beat and belabour him by their utterly different lifestyle: any dissent is plainly disapproval.

9 What is done to attack men is really no great surprise, since even people 'established in hope'[42] and well aware of God have risen against God himself for the same reason, and the just are pursued with the same inevitability that destroyed the creator of justice himself. 10 So the harassment and torment goes on, and the forms of torture are refined; they think that killing those they hate is no good unless their cruelty also toys with their victims. 11 As for those who, for fear of pain or death or out of their own perfidy, forswear the sacred mystery of heaven and consent to ruinous sacrifices, they praise them and heap them with honours, to lure the rest on by their example; 12 as for those who prize their faith highly and do not deny their worship of God, they lay into them with all of a butcher's energy, as if they were thirsty for blood, and call them desperate men for having so little care for their bodies, as if anything could be more desperate than twisting and tearing apart a person you knew to be innocent. 13 That is the extent to which persecutors have no shame at all at their complete lack of humanity: they fling at the just the abuse that perfectly fits themselves, 14 calling them impious, as if they themselves were pious and shrank from human blood; but if they were to consider their own actions beside those of the people they condemn as impious, they would quickly see what liars they are, and how much more worthy themselves of all those things they say and do to attack the good.

15 It is always men of theirs, not of ours, who beset the highways in arms, who play pirate on the seas, or, if they cannot pillage openly, brew poisons in secret; who kill a wife to have the dowry, or a husband to wed the adulterer; who either strangle their own children or, if they are too pious for

---

42 Ps. 4:8 (Ps. 4:10 in the Vulgate).

BOOK 5: JUSTICE

that, expose them;[43] 16 who fail to contain an incestuous lust for a daughter or sister or mother, or a priestess; who conspire against country and fellow-citizens; who even have no fear of the parricide's sack; who commit sacrilege and rob the temples of the gods they worship, and who (to mention items that are trifling and commonplace) grab at legacies, plant false wills, remove or shut out rightful heirs, trade their own bodies for sex; 17 who forget what they were born for and vie with women for the lower berth, and pollute and profane the holiest part of their own body against every sanction; who slice off their genitals with swords, and all (which is worse) to be high priests of a cult;[44] who have no respect even for their own lives but sell their own souls to be wiped out in public;[45] who sit on the bench and either condemn the guiltless for a bribe or dismiss the guilty scot-free;[46] who aim at heaven itself with their magic spells, as if the earth could not contain their evil. 18 These, I repeat, and worse than these are the crimes committed by the worshippers of gods.

Amid all this great welter of crime, what space is there for justice? And I offered only a few examples out of many, to make my point merely, not to prove it. 19 Anyone who wants to know the full tale should pick up the works of Seneca, who was a very accurate depictor, as well as a relentless hound, of public misbehaviour. 20 Lucilius has also described that dark sort of life neatly and briefly in these verses: 'As it is, from dawn to dusk, workday or holy day, all the people and senators all mill around in the forum, never leaving it, all of them devoted to one and the same passion: the art, that is, of swapping insults as cannily as they can, sparring sly, flattering competitively, aping the good man, laying traps, as if all were against all.'[47] 21 None of this can serve as objection against our people: our whole religion is to live without stain of wrongdoing.

22 Since they can see that they and their sort behave as we have said while our people practise only what is fair and good,[48] they could perceive

---

43 Cf. 6.20.18–25 with note *ad loc.*

44 These are the Galli, priests of the Great Mother. See 1.17.7n.

45 L. has in mind gladiators; cf. *Epit.* 58.4, where they are mentioned explicitly.

46 L. is uncomplimentary towards judges; see also 6.20.16, on the bringing of a capital charge as an act of attempted murder.

47 Lucil. fr.1145–51 (Warmington) = H 41 (Charpin) = 1228–34 (Marx).

48 L.'s *aequum et bonum* evokes the introduction of Ulpian's *Institutes* cited in *Digest* 1.1.1.1: '*ius est ars boni et aequi.. boni et aequi notitiam profitemur*' (Justice is the art of goodness and fairness.. we profess knowledge of goodness and fairness). For L., Christianity, embodying divine law, represents a new, more perfect justice. For Ulpian see note on 11.19 below.

from this, if they had any sense, that those who do good are the pious and they themselves are the impious, for doing wrong. 23 It is impossible that those who do no wrong in any action of their lives should go wrong in its most important act – in religion, that is, which is chief of all things. If impiety were adopted in what is the most important thing, it would spread through everything else without exception. 24 It is correspondingly impossible that people who go wrong in all the rest of their lives are not wrong in religion as well, for in sustaining its standard in the most important thing, piety would also preserve its pattern of conduct in everything else. Thus it comes about that the nature of the whole itself can be learnt from the state of affairs in existence on each side.

Pagan piety exposed

10.1 It is worth while getting to know their sort of piety, so that from what they do in kindness and piety we can understand the nature of what they do against the rules of piety.[49] 2 To avoid the impression that I'm going in for crude abuse, let me adopt a person from poetry to be the perfect example of piety. 3 What lessons in justice does that king in Vergil present? 'Never was a man more just, more pious, or more adept in warlike arts' [*A.* 1.544–40]. 'Manacled captives there were, consigned to be gifts to the dead, victims whose blood would be sprinkled on the altar flames' [11.81–82]. 4 What can be kinder than that pious deed, sacrificing human victims to the the dead and feeding fire with human blood as if it were oil? 5 But perhaps that was not the hero's fault but the poet's: he besmirched a hero 'of spectacular piety' [1.10] with that spectacular crime. So where is the piety, mister poet, which you praise so very often? Behold the 'pious Aeneas': 'Now he captured alive four warrior sons of Sulmo and four whom Ufens had reared, designing to sacrifice them to the ghost of Pallas and to sprinkle his funeral pyre with the blood of these captive youths' [10.517–20]. 6 So why did he say, at the very same moment that he was despatching them in chains to be sacrificed, 'Believe me, I'd like to have made peace with the living' [11.111], when he was ordering living people, whom he had in his power, to be killed like cattle? 7 But, as I said, it wasn't Aeneas' fault: he probably hadn't learnt his ABC; it was your fault. You had an education, and yet you did not know

---

49 After claiming *aequitas* for Christianity, L. does the same for *pietas*, the other primary element in justice as he defines it. These two virtues feature most commonly among the virtues of emperors on denarii between 69 and 235.

what piety was; you believed that what he did, so wickedly and so horribly, was an act of piety. People call him pious for one reason only, I take it, that he loved his father. 8 What about 'the good Aeneas' murdering people who 'were making prayers that deserved his regard' [11.106]? When he was begged in his own father's name, and by his 'hopes of upspringing Iulus' [7.523], he showed no mercy at all, 'inflamed with wrath and madness' [12.946]. 9 Could anyone think he had a particle of virtue in him, when he blazed in frenzy like stubble, unable to bridle his wrath, forgetting the spirit of his father, in whose name he was entreated? Not pious, then, no way: he killed not only those who yielded without resistance but even those who prayed to him.

10 At this point someone will say, What then is piety? Where is it? What is it like? It exists where people know nothing of wars, live in concord with all, are friendly even to enemies, love all men like brothers, know how to curb their anger and how to soothe all strong emotions with a tranquillising control.[50] 11 What then must be the darkness, the cloud of gloom and error, which blocks the hearts of those who become perfectly impious exactly when they think they are perfectly pious? The more devotedly they serve these earthly images of theirs, the more criminally they stand out against the name of true divinity. 12 In reward for their impiety they are often tormented by nastier troubles, and because they don't know the reason for it, they ascribe all the blame to luck, and then Epicurus' philosophy comes in: he thought the gods beyond reach, untouched by gratitude and unmoved by anger, because they behold those who scorn them often prosperous and those who worship them often in misery. 13 This occurs because, religious as these people are and good by nature, they are not thought to deserve the sort of thing that often happens to them. They console themselves, however, by blaming Lady Luck, not realising that if she existed she would never hurt her flock. 14 Piety of that sort earns its punishment rightly: offended by the wickedness of people whose worship is all wrong, the godhead lands them a painful surprise. They may be living a life of holiness in utter faith and innocence, but because they worship gods, and the true God hates that profane and impious ritual, they remain strangers to justice and to the name of true piety.

15 It is not difficult to explain why worshippers of gods cannot be good and just. When they worship gods of blood like Mars and Bellona, how will

---

50 A strong statement against war and all public and private violence, which are found to be incompatible with the worship of God (which is piety).

they keep from blood themselves? How will they be merciful to their parents, given Jupiter who drove out his father, or to their own children, given Saturn? How will they maintain their modesty when they worship a goddess who is naked and adulterous, the prostitute of Olympus? 16 How will they keep from robbing and cheating when they know the thefts of Mercury, who proves that deceit is not a matter of fraud but of cleverness? How will they curb their sex-drive when they venerate Jupiter, Hercules, Bacchus, Apollo and all those others whose rapes and adulteries against men and women are not just known to scholars but are acted out in theatres and put into songs, so that everybody knows them all the better? 17 How can they possibly be just people amid all this? Even if they were born good, they would be brought up to injustice, precisely by those gods. To please the god you worship you need what you know makes him happy and joyful. 18 Thus it is that a god shapes the life of his worshippers after the nature of his own spirit; the most devoted worship that exists is imitation.

Pagans, following the example of their gods, are vicious

11.1 These people who so match the behaviour of their gods find justice to be a harsh and bitter thing: hence they practise against the just, with great violence, that same impiety of theirs that they exercise on everything else. The prophets were quite right to call them animals.

2 Cicero put it well: 'If there is no one', he says, 'who would not rather die than be turned into some sort of animal, even though he kept his human mind, imagine the misery of being in human form with a mind gone wild. In my view, that would be as much more awful as mind is better than body.'[51] 3 Animal form is thus despised by people of more than animal savagery themselves, who are very glad to be born human when there is nothing human about them except outward form and features. 4 What Caucasus, what India, what Hyrcania ever reared animals as ghastly and as bloody? Since the fury of wild animals works only to meet the needs of the belly and quietens down as soon as hunger is satisfied, 5 the true beast is the one at whose single command 'black blood is shed on every side; bitter grief and panic are everywhere, and every form of death.'[52] 6 A fit description of this great beast's savagery is impossible; though its lair is in one place, yet the

---

51 This text is regularly assigned to Cic. *Rep.* 4.1.1. So Ziegler, *rep.* p. 107. Monat (1973) *ad loc.* is sceptical. For a similar idea, see Cic. *Off.* 3.82; *Rep.* 2.48; L. *Op. Dei* 1.11–13.
52 Verg. *A.* 11.646 and 2.368.

ferocity of its ferrous teeth is at work throughout the world, not just pulling humans limb from limb, but grinding up their very bones and raving at their ashes so that no place of burial even exists – as if the aim of those who confess God were to have lots of visits to their own tombs, rather than go to God themselves! 7 What wildness is it, what madness and insanity, that has denied light to the living and earth to the dead? Therefore I say, there is no greater misery than that of people found or forced necessarily to be agents of another's madness, stooges obeying an impious command. 8 There was no honour in it, no promotion of worth; it was man's condemnation to butchery and God's to eternal punishment. 9 What individuals have done all over the world is beyond telling: how many volumes will it take to contain such an infinite variety of cruelty? Given the opportunity, each man's ferocity matched his nature. 10 Some exceeded orders recklessly, out of excessive fright; others did so because of their own peculiar hatred of the just; some acted from a natural brutality of intent, and some to find favour and so to launch themselves on a career to higher things; some plunged headlong into massacre, like one individual in Phrygia, who burnt a whole community together with their meeting-place.[53]

11 The more cruel he was, however, the more merciful he turns out to be. The worst sort is a man who lulls you with a bogus appearance of mercy; the butcher who decides to kill no one is the really harsh and cruel man. 12 It is impossible to say how numerous and harsh the various tortures were that judges of this sort invented to achieve what they intended. 13 But they don't act like this simply to be able to boast that they put no innocent person to death (I've heard some, boasting that in this respect their administration had been bloodless); they act also in jealousy: either they themselves must not be the losers, or Christians must not justify their proud claim to virtue. 14 All they have in mind in thinking up the different torments is winning; they know there's a contest on and a fight. 15 I have seen a governor in Bithynia myself quite transported with joy, as if he had conquered some tribe of barbarians, because one individual who had resisted with great virtue for two years finally appeared to give way.[54] 16 Hence their efforts to win, and the extraordinary tortures they inflict, stopping short of nothing except the death of their victims – as if death were the only way to bliss, and even torture could not bring sufferers a glory in their virtue as great as the torture was hideous. 17 In their resolute stupidity they give instructions for their

---

53 See Euseb. *Hist. Eccl.* 8.11.1.
54 This detail points to the composition of this book c. 305.

victims to be carefully tended, so that their limbs are restored for further torture and fresh blood is there for punishment. What treatment can be as pious, as kind and humane as that? They could not have tended their own loved ones with such care.

18 And that is what gods teach: those are the works they train their worshippers for, and that is the sacrifice desired. Why, even the most criminal of murderers have constructed impious laws against the pious: legislation can be read which is sacrilegious, and lawyers' debates which are unjust. 19 Domitius[55] in book 7 of his *Duty of a Governor* gathered some outrageous imperial rescripts in order to show what penalties it was proper to apply to those who declared their worship of God.

But truth with suffering is always preferable to prosperous evil

12.1 What are you to do with people who call it law when elderly tyrants turn butcher and go rabid against the innocent? They are teachers of injustice and cruelty, and yet they want to seem just and wise[56] when they are blind and stupid, and ignorant of facts and truth. 2 Is justice something you hate so much, you poor lunatics, that you set it on a par with the greatest of crimes? Is innocence so dead among you that you think it undeserving of even a simple death, and that confessing to no crime and presenting a soul clean of all contagion is to be counted the crime above all crimes?

3 Since this is a mutual discussion with you worshippers of gods, permit us to do you a service. It is our law, our task and our religious duty to do so. If you think us wise, copy us; if foolish, reject us, or even mock us if you will: our folly is to our advantage. 4 Why torture us? Why harass us? We are not jealous of your wisdom: we prefer this folly of ours, we embrace it, we think it does us good to love you and to offer you all we have, yes, you, the very people who hate us.

5 There is a passage in Cicero [*Rep.* 3.27] not too far from the truth, in the disputation of Furius against justice.[57] 'I have a question', he says: 'if there were two men, of whom one was an excellent man, very fair, utterly

---

55 Domitius Ulpianus from Tyre, jurisconsult, was a leading civil servant under the Severan dynasty, holding the pretorian prefecture, but not for long (222–23) before he was assassinated. His juristic works make up about one sixth of the *Digest* of Justinian. The treatise named in the text is largely lost.

56 *Prudentes*, i.e., jurisconsults, to whom allusion is made in 1.1.12.

57 D. Furius Philus (cos. 140 BC) is given the task of arguing the case for injustice in Cicero's *Republic*. See 14.3ff. below.

just, especially loyal, and the other a man noted for his outrageous wickedness, and if their community were in such confusion that it thought the good man to be a wicked and nefarious criminal, while it reckoned that the actual villain was a man of the utmost probity and trustworthiness, and if in accordance with this conclusion of all citizens the good man were harassed and seized, his hands cut off, his eyes put out, he himself condemned, imprisoned, branded, cast out, impoverished, 6 and everyone concluded that he was quite rightly in such depths of suffering, whereas the wicked fellow were praised and flattered, loved by all, and all positions of authority civil and military together with all financial resources were bestowed on him by everyone, and in conclusion he were judged to be the best of men and thoroughly worth all his fortune: who so mad then as to doubt which one he would rather be?' 7 When he posed his model, Furius must have guessed what evils would come upon us, and how, because of justice. This is what our people suffer, all of it due to the wickedness of people confused. 8 Here is our country, or rather, the whole wide world, in such a state of confusion that it persecutes good and just men, and does so as if they were evil and impious, torturing, condemning and killing them. 9 When Furius says that no one is so mad as to hesitate which he'd rather be, he at least, *qua* speaker against justice, has realised that a wise man would rather be bad and well esteemed than good and poorly thought of. 10 We, however, must put away this madness of preferring false to true. The quality of our good is not to be measured by people all astray, but by our own consciences and the judgment of God, and no happy moment should ever lure us away from preferring real goodness with all ill over a false goodness with all prosperity. 11 'Let kings secure their kingdoms and wealthy men their wealth', as Plautus says [*Cur.* 178]; and let prudent men secure their prudence: let them leave us our folly, which is plainly wisdom anyway, to judge by how they envy us for it.[58] 12 No one would envy a fool unless he were an absolute fool himself. They, however, are not so foolish as to envy fools: by their precise and energetic persecution of them they acknowledge they are not fools. 13 Why would they act so savagely unless they are scared of being left behind with their own decaying gods as justice grows stronger day by day? If the worshippers of gods are wise and we are foolish, why should they worry that the wise will be duped by fools?

---

58 The distinction between *prudentia* and *sapientia*, prudence and wisdom, is important: *prudentia* as Furius uses it means good sense, or acting in one's own interest; only *sapientia* stands for wisdom.

Religion is boosted by persecution

13.1 Since our numbers are always being supplemented by ex-worshippers of gods, and the numbers never go down even in a time of persecution – people can sin, after all, and be made unclean by sacrifice, but they cannot be distracted from God, since truth has its own power to prevail – who can remain so mindless and so blind as not to see which side wisdom is on?

2 Worshippers of gods are made blind by malice and rage. The fools in their estimation are those who, having it in their power to avoid torture, nevertheless prefer to be tortured and to die; albeit they could perceive from that very fact that something which has the unanimous consent of so many thousands of people all over the world is not a piece of folly. 3 If women waver, from the weakness of their sex – from time to time our faith is maligned as a womanish superstition, fit for grannies – men at least have sense; if children and adolescents think in the short term because of their age, at least adults and the elderly have stable judgment; 4 if a single community loses its wits, all the countless others surely cannot be fools; if one whole province, or one whole nation, runs out of sense, all the others are bound to retain their understanding of right. 5 But now that God's law has been adopted from the rising of the sun to its setting, and now that every sex, every generation, every family and district serve God in perfect unanimity with the same endurance and the same disdain of death everywhere, persecutors should have realised that there is a logic in it which is being defended to the death not without good cause, and that there is a solid base to it which not only keeps the religion from breaking up despite the constant injustice it suffers, but is for ever expanding it and strengthening it.

6 Their malice is also exposed by the fact that they think they have utterly subverted the religion of God if they muck up God's people: yet God can still be satisfied, and none of his worshippers is so bad that they will not, given the chance, revert to satisfying him with even greater devotion. 7 Knowledge of having sinned and fear of being punished makes them more faithful; there is always much greater strength in a faith restored by penitence. 8 If it is their own belief that their gods are satisfied by gifts, sacrifice and incense when seen to be angry with them, whatever reason can they have for imagining that our God is so relentlessly implacable that having made libation to their gods, under compulsion and unwillingly, one cannot continue a Christian? Perhaps they think that people once so tainted will switch their determination and begin to do freely what they did before under torture. 9 Would anyone freely take on a duty which begins in injustice? Could anyone

see the scars on his body and not hate those gods all the more that are the cause of his bearing those everlasting marks of punishment scored in his flesh? 10 The fact is that, on God's terms of peace, all who fled him come back, and a new group comes over in addition, in amazement at our virtue.

11 When ordinary people see men being torn apart with different sorts of torture and yet maintaining their endurance unbowed while their tormentors grow weary, they come to the conclusion, quite rightly, that the resolute consensus of so many people dying is no empty thing, and that endurance itself could not survive so much agony without God. 12 Robbers, and other men of sturdy physique, cannot bear torture of that sort; they utter cries and lamentations, and give way to the pain: no spirit of endurance has been granted to them. Our people, however – and I will leave out our men – our women and children triumph over their tormentors without a sound; even fire cannot force a groan from them. 13 Romans can come and boast of their Mucius or their Regulus (Regulus gave himself up to the enemy to be killed because he was ashamed to live on in captivity, and Mucius, once captured by the enemy, saw he could not escape death and so thrust his hand into the fire, to satisfy his foe for the crime of murder he meant to commit, earning by the penalty a pardon he had not deserved): 14 look at our weaker sex, and look at our children in their weakness, enduring the torture of every limb and the torture of fire, not because they must – they could avoid it if they wished – but willingly, because they trust in God![59]

15 That is the true virtue, the virtue boasted of by vainglorious philosophers too, but in empty words, not fact, when they argue that nothing is so proper to the seriousness and self-consistency of a wise man than his capacity to be unmoved in his opinions and purposes by any threats, and that it is very important to be tortured to death in order not to betray a trust, not to decline a duty, not to do any unjust deed for fear of death or pain: 16 unless perhaps they see Horace as plainly mad when he says in his lyrics [*Carm.* 3.3.1–4] 'The just man who holds to his purpose is not swayed by commands from his fellows given in a wrongful passion, nor by a looming tyrant's countenance: his mind stays firm.' 17 No truer word can be said than

---

59 This passage, stressing the martyr's virtue of *patientia* and embodying a comparison with Roman heroes, draws on Min. Fel. 37.1–5. C. Mucius Scaevola set out to assassinate the Etruscan king Porsena, but mistook his target; taken before the king he won his freedom after boldly thrusting his sword-hand into the flames of a brazier (see Livy 2.12.1; V. Max. 3.3); M. Atilius Regulus, captured by the Carthaginians and sent to Rome on parole with their terms, recommended the Romans to refuse and returned to be tortured to death rather than break his word (see Cic. *Off.* 3.99; Hor. *Carm.* 3.5.13–56; Livy 18 epit.).

that, if it is applied to those who, to avoid swerving from faith and justice, resist no tortures or death, and are not deterred by demands of tyrants or governors' swords from defending with utter constancy that real, substantial freedom which every wise man must guard upon this earth. 18 Who has such a lofty presumption as to tell me not to lift my eyes to heaven or to force upon me the worship of what I won't worship, or the non-worship of what I will? 19 What would our prospects be if this too, something which ought to be done freely, is to be forced out of us at someone else's whim? But as long as we have the virtue to despise death and pain, nobody will achieve that, and if we maintain our purpose, why are we thought foolish for doing what philosophers acclaim? 20 Seneca was right when he attacked inconsistency. 'People think,' he says, 'that the height of virtue is great courage, and anyone who despises death they also treat as lunatic: which is a piece, quite simply, of utter perversity.'[60] 21 All these devotees of empty cults make their objection with the same stupidity with which they fail to recognise the true God. The Erythrean Sibyl calls them[G] deaf and mindless,[61] since they neither hear God's message nor perceive it, but fear and worship clay which their own fingers have moulded.

Carneades undermined an empty justice; true justice is piety and fairness

14.1 Why the wise are thought foolish has a sound explanation (the misunderstanding is not without cause), and we must give it with care, so that these people can, if possible, at last acknowledge their mistake. 2 Justice has of its own nature a certain sort of foolishness, and I can confirm this from both divine and human evidence. But we shall probably get nowhere with them unless we use their own authorities to show them that no one can be just (being just is closely linked with true wisdom) unless he also appears to be foolish.

3 There was a philosopher of the Academic school called Carneades[62] (his force, eloquence and shrewdness in debate may be understood by anyone unaware of it from the writings of Cicero or Lucilius; it is in Lucilius that Neptune, debating a very tricky question, declares that it could not be sorted out, 'not unless Orcus sent back Carneades himself'[63]): this Carneades

---

60 Sen. F78, 194 (Vottero).
61 *Orac. Sib.* 8.397. L. quotes the Greek and then translates into Latin.
62 See on 3.30.6 above. For the incident see Macr. *Sat.* 1.5.
63 Lucil. fr.35 (Warmington) = 17 (Charpin) = 31 (Marx).

had been sent to Rome by the Athenians as their spokesman, and he discussed the topic of justice at length before an audience including Galba and Cato the Censor,[64] the best speakers of the day. 4 The next day, however, he overturned his argument with a contrary set of points, destroying the justice he had so commended the previous day: the seriousness of a philosopher was gone, whose views should be firm and steady, replaced by that rhetorical sort of exercise which was his usual practice, of speaking on either side, so that he could refute any view put by others.[65] 5 In Cicero the argument which overthrows justice is put by L. Furius; I imagine Cicero did it like that (he was writing on government after all) in order to set up the defence and celebration of what he thought indispensable to government. Carneades' intention, however, was to rebut Aristotle and Plato, the champions of justice; so he gathered all that was being said in its favour in his first speech so that he could overthrow it as he did later. 6 It was very easy to undermine a justice that had no roots; at the time there was no justice on earth, so that its nature and quality could not be identified by philosophers. 7 If only all those great men had had as much knowledge as they had eloquence and spirit, to supply a full defence of the supreme virtue, whose roots are in religion and whose essence is in fairness! But as they didn't know part one of the thing, so they couldn't even grasp part two.

8 I want to set out first, concisely and briefly, what justice is, so that people can see that the philosophers have had no awareness of it and in their ignorance could not have defended it. 9 Justice embraces all the virtues together, but there are two chief virtues which cannot be split off and separated from it, piety and fairness. Loyalty, self-control, uprightness, innocence, integrity and all other qualities of that sort can exist, whether naturally or thanks to one's upbringing, in people who do not know justice, just as such

---

64 Ser. Sulpicius Galba (cos. 144 BC), a younger contemporary of Cato, is best known for greed and cruelty at the expense of the Lusitanians; see App. *B.C.* 59–60. Cicero (*Brut.* 295) acknowledges his importance but airs doubts about his oratory. M. Porcius Cato (cos. 195, censor 184) was a highly influential figure in Roman politics in the first half of the 2nd century BC. He pressed consistently and determinedly for high moral standards in public life; in the last year of his life (149) he attempted unsuccessfully to have Galba condemned. A bitter opponent of Carthage, he was the prime mover in its eventual destruction (146). The whole of his *de Agricultura*, extensive fragments of his speeches, his historical work *Origines* and other writings survive.

65 L. overlooks the nature of Carneades' mission, which gave a serious point to his strategy. Athens had seized Oropus, a small town on its borders, and had been heavily penalised for it. Carneades evidently raised the question whether the Athenians should be judged by a different standard from the Romans in creating and expanding their empire. See Atkins (2000), 494.

qualities always have done; 10 the Romans of old, who habitually boasted of their justice, certainly boasted of those virtues, which can, as I said, come from justice and can also be distinguished from their source.[66]

11 The twin arteries of justice are piety and fairness, and all justice springs from these two. Its basic beginning is in that first source, piety, while all its intellectual energy is in the second source.

Piety is simply the knowing of God, as it is soundly defined by Trismegistus, as we observed elsewhere. 12 If, then, piety is to know God,[67] and the nub of getting to know God is to worship him, anyone without a cult of God simply does not know justice. How can he know it for itself when he does not know its source? 13 Plato said a great deal about a one and only god as the maker of the world, but he said nothing of his worship; he had dreamt his god: he did not know him. If he or anyone else had wanted to make a full defence of justice, he should first have cast out cults of gods, because they are contrary to piety. 14 That was what Socrates tried to do, and he got put in prison, so that it was clear even then what would happen to people who started to defend true justice and to serve the one God.

15 The second part of justice is fairness;[68] I mean not simply the fairness involved in good judgments, which is itself a laudable thing in a just man, but the fairness of levelling oneself with everyone else, what Cicero calls 'equality of status'. 16 God who created human beings and gave them the breath of life wanted all to be on a level, that is, to be equal, and he established the same conditions of life for everyone, creating all to be wise and pledging them all immortality; no one is cut off from God's celestial benevolence. 17 Just as he divides his unique light equally between all, makes springs flow, supplies food and grants the sweet refreshment of sleep to all, so too he bestows fairness and virtue on all. No one is a slave with him, and no one is a master, for if 'he is the same father to everyone' [Lucr. 2.992], so are we all his children with equal rights. 18 No one is poor in God's eyes except for lack of justice, and no one is rich without a full tally of the virtues; moreover, no one is illustrious except for goodness and innocence;[69] no one is most notable except for lavish works of charity; no one is most perfect

---

66 A concession to old Rome, except that boasting is not practising.

67 Cf. Cic. *N.D.* 2.153; NF *Corp. Herm.* 9.4.

68 The discussion of *aequitas* includes a striking criticism of social inequality, as practised by, among others, Greeks and Romans. See pp. 39–40.

69 *Innocentia*, rendered as innocence, means not doing harm; though in form the word is negative, L. gives it a strongly positive sense. Innocence is an unsatisfactory translation: readers are urged to remember its root meaning on all occasions.

BOOK 5: JUSTICE   311

except for having completed every degree of virtue.[70] 19 That is why neither Romans nor Greeks could command justice, because they kept people distinct in different grades from poor to rich, from weak to strong, from lay power up to the sublime power of kings. 20 Where people are not all equal, there is no fairness: the inequality excludes justice of itself. The whole force of justice lies in the fact that everyone who comes into this human estate on equal terms is made equal by it.

Virtue, not rank, counts with God

15.1 If these two sources of justice suffer any alteration, all goodness and truth are gone and justice itself goes back to heaven. Philosophers failed to find the true good because they did not know where justice sprang from or what it did. It has been revealed to our people alone.

2 Someone will say, 'Are there not some amongst you who are poor, and some rich, some slaves and some masters? Is there no distinction between individuals?' No, none; the only reason why we share the name of brother among us is our belief that we are equal. 3 Since we measure all things human spiritually and not physically, even though our physical conditions differ, yet we have no slaves: we both name them and treat them as brothers in spirit and fellow slaves in worship. 4 Riches also cause no distinctions except for their power to make people notable for good works; people are not rich by possession of wealth but by using it for acts of justice, and those who seem poor are yet rich because they need nothing and want nothing. 5 Though we are therefore all equal in humility of spirit, free and slave, rich and poor, yet in God's eyes we are distinguishable for virtue: the more just we are, the higher we stand with him.

6 If it is justice to level oneself with people even lower – that was his great achievement, bringing himself equal to those below him – nevertheless, one who bears himself not just on a level with them but even lower will achieve in the judgment of God a much higher degree of worth. 7 Since everything in this secular world is short-lived and bound to decay, so people push themselves before others and fight for position, which is horrible, arrogant and far removed from wisdom: all those earthly achievements are quite the opposite of things in heaven. 8 Just as the wisdom of men in God's

---

70 For 'illustrious', 'most notable' and 'most perfect' L. uses the words *egregius, clarissimus* and *perfectissimus*, which were the standard terms for designating the status of, respectively, an equestrian, a senator and an equestrian functionary of a particular rank.

eyes is the height of folly, and folly, as I have explained, is the height of wisdom, so anyone walking tall and conspicuous on earth is a low and abject thing before God. 9 To say nothing of the good things here on earth, which earn a great regard but are opposed to real goodness and merely sap our spiritual energies, nobility, wealth and power are of little effect when God can bring even kings themselves lower than the lowest. God in counselling us therefore set this sentence in particular among his divine precepts: 'He who exalts himself shall be brought low, and he who abases himself shall be exalted' [Mt. 23:12]. 10 The healthy message of that is that anyone who makes himself level with others and behaves with humility will have precedence and note with God. 11 That verse in Euripides is very sound which says 'What here are thought ills are in heaven goods.'[71]

Carneades overthrew both civil and natural justice

16.1 I have explained why philosophers could neither find justice nor defend it; now I return to my original aim. 2 Because of the weakness of what the philosophers were offering, Carneades was bold enough to refute it because he realised it could be refuted. 3 In summary he argued as follows [*Rep.* 3.21]: people have sanctioned laws for themselves because laws are useful; these laws vary, of course, to suit different lifestyles, and they are often changed within any one group to suit a changed situation; there is no natural law. All human beings and all other living things go for what is useful for them as their nature guides them; accordingly, either there is no justice, or, if there is any, it is the height of folly, since anyone working for the benefit of others would do hurt to himself. 4 To prove his case he added that if all the people who did well out of empire, including the Romans themselves who controlled the whole world, were anxious to be just, that is, to give back other people's property, they would have to go back to wattle and daub and lie in want and squalor. 5 Then, leaving communal issues to one side, he proceeded to individual ones [3.27]: 'If a good man,' he said, 'had a runaway slave or an unsound, unhealthy house, and he alone knew of these faults and so published a bill of sale, will he admit that he is selling a runaway slave or an unhealthy house, or will he conceal it from the buyer? 6 If he admits it, he will be adjudged a good man for failing to deceive, but he will also be considered a fool, since he will either sell at a poor price or fail to sell at all;

---

71 Eur. fr. 1100 (Nauck); but its attribution to Euripides is doubtful. L. gives the verse in a Latin trimeter.

if he conceals the information, he will be wise for consulting his own interest, but he will also be a bad man for the deception. 7 Again, if he were to find someone who thought he had copper pyrites for sale when it was actually gold, or lead when it was silver, will he hold his tongue to buy it cheap, or speak, and pay full cost? It plainly looks stupid to prefer the expensive option.'[72] 8 Carneades' intention was to show thereby that one who is just and good is a fool, and one who is wise is bad. And yet it is possible, without disaster, for people to be content with poverty.

9 He then proceeded to more serious instances, where no one could be just without risking his life. 'It is of course justice,' he said [3.29–31], 'not to kill someone, and certainly not to hurt a stranger. 10 So what will a just man do if he happens to be shipwrecked and someone weaker has seized a plank? Won't he push him off the plank so that he can climb on himself and survive by staying on it, especially when there is no witness, in mid-ocean? If he is wise, he will; if he doesn't, he must perish himself. If, however, he prefers to die rather than lay hand upon the other, he is now a just man but also a fool, because he fails to spare his own life and spares another's instead. 11 So too, if his own side is routed and the enemy start a pursuit, and our just man finds some wounded man sitting on a horse, will he spare him, to be killed himself, or will he push him off so that he himself can escape the foe? If he pushes him off, he is wise but also bad; if he doesn't, he is just but also, necessarily, a fool.' 12 He thus divided justice into two categories, calling one civil and the other natural, and he overthrew both, because the civil one is wisdom but not justice, whereas the natural one is justice but not wisdom.

13 That is subtle stuff, obviously, with a lurking threat, and beyond Cicero's powers of refutation: when he has Laelius[73] speak in response to Furius on behalf of justice, he leaves it all unchallenged, passing it by as if it were a trap, so that it looks as if Laelius defended not the natural sort of justice, which had been accused of stupidity, but the civil sort, which Furius had admitted was wisdom but not just.

Carneades refuted: folly and wisdom redefined

17.1 As was relevant to the present discussion, I have shown how justice has the semblance of folly, so that it is clear there is reason for the confusion of people who think that those of our religion are fools in appearing to do the sort of thing that Carneades proposed.

72 For the examples see Cic. *Off.* 3.54 and 89.
73 C. Laelius nicknamed Sapiens, friend of Scipio Aemilianus, consul in 140.

2 I now feel that something greater is demanded of me, to show why God wished to wrap justice up to look like folly and to withdraw it from the sight of mankind. First, however, I must answer Furius' case, since Laelius' response was so inadequate. Laelius may very well have been wise, as people called him, but he was no sort of advocate for true justice at all, not grasping the basic source of it. 3 The relevant defence is much easier for us to make, since by the kindness of heaven justice is something familiar to us and very well known: we know it for real, and not merely as a name. 4 Plato and Aristotle were full of good intentions in their desire to defend justice, and they might have achieved something if their good endeavours, eloquence and quality of mind had been aided by knowledge of things divine. 5 Without it their efforts were vain and fell flat: they could not persuade anyone to live by their prescription because their doctrine had no foundation from above. 6 Our efforts are bound to be more reliable because our instructor is God. They drew a picture in words of an imagined justice, one not there to see, and they could not confirm what they presented with live examples. 7 Their listeners could always answer that life could not be lived in the way they recommended in their discussions; indeed, it was so impossible that no one had yet existed who followed that sort of life. 8 We can show the truth of what we say, however, not just in words but in examples drawn from reality. 9 Carneades did sense what the nature of justice is, except that he did not see deeply enough that it is not folly[74] – but I think I understand his mental process. He did not really think the just man was a fool, but though he knew he wasn't, and yet did not understand even so why he appeared to be, he wanted to prove that truth lurked in obscurity so that he could preserve that tenet of his doctrine summarily expressed as 'Nothing can be known.'

10 Let us see then whether justice can have any bond with folly. 'If a just man,' he says, 'fails to take a horse from a wounded man or a plank from a shipwrecked man in order to save his own life, he is a fool.' 11 First: I entirely deny the possibility of an event of that sort happening to a just man *qua* just, because the just man is the enemy of no man born and has absolutely no desire for what belongs to someone else. 12 Why would he go to sea,[75] or what would he want from other people's lands when his own sufficed? Why go to war and tangle himself in other people's lunacies when his heart was full of peace with everyone eternally? 13 A delight in overseas

---

74 Some text may be missing.
75 Cf. 6.4.20. L. may be aware of Tert. *idol.* 11; cf. *ibid.* 19, where military service is attacked, on which see 6.20.15–16. The evils of trade for enrichment, however, were a rhetorical topos and also feature in poetic discussions of the Golden Age.

trade or human blood will hardly mark out the man who doesn't know how to look for profit, is perfectly well fed, and thinks murder a sin not only for him to do but also to assist in and to watch. But I leave all that to one side, since it is possible a just man might be compelled, even against his will, to undergo the experience.

14 Do you think then, my dear Furius – or rather, my dear Carneades, since it's your speech entirely – that justice is so empty a thing, so unnecessary and so contemptible in God's eyes, that it is powerless and has nothing in it capable of working to its own protection? 15 Of course: knowledge of the force of justice is impossible for people who relate everything to this temporary life because they don't know the mystery of man. 16 Despite their understanding that virtue is full of distress and sorrow, when they discuss it they do say that it is something to seek out, but for its own sake, since they wholly fail to see its rewards, which are eternal and immortal. Thus it is that in relating everything to this present life they reduce virtue to folly, since its support of all the labours of this life is vain and empty.

17 I will deal with that at greater length elsewhere; in the meantime, justice is the topic, as at the outset, and its power is so great that when it lifts its gaze to heaven, it earns all that God can give it. 18 Horace was right to say [*Carm.* 1.22.1–8] that the power of innocence is so great that it needs neither weapons nor muscle for its own protection: wherever he goes, 'the man of honest life, clean of crime, needs no Moorish darts, nor bow, my dear Fuscus, and quiverful of poisoned arrows, whether he journey across the stormy Syrtes or through the hostile Caucasus or where the renowned Hydaspes licks the land'. 19 It is therefore impossible for any just man to lack divine protection amid the perils of storm and war: even if he sails with parricides and criminals, either they too will be spared in order that the one just and innocent soul is saved, or at least that soul will be saved alone though all the rest perish.

20 Let us admit, however, the possibility of Carneades' hypothesis: so what will the just man do if he comes across a wounded man on a horse or a shipwrecked man on a plank? I say without a qualm, he will rather die than kill. 21 That is no reason why justice, man's sole good, should be called folly. What better, more precious thing could mankind have than innocence? Obviously it is all the more perfect a thing if you take it to its extreme, if you would rather die than see the principle diminished. 22 'It is folly,' he says, 'to spare the life of another to the detriment of one's own.' So you'll think it foolish to die even for friendship's sake, will you? If so, why praise those members of the Pythagorean sect, one of whom surrendered himself to the

tyrant as earnest for the other, and that other then turned up himself at the appointed hour when his guarantor was being led off, and freed him by his intervention? Their virtue, in being willing the one to die for his friend and the other to die for his pledge, would not be held in so much honour if people thought them foolish. 23 And then, precisely because of that virtue of theirs, they had a tyrant's congratulations on saving each other, and a very cruel man had his own nature reformed. Why, he is even said to have begged them to make him a third in their friendship, clearly not seeing them as fools, but as men of goodness and wisdom. 24 Since it is counted a supreme glory to die for friendship and faith, I do not see why it is not also to a man's glory to die for the sake of innocence. People who call it a crime in us to be willing to die for God are very foolish when they themselves praise to the skies anyone willing to die for a fellow human being.

25 To conclude my argument: reason itself points out that one and the same person cannot be both just and foolish, or both wise and unjust. Fools cannot know what is good and just and that is why they always go wrong. Fools are led by their vices like captives: they cannot resist because they lack a virtue they know nothing of. 26 The just keep away from all sin, however, because they cannot act as if they had no knowledge of right and wrong. And who can tell right from wrong except the wise? The conclusion is that a fool can never be just, and the unjust can never be wise.

27 If that is absolutely sound, then it is plain that anyone failing to take a horse from a wounded man or a plank from a shipwrecked man is not a fool because to do that is a sin, and a wise man keeps from sin. 28 He looks a fool, however, I do admit, because of people's ignorance: they don't know what is appropriate in each case. The whole question is best resolved not by instances but by definition.

29 Folly, then, is a straying in deed or word caused by ignorance of right and wrong. It is not folly to fail to spare oneself in order to avoid harming one's neighbour (which is bad). That is what reason and truth prescribe us. 30 In all animals we see a nature which is, because of their lack of wisdom, self-preserving: they hurt others to help themselves; they do not know that it is bad to cause hurt.[76] 31 But because man has knowledge of good and evil,

---

76 Worth note here is the unique *quia* + indic. (*nesciunt quia malum est nocere*) used instead of acc. + infin. (NB the instance at 7.4.17 is in a quotation from Asclepiades.) Petronius gives us the earliest instances of this construction, as might be expected (45.10, 46.4); for as good a Ciceronian as Lactantius to admit such a latterday structure is astonishing. He is regularly unclassical, however, in his pairing in conditional sentences of pres. subj. in the protasis with fut. indic. in the apodosis.

he refrains from causing hurt, even to his own disadvantage, which an animal, being irrational, cannot do; that is why innocence is counted among the supreme human virtues.[77] So it becomes plain that the wisest man is the one who prefers to die to avoid causing hurt: he thus maintains a sense of duty which distinguishes us from the dumb beasts. 32 As Carneades wished us to see, the man who refuses to point out the seller's mistake in order to buy gold cheap, or to say that he's selling a runaway slave or an unhealthy house with an eye to his own profit, is not wise, but shrewd and clever.[78] 33 Shrewdness and cleverness exist in dumb beasts too, when they lie in wait, for instance, or use a trick to catch and eat, or when they deceive the traps of others in various ways; wisdom, however, falls to man alone. 34 Wisdom is intelligence applied either to doing good and right or to refraining from unsound words and deeds. No wise man ever aims at gain, because he has a contempt for the goods of this world; nor does he let anyone be deceived, because it is the duty of a good man to put people right when they are wrong and to bring them back in line; it is human nature to be sociable and generous. That is the unique basis for man's kinship with God.

The key: there is life after death, rewards and punishments

18.1 The apparent folly of a man who prefers to be in need or to die rather than cause hurt or seize another man's property is caused no doubt by the fact that people think death destroys a man. That belief is the source of all the confusion, on the part of philosophers as much as of ordinary people. 2 If we are nothing after death, then certainly it is the mark of a very great fool not to consider how this life may last as long as possible and be full of every advantage. 3 Anyone so doing is bound to depart from the rule of justice. But if a longer and better life awaits us, which is what we learn from the arguments of great philosophers, from the response of the poets and from the divine utterance of prophets, then it is the mark of the wise to despise this temporal life with its goods; every loss of this life is repaid with immortality.

4 In Cicero [*Rep.* 3.40], the defender of justice – Laelius, as ever – observes: 'Virtue in effect wants honour; it has no other reward.' But it has, my dear Laelius, and it is a reward entirely worthy of it, one which you could never suspect, for you had no knowledge of divine literature. 'It receives its reward without fuss,' he says, 'and requests it without bitterness.' You are

---

77 High praise; cf. L. on *patientia*, with which *innocentia* is closely linked: 22.2–3 below.
78 Cf. Cic. *Off.* 1.63, drawing on Plato (*Men.* 246e).

very wrong if you think that a human reward for virtue is possible, since you yourself have said elsewhere, quite rightly, 'What riches or powers or kingdoms can you offer this fellow who counts all such stuff human and reckons his goods are heaven-sent?' 5 No one would think you wise, my dear Laelius, when you contradict yourself, and a little later you deprive virtue of what you gave it. It is ignorance of the truth, of course, which makes your judgment so vague and wobbly.

6 Now for your next sentence. 'But if virtue is denied its rewards by general ingratitude or widespread envy or hostile power...' 7 O how fragile, how empty a virtue it is that you present, if it can be denied its own reward! If it 'reckons its goods are heaven-sent' (I quote), how can there be people with such ingratitude, such envy, such power that they can deprive virtue of the goods which have been divinely appointed for it?

8 'Many,' he says, 'many are the consolations that give it joy, and it is sustained by its own beauty most of all.' What consolations? What beauty? Beauty often enough stands accused, and then convicted.

9 What if it were, as Furius said, 'to be seized, harassed, cast out, in poverty, its hands cut off, its eyes put out, condemned, imprisoned, branded, killed in miserable fashion'? Will virtue lose its reward, or even perish? No: it will receive its reward at God's judgment and it will live and thrive for ever. 10 Take that away, and there is nothing in human life capable of seeming so useless and futile as virtue; but its own natural goodness and honesty can teach us that the soul is not mortal and has a divine reward appointed for it by God. 11 But God had three aims in wanting virtue to be hidden under the guise of folly: that the mystery of his truth and his religion should be secret, that the cults and the cleverness of this earth that exalts itself so much and is so very pleased with itself should be condemned for emptiness and error, and finally that things should be difficult, the path that leads to the sublime reward of immortality being very narrow.

12 I have explained, I think, why our people are thought fools by fools. To prefer to be tortured and killed, rather than pick three fingers of incense and cast it on a fire, does seem as foolish as caring more at a moment of peril for someone else's soul than one's own. 13 They don't know how wicked a thing it is to worship anything besides God 'who founded earth and heaven', who created the human race, and gave it breath and light. 14 But if the wickedest of servants is the one who runs away from his master and is judged to deserve beating, imprisonment, the chain gang, crucifixion and every sort of misery, and if in the same way a son is considered depraved and impious who deserts his own father in order not to obey him, and for that

reason is thought fit to be disinherited and to have his name deleted from the family for ever, how much more so the man who deserts God, in whom two titles of equal worth and honour combine, master and father? 15 The man who buys a slave at market does him no more good than to feed him, and he does it for the sake of the slave's use to him; the man who sires a son has no control over the conception, birth and life of that son, and thereby is plainly not the father, but merely the instrument of generation. 16 So if a man deserts the one who is both true master and true father, what are his due penalties if not those that God himself has established in preparing eternal fire for unjust spirits, in line with the threat to the impious and rebellious which he delivers through his prophets?

Persuasion preferable to force and freedom to coercion; pagan and Christian religions compared

19.1[79] Let them learn, then, those murderers of their own and others' souls, how unforgiveable a crime they commit, first in throttling themselves in serving such awful demons which God has condemned to eternal punishment, and secondly in not even allowing God to be worshipped by others, striving instead to direct people to cults of death and making such strenuous efforts to prevent any soul abiding on earth intact to gaze at heaven in utter safety. 2 What else can I call them but wretched, obedient as they are to the behests of their own plunderers whom they think gods? They do not know the state of those gods, or their origin, or their names; they cannot account for them; they roam at random, in the grip of vulgar belief and indulging their stupidity. 3 If you asked them to account for their belief, they couldn't do it. They would seek refuge instead in the opinions of their ancestors: they were the wise ones, they put it to the test, they knew what was best. Thus they fail to use their own wits, and for as long as they believe in others' mistakes, they abdicate reason. 4 Wrapped in a total ignorance, they know neither themselves nor their gods. If only they would keep their mistakes and stupidity to themselves! Yet they even grab at others to be partners in their wickedness, as if they meant to find solace in bringing many down with them. 5 It is exactly this ignorance which makes them so evil in persecuting the wise, when they pretend that they are acting in their interests and want to recall them to a right understanding.

---

[79] In this chapter and the next L. makes a spirited and eloquent case for the freedom of religion, and for the use of persuasion rather than force in religious disputes.

6 Do they try to do this by talk, or by offering any kind of argument? Not at all: they use violence and torture. What an extraordinary blind madness! Evil intent is presumed to exist in the people who try to keep their faith, and a good intent in their butchers! 7 Is there evil intent in people who suffer tortures contrary to all the rights of man and every ordinance of God, or is it in those who do to the bodies of the innocent things not done even by the cruellest of robbers, the angriest of enemies or the most ferocious of barbarians? Do they lie to themselves so much that they cross the words good and bad over and switch their meanings? 8 Why don't they call day night and sun darkness? Anyway, it is equally outrageous to label good bad, wise foolish, and just impious; if they have any confidence in philosophy or rhetoric, why don't they equip themselves to rebut these words of ours if they can, meeting us face to face and arguing every detail? 9 They really ought to take up the defence of their gods; otherwise, if our arguments prevail, as daily they do, their gods will be abandoned along with their shrines and other rubbish. Since they get nowhere by violence – worship of God increases the more they try to suppress it – let them operate instead by talk and exhortation.

10 Let them come out into the open, pontiffs great and lesser, flamens, augurs, kings of sacrifice, and all who are priests and spokesmen of the cults, and let them invite us to a meeting and encourage us to adopt cults of gods; let them convince us that these gods by whose power and foresight all things are controlled are many in number; let them reveal how gods and their rites were presented to mankind in the beginning, let them explain the source and the system, let them set forth what profit there is in worshipping so and what penalty for contempt of it all: why their gods wish to be worshipped by human beings, and, if they are blessed already, what they will gain from such human piety; and let them confirm all this, not by mere assertion – the authority of a mere mortal is worthless – but with proofs from heaven, as we do. 11 There is no need for violence and brutality: worship cannot be forced; it is something to be achieved by talk rather than blows, so that there is free will in it. They must unsheathe the sharpness of their wits: if the reasoning is sound, let them argue it! We are ready to listen if they would tell; if they keep silent, we simply cannot believe them, just as we do not yield when they use violence. 12 Let them copy us, and so bring out the reason in it all; we use no guile ourselves, though they complain we do; instead, we teach, we show, we demonstrate. 13 No one is detained by us against his will – anyone without devotion and faith is no use to God; but when truth detains, no one departs.

14 If they have any confidence in their truth, let them teach it to us: let

them talk, let them just utter, let them have the nerve, I say, to engage in debate of some such sort with us; at once, I'm sure, from our old women, whom they despise, and from our children too, there will be gales of laughter for so stupid an error. 15 They have great expertise; they know their gods' genealogies, achievements and powers, their deaths and burials by the book;[80] they know that the rituals in which they were initiated arose out of the achievements or mishaps, or even deaths, of men: so it's a piece of incredible lunacy to think that those who they dare not deny were mortal are gods – or if they were so impudent as to deny it, what they and their friends have written would prove them wrong, and the way their rituals began would be the overwhelming proof. 16 Let them understand from that how great the distinction is between true and false, since for all their eloquence they themselves fail to convince, while tiros of no education succeed because the truth of our facts speaks for itself.

17 So why do they behave with such savagery? To increase their folly while wanting to lessen it? The butcher's trade and piety are two very different things; truth cannot be partnered with violence, nor justice with cruelty. 18 They are quite right not to risk any explanation of things divine, in case they are mocked by our people and abandoned by their own. 19 If ordinary people, whose judgment is simple and straightforward, came to know that those mysteries of theirs were established in memory of the dead, they will vote against, I guess, and look for something else more sound to worship. Hence the institution by shrewd operators of 'the hush of the faithful at sacrifice,'[81] in case people should know what they are worshipping.

20 Since we are well versed in their doctrines, why do they not either believe us because we know both systems, or envy us because we have put truth before falsehood? Oh, but cults in the public domain, they say, must be defended. 21 Poor things! It's such a decent ambition, and so wretchedly wrong! They realise that nothing matters more in human affairs than religion and that it ought to be defended with every endeavour, but they are just as deceived in the religion itself as they are in how to defend it. 22 Religion must be defended not by killing but by dying, not by violence but by endurance, not by sin but by faith: that is the contrast between bad and good, and in religion the practice must be good, not bad. 23 If you want to defend religion by bloodshed, torture and evil, then at once it will not be so defended: it will be polluted and outraged. There is nothing that is so much a matter of

---

80 Here Euhemerism, the idea that gods were promoted men, is slyly introduced.
81 Verg. *A.* 3.112.

willingness as religion, and if someone making sacrifice is spiritually turned off, then it's gone, it's nothing.

24 The argument is therefore right that you defend religion with endurance or death; conservation of faith by that means is acceptable to God and adds authority to the religion. 25 If a man who serves in an army here on earth keeps his pledge to his king while doing some notable deed which he survives, he is prized and favoured greatly, and if he dies, for having undergone death for his leader he gains the greatest glory: all the more need, therefore, to keep faith with God who is commander of us all; for God can reward virtue not only in the living but also in the dead. 26 Since worship of God is an act of heavenly service, it needs the maximum of devotion and loyalty. How will God love a worshipper if the worshipper doesn't love him, and how will he grant the request of a suppliant who comes to make his prayer without heartfelt commitment?

27 When these people come to make sacrifice, they offer their gods nothing intimate or special, no cleanness of mind, no reverence, no awe.[82] When the sacrifice is over in all its emptiness, they leave their religion as they found it, in the temple and with the temple; they bring none of it with them and they take none of it away. 28 Hence the fact that religions of that sort cannot make people good and cannot be reliable and stable, and people can easily detach themselves from them, as there is nothing there to be learnt that is relevant to life, wisdom and faith. 29 What gives these gods their hold? What is their power, their teaching, their origin, reason, basis or substance? What's the aim of it and what's the promise, for a man to be able to observe it faithfully and defend it bravely? All I see in it is a ritual of mere fingertip relevance. 30 Our religion, however, is solid, strong and changeless, because it teaches justice, it is always with us, it is entirely in the mind of the worshipper, and it treats the mind itself as the sacrificial offering. There, all they ask is blood of cattle, smoke, and silly libations; with us it is a good mind, a pure heart, and a life of innocence. There, there is an indiscriminate congregation of shameless adulteresses, pert brothel madams, foul whores, gladiators, brigands, thieves and poisoners, and all they pray for is to commit their crimes unpunished. 31 What would a robber or a gladiator ask for in making sacrifice, except to kill? Or a poisoner, except to deceive? Or a whore, except to sin full-time? Or an adulteress, except either her husband's death or the concealment of her own unchastity? Or a pimp,

---

[82] In these paragraphs L. offers a neat (and rhetorical) comparison of pagan and Christian religion.

except plenty of clients to pluck? Or a thief, except bigger takings? 32 With us there is no place at all even for minor, common sins; anyone coming to worship with an unsound conscience hears God's threat against him, for God sees the secret places of the heart, God is always implacable on sin, God requires justice and demands faith. What room is there here for a dissident will or reluctant prayer? 33 But those poor wretches don't see even from their own wickedness how bad what they worship is, because they come to prayer contaminated by all their misdeeds, and they think they have made God a pious sacrifice if they wash their hands – as if the lusts pent up in the heart could be scoured out by even a river or purified by an ocean. 34 It is so much better to cleanse instead the mind, which gets soiled by evil desires, and to drive out all the vices together in the one bath of virtue and faith! He who does that, however foul and dirty his body, is pure enough.

The persecutors have no confidence in their gods and the persecuted have faith in God's power

20.1 Because these people do not know what or how to worship, in their blindness and thoughtlessness they go to the other extreme. They worship their enemies, they placate their robbers and murderers with victims, and they lay their own souls on loathsome altars to be burnt up with the very incense. 2 They even get cross, poor things, that others are not perishing as well. The dimness of their thinking is incredible. What are they to see, when they can't see the sun? As if their gods, if they did exist, would need any human help against their mockers! So why do they get cross with us, if their gods are powerless? In fact, by not believing in their gods' powers they destroy their gods themselves, which is being more irreligious than a total atheist. 3 In his work *de Legibus* Cicero says [2.19], in recommending that people go to sacrifice 'in purity, they shall present piety and lay wealth aside; him who doeth otherwise god himself will arraign'. 4 Quite right: it is not proper to despair of God: you are to worship him because you think him powerful. How can he right a worshipper's wrong if he cannot right his own? 5 We may then ask these people whom they think they most serve in forcing the unwilling to sacrifice. The people they compel? A kindness unwanted is no kindness. 6 Oh, but when people don't know what is good, they must be counselled against their will. But if they want them to be safe, why harass and torment them into helplessness? Alternatively, where does such an impious piece of piety come from that has them either ruin or disable, in miserable fashion, people they would like to counsel? 7 Or is it their gods they serve? An unwilling sacrifice is no sacrifice. Unless it come from the heart spontaneously, it is blasphemy when people act under threat of proscription, injustice, prison or torture. 8 If those are gods that get worshipped like that, they are not fit to be worshipped for the single reason that they want to be worshipped like that; gods who get libations of tears of lamentation and blood flowing from every limb are very proper objects of mankind's detestation.

9 We by contrast make no demand that our God, who is everyone's God willy nilly, be worshipped by anyone unwillingly, and we do not get cross if he is not worshipped. We are confident of his supreme power; he can avenge contempt of himself just as he can avenge the unjust sufferings of his servants. 10 That is why when we suffer outrage, we do not fight back even verbally, but submit the redress to God, which is not what they do: in their desire to appear as defenders of their gods, they go berserk against non-worshippers. 11 Out of that comes the understanding of how bad it is to worship gods, since people should rather be brought to good by good, not by bad; but because it is bad itself, any observance of it is bad.

12 But, it will be said, people who wreck religions must be punished. Are we worse wreckers than the Egyptians, who worship the most offensive figures of animals both wild and domestic, and adore as gods certain things not fit even to mention? Are we worse than these worshippers of gods themselves, who say they do worship their gods but then mock them in public disgustingly, letting them be put on stage amid hoots of laughter? 13 What sort of religion is it, and what respect can it command, when it gets worship in the temples and mockery in the theatres? And the people who mock it don't pay the price for the outrage they do it, but depart with honour and acclaim. 14 Are we worse wreckers than some philosophers, who say there are no gods at all, that everything came into being of its own accord, and that everything that happens does so at random? Are we worse than the Epicureans, who say there are gods but deny they take any interest, neither getting angry nor feeling gratitude? 15 That is simply an incitement not to worship them at all, since they neither defend their worshippers nor threaten their non-worshippers. Besides, when they argue against fear, all they are trying to achieve is non-fear of gods. Yet people listen to these things with pleasure, and discuss them with impunity.

Evil spirits are at the bottom of it; why God tolerates them and the superficial prosperity of our enemies

21.1 The rage that is abroad against us is not because we do not worship those gods – plenty of people don't worship them – but because the truth is with us and, as has been very soundly said, 'Truth gives birth to hatred.'[83] 2 So what shall we conclude, except that these people don't know what's hitting them? There is a blind and irrational madness at work; we can see it for what it is, and they cannot. 3 They do not do the persecution themselves: they have no reason to get angry with the innocent; it is those unclean, desperate spirits who know the truth and loathe it, insinuating themselves into their minds and egging them on to mad acts in their ignorance. 4 As long as there is peace among the people of God, these spirits keep shunning the just for fear of them, and whenever they try to occupy a body and torment its soul, they are exorcised by the just and are put to flight in the name of the true God, 5 and when they hear that name, they tremble and cry out, and say they are being branded and beaten, and when asked who they are and when they came and how they got into a man, they confess it all. Racked and tormented so, they are forced away from the virtue of the divine name. 6 It is those beatings and threats which cause their constant hatred of just and holy men, and because they cannot hurt them of themselves, they whip up a public hatred against people they see as harsh on them, and they practise their ferocity as savagely as they can, either to weaken those people's faith through pain or, if they cannot achieve that, to remove them altogether from the earth, so that no one shall exist with the power to repress their evil.

7 I am well aware[84] of the response that can be made from the other side: why does that one and only God of yours, that great God, lord of all things and master of all people as you call him, permit such things to happen and not either avenge or protect his worshippers? Why are people who don't worship him rich, powerful and happy, in power as magistrates and kings, holding those very worshippers of his in subjection to their own dominion and might? 8 This too must have its explanation, so that no confusion remains. First, this is the reason why worship of God is thought to be ineffective: people are led astray by the way the immediate goods of this earth look, which are quite irrelevant to care of the soul. Because they see the just are without these things and the unjust amply provided, they conclude that

---

83 Repeated from 9.6.

84 At this point L. returns to the main question: why are the just persecuted while the unjust prosper?

worshipping God is futile as they can't see those goods in it, and they think too that worship of gods is sound, since their worshippers enjoy wealth, position and kingship. 9 But people of that persuasion are not looking deeply enough into the point of human existence, which is totally spiritual, not physical. 10 All they can see is the visible: the body, that is. Now the body, in being available to sight and touch, is weak, fragile and mortal. All its goods are things of desire and admiration – wealth, position and power, for instance – because they bring a physical gratification, and for that reason are as perishable as the body itself. 11 Since the soul, in which alone man has his being, is not susceptible to sight, so neither can its goods be seen, and they have their being in virtue alone; for that reason the soul is bound to be as stable, consistent and lasting a thing as virtue itself is, and the good of the spirit has its being in virtue.

Persecution gives rise to virtues of patience and innocence, and swells the numbers of the faithful

22.1 There are goods whose enjoyment by the unjust causes worship of gods to be thought sound and effective; it is a long task to set out all the sorts of virtue there are in order to explain in each case why the wise and just man must keep his full distance from those goods. 2 With reference to the present enquiry it is sufficient to prove what we mean by taking one virtue.

One important and principal virtue is certainly endurance. It wins high and frequent praise equally in the talk of ordinary people and from philosophers and orators. 3 Its very high position among the virtues cannot be denied; but the just and wise have to be in the power of the unjust in order to develop it, endurance being the bearing with equanimity of ills whether imposed or accidental. 4 Because a just and wise man is virtuous, so endurance is with him already: but it will be missing entirely if he suffers no adversity. 5 By contrast, a man prospering is non-patient, and so lacks this most important virtue: by non-patient I mean he has nothing to endure.

Innocence too such a man cannot have, because it too is a virtue peculiar to the just and wise; 6 instead, the man without innocence causes frequent harm by coveting other people's property and grabbing what he wants unjustly: he has no part in virtue, he is subject to vice and sin, and he aims to lord it over the free because he has no self-control; he forgets his own weakness and grows monstrously big-headed.

It follows that the unjust and those ignorant of God do very well for wealth, power and position, which are all rewards of injustice but cannot last, sought as they are through greed and violence. 7 Because the just and wise man, as Laelius puts it, 'judges all those things to be human in origin while his proper goods are god-sent,'[85] so he wants nothing of anyone else's in case of harming anyone in contravention of the rights of humanity, and he seeks no position of power in case of doing someone an injustice – he recognises that all were born of the same God in the same state and all are bound by the rights of brotherhood – ; 8 instead, he is 'content with what is his, however slight'; mindful of his weakness he seeks no more than enough to maintain life and from the store of his possessions he even shares with have-nots because he is pious; and piety is the supreme virtue. 9 In addition, he despises all pleasures that are temporary and vicious, and cause the pursuit of wealth, because he is self-controlled and master of his desires. Equally, he acts without swagger or exaggeration, he doesn't vaunt himself, he doesn't behave arrogantly, but is peaceful, agreeable, open and frank, because he understands his own estate. 10 Since he does no one an injustice, desires nothing of anyone else's, and does not even defend what is his if it is taken from him by violence, and since he also knows how to endure any injustice he may suffer with self-control because he has the gift of virtue, so inevitably the just are subjected to the unjust and the wise endure the jibes of the foolish: the one lot sin because they are unjust, and the others stick to virtue because they are just.

11 If anyone wants to know more fully why God permits the wicked and the unjust to become powerful, happy and rich whereas the pious exist in lowliness, misery and poverty, he should take that book of Seneca's called 'Why good men meet much ill despite the existence of providence.' He has much to say there, with a wisdom almost divine, well above the usual secular ignorance. 12 'God,'[86] he says, 'treats people as free, but he permits the corrupt and vicious to live in luxury and refinement because he doesn't think them worth his correction. The good, however, whom he loves, he chastises quite often, and gives them constant troubles to exercise their virtue, not allowing them to become corrupt and depraved by goods that are perishable and mortal.' 13 No one ought then to think it surprising if we are often chastised for our faults by God. Indeed, it is when we are being particularly hard pressed that we must give thanks to our father for his great kindness in not permitting our corruption to proceed any further, putting us right with

---

85 Cf. 18.4.

86 The consensus is that this is not a fragment of a lost work, but a paraphrase, done in the style of Cicero, of passages in Sen. *prov.*: e.g., 1.6; 2.5–6; 3.3. See Monat (1973), *ad loc.*

blows and beatings. That is how we know we matter to God: he gets angry when we sin.

14 He could bestow both wealth and kingship on his people, as he once did on the Jews, whose heirs and successors we are; but he wanted the Jews to live under someone else's exercise of power so that they should not be spoilt by the happy fortune of prosperity and slide into luxuriousness, despising his instructions as our ancestors did: yet the good things of this world for all their fragility often unstrung them, so that they wandered off the path of discipline and broke the bonds of law. 15 He took a good precaution, therefore, in providing peace for his worshippers if they kept his commandments and in correcting them, however, if they did not obey his word.

16 To prevent them from being corrupted by peace as their fathers were by licence, he was content for them to come under pressure from those into whose hands he put them in order to strengthen backsliders, to restore the corrupted to full strength and to test and try the faithful. 17 How can a general test the martial virtue of his men unless he has an enemy? In his case opponents emerge despite his wishes because he is mortal and capable of being conquered; God, however, cannot be resisted, and so he creates adversaries for his name himself, not for them to fight against him as God, but against his soldiers, so that he may prove or strengthen the faith and devotion of his people until the blasts of oppression have restored their errant discipline.

18 There is a further reason why he lets persecution come upon us: it increases the number of God's people, and it is not difficult to show why or how that happens. 19 First, many are put off the worship of gods by their loathing for cruelty; who wouldn't shudder at sacrifice like that? Second, some are simply content with virtue and faith. A certain number suspect there is good reason for worship of gods being thought bad when so many people who do think so would rather die than do what others do in order to live. 20 Someone else wants to know what that good is which is defended even unto death and which is preferred to all the happy precious things there are in this life, and which people aren't put off by loss of goods or life or by pain and disembowelling. 21 All that has great effect, but the principal reasons for growth in our numbers have always been these: first, people standing by hear us say amidst the tortures that we do not sacrifice to stones shaped by human hands but to a living God who is in heaven. Many realise this is true and take it to heart. 22 Second, as tends to happen when things are unclear, and people are asking each other what the cause can be of this great determination, lots of things get learnt of relevance to the faith which are

spread around and picked up as rumours, and because they are good things, they are bound to satisfy. 23 Further, when vengeance follows, as it always does, that is a strong encouragement to believe. A reason of no small weight is this, that when unclean spirits of demons burrow, by permission, into the bodies of many people and then get ejected, all who are restored to health stick by the faith whose effectiveness they have experienced. 24 All these reasons combined bring a great many people to God, in wonderful fashion.

Punishment is in store for the wicked

23.1 All the contrivances against us of evil princes, therefore, take place with God's permission. Even so, those wicked persecutors who rail at God's name and mock it are not to think that they will get away with having been the instruments of his wrath against us. 2 God will judge and punish those who took his power and abused it without human limit, insulting even God in their arrogance, and subjecting his eternal name to the wicked and godless trampling of their own footsteps. 3 Besides, it is his promise is to be avenged upon them swiftly and to 'drive out evil beasts from the land' [Lev. 26:6]. Despite his custom of avenging the torments of his people, however, even here in this world, nevertheless he bids us await with endurance the day of divine judgment when he himself will reward or punish each man according to his deserts. 4 Those sacrilegious souls should not therefore hope that the people they so oppress will go neglected and unavenged. Those rabid, ravening wolves shall have their proper wages for torturing just and honest souls who did no wrong.

5 Let us work, then, to ensure that by men we are punished for our justice, and only for our justice; and let us work with all our strength to deserve of God both the avenging and the reward of our suffering.

BOOK 6: TRUE WORKSHIP

God requires worship from the innocent, not sacrificial offerings from pleasure-seekers

1.1 With God's spirit informing me and truth itself assisting I have now fulfilled my duty towards the task I undertook. Reason for claiming and clarifying truth was given me by my knowledge, by my faith and by our lord himself, without whom nothing can be known, nothing can be explained.[1] 2 I now come to the most important part of this work, my explanation of the ritual and sacrifice appropriate to worship of God.[2] Worship is the duty of man; the sum of things, and the entire aim of the life of bliss, consists in worship alone; that is why we were created and given breath by him, not to see the heaven and the sun, as Anaxagoras thought,[3] but to worship in pureness and wholeness of mind the maker of the sun and the God of heaven.

3 In the preceding books I have defended truth to the best of my poor ability, but now it can shine out in all its brilliance through worship itself. 4 All that is wanted from man by that holy and unique majesty is innocence.[4] Anyone who offers God innocence will be worshipping with piety and religion enough, 5 but men neglect justice and befoul themselves with all manner of wickedness and crime, and so think they are religious if they go smearing temples and altars with the blood of victims and drenching hearths with a profusion of fragrant old wine. 6 They even lay on sacred feasts and offer up choice banquets as if there were something in it for their would-be guests. Anything rarely seen, anything expensive to make or smell, they assume is precious to their gods, judging not by any understanding of divinity (which they do not have) but by their own desires; they do not realise that God has no need of earthly wealth. All their wisdom is earthbound, and they measure good and evil by the sensation of physical pleasure alone: 7 that dominates their view of religion, and it also controls their actions all their lives.

---

1 Cf. 5.4.1.
2 It is the centrality of sacrifice in the cult of the pagan gods which makes it essential that L. tackle the subject.
3 Cf. 3.9.4. Anaxagoras was introduced at 1.5.18.
4 Innocence was signalled as a key virtue in 5.17.21, 24 and 31. See also note on 5.14.18.

Once they had moved away from contemplation of the sky and had subdued their sense of heaven to the body, they gave free rein to their desires as if they were going to carry pleasure off with them entirely: it is their pressing aim every moment, even though the soul ought to have the body in its employ and not the body the soul. 8 In their judgment the greatest good is wealth: if they cannot acquire it by good means, they acquire it by evil means. They cheat, steal and rob, they lay traps and break their word, they have no self-control or scruples, provided only that they can glitter with gold and gleam in silver and jewelled clothes, and heap up wealth insatiably and walk surrounded by crowds of slaves with the people at a distance. 9 By such helpless submission to pleasure they destroy the power and vigour of their minds, and plunge headlong towards death even while they think they are living life to its full. 10 As I explained in book 2,[5] the business of heaven is with the soul and the business of earth with the body. People who neglect the good of the soul and go for the good of the body are busy with darkness and death, which belong to earth and body, because life and light are from heaven. In their enslavement to the body they know nothing of heaven: hence their remoteness from any understanding of things divine. 11 Poor things, the same blindness afflicts them everywhere. They no more know what true worship is than they know who the true God is.

Their worship is earthly, while ours embodies justice, which to teach is our duty and glory

2.1 So they slaughter fine fat victims as if God were hungry, they pour out wine as if he were thirsty, and they light lamps as if he were in the dark. 2 If they could imagine or understand what those heavenly goods are whose greatness we cannot perceive, wrapped up as we are in our earthly bodies, they would instantly know their own folly in these empty performances, 3 or if they were willing to gaze at the heavenly light which we call the sun, they would instantly realise how little God needs their lights when he himself is donor of a light so bright and pure for the use of men. 4 Its orb is small, and because of its distance from us it seems no larger than a man's head, and yet it has such brilliance that mortal eyes looking at it cannot sustain their gaze, and if you stare even briefly, your eyes are dulled and a dark fog comes over them: what brilliance of light must we think exists where God himself is, with whom there is no night at all? He kept that light under such control that

---

5 2.12.3.

it did no damage to living things with too much dazzle or too fierce a heat; instead he granted them just as much light and heat as mortal bodies could take or as the ripening of the crops required. 5 So if someone makes an offering of candlewax to him who is the creator and giver of light himself, are we to think the donor is in his right mind? 6 God requires of us a different light, not a smoky light, but, as the poet says, a clear, bright light, the light of the mind (that is why poets call us[G6] *photes*[7]): but that light can be displayed only by the man who knows God. 7 Because their gods are of earth, they need light to avoid being in darkness; because such worshippers have no heavenly wisdom, they are brought to earth by the very cults they practise: earth needs illumination, because its own form and nature are of darkness. 8 Hence they credit their gods with a human, not a heavenly perception, thinking the gods find the same things needful and enjoyable as we do, who need food when we are hungry, drink when we are thirsty, clothes when we are cold, and light when the sun goes down in order to see.

9 The fact that those gods are dead men who once were alive is best proved and best made intelligible by their worship, which is entirely of the earth. There cannot be heavenly good in the effusion of animal blood that fouls their altars, unless they think perhaps that gods feed on what men are too disgusted to touch. 10 As for the man who proposed this heavy diet, whether highwayman, adulterer, poisoner or parricide, he'll have a life of utter bliss: he's the one they love and cherish, offering him everything he could want. 11 Persius was right to mock superstitions of this sort in his usual way [2.29–30]: 'What will your bribe be,' he says, 'to buy the gods' attention? Larded lights and intestines?' 12 As he obviously realised, there was no need of meat to placate the heavenly majesty but a mind of purity, a soul of justice, and 'a heart,' as Persius also says [2.74], 'rich with natural honesty'. 13 The religion of heaven is not composed of things corrupt but of the virtues of the soul which is the product of heaven, and true worship is the worship in which the worshipper offers to God his own mind as his spotless victim. 14 How that can be achieved and established will be explained in the course of this book's argument.

Nothing can be so glorious and so proper for a man as educating people to be just. 15 In Cicero, Catulus says (in the *Hortensius*, when advancing philosophy's claims above all others) that he would prefer one little book on

---

6 G indicates that L. uses or quotes Greek.

7 See note at 1.21.7. *Phôtes* is plural of *phós*, a man (or wight: the word is poetical); the word for light is *phôs*. Confusion of the declensions enabled L. to make a meaningful pun.

duty to a long speech for the rebel Cornelius.[8] This view is not to be thought of as simply Catulus', who probably never delivered it, but Cicero's own, and he wrote it, I imagine, as a trailer for the books on duty he was about to write, in which he actually says that there is nothing in all philosophy better and more rewarding than offering advice on life.[9] 16 If it is done by people who do not know the truth, however, all the more burden on us to do it, since we have been trained and illuminated by God and we can offer advice which is true. Not that our teaching will be of the sort to take people back to the basic elements of virtue, which is an infinite task; let us adopt for instruction instead someone they think to be perfect already. 17 The advice they usually offer on uprightness can stay (it is sound); we shall be adding a superstructure which they don't know about, for the perfection and consummation of justice; that is quite outside their grasp. 18 In fact I shall ignore things we may have in common, in case it looks as if I am borrowing from people whose errors I am determined to refute and expose.

Two paths, one leading to heaven and the other to hell

3.1 There are two paths, o emperor Constantine, along which human life must proceed: one leads to heaven and the other plunges to the underworld. Poets have presented them in their poetry, and so have philosophers in their debates.[10] 2 The philosophers at least have been happy for one path to be the path of the virtues and the other the path of the vices, and for the one assigned to the virtues to be initially steep and rough going; if anyone overcomes its difficulty and emerges on top, for the rest he has a level road, and beautiful open country, and he reaps a fine, rich reward for all his labours; 3 but anyone deterred by the difficulty of the start slides off on to the path of vice, which is a pleasant path to begin with, and much more well trodden, but after a little more progress, its pleasant appearance suddenly fades, and it becomes precipitous, rough with rocks at one moment, overgrown with brambles at another, and broken by fast flooding streams at a third, so that strain, stalling, slipping and falling are inevitable.

4 All this is written up to a point where it is obvious that adopting the virtues is very hard work, but once they have been adopted they are very

---

8 Cic. *Hort.* fr. 34 (Straume-Zimmermann).

9 Cic. *Off.* 2.6; 3.5; cf. 1.4.

10 See Verg. *A.* 6.540 (cited below); Plato, *Gorg.* 524a; and the famous story of the choice of Hercules, attributed to the sophist Prodicus, in Xen. *Mem.* 2.1.21–34. The idea is as old as Hesiod: see *Op.* 287–92.

rewarding, bringing pleasure that is solid and unassailable, whereas the vices use their natural powers of beguilement to entrap people's souls, and once people have been caught by pleasures that turn out to be empty, they are drawn on into miseries of great bitterness and anguish. 5 The distinction is shrewdly made, if only the form and end of the virtues themselves were known. What the virtues are, however, and what reward God keeps for them had not been learnt. We shall explain that in these two final books.

Because they did not know or were unsure that men's souls are immortal, so they measured both virtue and vice in terms of earthly rewards and punishments. 6 All this debate about the two paths has as its objects frugality and luxury. The philosophers say that the path of human life is like the letter Y;[11] every human being, upon arrival at the threshold of adolescence, at the place 'where the road splits in both directions',[12] will pause and dither, and won't know which direction to prefer; 7 if he has a guide to point him in the better way as he dithers – if, that is, he studies either philosophy or oratory or some respectable skill which develops him successfully, and only very hard work will achieve that – then, they argue, he will live his life through in honourable plenty; 8 but if he does not find a teacher of frugality, then he tumbles on to the bad road, which belies its appearance of being the better: that is to say, he surrenders to sloth, idleness and self-indulgence, which look attractive at the time if you don't know the true good; later, when your reputation and property are all gone, you will live in total misery and shame.

9 The philosophers thus understood the destinations of the two paths physically, relating them to the life we live on earth. The poets have possibly done better in wanting the division of ways to be in the underworld, but they are wrong in claiming that the paths are for the dead. Both ideas have some truth in them, but neither is right, since the paths themselves should have been related to life and their destinations to death. 10 We can manage a better truth content: we say those two paths are the paths to heaven and to the underworld because just men have immortality ahead of them and the unjust have eternal punishment.

11 How the two paths either raise us to heaven or plunge us to the nether regions I will now explain, and I shall reveal what the virtues are which the philosophers do not know; then I shall set out their rewards, and also what

---

11 The symbolic use of the letter was attributed by Latin authors to Pythagoras. See Pers. 3.56–57; Auson. *Technopaegn.* 13.9; *Prof.* 11.5; Martian. Cap. 2.102; *Anth. Lat.* 632 (Riese); Isid. 1.3.7.
12 Verg. *A.* 6.540.

the vices are and the punishments for them. 12 It might be expected that I would speak of the vices and virtues separately, since whether my discussion was of good or of evil, its contrary could also be grasped. 13 Bring in the virtues, and the vices will spontaneously withdraw; take away the vices, and the virtues will be free to emerge. The nature of things good and evil is so constituted that they attack each other and try to drive each other away in a constant ding-dong. Thus, the vices cannot be removed without the virtues, and the virtues cannot be brought in without removal of the vices.

14 We think of these paths very differently from the way the philosophers usually do. We say first that each path has its own immortal guide, the one guide being honoured for having virtue and good in his charge and the other damned for having vice and evil in his. 15 The philosophers posit a guide for the righthand path only, and not just one guide, nor a constant one, since they assume that any teacher of a respectable skill will do who can rescue people from idleness and teach them to be thrifty. But the only travellers they imagine on the path are boys and adolescents, presumably because that is the time for learning such skills. 16 We bring to this heavenly path people of every sex, race and age, because God who is lord of the path denies immortality to no man born. The layout of the paths too is not what they think. 17 What is the point of a Y for things that are quite contrary to each other? The one path, the better path, faces the rising sun, and the other, the worse one, faces west, because he who follows truth and justice will receive the reward of immortality and will gain everlasting light, while the man ensnared by that evil guide, the man who puts vice before virtue and lies before truth, is bound to go west, down to eternal darkness. 18 I shall therefore give a description of each path, demonstrating their particular features.

4.1 There is, then, one single path of virtue and good, leading not to the Elysian fields, as the poets have it, but to the very citadel of the world. 'But the lefthand path works the punishment of the evil, and despatches them to wicked Tartarus',[13] 2 and that belongs to the great accuser, who institutes evil religions, diverts men from the heavenly way and sets them on the road to perdition. 3 This path is presented to our gaze in such a form that it seems smooth and open, and delectable with all sorts of flowers and fruit. God has planted on it all the things that are treated on earth as good things: riches, I mean, and distinction, peace and quiet, pleasure, all the usual traps; but

13 Verg. A. 6.542–43.

amongst them he has also set injustice, cruelty, arrogance, treachery, lust, greed, discord, ignorance, lies, folly, and the other vices. The exit from this path is as follows: 4 when the end is reached (and turning back is not now permitted), a cut through all the prettiness is made so suddenly that no one sees the deception until he is tumbling head over heels, a vast depth down. 5 Anyone caught by the shimmer of immediate goods, busy acquiring and enjoying them, unalert to what will follow after death and dividing himself from God, will be hurled to the world below to be condemned to eternal punishment.

6 The path to heaven, however, is presented as difficult and steep, rough with bristling thorns or obstructed by blockage of rocks, so that everyone must proceed with huge effort and torn feet, taking great pains not to fall. 7 On this path God has planted justice, self-control, patience, loyalty, chastity, abstinence, concord, knowledge, truth, wisdom, and the other virtues; but among them he has also set poverty, degradation, hardship, pain and all sorts of bitterness. 8 Anyone projecting his hopes into the future and preferring the better way of life will do without the goods of earth in order to travel light and so to defeat his journey's problems. No one surrounding himself with the trappings of royalty or loading himself with wealth could enter those straits and keep his foothold. 9 Hence the perception that for men of evil and injustice, their desires progress more easily because their path slopes down, while good men's hopes go forward with difficulty because they tread a steep and difficult path.

10 Because the just man has taken on a tough and uncomfortable journey, he is bound to be the object of contempt, derision and loathing. All people drawn unstoppably by desire or pleasure are jealous of a man who has been able to grasp virtue, and they take it as unfair that he has something which they do not. 11 He will be poor, humble, unimportant,[14] and open to attack, and yet he will also be patient of all the unpleasantness; if he maintains that patience unbroken through to the final stage, however, he will be given a crown for his virtue, and for the sufferings he endured in life for justice's sake he will be rewarded by God with immortality.

12 These are the paths that God has marked out for human life. On each he has displayed both good and bad, but in reverse order. On his own path he has shown temporary evils first, together with goods for ever, which is the

---

14 L.'s adjectives, *pauper, humilis, ignobilis*, repeat Cicero's nouns (*Tusc.* 5.29): *paupertas, ignobilitas, humilitas*. What had been base qualities for Classical writers are in patristic literature the hallmarks of a true Christian.

better arrangement, and on the other path he has shown temporary goods first, together with eternal evils, which is the worse arrangement, so that anyone choosing immediate evil together with justice will attain goods that are greater and more sure than those he rejected, while anyone putting immediate good before justice will tumble into evils which are greater and longer lasting than those he avoided. 13 Because this life of the body is short, so its evils and its goods are bound to be short too, whereas because the life of the spirit, which is the opposite of this earthly life, is for always, so its goods and its evils are sempiternal too. 14 The pattern is that brief good is succeeded by evil for ever, and brief evil is succeeded by good for ever.

Since, then, man has goods and evils before him, each individual should sort out with himself how much more satisfactory it is to weigh brief evils against perpetual goods rather than endure perpetual evils in return for brief and perishable goods. 15 In this world, when there is a fight before you with some enemy, you must work hard at the start in order to have peace thereafter, and you must go hungry and thirsty and put up with heat and cold, and sleep on the ground, keep watch and take risks in order to keep your children, home and family safe and then be able to enjoy all the good things of peace and victory to their full; 16 but if you prefer peace now to the hard work, you are bound to cause yourself maximum evil: your foe will seize the initiative if you don't resist, your fields will be laid waste and your home pillaged, and your wife and children will become his prey and you yourself will be killed or captured; to avoid all that you must put off immediate comfort so that a greater and more lasting comfort is produced in the end.

17 So it is throughout our life here. Because God kept a foe for us so that we could acquire virtue, immediate pleasure must be set aside in case the adversary strikes; you must keep watch and post guards, you must go out campaigning like a soldier, and shed your blood to the last drop; you must put up patiently with all manner of foulness and pressure, and all the more readily because God our commander-in-chief has given us eternal rewards for our hardships. 18 Since people on the earthly campaign use up all their energies only to get themselves what can perish the way it was won, we certainly must shirk no labour: we are winning what cannot possibly be lost.[15]

---

15 The idea of life on earth as a spiritual struggle in the *militia Dei* was introduced in earlier books. See 4.4.15–17; 5.19.25–26. This is the only 'warfare' that L. allows. For condemnation of soldiery as a profession, see 20.16 below; cf. Tert. *coron.* 11, *idol.* 19, etc; in general, Pucciarelli (1987).

19 That is the service that man was made for: God wanted him to stand in the front line stripped for action, watching with fierce intensity the manoeuvres or the open assaults of his one and only foe. Our adversary is for ever doing what skilled and practised generals do, trying to catch us with different tricks and adapting his ferocity to our individual behaviour patterns. 20 Some he infects with an insatiable greed, in order to bind them with the fetters of their wealth and so knock them off the path of truth; others he provokes with pricks of wrath, to make them concentrate on hurting people and to wrench them away from contemplation of God; others he drowns in uncontrollable lust, so that their obedience to the pleasures of the flesh prevents them keeping focussed on virtue; others he inspires with envy, so that they are busy tormenting themselves, thinking only of their hated objects' happiness. 21 Some he puffs up with ambition: they devote all their life's effort and energy to exercising public office, so that they stand in the annals and give their name to the year. 22 Some in their greed aim higher, not wanting to be briefly military commander of some province, but to be called lords of the whole human race, with infinite and perpetual power.[16] 23 Any he sees to be pious he entangles in a variety of religions, to make them impious. Those who seek wisdom he dazzles with philosophy, to blind them with the semblance of light in case they grasp the truth and stick to it. 24 Thus he tries to block off all our approaches and obstruct all our paths, jubilant to see us go astray. But God gave us light and armed us with the true, celestial virtue so that we could shake off our misdirections and overcome the author of evil himself. That virtue is now my topic.

Knowledge is not virtue: it precedes virtue

5.1 Before I start to set out the virtues one by one, however, virtue itself must be defined. The philosophers were not right about what it was or its circumstances, or what its work and its business were. All they kept of it was its name; its force, reason and effect they lost. 2 Everything they usually say by way of definition is well summarised in a few verses of Lucilius; to avoid being overlong in my refutation of many people's views, I have chosen to quote them here.

> 3 Virtue, my dear Albinus, is the power
> to pay the true price for our way of life.

---

16 Here L. is disparaging about political and military ambition.

BOOK 6: TRUE WORSHIP

> It is to know what each thing has for us;
> to know what's useful, honourable and right,
> what's good, what's bad, useless, dishonest, foul;
> to know the aim and end in all you seek;
> the power to pay the price that wealth is worth;
> to give to honour what it's truly owed;
> to be a bad man's enemy and foe,
> but also to defend the honest man,
> prizing him, wishing him well, befriending him;
> then, to believe your country's needs come first,
> your parents' next, and third and last your own.[17]

4 Cicero derived his *Officia* from these brief definitions of the poet, following the Stoic Panaetius, and wrote them up in three volumes.[18] We shall see in a moment how mistaken they are, which will show how much divine regard has favoured us in revealing us the truth. 5 Virtue, said the poet, is knowing what's good and bad, what's foul, what's honourable, what's useful and what's not. He could have put it more briefly if he had said just good and bad, because nothing can be useful and honourable without it also being good, and nothing can be useless and foul without it also being bad. Such was the philosophers' view, and so said Cicero, in Book 3 of the work mentioned.

6 Knowledge cannot be virtue, however, because it does not exist within us: it comes to us from outside. Anything with the power of passing from one person to another cannot be virtue since virtue is personal. Thus knowledge is dependent on someone else's goodness because it depends on listening, whereas virtue is entirely our own because it depends on the will to do good. 7 Knowing the route is no use in undertaking a journey unless the will and strength to walk are there; likewise, knowledge is no use if the personal virtue is missing.

8 Even sinners pretty well know, however imperfectly, what good and bad are, and every time they do something wrong they know they are sinning, and that's why they try to conceal it. 9 Although the nature of good and evil does not escape them, nevertheless they are victims of an evil desire, so that they sin because they lack a virtue, the virtue of wanting to act rightly

---

17 Lucil. fr. 1196–1208 (Warmington) = 23 (Charpin) = 1326–1338 (Marx).
18 One may be sceptical of the alleged influence of Lucilius on Cicero's *de Officiis*; the debt to Panaetius is acknowledged at *Off.* 2.60 and 3.7.

and honestly. 10 That knowledge of good and evil is one thing and that virtue is another is plain from the fact that knowledge can exist without virtue, as has been the case with so many philosophers. And since it is rightly a matter for blame not to have done what you knew you should, so it is right for a corrupted will and a vicious soul to be punished; ignorance is no excuse. 11 Virtue is thus not knowing good and evil; it is, rather, doing good and not doing evil.

And yet, knowledge is connected to virtue in such a way that it precedes virtue and virtue comes after, because knowing is no use unless doing follows it up. 12 Horace put it a little better: 'Virtue, and the prime wisdom, is to flee vice.'[19] Even so, he puts it poorly; he has defined virtue by its contrary, as if he were saying 'Good is what is not bad.' When I don't know what virtue is, then I don't know what vice is either; thus each term lacks definition, because the nature of the situation is such that either both or neither must be intelligible.

13 Let us do Horace's work for him, however: 'Virtue is to contain wrath, to control desire, to restrain lust: that is to flee vice.' Nearly all unjust or evil actions arise from those impulses. 14 If the energy in the emotion called wrath were blunted, all men's evil quarrels would be put to sleep, no one would lay traps, and no one would leap out to cause harm. 15 Likewise, if greed were controlled, no one would go robbing on land or sea and no one would create an army to go pillaging and wrecking what belongs to other people; 16 likewise, if the passion of lust were suppressed, every age and sex would retain its own sanctity and no one would either suffer or commit any act of shame.[20] 17 If these impulses were laid to rest by virtue, every possible crime and wickedness would be removed from people's lives and behaviour. This allaying of our emotional impulses has as its purpose that all our actions are right actions. 18 The whole business of virtue is thus not to sin. Anyone ignorant of God is incapable of carrying this out, of course, because ignorance of the source of our good is bound to make such a person unaware with regard to vice. 19 To put the shortest and most meaningful label on the chief business of each, knowledge is knowing God, and virtue is worshipping him: wisdom is contained in the one, and justice in the other.[21]

19 *Ep.* 1.1.41. L. has stopped in mid-sentence: Horace added, 'and the prime wisdom is to be free from stupidity'.

20 An early glimpse in this book of L.'s anti-imperialist sentiments. The juxtaposition of public greed and private lusts is striking.

21 In joining together wisdom and justice (as worship), L. has returned to the theme of Book 1, the unity of *sapientia* and *religio*.

Only the just and wise know the nature of virtue

6.1 I have made my first point, that knowledge of good is not virtue, and my second point, about the nature and content of virtue; it follows that I must now briefly demonstrate the ignorance of the philosophers about the nature of good and evil too. This was more or less set out in book 3, when I was discussing the supreme good.[22] 2 People ignorant of the supreme good are bound also to be in error about the other goods and evils which are not supreme; a true judgment of them cannot be made by anyone not grasping the source from which they come down to us.

3 The source of good is God, and the source of evil is of course that constant enemy of the divine name, of whom we have often spoken. These are the twin origins of good and evil. 4 What comes of God has as its purpose the preparation of immortality, which is the supreme good. What comes of that other has as its business the separation of man from things celestial, his immersion in things earthly and his killing, with a view to his punishment for ever, which is the supreme evil. 5 Without a doubt, all those philosophers who did not know God and God's adversary must also have been ignorant of what good and evil are. 6 No wonder they related the purpose of good to our brief life in the flesh (which is obviously bound to break up and collapse) and got no further; all their advice, and all the good things they infer belong to earth and stick to it, because when the body (which is earth) dies, they die too. 7 That sort of good has nothing to do with gaining a man life: it is focussed on finding and augmenting wealth, distinction, fame and power, and those are all mortal things, just as much as the man who toiled to achieve them is. Hence the phrase 'Virtue: to know the aim and end in all you seek.' 8 The philosophers give advice on the methods and skills appropriate for getting going in life because they see it is something usually done badly; but that is not the sort of virtue a wise man contemplates: virtue is not the quest for wealth; finding wealth and keeping it is not within our power. Hence the fact that wealth is easier for bad men to find and keep than for good men. 9 Virtue cannot therefore exist in seeking out those things which its own power and purpose plainly despise, nor will it switch to exactly what it is eager to trample high-mindedly underfoot, nor is it right that a soul intent on goods of heaven should be diverted from its proper immortal wealth to earn itself stuff so fragile. The point of virtue really consists most of all in achieving those things which no man, nor even death, can take away from us.

22 3.7–12.

10 This being so, the next line is true: 'Virtue: the power to pay the price that wealth is worth.' This has more or less the same meaning as the first two lines. But neither Lucilius nor any of the philosophers had the power to know what the price was, or its nature. He and all the people he followed thought it meant using one's wealth properly, being frugal, that is, not laying on lavish parties, not being recklessly generous, not wasting one's substance on unnecessary or unworthy objects.[23] 11 Someone will say perhaps, 'What about you? Don't you think that is virtue?' I do, because if I said no, it would look as if I approved of the opposite; but I also say it is not the true virtue, because it is not the celestial one but is wholly of earth, because it produces only what stays on earth. I shall set out more plainly what the proper use of wealth is and what its fruits should be when I start my section on the duties of piety.

12 All the continuation is also entirely untrue. Declaring hostilities against the wicked or undertaking the defence of the good can both be actions shared with bad people. 13 Some work their way to power by pretending to be good: they do a great deal that good people usually do, and all the more readily because they are doing it in order to deceive. If only it were as easy to practise goodness as it is to pretend it! 14 But once these people begin to get their target in their sights, and have taken the ultimate step to power, they lay aside pretence and reveal their true colours: it's smash, grab and harry everything, and even attack the good people themselves whose defence they once undertook, and the steps they climbed they now cut off, in case anyone else should have the power to copy them against themselves.

15 Let us assume, however, that this duty of defending the good belongs only to the good man. It is an easy task to take up, but a difficult one to fulfil. When you commit yourself to the struggle and the contest, the victory is in God's power, not in yours, and often the wicked are more powerful than the good both in number and in combination, so that their defeat depends not so much on virtue as on luck. 16 Everyone knows, I take it, how often the losers are the better and the juster party. That is why communities have always been subject to vicious tyrannies. 17 All history is full of examples, but we will be content with one. Pompey the Great set out to be defender of the good, since he took up arms on behalf of the republic, the senate and liberty. But he was conquered, and fell with liberty itself, and was left headless and graveless by Egyptian eunuchs.[24]

23 Cf. Cicero's discussion of *liberalitas* in *Off.* 2.52–65; and ch. 11 below.
24 On Pompey, cf. 7.15.16. In favouring Pompey and being hostile to Caesar (called killer of his country at 1.15.29), L. is perhaps following the line taken by Lucan in his epic poem on the Civil War.

18 Virtue is thus not a matter of being enemy of the bad or defender of the good, because virtue cannot be subject to uncertainty. 'Virtue: to believe your country's needs come first' is, in the absence of human discord, utterly without substance. 19 What are a country's interests other than the disadvantage of some other community or people? Working land stolen from others by violence, for instance, expanding one's own power and levying heavier taxes: none of those is a virtue; they are the overthrow of virtue.[25] 20 First of all, the ties of human society are removed, and so is innocence, and abstention from property of others, and justice itself: justice cannot endure division in the human race. Wherever the weapons flash, there is her inevitable rout and expulsion. 21 What Cicero said [*Off*. 3.28] is true: 'People who want citizens' interests heeded and those of non-citizens denied are dismissing the fellowship we share as human beings, and when that goes, so do kindness, generosity, goodness and justice in their entirety.' 22 How can a man be just who does harm, who hates, who ravages, who kills? And all those are actions of people striving to do their country good. People who think that the only useful or advantageous thing is something you can grasp simply do not know what doing good is. But what you can grasp, another can grab. 23 So anyone who goes for these 'goods of his country', as they themselves call them – anyone, that is, who destroys communities, wipes out nations, fills the treasury with money, grabs land and makes his fellow citizens richer – is lauded to heaven, and people think he is the embodiment of perfect virtue.

This is a mistake made not only by the ignorant mob but also by philosophers; they also give their advice on injustice, in case folly and malice should lack the authority of discipline. 24 So when they debate the duties relevant to time of war, nothing they have to say is aimed at justice and true virtue: it is all aimed at the life and behaviour of citizens present, which is not justice, as reality shows and as Cicero himself bears witness. 25 'We have,' he says [*Off*. 3.69], 'no firmly shaped model of true law and genuine justice; we work with a vague outline. If only we followed it! It comes from the best examples in nature and truth.' So what they thought justice is only a shadowy approximation of it! 26 Well? Doesn't Cicero also admit that there is no wisdom among the philosophers? 'Or when Fabricius [or Aristides] is called just,' he says [*Off*. 3.16], 'either they offer a model of

---

25 This discussion is derived, as is 23 below, from a missing section of Furius' speech against justice in Cic. *Rep.* 3.12.20. See Ziegler, *rep., ad loc*. L. draws for his own purposes on what were ultimately arguments of Carneades.

courage or he offers a wise man's model of wisdom.[26] None of them was wise in the sense in which we want wise to be understood;[27] 27 Cato and Laelius weren't wise, despite being treated so and being called so; nor were the Seven Sages wise, though they performed many middle level duties and so had the look of wise men.' 28 If then wisdom is denied to the philosophers on their own admission, and justice is denied to those treated as just, all those descriptions of virtue are bound to be false, since only a just and wise man can know what true virtue is. But the only just and wise man is the one educated by God with instruction from heaven.

Both paths can mislead the unwary

7.1 All the people who through the admitted stupidity of others are thought to be wise are clad in a semblance of virtue, but are grasping at a vague outline, not at what is true. It happens like that because the path that goes west is a deceiving path, with many lanes leading off it because of the great diversity of study and learning;[28] some human studies actually go in opposite directions. 2 The path of wisdom bears some resemblance to that of folly, as we showed in the previous book; so too, though the path of folly is totally the path of folly, it has some resemblance to that of wisdom (those who think folly is universal are welcome to the idea); its vices are obvious, but it also has some apparent resemblance to virtue; its badness is clear, but it also has some of the appearance of justice. 3 How could our precursor on the path, whose whole driving force lies in deception, draw everybody into his deception unless he offered them something looking like truth? After all, to keep his immortal secret under cover[29] God put things on his own path for people to shun as if they were disgracefully bad, so that when they had wandered off wisdom and truth (which they were looking for with no guide at all) they would tumble into exactly what they wanted to avoid and escape. 4 Hence all the twists and turns on the road to perdition and death, put there to match the multiplicity of lifestyles or else the multiplicity of gods being worshipped.

---

26 Aristides' place in Cicero's text is doubted. In 'either they offer a model of courage', 'they' refers to the Decii and the Scipios mentioned at the start of Cicero's sentence but the pronoun is irrelevant in L.'s context and so omitted.

27 Cf. *Off.* 1.46; 2.35.

28 This appears to be a tilt at the educational system of which L. was himself a leading light; cf. 3.7 above.

29 For the idea that God has hidden the truth, cf. 2.3.21; 4.8.8.

5 In order to show some difference between falsehood and truth and between evil and good, our conspiratorial and treacherous guide takes everybody to his road by different ways, sybarites one way and the frugal another; so too the ignorant and the educated, the lazy and the energetic, the fools and the philosophers (not that philosophers all go the same way!). 6 Those with no qualms about pleasures and riches he marshals at a little distance from this busy highway, while those earnestly pursuing virtue and professing a contempt for possessions he hauls over sheer rocky drops. 7 Nevertheless, all these routes which appear to lead to good are not different roads, but side-turnings and byways; they look different from the main road, as if they bore off to the right, but they all come back to it in the end; every one of them has the same outcome. 8 Our guide brings everybody together at the point where separation must be made of good from evil, of brave from cowards, of wise from foolish, and that point is worship of gods, and there he kills them all with a single stab because they were fools without distinction, and plunges them into death.

9 The road, however, which is the path of truth, wisdom, virtue and justice (all of which have one and the same origin, one and the same force and one and the same home) is not only a simple road on which we may follow and worship the one God with like minds in total concord, but also a narrow road, because rather few have the gift of virtue, and also a steep road, because without the utmost toil and trouble the good which is the supreme and sublime good cannot be reached at all.

To follow God's law is to follow the right road

8.1 This is the road the philosophers seek, but because they seek it on earth, where it cannot appear, they fail to find it. 2 They are like people all at sea, not knowing where they are going, because they cannot see their right course and they follow no guide. 3 This path of life is one to be sought in the same way that ships seek their courses at sea: if they have no light in the sky to watch, the course is not clear and they stray. 4 Anyone striving to keep on the right course must not look at the land but at the sky; to put it more plainly, he must follow not man but God, he must submit not to these earthly images but to God in heaven, he must not relate everything to the body but to the mind, and he must not heed this life but the eternal life. 5 If you kept your gaze fixed on heaven and watched where the sun rises, using it as your life's pilot, your feet will find their path of their own accord, and that light of heaven which is a far brighter sun to sane minds than this sun we see in our mortal flesh will so guide you and steer you that it will bring you without any straying at all to the ultimate haven of wisdom and virtue.

6 God's law is therefore the one to adopt to bring us on to this course, that sacred and heavenly law which Cicero described in almost godlike terms in book 3 *de Republica*. To avoid prolixity I quote his words [3.33]. 7 'True law is right reason, in accord with nature, universally distributed, consistent, perpetual, summoning men to their duty and deterring them from deceit with orders positive and negative; its orders whether positive or negative are not wasted on good men, nor do they change the behaviour of bad men. 8 It is not right for this law to be superseded; no subtraction from it is permitted; no suspension of it is possible: we cannot be released from it either by senate or by people, and no Sextus Aelius[30] is needed to explain it or to interpret it; 9 it will not be one law in Rome and a different law in Athens, one law now and different at a later date; all nations will be bound by it at all times, for it is one, eternal and immutable, and there will be one god, the common master and commander of us all; he was the one who wrote this law, explained it and enacted it. Anyone not obedient to him will be in flight from himself, and even if he avoids all other punishments imaginable, for defying his human nature he will pay the supreme penalty.' 10 No one with knowledge of God's mystery could possibly set forth God's law as meaningfully as that is expressed, and expressed by a man far from knowledge of the truth. My view of people who speak the truth unawares is that they divine it by some spiritual instinct. 11 But if Cicero had also known or explained what instructions the holy law itself consists in as clearly as he saw its force and reason, he would have fulfilled the role not of a philosopher but of a prophet. 12 That, however, he could not do, and so we must: it is to us that the law has been given by that one God who is master and commander of us all.

Knowledge of God is the head, and the practice of justice is the limbs; the promise of eternity justifies a life of virtue

9.1 The principal head of this law is to know God himself, to obey him alone and to worship him alone. No one can understand the meaning of man who fails to know God as parent of his soul. That is the supreme wickedness. That is the ignorance which makes a man serve other gods, and no worse crime

---

30 Sextus Aelius was a famous statesman and jurist of the early 2nd cent. BC. See Cic. *de Orat.* 1.198 (citing Ennius); 240.

can be committed than that. 2 Ignorance of the true and unique good makes the step from here to evil an easy glide: goodness comes from the very God whom men shrink from knowing.[31] Or if they want to pursue justice, nevertheless in their ignorance of God's law people will embrace their own laws as if they were the true law, when they are simply the product of expediency and not of justice. 3 Why are there so many different legal systems all over the world, unless it is because each individual nation endorses what it thinks beneficial to its own interests? 4 The gap between justice and expediency is well demonstrated by the people of Rome, who got themselves control of the whole world by using Fetials[32] to declare wars and by using forms of law to cover their wrongdoings and to seize and take other people's property. 5 These Romans think they are just if they do nothing against their own laws; but that can be put down to fear, if they kept from crime for fear of instant punishment. 6 Let us grant, however, that they do what their laws compel them to do naturally or, as the philosopher puts it, spontaneously.[33] Does obedience to human institutions make them just, when human beings themselves have been quite capable of error or injustice, like the authors of the Twelve Tables, or have certainly bowed to public convenience to suit the situation? 7 Civil law, which varies everywhere according to custom, is quite different from true justice, which is uniform and simple, being God's provision for us all; and anyone ignorant of God is bound to be ignorant of true justice also.

8 Let us imagine, however, the possibility of someone grasping the true virtues by some natural, inborn good: the sort of man we hear that Cimon was in Athens, who gave food to the needy, took in the poor, clothed the naked;[34] and yet, when that one thing of supreme importance is missing, the knowledge of God, all those good things are suddenly superfluous and futile, so that he laboured to achieve them in vain. 9 All his justice will be like a human body without its head: though every limb keeps place and form and use, nevertheless for want of the most important piece of all, life and sensation are utterly missing. 10 Those limbs thus have only the appearance of limbs without the use, much like a head without a body. So too with a

---

31 See note on 6.19. The next three sentences probably have the same origin.

32 In theory, the Romans did not wage war without an ultimatum, delivered by the priesthood of the Fetiales, demanding of the enemy restoration or compensation. See Cic. *Off.* 1.34–36 and 80; *Rep.* 2.31 (cf 26 on Numa). Despite Cicero's claim, it is clear that the fetial procedure was manipulated in the cause of Roman expansionism.

33 Cf. Cic. *Rep.* 1.3; *Leg.* 1.49.

34 See Athen. *Deipn.* 533a–c (citing Theopompus); Plu. *Cim.* 10.1–2; Millett (1989), 23–25.

person who is not ignorant of God but who is living without justice: all he has is the most important piece, but it is no use, because it is missing the limbs, the virtues. 11 For a body to be alive and to have sensation, knowledge of God is necessary as head, and all the virtues are necessary as body. That will produce a man live and perfect, but the sum total of him depends on the head, since it cannot exist in the absence of all the other parts, but it can exist in the absence of some. 12 It will be a faulty, handicapped creature, but it will live, just like someone who knows God and is in some respect a sinner; there is forgiveness from God for sins. Life is thus possible without some limbs, but quite impossible without a head.

13 Hence the phenomenon of philosophers who are good enough by nature but have no knowledge or wisdom. All their learning and virtue lacks a head, because they do not know God who is the head of virtue and learning. Someone who does not know God may be able to see, but he is blind; he may be able to hear, but he is deaf; and he may be able to speak, but he is dumb. 14 But when he does know the founder and father of the world, then he will see and hear and speak: he begins to have a head, in which all the senses are located, the eyes, that is, the ears and the tongue. 15 For seeing is most surely seeing when the eyes of the mind see the truth in which God exists or God in whom truth exists, and hearing is most surely hearing when God's words of advice on life are stamped upon the heart, and speech is most surely speech when talk of things celestial leads to talk of the virtue and majesty of the one and only God.

16 The impiety of those who do not know God is thus certain; all the virtues which they think they have and hold may be found on the path of death, which is wholly made of darkness. 17 There is no reason for anyone to congratulate himself upon obtaining these futile virtues; such a person is bound to be not only wretched in lacking immediate goods but also stupid in toiling so hard through life to no effect. 18 If the hope of immortality which God promises to those who practise his religion is taken away – and it is for the sake of acquiring immortality that virtue must be sought and all incidence of evil be endured – then it will certainly be a great piece of silliness to bind oneself deliberately to those virtues which bring man calamity and trouble to no purpose.[35] 19 If it is virtue to undergo need, exile, pain and death, which everyone else is afraid of, and to bear them with courage, what good has virtue in itself to make philosophers say that it should be sought for its own sake? People are surely taking pleasure in pains that are superfluous

---

35 Cf. 5.18.1–11.

and futile, when they could be living in peace. 20 If souls are mortal, and no virtue will exist when the body disintegrates, why do we shun the good things provided for us as if we are not glad or fit to enjoy God's gifts? In order to have these goods we must live in crime and irreligion, because virtue – justice, that is – is followed by poverty. 21 A man must be mad who has no greater hope before him and yet puts toil, torture and misery in front of the good things which everyone else enjoys in life.

22 If, however, virtue is to to be sought, as they most correctly say, on the grounds that man was born to that end, there ought to be some greater hope, to bring great and notable comfort for the evils and difficulties which it is virtue's part to endure. Virtue is hard enough already: it cannot be held a good thing unless its harshness is balanced by some very great good. 23 Equally, abstention from immediate goods is impossible unless there are other, greater, goods which make it worthwhile to miss out on pleasures and to put up with all manner of evil. But there are no other goods, as I explained in book 3, except those of life everlasting. And only God can provide life everlasting, the God who has put virtue before us. 24 Everything therefore turns on recognition and worship of God. That is the key to all man's hope of salvation; the first step to wisdom is to know who our true father is, to worship him alone with due piety, to obey him, and to serve him with utter devotion; our every deed, every thought, every effort must be aimed at earning his approval.

Society is based on mutual love and care

10.1 So much for what is due to God. Now I shall say what is due to man – though whatever you grant to man, you also grant to God, since man is the likeness of God. 2 Nevertheless: the prime activity of justice is connexion with God; then comes connexion with man. That first activity is called religion; the second is termed compassion, or humanity. It is an especial virtue of the just and the worshippers of God, because it alone contains the meaning of our life together.

3 God did not endow the rest of his creation with wisdom, but he made them comparatively safe from attack and danger by giving them natural defences. Man on the other hand he created naked and frail: in order to equip man in particular with wisdom, he gave him this emotion of piety in addition, so that man would protect man, and they would love and cherish each other and give each other help against all dangers. 4 The greatest bond between people is their humanity; anyone who breaks that tie must be

considered an evil man and a parricide. If we all spring from the one man[36] whom God made, then we are certainly linked by blood: hence the great crime it must be to hate someone, even one who causes harm. 5 God presumably said that we must never rouse up enmity but always try to remove it so that we can remind any who are our enemies of their relationship with us and so moderate their feelings. 6 So too, if we have all been given the breath of life by one and the same God, we must all be brothers, and closer than brothers too, being brothers in spirit rather than in the flesh. 7 Lucretius is right when he says [2.991–92]: 'Finally, we are all sprung from celestial seed, and all share an identical father.' 8 People who do harm to a man are to be seen as savage beasts therefore; contrary to all law of humanity and all that is right they rob, they torture, they kill and they banish.

This sibling relationship is why God instructs us to do evil never and good always. 9 Exactly what doing good is he has prescribed himself: it is to give help to people in sorrow and trouble and to share food with those who have none. 10 God deliberately made us a social animal because of his own piety; we need to see ourselves in others. We deserve no liberation from danger if we give no help ourselves, and we deserve no help if we deny it to others. 11 The philosophers have no advice to give in this area because they are victims of a bogus virtue; they have removed pity from man,[37] and despite a desire to heal him they have corrupted him. 12 They do generally admit that the ties of human fellowship should be maintained, but it is obvious that they detach themselves from them by the rigour of their own inhuman virtue. That is yet another mistake to be exposed in those who think nothing should be shared with anyone.

13 Philosophers have put forward more than one reason for the founding of cities. Some say that the people who were first born of earth led a nomadic life in forest and field and had no common bond of speech or law to keep them together; they used leaves and grass for beds, and caves and grottoes for homes, and they fell prey to wild beasts and more powerful animals. 14 The ones who were mauled and escaped, or who saw their neighbours being mauled, then ran to other people, aware now of their peril, and begged for help; at first they indicated their wishes by nodding; later they made first attempts at speech; by giving names to individual objects they slowly perfected a system of talking. 15 When people saw how many there were to

---

36 In introducing Christian charity as something derived from the virtue of piety, L. is Christianising a traditional Classical theme, as he did in ch. 3 above.

37 L.'s target is Stoicism. See ch. 11 below.

be protected against wild beasts, they began to build towns, to keep their nights safe and quiet or to keep the raids and incursions of the beasts at bay, not by fighting but by throwing up barriers.[38]

16 Nonsense like that is unworthy of human intelligence. What poor and sorry people, to record their folly in writing! 17 They could see that the dumb beasts also had a natural ability to come together for mutual help, to avoid danger, to watch out for harm or to make lairs and retreats for themselves, and yet they thought that only example could warn man himself and teach him what he should fear and flee and do; otherwise men would never have come together, nor found a cause for speech, if the beasts hadn't gobbled them up! 18 Others thought this was crazy, which it was, and they said that being mauled by beasts was not the cause of people uniting; humanity itself was rather the cause, and that was why people met: it was human nature to shun loneliness and to seek out company and fellowship.

The disagreement between them is not great; though their reasons are different, the outcome is the same. 19 Both points of view are possible because there is no contradiction between them, but neither is true at all, because all over the world people are not born from earth as if they were seeded from the teeth of some dragon, as poets say; rather, one man was created by God, and from him and him alone the whole earth has been filled with human stock, in the same way presumably that it was filled again after the flood, and that is a fact they cannot deny. 20 There was thus no initial meeting between men on that basis, and anyone capable of reason will understand that there have never been people on earth who couldn't speak except as infants. 21 We can pretend, however, that what old folk say in their idle folly is true, so that we can refute them best of all with their own perceptions and arguments.

22 If people came together in order to shore up their own feebleness by exchange of aid, then help must go to the man who needs it. 23 For since men have set up and endorsed association with their fellow men for the sake of protection, then violation or non-preservation of that association, observed as it is among men since its first coming, must be considered the supreme sin. 24 Anyone who withdraws from offering help is bound to withdraw from receiving help as well: anyone denying his own assistance to a neighbour must think he needs no one else's himself. 25 Anyone who detaches

---

38 Cf. Cic. *Rep.* 1.39ff.; Scipio finds the origin of communities not in weakness but in a natural human tendency to forgather, *naturalis quaedam hominum quasi congregatio.* L., however, finds a role for weakness in its provision of opportunity for charitable giving (see 22 below).

himself from society and keeps apart must live like the wild beasts and not like a man. But that is impossible; and so the bonds of human fellowship must be maintained, because no way can man exist without man. Maintenance of fellowship is sharing: offering help, that is, in order to be able to receive it. 26 But if people come together for the sake of humanity itself, as those others argue, then man must certainly acknowledge man. 27 But if that has been done by people ignorant and still uncivilised, and done when a system of speech had not yet been established, what are we to think should be done by people of education, linked to each other by exchanges of conversation and everything else, who cannot endure loneliness because they are used to their fellow human beings?

Charity looks for no return

11.1 Humanity must then be maintained if we want to be worth our name of human being.[39] And the maintenance of humanity is quite simply loving people because they are human and the same as we are. 2 Quarrels and disagreements are contrary to the meaning of man, and what Cicero said [*Off.* 3.25] is true: 'A man obedient to his nature cannot harm another.' If it is unnatural to hurt someone, it must be in accord with nature to do good to someone. 3 Anyone not doing so strips himself of the name of man, because it is the business of humanity to rescue men in need and peril. 4 If someone had been grabbed by a wild animal and were begging the help of a man with weapons, should he be helped or not? I wonder what the opinion would be of those who think a wise man has no business to be persuaded into pity. They are not be so brazen as to say that what humanity begs, nay, demands, must not be done. 5 So too, if someone were to be hemmed in by fire, crushed under a fall, drowned at sea, swept away by a flood, would they think it a man's business not to help? If they did think so, they wouldn't be men themselves; no one can avoid the risk of that sort of danger. I'm sure they will actually say that saving people in peril is exactly the business of a man, and of a brave man too.

6 If, then, in misfortunes of that sort they admit that it is humanity's business to go to the rescue because there is a threat to someone's life, what is their reason for thinking that help is not to be given if someone is hungry, thirsty or in pain? These are conditions naturally on a par with the other

---

39 In this chapter L. stages an effective confrontation between pagan and Christian attitudes to giving.

BOOK 6: TRUE WORSHIP

chance misfortunes of life, and they need one and the same humanity; and yet people distinguish them because they are measuring everything by immediate advantage and not by the true measure. 7 They hope that the people they rescue from danger will return the favour; they have no such hope of people in need, and they think that whatever they share with them of that sort is a waste. 8 Hence that detestable passage in Plautus [*Trin.* 339–40]: 'Give a beggar food to eat, and win no favours; what you give is wasted, and it only prolongs his misery.'[40] 9 Oh, but the poet wasn't speaking in his own person! Wasn't he? Isn't that exactly what Cicero recommends in his books *On Duties*, that largesse should not be universal? He put it thus [2.52]: 'Largesse drawn from one's own resources exhausts the well of generosity itself. Generosity is killed by generosity. The more people you help, the less you can help so many.' 10 A little further on he says: 'How stupid it is to get yourself into a position where you can no longer do what you were glad to do!' In advising people to look after their own resources with care and to put maintenance of purse before maintenance of justice, our pretender to wisdom is plainly restraining them from humanity. 11 As soon as he saw it was unkind and wrong, in a fit of remorse he says in another paragraph [2.54]: 'Largesse should be practised sometimes; this sort of generosity is not to be absolutely rejected; a contribution from your own resources can often be made to suitable people in need.' 12 What does suitable mean? Those who can repay and return the favour. If Cicero were alive today, I would certainly cry out, 'Here you have strayed from true justice, my dear Cicero; you wiped it out with one word, the moment you measured works of piety and humanity by their expediency.'

13 Suitable people are not the proper object of largesse: it is as far as possible for the unsuitable, because a deed done with justice, piety and humanity is a deed you do without expectation of return. This is the real and true born justice, of which you say there is no model of clear-cut shape.[41] 14 You insist at many points[42] that virtue is not for hire, and you acknowledge in your books *de Legibus* that generosity is for free, as follows [*Leg.* 1.48]: 'There is no doubt that anyone called liberal and generous is pursuing duty and not reward.' So why give to the suitable, except to reap a return later? 15 Anyone not suitable will thus on your authority as adviser on justice die

---

40 L. might have cited Sen. *Beata Vita* 24: 'To some I shall not give, although they are in need, because even if I did give, they would still be in need.'
41 Cf. *Off.* 3.69, quoted in ch. 6.25 above.
42 E.g. *Arch.* 28; *Mil.* 35, 96.

of his nakedness, thirst or hunger, and people of means, people even wallowing in wealth, will bring him no help in his extremity.

16 If virtue asks for no reward, if it is to be sought, as you say, for its own sake, then measure justice, which is mother and head of the virtues, at its own price and not by its advantage to you; offer it most of all to someone from whom you can expect nothing. 17 Why pick special people? Why check for looks? If someone prays to you because he thinks you are a human being, then you must treat him as a human being too. 18 Cast off all the shadows, the vague outlines of justice, and grab hold of true justice in its full form. Give to the blind, the sick, the lame and the destitute; if you don't, they die. Men may have no use for them, but God has: he keeps them alive, gives them breath and honours them with light. 19 Cherish them as much as you can, and sustain their souls with humanity so that they do not die. Anyone who can help a dying man but doesn't is his murderer.

20 There are people, however, who don't maintain their natural humanity and don't know the reward there is in doing so; in the middle of fearing a loss they suffer it, and they tumble into the trap they feared most, which is that all their giving is either completely wasted or serves their interest only very briefly. 21 The people who refuse a minimal dole to those in need because they are reluctant to maintain humanity without loss to themselves are actually throwing away their inheritance and getting in return either perishable and fragile stuff or else nothing at all, at enormous loss. 22 What is to be said of the people who succumb to the popular taste for trivia and spend wealth that would support great cities in giving games, except that they must be raving mad to offer people what they themselves lose and what none of those being offered it gains? 23 All pleasures are brief and fading, especially those of eye and ear: people either forget, and show no gratitude for the other fellow's spending, or even get cross if it failed to answer popular fancy (very stupid donors in consequence have even won themselves evil for their evil), or else, if they did find favour, all they gain is a futile popularity and a few days' gossip. The fortunes of shallow men are wasted in this fashion on superfluities every day.

24 Is there any more wisdom in those who offer their fellow citizens something more useful, of greater duration? I mean the people who seek some immortality by erecting public buildings. Even they get it wrong: they are burying their goods in the earth twice over, because being on the record is no use to the dead and the works don't last for ever: one earthquake shatters them and they collapse, or they go up in an accidental fire, or some enemy attack destroys them, or else they succumb to old age and so tumble

down. 25 As the orator says [Cic. *Marc.* 11], 'There is no work of man's making which old age will not end and consume, whereas this justice and mercy[43] will bloom more strongly every day.' 26 Those who make gifts to fellow tribesmen and clients do better: they are offering something to people and are doing them good; but it is still not an act of true and just giving. Giving is nothing where there is no necessity for it. 27 Anything given for favour's sake to people not in need is wasted, or else it comes back with interest added, and so will not count as a gift. Even if the recipients like it, it is still not a just gift, because if it were not made, no evil ensues.[44] 28 The only true and certain obligation of generosity is to feed the needy and the useless.

Provide for outsiders and the truly needy, and do not fear poverty

12.1 This is the perfect justice which guards that human fellowship of which the philosophers speak, and these are the greatest and truest fruits of wealth: not to use it for one person's own pleasure but for the rescue of many, and not for one's own immediate reward but for justice, which alone does not perish. 2 It needs to be fully understood that hope of a return must be absolutely missing from the exercise of mercy: only God may look for reward from this particular work. If you looked for it in a man, then it will not be humanity but the interest on a benefit; it is impossible for anyone who does what he does for himself and not for another to have earned any credit. And yet there is a return: what a man does for another expecting nothing back from it he does do for himself because he will have his reward from God. 3 So too God requires that if we give a party at any time we invite to share the food people who cannot invite us back on equal terms, so that every act of our lives is charged with its duty of mercy.[45] 4 But no one should think that he is forbidden the company of friends or the love of neighbours; God has made known to us what our true and just task is: we ought to live with our neighbours on a basis of knowing that one thing belongs to man in the relationship and another to God. 5 Hospitality is therefore a special virtue, as the philosophers also say, but they divorce it from true justice and force it under expediency. 'It is right,' says Cicero [*Off.* 2.64], 'that Theophrastus

---

43 Cicero was appealing to the clemency of Julius Caesar. His text says 'this justice and mercy of yours'.

44 An extraordinary condition for justice: L. pushes to the limit Cicero's linking of *utilitas* and *liberalitas* in *de Officiis*.

45 Luke 14:12.

commends hospitality. It is very attractive, in my own view too, for the homes of distinguished men to be open to distinguished guests.' 6 But he was wrong, in the same way that he was wrong when he supported 'largesse to suitable people'. A just and wise man's house ought to be open not to the distinguished but to the poor and desperate. Distinguished and powerful people cannot be in need of anything, since their wealth protects them as well as distinguishing them.

7 A just man should do nothing which is not a good deed. If the good deed is returned, however, it is over and done with; we cannot treat as clean and whole something with a price on it that we have been paid. 8 The purpose of justice is at work only in those good deeds which stay whole and uncorrupted, and they stay so only if they are done to people who cannot possibly be useful back. 9 In entertaining distinguished men Cicero looked only to his own advantage; for all his intelligence, he failed to conceal what he expected from it. As he says [2.64], 'Anyone doing that will be powerful abroad because of the favour of the important people whose interest he has secured by exercising hospitality and friendship.'

10 How many, many arguments I could make (if that were my aim) to expose the inconsistency of the man! And it would be his own words refuting him, not mine. After all, he it is who says [*Leg.* 1.49] 'The more a man refers all his actions to the service of his own interests, the less he is a good man.' 11 He also says 'It is not the business of an open, honest man to go canvassing, to pretend or to drop hints, to look as if he's doing one thing while actually doing another, to suggest he is doing something for another when he's doing it for himself; those are the actions of someone malign, crafty, deceitful and treacherous.'[46] 12 So how would he argue against hospitality of that self-seeking sort being malign? I mean, would you go frequenting all the city gates to invite the chief men of other nations and cities to your home as they arrived, in order to gain some consequence through them with their people? Would you expect to look just, humane and hospitable when pursuing your own advantage? 13 Cicero acts here not incautiously – that would be very untypical of him – but he has entangled himself in this trap wittingly and knowingly, in ignorance of true law. 14 In mitigation, he did say that he was not giving advice with a view to actual justice, which he didn't possess, but only for a hazy outline of it.[47] So let's excuse our vague and hazy adviser, and not demand the truth from one who admits he doesn't know it.

---

46 See Cic. *Off.* 3.57.
47 See note on 11.13 above.

15 A great and notable work of justice is the ransoming of captives. Cicero approved of it too. 'Kindness of the following sort,' he says [*Off.* 2.63], 'is also of service to the state: ransoming captives from slavery, enriching those of slender means. I put this pattern of generosity a long way in front of lavish public shows and games; it is the mark of serious men and great men.' 16 So: the proper business of just men is feeding the poor and ransoming prisoners, since the people who do this are called serious and great by the unjust; for it is very much a matter of praise that benefactions are made to people who were not expected to be recipients. 17 Benefactions to a kinsman, neighbour or friend earn no praise at all, or certainly not much, because they are a duty, and not to do what nature and kinship demand of a man would mark him impious and loathsome, whereas if they are done, it is as much to avoid censure as to gain glory. 18 It is benefactions to the outsider that truly deserve praise, because such acts come of humanity alone. Justice thus exists wherever there is no tie of necessity requiring a good deed. 19 Cicero should not have even preferred this duty of kindness to giving games, because it implies a comparison, a selection of the better of a pair of good things, 20 and the giving of people who waste their inheritance on shows is trivial and futile, and has nothing to do with justice at all. Gift[48] shouldn't even be the word when the only recipients are wholly undeserving.

21 A work of justice no less important is that of guarding and defending children and widows who are destitute and in need of aid. This is a universal prescription of divine law, since all good judges reckon it part of their duty to help such people and to try to do them good, from natural humanity. 22 In fact such works are especially ours to do, because we have received the law and the words of God himself instructing us. Others may well feel that it is naturally just to protect those who lack protection, but they do not see why. 23 God's kindness is unremitting: he thus requires widows and children to be defended and cherished, in case anyone should be held back, through regard and pity for his own children, from accepting death in the cause of justice and faith; he should meet it without flinching and with courage, knowing that he is entrusting his dear ones to God, and they will never lack for protection.

24 Looking after the sick, too, who have no one to support them, and cherishing them is a work of the greatest humanity and a great devotion of effort; anyone acting so will gain God a living sacrifice, and what he gives to his neighbour for now he will receive himself from God for ever.

---

48 L. is working two senses of *munus*, gift and public entertainment.

25 The last and greatest duty of piety is burial of strangers and paupers, something which those experts in justice and virtue have never discussed. They measured all duties by the advantage to them and so they could not see it. 26 In all the other duties mentioned above they failed to hold to the true path, but because they grasped some element of advantage in them, they strayed only slightly, kept in touch by a sort of sniff of the truth; but because they could see no profit in this duty they abandoned it altogether. 27 There have even been people who treated burial as superfluous, saying there was no harm in lying unburied and discarded. Their impious wisdom is rejected not only by the whole human race but also by the word of God, which requires it. 28 They don't dare to say that it is not to be done; rather, that if it weren't, there is no harm done.

They are thus fulfilling the role not so much of advisers on this issue but of comforters, so that if a wise man missed out on burial he wouldn't think himself wretched because of it. 29 We, however, are not discussing what is tolerable for a wise man but what his duty is. We are not therefore asking right now whether the whole idea of burial is useful or not: even if it is futile, as they think, nevertheless it is to be done for this reason alone, that it appears to people to be a good and humane action. What is wanted is feeling; what is in the balance is an idea. 30 We will not therefore permit a creature made in God's image to fall prey to wild beasts and birds: we will return it to the earth whence it came; unknown to us he may be, but we will fulfil his kinsmen's duty; in their absence humanity will step in, and where a man is mourned, there we shall reckon our duty is needed.

31 The whole point of justice consists precisely in our providing for others through humanity what we provide for our own families through affection. This kindness is much more sure and just when it is offered not to people, who are beyond perceiving it, but to God alone, for whom an act of justice is a most precious sacrifice. 32 Perhaps someone will say, 'If I do all this, I shall finish with nothing. I mean, if some great quantity of people falls upon need, sickness, captivity or death, so that anyone doing all this would be bound to be stripped of his inheritance in even a day, am I to waste the family fortune, whether it comes of my own or my ancestors' efforts, and then have to live life myself on the mercy of others?'[49] 33 Well? Are you so faint-hearted as to fear poverty? Even your philosophers approve of that, declaring there is nothing safer, nothing more peaceful! What you are scared of is

---

49 Cyprian in *de op. et eleem.* 9ff. raises this anxiety, but only to belittle it; and unlike L. in 37 below, he allows no compromise.

the haven of all cares. 34 Or don't you know how many dangers and how many accidents you are liable to with all this evil wealth? It will be dealing kindly with you if it all goes without shedding your blood. Yet you stroll around laden with booty, wearing spoils which may provoke the tempers of your own family even. 35 Why hesitate to lay out properly something which may be snatched from you by a simple act of robbery, a sudden proscription or some enemy raid? Why fear to make a loose and fragile good eternal, or to entrust your treasures to God to guard, where you need fear no thief or robber, no decay, no tyrant? A man rich with God can never be poor.[50]

36 If you think justice so important, throw away the burdens that oppress you and follow it; free yourself of their fetters and chains, and run to God unencumbered. Despising and trampling on mortal things is the mark of a soul that rides high.[51] 37 If, however, you cannot seize this virtue, I will free you from anxiety so that you can bring your wealth to God's altar and can get yourself something surer than its fragility. All this good advice is not for you alone: it is for the whole community that is united in mind and sticks together as one. 38 If you cannot manage great deeds on your own, practise justice as best you can, but do it so that your effort compared with the rest matches your means compared with the rest. 39 You are not to think that you are being urged to diminish your estate or to use it all up now, but rather to switch to a better purpose what you were about to spend on rubbish. What you buy wild animals with, free captives with; what you feed the animals with, feed the poor with; what you buy gladiators with, bury the innocent dead with. 40 What is the point of making rich men out of animal fighters and of equipping them for crime? They are hopelessly wicked anyway. Turn what is about to go to awful waste into a great sacrifice, so that these true gifts may win you the eternal gift from god. 41 The reward of mercy is great: God promises that for mercy all sins shall be remitted. 'If you heed the prayers of your suppliant,' he says,[52] 'I also will heed yours; if you pity sufferers, I too will pity your suffering. But if you do not take heed and do not help, I too will stir your sympathies against you and will judge you by your laws.'

Giving compensates for evil acts, thoughts and words

13.1 Whenever they beg of you, therefore, imagine that God is testing whether he should hear you. Examine your conscience, and heal its wounds as far as

50 Cf. Mt. 6:19ff.; 12:33.
51 Cf. Cic. *Off.* 3.24.
52 The source of this passage is unknown.

you can. Do not think you have licence to sin because sins are removed by generosity: sins are wiped out if you are generous because you have sinned. 2 If you were to sin from a confidence in your generosity, then they are not wiped out. God is very eager for man to be cleansed of his sins: hence his requirement of penitence; being penitent is simply declaring and promising that you will sin no more. 3 Pardon is granted therefore to those who slip carelessly or incautiously into sin, but there is no forgiveness for those who sin knowingly. No one should think, however, that if he has been purified from all stain of sin he is excused the work of giving because he has no sins to wipe out. 4 No! This is the moment for an even greater practice of justice, now that he has become a just man, so that what he did before to heal his wounds he can now do for the praise and glory of virtue. 5 Moreover, no one can be without a fault as long as he is burdened with his garb of flesh. He is liable in its weakness to the triple dominion of sin in deed, word and thought. They are the steps by which justice climbs to its topmost peak.

6 The first step of justice is to abstain from evil deeds, the second is to abstain also from evil words, and the third is to abstain even from thought of evil. 7 Those who climb the first step are fairly just; those who climb the second are already people of perfect justice since they are at fault neither in deed nor in word; those who climb the third step have clearly achieved likeness with God. 8 It is almost beyond the capacity of man not even to admit into one's thoughts things that would be evil to do or wrong to say. 9 Even just men, with the power to restrain themselves from unjust acts, nevertheless are sometimes overcome by their weakness, and they say something evil in a moment of anger or silently long for something evil at the sight of something desirable. 10 But if our mortal condition prevents us from being clean of every stain, then the sins of the flesh should be wiped out by constant giving. 11 The one need for a man who is wise, just and healthy is to ground his wealth in justice alone: be he richer than Croesus or Crassus, if he lacks justice, then he must be reckoned poor, naked and destitute.[53] 12 We must work to put on the garment of justice and virtue, therefore, of which no man may strip us and which will keep us clothed for ever. 13 If worshippers of gods attend to insensible statues and load them with all the precious things they have, which those gods cannot use and cannot be grateful to receive, how much more just and true it is to attend to living images of God in order to earn the living God's favour! 14 Just as people use what they

---

[53] Croesus the last king of Lydia (overthrown 546 BC) and Crassus the Roman politician (d. 53 BC) are coupled euphoniously as exemplars of enormous wealth.

receive and are grateful, so God, in whose sight you did your good deed, will approve it and will pay you full reward for your piety.

Stoics are in error in denying natural feelings

14.1[54] If then pity is a notable and excellent good in man, and if it is judged to be so both on evidence from God and in the thinking of good and bad men alike, then the philosophers are plainly well off course in recommending nothing of that sort or doing anything; indeed, they have always treated as a vice what is pretty well man's distinctive virtue. 2 This is a good moment to mention a particular philosophical point; then we can make full refutation of the mistakes of the ones who call pity, desire and fear ailments of the spirit. 3 They are trying to distinguish virtues from vices, which is very easy to do. Anyone could mark off generosity from prodigality as they do, or frugality from meanness, or quiet from sloth, or caution from fear, because all these goods have their limits, and if the limits are exceeded, they slide into being vices; constancy not undertaken for the sake of truth turns into stubbornness. 4 Likewise, where there is no necessity forcing the issue or no good cause for which to risk danger, bravery turns into foolhardiness. If freedom goes on to the attack itself instead of just resisting attackers, it becomes bullying. If firmness fails to stick to punishments that fit the criminal, it becomes mere cruelty. 5 Hence the philosophers' line, that people who seem bad do not sin deliberately and do not choose evil for preference, but tumble into evil because what looked good made them slip when they could not tell the difference between good and bad.

6 That is not wrong, but it is all related to our physical world. It is virtuous to be frugal, steady, cautious, quiet, brave or firm, but they are virtues of this temporal existence. We who despise this life have other virtues before us, of which philosophers could never have dreamt. 7 In this way they have treated some virtues as vices and some vices as virtues. The Stoics deny man all the feelings that stir the soul, desire, joy, fear and sorrow (the first two come from goods either present or yet to come, the two latter from evils).[55] 8 So too, they call these four feelings ailments, as I said, not inherent by nature so much as adopted by mistaken analysis, which is why they think they can be eradicated from the system if this wrong analysis of good and evil can be removed. 9 For if a wise man deems nothing good and

---

54 Cf. 3.23.8–10.
55 Cf. Cic. *Tusc.* 3.24ff.

nothing bad, he won't get hot with desire, he won't bubble with joy, he won't be atremble with fear and he won't be doubled up with illness. 10 We shall soon see whether they can do what they want, or indeed what they can do; meantime it is a presumptuous idea, and they must be almost insane to think they can act as healers and work against the power and system of nature.

Stoics cannot abolish feelings by renaming them

15.1 The naturalness of these feelings is proved by the fact that all living creatures exist on a model in which all these feelings operate anyway; they are not something willed. 2 The Peripatetics are thus nearer the answer: they say none of these emotions can be removed because they co-exist with us from birth; they try to demonstrate how providentially and how necessarily God – or nature, as they put it – has equipped us with our emotions. But because these feelings generally turn bad if they are excessive, they can be healthfully controlled by man to a limited extent, so that man is left with as much of them as nature needs. 3 This is not a stupid contention, provided, as I said, that everything is not related to this life. The Stoics are therefore mad for seeking not moderation but removal; the feelings are there by nature, and yet they want in some fashion to castrate people of them. That is like wanting to take fear out of stags, poison from snakes, wrath from wild beasts or placidity from cattle. These qualities which have been granted to dumb animals by species have been granted to man all together. 4 But if the feeling of joy is in the spleen, as doctors say, and wrath is in the gall bladder, lust in the liver and fear in the heart, it is easier to kill the whole animal than to make some partial excision. That is to want to change the animal's nature.

5 These are intelligent people, yet they do not realise that when they take vices out of a man they take out virtue as well, for which they were trying to make space on its own.[56] If it is a virtue to restrain and repress oneself in mid impulse to be angry, which they cannot deny, anyone deprived of anger is also deprived of virtue. 6 If it is a virtue to limit physical desire, then anyone without the lust he is trying to control is bound to lack virtue. If it is a virtue to rein in a greed for acquiring someone else's property, then possession of the virtue is impossible for someone without the emotion whose control depends on having it. 7 Where there are no vices, there is no room for virtue either, just as there can be no victory where there is no adversary. So it is that

---

56 Thus L. links his stance on human emotions to his favoured thesis on the necessary co-existence of virtue and vice (which is not a Peripatetic argument).

good cannot exist in this life without evil. 8 Emotions are a sort of natural exuberance of souls: fields which are naturally fertile grow a wealth of brambles, and in the same way any untilled soul chokes itself with vices that flourish like thorns. When the true farmer comes, however, at once the vices give way and the fruits of virtue spring up.

9 When God first made man, with marvellous foresight he bred in him first the sort of feelings which would enable him to acquire virtue as a land gets cultivation, and he planted the stuff of vice in the emotions and the stuff of virtue in the vices. Either virtue will not exist at all, or it will not be available for use if its power lacks visibility, or at least substantiation. 10 Let us now see what is achieved by these dear people who try to excise the vices entirely.[57] They know that the four emotions which they think develop from contemplation of good and evil, emotions whose removal they think necessary for restoring a wise man's soul to health, are in man by nature, and without them he can neither act nor react; in their place, therefore, and in their stead they try to put something else. For desire they substitute inclination, as if it was scarcely more significant to desire good than to wish it; so too, for joy they substitute gladness, and for fear, apprehension. 11 In the case of the fourth emotion they have no idea how to change the word, and so they remove sickness – sorrow, that is, and grief of soul – entirely, which is quite impossible. 12 No one could fail to grieve if his country were ravaged by pestilence, ruined by enemies or wracked by a tyrant; no one can fail to lament if he sees his freedom taken away, his friends and neighbours and all good men either banished or killed with great cruelty – unless his mind has been so shocked that all feeling has gone from it.

13 Either the whole lot ought to go, or else this feeble and defective argument should have been properly completed. That is to say, something should have been supplied in place of sickness, because to do so was a necessary consequence of the preceding adjustments. We grieve and sorrow at immediate evil just as we rejoice at immediate good. 14 If they found another name for joy because they thought it was a vicious thing, so they should have put another label on sickness, because they think it too is vicious. It is clear from this that what they were missing was a word, and not the emotion, and for lack of a word they were willing, quite contrary to what nature allows, to do away with a whole emotion which is actually very important. 15 I could have refuted those changes of name at greater length;

---

57 Cf. Cic. *Tusc.* 4.12ff. Augustine's critique of Stoic views is along the same lines as that of L. See *civ.* 14.8, with O'Daly (1999), 155–56.

I could have shown that a multiplicity of words for the same thing either was due to the desire to decorate the sentiment or to increase vocabulary, or certainly produced very little difference of meaning. Desire starts in inclination, apprehension arises out of fear, and joy is simply gladness expressed. 16 Let us assume, however, that they are different, as the philosophers want. Obviously they will say that desire is a continuing and uninterrupted inclination, that joy is a gladness raising itself to an unusual degree, and that fear is an overgreat apprehension that exceeds the limit. So: what they think should be removed is not removed but merely moderated, since only the names change and the emotions themselves abide. 17 All unawares they return to the point which the Peripatetics reach by reason: vices cannot be removed, and so they are controlled to a moderate degree. They are mistaken, then; they cannot achieve what they want, and back they come to the same old path by a long, hard, roundabout route.

Emotions require not extirpation but direction

16.1 I do not myself think that even the Peripatetics have reached the truth: they admit the existence of the vices but control them only up to a point; even modest vices are something we should eschew. 2 The first thing to aim for was no vices at all: nothing is born vicious, but vices can develop if we exercise the affections badly, and virtues can if we exercise them well. 3 Next it needs to be shown that it is not the affections themselves but what causes them that needs to be controlled. 'One should not get too happy,' they say; 'just moderately and in a controlled fashion.' That is as if they were to say one should not run in haste, but walk gently. But walkers can go astray, and runners can keep to the right course. 4 Well? If I prove that there is a situation in which it is a vice to rejoice for a moment, never mind moderately, and that there is another situation when a great outburst of joy is not at all a chargeable offence, what use will all this moderation be to us? 5 I wonder whether they think a wise man should rejoice if he sees some harm befall his enemy or whether he should curb his delight if the enemy are conquered, or a tyrant put down, and liberty and safety are restored to his fellow citizens. 6 No one doubts that it would be very bad to rejoice even a little in the first instance, and too little in the second, and the same goes for the other emotions.[58]

---

58 Aristotle would have approved of this argument, even if it exposes an ambiguity in his concept of the mean.

7 As I said, however, wisdom is not concerned with control of these feelings but in the control of what causes them, because emotions are stirred from the outside, and putting curbs on them is particularly inappropriate, since they are capable of being slight where there is much wrong and of being huge where there is nothing wrong; they should have been related to particular times, circumstances and places, in case feelings which one may correctly exercise become vices. 8 It is good to walk straight and bad to go astray; so too it is good to be emotionally moved in the right direction, and bad in the wrong direction. 9 If lust does not stray outside its lawful bed, it may be very strong but it is not culpable, whereas if it does seek another's bed, it may be a modest lust but it is a very great vice. 10 It is not thus a sickness to have feelings of anger or greed or lust, but it is a sickness to exercise them. Anyone given to anger can exercise his anger on someone he shouldn't or at an inappropriate time; anyone given to greed can even get greedy when there is no need; anyone given to lust can even attempt what is illegal. 11 The whole thing ought to have turned on the fact that since the impulse to these things cannot be checked nor ought to be, because it needs to be there to maintain our sense of duty, it should be aimed in the right direction, so that even those who run avoid the risk of stumbling.[59]

Virtues and vices need redefinition in the light of true religion

17.1 In my enthusiasm to refute the philosophers I got carried away; it was my intention to show that what they thought were vices were not vices at all but actually great virtues. Of these vices I shall take for purposes of instruction the ones that I think most relevant. 2 They treat fear, or panic, as a very great vice, and think it the supreme weakness of the mind; its opposite is bravery, and if there is bravery in a man, there is no space for fear. 3 Does anyone think it possible for fear also to be supreme bravery? No. Nature appears not to accept that anything can turn into its contrary. 4 And yet I'm not going to use any subtle conclusions such as Socrates does in Plato, forcing the people he is arguing with to admit what they had denied; I shall simply show that supreme fear is a supreme virtue.

5 Everyone agrees that fear of pain, want, exile, prison or death is the mark of a weak and timid mind; anyone not afraid of all of them is considered very brave. But anyone who fears God is not afraid of any of them.

---

[59] A similar argument is advanced in Aug. *civ.* 9.5, as acknowledged by O'Daly (1999), 119–20.

6 There is no need of arguments to prove the point: all over the world the punishments for those who worship God have always been conspicuous and still are: torments novel and monstrous have been invented for their torture. 7 The mind shudders to think of the different sorts of death; butchery done by wild beasts has raged beyond death itself. Yet these revolting dismemberments have been endured without a groan by a happy and invincible endurance. 8 This virtue has caused huge admiration among people in all areas, and even among the torturers themselves, because their cruelty was beaten by endurance. 9 And yet this virtue was born direct from fear of God. Fear therefore, as I was saying, is not to be rooted out, as the Stoics say, nor controlled, as the Peripatetics say, but directed to the true path; fears are to be removed but in such a way that this fear remains as the only one, and since it is a true and lawful fear, all on its own it prevents fear of anything else.

10 Desire is also counted a vice. If it involves a desire for things that are earthly, then it is a vice, whereas if its objects are celestial it is a virtue. Anyone desirous of achieving justice, God, everlasting life, perpetual light, and all those things which God promises to man will despise your wealth, distinction, power and kingship. 11 A Stoic will possibly say that to achieve these things needs an inclination, not a desire. Far from it: an inclination is too slight. Plenty of people are inclined, but when pain reaches the guts, inclinations fade, whereas desire persists, and if it causes everything that others desire to be matter for contempt, then it is a supreme virtue, since it is the mother of self-control. 12 That is why we ought instead to arrange for our feelings, which it is a vice to misuse, to be aimed in the right direction.

13 All these emotional excitements are like a chariot in harness: in keeping it straight the driver's chief business is to know the course; if he can hold the line he won't hit anything however energetically he goes, but if he strays, however quietly and gently he's going, he will either be wrecked on a rocky bit or plunge over the edge, or at the least he'll arrive where he has no need to arrive. 14 The chariot of life is drawn by the emotions as if they were vigorous horses: it will do its job if it keeps a straight road. If fear and desire are focussed on the earth, they will turn into vices; if they are related to things divine, they will turn into virtues.

15 Thrift, on the other hand, they treat as a virtue. If it is a desire for possession, it cannot be a virtue, since its whole concentration will be on increasing or protecting earthly goods. We, however, do not relate the supreme good to the body: we measure its whole business by its preservation of the soul alone. 16 But if, as I explained earlier, the maintenance of humanity and justice requires no sparing of one's inheritance, then it is not a virtue to be

frugal: it looks like a virtue, but the label is misleading. 17 Frugality is abstinence from pleasures, but it is a vice in that it is derived from love of possessing; and yet, we ought to abstain from pleasures but also not be economical with our money. Using money meanly or thriftily is a pusillanimous act: either you are scared of being without, or doubtful you can make good again, or you have no contempt for earthly things.

18 Again, philosophers use the word prodigal for someone unsparing of his family fortune. They distinguish between liberal and prodigal as follows: a liberal person is one who gives largesse to those who deserve it, who gives when it is appropriate, and who gives as much as suffices; a prodigal is one who pours it out on those who don't deserve it, when there is no need, and without regard to his means. 19 So: if someone bestows food on the needy out of pity, shall we call him prodigal? And yet it makes a big difference whether you bestow money on prostitutes out of lust or on the poor out of humanity; whether you let panders, gamblers and pimps plunder your purse, or you spend on piety and God; whether you pour it down your gullet and belly, or lay it up in the treasury of justice. 20 It is a vice to spend money to a bad end; correspondingly, it is a virtue to spend it well. If it is a virtue not to spare resources which can be restored in order to maintain a human life which cannot be restored, then thrift is a vice.

I have to call it madness when people deprive man, a gentle, social animal, of his name; 21 they remove the natural affections of which all humanity is composed and seek to reduce us to an emotionless mental stupor, while at the same time wanting to free the mind from trouble and to make it, in their own words, peaceful and tranquil. 22 It is not just that it cannot be done (the emotions are the context of rational effort); it ought not to be done even, because just as water which is stagnant is unhealthy and muddy, when the mind is motionless and torpid it is useless even to itself: it cannot safeguard its own existence, because it won't be doing or thinking anything – after all, thinking is itself a mental excitement. 23 In sum, those who press for immobility of mind really want to deprive the mind of life, because life is full of movement, and death is still.

24 There are some things which philosophers rightly treat as virtues, but they do not keep them all in proportion. Constancy is a virtue, not in resisting those who try to injure us (yielding is the right thing to do there, and I will explain why it is in a moment), but in not being frightened away from putting God's commands before those of men as a result of any threat or act of torture from people telling us to go against the law of God and against justice. 25 It is also a virtue to despise death, but not so as to seek it out and

bring it upon ourselves deliberately, as many philosophers, often the greatest ones, have done, which is a wicked, criminal deed;[60] rather, we should prefer to undergo death if we are being forced to desert God and to betray our faith; we should defend our liberty against the foolish and lunatic violence of the impotent, and we should challenge all the threats and terrors of this world with spiritual courage. 26 In this way we shall trample down what others fear, pain and death, with a lofty invincibility. That is the virtue, that is the true constancy, to be safeguarded and preserved on this basis alone, that no terror and no violence can possibly separate us from God. 27 Cicero's perception is right [*Off.* 2.38]: 'No one can be a just man who fears death, pain, exile or want.' 28 Seneca's view is also right; he says in his books of moral philosophy, 'Your honest man is a man of this sort: he is not marked out by diadem or purple, or the attentions of lictors; he does not fall short in any way; when he sees death close at hand he is less perturbed than if he saw some novelty; if he has torture of his whole body to endure or flame to swallow or his hands to be stretched on a cross, he asks not what he is to endure but how well.'[61] 29 A worshipper of God endures these things without fear: therefore he is just. So it comes about that neither the virtues nor their precise bounds can be either known or kept by any person who is estranged from the religion of the one God.

The just man is innocent and patient, and does not retaliate

18.1 Let us leave the philosophers; either they know nothing at all, and promote exactly that as the supreme knowledge, or else they do not even understand what they do know, or, because they think they know what they don't know, they are futile and presumptuous in their ignorance. 2 Let us return to our purpose; God has revealed his truth and has sent his wisdom from heaven to us alone; so let us carry out the commands of God our enlightener. Let us sustain the difficulties of this life and endure them by helping each other; at the same time, if we do a good work, let us seek no glorification from it.

3 God recommends that the doer of justice should not go boasting, in case it may look as though he has performed his duty of humanity not from any enthusiasm to obey the instructions of heaven but out of keenness to please, and that he already has the prize of fame which he wanted and would

---

60 For L. on suicide, see 3.18.5–12. The Stoic position, to which allusion is made here, is encapsulated in Cic. *Fin.* 3.60–61 (speech of Cato); cf. D.L. 7.130.
61 Sen. F96, 208 (Vottero).

not accept the reward of God's own celestial thanks. 4 Everything else that the worshipper of God should abide by is easy if these virtues are grasped. He must never tell lies in order to deceive or hurt. 5 It is wrong for anyone devoted to the truth to be deceptive in anything and to depart from the absolute truth which he pursues: on this path of justice and the virtues, there is no room for a lie. 6 The true and just traveller will therefore not quote that verse of Lucilius, 'It's not my way to lie to a close friend.'[62] He will reckon it is not his business to lie even to an enemy or to a stranger, and he will never allow his tongue, the interpreter of his soul, to diverge from his feelings and his thinking. 7 If he lends money, he will accept no interest on it, on two grounds: the kindness with which he succours someone's need will thus be unqualified and he will take no toll of property not his. 8 In observing a duty of this sort he must be content with his own; in any case, in order to do good, he should even not refrain from lightening his own purse; and it is unjust to take more than you give. Anyone doing that is laying a sort of ambush, to gain by someone else's need.

9 The just man will never forgo the chance to act mercifully, and he will never befoul himself with profit in such a case; he will arrange for the grant itself to count among his good works without any restitution. 10 He is to accept no gift from a poor man, so that anything he himself gives will be good because it was free. He is to answer a curse with a blessing; he himself should never curse, so that no evil word may proceed out of the mouth of one who reveres the good word. 11 He should also take great care never to create an enemy by fault of his own, and if there is someone so aggressive as to do harm to a good and just man, the good and just man should put up with it in a forgiving and self-controlled fashion, exacting no revenge of his own but leaving it to the judgment of God.

12 He should preserve his innocence at all times and in all places. This advice is not just to prevent him being the cause of harm himself, but also to prevent him seeking redress when harm is done to him. The greatest and fairest of judges is in perpetual session, watcher and witness of all: let him be preferred before any man to pronounce on any suit. His verdict is beyond evasion, whether by fine pleading or by favours. 13 And so it comes about that a just man earns everyone's contempt; because he will be seen as incapable of defending himself, he will be treated as slow and useless. Anyone who takes vengeance on his enemy, however, will be thought brave and vigorous, and everyone will fear and honour him. 14 The good man is capable of

---

62 Lucil. fr. 695 (Warmington) = 8 (Charpin) = 953 (Marx).

helping far more people; and yet they look up to the man who can hurt them and not to the one who can help them.

The wickedness of people cannot deprave the just man, however, or spoil his enthusiasm for obeying God and preferring people's contempt upon condition that he is always doing the good man's duty and never the bad. 15 As Cicero says in his own work on duties [*Off.* 3.76], 'If a man were willing to unpack the folds of his thinking, he would soon teach himself that a good man is one who would help those he could and would harm no one unless provoked by mistreatment.' 16 What a sound and simple sentiment he has ruined by adding a couple of words! What need was there to add 'unless provoked by mistreatment', pinning vice on to a good man like an awful tail, and denying his patience, which is the greatest of all the virtues? 17 A good man would do harm if he were provoked, he said: if a good man does do harm, he's bound to lose his name thereby. It is no less of an evil to return harm than it is to initiate it. 18 Where do quarrels between people come from, and how do their fights and squabbles arise, except that when impatience encounters crooked dealing it often stirs up big storms? 19 If you match dishonesty with patience – and there is no truer virtue than patience, and none more worthy of man – the evil will be put out there and then, like putting water on a fire. But if dishonesty in all its provocativeness gets impatience as its mate, then it will flare up as if drenched in oil, and no river at all will extinguish the blaze, but only bloodshed.

20 Patience has a huge point to it therefore, and yet the wise man has deprived the good man of it. It is the only means whereby no evil can happen; if it were granted to everybody, there would be no crime and no trickery among men. 21 For a good man, nothing could be more disastrous and more contrary to his interests than to relax the control of anger; that would strip him not only of the name of good but also of the name of man, since to harm another, as Cicero says so firmly, is not in accord with human nature.[63] 22 Even cattle fight back with hoof and horn if you provoke them, and if you don't pursue wild beasts and snakes to the death, they offer no trouble; to revert to human examples, if ignorant and stupid people suffer hurt at any time, a blind and irrational fury takes over and they try to get their own back on their assailants.

23 So what is the difference between a wise and good man on the one hand and evil and stupid people on the other, except that he has an invincible patience which fools lack? He knows how to control and reduce his own

---

63 Cic. *Off.* 3.25.

anger, while they, for lack of virtue, cannot control theirs. 24 Obviously Cicero was deceived: when he spoke of virtue, he thought it was the business of virtue to win, whatever the point at issue, and he simply could not see that a man could not maintain a duty of virtue if he succumbed to grief and anger and gave in to those feelings which he ought rather to resist, rushing off wherever a piece of dishonesty set him a challenge. 25 Anyone trying to repay a hurt is trying to imitate the man who hurt him. Anyone imitating a bad man thus cannot be good on any understanding. 26 In two words he deprived a good and wise man of two most important virtues, innocence and patience. But he was a practitioner of that canine eloquence, as Sallust says Appius called it; hence his wish for man to live like a dog, so that he can snap back when provoked.[64]

27 As for the damage done by retaliation, and the disasters it usually causes, no more suitable example will be found than in the utterly dismal fate of its recommender Cicero: in his enthusiasm to live by the advice of the philosophers he destroyed himself. 28 If he had kept his patience when provoked, if he had learnt that it is the business of a good man to dissemble and to endure insults, if those fine speeches, labelled with another's name, had never issued from his impatient mad folly, then his head would never have bled on the rostra where once he flourished, and his proscription would never have brought such total ruin to the republic.[65] 29 It is not the business of a wise and good man to look for quarrels and to put himself at risk, because victory is not within our power and all quarrels are uncertain of outcome; it is, however, typical of a wise and excellent man to want to be rid not of his adversary (which is impossible without risk of doing wrong) but of the quarrel itself, which can be done both usefully and justly. 30 Patience is therefore to be treated as the supreme virtue; for a just man to attain it God was willing for him to be despised as a sluggard, as said above. For if he is not belaboured with insults, it will never be known what fortitude he exercises in restraining himself. 31 But if, provoked by injury, he starts to chase his attacker he is the loser: the man who uses reason to suppress that reaction is plainly in command of himself; he can rule himself.

32 This control of his is rightly called patience; patience is the one virtue opposed to all vices and emotions. It recalls a troubled and wobbling soul to its calm, it soothes it, and restores man to himself. 33 Since any resistance to

---

64 Sal. *Hist.* 4.54 (Maurenbrecher).

65 The story of Cicero's proscription and death, which were Mark Antony's revenge for the *Philippics*, is told in Plu. *Cic.* 47–49.

nature which would reduce our reactions to nil is impossible and unprofitable, emotions which might spring up damagingly (something which can happen rather quickly) do need to be laid to rest before they cause harm. God says that the sun should not go down upon our wrath,[66] in case a witness of our folly may slip away. 34 Finally, Cicero (contrary to his own advice, of which I spoke earlier) counted the forgetting of injuries among the great credits. 'I hope,' he said to Caesar [*Lig.* 35], 'that you with your habit of forgetting nothing except injuries...' 35 If Caesar could do that, a man utterly remote from political and personal justice,[67] never mind the justice of heaven, how much more should we be doing it, when we are candidates for immortality?

The proper limits of anger, greed and lust

19.1 The Stoics try to eradicate human emotions as if they were diseases, but the Peripatetics resist the argument, not just retaining them but even defending them: they say there is nothing in man that is not deliberately and providentially innate.[68] That is right, provided they knew the true ends of every matter. 2 Anger, they say, is the whetstone of virtue, as if no one could fight bravely against a foe without being worked up by anger. 3 That way they make it plain that they do not know what anger is, nor why God put it in man. If it has been given us for killing people, what could be nastier than man? We should have to think of the very creature which God made for community and innocence as more akin to the wild beasts. 4 There are thus three emotions which can drive man headlong into all manner of crime: anger, greed and lust. The poets have observed in parallel that there are three Furies[69] which can excite people's minds: anger wants revenge, greed wants wealth, and lust wants pleasure. 5 But God has fixed limits for them all, and if people cross those limits and overreach themselves, they are bound to corrupt their nature and to become diseased and vicious.

What those bounds are is no great task to explain. 6 Cupidity has been given us for the acquiring of those things necessary for life, lust for the propagation of children, and the emotion of anger to check the misdeeds of those within our power: that is, for training the young by tight discipline to be upright and just. If young people are not constrained by fear, their

66 Eph. 4:26.
67 On Julius Caesar, see 1.15.29; 3.18.12.
68 Cic. *Tusc.* 4.43.
69 Cf. Cic. *Tusc.* 3.25.

freedom will produce insolence, and it will erupt in all manner of outrageous and evil action. 7 It is both just and necessary to use anger against the young; by the same token it is destructive and impious to do so against your equals, impious because humanity is assaulted, and destructive because if they resist, either you destroy them or you perish yourself. 8 The reason I have given for man having the emotion of anger can be seen in the precepts of God himself: he says we should not get angry with those who attack us, verbally or otherwise, but we should always have the upper hand over the young, in order to correct them with instant beatings when they sin, so that futile affection and over-indulgence do not rear them to evil and fatten them up for vice. 9 Inexperienced people, however, ignorant of God's intention, have set aside these feelings that were given to man for good ends; they are further off course than His purpose requires. 10 Hence the injustice and impiety of their lives.

People vent anger on their equals: hence division and banishment, and the wars that arise against justice. They exercise greed to heap up wealth: hence fraud, robbery, and all manner of crime. They practise lust merely to get pleasure: hence rape and adultery, and all sorts of depravity. 11 Anyone who brings these feelings back within their proper bounds (something which those ignorant of God cannot do) is patient, brave and just.

Ocular pleasure – games, theatre, circus – and God's prohibition of killing

20.1 It remains for me to speak against the pleasures of the five senses, but given the length of this book by now I must be brief. Since the pleasures are all vicious and deadly, they need to be conquered and suppressed by virtue, or, as I was saying earlier of the emotions, to be recalled to their proper purpose. 2 The other animals know no pleasure apart from that of reproduction. They use the senses therefore for their natural needs: they see in order to get what they need for safeguarding life; they hear each other and pick each other out in order to be able to meet together; anything useful as food they find by smell or perceive by taste, and things not useful they spit out and refuse; they measure their eating and drinking by the fullness of their bellies. 3 Man, however, thanks to the foresight of his most skilful creator has been given pleasure which is without limit and topples over into vice, because he has also been offered virtue, to wage perpetual war on pleasure as if it were the enemy within. 4 Cicero in his *Cato Major* says [*Sen.* 40]; 'Rape, adultery and all such outrageous acts are provoked by the temptations of pleasure, nothing else. Man has, whether from nature or from some god, the remarkable gift of mind; nothing is more the enemy of this divine gift and endowment than pleasure. 5 For when lust is lord there is no room for moderation, and virtue cannot exist under the kingship of pleasure.' On the contrary, however: God's gift of virtue was meant to take pleasure by storm and defeat it, keeping it inside the line when it tried to escape its given bounds, in case it should beguile man with its sweetness and make him its prisoner, bringing him under its own control and punishing him with everlasting death.

6 Ocular pleasure is complex and various; it comes from the look of things in common use which, naturally or artificially, give delight. The philosophers have rightly rejected this pleasure. 7 They say that it is much better and much more worthy of a man to gaze at heaven than at objets d'art;[70] better to marvel at that beautiful piece of work set with the light of its stars twinkling like flowers rather than gape at stuff painted, crafted and stuck about with jewels. 8 They urge us with eloquence to a contempt for earthly things and to contemplation of heaven, but they have no contempt for the great spectacle of the games.[71] 9 They are delighted with them and happily attend them too, but since these games offer great incitement to vice and are very powerful in corrupting the soul, we must abolish them: they don't just have nothing to give to the life of bliss, they actually do it great damage. 10 Anyone thinking his pleasure is served by the spectacle of someone being put to death, however deservedly condemned, pollutes his own conscience as much as if he were also taking part in the killing of which he is spectator. 11 And they call them games, when human blood is being shed! Humanity has got so far away from actual people that they think it's a game when they are trying to kill human souls: they are more guilty themselves than ever the people were whose murder they treat as pleasure.

12 I now put the question whether people can be pious and just if, when their victims are under sentence of death and are begging for mercy, they don't just let them be killed but actually press for it and add cruel inhuman tortures on the way, dissatisfied and discontented with the bloodshed so far. They even ask for more beatings, when the victims lie there beaten already; they want the corpses to break up under the blows, in case anyone is trying to trick them with a sham death. 13 They also get cross with gladiators if one of the pair isn't killed quickly; they hate delay as if they were thirsty for human blood. Then they demand fresh partners for the survivors, to sate

---

70 L. is working a pun on *caelum*, heaven, and *caelare*, to emboss, engrave.
71 Condemnation of games and other spectacles is standard among Christian apologists, including those of African origin. See Tert. *spect.*; *apol.* 38.4; Min. Fel. 12.5; Cypr. *donat.* 7ff.

their eyes as fast as possible. Imbued with a habit like that, they destroy humanity. 14 So they fail to spare even the innocent; what they learnt in the slaughter of criminals they practise on everyone.

15 For people trying to keep to the path of justice it is thus not appropriate to be aides and participants in these public killings. When God forbids killing, he doesn't just ban murder, which is not permitted under the law even; he is also recommending us not to do certain things which are treated as lawful among men. 16 A just man may not be a soldier,[72] since his warfare is justice itself, nor may he put anyone on a capital charge:[73] whether you kill a man with a sword or a speech makes no difference, since killing itself is banned. 17 In this commandment of God no exception at all should be made: killing a human being is always wrong because it is God's will for man to be a sacred creature. 18 Let no one think there is even a concession which permits the smothering of newborn babies;[74] that is the greatest of impieties, because God puts breath into souls for life, not death, 19 whereas these people, in case there should be any evil deed they fail to foul their hands with, are denying a light that is not in their gift to souls still new and undeveloped. 20 People who do not spare their own blood cannot be expected to spare the blood of others. They are, beyond argument, criminal and unjust.

21 What of those who use exposure, pressured by a mistaken piety?[75] Can people be thought innocent who offer up their own flesh and blood as prey for dogs, and kill as best they can more cruelly than if they had smothered the babies? 22 When space is made for the pity of others to operate, the name for that beyond doubt is impiety. Even if the exposer's aim were achieved, of getting the baby reared, he has certainly condemned his own blood to slavery or the brothel.[76] 23 Everybody knows very well what can and often does happen to children of either sex in error. The tale of Oedipus alone shows that, criminally compounded twice over. It is thus as

---

72 See note on 4.18.
73 Condemnation of killing is total in L. Christian writers are more usually sensitive to the risk of the innocent meeting their death in consequence of a judicial sentence. See e.g. Aug. *civ.* 19.6; anon. *de divitiis* 6.2 (P.L. suppl. 1.1385, tr. Rees (1998), at 6.4).
74 Christians were commonly accused of infanticide (sometimes coupled with cannibalism). See Just. *apol.* 1.26; Euseb. *Hist. Eccl.* 5.1.1–4, 25–26; Orig. *Cels.* 6.27; Tert. *apol.* 8.2ff.; *ad nat.* 1.7, 23ff.; Min. Fel. 9.5, 28.1. Here L. turns the charge against the pagans. For Christian attitudes to abortion and to abandonment of children (*expositio*), see next note.
75 See also Just. *apol.* 1.27; Orig. *Cels.* 8.55; Tert. *apol.* 9.7ff.; Min. Fel. 30.1–2; with Boswell (1988), 138–79; Evans Grubbs (1995), 325, and 338 on laws of Constantine, which do not directly condemn abandonment of babies.
76 Cf. Just. *apol.* 1.27.

wicked to expose as to kill. 24 These parricides protest their scanty means, of course, and claim they cannot manage the upbringing of too many children:[77] as if means were in the power of those who have them anyway, or as if God were not making poor out of rich and rich out of poor every day. 25 If a man is too poor to bring up his children, it would be better if he kept away from intercourse with his wife rather than destroy works of God with his own criminal hands. 26 If then murder is not allowed in any form, even to be at one is completely impermissible, in case any bloodshed swamps one's conscience; the blood is, after all, being offered to the people.[78]

27 A more vicious corruption may occur in the theatre.[79] Comedies talk of the rape of girls or the love affairs of prostitutes, and the more eloquent the authors of these outrages are, the more persuasive they are with the elegance of their language; harmonious and well-wrought verse sticks in an audience's memory all too easily. 28 So too the plots of tragedy put bad kings before our eyes, busy at parricide and incest; evil deeds are paraded on high heels. 29 As for indecent posturing of the actors, that simply teaches and stirs up lust. Their bodies go soft and willowy, with gait and gestures that are effeminate, and they do bogus imitations of immoral women with movements of great immodesty. 30 And what about mimes, which offer classes in corruption, teaching adultery even as they present it, preparing the way to the real thing by images of it? What are boys and girls to do when they see these shows being put on without shame and being watched with pleasure by all? 31 Frankly, they are being told what they can do; they are being inflamed with lust, and lust is most excited visually; according to their sex they can see themselves in the acts, in laughing at them they are accepting them, and they go back home to bed all the more corrupted with the vices clinging close, and I don't mean just boys, who ought to be kept out of vice early on, but even old men, who ought to be beyond such misbehaviour by now.

32 What is the purpose of the games in the circus if not a trifling and empty-headed silliness?[80] People's spirits are stirred to a frenzy with the same energy as goes into the races; once they start shouting and raving and

---

[77] At least there is a slight recognition here that poverty might be a motive for the abandonment of children.

[78] L. has been carried away; here he returns to his starting point, the corrupting influence of ocular pleasures.

[79] Another standard target of Christian apologists. See e.g. Tert. *spect.* 16–17; *apol.* 38.4; Cypr. *donat.* 8; Min. Fel. 37.12; cf. Aug. *civ.* 2.8–13; 6.5–7, etc. O'Daly (1999), 239 finds Cic. *Rep.* 4 (which survives only in fragments) a source for Christian polemicists.

[80] For criticism of the circus, see Juv. 11.193ff.; Pliny, *Ep.* 9.6; Tert. *spect.* 9.5, 16.1ff.; etc.

jumping up and down, there is more of a spectacle to be had from the people who go to watch. 33 All such spectacles are to be avoided therefore, to prevent not just any element of vice getting settled in hearts that ought to be calm and peaceable, but any habit of pleasure softening us and diverting us from God and good works. 34 Celebrations of games are festivals of gods, since they were instituted in dedication of new temples or for their birthdays. 35 Saturn had animal-hunts, called shows, allotted to him from the start, as Bacchus had stage shows, and Neptune the circus games. Little by little, however, the same honour began to be paid to the other gods and individual games were consecrated to them by name, as Sinnius Capito explains in his book on shows.[81] 36 Anyone therefore partaking in games being held for religious reasons has abandoned the worship of God and has gone over to those gods whose birthdays and festivals he has celebrated.

Aural pleasures

21.1 Aural pleasure comes from the sweetness of words and songs. This is just as vicious a pleasure as that of the eyes which we have mentioned. 2 A man who practised theatre at home would be seen as a silly wastrel, but it makes no difference whether the extravagance is practised on your own at home or with others in a theatre. 3 Shows have already been dealt with. We have one thing left to conquer, in case we fall captive to something which goes to the heart of our sensibilities. All wordless stuff, all the sweet sounds of metal and strings, can be comfortably ignored because it doesn't stick and can't be written down. 4 But songs and speeches that run sweetly are entrancing, and they can press people's minds to anything. Hence the reduced faith of educated people who have come to the worship of God through the teaching of someone comparatively uneducated. 5 Accustomed as they are to oratory and poetry that is sweet and refined, they treat the simple, common language of divine literature as low quality, and they despise it.[82] They want something to beguile the senses; it takes something sweet to persuade them, something so delightful that it settles deep into the soul. 6 Is God then, creator of mind, voice and tongue, incapable of eloquence? No: it was His supreme foresight to make divine things plain deliberately, so that His universal message would be universally understood.

---

81 Sinnius Capito was a Roman grammarian and antiquarian of the 1st cent. BC.
82 Cf. 5.1.15ff.

7 Anyone keen on the truth, therefore, and not eager to ruin himself, should throw away those hostile, damaging pleasures which ruin a soul the way sweet food ruins a body. Truth must be put before falsehood, eternity before things transitory and use before beauty. 8 There should be nothing attractive to look at except what you see done with justice and piety, and nothing sweet to the ear except what feeds the soul and improves you, and this sense especially must not be twisted into a vice, for it was given us to learn the teaching of God. 9 If it is a pleasure, then, to listen to songs and poetry, it must be a pleasure to sing and hear the praises of God. 10 This is a true pleasure in being a companion and ally of virtue; it is not doomed to a short life like the pleasures sought by people who are slaves to the body like animals; this pleasure is for ever, and it gives delight without cessation. 11 Anyone transgressing its limits and seeking only pleasure itself from pleasure is busy with his death, because death is in pleasure just as life eternal is in virtue. 12 He who prefers the temporalities will lose out on eternity, and he who prefers the things of earth will not have those of heaven.

Pleasures of taste and smell

22.1 As for the pleasures of taste and smell (which are entirely physical), there is nothing for us to discuss, unless perhaps someone wants us to say that it is a disgrace to a wise and good man to obey his belly and throat and to walk about smeared in scent or wreathed in flowers. Anyone doing that is simply stupid and silly, worthless: even the scent of virtue will not reach him. 2 Someone may possibly say, 'What are they there for then, if not for our enjoyment?' It has been said often enough by now that no virtue could exist unless it had something to suppress. God's purpose in His creation was to set up a struggle between two things. 3 Those allurements to pleasure are the weapons of him whose sole task it is to force out virtue and to shut justice off from mankind. Those are the tempting delights with which he titillates our souls. He knows that pleasure is the craftsman of death. 4 Just as God invites men to life only through virtue and toil, so the other one invites him to death through delights and pleasures; just as true good is reached by way of bogus evils, so true evil is reached by way of bogus goods. 5 All those temptations need as much wariness as traps and nets do, in case the refinement of the pleasures involved deceives us and we fall under the dominion of death together with the very body to which we enslave ourselves.

BOOK 6: TRUE WORSHIP

Pleasures of touch: lust is natural, but leads one astray all too easily

23.1[83] I come now to the pleasure to be got from touch: this is a sense which belongs to the whole body. I don't think I need to speak of clothes and adornment; lust alone is the topic, and lust must be ferociously repressed because it is ferocious in its damage.

2 When God thought up the idea of two sexes, he arranged for each to seek the other and to rejoice in the conjunction. He therefore put in the bodies of all living creatures a burning desire, so that they would plunge into this emotional state with great avidity and so families would be propagated and multiplied.[84] 3 This desire, or appetite, is found to be stronger and fiercer in man, either because God wanted the number of human beings to be greater or because only man received God's gift of virtue, so that man should have the praise and glory for containment of his pleasures and for self-control.[85] 4 That adversary of ours therefore knows how great the strength of the desire is (some people call it a need) and he tries to divert it from what is right and good to what is wrong and evil. 5 He inserts unlawful longings, so that people who could enjoy their own proper desires without sin are corrupted by their yearning for the joys of others.[86] He puts before our gaze provocative shapes, supplying comforts and feeding our vices. 6 Then he stimulates in our inmost hearts all sorts of teasing feelings, working up the natural passions we have and inflames us, until we are entangled, trapped and betrayed. 7 He also set up brothels, so that no one need keep from others' property for fear of punishment, and he prostituted the modesty of unfortunate women, to make mock of the men who indulge as much as of the women who endure perforce. 8 With obscenities of this sort he has overwhelmed souls born to sanctity in a maelstrom of mud; he has wiped out shame, and importuned chastity.

He even fitted male to male and contrived outrageous coitus contrary to nature and God's institution. Such was his pollution of men and their preparation for every wickedness. 9 What can be sacred to those who take young people in their weakness when they have no protection, and lay them

---

83 The Revd Dr Fletcher, whose translation was first published in 1850, said in a footnote at this point, 'It has been judged advisable to give this chapter in the original Latin.'

84 That sex is for procreation only is emphasised in the Christian and Judaic traditions. See e.g. Clem. *Strom.* 2.18.88.4, 2.7.58.2 etc.; Just. *apol.* 1.29; Jos. *ap.* 2.199, 2.202. The Stoic Musonius Rufus held the same view. See Lutz (1947), 86.

85 Again, lust is present, in part, to give virtue work to do.

86 Cf. Minucius Felix's fierce attack on prostitution and homosexuality (and on other sexual irregularities) at 28.10–11.

out for the ravages of their own corrupting lust? 10 No tale of this can be told that fully matches its wickedness. I can only call such people parricides, and impious, when they have to supplement the sex God gave them with treacherous, lecherous same-sex profanities. Yet they treat it as something trifling, as virtually respectable.

11 What can I say of those who practise an abominable lust – or rather, an abominable madness? It is revolting to mention it, but are we to think it will be so to people who are not revolted to practise it? It has to be mentioned, nevertheless, because it happens. I speak of people whose loathsome lust, whose detestable frenzy does not even spare life. 12 What words can I use to attack so great a wickedness as this? What must my indignation be? The evil is so great that it overwhelms my duty to speak. Since it is lust which causes such deeds and lust which plans such crimes, we must arm ourselves against it with the greatest virtue. 13 Anyone unable to restrain such feelings should restrict them to the measure of his lawful bed, so that he not only achieves what he wants so greedily but also keeps out of sin. 14 What do these wretches want, anyway? Pleasure is a natural consequence of good deeds; if they seek pleasure on its own, then the pleasure they can enjoy is a just and legitimate one, 15 but if it is a pleasure prevented by some necessary bar, then virtue must be applied very firmly, so that self-control can win the struggle against greed. It is not just other men's beds and other things impermissible but the bodies of public prostitutes from which God also requires abstention: he tells us that when two bodies are joined together they make one body.[87] 16 He who dips himself in mud is bound to come up smeared in mud. A body can be washed clean quickly, but a mind corrupted by contact with an unclean body can only be cleansed from the filth that clings to it over a long period of time and after many good works.

17 Everyone should therefore conclude that union of the two sexes was provided for living creatures for the sake of procreation, and that this is a law laid down for our emotions to ensure our continuity. 18 But just as God gave us eyes not to gaze and grab at pleasure but to see for the sake of those actions relevant to the needs of life, so too we have been given the genital part of the body, as the word itself indicates, merely for the creation of offspring. 19 This law of God needs an obedience of the utmost dedication. All those expecting to profess themselves God's disciples should be so organised morally that they can exercise command over themselves. 20 People who indulge in pleasure and follow the whim of their lust enslave

---

[87] Cf. I Cor. 6:16.

their soul to their body and condemn it to death, because they have surrendered to the body, where death holds sway. 21 Every individual should therefore, as far as he can, model himself on modesty, cultivate a sense of shame and guard his purity in mind and conscience; one who follows the law of God should not just obey the public laws, but be superior to all such laws. 22 If he conforms himself to these goods, he will soon be ashamed to degenerate to something less good. Let him just be content with what is right and honest, which is of more joy to good people than depravity and dishonesty are to the bad.

23 I have not yet completed all the duties of chastity. Its bounds are set by God to be not the walls of one's own dwelling but actually the edge of one's own bed, so that anyone with a wife should not want to have a further woman, slave or free, but should be true to his marriage.[88] 24 In public law the rule is that adultery applies only to the woman who has another man; the man is acquitted on a charge of adultery even if he has several women.[89] 25 Not so in God's law. God's law joins two people together in matrimony (into one body, that is) on equal terms: whichever one extends the physical bond elsewhere is treated as an adulterer. 26 This explains why God deliberately made all other female creatures reject their partners after giving birth, but made woman alone of them all continue with her husband; otherwise (presumably), if husbands were rejected, lust would drive them to look elsewhere, and if that happened, they would not sustain any claim to chastity. 27 But the virtue of chastity would be equally impossible for a woman, if she were unable to sin: who calls a dumb beast chaste just for rejecting the male after parturition? The animal does it because if she admits the male, she will necessarily come to pain and peril. 28 There is no praise for failing to do what you could not do anyway. Chastity is praised in a human being, however, because it is not natural but deliberate. 29 Each partner must therefore be true to the other; indeed, a wife must be taught her chastity by the example of his self-control. It is unfair to make a demand of what you could not produce yourself. This unfairness has certainly caused adulteries, when women take it badly that they are being faithful to partners who do not show a love to match.

30 There is, finally, no adulterous woman of such a desperate shamelessness that she won't excuse her vices by saying she does no injustice by her

---

88 This general attack on all extra-marital relationships includes concubinage, which was common and socially acceptable. See Evans Grubbs (1995), 309–16; Arjava (1996), 205–17.

89 On the double standard, which persisted under Constantine and other Christian emperors, see Arjava (1996), 202–05.

sin, but is merely retaliating. This has been very well put by Quintilian: 'A man,' he says, 'not abstaining from another's marriage, nor protective of his own.'[90] The two things are naturally connected. 31 A husband who concentrates on seducing other men's wives cannot make space for the sanctity of the home, and when a wife is caught in a marriage of that sort, she is encouraged by his example to think either of copying him or of getting her revenge. 32 We must take care therefore as husbands not to let lack of self-control on our part give occasion for vices of theirs: married couples should adjust themselves to a joint morality and accept the union in a spirit of equality; we must imagine ourselves in the other. In fact the sum of justice virtually consists in not doing to the other what you yourself would not want the other to do to you.[91]

33 These are the instructions God gives for development of self-control. Nevertheless, in case anyone should think that he can frame divine precepts himself, there are others (so that all false claims and opportunities for deception can be removed): anyone who marries a woman divorced by her husband is an adulterer;[92] so is anyone who divorces his own wife (except on a charge of adultery) to marry another. God did not intend the united body to be divided and split into two. 34 Further, not only is adultery to be shunned, but so is even thought of it:[93] no one is to look upon someone else's wife and lust for her mentally; the mind becomes an adulterer if it even paints itself a picture of its pleasure. 35 It is certainly the mind which sins; all the evil and all the misconduct lies in the mind which embraces in its thinking the fruits of uncontrolled lust. 36 Even if the body were spotless, if the mind is impure the meaning of chastity fails, and where greed sullies conscience, chastity plainly cannot be whole.

37 No one should think, however, that it is difficult to put the brakes on pleasure and when it roams to shut it in within the bounds of chastity and modesty, since man's appointed task is to conquer it, and very many have maintained a blessed and uncorrupted integrity of body, and there are many who enjoy this celestial style of life in utter bliss. 38 God does not give his commands for this as if he were creating restrictions (children do need to be born), but as if he were making space for it. He knows what pressure he has put on these feelings of ours. 'If any man can do this,' he says, 'he will have

---

90 [Quint.] *Decl.* (Ritter, pref. III, n. 17).
91 Cf. Mt. 7:12.
92 Cf. Mt. 5:32; 19:9.
93 Cf. Mt. 5:28.

an extraordinary reward, a reward beyond compare.'[94] 39 This sort of self-control is the pinnacle and consummation of all the virtues. If a man can strain and struggle through to it, our lord will acknowledge him as his servant, and our master will acknowledge him as his disciple: he who achieves the virtue of God will triumph over the earth, and he will be like unto God. 40 These things may seem difficult, but we speak of the man who has a path to heaven being prepared for him when he tramples down all earthly things. Because virtue lies in recognition of God, everything is difficult when you are in ignorance, while all is easy when you know. If we aim, as we do, at the supreme good, we must get to it through difficulty itself.

Penitence wins God's forgiveness

24.1 No one should give up, however, or despair of himself if he slips on to the path of injustice when overcome by greed, driven by lust, tricked by a mistake or compelled by force. He can be restored to freedom if he repents of his acts and satisfies God by turning to better things.[95] 2 Cicero thought this impossible; in his third *Academic* his words are: 'If it were possible for those who went astray upon their journey to repent and to correct their mistake after following the wrong path, then amendment of their carelessness would be easier.'[96] 3 Plainly it is possible. If we see our children sorry for their faults and we think they are right again, and if we then pick them up and cuddle and embrace them in their sorrow and submission, why should we despair of our true father's clemency being open to our penitence? 4 He who is our most indulgent lord and parent promises forgiveness of sins for those who repent: He will wipe out all the iniquities of anyone who starts to practise justice again. 5 The uprightness of his previous life is no good to one living badly now, because the new wickedness overrides his old acts of justice; likewise old sins are no impediment to one who has been put straight, because his new justice has wiped out the stain of his earlier life.

---

94 The passage L. appears to be quoting is not known.

95 There had been an important debate over penitence in the African church arising from the Decian persecution (249–50). See Cypr. *de lapsis*; *ep.* 55; with Clarke (1986), vol. 3 *ad loc*. L. would have applauded *ep.* 55.16.1, where Cyprian confronts the Stoic disapproval of pity with the Christian idea of divine clemency. L. does not here specifically evoke the theme of how to deal with Christians who abandon the faith or who have compromised themselves in time of persecution. The issue was shortly to rise to the surface again, and to tear apart the African church, in the Donatist schism.

96 Cic. *Ac.* fr. 24.12 (Plasberg).

6 Anyone repenting his misdeeds understands his former error; the Greeks call this[G] metanoia, which is better and more meaningful than we can manage in Latin by calling it resipiscence. Resipiscence, or recovery of mind from a sort of madness, marks the person irked at his mistake: he chastises himself for his idiocy and encourages his soul to live a better life; in particular he also develops a wariness of tumbling into the same trap again. 7 Moreover, when dumb animals are tricked and caught, they too, if they can extricate themselves somehow and escape, become more wary thereafter, and they always avoid anything in which they feel some treacherous trap has been laid.

8 Penitence thus makes people cautious and careful about avoiding any sins into which they once tumbled when deceived. 9 No one can be so far-sighted and so watchful as not to slip at some time. That is why God in His knowledge of our frailty revealed to man, out of his compassion, the haven of salvation, so that the healing power of penitence could rescue us in the need to which our frailty is subject. Let anyone who has gone astray retrace his steps and recover and reorder himself as soon as he can. 10 'To recall one's steps, to escape to the upper air: that is the task and that is the toil.'[97] When people have tasted of pleasures misleadingly pleasant, they can scarcely be prised away; they would follow the right more easily if they had never experienced those sweets. If they could but spring themselves out of such evil servitude: every mistake will be forgiven if they correct their mistakes by living better.

11 No one should think he profits if he has no witness of his fault: everything is known to him in whose sight we live, and even if we can fool all men we cannot fool God, from whom nothing can be hid and nothing can be secret. 12 Seneca ended his *Exhortations* with a splendid sentence. 'There is some great divine power, greater than can be imagined, and we give our best efforts to living for him. Let us make ourselves acceptable to him. It is no use to keep one's conscience closed: we are open to god.'[98] 13 Even a man who did know God could not have said anything truer that, and that was said by a man ignorant of true religion. He has expressed the majesty of God by saying it is greater than the capacity of the human imagination can grasp, and he has also reached the source of truth itself in his perception that human life is not something superfluous, as the Epicureans propose, but that if people live justly and piously they are living for God as best they can. 14 Seneca

---

97 Verg. A. 6.128–29.
98 Sen. F89, 202 (Vottero).

could have been a true worshipper of God if anyone had shown him how, and he would surely have despised Zeno and his own master Sotio had he found the guide to true wisdom.[99] 15 'Let us make ourselves acceptable to him,' he said: that is a simply celestial remark, if only the admission of his ignorance did not precede it. 'It is of no use to keep one's conscience closed: we are open to god.' No room, then, for lying, no room for dissembling: the eyes of man are frustrated by walls, but the divinity of God cannot be frustrated even by stomach walls from seeing and knowing a man all through.

16 In book 1 of the same work Seneca also says, 'What are you up to? What are you trying to do? Why are you hiding? Your guardian is close behind you. Emigration loses you one friend, death another, and poor health loses you a third; yet one whom you can never lose abides. 17 Why pick a secret place and remove all witnesses? Suppose you have had the luck, you idiot, to escape everyone's eyes: what's the use of no witness when you still have a conscience?'[100] 18 Cicero speaks in no less remarkable a way of conscience and God. 'Let him remember,' he says [*Off.* 3.44], 'that he has God for witness; that is to say, in my opinion, he has his mind, and God has given man nothing that is more godlike.' 19 So too, when he was speaking of the just and good man, he said [3.77], 'Such a man, therefore, will never venture to think, to say nothing of doing, anything that he would not dare proclaim openly.'

20 So let us purify our consciences, which are wide open to God's eyes, and, as Cicero says [*Ver.* 2.28], 'Let us always live in such fashion that we think we have an account to render,' and let us reckon that at every moment we are being looked down upon not by men [*Ver.* 5.35] 'in some theatre of the world,' but by him who will be our judge and also our witness, and when he asks for the account of our life we shall not be allowed to deny what we have done. 21 It is therefore better either to flee from our awareness or else to open our souls of our own deliberate accord and drain off any poison by re-opening our wounds. No one else has the power to heal them but he alone who restored the lame to walking and the blind to sight, cleansed polluted limbs and resurrected the dead.[101] 22 He will slake the fires of our desire, root out lust, take away envy, and soften wrath; he will restore a true and

---

99 Cf. 1.5.26 and note. This Zeno is presumably the founder of the philosophy that Seneca followed, Stoicism. See 1.5.10; 3.4.1ff.; 3.6.7 ('Zeno the leader of the Stoics'). Sotio, a Pythagorean, taught Seneca in the early years of Tiberius' reign (14–37); under his influence Seneca became a vegetarian, for a time. See Sen. *Ep.* 49.2; 108.17–21.
100 Sen. F81, 196 (Vottero).
101 Cf. Mt. 11:5.

lasting health. 23 This healing is one for all to seek, because the soul is beset by greater peril than the body is, and care is needed for its lurking diseases as an absolute priority. 24 Even if someone had clear sight in his eyes, all his limbs in good order, the health of his whole physique utterly sound, I still would not call him healthy if he were carried away by anger, swollen with pride, the slave of his lusts and hot with desires, 25 whereas a man who did not set his gaze on another man's prosperity, did not prize wealth, looked at another man's wife with respect, went after nothing at all, wanted nothing of anyone else's, envied none, despised none, was humble, merciful, generous, gentle and humane, with peace perpetual reigning in his soul: that is the healthy man, that is the just man, and that is the perfect man.

26 The true worshipper of God is therefore anyone who obeys all these commandments of heaven: his sacrifices are gentleness of soul, a life of innocence, and good deeds. 27 He who displays all these does sacrifice every time he does any good and pious deed. God has no desire for a victim made of dumb animal or death and blood, but one made of man and of a man's life. 28 For this sacrifice there is no need of sacred branches or expiatory offerings or altars of turf; they are utterly pointless. Only what comes from the inmost heart is needed. 29 The greatest altar is truly that of God; placed as it is in the heart of man it cannot be defiled by blood; on it are laid justice, patience, faith, innocence, chastity and abstinence. This is the truest ritual, and this is 'that law of God,' as Cicero put it, 'famous and god-given, which always requires what is right and honest and always forbids what is depraved and filthy.'[102] A man who obeys that most sure and holy law is bound to live in justice and lawfulness. 30 I have set forth only a few chapters of it because I promised I would say only those things which completed the topping out of virtue and justice. 31 Anyone who wants to grasp the rest that could be said should seek it at the very fountainhead from which this stream has flowed to us.[103]

God requires as sacrifice purity of soul and devout worship

25.1 Let us now say a few words about sacrifice. 'Ivory,' says Plato [*Lg.* 956a], 'is not a chaste offering to a god.' Well? Are paintings and cloth precious then? There is no chaste offering to be made to God out of anything that can

---

102 Cic. fr. 107,22 (Garbarino); cf. *Leg.* 1.18; 2.8.
103 L. here acknowledges that for all his parading of poets, philosophers and oracular literature, he can turn if need be to the ultimate written authority, the Bible.

be spoilt or stolen. 2 But if Plato could see that nothing should be offered to a living being made of dead matter, why did he not see that no corporeal offering should be made to the incorporeal? 3 Seneca put it much better, and more truly: 'Do you people want to think of god as great, peaceful, reverend in an easy majesty, as a friend and always close by, not someone to worship with sacrificial beasts and quantities of blood – what pleasure is there in the slaughter of the undeserving? – but with a pure heart and a good and honest determination? He needs no temples built with stone piled high; each man must keep him sacred in his heart.'[104] 4 Anyone thinking that God values clothes and jewels and the other stuff treated as precious clearly does not know what God is; he thinks God finds pleasure in things that a mere man would rightly be praised for disdaining.

5 There is no chaste offering and none worthy of God except what he has required in his famous holy commandment. There are two things which are due as offerings, gifts and sacrifices: a gift is for ever and a sacrifice is for the while. 6 For those people who have no notion of the nature of divinity, a gift is anything made of gold and silver or anything woven of purple and silk, and a sacrifice is a victim and anything burnt upon an altar. 7 But God has use for neither, because he himself is uncorrupt and all that stuff is corruptible. God must therefore be offered the pair of incorruptibles: that pair he can use. Integrity of soul is the gift, and praise and hymns are the sacrifice. Since God is not visible, he must be worshipped with things invisible. The only true religion is the one founded on virtue and justice.

8 How God puts man's justice to use is easy to understand. If a man is just, he will receive immortality and will serve God for ever. 9 Man's destiny of justice is an idea scouted not only by ancient philosophers but also by Cicero. In discussing the laws he says [*Leg.* 1.28]: 'Of all the ideas that are regularly debated by learned men nothing surely is more noteworthy than the clear understanding that we are born to be just.' We ought therefore to show and present to God only the sort of behaviour for whose achievement he created us.

10 The absolute soundness of this double sort of sacrifice is well attested by Hermes Trismegistus, who agrees with us (with the prophets whom we follow, that is) in fact as in word. He speaks of justice as follows: 'Adore this word, my son, and worship it. There is only one worship of god, not to be evil.'[105] 11 So too in that perfect address of his, when he heard Asclepius

---

104 Sen. F88 202 (Vottero).
105 NF *Corp. Herm.* 12.23.

asking his son whether he agreed to incense and other fragrances being offered to his father by way of sacrifice to god, he cried out, 'Speak words of good omen, Asclepius, of good omen. It is the very greatest impiety to have any such thing in one's mind concerning the one and only good. These things and their like are not agreeable to him. He is replete with all that exists, and of all that exists he has minimal need. Let us give thanks and adore him. The only sacrifice for him is a benediction.'[106] And quite right too. 12 God should be made sacrifice by word, since the word is God,[107] as he himself has declared.

The supreme rite in worshipping God is praise directed to God from the mouth of a just man; for it to be acceptable to God itself, however, there is need of the greatest humility, awe and devotion, in case one should incur a charge of pride and arrogance when behaving in the confidence of one's integrity and innocence, thereby losing the grace of virtue. 13 In order to be precious to God and free from all stain, a man should beg continually for God's mercy and should pray only for forgiveness of his sins, even if they be none. 14 If he wants for anything further, it needs no saying to him who knows our wishes: if he has good fortune, he should give thanks, and if bad, he should render satisfaction, and admit that it happened so because of his sins. And yet he should also give thanks in misfortune, and should render satisfaction for good fortune, so that he may be the same at all times, steady, unchangeable and unshaken. Nor should he think that such action is only for the temple; he should act so at home too, and even in his own bed. 15 Let him finally keep God always holy in his heart, since he himself is a temple of God. 16 If he serves God his father and lord with this constancy, obedience and devotion, that is the consummation and perfection of justice, and he who maintains such justice is, as we declared above, obedient to God and has satisfied the claims both of religion and of his own duty.[108]

106 NF *Corp. Herm. Asclep.* 41.
107 Jn 1:1.
108 Throughout this book L. has been in dialogue with Cicero *de Officiis*. It is fitting that he should end with an evocation of that work and a tacit assertion of the main source of its deficiencies, its neglect of religion.

BOOK 7: THE LIFE OF BLISS

On the nature and destiny of the world and man

1.1 'Good: the foundations are laid,' in the words of the great orator [Cic. *Mur.* 14]. We have not only laid foundations, however, to be strong and fit for the work ahead; we have also advanced the whole building, of great and sturdy mass, nearly to its top. 2 What remains, to roof it or to decorate it, is very easy by comparison; without it, however, our previous labour is waste and goes unrewarded. 3 What use is it, either to be liberated from bogus religions or to understand the true one? What use is it, either to see through the emptiness of bogus wisdom or to get to grips with the true wisdom? What use is it, I repeat, to defend the justice of heaven and to sustain one's worship of God despite great difficulties – that is the supreme virtue – unless it is followed up by God's reward of perpetual bliss?

4 That is our subject for discussion in this book; otherwise, all our previous work will look vain and fruitless, as it would if we left unclear the reason for the work being undertaken. No one must think that a task so great is being done to no effect; he will misdoubt the heavenly reward for it which God has established for all who despise these sweets of earth in favour of virtue pure and simple. 5 We must provide the satisfaction now due, using not only evidence from holy scripture but also arguments plausible in themselves, so that it is equally clear that future is more important than present, heavenly than earthly and eternal than transient: the rewards of vice are temporal, and the rewards of virtue eternal.

6 I shall therefore set forth the explanation of the world, so that the time of its making by God and God's reason for making it can be easily understood, something which Plato, who discussed the making of the world,[1] could neither know nor explain. He did not know the mystery of heaven, which cannot be learnt without the instruction of the prophets and of God; that is why he said it had been made in perpetuity,[2] which is well off the truth: anything of dimensions and weight which had a beginning at some

---

1 L. probably had before him Cic. *Ac.* 2.118, behind which lies Plato's *Timaeus*.

2 Later Platonists contested whether Plato believed this or agreed with Aristotle. For a critique of Plato, see Cic. *N.D.* 1.20.

point must also have an end. 7 Aristotle could not see how such a huge thing as the world could perish; in his desire to escape this requirement, he said the world had always existed and always would.[3] 8 He was quite blind, because every existing thing must have had a beginning at some point, and nothing can be in existence without having started existence. Since we can see earth, water and fire, which are simply ingredients of the world, disintegrating, being consumed and put out, so we understand that a whole whose parts are mortal is mortal itself.[4] Anything capable of perishing has thus had a birth. 9 Everything that becomes visible to the eyes must also be, as Plato says,[5] both corporeal and destructible. 10 Only Epicurus, therefore, upon the authority of Democritus, has told the truth of this: he said it arose at a certain point in time and would perish at a certain point in time.[6] He could give no reason, however, why this great work should be undone or when. 11 Since God has revealed it to us, and since we grasp it not by guesswork but by gift of heaven, we will explain it with care, so that those eager for the truth may see clearly at last that the philosophers neither saw nor understood the truth, but had scented it on the wind – though they wholly failed to realise where that scent of wisdom came wafting from in all its delicious sweetness.

12 Meantime I think it necessary to warn my readers that our tradition of knowledge will either not be understood at all by minds depraved and vicious, whose sharpness is blunted by their earthly desires, which dull and enfeeble all their senses, or if it is, they will pretend not to understand and will refuse its truth, because they are drawn by vice into a conscious preference of their own evil; they are trapped by the sweetness of it and abandon the way of truth, put off by its bitterness. 13 Because they are aflame with avarice and an insatiable thirst for wealth, because they cannot sell what they love or bestow it around and live a life of straitened means, of course they prefer to disbelieve the reality of what compels them to forsake their desires. 14 Hence too the claim of people spurred on by the pricks of lust till they 'plunge into madness and fire,' as the poet says:[7] they say that what we offer them is quite incredible, because our recommendations for self-control hurt their ears and bar them from the pleasures to which they have surrendered themselves body and soul. 15 Whether swollen by ambition or inflamed by

---

3 Cf. Cic. *Ac.* 2.119. Aristotle's *de Caelo*, where this doctrine is expounded, was unavailable to Cicero (or to L.).
4 Cf. Philo, *aet. mundi* 124–29.
5 See *Phd.* 80c.
6 Epic. fr. 304 (Usener); cf. 2.10.24 above.
7 Verg. *G.* 3.244.

love of power, they have devoted their efforts to acquisition of honours: not even if we held the sun itself in our hands would they fit their faith to a teaching which bids them despise all power and honour and live humbly, so humbly indeed that they could accept injury and would refuse to retaliate even if they did suffer. 16 These are people who shut their eyes and yap against the truth in any fashion, whereas people who mean to be healthy – people, that is, not so deeply into vice that they cannot be restored to health – will believe it and will gladly accept it; what we say will seem to them to be open, plain and simple, and also (which is the big need) true and incontrovertible. 17 No one favours virtue who lacks the capacity to pursue it, and the pursuit is not easy for all: it is possible for those well acquainted with poverty and need, experiences which make them capable of virtue. 18 If virtue is toleration of evil, then people for ever in good circumstances do not acquire it: they have never experienced evil and they are too used to good to endure it; good is what they desire because it is all they know.[8]

19 Hence the fact that belief in God is easier for the poor and lowly, who travel light, than for the rich, who are cumbered with too much baggage. Indeed, they are chained and fettered by it, and bow to the nod of my lady Greed, who has snared them in bonds inextricable, and they cannot gaze at heaven because their minds are face to the earth and fixed to the ground. 20 The road of virtue has no room for people with great loads: it is a very narrow path by which justice guides man to heaven, and its course can only be kept by a man stripped and unencumbered. 21 Those rich people, laden as they are with a host of vast boxes and bundles, are treading the path of death, which is a very wide path because ruin keeps wide empire upon it. 22 God's recommendations to them on justice, and our own treatment under God's guidance of virtue and truth, are bitter, and poisonous. If they are going to risk a repudiation of them, then they necessarily admit themselves to be enemies of virtue and of justice.

23 I will now come to what remains, so that this work may come to its end, and it remains to discuss the judgment of God. This judgment will take place when our lord returns to earth to pay each individual his reward or his punishment according to his merit. 24 We spoke of his first coming in Book 4;[9] in this book we shall relate his second coming, which the Jews also acknowledge and expect, but in vain, since he is bound to return merely to

---

8 L.'s favourite idea of the mutual dependence of virtue and vice, with virtue attainable only through the overcoming of evil, resurfaces here. See, in more detail, 5.27a–q below.

9 See 4.12.22.

console them, not to summon them, as he first came to do. 25 They treated him in his humility with gross impiety: they will behold him a conqueror in power. When God weighs them in the balance they will suffer all those things they read and do not understand: stained with all their sins and soaked too with his holy blood, they are doomed to everlasting punishment by the very one on whom they laid their wicked hands. 26 The material in which we shall convict the Jews of their criminal error we shall, however, keep separate.

The end of evil and the age of bliss beyond the comprehension of philosophers

2.1 Now to teach the people who do not know the truth. It was ordained by will of God most high that when due space of time had passed, this unjust generation should be ended, and as soon as all wickedness had been wiped out and the souls of the pious recalled to the life of bliss, an age of tranquillity, peace and quiet should bloom under the kingship of God: as the poets call it, a golden age.

2 The cause of all the philosophers' mistakes was principally the fact that they did not grasp the explanation of the world; and the whole of wisdom lies in that explanation. 3 Indeed, it cannot be grasped by any private sense or inner understanding; yet they wanted to achieve that understanding by themselves, without a teacher. So they fell into a variety of opinions which were often at odds with each other, and they could find no way out; they all stuck in the same mud, as the comic poet says,[10] because naturally the explanation did not match their assumptions, which were sound enough, but could not be confirmed or proved without knowledge of the truth and of things celestial. That knowledge cannot exist in a man, as I have said many times now, unless it has been understood through the teaching of God. 4 For if a man could understand God's work, he could also do it: to understand a thing is to follow in its footprint. But man cannot do what God does because man has a mortal body; hence he cannot even understand what God does, and the possibility of any such understanding is easy for anyone to estimate, from the immensity of God's activity in creation. 5 If you would just gaze at the world, together with everything in it, you would surely understand how much God's achievement exceeds man's. The difference between God's works and man's works is the same as the distance between God's and man's wisdom. 6 Because God is uncorrupt and immortal, and therefore perfect, and

---

10 Ter. *Ph.* 780. See 2.8.24.

because he is everlasting, so his wisdom is as perfect as he is, and nothing can obstruct it because God himself is subject to nothing. 7 Man, however, is subject to passion: so his wisdom is subject to error, and since many things prevent a human life from being everlasting, so human wisdom is necessarily prevented by many things from a perfect perception of the truth in its fullness.

8 There is therefore no human wisdom if it must make its own efforts in the direction of knowledge and the understanding of truth, since the mind of a man is bound in with his frail body, enclosed in a dwelling of darkness, and it cannot roam free or see the truth with clarity: knowledge of the truth is a mark of divine status. God's achievements are known to God alone. 9 Man cannot attain that knowledge either by thinking or by discussion, but only by learning and listening to him who alone has power to know and teach. 10 That is why Cicero [*Tusc.* 1.99] borrowed Plato's report of what Socrates said: a time had come for him to leave this life, while those before whom he pleaded his case would live on; 'Which is better,' he said, 'is known to the immortal gods. I think that no man knows it.'[11] 11 All philosophical sects are therefore bound to be remote from the truth because it was men who established them; in having no support from any oracular pronouncements of God they can have no foundation or solidity.

God made the world, God governs it, and God will bring it to an end

3.1 The Stoics (we are speaking of philosophers' errors) divide nature into two parts, one creative and the other to be available for creation.[12] They say the capacity for thought lies in the first part and matter in the second, and neither has any power without the other. 2 How can there be identity of the worker and his work? If anyone said that the potter was the same thing as the clay or vice versa, he would surely be plainly mad. 3 Yet in the one word 'nature' they include two completely different things, God and the world, the craftsman and his work, and they say that the one has no power without the other, as if God were naturally mixed in with the world. From time to time they get things so confused that God is himself the mind of the world and the world is God's body, as if God and the world could have begun to exist together and God had not actually made the world. 4 That is something they admit elsewhere, however, when they declare that the world was constructed

---

11 See Plato, *Ap.* 42a: Socrates' last words to his judges. L. is close to Cicero.
12 D.L. 7.134 (= LS 44B; also C-E).

for the sake of mankind,[13] and God could exist without the world if he wished, since God is divine and everlasting mind, released from body and free. 5 Hence that sentence of Vergil's [*A.* 6.726–27], 'Infused throughout its limbs, mind drives the whole mass, and permeates the great body.' 6 So where does that leave their statement that it was made by divine providence and is also governed so? If he made the world, then he existed without it; and if he rules it, then he does so not simply the way mind rules body but as a master rules his house, a helmsman his ship and a charioteer his chariot, all without being part of what they rule. 7 If all these things that we can see are limbs of God, then because the limbs lack sense God too must be insensible, and because the limbs are mortal as we see them to be, he also must be mortal.

8 I could list many occasions when lands have been shaken by sudden movements, and have cracked open or collapsed into a hole, when towns and islands have been drowned by waves and disappeared into the deep, when waters have inundated good agricultural land, and rivers and lakes have dried up, and mountains have shattered and tumbled down or been levelled with the plains; many regions, including the foundations of many mountains,[14] are eaten away by fire lurking inside. 9 Waste of his limbs on God's part is irrelevant, were it not that man has some licence to damage them. We build out into the sea, we hack down mountains, we dig up the entrails of earth to extract the riches;[15] even ploughing can't be done without scarring the divine body, and thus we are wicked and impious creatures, because we do hurt to God's limbs. 10 So does God permit his body to be tormented, and does he bring about his own enfeeblement, or at least let man weaken him? Or did that divine capacity of his to feel, which is mixed in with the world in every part, abandon earth's top layer and plunge to the lowest strata in order to avoid all feeling of pain from the constant torment?

11 If that is absurd nonsense, which it is, then the Stoics have been as short of sense as it is: they have failed to perceive that the divine spirit is diffused in all directions, and everything is contained within it, but not to the extent that God himself, who is incorruptible, can be mixed in with elements that have body and are corruptible. 12 What they took from Plato is sounder, that the world was made by God and is governed by his providence. Plato and people of like mind ought then to give us the reason, or the plan, that

13 Cf. *de ira* 13.9. See Cic. *N.D.* 2.133; Porph. *Abst.* 3.20.1 (both citing Stoic authorities).
14 Cf. Sal. *Cat.* 20.1.
15 Cf. Ovid, *Met.* 1.138ff.

there was for creating such a work: why did he do it, and for whose sake? 13 Our friends the Stoics say, 'The world was made for the sake of men.' Yes. Who made those men, however, and why, is beyond Epicurus' knowledge. When Lucretius said that the world was not constructed by the gods, he put it thus [5.156–57]: 'To say, further, that man was the cause of their wish to provide the world in all its glory is,' he then added [165–67], 'stupid. What advantage could thanks of ours bestow on immortals in their bliss that they should set out to do anything for our sake?' Rightly said. 14 The Stoics could offer no reason for the human race being created or established by God. It is our duty to explain the mystery of the world and of man; they knew nothing of that, and could neither reach nor see the shrine of truth.

15 Though they had assumed, as I said a little earlier, what was in fact the truth, namely that the world was made by God and that it was made because of man, they could not defend it because the reasoning failed them in their subsequent discussion. 16 To avoid treating God's work as feeble and liable to ruin, Plato said it would abide for ever. Now if it was made for men, and was so made that it would last for ever, why are the beings for whose sake it was made not eternal themselves? Whereas if the beings it was made for are mortal, then it too is mortal and perishable: it is not worth more than the people for whose sake it was made. 17 If he could think it through, he would understand that it would perish because it was made; only the intangible can abide for ever.

18 Anyone denying that it was made for man speaks irrationally. If he says that the creator put all these great works in motion for his own sake, then why were we born? Why do we enjoy the world? What is the meaning of the creation of the human race and of all other living things? Why do we usurp the advantages of others? Why do we grow, decline and die? 19 What is the point of procreation, and of the preservation of species? Presumably God wanted to go on seeing and making his little likenesses, as it were, in their own various images for his pleasure; and yet, if that were so, he would be treating living things as important, and especially man, in having put everything under man's control.

20 As for those who say that the world has always existed (I ignore the fact that it cannot exist without some beginning, and they cannot get out of that problem), I say this: if the world has always existed, then it can have no reason. 21 In something which had never had a start, what could reason construct? Before things get made or built, you need a plan, so that the method of construction can be sorted out, and nothing can be started without reasoned preparation. 22 Before every creation comes its reason: what never

got made has therefore no reason. And yet the world does have its reason, because the world is a construct and is under control. Therefore it was made. And if it was made, it will also be unmade. 23 So let them produce an explanation, if they can, either of why it was made in the beginning or of why it will be unmade in due course.

That was beyond the power of Epicurus (or Democritus) to explain; that is why he said it was born of its own accord, of seeds meeting each other at random, and that when the seeds broke apart again, its disintegration and death would follow.[16] 24 Epicurus misinterpreted what he had been right to see, and in his ignorance of the plan he destroyed it entirely, reducing the world and everything in it to the likeness of some meaningless dream, since human activity would make no sense. 25 But the world and all its elements run to a wonderful system, as we see; order in the heavens, the measured progress of the stars and lights of heaven within their variations, the regular and remarkable differentiation of the seasons, the diverse fruitfulness of the land, the level plains, the ramparts and ridges of mountains, the greenness and richness of forests, the vital emergence of springs, the seasonal overflow of rivers, the rich and abundant intervention of the seas, the winds in their different useful quarters, and everything else, are all constructed to a supreme plan: so who can be so blind as to think that something which simply radiates the wondrous provisions of a providential plan was produced without a cause? 26 If nothing exists and nothing at all can be made without a cause, if the foresight of God most high is manifest in the disposition of things, his virtue in their greatness and his power in their control, then those who said there is no providence are obtuse, and mad. I would not disapprove if they denied the existence of gods in order to speak of one god, but when they do it to speak of no god at all, anyone thinking they are not mad is off the rails himself.

God made the world for man and gave him reason

4.1 We spoke of providence adequately in book One; if it exists, as is plain from the remarkable nature of its effects, then it is inevitable that the same providence created man and the other living creatures. 2 Let us then see what the reason was for creating the human race, since the point the Stoics make is agreed, that the world was made for the sake of men, though the Stoics go wrong some way in saying for the sake of men, not man: use of the singular embraces the whole human race. 3 They go wrong because they do not know

---

16 See Epic. fr. 382 (Usener).

that God did first form one man alone; they think men developed like mushrooms in fields all over the world, but Hermes was well aware that man was made both by God and in God's image.[17]

I return to my purpose, however. 4 There is, I think, nothing that can be made for its own sake: anything that is made at all must be made for some end. No one would be so stupid or so futile as to attempt, unsuccessfully, to make something for which he expected no use and no profit. 5 A builder doesn't build just for a house to exist, but so that he can live in it; a shipbuilder doesn't start on his task just to have a ship appear but so that sailing in it happens; 6 so too, anyone who throws a pot doesn't do it just to prove he did it but so that when it is made it can contain something he wants. It is the same with all the other things that get made: they are not made to be superfluous but for some useful purpose.

7 The world was therefore made by God not just for the sake of the world itself: since it lacks the capacity to feel, it does not need the heat of the sun, the light of the moon, the blowing of the winds, the moisture of the clouds or the sustenance of crops. 8 Equally it cannot be said that God made the world for his own sake, because he can exist without the world, as he did before it, and none of the things that are in the world and are bred in it are used by God himself.

9 It is therefore clear that the world was made for the sake of living things, since living things enjoy what the world is made of: all the things necessary for them to live and maintain existence are supplied in due season. 10 It is also clear that the other living things were created for the sake of man from the fact that they serve man, and they have been given to him for his protection and his use, since, whether they are creatures of land or sea, they do not understand the plan of the world as man does.

11 At this point a reply is owed to the philosophers, and most of all to Cicero, who wonders [*Ac.* 2.120] 'why god, in making everything for our sake, gave such power to water-snakes and vipers, and why he spread so many sources of plague over land and sea'. 12 The room for debate is enormous, but we are skimming and must keep it brief. Since man has been shaped out of two different elements opposed to each other, soul and body – heaven and earth, that is – tenuous and graspable, eternal and temporary, responsive and unresponsive, enlightened and dark, the plan itself necessarily required that he should be offered both good and evil, good to use and evil to avoid and shun.

17 NF *Corp. Herm.* 1.12.

13 Man was given wisdom in order that he should learn the nature of good and evil and exercise the power of his reason both in seeking good and in avoiding evil. The other animals were not given wisdom, but received a natural protective clothing of armour instead; man's special gift from God to match all that was reason alone. 14 God made man naked and weaponless in order to protect him with a cloak of wisdom; man's armour for self-defence was put within, not without: not over his body but in his heart. If there were no evil for him to beware and to distinguish from things good and useful, his wisdom would not be needed. 15 Cicero should realise that either man was given reason in order to catch fish for his sustenance and in order to avoid water-snakes and vipers for his survival, or else he was challenged with good and evil because he had wisdom, and all the power of wisdom is occupied in distinguishing good and evil.

16 The strength, reason and capacity of man is therefore great, right and wonderful: God made the world itself and everything there is for man's sake and did him the great honour of putting him in charge of it all because only man could show wonder at God's achievement. 17 My friend Asclepiades,[18] who discusses the providence of God most high in the book which he wrote and sent me, puts it well: 'One may reckon,' he says, 'that divine providence was right to grant position next itself to a creature which would understand its arrangements. 18 There is the sun: who sees it in such a way as to understand that it is the sun, and what influence it has on everything else? There is the sky: who looks up at it? Here is the earth: who works it? Here is the sea: who sails it? Here is fire: who uses it?' 19 Nothing has been set up by God on his own account because God needs nothing; God set everything up for man because man could use it all fittingly.

Man is immortal but made for immortality, which is the reward for nourishing soul rather than body

5.1 Let us now give the reason for God's creation of man himself. If the philosophers had known it, they would either have defended the truth they found or not have fallen into such huge error. 2 This is the main point, the pivotal point, and anyone who fails to grasp it loses all hold on truth; this is, indeed, what caused God's purpose to make no sense to them. If they had seen its light, if they had known the whole mystery of man, the Academy would never have throttled the philosophers' debate and thwarted all

---

18 See Jerome *uir. ill.* 80. L. addressed two books to Asclepiades.

philosophy. 3 As God did not make the world for his own sake, not needing its goods, but for the sake of man, and man it is who uses it, so he made man for his own sake. 4 'What use was man to god,' says Epicurus, 'that god made him for his own sake?'[19] For there to be someone who understood God's achievement, of course, someone who could admire intellectually and proclaim verbally God's foresight in planning him, his thought in making him and his virtue in completing him; and the sum of it all is that man should worship God. 5 Worship follows on understanding: measure the virtue of his greatness by what it takes you to plan, to start and to finish your own works, and then you will observe the creator of the universe, your own true father, with the adoration he deserves.

6 No clearer argument for God having made the world for man's sake and man for his own sake can be presented than that man alone of all living things is so shaped that his eyes are directed at heaven, his face gazes at God, and his countenance is shared with his creator, and that God has clearly stirred man to contemplation of him by lifting him from the ground with outstretched hand. 7 'So what,' says Epicurus, 'does the worship of man confer on god in his bliss and utter self-sufficiency? Or if he had so much respect for man that he built the world for him, equipped him with wisdom, made him lord of living things and loved him like a son, why did he make him frail and mortal? Why expose his beloved to all evil, when man ought as god's close companion to be in bliss, everlasting even as god is, for whose worship and contemplation he was formed?'[20] 8 We have explained this here and there in earlier books, but because there is now specific demand for it, our theme being discussion of the life of bliss, we must sort out Epicurus' points with more care and clarity, so that God's plan, and his work and purpose, can be known.

9 God had the power to create countless souls from his own immortal spirits, just as he created the angels, who have their immortality quite free of peril or fear of evil. Nevertheless, he planned something beyond all telling, the creation of an infinite host of souls; he would set them up initially with bodies of frail and feeble constitution midway between good and bad, and nature would put virtue before them in their ambivalence, in case they should come to immortality softly and comfortably; they were to achieve the inexpressible reward of eternal life with the greatest difficulty and huge effort. 10 In order therefore to burden the souls with clumsy and troublesome

19 Epic. fr. 371 (Usener); cf. Lucr. 5.165–67.
20 Epic. fr. 371 (Usener); not apparently in Lucretius.

limbs, he decided first, since they could not exist in the middle of a void when their own bodyweight was pressing them downwards, that they should have some place of residence established. 11 He therefore began, of his own ineffable virtue and power, the wonderful work of the world. He hoisted light elements on high and heavy ones he set down low, fixing the heavens and establishing the earth. 12 There is no need to follow out the creation in detail since we did it in its entirety in book 2.[21] He put lights in the sky, whose pattern, brightness and motions are excellently adapted to use by living beings, and to the earth, which he meant to be their home, he gave fertility for bearing and producing all manner of things, so that a wealth of fruit, grain and greenstuff could supply nourishment to match the nature and practice of every species.

13 When he had set up everything appropriate to the state of the world, he made man out of earth itself, the earth which he had prepared for him as his dwelling place from the start: that is, he endued and wrapped his own spirit in an earthly body, so that in its own combination of diverse and contradictory materials it could take up both good and evil. 14 The earth is fertile for the production of its fruits; so too the body of man, being drawn from earth, has taken up a power to create and a capacity to bring forth offspring, so that despite its inability to last for ever (shaped as it is from degradable material), it could yield place when its own span of life was up, and renew in a perpetual succession the frailty and weakness of its own creation.

15 So why did he make man mortal and frail when he had made the world because of him? His first purpose was to have an infinite force of souls produced to fill the earth with its multitude; his second was to face man with virtue: that is, endurance of evil and toil as the path to the prize of immortality. 16 Man is made of two stuffs, body and soul; one is earthly and the other is heavenly: so man has been granted two lives, one temporal and assigned to the body, and the other eternal, related to the soul. 17 We take on the one by being born; the other we achieve by toil, to prevent, as we said earlier, man coming to immortality without any toil and trouble. The one life is earthly, like the body, and so is finite, but the other is celestial, like the soul, and so has no limit. We receive our first life in ignorance, our second in knowledge. It is the reward of virtue, not of nature, because God wanted us to win life for ourselves in life. 18 He has given us this present life so that either we lose the real and everlasting life by our vices or we earn it by our virtue. The supreme good does not exist in this temporal life because, being

21 2.9ff.

granted us by divine necessity, it is likewise undone by divine necessity: because this life has an end, so it does not possess the supreme good. 19 The supreme good is to be found, however, in the spiritual life to come, which we win for ourselves by ourselves, because it cannot contain either evil or end.

Proof of this comes from the nature and purpose of the body. 20 All the other animals bend towards the earth because they are of earth and without immortality, which is of heaven, while man is erect and contemplates the sky because he has immortality before him (though it does not come to him unless granted by God; otherwise there would be no difference between just and unjust, since every man born would become immortal). Immortality is not therefore a natural consequence but the reward and prize of virtue. 21 Finally, man does not walk upright from the moment of birth: first he goes on all fours, because the pattern of body and this present life is shared by us with the dumb beasts; our body becomes upright when its strength is developed, and its tongue is released into speech and it ceases to be a dumb animal. 22 This shows that man is born mortal, but then becomes immortal at the point when he starts to live of God, that is, to follow justice, which is entailed in worship of God, when God stirs man to gaze at heaven and himself. That happens when man is cleansed in the heavenly basin,[22] laying aside his infancy together with every stain of his life hitherto; with the increment of God's strength, he then becomes a man full and perfect.[23]

23 Virtue is the challenge that God puts before man. Body and soul may go together, but they are opposites, and they quarrel, turn and turn about. The goods of the soul are the evils of the body: avoidance of wealth, that is, the bar on pleasures, and contempt of pain and death. Likewise, the goods of the body are the evils of the soul: greed and lust, that is, which encourage pursuit of wealth and the attractions of pleasures of all sorts, which unmuscle the soul and kill it. 24 It is necessary for the just and wise man to live amid all evils because the conqueror of evils is courage, whereas the unjust man must live amidst wealth, esteem and power: these are corporeal and earthly goods, and the unjust live their earthly life incapable of aiming at immortality because they have succumbed to pleasures which are the enemy of the soul. This temporal life is thus bound to be subject to the eternal one to come, just as body is subject to soul.

25 Anyone therefore who prefers the life of the soul must despise the life of the body; such a man will not be able to aim for the highest unless he has

---

22 i.e., baptised.
23 Cf. I Cor. 13:11; Eph. 4:13.

despised the lowest. Anyone who embraces the life of the body and aims his desires at the earth cannot achieve the superior life. 26 He who prefers to live well for eternity will live poorly for a time, suffering all manner of trouble and hardship as long as he lives on earth in order to have God's heavenly comfort, and he who prefers to live well for now will live poorly for ever; for putting earthly goods before heavenly, he will receive God's sentence of eternal punishment. 27 God's wish to be worshipped and honoured as father by man is deliberate: man shall have thereby virtue and wisdom; wisdom alone creates immortality. There is no one apart from God who can give it; he is its only possessor. Man's piety, his means of honouring God, has the reward from God that man shall be in bliss for ever, being in God's house and with God always.

While soul and body cohere, so must good and evil

27a[24] 1 No one should now seek refuge in the argument that God is at fault for setting up good and evil. Why did he want evil if he hates it? Why did he not just make good, so that no one should sin and no one do evil? Though I have explained this in almost every previous book, and touched on it in the last book albeit lightly, nevertheless a word of warning is due now because the whole idea of virtue depends upon it. 27b Virtue could not exist if God had not made opposites, and the effect of good simply cannot be seen except by comparison with evil; that is the extent to which evil is simply the illumination of good. Take away evil, and good must go too. 27c If you cut off your left hand or foot, your body will not be whole, and life itself will not stay steady; that is the extent to which left is very properly combined with right, to balance your physical frame. 27d So too, if you make chessmen all the same, no one will play; if you fix on one colour at the circus, no one will think it worth going: all the pleasure of the games will be removed. The emperor who first instituted the games backed one particular colour, of course, but he created the other to be its rival, so that there would be competition, and some partisan element in the show. 27e So when God fixed good and presented virtue, he also fixed their opposites so that they could come into conflict. If there were no fight and no enemy, there is no victory.

24 The problem of evil is, as L. allows, a recurrent theme of this work. There now follows L.'s fullest discussion of it, and his distinctive resolution of it. Augustine went off in a different direction in developing his doctrine of grace. Because this passage occurs only in MSS S and g (R does not survive here) and because of its alleged dualistic content, it was regarded by Brandt as a later addition and was relegated to a footnote. See pp. 27–28 n. 106.

Remove competition, and even virtue is nothing. How many competitions men go in for with each other, and how cleverly constituted they are! Yet no one would be judged braver or faster or better if he had no adversary to compete with. Where there is no victory, there has to be no glory and no prize for victory either. 27f Hence God's provision of both together, so that he could strengthen virtue by constant practice and bring it to perfection through its conflict with evil: the one cannot maintain its effectiveness without the other. Hence a system of opposites: the whole idea of virtue relies upon it.

27g I am well aware what objection clever people can make at this point. If good cannot exist without evil, how can you say that the first man existed in a context of good alone before offending God and how will he do so again? This is a problem we must sort out, since I passed it by in earlier books in order to give it its due here. 27h We said earlier that human nature is composed of contradictory elements. The body, derived of earth, is tangible, time-bound, brutish and unenlightened, whereas the soul, derived from heaven, is intangible, eternal, sensitive and bright. 27i Because these elements are opposites of each other, man is inevitably subject to good and evil: good is attached to soul because soul is imperishable, and evil is attached to body because body is perishable. So, since body and soul are thus allied and conjoint, good and evil must also cohere and cannot be separated from each other except when body and soul split up. 27j Finally, knowledge of good and evil were given to the first man together. Once he had that knowledge, he was immediately banished from the holy place, where evil does not exist. He had been there in a context of good alone; he therefore did not know that it was good. Once he had taken on the understanding of good and evil, however, it was wrong for him to remain in a place of bliss, and he was banished to this world we all share so that he could experience together the two things he had learnt together.

27k It is thus plain that man was given wisdom in order to distinguish good from evil, benefit from disbenefit, and useful from useless, in order to exercise judgment and consideration of what he should beware and what he should seek, what to shun and what to pursue. Wisdom cannot therefore be established without evil; that first member of the human race lived in a context of good alone for as long as he did live in it like a child, knowing neither good nor evil.

27l In the end, it may be said, man has to be both wise and blessed without any evil at all, and that cannot happen as long as his soul is housed in the flesh. Evil will be separated from good, however, when the divorce of body and soul has been made, and just as the body dies and the soul remains, so evil will perish and good survive. Then man will take on the garment of immortality and he will be wise, and free of evil, as God is.

27m Anyone, therefore, who wishes us to exist in a context of good alone is simply wanting us to live without our bodies where the evil is. But if body were removed, then man will either lose wisdom (as I said) or body: if wisdom, he will not recognise evil; if body, he will not feel it. As it is, man being equipped with wisdom in order to know and with body in order to feel, God's purpose was for each to exist on equal terms in this life so that his plan for virtue and wisdom could take place. 27n He put man midway between the two so that he should have licence to pursue evil or good, but with the evil he mixed in some apparently good things, an assortment of attractive delights, that is, to draw man on by the temptations in them to the latent evil, and with the good he mixed in some apparent evils, pain, misery and toil, that is, whose harshness and unpleasantness might depress the spirit into shrinking from latent good. 27o This is where the use of wisdom comes in: we need to see more with our minds than with our bodies, something very few can do, because virtue is hard and rare while pleasure is something many share. 27p The wise man must therefore be treated as a fool: while he seeks out goods that are not visible, he dismisses out of hand those that are, and while he avoids evils that are not visible, he tumbles into evils right under his nose. That is our experience too: we refuse neither torture nor death for our faith when we are being compelled towards the supremely wicked act of betraying that faith, denying the true God and making libation to gods which are dead and deadly. 27q That is the reason why God constructed the world for man's sake, and yet made him mortal and also subject to evil: obviously, it was so that man could go for virtue and his virtue could give him immortality. And virtue, as we have shown, is worship of the true God.

Worship of gods is pointless

6.1 Let us now stamp a brief definition on the whole argument. The world was made in order for us to be born; we get born in order to acknowledge its maker and our God; we acknowledge him to worship him; we worship him to receive immortality as the reward of our labours (worship of God requires huge labours); we are granted the prize of immortality to become like the angels, to serve our father and lord most high for ever and to be God's eternal kingdom. 2 That is the sum of it all: that is God's secret and the mystery of the world, and those who chase after present pleasure are quite outside it, devoting themselves to earthly and fragile goods and plunging their souls, which were born for things celestial, into the mud and muck of joys that are lethal.

3 Let us see instead whether there is any sense in worship of gods. If they are numerous, and if they are only worshipped by men so that men can bestow on them wealth, victories, honours, and other things of only present validity; if we are born without cause, if there is no providence in the procreation of human beings, if we are born to ourselves by chance and for our own gratification; if after death we are nothing: then what can be so superfluous, so insignificant, so empty as humanity and the world itself, when it has such incredible greatness and such a wonderful construction and yet is open to such silly nonsense? 4 Why should clouds move at the breath of winds? Why should lightning flash, thunder roar, and rain fall? Why should earth produce its fruits and feed its various offspring? Why indeed should all nature toil to ensure no dearth of what keeps man alive if man is futile and we die for nothing, if there is nothing in us of greater profit to God? 5 But if it is wrong to say that, and it is not to be thought possible that something which you can see has been constructed to an excellent plan was nevertheless not constituted to any plan, what reason can exist in these religions of confusion and corruption, and in this belief of philosophers that makes them think souls die? Absolutely none at all. 6 What reason can they give for gods demonstrating all these things so carefully to men in due season? Is it so that we can give them barley and wine, and the smell of incense and the blood of cattle? Immortals can take no pleasure in that because it is all perishable, and it is of no use to beings without bodies because it is all for the use of beings with bodies; and anyway, if that was what they wanted, they could supply themselves whenever they wished. 7 Whether souls die or last for ever, what is the sense in worship of gods? Alternatively, who made the world? Why were men created, or when, or how long for? For what end and purpose? Why do they get born, die, succeed each other and get renewed? What do the gods get from the worship of beings who are going to be nothing after death? What offers and promises do the gods make, and what threats that are worthy of men or gods? 8 Or if souls survive after death, what do the gods do, or what are they going to do, with them? What is their need for a stockpile of souls? Where do they spring from themselves? How, why and whence are they so numerous? 9 If you stray from the summary of the situation just given above, the result is that all reason disappears, and everything collapses into nothing.

Philosophers have pieces of the truth at best

7.1 Because philosophers have not grasped this summary, so they have not been able to find the truth either, even though they have more or less seen and accounted for what makes up the summary. Various of them have presented it all in various ways, without linking together the causes, consequences and systems of things so as to give that all-embracing summary its proper frame and content. 2 It is easy to show that truth has been divided almost in its entirety by philosophers and sects. We don't go undermining philosophy the way the Academics usually do, required as they are to respond to everything (though what they really do is to nitpick and quibble); we point out that no sect has been so astray and no philosopher so witless as not to see something of the truth, 3 but the Academics, in their mad determination to contradict, in their defence of their own views even when wrong and in their attack upon the views of others even when right, have not just lost hold of the truth which they claimed to be seeking; they have lost it altogether, by their own fault. 4 If there were anyone at all who could have collected together and restored to its parent body the scatter of truth dispersed among individuals and sects, he would certainly not disagree with us. But no one can do that without an expert knowledge of the truth, and knowledge of the truth requires a man to be taught by God. 5 There is no other way of rejecting what is false and picking out and proving what is true; but if that did happen, even by chance, it would be a philosopher's act, and though the fellow could not defend the truth with evidence from God, even so, the truth would shine out with its own light itself.

6 Their confusion is unbelievable. They back a particular sect and give it their allegiance, and then condemn the others as false and empty; they equip themselves for war without knowing what they ought to defend or what they ought to refute, and they sail into the attack all over the place, with no discrimination, against everything proposed by anyone who disagrees with them. 7 This determined quarrelsomeness of theirs has led to there being no philosophy which gets any nearer the truth: their own grasp of the truth is entirely piecemeal.

8 Creation of the world by God was asserted by Plato; the prophets say the same, and so it appears from the verses of the Sibyl. It is an error therefore to say that everything was born of its own accord or from minute seeds getting clotted together, since something so extensive, so detailed and so great could not be created or arranged and ordered without some very intelligent creator, and the very system by which everything is perceived to hold

together and to be under control argues a creator of the shrewdest understanding. 9 The Stoics say that the world and everything in it was made for the sake of men; holy scripture tells us the same. Democritus was therefore wrong to think that people oozed out of the earth like worms, with no creator and no pattern. 10 The reason for man's creation belongs to the divine mystery; Democritus could not know that, and so he reduced human life to nothing. 11 Aristo[25] taught that men were born to seek virtue; we are told so and taught so by the prophets. Aristippus[26] is therefore deceived in making man subject to pleasure – to evil, that is – like an animal. 12 Pherecydes[27] and Plato argued that souls are immortal; in our faith, that is established doctrine. Dicaearchus[28] was therefore as wrong as Democritus in arguing that the soul perishes and breaks up with the body. 13 The existence of a world below was the teaching of the Stoic Zeno, with different abodes in it for the pious and the impious, the pious dwelling in areas of peace and delight and the impious paying their penalties in areas of darkness and ghastly pools of mud; the prophets put the same picture to us. Epicurus was therefore wrong in thinking it a figment of the poets and in interpreting the well-rehearsed punishments of the world below as events of this life.[29]

14 The whole truth, therefore, and the full mystery of God's religion were things with which the philosophers made contact, but because the reason for them did not accord with the views of any of them individually they could not defend their discoveries against the objections of others. They could not fit the truths that they had perceived into the sum, as we did above.

The supreme God and immortality are connected inextricably

8.1 The one supreme good is therefore immortality: we were formed in the beginning to acquire it and we were born so too. That is what we aim at, that is what human nature gazes at, that is what virtue brings us to, and because we have our hands on this good thing, all that remains is to speak of immortality itself. 2 Plato's arguments have a considerable contribution to make, but they have too little reliability to establish the truth and fill it out: the sense of the whole great mystery missed its consummation in him; he failed

---

25 Aristo of Chios (*fl.* early 3rd cent. BC) was an unorthodox pupil of Zeno of Citium.
26 For Aristippus, see 3.7.7.
27 Pherecydes of Syros (*fl.* mid 6th cent. BC), an early prose writer in Greek (possibly the earliest), wrote on the origin of the gods and the universe.
28 For Dicaearchus, see 3.17.34.
29 Epic. fr. 341 (Usener).

to bring it together; he had not understood the supreme good. He may have come to a sound conclusion about the immortality of the soul, but he did not discuss it in the way he discussed the supreme good.[30] 3 We are therefore in a position to identify the truth with greater confidence; we can do so without uncertainty and surmise because we have come to know it by gift of God.

4 Plato argued as follows:[31] whatever perceives of itself and always moves of itself is immortal; what has no initial motion will have no end of motion because it cannot abandon itself. This argument would grant eternity to dumb animals as well, if he had not made the distinction by tacking on wisdom. 5 To avoid the link he added:[32] it is impossible for the human spirit not to be immortal; man's extraordinary powers of invention, his speed of thought, his ready ability to understand and learn, his recollection of the past and his anticipation of the future, his knowledge of countless skills and other things, a knowledge which other animals lack, is plainly divine and heavenly, 6 because a soul which grasps so much and retains so much can have no origin on earth since it has no admixture of anything earthy in it. Inevitably the solid elements in man, which break up, return to earth, but the light elements, which are very fine, are indivisible, and when released from the prison of abode in the body fly off in pursuit of heaven and their own nature. 7 That is an abbreviation of Plato's thinking; in Plato himself it is set out at length. Pythagoras before Plato was also of the same opinion, and so was Pythagoras' teacher Pherecydes, of whom Cicero reports[33] that he was the first to debate eternity of life for souls. 8 All these people may have excelled in eloquence, but in this clash, so to put it, there was just as much authority in the expression of the contrary views, by Dicaearchus first, then by Democritus and finally by Epicurus, enough indeed to call into doubt the very issue at the heart of their quarrel.

9 Finally Cicero: he set out the ideas of all these people on immortality and death and then declared that he did not know which was true. 'Which of these opinions is true,' he says [*Tusc.* 1.23], 'some god may see.' Again elsewhere: 'Since each of these two views,' he says, 'has persuaded experts of considerable authority, and their soundness cannot be divined...'[34] 10 We,

---

30 This is a surprise, since Plato does discuss the immortality of the soul in *Phaedo*. What he does not do is to connect *summum bonum* with immortality.

31 *Phdr.* 245c; cf. Cic. *Tusc.* 1.53.

32 Cic. *Tusc.* 1.66, citing his own *Consolatio.*

33 In *Tusc.* 1.38 Pherecydes is said to have been the first simply to state that the souls of men were eternal.

34 Cic. fr. 107,23 (Garbarino).

however, have no need of divination; the divinity itself has revealed us the truth.

Immortality of soul proved by nature of God and man

9.1 There are thus other arguments, undiscovered by Plato or anyone else, by which the everlastingness of souls can be proved and understood. I will assemble them without elaboration since my text is fast approaching the account of God's supreme judgment; the end of time is coming, and that judgment will be celebrated on earth. 2 Most importantly, since God cannot be seen by man, in case anyone should doubt the existence of God simply because he is not visible to mortal eyes, there are many miracles he did among the rest of his activities whose effect is plain but there is nothing to see of substance. The same applies to speech, smell, and wind, and they provide argument and example for God not coming within our gaze but being visible nevertheless in the forceful effect of his works. 3 What is more audible than speech, or fiercer than wind, or stronger than smell? Yet when they travel through the air and reach our senses and impinge upon them with all their power, no sharpness of sight beholds them: they are felt by other senses of the body. 4 So too God is not to be grasped by sight or any other feeble sense of ours: he must be seen with the mind's eye, since it is his great and wonderful works that we behold.

5 Those who said there was no god at all are in my view not just not philosophers but not even human beings: they are identical with dumb beasts, composed of physical matter only, seeing nothing with their minds and relating everything to their physical senses; they thought that only what they could see by eye existed. 6 Because they saw bad things happening to good men, and good things to bad men, they concluded that all things happened fortuitously, and that the world was constructed by nature, not by providence. On that basis they promptly tumbled into the absurdities that were bound to follow. 7 But if God is incorporeal, invisible and eternal, then it is not credible that the soul perishes simply because it is unseen after it leaves the body, since it is agreed that there is something sentient and alive which fails to come into view anyhow. 8 But, they say, it is hard to understand how the soul can retain a capacity to feel without the parts of the body where the capacity is lodged. 9 What about God? Is it easy to understand how he thrives without a body? If people accept the existence of gods who, if they exist, are simply souls without bodies, then by the same reasoning there must be human souls as well: it is as a result of reason and foresight themselves that

a certain resemblance between man and God is understood to exist. 10 The argument which even Cicero saw [*Leg.* 1.24] is conclusive enough, that the eternity of the soul can be understood from the fact that there is no other animal which has any knowledge of God, and religion is almost the only thing which distinguishes man from the dumb creation; the uniqueness of religion in man is certainly good evidence that we affect, desire and worship something which is going to be intimately related to us.

11 When the nature of the other living creatures is taken into account – the providence of God most high has made them lowly, with their bodies prone and flat to the ground, so that their lack of relationship with heaven is obvious – can anyone fail to realise that man is the only divine and celestial creature of them all? With his body raised up from the ground, his face uplifted and stature erect, he is looking for his origin, striving upwards as if he despised the lowness of earth; he senses that the supreme good must be sought on high, and he gazes in the direction of his creator because he recalls the remarkable status his creator gave him. This gaze of his is called[G35] 'theoptia' (godsight) by Trismegistus,[36] and rightly so too; in dumb creatures it is non-existent. 12 Since wisdom, which only man has been granted, is simply knowledge of God, plainly the soul does not perish or disintegrate, but abides for ever because it seeks and loves the ever-living God, sensing at the instance of nature herself whence it sprang and where it will return.

13 There is no small further argument for immortality in the fact that use of the element of heaven is peculiar to man. Since things are naturally composed of two elements which are contradictories and enemies of each other, fire and water, and one of them is ascribed to heaven and the other to earth, the other creatures, being of earth and mortal, avail themselves of the element which is earthy and heavy, while man alone makes use of fire, the element that is lofty, light and celestial. 14 Heavy things press us down to death, and light things elevate us to life, because life is on high and death is below. There cannot be light without fire: so, there cannot be life without light. Fire is therefore the element of life and light, from which it is clear that man its user has immortality for his allotted state because the element which causes life is one that is familiar to him.

15 Another proof of the immortality of the soul is the fact that virtue has been granted to man alone, and will not follow its natural course if the soul is extinguished: it is this present life which is hurt by it. The life on earth

---

35 G indicates that L. uses or quotes Greek.
36 NF *Corp. Herm.* vol. 4, fr. 14.

which we share with the dumb animals both seeks pleasure, taking delight in its various attractive rewards, and shuns pain: the harshness of pain assaults the nature of living things with sharp sensations, pressing them towards death and disintegration. 16 If then virtue keeps man away from the goods which are his natural aim and forces him to endurance of evils such as he naturally evades, then virtue is an evil, and an enemy of nature, and anyone pursuing it must be reckoned a fool, because he is hurting himself both in avoiding present goods and also in aiming at evils without hope of a richer reward. 17 When we are free to enjoy the most delightful of pleasures, we should plainly lack all sense if we preferred to live abjectly, in need, contempt and ignominy, or even not to live at all but to be tortured and die in agony, getting nothing extra from our miseries by which to gauge the pleasure lost; 18 but if virtue is not an evil and deals honourably in despising pleasures which are foul and vicious, and bravely in fearing neither pain nor death in order to do its duty, then it must be achieving some good which is greater than the things it despises. But once death has happened, what further good is there to hope for than eternity?

Virtue is enduring and carries rewards after death

10.1 Let us now move to the things which offer resistance to virtue, so that they too can be made to argue for the soul's immortality. 2 All vices belong in time: they are provoked in the present. The violence of anger is stilled once vengeance is obtained; lust ends in the body's pleasure, greed is over when it is sated with what it wants or when other emotions arise, and ambition decays once the honours it sought are achieved; the rest of the vices likewise cannot abide and hold firm but are terminated by the very satisfaction they seek. They therefore come and go, 3 whereas virtue endures for ever without a break; it cannot withdraw from the man who has once obtained it. If it were to have a gap, if we could be without it for a period, then we should have the instant return of those vices that are always assailing virtue. 4 If it does go, if it does ever withdraw, then it was never securely there; whereas once it has built a safe abode, it takes part of necessity in every act, and it cannot drive out vice and put it to flight for sure unless it builds a perpetual fort in the heart where it settles. 5 The perpetuity of virtue is thus a mark of the permanence of the human spirit once it has attained virtue, because virtue is perpetual, and only the human spirit attains it.

6 Since, then, the vices are in opposition to virtue, their whole system must be also. As the vices are disturbances, or perturbations, of the spirit, so

virtue, contrarily, is a smoothing, or pacifying, of the spirit; because the vices are time-bound and short-lived, so virtue is perpetual, constant and ever self-consistent; because the rewards of the vices, the pleasures, that is, are as short-lived and time-bound as the vices are, so the reward and prize of virtue is for always; 7 because the advantage of the vices is immediate, so the advantage of virtue is in the future.

Thus it is that there is no reward for virtue in this life because virtue lives on too. 8 Just as the vices cease upon their performance, to be followed by their pleasure and their rewards, so once virtue is completed it is followed by its reward. But there is no completion of virtue except in death: the supreme business of virtue lies precisely in the undertaking of death. The reward of virtue therefore comes after death. 9 Cicero in his *Tusculan Disputations* realised, however uncertainly, that man attains his supreme good only after death [1.110]: 'A man will go to his death, if events so conspire, in a spirit of confidence, and we know that in death there is either the greatest good or else no evil.' So death does not extinguish a man: it escorts him to the reward of his virtue. 10 But anyone who, as Cicero also says, has fouled himself with vice and wickedness, and has yielded to pleasure,[37] is damned, and will pay the everlasting penalty, what holy scripture calls the second death:[38] it lasts for ever and is full of excruciating pain. 11 Just as man has two lives before him, one the life of the soul and the other the life of the body, so he also has two deaths before him, one relevant to the body, a death which all men must die in obedience to nature, and the other relevant to the soul, a death which crime can obtain and virtue can avoid. As this life is time-bound and has fixed limits because it is the life of the body, so too death is equally time-bound and has its appointed end because it applies to the body.

Body pursues the mortal and soul the immortal

11.1 Death itself will be ended when the times appointed by God for death have been completed. And because life in time is followed by death in time, it follows that souls rise again to perennial life, because death in time has received its end. 2 Again, just as the life of the soul is for always, and it obtains the divine and inexpressible reward of its own immortality in that life, so the death of the soul is bound to be for always, and it pays the everlasting penalty of infinite torment for its sins in that death.

---

37 Cf. *Tusc.* 1.2.7; *Rep.* 6.29.
38 *Rev.* 2:11. See also Aug. *civ.* 21.3; *trin.* 4.5.3; *c. Iul.* 6.31.36.

3 The situation is such that people who are in bliss in this corporeal and earthly life are going to be in misery eternally because they have already obtained the goods they preferred; that is what happens to those who worship gods and neglect God. 4 Those who have been in misery in this life by following justice, however, despised and helpless as they are, and often pursued with insult and injury precisely because of their justice (because that is the only way that virtue can be grasped), are going to be in bliss for ever, so that they have their enjoyment of good because they have already endured their evil; that is simply what happens to those who despise gods of earth and perishable goods and follow the heavenly religion of God, whose goods are as eternal as he himself the giver is.

5 Proof that the soul has no part in death is surely very plain in what body and soul achieve. The body is frail and mortal: hence whatever it strives to accomplish is equally liable to fail. Cicero says[39] 'There is nothing made by human hand which is not eventually brought to collapse, whether by assault of man or by old age itself, the destroyer of all things.' 6 The achievements of the soul, on the other hand, are eternal, as we see. Everyone who practises a keen contempt of things present and leaves something behind him to recall his great talents and accomplishments has obviously aimed at a name for intelligence and virtue that will not be wiped out. If then the body's achievements are mortal because the body is, it follows that the soul can be seen as immortal because its achievements are seen to be not mortal. 7 In the same way too, the desires of body and spirit demonstrate that the one is mortal and the other eternal. The body desires only temporal stuff, food and drink, that is, and clothes, rest and pleasure, and yet it can neither desire them nor get them without the assent and assistance of the spirit. The spirit, however, has many desires of its own which do not concern the business of the body and its reward, and they are not feeble but eternal, like the glory of virtue and the remembrance of a name. 8 Worship of God, which is based on abstention from desire and lust, endurance of pain and contempt for death, is pursued by the soul even in spite of the body. To think that the soul does not die but is separated from the body thus makes sense, because body without soul can do nothing, whereas soul without body can do much, and much of note. 9 What about the fact that things visible to the eye and touchable by hand cannot be eternal because they are subject to external action, whereas things not subject to touch or sight (it is only their energy, aim and effect which are

---

39 L.'s citation contains a word (*confectrix*) not recorded in OLD; it is recorded, without attribution however, in Souter. L. may be reworking a sentence of Cicero's quoted at 6.11.25.

obvious) are eternal because they suffer no force from without? 10 If body is mortal because it submits equally to sight and touch, then the soul is equally immortal precisely because it can neither be touched nor be seen.

On the alleged shared fates of body and soul

12.1 Let us now expose the arguments on the other side, which were pursued by Lucretius in his third book. Since the soul shares its birth with the body, he says [3.445–6], necessarily it shares its death with the body. 2 But the same reasoning does not apply in each case. Body is solid and graspable, by hand and by eye, but soul is insubstantial and evades touch and sight.

Body is made and compacted of earth; soul has nothing solid in it – no weight of earth, as Plato argued.[40] Nor could it have its great skill, power and speed unless its origin were in heaven. 3 Since body is constructed of heavy and unstable material and can be touched and seen, so it breaks up and collapses, and because it is subject to sight and touch it cannot resist attack, whereas soul cannot be undone by any act of violence because its insubstantiality enables it to escape all contact. 4 Thus, though they come into being yoked as mates, and the one is the other's container, the one being formed from earth compacted and the other being a product of celestial fineness,[41] when any act of violence divides them (the division being what we call death), each one withdraws into itself: what was earthly is resolved into earth and what came of the heavenly spirit holds its own and keeps its vigour because the divine spirit is everlasting. 5 Even Lucretius forgot what he was arguing and what principle he was defending when he composed the following verses [2.999–1001]: 'What was previously of earth gives way likewise and returns to earth, but what came from the coasts of sky is restored to the gleaming temples of heaven.' Someone arguing that souls perish with bodies had no business to say that, but truth prevailed, and the true analysis slipped in unperceived.

6 Besides, the inference that he draws that the soul breaks up (which is what perishing with the body means) because the two were born together is wrong, and it too can be controverted. The body does not break up at the moment of death: the soul withdraws, but the body stays whole for several days, and if treated can often last a very long time. 7 If they perished together

---

40 *Phd.* 80d.
41 The idea of soul as very fine matter recalls Chrysippus in Calcidius 220 (= LS 53G); Epic. *Ep. ad Hdt.* 63ff (= LS 14A), cf. Lucr. 3.417–62 (= LS 14F); and Tert. *anim.* 5ff., who is criticised by Aug. *gen. ad litt.* 10.25.40ff.

BOOK 7: THE LIFE OF BLISS

in the same way that they were born together, the soul would not abandon the body and suddenly depart; each would instead disintegrate at one and the same moment, and even the body would go liquid and perish with the soul still in it as quickly as the soul withdrew; indeed, upon the disintegration of the body the soul would vanish like liquid spilling from a broken jar.[42] 8 If our frail and earthly body does not dissolve immediately after the withdrawal of the soul and ooze into the earth which is its origin, then the soul, which is not frail, lasts for ever because its source is everlasting. 9 Since mind, he says, expands in children, flourishes in the young and dwindles in the elderly, it is plainly mortal.[43]

First: soul and mind are not the same.[44] We live by the one and we think by the other. When we sleep, the mind rests but not the soul, and in madmen mind is wiped out but not the soul; hence their labelling as witless, not lifeless. 10 It is the mind, then, or the intelligence, that grows or declines with age; the soul is always in its own state: it remains the same from the moment when it receives its opportunity to breathe till its last moment, when it leaves the confinement of the body and flies back to its own abode.

11 Next: though the soul receives its breath from God, nevertheless, shut up as it is in a dark home of earthly flesh, it does not have the knowledge that belongs to divinity. 12 Everything comes to it by hearing and learning: they are the means of developing its wisdom. Old age does not diminish wisdom, but increases it, if, that is, the period of youth was spent virtuously; and if extreme old age does weaken the limbs, it is no fault of the soul that sight fades, the tongue goes dull and hearing thickens:[45] they are failings of the body. 13 But memory fails, it is said.[46] No wonder, if the intellect has to suffer its home collapsing in ruin, and so forgets the past: it will never become divine unless it escapes the prison that confines it.

14 But the soul is also subject to pain and sorrow, says Lucretius,[47] and goes witless with drunkenness: hence it is obviously frail and mortal. 15 Virtue and wisdom are necessary precisely in order that grief, which comes of suffering and of seeing humiliations, may be repelled by courage, and so that pleasure (the pleasure not only of drinking but of everything else too) may be beaten by abstinence. If the soul lacked virtue, if it were devoted to the

42 The image is Lucretian: 3.434–35.
43 Cf. Lucr. 3.445ff.
44 This was also Lucretius' position, however. See 3.138–44.
45 Cf. Lucr. 3.451ff.
46 Cf. Cic. *Sen.* 7.21.
47 Cf. Lucr. 3.459–86.

pleasures and went soft, it would become subject to death, since virtue, as we explained, is the creator of immortality, and pleasure is the creator of death. 16 As I have shown, death is not an utter destroyer: it applies eternal torments. The soul cannot just die, because it has its origin in the spirit of God, which is everlasting. 17 The soul, says Lucretius,[48] can even feel a physical ailment and lose awareness of itself; yet though it may sicken, it can often be healed. 18 That is why virtue should most be applied, in case the soul should crack under any physical pain: losing self-awareness should be the experience of the mind, not of the soul. The mind has 'its own place in the body' [3.610], and that is why it shifts when some disease ravages the area: it migrates as if its home had been 'shattered' [3.600], though it will return of course when treatment and recovery have restored its proper abode.

19 If the soul lacks virtue, then because it is linked with the body, it grows weak at the contact, and the debilitating effect of the link spreads to the mind; whereas upon separation from the body it will thrive of itself and will not now be under attack from any context of enfeeblement, having thrown off its garment of frailty. 20 Just as an eye, says Lucretius,[49] can see nothing when torn out of the body, so too the soul can receive no sensations when separated from the body because it too is part of the body itself. 21 That is wrong; the comparison does not hold. The soul is not a part of the body, but merely in the body. The contents of a jar are not part of the jar; the contents of a house are not part of the house; so too the soul is not part of the body, because the body is the container, or the receptacle, of the soul.

22 Much sillier is his argument[50] saying that the soul is plainly mortal because it is not released from the body at speed but disentangles itself from all the limbs little by little, starting with the feet. If it were everlasting, I suppose he means, it would burst out of the body all in a moment, as happens to those who die by the sword! But people who die of disease are longer in breathing out their spirit: the soul departs little by little as the limbs grow cold. 23 The substance containing the soul is the blood (as oil is for light); when the heat of fevers exhausts it, the outermost limbs are bound to grow cold, because the veins which reach the body's extremities are narrower; when the flow of a spring dwindles, it is the little, distant streams that dry up. 24 We must not imagine, however that the soul's ability to feel is utterly extinguished just because the body's ability fails. It is not the soul that

---

48 Lucr. 3.487–522.
49 Lucr. 3.548–79.
50 Lucr. 3.526–47.

'grows brutish' [3.545] when the body fails, but the body when the soul departs, because the soul takes the capacity to feel away with it. 25 Since it is the presence of the soul which gives the body its capacity to feel and makes it live, it is impossible for the soul not to live and feel of itself, since it is itself life and feeling.

26 As for Lucretius saying [3.613–15], 'But if our mind were immortal, it would not so much complain of dissolution at its death as go off and shed its garment like a snake,' 27 I have never seen anyone complaining of his dissolution at death; but perhaps Lucretius had seen some Epicurean philosophising while he died, discussing his own dissolution with his last breath. 28 How can it be known whether a man feels himself breaking up or feels himself being freed from the body? At death the tongue goes dumb! While he still has feeling and speech, he has not yet broken up, and when he has broken up he can feel and speak no longer; so complaints about dissolution are either not yet possible or not now possible. 29 But before he gets broken up, it will be said, he realises that he is going to be. What of the fact that we see plenty of people who are dying not complaining of dissolution, as Lucretius says, but declaring they are departing, and are setting out and walking, and they indicate as much either by gesture or, if they still can, even by saying so out loud? It is obvious from this that no break-up is taking place, but a separation, which makes it plain that the soul persists.

30 All the other proofs of the Epicurean system are at odds with Pythagoras' position: he says that souls migrate from bodies that are worn out by age and death, and they insert themselves in new ones, just born, and it is the same souls that go on being born, sometimes in a man, sometimes in a domestic animal, or in a wild beast, or in a bird, and they are immortal in the sense that they frequently change abode in a variety of different bodies. 31 That is the view of a lunatic: it is ludicrous; it belongs better on stage than in a school of philosophy, and it is not worth serious refutation because that would suggest a worry that someone might actually believe it. 32 Everything spoken against error in error we must leave to one side; it is quite enough to refute the arguments against truth.

The testimony of prophets and oracles

13.1 I have in my view demonstrated the indestructibility of the soul. It remains to quote the evidence whose authority will confirm the proofs. 2 I shall not at this point call in the witness of the prophets, whose pattern of divination depends entirely on their teaching that man was created for worship of God and for receipt of immortality from God; instead I shall call upon people who simply have to be believed by those who reject the truth.

3 In describing the nature of man, Hermes introduced the following words in order to explain how man was made by God:[G] 'The same power created the nature of man to be one nature composed from two natures, the immortal and the mortal, making the same creature partly immortal and partly mortal, and he set him up midway between the divine and immortal nature and the mortal and mutable, so that he could see everything and admire it all.'[51]

4 It may be that Hermes should be counted among the philosophers, even though he was translated to the gods and is honoured under the name of Mercury by the Egyptians; perhaps he deserves no more attention than Plato and Pythagoras. 5 We should then be looking for a more important piece of evidence. A certain Polites consulted Apollo of Miletus whether the soul lived on after death or broke up, and Apollo replied in verse as follows:[G] 6 'As long as a soul is bound by fetters to the body, in feeling perishable pains it yields to mortal anguish. But when it has found that mortal dissolution of great speed for itself, after the body has decayed, it is entirely borne up into the sky, ageless for eternity, and it survives unscathed for ever. God's firstborn providence so appointed.'[52]

Well? Don't the Sibylline verses make the same point when they declare that a time will come for God's judgment upon the living and dead? We will produce examples in a while. 7 The view of Democritus, Epicurus and Dicaearchus on the dissolution of the soul is therefore wrong. They would of course not venture to discuss the death of souls if any Magus were present with his knowledge that souls get summoned from the underworld by spells, and come and present themselves to human sight, and speak in prediction of the future; if they did so venture, they would be confounded by the facts and the evidence presented. 8 They said that souls perish because they could not see the soul's fine structure, a structure so fine that it cannot be seen by the human mind.

9 What about Aristoxenus,[53] who said there is absolutely no soul at all, even when it is alive in the body? He made comparison with stringed instruments, saying that a power of perception exists in bodies as a result of the structure of the guts and the vitality of the limbs in the same way that a harmonious sound, the harmony that musicians speak of, can be produced

---

51 NF *Corp. Herm.* vol. 4, fr. 15.
52 *Orac. Apoll.* fr. 50 (Fontenrose).
53 Aristoxenus, musician and philosopher (b. Tarentum c. 375–60), studied with the Pythagoreans and with Aristotle. Cicero (*Tusc.* 1.19) refers to his view of the soul as a 'tuning' of the body; cf. Plato, *Phd.* 89.

from tensioning the strings of an instrument. Nothing can be madder than that. 10 Aristoxenus' eyes were sound enough, but his heart was blind: he failed to see he was living by his heart, and did possess a mind, the mind with which he had done his thinking. 11 Philosophers commonly disbelieve in the existence of anything not visible to the eye, though their ability to see mentally things whose force and aim are felt rather than seen ought to be much greater than their ability to see physically.

Six thousand years, and one thousand

14.1 Now that we have discussed the immortality of the soul, it follows that we should explain how far it is granted to man, and when, so that on this point too the mistakes of their own perversity and folly can be seen by those who think that certain mortals are gods by decree and decision of men, whether for their discovery of arts and crafts or their indication of the use of certain plants or their production of things useful to human life or for destroying dangerous beasts. 2 How far distant these worthy actions are from immortality has been explained in our previous books, and we will explain it now too, so that it is clear that only justice creates eternal life for man and the prize of eternal life is bestowed by God alone. 3 There are people said to have become immortal for their good deeds; but there was no justice in them, and no true virtue either, and because of their sins and lusts they have achieved death for themselves, not immortality; they have earned not the prize of heaven but torment for ever, and they will pay just as all those who have worshipped them will pay. I shall show that the time of this judgment is approaching when the just are paid the reward they deserve and due punishment is imposed upon the impious.[54]

4 Plato together with many another philosopher did not know the origin of things and that final moment when the world would be completed. They said that many millennia had gone by since this beautiful world was in full primal form; perhaps they were following the Chaldeans, who, as Cicero reports in book 1 *de Diuinatione* [36] say they have 470,000 years stored in their records, which is mad.[55] They assumed they were free to lie because

---

54 The sources of L.'s eschatology are a puzzle. There are contributions to it, by way of unnamed intermediaries, from early Christian treatments of it, in the first instance from *Revelation* (named only in *epit.* 37.8), from Old Testament prophecy, from Jewish apocalyptic, and from the Iranian religious and astrological tradition going back at least to Zoroaster (L. twice cites the oracles of the Median seer Hystaspes). For a bibliography, see pp. 45–46 n.

55 Cic. *Div.* 1.36; 2.97. Many different figures were offered. See Pease (1920–23) *ad loc.*

they thought they could not be disproved. 5 We who are educated in knowledge of the truth by holy scripture, however, we know the beginning of the world and its end, and it is the end we shall discuss now, at the end of this work; we explained the beginning in book 2. 6 The philosophers who count the centuries in thousands since the world began need to know that the year 6000 has not yet come; when it does come, there will be the inevitable consummation, and the state of human affairs will inevitably be resolved into something better. First, proof of this must be given, so that the pattern is clear.

7 God completed the world and this wonderful work of creation within the space of six days, as is contained in the secrets of holy scripture, and the seventh day, when he rested from his labours, he made sacred.[56] 8 This is the day called sabbath, which takes its name in the Hebrew language from the number; hence the number seven is a lawful and full number, for there are seven days in whose cycle of revolution the cycles of years are completed, there are seven heavenly bodies which do not set, and there are seven stars called wanderers whose uneven orbits and incompatible movements are thought to account for the variations in seasons and circumstances.[57] 9 Since all God's works were done in six days, the world is bound to abide in its present state for six periods of time; six thousand years, that is. A great day of God is completed when a cycle of a thousand years is completed, as shown by the prophet who says [Ps. 90:4], 'Before thine eyes, o lord, a thousand years are as one day.'[58] 10 Just as God laboured for those six days at his great work of creation, so his religion and his truth must labour these six thousand years, while evil is prevalent and dominant. 11 Again, because he rested on the seventh day when his works were done, and blessed it, it is inevitable that at the end of the year 6000 all evil will be swept off the earth and justice will reign for a thousand years[59] and there will be peace and rest from the labours that the earth has endured for so long. 12 I will explain how that will happen.

We have often said that little things, slight things, are signs and foreshadowings of great things; so, this dayspan of ours which is bounded by the rise and set of the sun bears a likeness to that great day which is defined by the revolution of a thousand years. 13 In the same way the shaping of man

---

56 Gen. 2.1–2.
57 L., following Theophil. *Autol.* 2.12 (and no one else), attaches the name of Sabbat to the Hebrew Sheba', 7, by a false etymology. On the number 7, see Gel. 3.10., drawing on Varro's *Hebdomadis*, or *Imagines*. See also Cypr. *ad Fort.* 11.
58 The millenarian reading of Ps. 90:4 is already in 2 Pet. 3:8; Barn. *Ep.* 15.4; Iren. 5.23.2, 28.3; Justin. *dial.* 81.3. See Nicholson (1985), 294–95, n. 21.
59 Cf. Rev. 20.1–10.

from earth was a sign for the future of the creation of the people of heaven. When everything that God contrived for the use of man was ready, on the sixth day he finally made man himself and introduced him into this world as if it were his house now carefully built; just so, on the sixth great day true man is being fashioned by the word of God; that is to say, the holy people is being shaped for justice by the teaching and precepts of God. 14 Just as original man was made mortal and imperfect out of earth, to live in this world a thousand years,[60] so now from this earthly generation perfect man is being fashioned, to be given life by God and to be master in this same world a thousand years. 15 How the consummation will take place and what sort of end is looming for human affairs will be found by inspection of holy scripture. 16 Utterances by prophets of this world, in agreement with prophets of heaven, announce an end of things, and shortly after, their ruin; they describe a sort of extreme old age for a world exhausted and collapsing.[61] 17 But as for what the seers and prophets say will happen before that final conclusion supervenes, I will search all sources and present it in its totality.

Approaching the end of the world, and of Rome

15.1 It says in the secrets of holy literature that the leader of the Hebrews with all his household and family crossed into Egypt when pressed by lack of corn.[62] 2 His descendants spent a long time in Egypt, and became a great nation; when they were oppressed by a heavy and intolerable yoke of slavery, God struck Egypt with an incurable disease, and liberated his people by guiding them through the middle of the sea, the people walking on dry ground when the waves had been parted and pushed to either side. 3 The king of the Egyptians attempted to pursue them as they fled, but when the sea returned to its natural state he was trapped with all his forces. 4 This was a remarkable event, an event of great note; in the immediate context it displayed the virtue of God to mankind, but in its meaning it was the foreshadowing of a greater event, which God was going to accomplish at the final consummation of time: for then he will free his people from their oppressive enslavement to the world.[63] 5 At the time there was only one

---

60 The shortening of man's lifespan after the flood to 120 years was a consequence of sin (2.12.21–23; *epit.* 27.5; *Gen.* 6.3). Here L. uses the original dispensation of a thousand years to boost the argument for a millennium in which the faithful rule the earth with God.

61 See 15.14 below; Lucr. 2.1144ff.; NF *Corp. Herm. Asclep.* 25ff.

62 Gen. 47–50; Exod. 1–14.

63 A different explanation is given in 4.13.22–23. Cf. Cypr. *Quir.* 2.11.

people of God and only one nation accommodating them; so Egypt alone was blasted; now, however, God's people are a congregation of all tongues dwelling among all nations and they are oppressed by the tyranny of these nations, and so all nations, the whole world, that is, must be beaten by blows from heaven in order to liberate the people who are just and who worship God. 6 Just as signs were made at the time to warn the Egyptians of the disaster threatening them, so at the end of time there will be extraordinary portents in every element of the world so that all nations may know of the imminence of the end.

7 As this period approaches the end, therefore, the state of human affairs is bound to be altered; as wickedness grows stronger, so things will get worse, so that these times of ours, when iniquity and evil have grown to their highest degree, can be deemed happy, virtually golden, by comparison with the incurable evil then.[64] 8 Justice will grow so rare and impiety, covetousness, greed and lust will grow so frequent that all good men who happen to exist at the time will fall prey to criminals and will be attacked on all sides by the unjust, and only the evil will be rich, while good men are beset by all manner of insult and indigence. All rights will be overthrown and all laws will perish. 9 No one will hold on to anything unless he seeks or defends it with force; violence and outrage will be in control of everything. There will be no faith among men, no peace, no generosity, no shame, no truth: and thus there will be no security, no order and no respite from evil. 10 All the earth will be in upheaval, wars will rage everywhere, all nations will be in arms attacking each other by turns; neighbour cities will fight each other, and Egypt will be the first to pay the penalty for its stupid superstitions, and will be covered with rivers of blood.[65] 11 The sword will traverse the globe reaping all in its path, laying all low in its harvest,[66] and the cause of the devastation and confusion will be this: the name of Rome, by which the world is presently ruled – I shudder to say this, but I will say it even so, because it will happen so –, the name of Rome will be razed from the earth, power will return to Asia, and once again East will be master and West will be servant.[67]

 64 Cf. *4 Ezra* 6–7.
 65 Cf. *Orac. Sib.* 5.54ff., 77, 197ff.
 66 *Orac. Sib.* 3.316ff., 350ff.
 67 The fall of Rome coincides with the end of the world (cf. 25.6ff. below), and L. welcomes it no more than Tertullian did (*apol.* 32.1); not so the author of Revelation (cf. 13–14) and Hystaspes (see 19 below). The idea that Rome and the world would end together was widespread among Christians, however they viewed the Roman state. Augustine broke with this tradition. See Mommsen (1959), 265ff.

BOOK 7: THE LIFE OF BLISS

12 It should be no surprise to anyone if an empire founded on such a base, expanded so long and so widely and buttressed by such great resources should eventually collapse. There is nothing constructed by human effort which cannot also be felled by human effort, because the achievements of mortals are mortal. 13 Other empires flourished before now even longer, yet none the less they fell. It is recorded that the Egyptians, the Persians, the Greeks and the Assyrians all had the governance of the world; all were destroyed and supreme power came to the Romans in their turn. The more they outreach other empires in greatness, the further will be their fall, because what towers above the rest has more mass for its fall. 14 Seneca[68] divided the ages of Rome into periods very shrewdly. He said that 'its infancy came first, when Romulus was king; Rome was born and brought up by Romulus; then came its childhood under the other kings, who developed it and gave it shape with more extensive education and advice; but when Tarquin was king, and Rome was virtually grown up, it refused servility and threw off the yoke of an arrogant rule, choosing to obey laws rather than kings; when this period of its adolescence was terminated by the end of the Carthaginian war, then at last it came to its strength and began its young manhood.' 15 Once Carthage was put down, so long her rival in empire, Rome stretched out her arm over all the earth by land and sea, until with all kings and peoples brought under her yoke any cause for campaigns now failed; she could not use her strength well, and exhausted herself thereby.[69] 16 That was the start of her old age: torn by civil wars and weighed down by internal evil she reverted to one man rule as if she had returned to her infancy. When the freedom was gone that she had preserved under Brutus' lead and inspiration, she grew old: she seemed not to have the strength to keep going without rulers to prop her up.

17 If that is so, then what is left to follow old age but death? Death soon is indeed what the prophets say in public, but they disguise it under other names to prevent easy understanding. 18 The Sibyls say openly that Rome will perish, and by judgment of God, because she held God's name in hatred and in her hostility to justice slew the people brought up to truth.[70] 19 Hystaspes also, king of the Medes long ago, who gave his name to the river now called Hydaspes, put on record for posterity an extraordinary dream as interpreted by a boy prophesying: long before the founding of the Trojan race, he said that the power and name of Rome would be removed from the world.[71]

---

68 Seneca the Elder, Hist. F1 (Peter, vol. 2, 91–92), with Vottero 77–78.
69 Cf. Sal. Cat. 10.
70 *Orac. Sib.* 8.9ff., 165, 171–73.
71 *Orac. Hyst.* fr. 13a in Bidez and Cumont (1938), vol. 2, 366–67.

The reign of evil

16.1 I will explain how this will come about, in case anyone thinks it incredible. First, Rome's kingship will be extended, and her supreme authority will be split up and spread amongst many, to its diminution. Next, there will be constant dissemination of civil strife and no rest from destructive wars, until there are ten rulers at one time who will share out the earth, not to rule it but to wreck it. 2 They will get themselves huge armies, abandon all agriculture (which is the beginning of revolution and disaster), and lay everything waste, breaking it all up and devouring it. 3 Then an enemy of great power will suddenly rise up against them, from the furthest bounds of the north,[72] and after destroying three of the kings who will then be in occupation of Asia he will be taken into alliance by the rest and be made chief of them all. 4 He will exercise an oppressive tyranny over the earth, making no distinction between human and divine, attempting things unspeakable and loathsome, plotting revolution in his heart to establish his own private rule, changing the laws and authorising his own, with pollution, plunder, theft and murder. Finally he will change his name and move the seat of government, and then the confusion and ruin of the human race will follow.

5 Then there will truly be a time to detest and abominate, when life will be enjoyable for no one. Cities will be wrecked to their roots; they will die not just by fire and sword but by constant earthquakes, floods, chronic disease and frequent famine.[73] 6 The air will grow foul and will become corrupt and pestilent, partly from unseasonable rain and partly from futile drought, partly from great cold and partly from great heat, and men will have no fruits of the earth: cornfield, orchard and vineyard will bear nothing; they will offer great hope in the flower and betray it in the bud. 7 Springs will dry up, together with rivers, so that there is no drink, and water will turn to blood or brackishness. 8 Hence there will be no cattle on earth, no birds in the sky and no fish in the sea.

There will also be extraordinary signs in the sky, fretting men's minds with great panic, comets with tails, a dark sun, the moon changing colour and shooting stars descending. 9 These things will not happen in their usual way: unknown stars will suddenly appear, unfamiliar to sight. The sun will

---

72 From the north: frequent in OT prophets, e.g., Jer. 1.13–15; Ezek. 1.4.

73 The influence of *Orac. Sib.* 8 in the following section has long been noted; Bidez and Cumont (1938), 368ff., label it a fragment of *Orac. Hyst.* (fr. 14). Nor should Jewish apocalyptic be neglected: see e.g. *4 Ezra* 5.1–12, the Syriac Apocalypse of Baruch 25ff, and Jubilees 23 (all in Charlesworth (1983), 517ff., 615ff.; (1985), 35ff.).

be overcast for good, so that distinction of night and day will scarcely occur, and the moon will go into eclipse not just for three hours but with a lasting veil of blood and extraordinary irregularity of orbit, so that people will not be able to recognise the courses of the heavenly bodies or the pattern of the seasons; there will be summer in winter or else winter in summer. 10 The year will shorten, the month will lessen, and the day will be squeezed into a small span, and stars will fall in great frequency, so that the whole sky will look blind, with no lights in it. 11 The loftiest mountains will also tumble and be levelled with the plains, and the sea will become unnavigable.

To prevent anything being missing among the evils of men and earth, a trumpet will sound from the sky; the Sibyl declares it thus:[G] 'A trumpet shall launch its voice of long lament from heaven.'[74] All will tremble and shudder at that note of grief. 12 Then, because of God's anger against the people who do not acknowledge justice, sword, fire, famine and disease will rage, and above them all an ever-looming panic. Then they will pray to God and he will not hear them; death will be their prayer and it will not come. Not even night will give them respite from fear, nor will sleep come to their eyes; worry and wakefulness will exhaust men's spirits; they will weep and wail and gnash their teeth, congratulating the dead and lamenting the living.[75] 13 At these evils, and many more, there will be desolation on earth, and the world will lose shape and population, as is observed in the Sibylline verses:[G] 'The world will lose its order as people perish.'[76] 14 Thus the human race will be finished off, and scarce a hundred will go where a thousand once went. Two thirds will die even of God's worshippers; one third will survive, those that were put to the proof.[77]

Good and evil in combat

17.1 I will explain more directly how this will happen.[78] When the ending of time is imminent, a great prophet will be sent by God to convert people to acknowledgement of God, and he will take on the power to do miracles. 2 Wherever men do not hear him, he will close the sky and take away the

---

74 *Orac. Sib.* 8.239.
75 Cf. *Orac. Sib.* 8.352–56; 2.306–11.
76 *Orac. Sib.* 7.123.
77 Cf. *Orac. Sib.* 3.544; Rev. 9.15, 18.
78 Aune (1998), vol. 2, 590–93, 726–28, notes similarities in this chapter with Rev. 11:1–13, 13:11–16, but also differences, which he ascribes to the Oracle of Hystaspes. Cf. Bidez and Cumont (1938), fr. 15, pp. 370ff.

rainclouds, he will turn water into blood, and will torment people with hunger and thirst, and if an attempt is made to assail him, fire will proceed from his mouth and will burn up the man. By such portentous acts of virtue he will convert many to worship of God.

When all his works are accomplished, a second king will arise in Syria, born of an evil spirit, the wrecker and destroyer of the human race, who will wipe out the remnants of previous evil together with himself. 3 He will fight against the prophet of God, and will defeat and kill him, and will leave him to lie unburied, but after the third day the prophet will come back to life and will be swept up into heaven before the admiring gaze of all. 4 That second king will certainly be very ghastly in himself, but he will also be a liar: he will set himself up as god, and will call himself god, and will give orders to be worshipped as god's son. He will be given power to do signs and prodigies, and when they are seen, men will be ensnared into adoration of him. 5 He will command fire to descend from heaven, the sun to halt in its course and an image to speak, and these things will happen at his word;[79] very many even of the wise will be drawn to him by these miracles. 6 Then he will try to overthrow the temple of God, and he will pursue the just people, and there will be persecution and pressure such as there has never been, not since the beginning of the world.

7 All those who believe him and go over to him will be marked by him like cattle,[80] while those who refuse his mark will either escape to the hills or get caught and killed with special tortures. 8 He will wrap the just in the writings of the prophets and cremate them so. He will be given power to lay the world waste for 42 months.[81] 9 In that time justice will be in exile and innocence will be hated, and the evil in their hatred will plunder the good like foes. Neither law nor order nor military discipline will survive, none will respect grey hairs or acknowledge the duty of piety, or show pity to women or children; everything will be confounded and confused, contrary to right, contrary to the laws of nature. The whole earth will be wasted as if in a single act of communal depredation. 10 When this happens, the just and those who pursue truth will separate themselves from the evil and will flee to deserts, and when the impious man hears that, he will flare up in anger and will come with a great army, and he will bring up all his forces to surround the mountain where the just are living in order to seize them. 11 When they see themselves hemmed in on every side and under siege, they will cry to

79 Cf. Rev. 13.13–14.
80 Cf. Rev. 13.16–17.
81 42 is also the figure in Rev. 13:5.

God with a loud voice and beg for help from heaven, and God will hear them and will send them a great king from heaven to rescue them and to free them, and to destroy all the impious with fire and sword.

The evidence of oracles and seers

18.1 It is the common claim of all prophets who act on God's inspiration and of all seers who act at the instigation of demons that this will be so. 2 Hystaspes, whom I mentioned earlier, in describing the iniquity of this final generation says 'The pious and the faithful will separate themselves from the evil and will stretch out their hands to heaven with weeping and wailing, begging for Jupiter's promise; Jupiter will look upon the earth, hear the voices of men and destroy the impious.'[82] All that is true except for one thing: he said Jupiter would do what God will do. 3 Yet even the sending of God's son by his father to destroy all the evil and to liberate the pious has not been omitted without some devilish deception, though Hermes, however, has not practised dissimulation. In his book entitled *Perfect Discourse*, after enumerating the evils we have spoken of, he added this:[G] 4 'When this happens, my dear Asclepius, then the lord and father and god and creator of the first and only god will look upon events and will defy disorder with his own will, which is goodness; he will end exile and will purify evil, partly by drenching it in water, partly by burning it with keen fire and sometimes by striking it with war and plague, and he will restore and re-establish his own world.'[83]

5 The Sibyls also reveal a similar future: the son of God will be sent by his father most high to free the just from the grip of the impious and also to wipe out the unjust together with their cruel tyrants. 6 One of the Sibyls reports thus:[G] 'He will come with a wish to destroy the city of the blessed. And a king sent against him from God will destroy all great kings and mighty men, and the judgment of the immortal one will be upon men.'[84] 7 Another says:[G] 'And then God will send a king from the sun who shall free the whole earth from evil war.'[85] 8 And a third says:[G] 'Behold, he will come in gentleness, to raise the unbearable yoke of slavery that lies upon our necks, and he will undo godless laws and the bonds of violence.'[86]

---

82 *Orac. Hyst.* fr. 15 in Bidez and Cumont (1938), 370–73.
83 NF *Corp. Herm. Asclep.* 26.
84 *Orac. Sib.* 5.107–10.
85 *Orac. Sib.* 3.652ff.
86 *Orac. Sib.* 8.326ff.

19.1 Since human resources are inadequate to dislodge a tyranny of immense power from a world oppressed – and once the world has been seized, that tyranny will maintain its position on top with vast armies of criminals – a calamity of such extent will need divine aid. 2 God will be moved both by the ambiguous peril of the just and by their pitiful appeal, and will therefore send his deliverer at once.[87] Then, at darkest midnight, the centre of heaven will open, so that the light of God descending is visible throughout the world like lightning. The Sibyl has announced this in verse as follows:[G] 'When he comes, there will be lurid fire at black midnight.'[88] 3 This is the night that we shall celebrate watching for the advent of our king and God. It has a double meaning: on that night he regained life after his passion, and on that night he will regain his kingship of the earth, 4 for he is deliverer, judge, avenger, king and God, and we call him Christ.

Before he descends he will give the following sign. 5 A sword will suddenly fall from the sky, so that the just may know that the leader of the holy army is about to descend, and he will come with angels accompanying him to the centre of the earth, and in front of him will go an inextinguishable flame, and the virtue of the angels will put into the hand of the just all that host which besieged their mountain, and the host will be killed from the third hour till evening, and blood will flow in torrents. When all his forces have been destroyed, only the impious one will escape, and he will be the destroyer of his own virtue. 6 He is the one called Antichrist, but he himself will claim that he is Christ, and he will fight against the true Christ. When he is beaten, he will flee; he will often renew the fight and he will as often be beaten, until in the fourth war, when all the impious have been finished off, he will be beaten down and taken, and at last will pay the penalty for his wickedness. 7 At the same time the other princes and tyrants who have devastated the world will be made prisoners with him and will be brought before the king, and the king will assail them and rebuke them, proving their own crimes against them, and he will condemn them and deliver them to well earned punishment.

8 When evil is thus wiped out and impiety suppressed, the world will have peace again; for so many years it has been subject to error and crime, and has endured a wicked servitude. 9 There will be no more worship of gods made by hand; their images will be turned out of their temples and off their couches and burnt, and they will burn together with their extraordinary

---

87 Cf. Rev. 19:11–21.
88 *Orac. Sib.* fr. 3.

BOOK 7: THE LIFE OF BLISS

offerings. The Sibyl is in agreement with the prophets in having predicted this too:[G] 'Let men cast off images with all wealth,' and the Sibyl of Erythrae has promised,[G] 'Forms of gods made by hand shall be burnt.'[89]

The first resurrection and how unjust souls can suffer

20.1 After this the underworld will open and the dead will rise, and the great verdict will be delivered upon them by the same king and God who has received from his father most high the supreme power both of judgment and of kingship. As for this judgment and kingship, in the Sibyl of Erythrae we find as follows:[G] 2 'When the fated day comes to its fulfilment, the judgment of the immortal God will come upon men; upon mankind will come great judgment and power.'[90] 3 In another Sibyl we find:[G] 'Then the earth will gape and reveal Tartarean chaos, and all shall come to the tribunal of God the king.'[91] 4 And in the same Sibyl elsewhere:[G] 'I will unroll the sky and open the vaults of earth, and I will resurrect the dead by undoing their fate and the sting of death. Then I will bring them to judgment, judging the lives of pious men and impious men.'[92] 5 Not all men will then be judged by God, however: only those well practised in God's religion.[93] Those who have not acknowledged God are already judged and condemned because no verdict upon them can result in acquittal; holy scripture bears witness [Ps. 1:5]: 'the impious will not be resurrected for judgment.' 6 Only those who know God therefore will be judged, and their deeds, their evil deeds, that is, will be weighed in the balance against their good deeds, so that if their good and just deeds are more numerous and significant, they will be despatched to the life of bliss, but if their evil deeds prevail, they will be condemned to punishment.

7 At this point someone may say, 'If the soul is immortal, how is it being treated as capable of suffering and of feeling punishment? If it is punished as it deserves, it will simply experience pain, and on that basis even death; if it is not subject to death, then it is not subject to pain either, and so is not capable of suffering.' 8 This question, or argument, is met by the Stoics[94] as

---

89 *Orac. Sib.* 8.224; 3.618.
90 *Orac. Sib.* 3.741ff.
91 *Orac. Sib.* 8.241ff.
92 *Orac. Sib.* 8.413ff.
93 Cf. Rev. 20:4–5 (the first resurrection).
94 For the Stoic doctrine of everlasting recurrence, see Nemesius 309.5–311.2 (= LS 52C): 'For again there will be Socrates and Plato and each one of mankind...'; cf. Alexander, *On Aristotle's Prior Analytics* 180, 33–6; 181, 25–31 (= LS 52F), citing Chrysippus; Euseb. *Praep. Evang.* 15.20.6 (= LS 54W).

follows: the souls of men do survive, and are not reduced to nothing by the intervention of death, but whereas the souls of the just return pure, free of suffering and blessed to the place in heaven whence they came (or are swept off to the so-called happy plains, where they have the joy of wonderful pleasures), 9 impious souls have befouled themselves with evil desires, and have developed an intermediate nature, between mortal and immortal; by contact with the flesh they have an element of weakness, from enslavement to its desires and lusts, and they are marked with a sort of ineradicable stain, a blemish of earth; over a long passage of time it gets deeply ingrained, and souls become of such a nature that though not totally extinguishable, being from God, nevertheless they do become liable to torment because of the stain of the body, branded upon them for their sins, and that produces the sensation of pain. 10 This view is put by the poet as follows [Verg. A. 6.735–40]: 'Why, when life at its last light leaves us, even so not all evil departs from us poor wretches; not all the plagues of the body depart forthwith; much that is customary continues to grow within, inevitably, over time, in mysterious fashion. Therefore are men disciplined by punishment, and they pay out the penalty for ancient evils.' 11 That is virtually true. When the soul makes its separation from the body, it is, as the same poet puts it [Verg. A. 6.702], 'one with the insubstantial winds, and very like fleeting sleep,' because it is spirit, and ungraspable precisely because of its insubstantiality; we cannot grasp it because we are corporeal, but God can, because it is God's part to be omnipotent.

How unjust souls can suffer (continued)

21.1 First therefore we say that God's power is so great that he can even grasp the incorporeal and can affect it as he wills.[95] The angels fear God because they can be chided by him in some unaccountable fashion; the demons are terrified of him because he can torture them and punish them. 2 So there is no surprise if souls are immortal and yet liable to suffering from God. Since they have nothing in them which is solid enough to take an impression, they cannot feel the force of things solid and corporeal; because they live in the spirit only, they are impressible only by God, whose virtue and effect is of the spirit. 3 Even so, holy literature tells us how the impious will pay their penalties. Because they committed their sins in the flesh, they

---

95 For Bidez and Cumont (1938), 373–74; this chapter contains Hystaspian material (= fr. 16).

will be reclothed in flesh, so that they make expiation in the body; but it will not be the flesh in which God clothes man, something similar to this earthly flesh of ours, but a flesh indestructible and everlasting, so that it can take torture and eternal fire (the nature of this fire is different from that of the fire we use for the necessities of life, which dies unless kept fed with fuel of some sort). 4 The divine fire lives all the time by its own means and thrives without any feeding; it has no contamination of smoke, but is pure and liquid, fluid like water; it is not forced upwards by something as our fire is, which is compelled by the stain of the earthly body that holds it and by its own admixture of smoke to leap up and fly upwards, fluttering and quivering to attain its heavenly nature.[96]

5 It is therefore that same divine fire, with one and the same power of effect, which will both burn the impious and remake them, and what it takes away from their bodies it will replace in full, and so keep itself supplied with constant sustenance (this is what the poets mean by the vulture of Tityus).[97] Without any loss to their self-renewing bodies it will thus simply burn them and make them feel the pain. 6 Yet when God judges the pious, he will test them too with fire. Those whose sins are excessive in weight or number will be scorched and burnt by the fire, but those who are fully imbued with justice and are ripe in virtue will not feel it, since they have in them an element of God to repel the effect of the flame and to reject it. 7 The power of innocence is so great that the fire retreats before it with no harm done because it has received its mission, of burning the impious and respecting the just, from God.[98] No one should think that souls are judged immediately upon dying, however; all are kept under one common guard until the moment comes when their merits are tested by the supreme judge. 8 Then the prize of immortality will go to those whose justice of behaviour is established, but there will be no resurrection for those whose sins and crimes are exposed; they will be buried in the same darkness with the impious, doomed to certain punishment.

---

96 Cf. Sen. *Nat.* 2.24.3.

97 Tityus suffered the perpetual laceration of his liver by vultures for having assaulted Leto (cf. Min. Fel. 35). The idea of a fire which does not consume what it burns is characteristic of Stoic thought, but is given a second life in Christian thinking on eternal punishment (see Tert. *apol.* 48.14).

98 *Orac. Sib.* 2.253–55; 8.410ff.

Poets are authorities for resurrection

22.1 Some people think this is a poetic fabrication; they say it is impossible because they don't know the poets' sources. Their view is not surprising. 2 What the poets report is inconsistent with reality; they may go much further back than historians and orators and other sorts of writers, but because they did not know the mystery of the divine promise, and mention of a future resurrection had reached them only as a faint rumour, they passed it on as a story without credibility, having heard it only casually. 3 And yet they also said they had no sure authority to follow, but only opinion; for instance, Vergil says [*A.* 6.266], 'May it be right for me to say what I have heard.' 4 Despite, then, their partial distortion of the secrets of truth, nevertheless the reality emerges all the more truly because of their partial agreement with the prophets, and that is sufficient for us as proof of the matter.[99]

5 There is, however, some sense in their mistake. The prophets had kept asserting that the judge of the dead would be god's son, and this was no covert pronouncement; but because they thought that the god who ruled the sky was Jupiter, they said it was Jupiter's son who was judge in the underworld, not meaning Apollo or Bacchus or Mercury, who are considered gods of heaven, but someone who had been both mortal and just, Minos or Aeacus or Rhadamanthus.[100] 6 They therefore exercised a corrupting poetic licence on the tradition – or else truth was altered by opinion, once it had passed through different lips in a variety of telling. 7 They said there was restitution to life after a thousand years in the underworld, with Vergil saying [*A.* 6.748–51], 'All these will be summoned to the river of Lethe in a great phalanx by god when they have worked their thousand year cycle, to see the curves of sky again without, of course, remembering them, and to kindle the desire of regaining their bodies', 8 but they got it wrong; the idea is that the dead will rise again not after a thousand years of being dead but to be restored to life again and to reign a thousand years with God. For God will come to cleanse this world of all stain, to revive the souls of the just in new bodies, and to raise them to eternal bliss. 9 Apart from the water of oblivion the rest is true; that particular story was meant to deal with the question why they had not then remembered that they had once been alive, or who they were, or what they had done. Nevertheless, it is not plausible, and the whole thing can be rejected as a wild and wanton fiction.

---

99 L. has explained and defended his use of poets as authorities in Book 1. See e.g. 1.5.4, 11.23ff. and 15.5.

100 See note at 3.20.17.

10 When we assert the resurrection, however, and explain that souls will return for a second life fully cognisant of themselves, in the same shape and with the same capacity to feel, there is opposition: 'So many centuries have passed; what resurrection has there ever been from the underworld, even one, for us to take that precedent as proof of the possibility?' 11 But resurrection is not possible as long as injustice is still in control. People are still being killed in this generation by the violence of sword, plot and poison; they are still suffering brutality, want, imprisonment, torture and proscription. 12 In addition, justice is hated, and all who wish to follow God are not merely loathed but attacked verbally and tortured physically in all sorts of ways, forced to an impious worship of manufactured gods not by reason and truth but by unspeakable physical violence.

13 Would it be right, then, for men to rise to all that again, or return to a life in which they cannot be safe? Since the just are treated with such contempt and are put out of the way so easily, what are we to think would have happened if someone did come back from the underworld and regained life with full restoration of rights? 14 He will certainly be whisked out of view, in case sight or sound of him made everyone abandon the gods and switch to the worship and religion of the one God. 15 Resurrection is therefore bound to happen once only, at the removal of evil, because it is not right for those who have risen again to die any more or to be attacked in any way, so that they can live the life of bliss with their death cancelled. 16 The poets knew that this generation abounded in every ill, but they set up a river of oblivion, in case souls remembered their difficulties and refused to return to the upper world. 17 Hence Vergil's lines [A. 6.719–21]: 'O father, must we think that some souls go hence aloft to heaven, and return to the tardy flesh again? Poor things, what is this dreadful longing for the light?' 18 They did not know the form or the time in which it should happen; they thought it was a second birth, and souls would return to the womb again and regress to infancy. 19 Hence even Plato says,[101] in discussion of the soul, that 'it can be understood that souls are immortal and divine from the fact that in children there is a flexibility of mind and a readiness in learning, because they grasp what they learn so quickly that they appear not to be learning from scratch but to be regaining knowledge from memory.' There you have an intelligent man foolishly putting his trust in poets.

---

101 Cf. Cic. *Tusc.* 1.57ff. (citing Pl. *Men.* 85c); *Sen.* 21.78.

Philosophers in confusion over resurrection

23.1 They will not be reborn because rebirth is impossible; they will rise again to be endowed by God with bodies, and they will remember their former lives and all their actions; they will have place among the goods of heaven, they will enjoy the pleasure of untold plenty, and will give thanks to God face to face because he has destroyed all evil and has raised them to his kingdom and to life eternal. 2 On the topic of resurrection, the philosophers have also attempted to say something, but with as much distortion as the poets. Pythagoras argued that souls moved into new bodies, but it was silly to argue that they moved from men into animals and from animals into men, and that he himself had been recreated from Euphorbus. 3 Chrysippus, called by Cicero a pillar of the Stoic portico, put it better: in his books on providence, in speaking of the renewal of the world, he said:[G] 'In these circumstances it is plain that we too could perfectly well return to the form we now have in some period of time after dying.'[102] 4 Let us move from the human to the divine. The Sibyl speaks as follows:[G] 'All the mortal race is hard of belief, but when the judgment of the world and men arrives, which god himself will give when he judges impious and pious alike, then he will despatch the impious to darkness in fire, but those who are pious shall live on the earth again, and god will give them breath, esteem and life.'[103] 5 If not only the prophets but also seers, poets and philosophers agree that there will be a resurrection of the dead, no one should ask of us how it can happen; no explanation can be given of God's works, but if God did institute man from the start in some fashion impossible to describe, then we may be sure that he who made new can also restore the old.

Judgement and the golden age

24.1 Now for the remainder. The son of God most high and most great will come to judge the living and the dead, as the Sibyl testifies when she says:[G] 'There will be confusion of men all over earth at the time when the almighty comes in person to his tribunal to judge the souls of the living and the dead and to judge the whole world.'[104] 2 When he has destroyed injustice and made his supreme judgment and restored to life the just who were so from the start, he will spend a thousand years with men and will rule them with

---

102 Cic. *Ac.* 2.75.
103 *Orac. Sib.* 4.40–43, 186ff.
104 *Orac. Sib.* 8.81–83.

great justice.[105] This is proclaimed by another Sibyl prophesying in a frenzy:[G] 'Hear me, o mortals: the everlasting king is reigning.'[106] 3 At that time, those alive in the flesh will not die but will produce children without number during those thousand years,[107] and their offspring will be holy and precious to God; those raised from the underworld will be in charge of the living like judges. 4 Other people will not be wiped out altogether; some will be left for God's victory, so that the just may triumph over them and put them into perpetual servitude. 5 At the same time even the prince of demons, who is the fabricator of all evils, will be put in chains and kept under guard for the thousand years of heaven's control, when justice will reign on earth, in case he tries to start any evil against God's people.[108] 6 After God's coming the just will gather from all over the world, and after his judgment the holy city will be set up at the centre of earth, and God himself will dwell in it with the just in control.[109] This city is what the Sibyl points to when she says:[G] 'This is the city that god desired, and he has made it brighter than the stars and sun and moon.' 7 Then the darkness that clouds the earth and blocks out the sky will be removed from earth, and the moon will take on the sun's brightness and not be reduced thereafter, and the sun will become seven times brighter than it now is.[110] The earth will disclose its fertility and breed rich fruit of its own accord, the rocks of the hills will ooze with honey, and the rivers will swell with milk; the world itself will rejoice and all nature will be glad at being plucked into freedom from the dominion of evil, impiety, wickedness and error.[111] 8 Wild beasts will not feed on blood in this period, nor birds on prey; everything will instead be peaceful and quiet. Lions and calves will stand together at the stall, wolf will not seize lamb, dog will not hunt, hawk and eagle will do no harm, and children will play with snakes.[112]

9 This will be the time for all those things to happen that the poets claimed for the golden age when Saturn was king. The mistake about them arises from the fact that prophets foretelling the future keep putting plenty

---

105 Cf. Rev. 20:1–6; *Dan.* 7:9, 22, 27; Isa. 11. See Jerome, *uir. ill.* 18 for Christian writers (including L.) who treated this topic. L., as was his custom, gives prominence to the Sibyl and to Vergil, but also draws on prophecy in the Old Testament in painting his own picture of the Millennium.

106 *Orac. Sib.* fr. 4.

107 Cf. Isa. 6:12.

108 Cf. Rev. 20:2.

109 For the city, see 26.1 below; Rev. 20:9; Justin, *dial.* 81.4, citing Isaiah and Revelation.

110 Cf. Isa. 30:26.

111 Cf. Ezek. 47:12; Amos 9:13ff.; Joel 4:18.

112 Cf. Isa. 11:6ff., 65:25; *Orac. Sib.* 3.619–23, 8.210ff.

forward like that, delivering it as if it has taken place.[113] Visions were put before their eyes by the divine spirit, and they saw things in their sight as if in process and completion. 10 Their words of prophecy were slowly spread by rumour, but those outside God's mystery did not know their scope; they thought it was all stuff over and done with long before, because it simply could not take place in the reign of a man.

11 When wrong religions have been destroyed, however, and crime has been suppressed, and the earth is subject to God, 'Merchants will leave the sea, ship's timbers will not haggle for bargains; all things will grow everywhere on earth. The soil will suffer no ploughshares, the vine no knife; the sturdy ploughman too will release his oxen from the yoke' [Verg. *Ecl.* 4.38–41]. Then too, 'The field will slowly turn yellow with soft awns, and the grape will hang reddening amid uncut brambles, and tough oaks will drip the dewy honey' [28–30]. 'Wool will not learn to copy different colours: the ram at pasture will vary his fleece himself, sometimes to a soft pink hue, sometimes to yellow ochre, and red dye will dress the feeding lambs of its own accord' [42–45]. 'Nanny goats will bring their milk-distended udders home themselves, and herds will have no fear of great lions' [21–22].

12 Vergil follows the Sibyl of Cumae in saying this. The Sibyl of Erythrae puts it thus:[G] 'Wolves and lambs will eat grass on the hills together, and leopards will feed with kids; bears will graze among calves and all cattle, the carnivorous lion will eat bran at the manger, and snakes will bed down with infants.'[114] 13 Elsewhere, on the fertility of nature:[G] 'Then god will give men great joy, for earth and trees and the countless offspring of earth will give men the true fruit of wine, sweet honey, white milk and grain, and that is for mortals the most beautiful of all things.'[115] 14 Again in like fashion:[G] 'The holy earth, abode of the pious alone, will produce all these things; a stream will flow from a rock dripping honey, and milk too from an immortal spring for all just men.'[116] 15 People will thus live lives of great peace and plenty, and will reign side by side with God; kings of nations will come from the ends of the earth with offerings and gifts to honour and adore the great king, and his name will be known and revered by all people under heaven and by all kings with dominion on earth.

---

113 Vergil, however, guided by the Sibyl, was not in error insofar as he looked forward to a Golden Age in the future.
114 *Orac. Sib.* 3.787ff.
115 *Orac. Sib.* 3.619ff.
116 *Orac. Sib.* 5.281ff.

BOOK 7: THE LIFE OF BLISS

No more than two hundred years remain

25.1 This is what the prophets said would happen. I have not thought it necessary to set out what they say in evidence because it would go on for ever; my book could not manage so much material when so many people are saying the same things in the same spirit, and I would not want to bore my readers by piling up stuff gathered from all of them; besides, what I would be saying would simply be confirmation drawn from the writings of others, not my own words, and I would be pointing out that the truth is kept recorded not just with us but also with those very people who keep persecuting us – though it is a truth which they refuse to acknowledge. 2 Anyone wanting to know this more precisely should go to the fountainhead itself: they will discover more wonderful things than I have managed to get into these books of mine.

3 Someone may now ask when these things will happen which we have spoken of. I have already pointed out above that the change should occur at the end of six thousand years, and that the supreme day of final conclusion is already approaching. 4 We can learn from the signs which the prophets have predicted: they have told us the signs by which we should expect the consummation of all time daily and also fear it. 5 The timing of it is set forth by those who have written upon timing; they have searched in holy literature and in various histories for the number of years gone by since the beginning of the world. They differ; their numbers vary somewhat; nevertheless, the universal expectation appears to be for a maximum of two hundred years more.[117] 6 The circumstances themselves make it clear that the slide into ruin will come soon, except that no part of it seems fit to fear as long as Rome is intact. 7 But when the chief city of the world does fall, and the rush[118] starts that the Sibyls predict, then the end will be there without doubt for deeds of men and for the whole world. 8 Rome is the city which has kept everything going so far, and we must pray to God in heaven with due adoration – if, that is, his statutes and decisions can be deferred – that the awful tyrant does not come sooner than we think, that loathsome tyrant with his great task to achieve and the famous light to put out, at whose death the world itself will collapse.[119] 9 Let us now return to following out the other things which will then ensue.

---

117 L. probably based his calculation on Theoph. *Autol.* 3.28 (5,695 years from the creation to the death of M. Aurelius in AD 180), but Theophilus was not here concerned with the end of the world. See Nicholson (1985).

118 L. uses the Greek word *rhúmê*, rush, to pun on Roma.

119 As in 15.11 above, L. represents the collapse of Rome as an undesirable event.

End of the Millennium, the last battle, the second resurrection

26.1 We said a little earlier that at the beginning of the holy reign the prince of demons would be put in chains by God. When the thousand years of the reign (which is seven thousand years of ours) begin to end, he will be set free again, and once released from custody he will go forth and gather all the nations then under the control of the just to make war upon the holy city.[120] A countless host of people will gather from all over the world, and they will surround the city and lay siege to it. 2 Then God's final wrath will come upon the nations, and he will campaign against them to their last man. First he will produce the strongest earthquake possible; as a result of it the mountains of Syria will crack, the valleys will slide away precipitously, and the walls of all cities will fall down. God will fix the sun not to set for three days; he will set it on fire, and excessive heat and great burning will descend upon warring and impious peoples, with clouds of sulphur, storms of hailstones and gouts of fire; people's breath will liquefy in the heat, their bodies will be smashed by hail and they will work their swords on each other; the hills will be full of corpses and the plains will be covered with bones.[121] 3 The people of God, however, will hide for those three days in hollows of the earth, until the wrath of God against the nations and his final judgment are done. 4 Then the just will emerge from their lairs to find everything covered with corpses and bones, but the whole population of the impious will be utterly dead, and there will be no nation on earth any more except the one people of God. Then for seven continuous years woods will be untouched and no timber will be cut from the hills; the weapons of the gentiles will be burnt, and there will be no more war: instead there will be peace and quiet for evermore.[122]

5 When the thousand years are over, God will renew the world, fold up the sky and alter the earth. He will transform men to look like angels, and they will be white as snow; they will be at all times in the sight of the almighty, and they will sacrifice to their lord and serve him for ever. 6 At the same time there will be that second, public resurrection of everybody, when the unjust will be ejected into eternal torment.[123] The unjust are those who worshipped things made by hand, who did not know or refused to acknowledge the lord and father of the world. 7 Their lord will himself be arrested

---

120 Rev. 20:7.
121 Cf. Ezek. 38:20, 22.
122 Cf. Ezek.. 39:9ff.; *Orac. Sib.* 3.724ff.; Rev. 20:10-15.
123 Cf. Rev. 20:11-13 (without specific reference to a second resurrection). For the first resurrection, of the faithful only, see 20.4 above.

BOOK 7: THE LIFE OF BLISS

with his servants and will be condemned to punishment, and with him the whole mob of the impious will be burnt for their sins for ever with perpetual fire in the sight of the angels and the just.

8 This is the teaching of the holy prophets which we Christians follow, and this is that wisdom of ours, which is derided as folly and emptiness by people who worship breakable things or practise futile philosophy just because we have no custom of defending or asserting it in public; God instructs us to be still and silent, keeping his secret under cover within our consciences, and not to fight with a bitter determination against these people who are right outside the truth, who make their vicious attacks on God and his religion not to learn anything but to quibble and mock. 9 It is a mystery, to be hidden away under cover as faithfully as possible, especially by us, since we have the name of faithful; 10 yet they see this silence of ours as cause to accuse us of an evil conscience. Hence their invention of certain outrageous attitudes towards people who are decent and innocent, and these inventions they readily believe.

10a[124] All fictions have now, most holy emperor, been laid to rest, ever since God most high raised you up to restore the abode of justice and to protect the human race. Now that you are ruler of the world of Rome we worshippers of God are no longer treated as criminals and villains; as the truth comes clear and is brought to light we are not put on trial as unjust for trying to do the works of justice. No one now flings the name of God at us in reproach, no one calls us irreligious any more, for we are the only religious people of them all: we scorn images of dead men; we worship the true and living God. 10b The providence of the most high godhead has promoted you to supreme power so that you can in the trueness of your piety rescind the wicked decrees of others, correct error, provide for the safety of men in your fatherly kindness, and finally remove from public life such evil men as God has ousted with his divine power and has put into your hands, so that all men should be clear what true majesty is. 10c They had sought to be rid of the worship of the one heavenly God in order to protect impious religions: now they lie defeated, and you, who defend his name and adore it, in the might of your virtue and prosperity enjoy your immortal glories in utter bliss. 10d They are paying, and have paid, the penalty for their wickedness; you are protected from all dangers by the powerful right hand of God, who gives you

---

124 The remaining text of this chapter appears in the MSS which carry it (S and g; see note on 5.27a above) two sections later than it is printed here, at the end of 27.2, but editors agree that it belongs here. On the invocations of Constantine, see pp. 48–49.

a tranquil and peaceful power of control amid expressions of great gratitude from all. 10e It was not wrong of the lord and ruler of the world to pick you out above all others through whom to re-inaugurate his holy religion, because you were the only one to demonstrate special qualities of virtue and holiness, and through them not just to equal but also, and most importantly, to surpass the glory of emperors of old, even though by reputation they are counted among the good emperors. 10f In their own natures they were perhaps the bare equivalent of just men; a man who does not acknowledge God as the controller of the universe may yet achieve a likeness of justice, but cannot attain the thing itself, 10g but you are the consummation of justice in your every act because of your inborn holiness of behaviour and your acknowledgement of truth and God. It was right therefore that in giving shape to the human race the godhead should make use of you as his advocate and minister. In our daily prayers we beg him first to guard you as his chosen guardian of the world and secondly to inspire in you a will to abide for ever in love of the divine name: for that is good for all men, for you, for your prosperity and for the rest of us for peace.

Endure evil and strive for virtue and its rewards

27.1 Seven laps of the work intended are done and we have come through to the finishing post; all that remains is to urge all people to adopt wisdom and true religion together. All the proper focus of wisdom is on despising earthly things, on discarding errors that held us previously when we were in thrall to things breakable and greedy for things fragile, and on aiming for the everlasting prizes of our treasure in heaven. To get them we must abandon as fast as possible the wrongful pleasures of this present life, which beguile men's minds with a ruinous delight. 2 There is such a fund of happiness in being freed from these stains of earth and in setting out towards that fairest of judges and kindest of fathers, who bestows peace instead of toil, life instead of death, light instead of darkness, goods eternal and celestial instead of goods earthly and brief; the bitterness and misery we suffer here on earth when we perform our acts of justice cannot be compared or matched at all with that reward. 3 If we want to be wise, if we want to have bliss, we must not only keep those words of Terence before us for contemplation [*Ph.* 249], that 'we must work at the mill, get flogged and carry fetters', but much worse than that: there are prison, chains and torture to bear, pain to suffer, and even death itself to be accepted and endured, for it is plain to our consciences that fragile pleasure will have its penalty and virtue will have God's prize.

4 Everyone should therefore make an effort to aim for the right path in life as fast as possible, or to adopt the virtues and practise them and work patiently through the troubles of this life to earn the presence of God for his consolation. 5 Our lord and father, who built the sky so strong and gave it the sun and other heavenly bodies, who poised the earth in all its extent, walling it with mountains, girding it about with sea and dividing it with rivers, who created and made out of nothing everything there is in this world of his: he saw the mistakes of men, and sent a guide to open the path of justice for us. 6 Let us all follow that guide, hear him and obey him with utmost devotion, for he alone, as Lucretius says [6.24-28], 'purged the hearts of men with words of truth, put an end to lust and fear and explained what the supreme good would be to which we all aspire, and showed us the path by which we could attain it, travelling straight on its narrow track.' 7 He did not just show us the path; he travelled it before us, in case its difficulty might cause some to shrink from the way of virtue. The path of perdition and deceit must be abandoned if at all possible: on it lurks death, concealed by the attractions of pleasure.

8 The more a man's years approach old age, and he can see the day coming when he must depart this life, let him consider how to be gone with purity and how to come to his judge with innocence, not as some do who lean on a blindness of mind; when their strength begins to fail, they use that warning of the closeness of ultimate necessity to go for the satisfaction of their desires ever more greedily and more ardently. 9 People must free themselves from that maelstrom while they can, while the chance is there, and turn themselves totally to God, to await that day in safety when God presiding as lord of the world will give judgment on the deeds and thoughts of each one of us. People should not just ignore the prizes of this world; they should shun them, reckoning their own souls more important than these deceptive goods. Possession of them is uncertain and short-lived, 10 because they shift daily, departing much more swiftly than they came, and even if we do have licence to enjoy them to the last moment, in the end they must be left to others. We can take nothing with us except a life well lived in innocence. 11 We come to God with plenty, we come with an abundance, if we come with self-control, mercy, endurance, love and faith. That is our inheritance, and it can neither be stolen from any man nor be bestowed upon another.

12 Who would like to make these goods ready for his own possession? Let the hungry come, to be filled with food of heaven and to lay aside long starvation; let the thirsty come, to drink with full throat the water of salvation from the everlasting spring. 13 With this food and drink of God the blind

will see, the deaf will hear, the dumb will speak, the lame will walk, the stupid will be wise, the sick will recover, and the dead will live again.[125] 14 All who use their virtue to trample down the corruptions of the earth will be raised to light and life perpetual by that supreme and truthful judge. 15 No one should put faith in wealth or instruments of authority, or even in royal power: they make no one immortal. Those who reject the whole purpose of man to pursue the immediate, prostrating themselves to the ground, will be punished as deserters of him who is their master, their commander and their father.

16 Let us therefore go for justice, our only and inseparable friend to lead us through to God, and 'while the spirit guides these limbs' [Verg. *A.* 4.336], let us fight the unwearying fight for God, manning his guardposts and keeping his watches, and let us close bravely with the enemy we know, so that in victory and triumph over our beaten foe we may win from our lord the prize for virtue which he himself has promised.

---

125 Cf. Mt. 11:5.

SELECT BIBLIOGRAPHY

EDITIONS OF *DIVINE INSTITUTES* AND OTHER TREATISES OF LACTANTIUS

Brandt, S. and Laubmann, G., *L. Caeli Firmiani Lactanti Opera Omnia*. *CSEL* 19 and 27 (Prague, Vienna, Leipzig, 1890–93)

Creed, J.L., *Lactantius: De Mortibus Persecutorum*. Ed. and trans. (Oxford, 1984)

Heck, E. and Wlosok, A., *Epitome Institutionum Divinarum*. Teubner (Stuttgart, 1994)

Ingremeau, Chr., *De Ira Dei*. SC 289 (Paris, 1982)

Monat, P., *Institutions Divines. Livre I*. SC 326 (Paris, 1986) (= Monat 1986)

Monat, P., *Institutions Divines. Livre II*. SC 337 (Paris, 1987) (= Monat 1987)

Monat, P., *Institutions Divines. Livre IV*. SC 377 (Paris, 1992) (= Monat 1992)

Monat, P., *Institutions Divines. Livre V*. 2 vols. SC 204–05 (Paris, 1973) (= Monat 1973)

Moreau, J., *De Mortibus Persecutorum*. SC 39 (Paris, 1954)

Perrin, M., *L'ouvrage du dieu créateur*. 2 vols. SC 213–14 (Paris, 1974) (= Perrin 1974)

OTHER WORKS

Amarelli, F. (1970), 'Il "de mortibus persecutorum" nei suoi rapporti con l'ideologia coeva', *SDHI* 36, 207–64

Amarelli, F. (1978), *Vetustas-Innovatio: Un'Antitesi apparente nella legislazione di Costantino* (Naples)

Arjava, A. (1996), *Women and Law in Late Antiquity* (Oxford)

Athanassiadi, P. and Frede, M. (eds) (1999), *Pagan Monotheism in Late Antiquity* (Oxford)

Atkins, E.M. (2000), 'Cicero', in C. Rowe and M. Schofield, eds, *The Cambridge History of Greek and Roman Political Thought* (Cambridge), 477–516

Atkins, E.M. and Dodaro, R.J. (2000), *Augustine: Political Writings* (Cambridge)
Aune, D.E. (1998), *Word Biblical Commentary: Revelation*. 3 vols (Nashville)
Barnes, T.D. (1976), 'Sossianus Hierocles and the antecedents of the Great Persecution', *HSCP* 80, 239–52
Barnes, T.D. (1981), *Constantine and Eusebius* (Cambridge, MA).
Barnes, T.D. (1994), 'Scholarship or Propaganda? Porphyry *Against the Christians* in its Historical Setting', *BICS* 39, 53–66
Barnes, T.D. (1996), 'Emperors, Panegyrics, Prefects, Provinces and Palaces (284–317)', *JRA* 9, 532–52
Barnes, T.D. (1998), 'Constantine and Christianity: ancient evidence and modern interpretations', *ZAC* ??, 274–94
Barnes, T.D. (2001a), 'Constantine's Speech to the Assembly of the Saints: Place and Date of Delivery', *JThS* 52, 26–36
Barnes, T.D. (2001b), 'Monotheists All?', *Phoenix* 55, 142–62
Barnes, T.D. (2002), 'From Repression to Toleration: The Evolution of Constantine's Religious Policies', *Scr.Cl.Isr.* 21, 189–202
Baynes, N. (1944), Review of K.M. Setton, *Christian Attitude towards the Empire in the Fourth Century ...*, *JRS* 34, 135–40
Beard, M., North, J. and Price, S. (1998), *Religions of Rome*. 2 vols (Cambridge)
Bidez, J. and Cumont, F. (1938), *Les mages hellénisés: Zoroastre, Ostanès et Hystaspe d'après la tradition grecque*. Vol. 2 (Paris)
Bochet, I. (1998), '"Non aliam esse philosophiam (...) et aliam religionem" (Augustin, *De Ver.Rel.*5,8)', in Pouderon and Doré, eds, 333–53
Bolkestein, H. (1939), 'Humanitas bei Lactantius: Christlich oder orientalisch?', in *Pisciculi: Studien zur Religion und Kultur des Altertums: Franz Joseph Dölger zum sechzigsten Geburtstage* (Münster in Westfalen), 62–65
Boswell, J. (1988), *The Kingdom of Strangers: The Abandonment of Children in Western Europe from Late Antiquity to the Renaissance* (London).
Bosworth, B. (1999), 'Augustus, the *Res Gestae* and Hellenistic Theories of Apotheosis', *JRS* 89, 1–18
Brandt, S. (1891), 'Über die Quellen von Laktanz' Schrift De opificio Dei', *WS* 13, 225–92
Brandt, S. (1922), 'Zu Lactantius', *Philologus* 78, 131–42
Brown, P. (1967), *Augustine of Hippo* (Oxford)
Bryce, Jackson (1990), *The Library of Lactantius* (New York)
Bryce, Jackson (1999), *Bibliography of Lactantius*,

ius.biblio.htm *http://www.carleton.edu/curricular/CLAS/lactantius.bibli.htm*
Buchheit, V. (1978), 'Goldene Zeit und Paradies auf Erden (Laktanz, Inst. 5.5-8)', *Wurz.Jahrb.Alt.Wiss.* 4, 161-85
Buchheit, V. (1979a), 'Idem', *Wurz.Jahrb.Alt.Wiss.* 5, 219-35
Buchheit, V. (1979b), 'Die Definition der Gerechtigkeit bei Laktanz und seinen Vorgänger', *Vig. Chr.* 33, 356-74
Cameron, A. and Hall, S.G. (1999), *Eusebius: Life of Constantine*. Trans., comm., introd. (Oxford)
Carusi, E. (1906), 'Diritto romano e patristico', *Studi giuridici in onore di Carlo Fadda pel xxv anno del suo insegnamento*. Vol. 2 (Naples), 71-97
Cavalcanti, E. (1996), 'Etica cristiana nei secoli III e IV: principali elementi di strutturazione', in *L'Etica cristiana nei secoli III e IV: eredità e confronti. Studia Ephemeridis Augustinianum* 53, 11-38
Centrone, B. (2000), 'Platonism and Pythagoreanism in the Early Empire', in C. Rowe and M. Schofield, eds, *Greek and Roman Political Thought* (Cambridge), 559-84
Chadwick, H. (1966), *Early Christian Thought and the Classical Tradition: Studies in Justin, Clement and Origen* (Oxford)
Charlesworth, J.H. (1983-85), *The Old Testament Pseudepigrapha*. 2 vols (London)
Clark, G. (2000), *Porphyry: On Abstinence from Killing Animals*. Trans. (London)
Clarke, G. (1974), *The Octavius of Marcus Minucius Felix* (London)
Clarke, G. (1986-89), *The Letters of St. Cyprian* (New York)
Cohn, N. (1970), *The Pursuit of the Millennium* (London)
Cohn, N. (1993), *Cosmos, Chaos and the World to Come: The Ancient Roots of Apocalyptic Faith* (New Haven and London)
Collins, J.J. (1998), *Encyclopedia of Apocalypticism. Vol. 1: The Origins of Apocalypticism in Judaism and Christianity* (New York)
Copenhaver, B.P. (1992), *Hermetica: The Greek* Corpus Hermeticum *and the Latin* Asclepius *in a new English translation, with notes and introduction* (Cambridge)
Crook, J.A. (1995), *Legal Advocacy in the Roman World* (London)
Cumont, F. (1931), 'La fin du monde selon les mages occidentaux', *Rev.Hist.Rel.* 102, 29-96
Daley, B.E. (1991), *The Hope for the Early Church: A Handbook of Patristic Eschatology* (Cambridge)
Daley, B.E. (1998), 'Apocalypticism in Early Christian Theology', in McGinn, ed., 3-47

Daniélou, J. (1948), 'La typologie millénariste de la semaine dans le christianisme primitif', *Vig.Chr.* 2, 1–16

Denis, A.-M. (1970), *Introduction aux pseudépigraphes grecs d'ancien testament* (Leiden)

De Ste Croix, G.E.M. (1954), 'Aspects of the "Great Persecution"', *Harv.Theol.Rev.* 47, 75–113

Digeser, E. De P. (1994), 'Lactantius and Constantine's Letters to Arles: Dating the Divine Institutes', *JECS* 2, 33–52

Digeser, E. De P. (1998), 'Lactantius, Porphyry, and the Debate over Religious Toleration', *JRS* 88, 129–49

Digeser, E. De P. (2000), *The Making of a Christian Empire: Lactantius and Rome* (Ithaca, NY, and London)

Doignon, J. (1963), '"Nos bons hommes de foi": Cyprien, Lactance, Victorin, Optat, Hilaire *(de docr. Christ.* 2, 40, 61)', *Latomus* 22, 795–805

Dolbeau, F. (ed.) (1996), *Augustin d'Hippone: Vingt-six sermons au peuple d'Afrique* (Paris)

Drake, H.A. (2000), *Constantine and the Bishops: The Politics of Intolerance* (Baltimore)

Edwards, M. (1999), 'The Flowering of Latin Apologetic: Lactantius and Arnobius', in Edwards, Goodman and Price, eds, 197–222

Edwards, M., Goodman, M. and Price, S., eds, (with Rowland, C.) (1999), *Apologetics in the Roman Empire: Pagans, Jews and Christians* (Oxford)

Evans Grubbs, J. (1995), *Law and Family in Late Antiquity: The Emperor Constantine's Marriage Legislation* (Oxford)

Fabrega, V. (1974), 'Die chiliastische Lehre des Laktanz', *JAC* 17, 126–46

Ferrini, C. (1894a), 'Su le idee giuridiche contenute nei libri V e VI delle Instituzioni di Lattanzio', *Rivista internazionale di scienze sociali e discipline ausiliarie* 5, 581–86 (= *Opere di Contardo Ferrini II. Studi sulle fonti del diritto romano a cura di E. Albertario* (Milan, 1929), 481–96)

Ferrini, C. (1894b), 'Le cognizioni giuridiche di Lattanzio, Arnobio e Minucio Felice', *Mem. Accad. Scienze Modena*, Serie II, 10, 195–210 (= *Opere di Contardo Ferrini...*, 467–92)

Festugière, A.-J. (1950), *La révélation de Hermès Trismégiste* (Paris)

Festugière, A.-J. (1967), *Hermétisme et mystique païenne* (Paris)

Fontaine, J. (1978), 'La conversion du christianisme à la culture antique: la lecture chrétienne de l'univers bucolique de Virgile', *Bull.Assoc. G.Budé* 1, 50–75

Fontaine, J. and Perrin, M. (eds) (1978), *Lactance et son temps: recherches actuelles. Actes du ive Colloque d'Etudes Historiques et Patristiques,*

Chantilly 21–23 sept. 1976 (Paris)
Fowden, G. (1986), *The Egyptian Hermes: A Historical Approach to the Late Pagan Mind* (Cambridge)
Frankfurter, D. (1998), 'Early Christian Apocalypticism: Literature and Social World', in Collins (1998), 415–51.
Fredouille, J.-Cl. (1978), 'Lactance historien des religions', in Fontaine and Perrin, eds, 237–52
Garnsey, P. (1984), 'Religious Toleration in Classical Antiquity', in W.J. Sheils, ed., *Persecution and Toleration. Studies in Church History* 21, 1–27
Garnsey, P. (2002), 'Lactantius and Augustine', in A.K. Bowman, H.M. Cotton, M. Goodman and S. Price, eds, *Representations of Empire: Rome and the Mediterranean World* (Oxford), pp. 153–79.
Garnsey, P. and Humfress, C. (2001), *The Evolution of the Late Antique World* (Cambridge)
Gaudemet, J. (1975), 'Lactance et le droit romain', *AARC* 2, 83–101
Geffcken, J. (1902), *Die Oracula Sibyllina* (Leipzig).
Gill, C. (1997), 'The Emotions in Greco-Roman Philosophy', in S.M. Braund and C. Gill, eds, *The Passions in Roman Thought and Literature* (Cambridge), 5–15.
Goulon, A. (1978), 'Les citations des poètes latins dans l'oeuvre de Lactance', in Fontaine and Perrin, eds, 107–56
Graf, F. (1993), 'Dionysian and Orphic Eschatology: New Texts and Old Questions', in T. Carpenter and C. Faraone, eds, *Masks of Dionysus* (Ithaca, NY, and London), 239–58
Guillaumin, M.-L. (1978), 'L'exploitation des "oracles sibyllins" par Lactance et par le "discours à l'assemblée des saints"', in Fontaine and Perrin, eds, 185–202
Hägg, T. (1992), 'Hierocles the Lover of Truth and Eusebius the Sophist', *SO* 67, 138–50
Hagendahl, H. (1958), *Latin Fathers and the Classics. A Study in the Apologists, Jerome and Other Christian Writers* (Göteborg)
Harris, R. and Mingana, A. (1916–20), *The Odes and Psalms of Solomon* (Manchester)
Hartog, F. (1988), *The Mirror of Herodotus: The Representation of the Other in the Writings of Herodotus.* Trans. J. Lloyd (Berkeley)
Heck, E. (1972), *Die dualistischen Zusätze und die Kaiseranreden bei Lactanz* (Heidelberg)
Heck, E. (1975), 'Die dualistischen Zusätze und die Kaiseranreden bei Lactanz', *Studia Patristica* 13, 185–88

Heck, E. (1978), 'Iustitia civilis-iustitia naturalis: à propos du jugement de Lactance concernant les discours sur la justice dans le "De re publica" de Cicéron', in Fontaine and Perrin, eds, 171–84

Heck, E. (1980), Review of R.Ogilvie, *The Library of Lactantius. Gnomon* 52, 572–74

Heck, E. (1988), 'Lactanz und die Klassiker. Zu Theorie und Praxis der Verwendung heidnischer Literatur in christlicher Apologetik bei Laktanz', *Philologus* 132, 160–79

Heim, F. (1996), '*Virtus* chez Lactance: du *vir bonus* au martyr', *Augustinianum* 36, 361–76

Hinnells, J.R. (1973), 'The Zoroastrian Doctrine of Salvation in the Roman World: A Study of the Oracle of Hystaspes', in E.J. Sharpe and J.R. Hinnells, eds, *Man and his Salvation: Studies in memory of S.G.F. Brandon* (Manchester), 125–48

Horsfall, N. (2000), *Vergil, Aeneid 7: A Commentary* (Oxford)

Hultgård, A. (1998), 'Persian Apocalypticism', in Collins, ed., 39–83

Inglebert, H. (1996), *Les romains chrétiens face à l'histoire de Rome: Histoire, christianisme et romanités en Occident dans l'Antiquité tardive (IIIe–Ve siècles)* (Paris)

Ingremeau, C. (1998), 'Lactance et la philosophie des passions', in Pouderon and Doré, eds, 283–96

Kolb, F. (1988), 'L'ideologia tetrarchica e la politica religiosa di Diocleziano', in G. Bonamenti and A.Nestori, eds, *I cristiani e l'impero nel iv secolo: colloquio sul cristianesimo nel mondo antico. Atti del Convegno, Macerata 17–18 Dec. 1987* (Macerata), 17–44

Lane Fox, R. (1986), *Pagans and Christians* (London)

Labriolle, P. de (1924), *Histoire de la littérature latine chrétienne*. 2nd edn (Paris)

Le Gall, J. (1953), *Le Tibre, fleuve de Rome dans l'antiquité* (Paris)

Lo Cicero, C. (1989), 'Omnium Stoicorum acutissimus: Seneca filosofo in Lattanzio: intertestualità e riscrittura', *Studi di filologia classica in onore di Giusto Monaco*. Vol. 3 (Palermo), 1237–61

Loi, V. (1965), 'I valori etici e politici della romanità negli scritti di Lattanzio', *Salesianum* 27, 65–132

Loi V. (1966), 'Il concetto di "iustitia" e i fattori culturali dell'etica di Lattanzio', *Salesianum* 28, 583–625

Loi, V. (1970), *Lattanzio nella storia del linguaggio e del pensiero teologico pre-niceno* (Zürich)

Loi, V. (1973), 'Il libro quarto delle *Divinae institutiones*: Fu da Lattanzio composto in Gallia?', *Mél. Christine Mohrmann: Nouveau recueil* (Utrecht), 61–79

Lutz, C. (1947), 'Musonius Rufus: The Roman Socrates', *YCS* 10, 3–147

MacCormack, S.G. (1998), *The Shadows of Poetry: Vergil in the Mind of Augustus* (Berkeley)

McGinn, B. (1998), *The Encyclopedia of Apocalypticism. Vol. 2: Apocalypticism in Western History and Culture* (New York)

Michel, A. (1996), 'Du *De Officiis* de Cicéron à Saint Ambroise', *Studia Ephemeridis Augustinianum* 53, 39–46

Micka. E.F. (1943), *The Problem of Divine Anger in Arnobius and Lactantius* (Washington, DC)

Millett, P. (1989), 'Patronage and its Avoidance in Classical Athens', in A.Wallace-Hadrill, ed., *Patronage in Ancient Society* (London), 15–48

Mommsen, T.E. (1959), 'St. Augustine and the Christian Idea of Progress: The Background of *The City of God*', in E.F. Rice, ed., *Theodore E. Mommsen, Medieval and Renaissance Studies* (Ithaca, NY), 265–98

Monat, P. (1978), 'La présentation d'un dossier biblique par Lactance: le sacerdoce du Christ et celui de Jésus, fils de Josédec', in Fontaine and Perrin, eds, 273–91

Monat, P. (1982), *Lactance et la Bible. Une propédeutique latine à la lecture de la Bible dans l'Occident constantinien.* 2 vols (Paris)

Mynors, A.R.B. (ed.) (1937) *Cassiodori Senatoris Institutiones* (Oxford)

Nicholson, O. (1982), 'Lactantius: Prophecy and Politics in the Age of Constantine the Great'. Unpublished DPhil thesis (Oxford)

Nicholson, O. (1984a), 'The Wild Man of the Tetrarchy: A Divine Companion for Galerius', *Byzantion* 54, 253–75

Nicholson, O. (1984b), 'Hercules at the Milvian Bridge: Lactantius, *Divine Institutes*, I, 21,6–9', *Latomus* 43, 133–42

Nicholson, O. (1985), 'The Source of the Dates in Lactantius' *Divine Institutes*', *JThS* 36, 291–310

Nicholson, O. (1989), 'Flight from Persecution as Imitation of Christ: Lactantius' Divine Institutes IV.18,1–2', *JThS* 40, 48–65

Nicholson, O. (1997), 'Doing What Comes Naturally: Lactantius and *Libido*', *Studia Patristica* 31, 314–21

Nicholson, O. (1998), 'Golden Age and the End of the World: Myths of Mediterranean Life from Lactantius to Joshua the Stylite', in M. Chiat and K. Reyerson, eds, *The Mediaeval Mediterranean* (S. Cloud, MN), 11–18

Nicholson, O. (1999), 'Civitas quae adhuc sustentat omnia: Lactantius and the City of Rome', in W.E. Klingshirn and M. Vessey, eds, *The Limits of Ancient Christianity: Essays in honour of R.A. Markus* (Ann Arbor, MI), 7–25

Nicholson, O. (2000), 'Constantine's Vision of the Cross', *Vig.Chr.* 53, 309–23

Nicholson, O. (2001a), '*Caelum potius intuemini*: Lactantius and a Statue of Constantine', *Studia Patristica* 34, 177–96

Nicholson, O. (2001b), 'Broadening the Roman Mind: Foreign Prophets in the Apologetic of Lactantius', *Studia Patristica* 34, 364–74

O'Daly, G. (1999), *Augustine's City of God: A Reader's Guide* (Oxford)

O'Donnell, J.J. (1979), *Cassiodorus* (Berkeley)

Ogilvie, R.M. (1978), *The Library of Lactantius* (Oxford)

Osborn, E. (1997), *Tertullian: The First Theologian of the West* (Cambridge)

Oxford Latin Dictionary. P.G.W. Glare, ed. (Oxford, 1968–82)

Panizza, L.A. (1978), 'Lorenzo Valla's *De vero falsoque bono,* Lactantius and Oratorical Scepticism', *Jl. Warb. Court. Inst.* 41, 76–107

Parker, R. (1995), 'Early Orphics', in A. Powell, ed., *The Greek World* (London and New York), 483–510

Pease, A.S. (ed.) (1920–23), *Cicero: de divinatione* (Urbana, IL)

Pease, A.S. (ed.) (1955–58), *M. Tulli Ciceronis de natura deorum* (Cambridge, MA)

Pellegrino, M. (1947), *Studi su l'antica apologetica* (Rome)

Perrin, M. (1981), *L'homme antique et chrétien. L'anthropologie de Lactance – 250–325* (Paris)

Piccaluga, G. (1996), 'Ius e Vera Iustitia (Lact.Div.Inst.VI 9.7). Rielaborazione cristiana di un valore assoluto della religione romana arcaica', *L'Etica cristiana dei secoli III e IV: eredità e confronti: Studia Ephemeridis Augustinianum* 53, 257–69

Pichon, R. (1901), *Lactance: étude sur le mouvement philosophique et religieux sous le règne de Constantin* (Paris)

Potter, D. (1990), *Prophecy and History in the Crisis of the Roman Empire* (Oxford)

Pouderon, B. and Doré, K. (eds) (1998), *Les apologistes chrétiens et la culture grecque* (Paris)

Pucciarelli, E. (1987), *I cristiani e il servizio militare: testimonianze dei primi tre secoli* (Florence)

Qasten, J. (1992), *Patrology. Vol. 2: The Ante-Nicene Literature after Irenaeus* (Westminster, MD; repr. of 1950 edn)

Rives, J. (1995), 'Human Sacrifice among Pagans and Christians', *JRS* 85, 65–85

Roots, P.A. (1987), 'The *De Opificio Dei*: The Workmanship of God and Lactantius', *CQ* 37, 466–86
Roots, P.A. (1988), 'De Opificio Lactantii: A Reassessment of the Work of L.Caecilius Firmianus Lactantius'. Unpublished PhD thesis (Cambridge)
Rose, H.J. (1927), 'De Iove Latiari', *Mnemosyne* 55, 273–79
Rougé, J. (1983), 'Questions d'époque constantinienne', in E. Frézouls, ed., *Crise et redressement dans les provinces européennes de l'empire*, Actes du colloque de Strasbourg 1981 (Strasbourg), 113–25
Rowland, C. (1982), *The Open Heaven: A Study of Apocalyptic in Judaism and Early Christianity* (London)
Schanz, M. (1922), *Geschichte der römischen Litteratur bis zur Gesetzgebungswerk des Kaisers Justinian*. Vol. 3, C. Hosius and G. Krüger, eds (Munich)
Schneweis, E. (1944), *Angels and Demons according to Lactantius* (Washington, DC)
Scullard, H.H. (1981), *Festivals and Ceremonies of the Roman Republic* (London)
Skutsch, O. (1985), *The Annals of Ennius* (Oxford)
Shaw, B. (1996), 'Body/Power/Identity: Passions of the Martyrs', *JECS* 4.3, 269–312
Simmons, M.B. (1995), *Arnobius of Sicca: Religious Conflict and Competition in the Age of Diocletian* (Oxford)
Sorabji, R. (2000), *Emotion and Peace of Mind: From Stoic Agitation to Christian Temptation* (Oxford)
Souter, A. (1949), *A Glossary of Later Latin to 600 AD* (Oxford)
Spanneut, M. (1957), *Le Stoïcisme des pères de l'église* (Paris)
Spanneut, M. (1969), *Tertullien et les premiers moralistes africains* (Paris)
Stevenson, J. (ed.) (1968), *A New Eusebius; Documents Illustrative of the History of the Church to AD 337* (London)
Swift, L.J. (1968), 'Lactantius and the Golden Age', *AJP* 89, 144–56
Syme, R. (1964), *Sallust* (Oxford)
Treggiari, S. (1991), *Roman Marriage*: iusti coniuges *from the Time of Cicero to the Time of Ulpian* (Oxford)
van Hooff, A. (1990), *From Autothanasia to Suicide: Self-Killing in Classical Antiquity* (London)
Weinstock, S. (1971), *Divus Julius* (Oxford)
West, M.L. (1983), *The Orphic Poems* (Oxford)
Windisch, H. (1929), *Das Orakel des Hystaspes* (Amsterdam)
Wlosok, A. (1960), *Laktanz und die philosophische Gnosis: Untersuchungen*

zu Geschichte und Terminologie der gnostischen Erlösungsvorstellung.
Abh. der Heidelberger Akad. der Wiss. Phil.-hist-Kl. (Heidelberg)

Wlosok, A. (1993), 'Lactance (L. Caelius *ou* Cae(cil)ius Firmianus Lactantius)', in R. Herzog and P.L. Schmidt, *Nouvelle Histoire de la Littérature Latine.* Vol. 5, G. Hauroy, ed. (Paris), 426–59

Young, F. (2000), 'Christianity', in C. Rowe and M. Schofield, eds, *The Cambridge History of Greek and Roman Political Thought* (Cambridge), 635–60

INDEX OF TOPICS

actors **1** 20.10; **6** 20.9ff; *see* theatre
Academics p.9; **1** 6.2; **2** 8.14; **3** 3.7ff, 4.11, 5.3, 6.5–20, 7.10, 15.3, 28.17–19; **7** 5.2, 7.2–3; *and see Index of Proper Names under* Arcesilaus, Carneades, Cicero, Socrates
adultery pp.30, 39–40; **1** 9.1ff, 10.4ff & 10ff; **6** 23.24ff.
advocates pp.2, 13–14; **3** 1.5, 13.12n; **5** 1.22
angels **1** 7.4, 8, 9; **2** 14.1, 3, 16.6–8; **4** 6.2, 8.6 & 9, 14.17; **7** 5.9, 6.1, 19.5, 21.1, 26.5
anger pp.32, 50–51; **6** 5.13–14, 15.3ff, 16.10, 19.2ff; *see* god, anger of; judgement, last
animals pp.8, 24, 25, 34; **2** 2.20, 8.37, 10.1, 13.11, 18.6; **3** 10.1ff; **4** 12.2; **5** 17.30–33; **7** 5.20
antipodes **3** 24
antiquarians **1** 12.8
apocalyptic, *see* eschatology
apologists for Christianity pp.12–14; their deficiencies **5** 1.21–2.1, 4; *and see Index of Proper Names under* Arnobius, Cyprian, Minucius Felix, Theophilus, Tertullian
apostasy **5** 9.11, 11.15
army, *see* empire, God as general, militia of God, soldiery, war
astrology **2** 16.1; **3** 25.11
atoms **3** 17.21–27; **7** 3.23ff, 7.8
augurs, augury **1** 22.4; **2** 7.7, 16.1; **5** 19.10

bliss, life of, *see* happiness
body pp.12, 22, 26, 35; **2** 2.24, 3.8, 8.68, 9.22, 12.3ff; **3** 6.3, 12.2, 27.15; **5** 21.10ff; **6** 6.6; **7** 2, 4.12, 5, 11–12; *and see* soul
burial **6** 12.25–30

cannibalism **1** 12.2–3; **6** 20.18n
causidicus, *see* advocates
chaos **1** 5.8–9
charity p.31; **6** 9.8, 10.9, 22–27, 11–12
chastity pp.11–12; **6** 22.2–23
children pp.29, 45 n.181; **4** 3.15–17, 4.1–2, 5, 28.7–9 & 13, 29.7–9; **5** 8.6, 13.3, 12, 18.14–15, 19.14; **6** 3.15, 12.23, 24.3; *see* exposure, infanticide
Christ, as son pp.15, 16, 18, 24; **4** 6–9, 29; incarnation p.32; **4** 12–13; as high priest **4** 14; his life and mission pp.9–10, 43; **4** 15; passion p.10; **4** 16–19, 26.17–42; resurrection **4** 19; return to Galilee **4** 20; ascension **4** 21; as teacher pp.9–10, 24, 46; **4** 11, 23–25; miracles of p.2; **4** 13.17, 15, 16.5, 26.1–16; **5** 3.7–10, 18–21; **7** 9.2; *see Index of Proper Names under* Christ
Christians pp.17, 22, 29, 31, 43, 45, 48, 49, 50, 53; **4** 30.10, 13; **5** 2.4, 13, 11.13, 13.8; **7** 26.8
Church pp.43–44, 47, 49–50; **4** 10.1n, 13.26–14.3, 21.2, 30.4, 11; **5** 2.2
circus **2** 7.20; **6** 20.32, 35
city of the millennium **7** 24.6, 26.1
cities, origin of **6** 10.13–15

citizens, Roman **1** 17.7n, 21.23n; **4** 18.10
compassion, *see* charity, pity
concubinage **6** 23.23
conscience **5** 1.12; **6** 24.11–21
constancy **6** 14.3, 17.24–29
creation **2** 8–11; *see* God as creator
cremation **7** 17.8
crucifixion, of Christ **4** 26.24–27.5; *see* Christ, passion
cult, cults, *see* religion, pagan, worship
Cynics/Cynicism **3** 15.20–21
Cyrenaics **3** 8.9, 15.15

death **1** 3.9; **2** 12.9, 20; **3** 18.1ff, 19.1–13; **4** 25.7, 27.16; **5** 17.20, 24; **6** 17.5; *see* suicide
demons **1** 7.9; **2** 14–16, 17.10–11; **4** 14.17, 27.1–18; **5** 19.1, 21.3–6; **7** 18.3, 21.1; *see* devil
devil p.37; **2** 1.13, 8.4–6i, 12.10–11, 17–18, 14.1–6; **6** 3.14, 4.2, 17, 6.5, 7.3–8, 22.3–5, 23.4–8; **7** 24.5, 26.1ff; *and see* evil
dialectic **3** 13.4–5
Donatists **6** 24.1n
dualism pp.27–28, n.106; **2** 8.3–6i, 12; *and see* virtue and vice, good and evil

earth **2** 2.24, 6.2, 12.3–11, 18.4–6; **3** 24.4ff; **6** 1.10–11; *see* world
education **6** 7.1–2; *and see* eloquence, oratory, rhetoric
eloquence **1** 1.9–11; **3** 1.1; **5** 1.15–20, 19.16; *see* oratory, rhetoric.
emotions p.32; **2** 5.34; **4** 22.3; **6** 15–23; *see* passions, pleasures
emperor-worship **1** 15.6 *see* ruler worship
empire pp.33, 37, 41, 45; **1** 18.8ff; **2** 16.16–18; **5** 16.4; **6** 4.18–23, 5.15, 9.4–5; **7** 15.11–16; *see* war
endurance pp.11, 28–29; **5** 7.6, 13.11ff,
22.2–5; **6** 18.19–32
Epicureanism/Epicureans pp.9, 12, 23 n.81, 29 n.111; **2** 8.60; **3** 17.2–3, 18.3, 20.15, 25.15; **5** 20.14–15; **6** 24.13; **7** 12.30; *see Index of Proper Names under* Epicurus
equality (*aequabilitas*) p.39; **5** 14.15–20; *see* fairness (*aequitas*)
equestrians **5** 14.18n
eschatology pp.7, 12, 14, 36 n.140, 45–46, 50 n.203; **7** 14ff
ethics pp.9, 25, 27; **3** 13.6–7
euergetism **6** 11.22ff, 12.19–20, 39–40
euhemerism **1** 11.33–15.33; **5** 19.15
evil pp.10–12, 25–27; **2** 8.6a-6i, 17.1; **7** 4.11–15, 23–24, 27a-q, 15.7–9, 16, 17; *see* devil, dualism, good
evocatio **2** 7.11
exposure, of children pp.11, 37; **5** 9.15; **6** 20.18–25

fairness (*aequitas*) pp.10, 30–31, 36; **5** 6.4, 14, 9–11, 15–20; in Plato 3.21; *see* charity, humanity, justice
fall, of man pp.8, 20; **2** 12.17–20; of Rome **7** 15.11, 16.1, 25.6–8
fate **1** 11.13–14; **2** 7.11, 16, 15.6, 16.11; **3** 8.18; **5** 10.12–13
father pp.9, 10, 32, 51; **4** 3.16–18
female/woman **1** 8.7–8, 11.26–27, 16.4–17; **2** 12.1; **5** 8.7; **6** 23.23–26; suffering persecution **5** 13.3, 12, 19.14; in Plato **3** 21–22; as philosophers **3** 25.5–7, 12, 15
Fetiales **6** 9.4; *and see* empire
fire **1** 11.16, 12.5–7; **2** 6.2, 9.10, 16, 18–27, 12.4–6,14; **5** 18.16; **7** 9.13–14, 21.3–7
flamen **5** 19.10
flood **2** 10.9–11, 23–24; 13.1–3; **6** 10.19
fools/folly pp.10–11, 32–34; **5** 14–18; **6** 7.2; *see* wisdom

INDEX OF TOPICS

fortune, *see* fate
free will **2** 8.4; *and see* freedom, of religion
freedom pp.9–10; **4** 23.3ff, 24.7; **6** 6.17; **7** 15.16; of religion pp. 11, 46–48; **5** 19–20
frugality **6** 3.8, 17.15–20

games **1** 20.10; **6** 11.22, 12.19, 20.6–36; *see* circus, spectacles, theatre
generosity **6** 6.10, 11, 21, 11.27n; *and see* charity, euergetism, pity.
gladiators **5** 19.30–31; **6** 20.10ff
God, Christian nameless p.16; **1** 6.4–5; one not many pp.7–8, 16, 30; **1** 3; **4** 3.13–22. 4.1–2, 7–10; eternal **2** 8.44; **4** 12.16; **7** 2.6; without sex **1** 8.5; perfect **1** 3.7, 11, 23; **7** 2.6; impassible **1** 3.23; **2** 8.44; anger of pp.50–51; **2** 17.2, 4–5; 5.22.12–13; **7** 26.1–3; as father (of Christ) **2** 8.3, 5; **4** 29; as father (of mankind) pp.24–25, 46, 52–53; **1** 11.42; **3** 9.19; **4** 29.14–15; **5** 6.12, 8.11, 22.13; **7** 5.5–6, 27; as lord p.16; **6** 1.1; as lord/master and father **1** 7.3ff; **4** 3.14–4.11; **5** 18.14–16; **6** 24.3ff; as creator pp.20, 24, 27–28 n.106, 30, 39; **2** 8–13; as ruler of the world **5** 8.5; **6** 8.12; **7** 27.9, 15; worshipped in golden age pp.30, 36–37, 52; **5** 5.3, 8.4; mankind created to worship God **3** 9.13–14; cf. **6** 1.2; what is due to God **6** 9; as teacher pp.41, 46–47; **1** 1.19; as judge pp.11, 50–51; **1** 1.15; **5** 23; **6** 24.20; **7** 27.2; forgiveness of **6** 24; as general p.47; **5** 22.17; **7** 27.15; as general and master **6** 8.12
gods, pagan pp.7, 8, 12–14, 17, 29; **1** passim; **2** 5–6; as men pp.7–8; **1** 8–22; **2** 2.2, 7.7; **4** 28.15–16; **5** 19.15–19; **6** 2.9; **7** 14.1; *and see Index of Proper Names under* Ennius, Euhemerus; gender of **1** 16.4–17; scandalous behaviour of **5** 10.15–18; images of **2** 4.13–20; cults as source of all evils **5** 8; numbers of **1** 7.7; *see* euhemerism; religion, pagan; worship, *Index of Proper Names under* Aesculapius, Apollo, Bacchus, Castor and Pollux, Ceres, Flora, Great Mother, Hercules, Juno, Jupiter, Mercury, Minerva, Neptune, Pluto, Proserpina, Saturn, Uranus, Venus, Vesta, Vulcan, Zeus
golden age pp.10, 36–40, 41, 42, 44; **1** 11.50, 13.11–12; **4** 12.21; **5** 5–7, 8.1–3, 8–9; **7** 2.1, 24
good **2** 8.5 ; **5** 7.5–10; **6** 6.1ff, 14.5ff; good and evil **5** 17.31; **7** 17ff; supreme (*summum bonum*) pp.9, 25–26; **3** 7.6–13.1; **4** 1.3; **6** 6.4; **7** 5.18–19, 8.1–2; *see* dualism, evil, knowledge, virtue
governor p.2; **1** 11.64n; **2** 16.7–8; **4** 18.4n; **5** 11.15, 13.17; **6** 4.22
grammarians **3** 25.10
greed pp.11, 30, 37, 38, 39; **5** 5.8, 6.1–3; **6** 16.10–11, 17.10–12, 19.4ff

happiness pp.25–29, 52; **3** 8.29, 12.12–17, 24–36; **7** 5.27, 27j; *see* good, supreme, heaven, immortality
heaven **2** 12.3–14, 18.4ff; **6** 1.10; book **7** passim; *see* happiness, immortality, paths of life
Hebrews **2** 13.8; **4** 7.7, 10.5–18, 26.37, 38; **7** 15.1; *see* Jews
heresy pp.3, 17, 54; **4** 30.1, 8–14
history/historians p.19; **1** 8.8, 11.33; **2** 10.9; **4** 5.8; **5** 4.6; **7** 22.2
homosexuality **6** 23.8ff
hospitality **6** 12.5–14

humanity **3** 9.19, 23.9–10; **5** 6.4; **6** 10–13; *see* charity, generosity, pity
humility **4** 16.13–17, 26.30; **5** 15.10; **6** 4.11

images **1** 11.5, 15.4, 15, 18, 27, 17.5, 20.11, 37; **2** 2–4, 6.6, 10.12–14, 16.3–4, 17.6ff, 18.2ff; **6** 13.13–14; **7** 19.9.
immortality pp.9, 12, 14, 25–26, 29, 34; **3** 13.1, 18.1–4, 19.1ff; **5** 18.1–4, 9–11; **7** 3–13, 20.7–11; *see* soul, virtue
imperialism, Athenian **5** 14.4n; Roman, *see* empire, Fetiales
incarnation **4** 12–13
infanticide **6** 20.18–20; *see* exposure
innocence pp.11–12, 34, 37–38; **5** 7.7, 14.18n, 17.18, 21–24, 22.5–6; **6** 1.4, 18.12ff
institutes pp.13–14 n.32; **1** 1.12; **5** 4.3

Jews pp.3, 17, 54; **4** 2.4–5, 5, 8, 7.4–7, 10.5–11.16; 12.13, 14.10–12, 15.1–2, 12–14, 16.12–13, 17, 18.3–6, 20–33, 19.1, 20, 21.5, 26.37–42; **5** 3.4, 17–19, 9.9, 22.14; **7**.1.24–25; *see* Hebrews, revolts, Jewish, Sabbath
judgement, in underworld **3** 20.17; **7** 22.5; last **2** 17.1–2; **7** 1.23–25, 14.3ff, 20–21, 24.1–5, 26
judges pp.50–51; **5** 5.11, 9.17; *see Index of Proper Names under* Hierocles
jurists p.2; **1** 1.12; **5** 11.18–12.1
justice pp.7, 9, 10–12, 24–25, 29–35, 37–38, 39, 40–42,44–45, 51–53; **3** 9.15–19; 21–22; **4** 12.15, 13.1,9; **5** 6.4, 6, 11–13, 7.1–3, 5–6, 10, and **5** passim; civil, **4** 2.15; **5** 16.12–13; **6** 18.35, *see* law, civil; natural **5** 16.12–13; heavenly **2** 12.14; **3** 9.15, 19; **5** 14.7–15.1,

6; **6** 9.7, 18.35, 25.7; **7** 1.3; *see* law, divine; works of justice **6** passim; **4** 14.16–20, 25.6ff.; *see* golden age, *Index of Proper Names under* Carneades

king/kingship pp.32, 42–43; **1** 3.5–6, 11.30ff, 15.1ff; of God **2** 10.2; **7** 14ff
knowledge p.26; **3** 3–6, 8.24–31, 12.27–30; of good and evil **2** 12.7–18; **5** 5.13, 17.31; **6** 5.10–12; of God **6** 9; *see* wisdom

Lactantius, life pp.1–3; **5** 2.2; as Christian apologist 4, 12–14; as ethical thinker 6, 25–35; as historian of religion p.41; as millenarianist p.45; as social and political thinker 29–51; as teacher of rhetoric 1, 4; **3** 13.12; as theologian p.4; on Constantine 3, 48–50; on the Tetrarchy 43–48; on the Principate 48–49; on old Rome 40–43; works: *Divine Institutes*, contents 7–12; genre 12–14; authorities 14–21; other works 3, 49–51
law, pp.33, 37–38, 41, 45, 50–51; civil pp.9, 10–11, 33, 37–38, 41, 48 n.195, 53; **1** 1.12; **4** 29.7; **5** 11.18–19; **6** 9.4–7, 23.24–25; divine pp.38, 45 n.181–2; **4** 10; **5** 8.8–10; **6** 8.6–12, 9, 23.21–25, 24.25–27; natural pp.33, 46 n.186; **4** 3.18; **5** 16.3, *see* justice, natural; of three children, **1** 16.10; *see* justice
lawyers, *see* advocates, jurists
lex Papia Poppaea **1** 16.10
lust pp.11, 32; **6** 16.9–11, 19.4–6, 23
lying **6** 18.4–6

INDEX OF TOPICS

magic **2** 14.10, 16.1, 4; **4** 15.4, 19; **5** 3.7–21, 9.17; *see* Christ, miracles of
marriage **1** 11.26, 16.10n; **3** 21–22; **6** 23.23–29
martyrs, martyrdom pp.29, 42; **4** 21.5; **5** 3.3, 13.2, 5, 11–20, 19.24, 22.18–24; *see* persecution
milk **1** 10.2, 22.19; **2** 11.2, 7; **4** 17.19; **5** 4.6, 5.7; **7** 24.7, 11, 13, 14
millennium **7** 14 ff; *and see* eschatology, golden age
miracles, *see* magic, Christ
murder pp.11, 34, 38; **1** 10.4; **2** 6.3; **5** 11.18; **6** 20.10–11, 15, 26; *see* suicide

nature **3** 28.3–5; *see* law, natural; philosophers, natural
necromancy **2** 16.1; **4** 27.18–19; **7** 13.7

opinion p.20; **3** 8.29; **7** 22.3; public pp.14–15; **1** 19.5–6; **2** 2.6, 16.4; **5** 18.1, 19.19
oracles pp.8, 15–21; **2** 7.7, 16.1, 13–14; **7** 13; *see also* prophets, *Index of Proper Names under* Apollo, Hystaspes, Sibyl
orators, oratory **1** 1.8–11; **3** 25.11; **5** 1.10, 24, 2.2, 14.4; *see* rhetoric

panegyrics **1** 15.13
parricide **1** 15.29; **3** 14.9; **5** 9.16
passions **4** 24.17; *see* emotions, pleasures
paths, of life **6** 3–4, 7–8
paterfamilias **4** 3.16–17; *see* father
patience, *see* endurance
patria potestas, *see* father, power
patronage **6** 11.26–27
peace **1** 13.12–13, 18.17; **5** 22.15–16; *see* war
penitence **6** 24.1–10
Peripatetics p.11, 32; **2** 8.48; **3** 7.7,
8.10, 16; **6** 15.2, 17, 16.1, 17.9, 19.1
persecution pp. 2–3, 11, 43–48; **4** 18.2; **5** 1.24n, 9.1–14, 11–13, 19.1, 6–9, 22–23, 20.1, 7–8, 12, 21.1–6, 22.18–24, 23.1; **6** 24.1n
philosophers, philosophy pp.2, 7–9, 12, 14–15, 16, 19, 21–27, 32–34, 51–52; **1** 1.9, 17–18, 2, 5.15–28; **2** 1.2–4; **3** passim; **4** 23.8–9; **5** 1. 10, 2.3–11, 14.3–16.1; **6** 5.1, 10. 6.1, 5–9, 23–28, 9.13, 10.11–13, 12.1, 14, 15.2, 3, 5, 10–12, 14– 17, 16.1–6, 17.1, 9, 15.18, 24, 18.1, 3; **7** 2.2–3, 3.1–7, 11–26, 5.1–2, 7; natural philosophers **3** 6.5, 6, 17, 20, 13.6; *see* Cynics, Cyrenaics, Epicureans, Peripatetics, Pythagoreans, Stoics; *and Index of Proper Names under* Anaxagoras, Anaximenes, Antisthenes, Arcesilaus, Aristippus, Aristo, Aristotle, Aristoxenus, Callipho, Chrysippus, Cicero, Cleanthes, Critolaus, Democritus, Diagoras, Dicaearchus, Dinomachus, Diodorus, Diogenes, Empedocles, Epicurus, Euclides, Heraclides, Heraclitus, Herillus, Leucippus, Panaetius, Philodemus, Plato, Porphyry, Protagoras, Pythagoras, Seneca, Socrates, Speusippus, Thales, Theombrotus, Theophrastus, Xenophanes, Zeno of Citium, Zeno of Sidon
piety pp.10, 24–25, 30; **3** 9.19; **5** 6.10, 7.2, 7, 10.1–14, 14.9–14, 22.8; **6** 9.24, 10.3, 12.25; *and see* justice
pirates **1** 11.32
pity pp.30–32; **3** 23.8–10; **5** 6.4; **6** 10.2, 14.1–2; *and see* charity
pleasures p.32; **2** 1.3; **3** 8.5–26, 11.6, 11–12, 14; 16.5; 17.38, 42; aural

458   INDEX OF TOPICS

6 21; ocular 6 20, of taste and smell 6 22; of touch 6 23
poets/poetry pp.7–8, 14–15, 19–20; 1 5.2–14, 11.17–38, 53–4, 15.13, 21.27, 29, 22.20; 2 10.9, 12; 4 12.21; 5 1.10, 5.1–8, 6.11, 10.2–9, 18.3; 7 22.1–4; *and see Index of Proper Names under* Ennius, Germanicus, Hesiod, Homer, Horace, Lucan, Lucilius, Lucretius, Orpheus, Ovid, Persius, Pindar, Plautus, Terence, Varro (P. Terentius Atacinus), Vergil
pontiffs 5 19.10
poverty/the poor pp.23, 39; 5 14.18–19, 15.1–5, 16.8; 6 4.11, 9.20, 12, 18.10, 20.24–25; *see* charity
power, divine 1 3.1–15; of Roman father 4 3.16–18
priests, pagan, *see* augurs, flamens, pontiffs
property, private pp.9, 11, 22–23, 38–40; 3 21.2–3, 22.3–4, 6–7; 5 5.7–8
prophecy/prophets pp.7–9, 15–21; 1 4–5.1; 2 10.11; 4 5.3–10, 11.1–10, 12.3–21, 13.6–10, 18–27, 14.1–17, 15.4, 13–14, 16.6–11, 13–16, 17.2–13, 16, 18.1, 13–33, 19.3–4, 8–9, 20.5–13; 5 1.15, 3.18, 11.1, 18.3; 7 7.8, 13.2, 17.1–8; *see* oracles
prostitute/prostitution 1 20.2ff; 3 15.15–19, 21.4; 6 20.21–22, 23.7
providence 1 2; 2 8.48–71, 10.15–16, 11.13–14; 3 23.9–10, 28.5; 5 22.11; 7 3.25–4.1, 9.11–12
prudence 5 12.11; *see* wisdom
punishment, eternal 7 20–21
Pythagoreans 2 8.48; 3 18.1; 5 17.22; *see Index of Proper Names under* Pythagoras

quindecimvirs 1 6.7, 13–14

ransoming of captives 6 12.15–16
religion, etymology of 4 28.3–5; pagan religions pp.7, 23, 40–41; 1 passim, and *see* gods, worship; Christian religion pp.4, 7–9, 26, 30, 46–47; 4 passim, *and see* Christ, Christians, God; Christian and pagan compared 5 19.27–34; freedom of pp.46–48; 5 19–20; religion and wisdom pp.21–25; 1 1.25; 4 2.6–5.1, 10.4; 5 1.11, 4.8
republicanism p.42; 6 6.17
rescripts, of emperors p.45; 5 11.19; *see* law
resurrection, of Christ 4 19; of humans 7 20, 22–23, 26.1–7
revolts, Jewish 4 21.5n
rhetoric, pp.1–6, 7, 14; *see* eloquence, oratory
Rome, *see* fall; *Index of Proper Names under* Rome
Romans, old pp. 40–43; 5 13.13, 14.9–10; *see* citizens, empire; *Index of Proper Names under* Cato, Decii, Mucius, Regulus, Romulus
ruler-worship 1 15.28–33; *see* gods, as men

Sabbath 7 14.8
sacrifice 5 13.1, 8, 19.10, 27–34, 20.3–8; 6 1–2, 25
sages, the seven 1 5.16; 2 8.49; 4 1.9; 6 6.27
scripture pp.14–16, 20–21; 2 11.15; 3 1.10–12; 4 5.9–10, 20.1–5; 5 1.15–21, 2.13–16, 3.1–3, 4.4–7; 6 24.31; 7 25.1–2; *see* prophets, and *Index of Proper Names under* Baruch, I Corinthians, Daniel, Deuteronomy, Ecclesiastes, Ephesians, Ezekiel, etc.
senate, senators pp.8, 40–41; 1 15.32,

INDEX OF TOPICS

20.7, 13, 22.6–8; **2** 6.14–16; **5** 14.18n; of the gods **1** 10.8
sex, *see* lust
slaves/slavery pp.33, 34, 39; **4** 3.16–18, 4.1–5; **5** 6.2, 14.17, 15.2–3, 18.14–15; slaves as philosophers **3** 25.15–16
soldiery, as profession pp.38, 51; **6** 20.16
soul **2** 2.6, 10.2, 12.3, 7–14; **3** 6.3, 12.2, 34, 13.16; **5** 21.11; **6** 1.10, 2.13, 14.2; **7** 5.9–10, 13, 15–19, 23–25, 27a-l, 11–12, 23; *see* body, immortality, necromancy, transmigration.
spectacles **6** 20.32–36; *see* games
spirit, *see* soul
Stoics/Stoicism pp.8, 9, 11, 14, 18, 19 n.69, 27, 29 n.111, 32; **1** 2.2–3, 5.19–21, 6.2, 12.3–10, 17.1–2; **2** 5.7–9, 19, 28–42, 8.23, 48, 10.15–16; **3** 4.1–2, 6.7, 7.8, 8.10, 12.12, 18.1–5, 11, 23.8–10, 14, 25.7, 27.4, 6; **6** 5.4, 14.7–9, 15.3, 17.9–17, 19.1; **7** 3.1ff, 11ff, 4.2, 7.9, 20.8–9, 23.3; *see Index of Proper Names under* Cleanthes, Chrysippus, Panaetius, Seneca, Zeno of Citium
suicide pp.42, 50; **1** 5.26n; **3** 18.5–12; **6** 17.25
summum bonum, see good, supreme
superstition **1** 1.12, 23, 15.18, 22.1; **2** 9.11; **4** 28.3–7, 13–16; **5** 1.1, 2.7, 13.3

toleration, *see* freedom
theatre **5** 20.12–13; **6** 20.27–31, 21.2
trade **5** 17.12–13
transmigration, of the soul **3** 18.1–3, 19.19–20
triumph **1** 10.8, 11.2

tyranny pp.28, 37–38, 42, 45; **2** 4.16ff, 27ff; **5** 6.5–6, 12.1; **7** 18.5–19.7
Twelve Tables p.41; **6** 9.6

usury **6** 18.7–9

vegetarianism **6** 24.14n
virgin birth, *see* incarnation
virtue pp.11–12, 25–35, 37, 41–42, 46, 52, 53; **1** 3.4, 7, 9.1, 18.3–4; **3** 8.31–42, 11–12; **4** 24.7, 19, 29.5–6; **5** 18.4–11; **6** 5–6, 9.8–11, 16ff; **7** 1.17, 5.15, 10; of God **1** 3.1, 8.2, 11.43; of Christ **4** 6.9, 23–25; interdependence of virtue and vice pp.27–28 n.106, 40; **2** 17.1ff; **3** 29.16ff; **5** 7.4–10; **6** 3.12ff, 5.11–13, 22.2ff; **7** 1.17–18, 5.27a-q; immortality as reward for p.29; **3** 12.7–36; **4** 25.5–10; **5** 18.1–11; **6** 9.17–24; **7** 1.3, 5.9–27; *and see* innocence, justice, patience, piety

war pp.30, 34, 37, 41, 45, 50, 51; **5** 8.6, 10.10, 17.12–13, 20, 22.17; **6** 4.15ff; **7**.27.15; *see* empire
widows **6** 12.23
wisdom pp.7, 12, 21–27, 34–37, 52; **1** 1.6, 23.8–9; **2** 3.23–24, 7.1–6, 8.71; **3** passim, esp. 1.9–10, 6.1–2, 8.31, 9.1, 6–8, 11.2–3, 16.10, 26.1; **4** passim; **5** 17.33–34; **6** 9.24; **7** 4.13; *see* philosophy, religion and wisdom
world, creation of **7** 1–4, 7.8–13; end of, *see* eschatology; worldly ambition **6** 4.21–22; **7** 1.15
worship, of gods **1** passim; **2** 1–4, 6; of God **6** passim; **7** 6; *and see* religion

INDEX OF PROPER NAMES

Underlining of references indicates that text is quoted, directly or indirectly.
In addition to names in L.'s text, names mentioned in the footnotes are also referenced when it seems significant.
Books of the Bible are printed in italics; virtually no other works are listed separately.

Academy, Academics pp.9, 23–24, 34, 44; **1** 2.3, 6.2, 12n; **2** 8.14; **3** 3.7, 4.11, 6.5, 8, 20, 7.10, 14.14, 15, 15.3, 28.17; **5** 14.3; **7** 5.2, 7.2, 3
Acestes **1** 22.25
Achilles **1** 23.3
Adonis **1** 17.9
Aeacus **3** 20.17n; **7** 22.5
Aegean sea **1** 11.59
Aelius, Sextus **6** 8.8
Aeneas pp.30, 31n.122, 37, 40; **1** 17.9, 22.25; **5** 10.3–9
Aesculapius/Asclepius p.8; **1** 10.1, 15.5, 23, 26, 17.15, 18.1, 21, 25; **2** 4.18, 7.13, 17, 15.7, <u>8</u>; **3** 20.16, 17; **4** 27.12; **6** 25.10, 11; **7** 18.4
Africa (North) pp.1, 2, 3, 17, 53
Africanus, P.Cornelius Scipio **1** 9.1, 18.11–13
Agamemnon **1** 23.3
Agathocles, king of Sicily **1** 21.13, 15
Agesilaus, *see* Pluto
Aglaosthene **1** 11.64
Agrarian law **3** 23.7n
Ajax **1** 23.3
Albinus **6** 5.3
Albunea **1** 6.12
Alcibiades **3** 19.24
Alcmena **1** 9.1
Alexander the Great **1** 6.8; **2** 7.19
Alexander I, king of Macedon **4** 14.11

Amalek **4** 17.12
Amalthea **1** 6.10, 21.38, 22.19
Amazons **1** 9.2, 5
Ambracia **3** 18.9
Ambrose pp.4, 35nn.138 & 139
Amos **4** 19.3
Amphitryo **1** 10.11, 15.20
Anacharsis the Scythian **3** 25.18
Anaxagoras of Clazomenae, philosopher **1** 5.18; **3** 9.4, 15, 18, 12.20, 23.11n, 28.12, 30.6; **5** 3.23; **6** 1.2
Anaximenes of Miletus, philosopher **1** 5.19
Anchises **1** 15.12, 17.9; **5** 10.8
Ancyra **1** 6.12
Anio, river **1** 6.12
Anniceris **3** 25.16
Anthropians (Christian sect) **4** 30.10
Antichrist **7** 19.6
Antisthenes, philosopher **1** 5.18; **3** 15.20n
Antonius, M., the elder **1** 11.32
Antonius, M., triumvir p.42; **1** 1.11n, 11.32n, 15.29–30, 22.11n; **2** 7.17; **3** 14.12n; **6** 18.28n
Apis **4** 10.12
Apollo pp.16, 19; **1** 7.1–2, 8–<u>9</u>, <u>10</u>, <u>13</u>, 8.4, 10.1, 3, 15.9, 13, 26; **2** 4.18; **4** 4.8, 13.<u>11</u>–15, 17, 15.6, 27.12, 14, 18; **5** 3.5, 10.16; **7** 13.5, <u>6</u>, 22.5

INDEX OF PROPER NAMES

Apollodorus **1** 6.9
Apollonius of Tyana pp.2, 15; **5** 3.7–10, 14, 16, 21
Appius **6** 18.26
Appius Claudius, Censor **2** 7.15, 16.11
Apuleius **5** 3.7, 21
Arabia **2** 13.6
Aratus **1** 11.64n; 21.28n; **5** 5.4
Arcesilaus, philosopher **3** 4.11–14, 5.3, 5, 8, 6.7–10, 30.6
Archimedes, scientist **2** 5.18
Areopagus **5** 3.6
Argonauts **1** 5.4, 9.10, 22.17
Argus **1** 6.2
Ariadne **1** 10.9n
Arician wood **1** 17.15, 22.2
Aristarchus of Samothrace **5** 2.17
Aristides, Athenian **3** 19.8
Aristides, Christian apologist p.12
Aristippus, philosopher **3** 7.7, 8.6, 15.15; **7** 7.11
Aristo, philosopher **7** 7.11
Aristophanes of Byzantium **5** 2.17
Aristotle **1** 5.22, 6.12n; **2** 10.17, 25; **3** 7.8, 8.38, 17.34n, 28.20, 21; **5** 3.1, 14.5, 17.4; **6** 16.6n; **7** 1.7
Aristoxenus, philosopher **7** 13.9, 10
Arnobius pp.1, 19, 51n.206; **1** 11.13n; **5** 1.21n
Artorius, doctor **2** 7.22
Asclepiades p.3; **7** 4.<u>17–18</u>
Asclepius, *see* Aesculapius
Asia **7** 15.11, 16.3
Asia Minor p.2; **1** 7.1
Assyria, Assyrians **1** 23.2; **7** 15
Ataburus **1** 22.23
Athenagoras p.12
Athens/Athenians **1** 10.4, 15.9, 20.3–4; **3** 12.22, 19.17, 22, 23, 20.16; **5** 14.3; **6** 8.9, 9.8
Atinius, Tiberius **2** 7.20–21, 16.11
Atlas **1** 11.58
Atticus, T. Pomponius **1** 15.26, 20.14 **3** 28.9n

Attus Navius, augur **2** 7.8
Augustine pp.4–6, 17n.54, 18, 22, 26, 35, 49n.197, 51, 53; **2** 4.10n, 13n, 15.7n; **3** 18.5n, 24.1n; **6** 15.10n, 16.11n, 20.27n; **7** 10.10n, 15.11n
Augustus, emperor p.43; **1** 11.64n, 16.10n, 20.5n; **2** 7.22
Aulacia **1** 11.65
Auses **4** 17.12
Autolycus **1** 23.2
Autronius Maximus **2** 7.20
Aventinus **1** 11.59

Babylon/Babylonians **1** 6.13, 23.2; **4** 5.7, 10.17
Bacchus **1** 8.4, 10.8–9, 15.5, 9, 13, 23, 26, 18.1, 18, 21.28, 22.15; **2** 13.4; **4** 3.12, 4.8; **5** 10.16; **6** 20.35; **7** 22.5.13
Bacis p.17
Baebius, consul in 181 BC **1** 22.5
Baruch **4** 13.<u>8</u>
Bellona p.41; **1** 21.16; **5** 10.15
Belus **1** 23.2
Bibaculus, *see* Furius Bibaculus
Bithynia pp.2, 3; **5** 2.2, 11.15
Boeotia **1** 22.15
Bona Dea **1** 10.14n, 22.11; **3** 20.4
Brutus, M., expeller of the kings **7** 15.16
Brutus, M., assassin of Caesar p.42n.170; **2** 7.22
Butes **1** 17.9

Cabirus **1** 15.8
Caca **1** 20.36
Cadmus **1** 15.20
Caelus **1** 12.10, 13.14, 18.18; **4** 4.8
Caesar, C. Julius p.42; **1** 6.7, 15.29–30, 21.3n; **2** 7.17, 16.11; **3** 18.5n, 11–12; **6** 11.25n, 18.34, 35
Caesar, L. Julius, uncle of the above **1** 15.30

INDEX OF PROPER NAMES

Caesars **1** 15.6
Callipho, philosopher **3** 7.7
Canaan/Canaanites **2** 13.6
Cannae **2** 16.16
Capitol **1** 6.11, 12, 14, 11.49, 20.27, 38, 40; **3** 14.10, 17.12, 14
Carneades pp.10, 32–35, 44, 53; **3** 30.6; **5** 14.3–5, 16.2–12, 17.1, 9, 14, 20, 32
Carthage/Carthaginians pp.1, 29; **1** 15.8, 21.13; **2** 16.18; **7** 15.14, 15
Cassiodorus p.13n.32
Cassius Hemina, annalist **1** 13.8 and n
Castor and Pollux **1** 5.4, 10.5–6, 15.5, 23, 26; **2** 7.9, 10
Catiline, L. Sergius Catilina **3** 19.8
Catina, in Sicily **2** 4.28
Cato, M. Porcius, Censor **3** 16.5n; **5** 14.3
Cato, M. Porcius, the younger pp.41, 42; **3** 18.5, 8, 10–12, 19.8; **6** 6.27
Catulus, Q. Lutatius, (in Cic. *Hort.*) **6** 2.15
Caucasus **2** 10.7; **5** 11.4, 17.18
Cecrops **1** 17.14
Celsus p.15, 17
Ceres **1** 14.2, 17.6, 18.1, 18, 21.24; **2** 4.28–30, 7.19, 16.11; **3** 20.4
Chaldeans **4** 13.11; **7** 14.4
Chiron **1** 10.2
Chloris **1** 20.8
Christ (see also Jesus) pp.5, 7, 9–10, 14, 15, 18, 24, 29, 46, 54; **4** 7.4, 7, 8.1, 10.2, 18, 19, 12.14, 17, 18, 13.9, 18, 14.1, 3, 15.27, 30, 16.4, 12, 14, 17.1, 10, 11, 12, 13, 18.1–9, 31, 20.3–5, 10, 23.10, 26.2, 3, 28, 39, 27.1, 14, 19, 29.11, 30.10; **5** 3.4, 7, 9, 10; **7** 19.4, 6
Christians **4** 30.10, 13; **5** 2.4, 13, 11.13, 13.8; **7** 26.8

Chronos **1** 12.9
Chrysippus, philosopher p.27n.105; **1** 2.2n, 5.20, 6.9; **3** 7.8n, 18.5; **7** 23.3
Chthon **1** 17.13
Cicero, M. Tullius pp.4, 8, 9, 11, 13, 14–15, 17, 19, 20, 21, 22, 23, 26–27, 31, 32–33, 34, 35–36, 42, 44, 49, 51, 53; **1** 1.11n, 12n, 2.3, 3.22n, 5.24, 25, 6.2–3, 7.4, 9.3–4, 10.2, 14, 11.40, 48, 12.3–4, 9–10, 15.5, 6, 16–18, 19–20, 21, 23–5, 27, 17.1, 2, 3–4, 18.13, 20.14, 16, 17, 19, 22, 21.28n; **2** 3.2–7, 24, 4.27, 31, 33–37, 5.7, 8, 9, 6.8, 8.10–11, 12–16, 20, 25, 45, 46, 53, 60, 65, 9.12, 10.15, 11.15–16; **3** 1.1, 8.32, 10.7–8, 13.10–11, 13, 14, 15, 16, 14.7, 8, 9, 11, 13, 15, 17, 20, 15.1, 9, 10, 16.2, 5, 6, 9, 12–13, 17.13, 14, 18.12, 18, 19.2, 5–6, 14, 25.1, 2, 12, 27.5n, 28.9, 12n, 20, 29.3, 4, 6, 7, 18; **4** 4.6, 15.27, 18.10, 28.3, 4–5, 10; **5** 5.5, 9, 6.12, 8.6, 10, 11.2, 12.5–6, 14.3, 5, 15, 16.5–7, 9–11, 13, 18.4, 6, 7, 8, 20.3, 22.7; **6** 2.15, 4.11n, 5.4, 5, 6.21, 24, 25, 26, 8.6, 7–9, 11, 11.2, 9, 10, 11, 12, 13, 14, 25, 12.5, 9, 10, 11, 13, 15, 19, 17.27, 18.15, 21, 24, 27, 34, 20.4–5, 24.2, 18, 19, 20, 29, 25.9; **7** 1.1, 2.10, 4.11, 15, 8.7, 9, 9.10, 10.9, 10, 11.5, 14.4, 22.19n, 23.3
Cimmeria **1** 6.9; **5** 23.3
Cimon, Athenian pp.40n.156, 49; **6** 9.8
Circe **1** 21.23
Circus **2** 7.20; **6** 20.32, 35
Cithaeron **1** 22.15
Claudia **2** 7.12, 16.11
Cleanthes **1** 5.19; **3** 18.5
Clement of Alexandria p.12
Clinic philosophers **3** 8.10 and n

INDEX OF PROPER NAMES

Cloacina **1** 20.11
Clodius, P. **1** 10.14
Clodius, Sextus, historian **1** 22.<u>11</u>
Cnossos **1** 11.46
Codrus, king of Athens **3** 12.22
Colophon, in Asia Minor **1** 7.1
Constantine, emperor pp.3–4, 18, 36, 43, 48–51; **1** 1.13, 14n; **2** 1.2; **3** 1.1; **4** 1.1; **5** 1.1; **6** 3.1; **7** 26.10a
Constantius, father of Constantine **1** 1.13n
1 Corinthians **5** 15.<u>8</u>; **6** 23.15; **7** 5.22
Cornelius, consul in 181 BC **1** 22.5
Cornelius (in Cic. *Hort.*) **6** 2.15
Cornelius Nepos, *see* Nepos
Corybantes **1** 13.5, 21.40
Corythus **1** 23.3
Cos **2** 7.17
Cotta, C. Aurelius (in Cic. *N.D.*) **1** 6.2; **2** 6.8, 8.55
Crassus, M. Licinius **6** 13.11
Crete/Cretans **1** 10.9, 11.46–8, 13.3, 14.10, 21.38–41, 22.19
Crispus, son of Constantine pp.3, 48
Critias **3** 19.24
Critolaus, philosopher **3** 30.6n
Croesus, king of Lydia **6** 13.11
Cronos/Kronos **1** 11.46, 12.9, 13.1, 11
Cumae in Italy p.17; **1** 6.10, 13; **7** 24.12
Cunina **1** 20.36
Cupid(s) **1** 11.1–3, 17.9, 20.14
Curetes **1** 11.46, 13.5n, 21.40–42
Curio, C. Scribonius **1** 6.14
Curtius **3** 12.22
Cynics **3** 15.20, 18.9n
Cynosura **1** 10.2
Cyprian pp.1, 4–5, 13, 16, 28; **5** 1.24, 26, 4.3, 5, 7; **6** 12.32n, 24.1n
Cyprus **1** 17.10, 21.1
Cyrenaics **3** 8.9, 15.15
Cyrus the Great of Persia **1** 6.12; **4** 5.7, 10.17, 11.5

Danae **1** 11.18
Daniel **4** 12.<u>12</u>, 21.<u>1</u>; **7** 24.2n
Dardanus **1** 23.3
Darius, king of Persia **4** 5.8, 14.11
David **4** 8.13, 14, 11.9, 12.7, 17, 13.9, 18, 21, 22, 24–27, 14.1, 4, 15.3, 16.6, 14, 18.14, 18, 26, 30, 31, 32, 19.8
Decii **3** 12.22
Delos **1** 15.9
Delphi **1** 6.7, 9, 7.1; **4** 27.14
Demetrianus, correspondent of Cyprian **5** 4.3, 4, 6
Demetrianus, pupil of Lactantius p.3; **2** 10.15
Democritus, philosopher p.23; **1** 1.4n, 2.2; **3** 17.23, 34, 18.6, 23.4, 28.13, 30.6; **7** 1.10, 3.23, 7.9, 10, 12, 8.8, 13.7
Demophile, *see* Herophile
Demosthenes, Athenian orator **3** 14.12n; **5** 2.15
Deucalion **2** 10.10, 23
Deuteronomy **4** 17.<u>6</u>, <u>9</u>, 18.<u>29</u>
Diagoras, philosopher **1** 2.2
Diana **1** 17.15n, 21.2
Dicaearchus, philosopher **3** 17.34; **7** 7.12, 8.8, 13.7
Didymus, commentator **1** 22.<u>19–20</u>, 27
Diespiter **1** 14.5
Dinomachus, philosopher **3** 7.7
Diocletian, emperor pp.2, 4, 36, 44; **1** 1.13n, 9.1n
Diodorus, historian **1** 13.8
Diodorus, philosopher **3** 7.7
Diogenes, philosopher **3** 25.16, 30.6n
Dionysius I of Syracuse **2** 4.16–20, 25–26, 27, 35
Dolabella, P. Cornelius, Cicero's son-in-law **1** 15.30
Domitian, emperor p.49; **5** 3.9
Domitius Ulpianus, jurist pp.13n, 45; **5** 11.19

INDEX OF PROPER NAMES

Ecclesiasticus **4** 8.15
Egeria **1** 17.15, 22.1–2
Egypt, Egyptians pp.5, 16, 42; **1** 6.2,
   3, 11.20, 15.8, 20.36, 21.20, 24;
   2 5.36, 12.22, 13.10; **3** 20.16; **4**
   2.4, 10.5–8, 11, 13.7, 20.6,
   26.37, 38; **5** 20.12; **6** 6.17; **7**
   13.4, 15.1–6, 10, 13
Eleusis **1** 21.24
Elijah **4** 11.6
Elysian Fields **6** 4.1
Emmanuel **4** 12.4, 6–7
Empedocles, philosopher **2** 12.4; **3**
   18.5, 28.12, 30.6
Ennius pp.5, 8; **1** 11.<u>34</u>, <u>35</u>, <u>45–46</u>,
   <u>63</u>, <u>64</u>, <u>65</u>, 13.<u>2</u>, <u>14</u>, 14.1, <u>2–6</u>, <u>7</u>,
   <u>10–12</u>, 15.<u>31</u>, 17.10, 18.<u>11</u>, 12,
   22.<u>21</u>; **5** 1.<u>5</u>
Ephesians **6** 18.<u>33</u>; **7** 5.22
Ephesus **5** 3.14
Epicureans pp.12, 23n.81, 29n.111; **2**
   8.60; **3** 17.2, 3, 18.3, 20.15,
   25.15; **5** 20.14; **6** 24.13; **7**
   12.27, 30
Epicurus, philosopher p.9; **1** 2.2; **2**
   8.49, 10.25; **3** 7.7, 12.<u>15</u>, 17.7,
   16, <u>17–25</u>, 28–30, <u>31</u>, <u>32</u>–35,
   41–42, 25.7, 13, 27.5, 6; **5** 3.1,
   10.12; **7** 1.10, 3.13, 23, 24, 5.<u>4</u>,
   <u>7</u>, 8, 7.13, 8.8, 13.7
Epidaurus **1** 10.2; **2** 7.13, 16.11
Epimenides p.17
Eratosthenes of Cyrene, scientist **1** 6.9
Erichthonius **1** 17.11, 13
Eris **1** 17.13
Erythrae/Erythrean **1** 6.9, 11, 13, 14–
   15, 8.3, 14.8; **2** 12.19, 16.1; **4**
   6.5, 15.27, 29; **5** 13.21; **7** 19.9,
   20.1, 24.12
Eryx **1** 17.9
Esdras/*Esdras* **4** 11.5, 18.<u>22</u>
Esus and Teutates **1** 21.3
Ethiopians **4** 13.7
Etna **1** 21.24; **3** 18.5

Euclides of Megara, philosopher **3** 12.9
Euhemerus pp.8, 15n; **1** 11.33, 65,
   13.14, 22.27
Euphranor, sculptor **2** 4.13
Euphorbus **3** 18.15; **7** 23.2
Euripides **1** 6.8; **5** 15.11
Europa **1** 11.19, 21
Eurystheus **1** 9.7
Eusebius, of Caesarea pp.3, 37n.141,
   43, 49
Eusebius, sophist pp.2–3
Ezekiel **7** 26.2n, 4n

Fabricius **6** 6.26
Faenia **1** 6.3
Fatua **1** 22.9
Faula **1** 20.5
Faunus **1** 15.8, 22.9, 11, 12, 13, 16, 17
Faustulus **1** 20.2
Febris, Roman cult of **1** 20.17n
Fenestella, historian **1** 6.<u>14</u>
Fenta Fauna **1** 22.9–11
Fetials, Roman priests p.41; **6** 9.4
Flora **1** 20.6–7
Floralia **1** 20.6–7
Florentinus, jurist p.13n.32
Fornacalia **1** 20.35
Fornax **1** 20.35
Fortuna **2** 7.11, 16, 16.11; **5** 10.13
Fulvius, M., Censor **2** 7.16
Furius Bibaculus **1** 21.47–48
Furius (L. Furius Philus) (in Cic. *Rep.*)
   pp.33, 44; **5** 12.5, 7, 9, 14.5,
   16.13, 17.2, 14, 18.9
Fuscus, Aristius **5** 17.18

P. Gabinius **1** 6.14
Galba, Ser. Sulpicius **5** 14.3
Galilee **4** 19.7, 20.1
Galli (priests) **1** 17.7; **5** 9.17
Ganymede **1** 10.12 and n, 11.19, 22,
   29, 23.3; **2** 16.17
Gauls **1** 20.27, 33, 21.3
Gavius in Cic. *Ver.* 5 **4** 18.10–11

INDEX OF PROPER NAMES

Gavius Bassus **1** 22.9
Gemini, consuls **4** 10.18
Genesis **2** 10.3; **5** 5.13
Gentiles **2** 13.12; **4** 11.8, 9, 12.14, 15, 15.2
Gergithium **1** 6.12
Germanicus, Ti. Claudius **1** 11.64, 21.28n, 38; **5** 5.4, 9
Glauce **1** 14.5
Gracchi **2** 4.29
Great Mother **1** 17.7n, 21.16, 25, 22.20; **5** 9.17
Greece, Greeks pp.6, 10, 12, 17, 22, 31, 39, 52; **1** 1.9, 6.7, 9, 11, 10.6, 11.59, 13.8, 15.14, 15, 24–25, 18.7, 20.14, 16, 17, 21.28, 31, 22.15; **2** 1.16, 4.16, 8.6, 6g; **3** 14.7, 16.16, 19.17; **4** 1.12, 5.8, 7.7, 9.1, 25.5; **5** 14.19; **6** 24.6; **7** 15.13

Hadrian, emperor **1** 21.1
Ham, son of Noah **2** 13.5–6
Hanging Gardens **3** 24.1
Hannibal **2** 16.17
Harmonia **1** 17.9
Hebrews **2** 13.8; **4** 7.7, 10.5–18, 26.37, 38; **7** 15.1
Helen **1** 10.6
Helicon **1** 5.10
Hellespont **1** 6.12, 11.59; **2** 4.4
Henna, in Sicily **2** 4.28, 29
Heraclides of Pontus, philosopher **1** 6.12
Heraclitus, philosopher p.17; **2** 9.18
Hercules pp.8, 44; **1** 5.4, 8.4, 9.1–4, 7, 10–11, 15.5, 23, 26, 18.1, 3–6, 13, 20.5, 36, 21.8, 31–37; **2** 7.15, 16.11; **5** 3.14, 10.16
Herillus, philosopher **3** 7.8
Hermaphroditus **1** 17.9
Hermes, *see* Mercury
Hermes Trismegistus pp.16–17, 18; **1** 6.2–3, 4, 7.2, 11.61; **2** 8.48, 68, 10.14, 12.4–5, 14.6, 15.6, 8; **4** 6.3, 4, 9, 7.3, 8.5, 9.3, 13.2, 27.19; **5** 14.11; **6** 25.10, 11; **7** 9.11, 13.3, 4, 18.3, 4
Hermopolis in Egypt **1** 6.3
Herod the tetrarch **4** 10.18, 18.6
Herophile **1** 6.10
Hesiod **1** 5.8–10; **2** 14.7
Hierocles, Sossianus pp.2, 15; **4** 15.26n; **5** 2.12, 3.4, 7
Hieronymus **3** 7.7
Hilary of Poitiers pp.4, 5
Hippolytus **1** 10.1, 17.15n
Homer **1** 3.17, 5.8, 6.9, 10.6; **4** 7.7, 27.15, 29.11
Honorius, emperor p.17
Honour, Roman cult of **1** 20.12
Horace **2** 4.1; **5** 13.16, 17.18; **6** 5.12, 13
Horeb, Mt **4** 17.4
Hortensius (in Cic. *Hort.*) **1** 7.4; **3** 16.9, 11, 12–13
Hosea/*Hosea* **4** 19.9, 29.11
Hostilius, *see* Tullus Hostilius
Hyacinthus **1** 10.3n
Hyperion **1** 21.30
Hyrcania **5** 11.4
Hydaspes, river **5** 17.18; **7** 15.19
Hystaspes, Persian king pp.18n.63, 19; **7** 15.11n, 19, 17.1n, 18.2, 21.1n.95

Iapetus **2** 10.7–8
Iasius **1** 23.3
Icarian sea **1** 11.59
Ida **1** 21.40
Idaean Mother (see also Great Mother) **2** 7.12
Ilium, *see* Troy
Illyricum **2** 7.16
Inachus **1** 11.20, 58
India **1** 10.8; **5** 11.4
Ino **1** 21.23
Institutes of Civil Law pp.13–14; **1** 1.12
Io **1** 11.20, 21

INDEX OF PROPER NAMES

Isaiah/*Isaiah* p.19; **4** 11.10, 12, 12.4, 8, 9, 10, 18–19, 13.7, 10, 19, 20, 15.13–14, 16.15–16, 17.8, 18.13, 16, 24–25, 20.12, 29.10; **7** 24.3n, 7n, 9n
Isis **1** 11.20–21, 15.8, 17.6, 21.20–21
Israel **4** 11.12, 13.7, 10, 17.9, 12, 18.32, 20.11, 29.10
Italy p.3; **1** 6.9, 11, 11.55, 13.6, 8, 9, 17.15
Iulus, son of Aeneas **5** 10.8

Jacob **4** 13.8, 10
Janiculum **1** 22.5
Janus **1** 13.7; **4** 3.12
Jeremiah/*Jeremiah* p.19; **4** 8.1, 11.4, 12–13, 13.8, 10, 17.8, 18.27, 19.4, 20.5–6, 7, 9, 10, 30.1
Jerome pp.1, 2n, 4, 5, 21
Jerusalem **4** 13.24, 14.7, 17.3, 8, 18.32
Jesse **4** 13.19–21
Jesus (see also Christ) **4** 7.4, 12.6, 13.16, 14.6–9, 11, 14, 16.13, 17.10, 11, 13, 18.5
Jesus, son of Josedech **4** 14.12
Jews pp.3, 9, 17, 54; **4** 2.4–5, 5.7, 7.4, 6, 10.18, 11.1–3, 5, 12, 12.5, 13, 13.17, 24, 14.10, 12, 17, 15.1, 2, 12, 30, 16.5, 12, 17.10, 21, 18.3, 4, 6, 21, 23, 19.1, 20.1, 2, 5, 11, 21.2, 5, 26.37, 39; **5** 3.4, 17, 19, 22.14; **7** 1.24, 26
John **4** 8.16, 26.31; **6** 25.12
John the Baptist **4** 15.2
Jordan, river **4** 15.2
Joshua **4** 5.6, 14.12, 17.9, 12
Joshua **4** 17.9
Juba **1** 15.8
Judaea/Judaeans **4** 10.14 and n, 18.4n
Judah **4** 10.14, 17.8, 18.20, 20.6, 10, 11
Judaism **4** 17.1
Judas **4** 19.3
Julian the apostate, emperor p.17

Julius Caesar, *see* Caesar
Julius Proculus, *see* Proculus
Junillus, jurist p.13n
Juno **1** 11.20, 39–40, 14.4, 15.9, 17.7, 8; **2** 7.11, 16.11, 16–18
Jupiter pp.8, 10, 30, 38–40, 44; **1** 5.7, 7.2, 8, 8.4, 10.8, 10–14, 11.2, 5–29, 30, 33–49, 62–65, 12.10, 13.1–4, 14.4–12, 15.12, 13, 26, 27, 16.5, 10, 17.7–8, 9, 12–13, 20, 20.33, 37–9, 21.1, 3, 9, 38–42, 22.3, 19, 21–23, 26–28, 23.3; **2** 1.7, 4.17, 5.2, 7.20, 10.12, 16.5, 11, 16; **3** 17.13, 14; **4** 3.12, 4.8, 10, 9.2–3, 27.12, 14, 15, 18; **5** 3.25, 5.9, 10, 12, 6.6, 11, 13, 10.15, 16; **7** 18.2, 22.5
Justin pp.12, 22
Justinian p.13n.32
Juturna **2** 7.9
Juvenal **3** 29.17

1 Kings **4** 11.6, 18.32–33
Kronos, *see* Cronus

Labryandus **1** 22.23
Laelius, C. Sapiens (in Cic. *Rep.*) pp.34–35; **5** 16.13, 17.2, 12, 18.4, 5, 22.7; **6** 6.27
Lamia, bogey **1** 22.13
Lampsacus **1** 21.25, 26
Laomedon, king of Troy **1** 9.10, 10.3, 22.17
Lara **1** 20.35
Larentinalia **1** 20.4
Larentina **1** 20.2
Lares **1** 20.35
Larunda **1** 20.35
Latinus **1** 22.17
Latins, Latium **1** 11.59, 13.9, 13, 15.8, 21.3, 6, 22.9; **2** 7.9; **5** 5.9
Latona **1** 17.6
Leda **1** 21.23
Lemnos **1** 15.9

INDEX OF PROPER NAMES 467

Lethe **3** 18.16; **7** 22.7
Leucippus, philosopher **1** 2.2n; **3** 17.23
Leucothea **1** 21.23
Leviticus **5** 23.3
Libanius of Antioch p.2
Liber (= Bacchus) **1** 10.9n; **4** 3.12
Libyans **1** 6.8
Licinius, emperor p.50
Lindos **1** 21.31–37
Lioness **1** 20.34
Livy p.17; **1** 11.49n, 20.2, 27n, 21.47n, 22.1n; **2** 7.8n, 11n, 12n, 13n
Locri **2** 7.18, 16.11
Lucan p.42n; **1** 21.20 (but see note), 21; **6** 6.17n
Lucian **1** 9.8
Lucilius, poet **1** 9.8, 22.13; **4** 3.12; **5** 9.20, 14.3; **6** 5.2, 3, 6.10, 18.6
Lucilius (Q. Lucilius Balbus) (in Cic. *N.D.*) **2** 5.7–8, 9, 15, 16, 6.8, 8.54
Lucretius **1** 16.3, 21.14, 48; **2** 3.10, 11, 11.1, 12.4; **3** 14.1, 2, 4, 16.14 and nn till 25, 34n, 17.10, 14, 28, 18.6, 27.10; **4** 28.13; **5** 6.12, 14.17; **6** 10.7; **7** 3.13, 12.1, 5, 7n, 9n, 14n, 17, 18, 20, 22, 24, 26, 27, 29, 27.6
Luke **4** 15.3; **6** 12.3

Manichees pp.17n.54, 27–28n.106
Macedon, Macedonians **1** 6.8, 15.8; **2** 7.10
Magi **2** 14.10, 16.4; **4** 2.4; **7** 13.7
Malachi/*Malachi* **4** 11.8
M. Marcellus **1** 20.12
Marcianus, jurist p.13n
Marcionites (Christian sect) **4** 30.10
Marcus Aurelius, emperor p.43
Marica **1** 21.23
Mark **4** 18.4
Mark Antony, *see* Antonius, M., triumvir
Marmessus (*sic*) **1** 6.12
Mars p.41; **1** 10.4, 15.26, 17.9; **4** 3.12; **5** 3.6, 10.15

Mater Matuta **1** 21.23
Matthew **5** 15.9; **6** 12.35n, 23.32, 33, 34, 24.21; **7** 27.13n
Maximian, colleague of Diocletian p.44; **1** 1.13n, 9.1n
Medes **7** 15.19
Mediterranean **1** 11.32
Melicertes **1** 21.23
Melissa **1** 22.19, 20
Melisseus **1** 22.19, 27, 28
Melito p.12
Memmius, C., **3** 14.2
Menoeceus **3** 12.22
Mercury (Roman god) **1** 6.2, 3, 8.4, 10.7, 11.61, 15.13, 26, 17.9; **4** 27.18; **5** 10.16; **7** 13.4, 22.5
Messene/Messenians **1** 10.2, 11.33, 20.29–30
Messiah **4** 7.7
Micah **4** 17.3
Miletus **1** 5.16; **2** 7.19, 16.11; **3** 14.5; **4** 13.11; **7** 13.5
Mind, Roman cult of **1** 20.13
Minerva **1** 11.39, 15.9, 17.12–14, 18.1, 23–24; **2** 7.22, 16.11
Minos **1** 22.3; **3** 20.17n; **7** 22.5
Minucius Felix pp.1, 4n.19, 13, 14; **1** 11.55, 62, 17.6n; **2** 4.1n, 7.8n; **5** 1.22, 13.14n; **6** 23.5n
Moon **1** 21.30
Moors **1** 15.6, 8; **5** 17.18
Moses **1** 4.8n; **4** 5.6, 9n, 10.6–7, 12, 13, 13.10, 14.12, 17.1, 4, 5–7, 9, 12, 13, 18.29, 20.2, 10, 26.40
Mucius, C. Scaevola pp.41–42; **5** 13.13
Mulvian bridge **1** 21.6
Musaeus p.17; **1** 21.39
Muses **1** 5.10
Muta **1** 20.35

Naevius, historian **1** 6.9
Nathan **4** 13.22
Naxos **1** 11.64, 15.9

468   INDEX OF PROPER NAMES

Nehemiah 4 11.5
Nemesis 1 21.23
Nepos, Cornelius 1 13.8; 3 15.10
Neptune 1 11.30, 32, 34, 14.5, 15.26; 2 6.2; 4 3.12, 27.18; 5 14.3; 6 20.35
Nero, emperor pp.17n.57, 49; 1 5.26n; 4 21.5
Nicanor 1 6.8
Nicomedia pp.2, 3
Nile, source of 3 8.29
Noah 2 13.1–8
Novatians (Christian sect) 4 30.10
Numa, Pompilius, king of Rome pp.40–41; 1 22.1–5, 9, 13; 2 6.15
Numbers 4 13.10, 18.29
Nun, father of Joshua 4 14.12, 17.9

Oceania 1 11.65
Oedipus 6 20.23
Oeta 1 9.11
Olympus p.41; 1 11.35; 3 17.14; 5 10.15
Omphale 1 9.7
Ops, *see* Rhea
Optatus p.5
Orcus 1 14.5; 5 14.3
Origen pp.12, 17
Orion 4 15.21
Orosius p.44n.177
Orpheus pp.17, 19; 1 5.4, 5, 6, 7, 14, 7.7, 13.11, 21.39n, 22.15, 17; 4 8.4, 5
Osiris 1 17.6, 21.20–22, 24
Otacilius, M., 1 6.14
Ovid, P. Ovidius Naso 1 5.13, 11.1n, 12.6, 13.6, 7, 16.12, 20.8, 35, 21.8, 9, 20 (see note), 25–6, 30, 40; 2 1.15, 5.1, 2, 24, 8.64, 9.20; 5 5.7

Palaemon 1 21.23
Pallas 5 10.5

Pan 1 15.13
Panaetius, philosopher 6 5.4
Panchaeus mountain 1 11.63
Panic and Paleness, Roman cult of 1 20.11
Paphos 1 15.9
Papian law 1 16.10
Paradise 2 12.15, 16, 19
Parthenia 1 17.8
Partheniae 1 20.32
Paul, apostle p.15n.44; 4 21.2, 5; 5 2.17, 3.1
Paul, jurist p.13n.32
Paulinus of Nola pp.4–5
Paulus (Paullus), L. Aemilius, victor of Pydna 2 7.10
Paulus (Paullus), L. Aemilius, consul, killed at Cannae 2 16.17
Perfect Discourse (of Hermes Trismegistus) 2 15.7; 4 6.3; 7 18.3, 4
Perillus 3 26.6
Peripatetics pp.11, 32; 2 8.48; 3 7.7, 8.10, 16; 6 15.2, 17, 16.1, 17.9, 19.1
Perseus, king of Macedon 2 7.10
Persia, Persians 1 6.8; 4 2.4, 5.7; 7 15.13
Persis 1 21.30
Persius, poet 2 2.18, 4.10, 11–12, 13; 3 16.15; 6 2.11, 12
Pescennius Festus, historian 1 21.13
Peter, disciple p.15n; 4 21.2, 5; 5 2.17, 3.1
Petilius 1 22.5
Petilius, Q. praetor 1 22.6
Phaedo 3 25.15
Phaenomena 1 21.28 and n
Phaenomena (attrib. to Ovid) 2 5.24
Phaethon 2 10.23
Phalaris 2 4.27; 3 19.8, 27.5
Pherecydes 7 7.12, 8.7
Phidias 2 4.13
Philip, king of Macedon 3 14.12n

INDEX OF PROPER NAMES

Philoctetes **1** 9.11
Philodemus **3** 20.15n
Phrygia **1** 6.12; **5** 11.10
Phrygians (Christian sect) **4** 30.10
Picus **1** 22.9
Pindar **1** 22.19
Piso, historian **1** 6.9
Piso, father-in-law of Julius Caesar **1** 15.30
Plato pp.16, 20, 25, 31, 39–40, 49; **1** 5.23, 6.12n, 8.1, 15.16, 23; **2** 4.26, 8.49, 10.4, 25, 14.6n, 9; **3** 14.13, 17.29, 18.8–10, 19.17–21, 24, 21.1, 2, 4, 5, 6, 7, 8, 11, 12, 22.2, 5–11, 25.1, 7, 16; **4** 2.4, 4.6; **5** 1.14n, 3.1, 14.5, 13, 17.4; **6** 17.4, 25.1, 2; **7** 1.6, 9, 2.10, 3.12, 16, 7.8, 12, 8.2, 4, 7, 9.1, 12.2, 13.4, 14.4, 22.19
Plautus, T. Maccius **5** 12.11; **6** 11.8
Pluto **1** 11.30, 31, 14.5
Polites **7** 13.5
Pollux, *see* Castor
Polyclitus, sculptor **2** 4.13
Pompey the Great p.42; **6** 6.17
Pompey, Sextus, son of Pompey the Great **1** 21.21
Pontius Pilate **4** 18.4–6
Porphyry p.2; **5** 2.3n
Portunus **1** 21.23
Potitii **2** 7.15
Priam, king of Troy **1** 10.6, 22.17, 23.3
Priapus **1** 21.25–30; **2** 4.1–4
Probus, correspondent of L. p.3
Proculus, Julius p.40; **1** 15.32
Prometheus p.8; **2** 10.5, 7–8, 10–12; **7** 21.5
Propertius **2** 6.14
Proserpina **1** 17.6, 21.24; **2** 7.18, 16.11
Protagoras, philosopher **1** 2.2, 5.17
Proverbs p.18; **4** 6.6-8
Psalms **4** 8.14, 11.9, 12.7, 17, 13.9, 18, 27, 14.4, 15.3, 16.6, 14, 18.14, 18, 26, 30, 19.8; **5** 9.9; **7** 14.9, 20.5

Pyrrhus **2** 7.18
Pythagoras p.16; **1** 5.17; **3** 2.6, 14.5, 18.15–17, 19.19; **4** 2.4; **6** 3.6n; **7** 8.7, 12.30, 13.4, 23.2
Pythagoreans **2** 8.48; **3** 18.1; **5** 17.22

Quirinus **1** 15.8, 23, 29, 32, 21.23; **4** 3.12
quindecimviri **1** 6.7, 13, 14
Quintilian **1** 21.17; **5** 7.6, 7; **6** 23.30
Quirites **2** 6.14

Red Sea **4** 10.7
Regulus, M. Atilius pp.29, 41–42, 49; **5** 13.13
Remus **1** 15.29
Revelation **7** 10.10, 17.1n, 5n, 7n, 8n, 20.5n, 24.2n, 6n
Rhadamanthus **3** 20.17; **7** 22.5
Rhea/Ops **1** 11.6, 27, 38, 13.2–3, 7, 14.2–7, 17.7n
Rhodes **1** 21.31
Robigo, Roman cult of **1** 20.17n
Rome/Romans pp.8, 10, 12, 17, 29, 30, 31, 35–51, 52, 53; **1** 1.14, 5.26, 6.11, 13, 14–15, 13.8, 29, 15.6, 8, 18.8, 20.1, 3, 4, 5, 17, 27, 33, 21.8, 26, 22.1, 9; **2** 4.29, 30, 7.10, 11, 12, 13, 16, 12.4, 16.11, 12, 16–18; **3** 12.22, 17.12, 18.8, 20.3; **4** 5.7, 7.6, 10.5, 21.2; **5** 13.13, 14.3, 10, 19, 16.4, 17; **6** 8.9, 9.4–6; **7** 15.11, 13, 14, 15, 18, 19, 16.1, 25.6, 8, 26.11
Romulus p.8, 40; **1** 15.29, 31, 33, 20.1, 21.23; **2** 6.13; **7** 15.14

Sabines **1** 15.8, 22.1
Sages, the Seven **1** 5.16 **2** 8.49; **4** 1.9; **6** 6.27
Salii **1** 21.45, 47n, 22.4
Sallust, C. Sallustius Crispus **1** 21.41; **2** 12.12–13; **3** 29.8, 10; **6** 18.26

Samos, Samians **1** 6.9, 15.9, 17.8
1 Samuel **4** 14.<u>5</u>
2 Samuel **4** 13.<u>22</u>
Sancus **1** 15.8
Saturn pp.8, 30, 36–40, 44; **1** 5.7, 10.10, 11.6, 7, 16–17, 27, 38, 46, 48, 50–62, 12.1–2, 8–10, 13.1–15, 14.2–12, 15.2, 16.10, 18.18, 20.37, 21.6–7, 9, 13, 22.9, 28, 23.2, 5; **2** 10.8, 13.4; **4** 3.12, 4.8, 10, 27.18; **5** 5.2, 3, 9, 10.15; **6** 20.35; **7** 24.9
Seneca (the younger), L. Annaeus pp.5, 20, 28, 41n.163, 49, 51; **1** 5.<u>26</u>, <u>27</u>, 28, 7.<u>5</u>, <u>13</u>, 16.<u>10</u>; **2** 2.<u>14–15</u>, 4.<u>14</u>, 8.<u>23</u>; **3** 12.<u>11</u>, 15.<u>1</u>, 2, <u>11–13</u>, <u>14</u>, 16.<u>15</u>, 23.<u>14</u>, 25.16; **5** 9.19, 10.15, 13.<u>20</u>, 22.11, <u>12</u>; **6** 17.<u>28</u>, 24.<u>12</u>, 14, <u>15</u>, <u>16–17</u>, 25.<u>3</u>; **7** 15.<u>14–15</u>
Serapis/Serapides **1** 20.22
Severus, correspondent of L. p.3
Sextus Aelius, *see* Aelius
Sheba **4** 13.7
Sibyl(s) pp.5, 16–21; **1** 6.7–12, 13, 14, <u>15</u>, <u>16</u>, 7.<u>13</u>, 8.<u>3</u>, 14.8, 15.<u>15</u>; **2** 10.<u>4</u>, 11.<u>18</u>, 12.<u>19</u>, <u>20</u>, 16.<u>1</u>; **4** 6.3, <u>5</u>, <u>9</u>, 13.<u>21</u>, 15.<u>9</u>, <u>15</u>, <u>18</u>, <u>24</u>, <u>25</u>, 26, 27, <u>29</u>, 16.<u>17</u>, 17.<u>4</u>, 18.13, <u>15</u>, <u>17</u>, <u>19</u>, <u>20</u>, 19.<u>5</u>, <u>10</u>, 20.<u>11</u>; **5** 13.21; **7** 7.8, 13.6, 15.18, 16.<u>11</u>, <u>13</u>, 18.5, <u>6</u>, <u>7</u>, <u>8</u>, 19.<u>2</u>, <u>9</u>, 20.1, <u>2</u>, <u>3</u>, <u>4</u>, 23.<u>4</u>, 24.<u>1</u>, <u>2</u>, <u>6</u>, 24.<u>12</u>, <u>13</u>, <u>14</u>, 25.7
Sibylline books pp.16–21, 51; **1** 6.10–11, 13–14, <u>15–16</u>, 11.<u>47</u>; **2** 4.29, 7.12, 8.48
Sicca Veneria p.1
Sicily/Sicilians **1** 6.7, 21.13, 24, 22.25; **2** 4.16, 27, 31, 33, 5.18
Sion **4** 17.3
Sion, Mt **4** 17.4
Sirach, see Ecclesiasticus
Silenus **1** 21.25; **3** 19.14

Sinnius Capito **6** 20.35
Socrates pp.9, 23; **2** 3.5, 8.49, 14.9; **3** 3.7, 4.2, 6.7, 7.10, 13.6, 17.29, 19.17, 23, 24, 20.1, 9, 12, 15–17, 21.1, 2, 28.17, 30.6; **5** 14.14; **6** 17.4; **7** 2.10
Solomon **4** 6.6, 8.13, 15, 12.3, 13.24–27, 16.7, 10, 18.32
Solon **1** 6.12
Sotio **6** 24.14
Spain **1** 21.8
Sparta/Spartans **1** 20.29–32
Sparti **3** 4.9
Speusippus, philosopher **1** 6.12n
Stercutus **1** 20.36
Stilicho p.17
Stoics pp.8, 9, 11, 14, 18, 19n.69, 27, 32; **1** 2.2 and n, 3, 5.26, 6.2, 12.3, 10, 17.1; **2** 5.7, 19, 28, 8.23, 48, 10.15, 16; **3** 4.1, 6.7, 7.8, 8.10, 12.12, 18.1, 5, 11, 23.14, 25.7, 27.4, 6; **6** 5.4, 14.7, 15.3, 17.9, 11, 25n, 19.1; **7** 3.1, 11, 13, 14, 4.2, 7.9, 13, 20.8, 23.3
Styx **1** 11.12, 19.3
Sulmo **5** 10.5
Syria **4** 10.14, 18.4; **7** 17.2, 26.2
Syrtes **5** 17.18

Tarquinius Priscus, king of Rome **1** 6.10–11; **2** 7.8
Tarquinius Superbus, king of Rome p.17; **1** 20.38; **4** 5.7, 14.11; **7** 15.14
Tarquitius Priscus, Etruscan antiquarian **1** 10.<u>2</u>
Tartarus **6** 4.1; **7** 20.3
Tatian pp.12, 22
Tatius, Titus, king of Rome **1** 20.11
Tauri, people of the Crimea **1** 21.2
Tellus **1** 22.28
Terence, P. Terentius Afer p.19; **2** 8.<u>24</u>; **3** 4.<u>7</u>, 18.<u>13</u>, 26.<u>4</u>; **5** 9.<u>6</u>, 21.<u>1</u>; **7** 2.3, 27.<u>3</u>

INDEX OF PROPER NAMES

Terminus **1** 20.37–41
Tertullian, Septimius pp.1, 4, 13, 22, 28, 31n, 46, 47; **5** 1.23, 4.3
Teucer **1** 21.1
Thales of Miletus, philosopher **1** 5.16; **2** 9.18; **3** 14.5, 16.13, 20.17n; **4** 10.18n
Thallus **1** 13.8, 23.2
Thebes **1** 22.15; **3** 12.22
Themis **1** 11.10
Themiste **3** 25.15
Theombrotus, philosopher **3** 18.9, 10
Theophilus of Antioch pp.12, 22; **1** 13.8n, 23.2, 5n; **7** 14.8n, 25.5n
Theophrastus, philosopher **6** 12.5
Thetis **1** 11.9
Thoyth **1** 6.3
Tiber **1** 13.6, 21.6; **2** 7.12
Tiberinus or Thybris **1** 11.59
Tiberius Atinius, *see* Atinius
Tiberius, emperor **1** 11.64n; **4** 10.18, 14.11
Tiberius Gracchus **3** 23.7n
Tibur **1** 6.12
1 Timothy **4** 12.17
Titan(s) **1** 10.10, 11.64, 14.2–3, 7, 9, 10, 21.39; **2** 10.8; **5** 6.7
Titus, emperor **4** 21.5n
Tityus **7** 21.5
Trajan, emperor p.46n.186
Tribonian p.13n.32
Trismegistus, *see* Hermes Trismegistus
Triumph of Cupid **1** 11.1
Troy/Trojans **1** 3.17, 6.9, 12, 9.10, 22.17, 23.4; **2** 16.18; **4** 5.6, 8.13; **7** 15.19
Tuditanus **3** 23.7
Tullia, daughter of Cicero **1** 15.16, 18.27; **3** 28.9
Tullus Hostilius, king of Rome **1** 20.11, 12
Turullius **2** 7.17
Tutinus **1** 20.36
Twelve Tables p.41; **6** 9.6

Tyndarus **1** 10.11, 15.20

Ufens **5** 10.5
Ulysses **1** 23.3
Urania **1** 15.8
Uranus **1** 11.61, 13.14, 15, 15.2, 22.28; **2** 13.4

Valentinians (Christian sect) **4** 30.10
L. Valerius **1** 6.14
Varro, M. Terentius, antiquarian p.17; **1** 6.7–12, 14, 13.8, 17.8, 21.7, 22.10–11; **2** 12.4, 21–22, 24; **4** 15.27
Varro, P. Terentius Atacinus, poet **2** 12.4
Varro, M. Terentius, surviving loser of Cannae **2** 16.16–17
Vatienus, P. **2** 7.10
Veii, town 10 miles N. of Rome **2** 7.11, 16.11
Venus p.41; **1** 10.4, 15.9, 17.9–11, 20.27, 32; **2** 4.12
Vergil, P. Vergilius Maro, poet pp.5, 6, 18, 19–21, 30, 38–39, 51; **1** 5.11, 12, 19, 8.8, 10.9, 14, 11.6, 12, 20, 13.9, 12, 13, 15.12, 17.15, 19.3, 20.38, 21.23n; **2** 4.4, 8.2, 10.16, 16.17, 18, 17.2; **3** 8.27, 29.8; **4** 10.7, 15.21, 27.3, 28.15; **5** 1.13, 5.5, 9, 10, 12, 9.4, 10.3, 5, 6, 8, 11.5, 19.9; **6** 3.6 4.1, 24.10; **7** 1.14, 3.5, 20.10, 11, 22.3, 7, 17, 24.11, 12, 27.16
C. Verres, governor of Sicily **1** 7.4n, 10.14; **2** 4.27, 30, 31, 33–37
Verrius, M. Flaccus, scholar **1** 20.5
Vespasian, emperor **4** 21.5
Vesta **1** 11.46, 12.4–6, 14.2–4, 21.25, 27; **2** 6.2; **3** 20.4
Vestal Virgins **1** 21.9, 26
Victorinus pp.4–5
Virbius **1** 17.15 and n
Virtus, Roman cult of **1** 20.12, 21.16

Vulcan **1** 12.7, 15.9, 26, 17.12–13, 18.21; **2** 6.2; **4** 4.8, 27.18

Wisdom of Solomon **4** 16.7–10

Xenophanes of Colophon, philosopher **3** 23.12

Zechariah/*Zechariah* **4** 5.8, 14.6–9, 11, 18.29

Zedekiah, king of Israel **4** 5.7
Zeno of Citium, philosopher **1** 5.20; **3** 4.1, 2, 6.7, 7.8, 8.20, 22, 18.5, 23.8; **4** 9.2; **5** 3.1; **7** 7.11n, 13
Zeno of Sidon, philosopher **3** 20.15; **6** 24.14;
Zephyrus **1** 20.8
Zeus (Zan, Zen) **1** 11.16, 46, 13.11; **2** 14.7

Appollonius of Tyana
Hermes Trismegistus